Forensic Structural Engineering Handbook

Forensic Structural Engineering Handbook

Robert T. Ratay, Ph.D., P.E.
Editor-in-Chief

MCGRAW-HILL
New York   San Francisco   Washington, D.C.   Auckland   Bogotá
Caracas   Lisbon   London   Madrid   Mexico City   Milan
Montreal   New Delhi   San Juan   Singapore
Sydney   Tokyo   Toronto

McGraw-Hill

A Division of The McGraw·Hill Companies

Copyright © 2000 by The McGraw-Hill Companies, Inc.. All rights reserved.
Printed in the United States of America. Except as permitted under the United
States Copyright Act of 1976, no part of this publication may be reproduced or
distributed in any form or by any means, or stored in a data base or retrieval
system, without the prior written permission of the publisher.

1 2 3 4 5 6 7 8 9 0   DOC/DOC   9 0 4 3 2 1 0 9

ISBN 0-07-052667-2

*The sponsoring editor for this book was Larry Hager, the editing supervisor was
Steven Melvin, and the production supervisor was Sherri Souffrance. It was set
in the HB1A design in Times Roman by Joanne Morbit of McGraw-Hill's
Professional Book Group composition unit, Hightstown, New Jersey.*

Printed and bound by R. R. Donnelley & Sons Company.

*Cover photos: Left photo by Robert T. Ratay; right photo by LZA technology, a
division of the Thornton-Tomasetti Group.*

This book was printed on acid-free paper.

McGraw-Hill books are available at special quantity discounts to use as
premiums and sales promotions, or for use in corporate training programs. For
more information, please write to the Director of Special Sales, McGraw-Hill,
11 West 19th Street, New York, NY 10011. Or contact your local bookstore.

Food for Thought

Structural failures are not just accidents, nor acts of God. They are the results of human error originating from oversight, carelessness, ignorance or greed.

With the advance of design sophistication and construction methodology came the proliferation of structural failures.

Early savings in design and construction costs often boomerang as later and larger costs of repair and litigation.

The vulnerable structures of the late 20th century will provide bread and butter to the forensic engineers of the 21st century.

RTR 1/1/2000

CONTENTS

Part III   Engineering Analysis of Structural Defects and Failures

CONTRIBUTORS

Howard W. Ashcraft, Esq., *Chair, Construction Group, Hanson, Bridgett, Marcus, Vlahos & Rudy, L.L.P., San Francisco, California* (CHAP. 9)

Mohammad Ayub, P.E., S.E., *Director, Office of Engineering Services, Directorate of Construction, Occupational Safety and Health Administration (OSHA), U.S. Department of Labor, Washington, D.C.* (CHAP. 3)

Kimball J. Beasley, P.E., *Principal and New York Branch Manager, Wiss, Janney, Elstner Associates, Inc., New York, New York* (CHAP. 14)

Glenn R. Bell, P.E., *Principal, Simpson Gumpertz & Heger Inc., Arlington, Massachussetts, San Francisco, California* (CHAP. 6)

W. Gene Corley, S.E., P.E., Ph.D., *Vice President, Construction Technology Laboratories, Inc., Skokie, Illinois* (CHAP. 12)

Daniel A. Cuoco, P.E., *President, LZA Technology, a Division of the Thornton-Tomasetti Group, Inc., New York, New York* (CHAP. 4)

Robert W. Day, P.E., G.E., *Chief Engineer, American Geotechnical, San Diego, California* (CHAP. 16)

John F. Duntemann, P.E., S.E., *Senior Consultant, Wiss, Janney, Elstner Associates, Inc., Northbrook, Illinois* (CHAP. 2)

Donald O. Dusenberry, P.E., *Principal, Simpson Gumpertz & Heger Inc., Arlington, Massachussetts* (CHAP. 9)

John W. Fisher, Ph.D., P.E., *Joseph T. Stuart Professor of Civil Engineering, Lehigh University, and Director, Center for Advanced Technology for Large Structural Systems (ATLSS), Bethlehem, Pennsylvania* (CHAP. 11)

Clayford T. Grimm, P.E., *President, Clayford T. Grimm PE Inc., Austin, Texas* (CHAP. 13)

Joshua B. Kardon, S.E., *Principal, Joshua B. Kardon + Company Structural Engineers, Berkeley, California* (CHAP. 7)

Michael C. Loulakis, Esq., *Senior Shareholder, Wickwire Gavin, P.C., Vienna, Virginia* (CHAP. 5)

Donald W. Neal, P.E., S.E., *President, Neal Engineering Associates, Beaverton, Oregon* (CHAP. 15)

Antraning M. Ouzoonian, P.E., *Principal, Weidlinger Associates, Inc., Consulting Engineers, New York, New York, Cambridge, Massachussetts, Los Altos, California, Arlington, Virginia* (CHAP. 1)

David S. Patterson, AIA, *Senior Consultant, Wiss, Janney, Elstner Associates, Inc., Princeton Junction, New Jersey* (CHAP. 14)

Alan W. Pense, Ph.D., *Professor Emeritus of Material Science and Engineering, Lehigh University, Bethlehem, Pennsylvania* (CHAP. 11)

David B. Peraza, P.E., *Senior Associate, LZA Technology, a Division of the Thornton-Tomasetti Group, Inc., New York, New York* (CHAP. 4)

Robert T. Ratay, Ph.D., P.E., *Consulting Engineer, R. T. Ratay Engineering, P.C., Manhasset, New York* (CHAP. 17)

Robert A. Rubin, Esq., P.E., *Partner, Postner & Rubin, New York, New York* (CHAP. 8)

David E. Thompson, P.E., *Chairman/CEO, Haley & Aldrich, Inc., Boston, Massachussetts* (CHAP. 9)

Dana Wordes, Esq., P.E., *Associate, Postner & Rubin, New York, New York* (CHAP. 8)

Joseph Zelazny, C.E., *President, Kreisler Borg Florman General Construction Company, Inc., Scarsdale, New York* (CHAP. 1)

Preface

Engineering investigation and determination of the causes of structural failures of buildings, bridges, and other constructed facilities, as well as rendering opinions and giving testimony in judicial proceedings, has become a field of professional practice of its own, often referred to as *forensic structural engineering*. Structural failure does not have to be a "catastrophic collapse," it may be a "nonconformity with design expectations" or "deficient performance." Collapse is usually attributed to inadequate strength and/or stability; deficient performance, or so-called serviceability problems, is usually the result of abnormal deterioration, excessive deformation, and signs of distress. In short, structural failure may be characterized as the unacceptable difference between intended and actual structural performance.

Well-rounded expertise and success in this field is the result of the combination of many components in an engineer's background: a good education in structural engineering and its related subjects; years or even decades of experience in analysis, design, construction, testing, inspection, condition assessment, and trouble-shooting; an understanding of the design-construction process; comprehension of legal implications; good communication skills; a knack for problem solving; a positive attitude to teamwork; a strong sense of ethics; self-confidence without arrogance; credible and confident disposition; and a high level of intellectual sophistication. Some of these traits can be learned but most are ingrained or acquired.

In my nearly 40 years of structural engineering practice and university teaching of structural design, analysis, and investigation of failures, I often felt the lack of a comprehensive practical reference on the practice and business of investigating failures. This book is intended to fill the need for a comprehensive and authoritative reference for guidance on forensic structural engineering, addressing technical as well as nontechnical and legal matters on the investigation of structural and construction failures.

Some of the most frequently asked nontechnical and legal-related questions by engineers embarking on an activity of forensic structural engineering are: "How do I go about it?", "How do I start?", "What is the right procedure?", "What should I watch out for?", "How do I deal with my client, with the other parties, with the other experts?", "Who are my allies, who are my adversaries?", "What are my duties and to whom?", "What is my expected, allowable and ultimate behavior?", "How do I work with the lawyers?", "What are the legal positions I need to be aware of?", "What is an affidavit, a deposition, a testimony?", "What do I do and how do I testify at arbitration, at trial?", and "How do I charge for my work?"

Strictly technical questions by both the novice and the experienced forensic engineer include: "What are the applicable codes and standards in this case?", "How do I define the applicable standard of care?", "What are the critical characteristics of this type of structure?", "What are the types and causes of common deficiencies and failures of this type of structure?", "What are the methods of observation, instrumentation and testing?", "What are the effective methods of analysis for this type of structure?", and "What are the workable temporary and permanent repairs for this type of structure?"

This book has been developed to answer these and many other questions.

This is not a "what happened" or "lessons learned" book — this is a "what I need to know," "what I need to do," and "how I need to do it" book.

In order for the forensic engineers to intelligently investigate the cause of a failure and subsequently to identify the parties responsible for it, they have to have an understanding of not only loads, strength and stability, but also of the business and practice of design and construction in order to know where, when, how, why, and by whom a cause of failure can originate. They have to know, of course, how to conduct the investigation appropriate to the case. Since nearly all structural deficiencies and failures create claims, disputes, and legal entanglements, forensic engineers need to have some familiarity with the relevant legal process and need to know how to work effectively with attorneys. Complete familiarity with the nature and consequences of loads, and of the critical characteristics and vulnerabilities of structures of different types and materials is the most basic requirement. A special feature of this handbook is its coverage in appropriate detail of the range of these topics that are all necessary for the successful practice of forensic structural engineering.

Seventeen chapters are grouped into three parts:

Part I—Design and Construction Practices provides the background for understanding the design-construction process, the design and construction codes, standards and regulations, and the legal relationships.

Part II—Investigation of Failures and Resolution of Claims contains six chapters that explain the technical and legal steps both immediately and later after a failure, the engineering investigation and reporting process, the standard of care, the litigation and dispute resolution procedures, and the practice and business of expert consulting and witnessing.

Part III—Engineering Analysis of Structural Defects and Failures begins with a chapter on the magnitude, nature, and consequences of loads and hazards, and then continues with seven chapters on the critical characteristics, most common types and causes of failures, methods of analyzing and testing, and remedial repairs of steel, concrete, masonry, building envelope, timber, foundation, and temporary structures, and presents case studies of nonperformance and failure of each of these seven classes of structures.

The book is intended for use primarily by structural engineers but also by geo-technical, civil, and construction engineers, contractors, attorneys, insurers, and owners and managers of constructed facilities. (Failure analysis and forensic investigation is an intriguing and stimulating subject, and it is expected that a number of engineers will acquire the book as a useful addition to their reference library even though they are not actively practicing in this field.) Although not written specifically as such, in the absence of a real textbook on the subject and given the logical progression of the topics, as well as the case studies included, it is expected that this handbook will stimulate the teaching of forensic structural engineering and will be embraced as the text in academic and continuing education courses.

No single author would have the wide-ranging expertise and credibility to write on all the topics that were necessary for this comprehensive reference book; therefore contributing authors were invited to prepare the individual chapters. The authors are not only experienced practitioners and competent writers but, in most cases, are also nationally and internationally recognized experts in their respective fields.

I am grateful to the contributing authors for accepting my invitation to partici-pate in this book and I thank them for their outstanding effort and cooperation. Without their contributions there would be no book.

I also owe thanks to the McGraw-Hill people, particularly to Larry Hager, Senior Editor of Civil Engineering and Construction in the Professional Book Division, for his valuable assistance and continuing cooperation in producing the book, to Steven Melvin for his able supervising of the editing, and to the production supervisor, copyeditor, illustrator, typesetter, and others whose work I much appreciate.

Robert T. Ratay, Ph.D., P.E.

CHAPTER 1
DESIGN-CONSTRUCTION PROCESS

Antranig M. Ouzoonian, P.E., and Joseph Zelazny, C.E.

INTRODUCTION

This chapter presents the sequence of events of a project from its design concept through the construction stage. It is intended to state and refresh the structural engineer's role and responsibilities in the design and construction process toward the common goal shared by the owner and the design professional: a quality project designed for its intended use and constructed within the budget and time restraints.

The structural engineer must bring into the forensic arena the academic training, practical knowledge, and experience (including successes and disappointments), and then use them in the role of a detective or investigative reporter. Every piece of evidence in the case including calculations, drawings, materials, and products should be documented for review as part of the information-gathering process for analysis prior to the commencement of formulating an opinion. When applicable, the forensic engineer should visit the site of the distressed area, visually examine the failures, photograph and document the components of the failure, and request certain tests to be performed, if and when applicable, before rendering an opinion.

Often forensic engineers will be retained as expert witnesses. When confronted during litigation by attorneys and/or opposing experts in court, they must demonstrate complete understanding of the forensic process, as well as the design-construction process, and possess the confidence and ability to formulate and deliver professional opinions that are ethically, morally, and technically correct.

To accomplish this mission, one must be totally familiar with the entire spectrum of events leading to building a project from its inception to final use.

The Council of American Structural Engineers (CASE) has identified the role of the structural engineer (SE) and that of the forensic engineer (FE) with subtle but poignant distinctions as follows: A structural engineer is "an engineer with specialized knowledge, training and experience in the sciences and mathematics relating to analyzing and designing of force-resisting systems for buildings and other structures." A forensic engineer is "a structural engineer who, through training, education experience and knowledge is recognized by their peers to possess specialized information on a given structural subject matter and who is experienced and versed in the ethical practice of forensic engineering and is generally knowledgeable with the dispute resolution processes."

A design is a product of one's idea or vision, which is then, in terms of buildings and structures, transformed to a scientific or artistic pattern from which details are derived for the construction of a project to meet the needs of an owner or the community.

The design of a structural component is performed through the use of simple principles of mathematics, physics, and engineering often with reliance on recognized industry handbooks ("cookbooks"). The detailing of these components to fit into the assembly of a structure requires the knowledge, experience, and applications in the field of structural engineering.

FIGURE 1.1 (*Left to right*) Antranig M. Ouzoonian, PE, Principal, Weidlinger Associates, Inc., and Joseph Zelazny, CE, President, Kreisler Borg Florman General Construction Company, Inc., inspecting a construction site in New York City.

The design of a structure must contain a support system with a clear line of load path to carry and resist the applied loads to a stable resistive foundation. To be viable, the structure should have redundancy and should be able to resist a progressive collapse scenario as set forth in the American Society of Civil Engineers (ASCE) Standard ASCE 7, Minimum Design Loads for Buildings and Other Structures, 1995.

In case of a building, the architect is the creator of the structure for its use and its aesthetic form, and has the responsibility to coordinate the design produced by retained consultants. The architect is similar to an orchestra leader conducting the musicians toward the completion of a satisfying event for the public. In the design of a project, the architect directs the consultants toward a successful project. The architect reviews and implements the owner's program for space allocation and use. In conjunction with the space requirements, the architect prepares various façade schemes including window types and wall materials for the owner's review and approval. Based upon instructions from the owner, the architect prepares sketches and/or drawings to present to consultants for their review and implementation into the design process. Consultants are licensed professionals in their respective fields. The structural engineer is responsible for the design of the floor framing systems, their supports and foundations. The mechanical engineer is responsible for the heating and ventilation systems, electrical and plumbing requirements, and life-safety systems. High-rise office buildings may require an elevator consultant whose expertise lies in programming the number and time duration for people movement and related equipment. The civil engineer, also known as the site engineer, is responsible for the site grading and drainage, access roads, and parking requirements. On certain projects there may be specialized consultants, such as acoustical, window, elevator, laboratory, and landscaping, to assist the architect for the particular needs of the project.

DRAWINGS AND SPECIFICATIONS

The design drawings and specifications comprise the documents from which the contractor will build the project.

Drawings

Drawings encompass the architectural, civil, structural, and mechanical professions, and they are the means of conveying diagrammatic detailed aspects of the design components of a structure.

Architectural Drawings.   Architectural drawings convey the aesthetic and functional aspects of the project and include the fire-rated classification of the structure, occupancy, exiting requirements, and conformance to Americans Disabilities Act (ADA). These drawings generally contain the following:

> *Title sheet:* In addition to the title and owner of the project, this sheet usually designates the project footprint, location and area coverage with respect to the total property area, key plan, the true north arrow or project/plan north arrow, applicable local building code references, classification of the building for occupancy and fire rating, and a list of consultants.

> *Plans:* These designate the project program space allocations, generally a service "core" which may contain elevators, stairs, toilets, and mechanical space requirements such as duct, piping, and electrical shafts; also, the plans include communication closets, mechanical rooms, the roof, penthouse (where applicable), and basements or cellars.

Elevations: These are a pictorial view of each façade of the building indicating windows, doors, etc.

Building sections: A detailed sectional view through the building is taken usually in the project north-south and east-west direction.

Sections and details: These are a larger-scale dimensional detailed presentation of pertinent construction components and their interface connections with other materials.

Civil Engineering Drawings. Civil engineering drawings indicate site and project locations, vehicle accessibility, topography, site drainage, and possibly landscape requirements, although this aspect may be performed by a licensed landscape architect rather than the project architect.

Structural Drawings. Structural drawings indicate the design loads and applicable building code criteria and define the structural framing systems and their supports and foundations. These drawings will contain the following:

Foundation plan: Generally drawn to $1/8'' = 1'$-$0''$ scale, it indicates the type of support foundation selected for the building and structure including the required soil bearing capacities, elevations, dimensions, concrete strengths, and reinforcing steel.

Framing plans: Generally drawn to $1/8'' = 1'$-$0''$ scale, they show the required floor and roof framing systems which include the locations of columns, locations and sizes of the floor deck (slabs), support beams/girders, or trusses. These drawings will generally indicate column and beam reactions, and member moments where applicable. Further, equipment loads imposed on the structure from other trades weighing more than 1000 lb should be designated and located on the drawings, indicating that these weights have been accounted for in the structural design.

Column schedule: A tabular matrix of the building columns indicating sizes and weights of steel and concrete columns with the required reinforcing steel, as well as the loads on a designated column at each floor level and the column splice location with change in column size (if applicable). Base plate sizes (for steel columns), reinforcing dowels from column piers, reinforcing steel for concrete columns, as well as the total load of the columns on the foundation are also indicated.

Elevations: These show the configuration of perimeter walls, shear walls, sizes of trusses, or vertical bracing systems, indicating forces in the members together with end moments (when applicable).

Sections and typical details: These are drawn to a larger scale and dimensioned, indicating detailed interfaces with the surrounding materials or components.

General notes: These indicate the design loading schedule which includes weights of materials; live, wind, and seismic loads; applicable codes; material designations; and instructions to the general contractor.

Mechanical Drawings. Mechanical drawings designate the heating, ventilating, and air-conditioning (HVAC) systems; electrical distribution requirements; fire and security systems; sprinklers and the necessary plumbing requirements. These drawings generally contain the ductwork sizes and locations and designate required openings in the structure for their paths. Flowcharts and riser diagrams are produced for electric conduit runs and plumbing lines including sprinkler-piping systems. Drawings are prepared for the mechanical equipment rooms indicating the selected equipment, the operating weights of the machinery, and weights of heavy piping which are detailed to be hung or floor-mounted.

Tables 1.1 through 1.3 are helpful "checklists" prepared by CASE which can be used by the forensic engineer to assist in establishing the available basic design information for the investigation.

Design Drawing Phases. The most common design drawing process has four distinctive phases.

1. Concept sketches (CS)
   The architect, generally in concert with the structural engineer, initiates a design which in some cases may require alternate structural framing systems as well as stability and constructibility schemes. This phase normally constitutes 10 percent of the total effort for the proposed project and consists of plan dimensions, general column locations, and architectural features including probable façade materials. This information is presented to the owner in the form of professional sketches or drawings, and occasionally it includes a rendering of the project.

2. Preliminary design (PD)
   Upon approval of the CS by the owner, the design enters the preliminary phase, wherein a selected scheme is developed into a more defined scope with the structural and mechanical consultants. In this phase, outline specifications for materials and their use in the construction are noted, from which preliminary budgets for financing requirements, scheduling, and construction are derived. The end of this phase normally is considered as 25 percent of project design completion and is presented in the form of hard-lined drawings (CAD) representing the basis of the project.

3. Design development (DD)
   The project now begins to take shape. The structural systems are finalized, the mechanical requirements are defined, the façade and interior finishes are being selected and incorporated, and the project cost estimates are more firmly defined. The end of this phase now represents 50 percent of project design completion. At this stage, drawings from the design team (architect, structural and mechanical engineers) provide sufficient information to professional estimators for them to evaluate costs within the owner's project budgetary guidelines.

4. Construction document (CD)

   All the disciplines of the design team are in the stage of finalizing, coordinating, and detailing their work toward 100 percent completion of the designs, in preparation for bids. However, with respect to the total project, the end of this phase represents 75 percent of the total design. The remaining 25 percent is assigned to the construction phase, also known as the construction administration phase. There are projects that terminate at the construction document phase. Therefore, coordination of the project drawings among the design disciplines is absolutely *paramount* when the architect or engineer, as the prime professional, assumes the responsible role of heading the team.

   Technical specifications are finalized in this phase by each discipline and are added to the general conditions including bid forms for distribution to prospective qualified bidders.

   After the design bid documents are released for bidding and subsequent addenda, if any, are issued, the design portion of the project is complete, and the project enters into the construction administration phase.

5. Construction administration phase (CA)

   When a contract is signed by the owner, or agency authorized to act on behalf of the owner, for the construction of the project, the design document terminology is changed to *construction documents* or sometimes called a set of *conformed documents* which includes addenda during the bid stage.

   This distinction is made because the contract for the construction of the project may have conditions or exceptions to the design documents. A conformed set of design drawings is issued with the approval of the prime designer (architect or engineer) which reflects the contract "conditions" so that all parties are working from the same set of *contract documents.*

   In the construction administration phase, the prime designer reviews the contractor's submittal of shop drawings, equipment, and material specification submittals; performs site visitations; attends meetings with contractors; responds to the contractor's request for information (RFI), and issues clarification sketches and owner-initiated changes to the project. (This process is discussed in greater detail later in this chapter.)

   It is important to note that there are many situations, particularly on government-generated projects, in which the project construction administration is performed by another design team or by a government agency, such as the Department of State or the General Services Administration.

Technical Specifications

Common use in the design profession is the Construction Specifications Institute format, which is basically divided into three parts for each trade or product: general, materials, and execution.

Brief highlights of the three parts are as follows:

Part 1—General

Consists of the general description of the scope of work for the section, or trade, for which the specifications are written.

Lists applicable codes and standards.

Lists and describes the required submittals, i.e., shop drawings, engineering calculations for items designed by the contractor, product specifications, and guarantees/warrantees.

Defines the contractor's quality assurance (QA) and quality control (QC) procedures.

Part 2—Materials

Describes the materials to be used in the construction.

Describes the equipment to be used in the project.

Part 3—Execution

Fabrication requirements and conditions.

Material delivery and protection prior to use.

Installation procedures and tolerances.

Testing requirements during fabrication and installation of specified items.

Specifications are and should be prepared by the project design disciplines and/or in conjunction with a professional specification (CSI) consultant for the particular project and not submitted as an off-the-shelf item. Each project is different and has its own unique qualities.

Pertinent Questions

Since the drawings and specifications are an integral part in the investigation of distressed structures, the forensic engineer should ask the client the following minimum questions regarding the construction documents:

Are the latest drawings available?

Are the drawings signed and sealed by a professional engineer/architect?

Are as-built drawings available?

Do they depict the constructed structure?

Do the specifications indicate materials for the project?

Are the specification performance-type specifications?

Were there sufficient quality control requirements performed, such as special inspections during shop and field fabrication of materials, and results of material testing for the project?

Bid Package

The project construction bid package consists of the following major parts:

Invitation to bid: A sample bid form similar to or the same as that in "Recommended Competitive Bidding Procedures for Construction Projects," EJDC 1910-18, by the Engineers Joint Contract Committee. The term *invitation to bid* is sometimes used interchangeably with *specifications,* but note that they are two distinct sections of the project documents.

Qualification of bidders: This requires documentation of the prospective bidder's and contractor's financial capability, construction bonding ability, sufficient insurance coverage—both general and property, listing of similar project experience, adequate supervision, and ability to meet the owner's schedule and budget.

Unit price schedule: Unit prices are stated by the contractor for alternates in the bid package and/or "add" and "deduct" in-place costs for authorized changes during the construction.

General conditions of the contract for construction: The commonly used document is Standard AIA A201-1997.

Supplementary conditions: These include additions or deletions to the general conditions of the particular project.

Design drawings: These are drawings, details, and instructions prepared by the design team for the construction of the project.

Technical specifications: They define the scope of work, materials or equipment usage, and their implementation for each trade.

SHOP DRAWINGS

Shop drawings reflect the contractor's understanding and interpretation of the construction documents for the fabrication and installation of the various components used in the construction of the project. These drawings are detailed to indicate the sequence of assembly of various components of the project as well as its final form or position within the project.

Shop drawings are submitted to the design team for *review* prior to the actual fabrication or assembly of construction components. Since time is of the essence, return of the shop drawings within a specified time is essential to the contractor. Delays in approval of shop drawings may impact the construction schedule and further prevent other trades from continuing their work. For example, the American Institute of Steel Construction Code of Standard Practice, Section 4 Shop and Erection Drawings, paragraph 4.2 states: "The fabricator includes a maximum allowance of fourteen (14) days in his schedule for the return of shop drawings." If the architect or the structural engineer does not take exception to the above during the bid period, then the architect/engineer (A/E) must abide by the above or take the risk of receiving a delay claim from the contractor.

There has been much discussion regarding the party who is legally responsible for steel connection detail during the *review/approval* process of the shop drawings, following the Hyatt Regency walkway collapse in Kansas City, MO, in 1981. The generally accepted version is that the structural engineer of record (SER) is responsible for the entire structure and its component parts unless the designer *specifically* provides sufficient information on the contract documents and instructs the contractor (detailer) to assume the responsibility for the design of certain designated connections and/or members. Further, the SER would be prudent to stipulate that items not so designed by the SER be designed by a professional structural engineer registered in the state where the project is constructed and that engineering calculations be submitted for the SER's review.

Table 1.4 is a checklist prepared by CASE and can be used by forensic engineers in their investigation. Figure 1.2 illustrates a typical shop drawing review stamp used by various structural engineering consultants upon the recommendation of insurance carriers, in particular DPIC. Figure 1.3 is a sample of a stamp used by a consultant to designate responsibility that is assigned to the contractor regarding "the means and methods of construction," which generally include the following:

Underpinning of existing adjacent structures

Design of formwork for concrete construction

Bracing, shoring, and reshoring of concrete work

Construction loads imposed on the structure during construction

Temporary bracing of the structure during construction for wind and other lateral loads

Loads imposed on the structure during construction such as cranes, storage, and temporary equipment loads

ARCHITECT'S AND ENGINEER'S LOGS

It is important for the design team to establish an ongoing record of the project for possible claims initiated by the contractor or even claims by the design team due to contractor's errors or owner changes. The architect's and structural engineer's documentations, often referred to as logs, for a project are basically similar. These logs should be organized and maintained in a safe and secured area and should include the following:

Design logs and records

Agreement and conditions between the design professional and the client.

Client's approval of the needs and criteria of the project.

SHOP DRAWING REVIEW

	A	NO EXCEPTIONS TAKEN		
	B	MAKE CORRECTIONS NOTED		
	C	AMEND & RESUBMIT		
	D	REJECTED SEE REMARKS		
	E	REVIEWED ONLY FOR LOADS IMPOSED ON THE STRUCTURE		

Corrections or comments made on the shop drawings during this review do not relieve contractor from compliance with requirements of the drawings and specifications. This check is only for review of general conformance with the design concept of the project and general compliance with the information given in the contract documents. The contractor is responsible for confirming and correlating all quantities and dimensions; selecting fabrication processes and techniques of construction; coordinating his work with that of all other trades and performing his work in a safe and satisfactory manner

Date_____By _____

FIGURE 1.2   Typical shop drawing review stamp.

NOT REVIEWED

THIS SUBMISSION IS THE SOLE RESPONSIBILITY OF THE CONTRACTOR AND HIS SUB-CONTRACTORS FOR MEANS AND METHODS OF CONSTRUCTION FOR THIS PROJECT.

BY _____   DATE

FIGURE 1.3   Sample stamp by consultant designating responsibility for "means and methods of construction."

Government applications and approvals.

Design calculations.

Correspondence, records, minutes of meetings, dates of all submittals to client and consultants.

A record copy of drawings and specifications of each design stage submittal (PD, DD, and CD documents).

Shop drawing submittals

A log of each drawing submittal, when received, when reviewed and released with appropriate actions. Table 1.5 is a sample of a consultant's log for recording shop drawings received from the contractor.

A record of product and sample submittals.

Minutes of meetings and personnel in attendance.

Construction administration

Results of construction material tests.

Written report of each site visit, distributed to interested parties.

Log of all field office memos (FOMs).

A log of all contractor's requests for information, when received, when and how responded.

Minutes of meetings.

A record of authorized change orders (COs) and bulletins.

What is the time duration for keeping records? The National Society of Professional Engineers (NSPE) publication 4046 explains the differences between statutes of limitation and repose as follows: "Statutes of limitation bar actions against design professionals after a certain period of time following the date of injury or discovery of the deficiency. Statutes of repose bar actions against design professionals after a certain period of time following the completion of services or the substantial completion of construction."

In the United States, 48 states have statutes of repose with certain local limitations and conditions. Two states, New York and Vermont, have not adopted a statute of repose for design professionals. New York State does have a statute of limitation that takes effect 3 years after the date of discovery.

EXISTING CONDITIONS

In many instances the structural engineer is retained to perform analytical investigations of existing structures. The engineer must be prepared to perform his or her investigation in a manner similar to a detective pursuing answers to questions in order to understand the behavior and facts of the case before a verdict can be reasonably readied. At a minimum, the following items should be on the structural engineer's checklist:

Acquire the latest structural drawings and/or shop drawings.

Perform a site visit.

Confirm and/or take measurements of pertinent structural components.

For concrete structures investigate the size and location of reinforcing, initiate a program for concrete core sampling and testing.

For steel structures check beam sizes and connections; and, if required, ascertain the type of steel in the structure by a program of test coupons recovered from selected beams for testing.

For masonry structures check the type of block or brick, whether cells are grouted and/or reinforced, mortar type and strength, bond beams, and joint reinforcement.

For timber structures check size, type, and grade of members; check moisture content and connections.

For foundations, probes or borings may be required to ascertain the size of footings and in some instances the soil-bearing capacity.

Observe and define the existing load path of the structure under investigation.

The engineer should be cognizant of the fact that it is always beneficial to take more field measurements and make more sketches than may be deemed necessary at time of the field investigation, since "paper is cheaper" than the revisit site time. Also, field notes should be transferred to hard office drawings or CAD as quickly as possible.

VALUE ENGINEERING

In the early 1980s the term *value engineering* became a part of the construction industry vocabulary, probably and partly because "construction managers" needed outside opinions and consultation from building design professionals to optimize project costs and schedules.

During the latter part of 1980 (the stock market "drop"), large general business corporations started to use the term *reengineering* for the corporate system, which has basically similar goals to value engineering: to decrease costs for the same work and to do it in less time.

Value engineering pertains not only to engineering but also to architecture and construction. The value engineer (VE) must be experienced in the respective discipline to serve as a nonadversarial participant in this process.

Note that peer reviews and value engineering reviews are opinions of outside professionals, and their recommendations may or may not be accepted by the project design professional. If the recommendations are accepted and implemented in the project, the design professional is still solely responsible for the work.

PEER REVIEW

At the 1983 Structural Failures Conference in California, suggestions were made by the participants to find means to reduce structural distress in major buildings and to prevent catastrophic failures. Thus, a *peer review* was conceived initially to be a voluntary process which would be performed by an independent structural consultant, and the review would be done upon completion of the contract documents, but prior to bid or construction.

Recently, it has been found that the peer review process could be more beneficial to the project if the process were started during the design development phase. Note that the concept of a peer review is not a substitute for value engineering.

It is important to note that the reviewing engineer is not responsible for the structural design and does not supplant the duties of the engineer of record (EOR). The review is intended to verify the design load criteria, local building code compliance, and that no major errors are apparent with respect to concept in the design, the load path, or in pertinent calculations.

The City of Boston, Massachusetts, and the State of Connecticut presently require peer reviews of large and special structures.

INSPECTION AND TESTING

Although the inspection and testing terms are used synonymously in the construction field, they have distinct roles in the building world.

Inspections during construction are required to be performed directly by a registered professional engineer or by an engineer under the supervision of a registered professional engineer.

Inspection during construction is presently a requirement of the following recognized building codes: BOCA (Building Officials Construction Association), UBC (Uniform Building Code), and SBC (Standard Building Code). Certain major populated cities such as New York City advocate local special inspection requirements that are generally visual and may be accompanied by mechanical and/or electronic aids.

The definition of inspection varies with the building code in effect at the time of construction. The following is a list of building codes that require inspection of structural components during construction.

Authority	Inspection nomenclature
Building Officials Construction Association	Special inspections
Uniform Building Code	Special inspections
Standard Building Code	Threshold inspection (Florida)
Administrative Building Code, New York City	Controlled inspection

Project specifications should require at least the following minimum requirements for inspection and testing of the subgrade, concrete, steel, masonry, and timber structures.

Subgrade. The following inspection and testing of the subgrade should be carried out:

Borings
- Subsurface investigations are a requirement for major structures. Alternatively, a "judgment call" may be made by the structural engineer of record or the geotechnical engineer of record (GER) for minor structures, particularly if evidence of the subgrade conditions is available at adjoining sites.
- National building codes require at least one boring for 2500 ft^2 for all buildings which are more than three stories or 40 ft in height. Whenever it is proposed to use float, mat, or any type of deep foundation, there shall be at least one exploratory boring to rock or to an adequate depth below the load-bearing strata.
- Some building codes, such as that of New York City, require the soil boring investigations to be under the supervision of a licensed professional engineer (preferably a geotechnical engineering consultant) registered in the State of New York.
- The standard test borings should be taken in accordance with ASTM D-1586.
- Subgrade investigations should ascertain the presence of the elevation of natural groundwater through the installation of piezometers for observation.

Inspections
- A geotechnical engineer should perform physical and laboratory tests to verify the safe soil bearing value for the specified foundation design.
- A geotechnical engineer should also perform inspection of the preparation of the subgrade prior to the foundation concrete pours.
- Pile driving operations and installation of caissons and other deep foundations should be done under the observance of a geotechnical engineer.

Testing
- It may be necessary to validate the safe bearing value of the subgrade by a soil bearing plate test method. The New York City Building Code, subchapter 11, article 5, provides the requirements and interpretation of a soil load-bearing test.
- Sieve analysis, plasticity, moisture content, and other tests should be performed by a qualified testing laboratory.

- Pile loads tests, when required, should be performed per ASTM D-1143.
- Inspection of caisson bottoms should be conducted either visually by a soils technician or by use of TV equipment.
- Compaction tests during backfill operations should be done in accordance with ASTM D-1557.

Concrete
Formwork inspection

Inspection of concrete work is particularly important because once the concrete is hardened, correction of problems is extremely difficult and costly.

- Formwork should be checked for proper dimensioning and tolerances.
- Formwork bracing and shoring are the contractor's responsibility; therefore the designer is not involved.

Reinforcing steel inspection

- The size, amount, and location of rebars should be checked; and the lengths and end termination requirements should be spot-checked.
- Tying and supports for the reinforcing steel are the contractor's responsibility; therefore the designer is not involved.

Concrete material inspection

- Concrete mix and strength requirements should be verified from batch plant tickets. Additives may have been added at the plant, or additives may be designated to be added in the field prior to the pour. Some states require inspection at the batch plant by a qualified testing laboratory.
- Concrete slump, air content, and temperature should be checked prior to the pour in accordance with ASTM C-172 and C-173.
- Method for conveying concrete to the forms should be checked.
- Test cylinders are to be cast in accordance with ASTM C-31 and tested per ASTM C-39.
- Sometimes "strip cylinders" are cast and cured adjacent to the pour location in order to schedule a form stripping and reshore cycle for the project. Means and methods of reshoring are the contractor's responsibility; therefore the designer is not involved since it is the contractor's means and methods for construction.
- Curing methods should be in accordance with the project specifications or at least conform to the American Concrete Institute Building Code Requirements for Structural Concrete (ACI 318-99).

Posttensioned Concrete

- Size, amount, and locations of strands must be verified prior to the concrete pour. "Deadend" anchor conditions must be checked.
- Tensioning equipment must be checked and calibrated.
- Concrete pour inspection is the same as under Reinforced Concrete.

- Concrete strength must be ascertained by standard test cylinders per project specifications prior to strand tensioning.
- Tensioning must be observed and recorded by the testing agency.

Precast-Prestressed Concrete

- Plant fabrication is certified by the manufacturer.
- Field connections should be checked by the testing agency, similar to structural steel inspection requirements, since generally connections of structural steel are either bolted or welded.

Structural Steel

- High-strength bolts should be checked in accordance with ASTM A325/490. This applies not only in the shop but also in the field.
- Many states require that inspection of welding procedures, and tests be performed not only in the shop but also in the field and checked in accordance with Structural Welding Code, AWS D1.1. The following is a recommended guide for inspection of welds:

  1. Welds should be prequalified in accordance with AWS. Weld preparation joints that are not previously qualified require a test procedure as stated in AWS.
  2. Welders should be certified and prequalified per AWS for the work they are performing. Certification should have been established within the past six months of the actual work performed.
  3. Major through-thickness welds of 1.5 in or greater require a welding procedure for the weld process which is generally submitted to the EOR for review and approval.
  4. Material for complete joint penetration (CJP) welds greater than 1.5 in in thickness should be checked by ultrasonic methods for delaminations or inclusions in the base material. This is particularly important for welds that are subjected to tension forces.
  5. All complete joint penetration welds should be 100 percent tested by either ultrasonic or radiographic methods. Experience has indicated that ultrasonic inspection can be interpreted more consistently than radiographic films.
  6. Fillet welds are usually checked by either magnetic particle or dye-penetrate test procedures. Unless otherwise stated in the contract documents, 10 to 15 percent of the lineal feet of weld should be checked.

Timber

- Size, location, and species of the members should be checked.
- Special wood composite members such as glued laminated members and wood-and-steel composites should be checked by reviewing the manufacturer's shop and mill certificates.
- Generally, special connections, bolting, and nail patterns require inspection.

PROJECT DELIVERY METHODS

To put into effect a proposed project, it is essential to first establish the method by which the design team, architect/engineer, contractor, and subcontractors will design and deliver the proposed project plan for use. Therefore, when one is participating in the selection of the delivery method, it is important to know, among other things,

- Established regulations for procurement when dealing with a public agency
- Who the owner is as well as her or his capability and experience to respond to the needs of a proposed project delivery method (personnel and budget constraints, construction management understanding)
- Owner's financial strengths and cash flow concerns
- Timely availability of all contract documents
- When use of premises is required
- Environmental and community concerns
- Special site conditions such as underpinning of adjacent structures and shoring and sheeting availability of utilities

Once the above items have been determined, along with other pertinent project requirements, the selection of the most suitable project delivery system can be made. The most common project delivery methods used in the industry are

- Design-Bid-Build (DBB)
- Design-Build (DB)
- Design-Build-Operate-Maintain (DBOM)
- Construction management with or without guaranteed maximum price (GMP)

Design-Bid-Build (DBB).   Under this scenario an owner retains a qualified architect/engineer to design a project for his or her needs and then submits the design for bidding to qualified contractors for the construction.

In this process the professional designer has the responsibility to design the project to the agreed requirements of the client in accordance with the local building code for the protection of the public. The contractor has the responsibility to build the project in accordance with the requirements of the contract documents. Although both the designer and the contractor have common allegiance to the owner, the relationship between them may be trying at times.

Generally, the owner requires a statement from the design professional that the project was built in accordance with the contract documents.

Design-Build (DB).   In the 1980s a new idea of "one-stop" shopping entered the construction industry. The owner now has the opportunity to contract with one entity (responsibility) for the design, construction, and guarantee of the project.

Previously, DB projects were also known as *turnkey* projects. Normally in the DB process a qualified contractor retains the design professionals and is in control of both the design and the construction of the project. On occasion a qualified design professional heads the DB process and retains either one general contractor or several contractors as needed for the project. At the completion of the project, the owner only requires certification from the design-builder. Many owners in the private sector and some government agencies do not require an acceptance of the project from design professionals because their contract is with the design-builder and this entity is the responsible source. Any disputes between the designers and constructors become an internal matter among them, which does not involve the owner. The owner requires certification from the design-builder that the project conforms to the contract requirements. Note that the designer is not part of this process.

Design-Build-Operate-Maintain (DBOM). The DBOM process is a relatively new way to construct a major public or utility project, with the idea being that the successful qualified entity will also be contractually responsible to *operate* the building systems and *maintain* them for a designated number of years.

The design professionals, especially the architect and the structural engineer and mechanical engineer must review the contractual requirements regarding their role in the operational and maintenance conditions of the DBOM contract with the design-builder, who is generally a contractor and the owner. Also, in this scenario the design professional is responsible to the design-builder who has control over the entire project.

Construction Management. A method evolved in the 1960s and 1970s whereby a construction manager (CM) acts as the owner's agent and advises upon the economy of the design systems. The overall project is grouped into trade contracts which are competitively bid on by prequalified contractors. All contracts are directly held by the owner. Subsequently the process evolved into *CM at risk* where the CM holds the contract (with the subcontractors) and provides a general maximum price (GMP) to the owner.

For a detailed review of the various delivery systems discussed above, refer to the articles in the *Proceedings of the ASCE Construction Congress V,* Minneapolis, Minnesota, October 4–8, 1997.

Partnering. Yet another form of establishing a relationship in the construction industry is *partnering,* which occurs when all interested parties of the project, including the owner, actually sign and agree to a statement or resolution (generally not legally binding) saying that all parties will respond to one another's needs in a timely, nonadversarial fashion in the interest of the project. The success of the partnering program relies upon a dedicated point of contact from each discipline, usually at the project management level, who is experienced in understanding timely needs of the members of the partnering team.

The design professional should be confident in his or her areas of expertise when agreeing to the partnering agreement.

CONTRACTING AND SUBCONTRACTING

Today's construction organizations, in providing their services, must be familiar with the latest technology, improved machinery, and sophisticated equipment, and most of all they must have the ability to deliver the project ahead of schedule. Success will depend on the contractor's competence in finding ways to increase profitability in an augmented competitive market. An understanding of the competitive forces one faces as well as the potential strategies available for responding to an invitation to bid is essential. The most important initial step for the contractor to take is to study the selected delivery method, in order to understand the risks involved, services to be provided, and how the delivery system works (who are the members of the team, their respective responsibilities, and what is required in order to perform the work).

It is important to know the specific requirements pertaining to procurement laws, prerequisites, and restrictions in each state. For detailed definitions of a general contractor and subcontractor, licensing requirements, and individual and state regulations, refer to "The Design Build Process, A Guide to Licensing and Procurement Requirements in the 50 States and Canada," by John R. Heisse, II, editor, *Forum on the Construction Industry,* American Bar Association, 1997. A *general contractor* is defined as "any person engaged in the business of construction, structural repair, structural restorations, dismantling, demolition or addition to a structure that exceeds the threshold limits contained in the state's general statutes and agency regulations."

A *major subcontractor* is defined as "any person who, under the direction of a General Contractor, performs any work that impacts upon the structural integrity of the structure or addition," including repairs, alterations, dismantling, or additions that exceed the threshold limits contained in the state's general statutes and agency regulations.

A reputable general contractor's organization must have the ability to perform estimation, procurement, scheduling and planning, contract administration, accounting services, and general administration.

The general contractor must have operating capital and the financial strength to provide bonding if and when requested by the owner. After winning a bid or successfully negotiating a contract, the general contractor is left alone in the construction arena. She or he must perform and complete the project on time and under budget, or it may be the last project the general contractor will ever do. The total dependency on the selected subcontractors and vendors for delivery of materials and services can make or break the project. It is therefore absolutely necessary for the general contractor to study the drawings and specifications in order to accomplish his or her goal: the construction of a safe and profitable project.

Provision of the means and methods of construction, guarantees and warranties, quality control, and safety measures is the fundamental responsibility of the general contractor.

In addition, the general contractor must comply with local laws and ordinances; obtain permits; provide shop drawings, equipment cuts, and material samples;

provide underpinning and shoring drawings and calculations, if required; provide fastening devices; effect overall construction coordination with other trades; provide workforce; prepare reports; prepare requisitions; plan the project; prepare and submit schedules; and provide general project supervision and administration.

All the foregoing is the general contractor's responsibility. The subcontractor is a "mini" general contractor and as such must perform the same tasks as the general contractor, but only within the subcontractor's own trade.

In conjunction with the construction team, a well-organized general contractor or construction manager will administrate and maintain project documents for years to come.

DOCUMENTS AT THE CONSTRUCTION SITE

To properly manage any construction project, seven basic categories of documents are required: design documents, contracts, submittals, contractor claims and credit documents, logs, schedules, and correspondence. The essence of the first six categories of these documents is highlighted below.

Design Documents

- Design drawings (signed and sealed) by the architect, structural engineer and mechanical engineer, and other consultants.
- Sketches issued by the architect, structural engineer and mechanical engineer, and other consultants.
- Specifications issued by the architect, structural engineer and mechanical engineer, and other consultants.

Contracts

- Contract with the owner—Executed official agreement between owner and construction manager, or between owner and general contractor.
- Subcontracts—Executed official agreements between owner and subcontractors, or with owner's agent, the construction manager and subcontractors, or general contractor and subcontractors.
- Purchase orders—Executed official authorizations to purchase certain materials and labor required for the project.
- Letters to and from all parties involved in the project.
- All documented communication (faxes, e-mails, memoranda, transmittals, etc.).

Submittals

- Shop drawings prepared by individual subcontractors, suppliers, and/or manufacturers providing labor and/or material to the project. They illustrate how their product is built and accomplishes the intended design function. Drawings are submitted to the general contractor or construction manager, who then submits them to the architect and/or engineers for review and approval for project conformance.

- Manufacturers' cuts or data sheets pertaining to the material and equipment made by the manufacturer which will be incorporated into the project. These are also submitted to the general contractor or construction manager for project conformance prior to their submission to the architect and/or engineers for review and approval.

Contractor Claims and Credit Documents

Daily Work Report forms are used by the general contractor or construction manager to verify the worker-hours and materials used to perform a subcontractor's work. These report forms are essential when a subcontractor states that work performed constitutes an addition to the contracted scope of work.

Backcharge Order forms of the general contractor or construction manager are used to verify the worker-hours and materials used to perform work which was included in a subcontractor's scope of work but had to be performed by others; or to verify work required to repair damage caused by another subcontractor.

Subcontractor and Vendor Claims are for extra costs incurred over and above the actual contract or purchase order amount due to work or material provided that was beyond the original scope of the contract or purchase order. These claims can be billed on a time-and-material basis with the accompanying Daily Work Report form, or billed on a lump-sum or unit-price basis.

Credits or Backcharges are requests for reduction in the costs owed a subcontractor or vendor for work or material eliminated, reduced by design, or to be performed or supplied by others. This includes the recovery of costs to repair damage to the work of other trades caused by a subcontractor. Credit or backcharge requests can be billed on a time-and-material basis with accompanying Backcharge Order forms, or on a lump-sum or unit-price basis.

Approved Change Orders are prepared as the legal, written adjustment to the subcontract or purchase order once a claim or credit is agreed to with a subcontractor or vendor. This form must be signed by the contractor or vendor and countersigned by the owner or general contractor or construction manager.

Anticipated Cost Report provides a financial overview of the project. It compares the original budget against the actual costs of contracts and purchase orders, claims, credits, change orders, and future anticipated costs not yet incurred or not yet received.

Logs.   Numerous logs are required to properly track and manage a construction project. Logs are used to track the processing of documents and building department processes, or to report on the status of material test report results, material status, etc. Although the logs required for each project may vary, the following are examples of typical logs used:

Daily Work Report is used to record daily weather conditions, subcontractor workforce, activities and material deliveries to the site. It also records visitors to the project and unusual incidents pertaining to the work. (See Tables 1.6 and 1.7.)

Permit Log is used to track the expiration dates of required building department and highway department permits. (See Table 1.8.)

Insurance Log is used to track receipt of contractor's insurance certificates, insurance amounts, and policy expiration dates. (See Table 1.9.)

Contract Log is used to track contracts, letters of intent, drafts, and status of each individual contract or purchase order. (See Table 1.10.)

Bond Log is used to track the receipt of required material and performance bonds requested from contractors and/or subcontractors.

Change Order Log is used to track the issuance and signing of change orders.

Material Status Log is used to track the status of required materials. It indicates whether the materials are approved and/or released, when they are required, and how recently the delivery date was confirmed.

Submittal Log This log is utilized by the construction manager/general contractor to track all submissions from contractors through design team. Submissions include shop drawings, catalog cuts (manufacturer's literature), and samples. To the construction manager/general contractor it is important to monitor the number of days a submission has been held at the design team's offices. The architect/engineer should be contacted immediately if a submission is being held for longer than 14 days (see Table 1.11).

Concrete Cylinder Strength Log is used to track laboratory strength tests performed on concrete cylinder samples taken from the project. (See Table 1.12.)

Mortar Cube Strength Log is used to track laboratory strength tests performed on mortar cube samples taken from the job site.

Concrete Stripping Log is used to track actual pours versus the anticipated pour schedule, as well as when shores can be removed, when stairs are poured, and the status of grinding and patching.

Winter Concrete Log is used to record daily temperatures, projected low temperatures, and whether winter concrete procedures were implemented.

Building Department Signoff Log is used to track processing and signoff of controlled inspections, fire alarm filing and inspection, elevator filing and inspection, etc., which are all required by the building department.

Turnover Log is used to track the receipt and turnover of warranties, guarantees, attic stock, operating and maintenance manuals, "as-built" drawings, etc.

A sample Warranty/Guarantee/Attic Stock Log is shown in Table 1.13.

Schedules.   Various schedules are maintained at the site.

Contract schedule is a base schedule for the entire project which represents the schedule agreed to by the owner and general contractor or construction manager that is to be met or bettered.

Working schedule is a schedule used by the general contractor or construction manager on a day-to-day basis for the entire project. It is kept current to reflect actual work duration and projections and is typically more detailed than the base contract schedule mentioned above.

Working "mini" schedule, a small working schedule, pertains to specific phases of the work rather than to the entire project. These mini schedules cover such aspects of the work as excavation and foundations, or drywall framing and sheetrock. The schedules are used for review with the subcontractors and are generally more "aggressive" than the base contract schedule.

The foregoing is a summary of the documents typically used to manage a construction project. Although specific requirements vary from project to project, the documents described above should only vary slightly.

REVIEW OF PROJECT HISTORY

The entire history of a project, as well as adherence to the design requirements, can be reconstructed by the forensic engineer by carefully studying the following records.

Contract documents
>   Drawings—dates and revisions
>   Specifications—dates and revisions
>   Addenda or bulletins
>   Contracts and riders

Construction field documents
>   Site mobilization plan
>   Permits
>   Site safety plan
>   Schedules
>   Daily reports
>   Correspondence
>   Logs
>   Claims
>   Violations, if any

Pictures

Surveys

Mill certificates

Material conformance certifications

Work progress records

Weekly, monthly reports

Requisitions

Controlled inspections

Quality control

Photographs of partial work in place

Substantial and final completion records

Signoffs, as per jurisdictional requirements

Temporary Certificate of Occupancy and/or Certificate of Occupancy

All "as-built" drawings, warranties, and guarantees

Punch list items

When a failure occurs, an experienced forensic investigator should be able to draw some conclusions by examining the aforementioned material. It is also essential to investigate postconstruction developments, if any, such as tenant complaints, frequent repairs, leaks, visible cracks, settlements, or movements reported. Nothing should be ignored when one is investigating a collapse or failure. Focus should not be limited to the materials used, or to structural analysis, but should extend to the means and methods of the contractor.

APPROVAL, ACCEPTANCE, AND CERTIFICATIONS

There is a continuing debate among the design profession, construction industry, the private sector, and government agencies as to the use of the word *approval* for construction-related items.

The structural engineer is often requested to review, but should not "approve," items that are not directly designed or supervised by the SER of the project. Some examples are contractor-initiated designs, material test results, shoring, temporary bracing, underpinning, and scheduling. The SER has a fiduciary responsibility to the client to perform these professional services and to pass judgment on the acceptability of the items for inclusion in the project. By accepting the reviewed items, the SER in effect states that these items are accepted as "fitness for purpose" and will serve the client for the intended use.

The structural engineer should not be in the position to certify or guarantee manufacturer's equipment or items constructed by a contractor.

This chapter represents the design and constructions process of a project. The forensic engineer should be aware of the various stages and responsibilities that are associated with the achievement of a constructed structure. Knowledge, eperience, and professional manner are paramount in the discovery of causes of a failure, which, when properly documented, will be invaluable to designers and constructors for the prevention of similar failures in the future.

TABLE 1.1 Council of American Structural Engineers Design Criteria Checklist

Project: Project Manager: Reviewer:

Project No.:   Engineer: Date:

Item	✔ Yes	✔ No	✔ N/A	Comment
I. Building Code				
A. Have we determined which building code is applicable to this project?				
B. Have we determined if there are any special design provisions mandated by local building officials?				
C. Type of construction determined?				
D. Occupancy determined?				
E. Fire assemblies supplied by architect for floor, roof, ceiling, and walls?				
F. Wind speed verified?				
G. Seismic zone verified?				
H. Dead loads verified with architect's drawings for materials utilized in floor, roof, and walls?				
I. Live loads verified with architect's drawings for occupancy and usage?				
J. Roof loads verified with building code?				
K. Have thermal loads been considered?				
L. Is design to be based on ICBO evaluation reports?				
II. Client-Supplied Information				
A. Geotechnical engineer retained by owner and soils report provided?				
B. Architect/client set budget for structural elements of project?				
C. Architect/client supply dimensioned floor plans and elevations in hardcopy format?				
D. Architect/client furnish mechanical equipment sizes, locations, and weights?				
E. Architect/client supplied site grading plan?				

Project: Project Manager: Reviewer:

Project No.:   Engineer: Date:

Item	✔ Yes	✔ No	✔ N/A	Comment
F. Architect/client provide special drawing standards and/or CAD format requirements?				
G. Architect/client provided drawings of adjacent structures?				
H. Have drawings of adjacent structures been verified for accuracy?				
I. Architect/client requested provision for future expansion?				
J. Has the architect/client provided any vibration criteria?				
III. Structural System				
A. Is the structural system appropriate for the project?				
B. Have all material properties been determined?				
C. Does structural system satisfy architect's/client's requirement for vertical and horizontal constraints?				
D. Has architect/client been apprised of both vertical and lateral movement potential in structure?				
E. Has structure been designed in accordance with geotechnical report?				
F. Has the client been apprised of potential for foundation costs to increase due to unforeseen soil conditions?				
G. Does structure possess a definable load path for transmission of lateral loads to foundation?				
H. Do structural walls span in direction assumed in design of main lateral load-resisting system?				

TABLE 1.1 Council of American Structural Engineers Design Criteria Checklist (*Continued*)

Project: Project Manager: Reviewer:

Project No.:   Engineer: Date:

Item	✔ Yes	✔ No	✔ N/A	Comment
I. Have design criteria been determined and specified for all structural elements that are to be designed by specialty engineer?				
J. Was selection of structural system based upon economics?				
K. Did architect/client sign off on structural system employed?				
L. Was architect/client provided with design criteria for design of doors and windows for wind?				
M. Was design of any structural elements based upon any special field observation, inspection, or testing requirements?				
N. Are any uncommon material properties or strengths utilized in design of any elements?				
O. Has architect/client been apprised of vibration characteristics of structure?				
P. Have serviceability considerations been considered?				
1. Concrete crack control				
2. Corrosion considerations				
3. Materials shrinkage				
IV. Documents				
A. Have design criteria been specified on drawings, i.e., live loads, snow loads, etc.?				
B. Have all material properties been listed on drawings?				
C. Do specifications reference the proper building codes?				
D. Do calculations list all design criteria, building codes, and material properties utilized in design?				

TABLE 1.2 Council of American Structural Engineers Calculation Review Checklist

Project: Project Manager: Reviewer:

Project No.:   Engineer: Date:

Item	✔ Yes	✔ No	✔ N/A	Comment
I. General				
A. Are calculations dated, numbered, and initialed by designer?				
B. Have design criteria been included in calculations?				
C. Does design have any unusual features that should be noted?				
D. Does design, in general, meet design requirements of the architect and other professionals?				
E. Is design complete?				
F. Is method of resisting lateral loads noted?				
G. Have computer models been graphically verified?				
H. Is design required by contract for miscellaneous items such as stairs, handrails?				
I. Does design appear visually correct, i.e., larger spans have larger members?				
J. Does design need to be based on specific ICBO evaluation reports?				
II. Structural System				
A. Has a statement of economic factors influencing the selection of structural system been provided?				
B. Is structure designed to be modular with repeating elements where possible?				
C. Does structure meet stated fire requirements, including minimum sizes of steel members?				
D. Does structure fit within space limitations of building, including seated connections and concrete haunches?				

TABLE 1.2 Council of American Structural Engineers Calculation Review Checklist (*Continued*)

Project: Project Manager: Reviewer:

Project No.: Engineer: Date:

Item	✔ Yes	✔ No	✔ N/A	Comment
E. Has structure been evaluated based on possible future occupancies that will relocate partitions and corridors?				
III. Vertical Loads				
A. Verified that there are no circuitous support paths for framing members?				
B. Has weight of cladding been included in design of members?				
C. Is distribution of loads logical?				
D. Have uplift loads been considered and noted?				
IV. Lateral Loads				
A. Is there a clear load path for all loading to foundations?				
B. Are horizontal elements capable of transferring loads to vertical elements?				
C. Does distortion of frame appear to be consistent with configuration of structure and loadings?				
D. Have proper dead loads been used to determine base shear?				
E. Have diaphragms been properly designed?				
F. Have relative rigidities been considered?				
G. Have overturning forces been properly considered?				
H. Have tie-downs and uplift forces been adequately addressed?				
I. Have loads been properly applied?				
J. Are all exterior walls capable of withstanding both inward and outward forces?				

Project: Project Manager: Reviewer:

Project No.:   Engineer: Date:

Item	✔ Yes	✔ No	✔ N/A	Comment
K. Have correct factors for wind and seismic forces been used in frame and individual elements analysis?				
L. Have interior partitions been designed for horizontal loads including code minimums?				
M. Are large changes in mass or stiffness accounted for in analysis?				
N. Are discontinuities accounted for in lateral load-resisting system?				
O. Have story and building drifts been calculated?				
P. Are expansion joints consistent with calculated horizontal displacement and code requirements?				
Q. Have nonstructural elements, i.e., piping, ceiling, roof-mounted equipment, been designed to resist both seismic and wind loads?				
V. Foundation				
A. Do foundation loads match loadings assumed by soils engineer?				
B. Have earth pressures, including effect of surcharges and sloping fill, been included in design?				
C. Has correct assumption of use of active or passive forces been applied?				
D. Do all wall elements have adequate resistance through friction, cohesion, or passive pressures?				
E. Have hydrostatic forces been applied to the wall, or have adequate steps been taken to remove pressures?				
F. Was weight of soil slabs and superimposed loads included in design of footings?				

TABLE 1.2 Council of American Structural Engineers Calculation Review Checklist (*Continued*)

Project: Project Manager: Reviewer:

Project No.: Engineer: Date:

Item	✔ Yes	✔ No	✔ N/A	Comment
G. Are elevations of foundation consistent with recommendations in soils report?				
H. Has foundation settlement or heave been addressed in design?				
I. Have horizontal forces, applied to deep foundations, been adequately addressed?				
J. Does pile spacing match requirements for soils report and pile cap design?				
K. Has settlement of large fills, adjacent to rigid members, been assessed?				
L. Can both downward and upward loads be transmitted from pile cap to piles?				
VI. Concrete Design				
A. Have unbraced lengths been included in design of all columns?				
B. If members do not meet requirements for minimum size by ACI, have deflections been checked, based on cracked sections?				
C. Have major elements and highly repetitive members been checked using code moments?				
D. Have restraining effects of walls and footings been included in design?				
E. Have effects of temperature, creep, shrinkage, and elastic shorting been included in design? (*Note:* Pay particular attention to these items in prestressed structures.)				
F. Have bar splice and lap lengths for special conditions been calculated where required?				

TABLE 1.2 Council of American Structural Engineers Calculation Review Checklist (*Continued*)

Project: Project Manager: Reviewer:

Project No.:   Engineer: Date:

Item	✔ Yes	✔ No	✔ N/A	Comment
G. Have all edge beams been designed and reinforced for torsion?				
H. Have intermediate bars been provided for beams greater than 30 in deep?				
I. Have minimum stirrups been required?				
J. Are *d* values used, consistent with expected tolerances at project site?				
K. Does bar spacing meet both minimum and maximum spacings?				
L. In two-way slabs has correct *d* value been used in both directions?				
M. Have minimum steel requirements for beams, slabs, and walls been met?				
N. Has construction sequence been considered in design of backfilled walls?				
O. If steel percentage exceeds 50% of allowable, have beam and column intersections been investigated for interference?				
P. Are proper splices called for in columns where percentage of steel exceeds 4%?				
Q. Has length of top reinforcing in cantilevers been calculated to extend past point of inflection?				
R. Has effect of creep and shrinkage been calculated in cantilever sections?				
S. Has cover depth for reinforcing been correctly maintained throughout calculations?				
VII. Masonry Design				
A. Have height-to-thickness ratios been checked for unreinforced walls?				

TABLE 1.2 Council of American Structural Engineers Calculation Review Checklist (*Continued*)

Project: Project Manager: Reviewer:

Project No.:   Engineer: Date:

Item	✔ Yes	✔ No	✔ N/A	Comment
B. Are correct masonry ties specified to distinguish between a cavity wall and a veneer wall?				
C. Are design stresses consistent with level of inspection for project?				
D. Have deflections of masonry elements been limited to L/600 or other appropriate criteria?				
E. Have bond beams been provided to distribute large vertical loads?				
F. Has a distinction been made in calculations between stack bond and running bond for wall reinforcing?				
G. Have all openings in masonry walls been adequately designed for both vertical loads on lintel and horizontal loads on jambs?				
H. Have special requirements of local building codes such as South Florida Building Code been met?				
I. Are control joints spacing calculated and shown on documents?				
J. Are control joints located beyond lintel bearing to allow for arching action?				
VIII. Steel Design				
A. Have equipment loads been included in design of floor and roof members?				
B. Have members been designed and braced for uplift loads?				
C. Have unbraced lengths been checked for primary and secondary compression members and beams?				
D. Has floor system been checked for vibration?				
E. Has roof system been checked for ponding?				

Project: Project Manager: Reviewer:

Project No.:   Engineer: Date:

Item	✔ Yes	✔ No	✔ N/A	Comment
F. Has effect of deflection of members and frames been considered on all elements of building?				
G. Has web buckling been checked on deep members and members with concentrated loads?				
H. Are connection eccentricities consistent with design assumptions?				
I. Have torsional loads been considered?				
J. Have tension sections been reduced because of boltholes?				
K. Have purlins on sloping roofs been designed for unsymmetric loads?				
L. Are end bearing areas adequate?				
M. Have members subject to frequent stress reversals been designed for fatigue?				
N. Have weld sizes, lengths, and returns been designed?				
O. Have complicated connections been designed and detailed on drawings?				
P. Have trusses been designed to meet width requirements of highway shipping?				
Q. Are bolt types and weld materials specified consistent with design calculations?				
R. Have anchor bolt lengths been calculated for uplift forces?				
S. Has unbraced compression flange length been used for design of cooling tower beams and lintels?				
T. Has rotation of beam bearings been considered in calculations and drawings?				

TABLE 1.2 Council of American Structural Engineers Calculation Review Checklist (*Continued*)

Project: Project Manager: Reviewer:

Project No.:   Engineer: Date:

Item	✔ Yes	✔ No	✔ N/A	Comment
U. Are there any special requirements for steel deck imposed by noncode agencies such as Factory Mutual?				
IX. Steel Joist and Joist Girder Design				
A. Does span-to-depth ratio exceed minimum for floor and roofs?				
B. Are loads noted for cantilever ends?				
C. If joist and girders are part of lateral load-resisting system, is moment of inertia correct?				
D. Has adequate bearing been provided for ends of joist and girders?				
E. Have connection details been shown where both joists and beams are to bear on tops of columns?				
F. Are uplift forces noted for joist and girders?				
G. Have joists been checked for ponding?				
H. Has special equipment, such as basketball goals, folding partitions, and mechanical units, been included in design?				
X. Timber Design				
A. Are types and stress grades of lumber adequately defined?				
B. Have unbraced lengths and slenderness been checked?				
C. Have criteria for fire-resistant construction been met?				
D. Have deflections of members and frames been considered in design?				
E. Have repetition and duration loads been considered in design?				
F. Have nailing schedules been calculated, or are code schedules adequate?				

TABLE 1.2 Council of American Structural Engineers Calculation Review Checklist (*Continued*)

Project: Project Manager: Reviewer:

Project No.:   Engineer: Date:

Item	✔ Yes	✔ No	✔ N/A	Comment
G. Have splices been kept to a minimum and do they occur at point of minimum stress?				
H. Have glue-laminated members been designed in accordance with Timber Construction Standard AITC 100?				
I. Have plywood walls, floors, and roofs been designed in accordance with American Plywood Association "Plywood Design Specifications"?				
J. Does design of connections adequately address direction of loads on individual members?				
K. Are forces at termination of truss bracing adequately resisted?				

TABLE 1.3 Council of American Structural Engineers Drawing Review Checklist

Project: Project Manager: Reviewer:

Project No.:   Engineer: Date:

Item	✔ Yes	✔ No	✔ N/A	Comment
I. General Drawing Format				
A. Title block: Sheet tiles match drawing list?				
B. Date, column no., and initials correct?				
C. Drawing numbers correct?				
D. Graphic scales included, if required?				
E. Firm's name stamp, if applicable?				
F. P.E. stamp, if applicable?				
G. Do plans show north arrow for orientation?				
H. Do title blocks match prime consultant's (project name, location, font, etc.)?				
II. Site Plan/Structural Coordination				
A. Verified from site plans that new or old underground utilities (power, telephone, water, sewer, gas storm drainage, fuel line, grease traps, fuel tanks) have been checked for interference with foundation?				
B. Verified property line and location of foundations and footings in relation to property lines/adjacent structure foundations?				
C. Checked retaining walls for location, height, and bearing condition?				
D. Checked old survey, if available, to determine if site has been filled in?				
E. Is there a geotechnical report and are recommendations included in design?				
III. Architectural/Structural				
A. Are all dimensions checked for consistency in themselves and in agreement with architectural drawings?				

Project: Project Manager: Reviewer:

Project No.:   Engineer: Date:

Item	✔ Yes	✔ No	✔ N/A	Comment
B. Verified property line dimensions on site plan against architectural drawings?				
C. Verified column lines on structural and architectural drawings?				
D. Verified all column locations and orientation are same on structural and architectural drawings?				
E. Verified perimeter slab on structural matches architectural?				
F. Verified all depressed or raised areas of slabs are indicated?				
G. Verified slab elevations?				
H. Verified perimeter roof line and slope with architectural roof plan?				
I. Verified all expansion joint locations against architectural drawing?				
J. Verified location of control joints in walls?				
K. Checked architectural drawings for lintels that are required, particularly in non-load-bearing walls?				
L. Checked for folding suspended partitions and their support?				
M. Designed stairs and landings and coordinated with architect?				
N. Coordinated elevator cells				
1. Shelf angles				
2. Divider beam				
3. Max. spacing of guiderail supports				
4. Hoist beam in penthouse				
5. Elevator beams				
O. Coordinated wall sections?				
P. Verified that brick ledges are properly shown?				

TABLE 1.3 Council of American Structural Engineers Drawing Review Checklist (*Continued*)

Project: Project Manager: Reviewer:

Project No.:   Engineer: Date:

Item	✔ Yes	✔ No	✔ N/A	Comment
IV. Mechanical/Electrical and Plumbing/Structural				
A. Checked storm drain system against structural floor and foundation plan?				
B. Checked HVAC floor plans against structural for floor and wall openings?				
C. Checked that all structural supports required for mechanical equipment are indicated on structural drawings?				
D. Verified all roof penetrations (ducts, etc.) have framing to support adjacent structure?				
E. Checked underground utility line locations for interference with foundations?				
F. Verified that toilet layout and penetrations do not conflict with beams and joist (both steel and concrete)?				
G. Does imbedded conduit conform to ACI 318?				
H. Checked light fixture interference with structural framing?				
V. Structural Drawings				
A. Are notes complete, showing design criteria, building code references, floor loads, material strengths, and allowable foundation pressure?				
B. Are requirements for special inspections included?				
C. Do drawings conform to design calculations and sketches?				
D. Are notes consistent with sections and details?				
E. Do notes provide necessary design information for prefabricated items?				

Project: Project Manager: Reviewer:

Project No.:   Engineer: Date:

Item	Yes ✔	No ✔	N/A ✔	Comment
F. Are dowels, brackets, and keys provided for future expansion in scope of work?				
G. Is nomenclature used throughout all drawings and specifications?				
H. Is list of abbreviations shown?				
I. Are floor and roof elevations given?				
VI. Preengineered Building				
A. Is a note included that foundations for preengineered buildings or for equipment shall not be placed until design loads and anchor bolt sizes and arrangement have been submitted on shop drawings and approved?				
B. Is the MBMA *Design Practices Manual* referenced for metal buildings?				
C. Are metal buildings required to be designed for unusual dead loads such as ventilation equipment, sprinkler system piping, ceilings, cranes?				
D. Is erection under observation of engineer of record or other registered engineers?				
E. Are design reactions shown on plan?				
F. Is manufacturer required to submit loads for building?				
G. Is it noted that shear devices are to be provided by metal building manufacturer?				
H. Is it noted that anchor bolt size, length, and location must be provided by metal building manufacturer?				

Project: Project Manager: Reviewer:

Project No.:   Engineer: Date:

Item	✔ Yes	✔ No	✔ N/A	Comment
I. Have appropriate sideway criteria been shown?				
VII. Foundations				
A. Are all footings located to provide concentric loading as closely as possible?				
B. Is footing schedule used for continuous wall footings and individual footings?				
C. Are tops of footing elevations shown?				
D. Are foundations placed at proper depth for frost line?				
E. Are all footing steps shown?				
F. Is standard footing step shown?				
G. Is there any top reinforcing in continuous footing? If so, note in standard detail.				
H. Are concrete piers required for structural steel columns?				
I. Are footings lowered near elevator/escalator pits to distribute bearing pressure below pits?				
J. Do elevator/escalator pits have sumps?				
K. Are water stops shown?				
L. Are all special notes requiring bracing and shoring included?				
M. Is wall reinforcing coordinated?				
N. Is basement wall backfill noted to be placed after lower slab and frame slab are in place?				
O. Is special detail for base of basement wall and slab on grade shown?				
P. Is footing steel located in bottom for spread footings and on top and bottom for combined footings?				

Project: Project Manager: Reviewer:

Project No.:   Engineer: Date:

Item	✔ Yes	✔ No	✔ N/A	Comment
Q. Provided supplementary reinforcing at wall penetrations and interruptions?				
R. Compare wall steel and wall height. Is more steel required for higher walls?				
S. Does foundation wall require steel in both faces?				
T. Are expansion joints in stems of retaining walls shown?				
U. Are backfill and drainage fill properly indicated?				
VIII. Drilled Piers				
A. Pier diameter shown?				
B. Bell diameter shown?				
C. Pier vertical reinforcing:				
1. Size, quantity, and length shown?				
2. Splices permitted?				
3. Staggered?				
4. Splices required?				
5. Dowels—size, quantity, length, and embedment length into pier—shown?				
D. Dowel or anchor bolt template details shown?				
E. Top of pier elevation noted?				
F. Pier bid quantities established?				
G. Pier cap size and reinforcement determined?				
H. Test holes—reference made to geotechnical?				
I. Typical pier details shown?				
IX. Pile Foundations				
A. Are pile specification requirements and pile sizes given in notes? Diameter and length for bidding?				

TABLE 1.3 Council of American Structural Engineers Drawing Review Checklist (*Continued*)

Project: Project Manager: Reviewer:

Project No.:   Engineer: Date:

Item	✔ Yes	✔ No	✔ N/A	Comment
B. Is pile capacity noted?				
C. Are concrete piles tied into footings with extended pile reinforcing?				
D. Are load-test piles shown?				
E. Are pile cutoff elevations indicated?				
F. Are pile splice details provided?				
G. Are single piles tied in two directions?				
H. Are two pile groups tied in two directions?				
X. Concrete Construction				
A. Type of splice or lap (A,B) splices or lap lengths shown?				
B. Are corner bars called out?				
C. If seismic detailing is required, has Appendix A ACI-318 been checked?				
D. Are column ties used in added column/beam or column/beam slab joints?				
E. Are accessories galvanized or plastic-tipped?				
F. Are stainless steel accessories used for sand-blasted or bash-hammered concrete?				
G. Is reinforcing in spandrel beams properly sized and detailed?				
H. Do lateral resisting frames have hooked and continuous bottom reinforcing?				
I. Do beam top bars extend into slab where possible?				
J. Are minimum cover requirements shown?				
K. Is corrosion-resistant reinforcing required?				

Project: Project Manager: Reviewer:

Project No.:   Engineer: Date:

Item	✔ Yes	✔ No	✔ N/A	Comment
L. Are classes of concrete for the various items of work shown in notes?				
M. Are specifications for reinforcing steel included in notes?				
N. Are base courses and capillary water barriers shown under floor slabs on grade and checked with foundation design criteria?				
O. Are slab-on-grade floor thicknesses given?				
P. Are crack control joints located in an interior and an exterior slab on grade?				
Q. Is a thickened slab on grade provided under masonry partitions?				
R. Are reentrant corners of floor slab cutouts noted?				
S. Is concrete cover over reinforcing shown or noted?				
T. Has reinforcement in slabs been specified in general notes or drawings for slab on grade and/or pan joist construction?				
U. Are depressed slabs shown for tile floors, etc.?				
V. Are cross-sectional details of depressed slabs shown with reinforcing details?				
W. Are perimeter felt joints and premolded joint filler correctly located and called out?				
X. Has reinforcing steel been detailed to avoid congestion? In beam/column joints?				
Y. Has steel been detailed to avoid lengths of bars extending from joints?				

Project: Project Manager: Reviewer:

Project No.:   Engineer: Date:

Item	✔ Yes	✔ No	✔ N/A	Comment
Z. Are diagonal bars provided at openings in walls, floors, and roof?				
AA. Have construction joints been provided for stairs so they may be constructed after floors are in place?				
AB. Is reinforcing on proper face for walls and slabs?				
XI. Masonry Construction				
A. Is value of f'_m specified?				
B. Are control joints spaced as required?				
C. Will all walls with reinforcing have cells at least 2 in × 2 in? Are cells with reinforcing filled with grout, not mortar?				
D. Are bar laps specified?				
E. Are lintel details provided for all openings?				
F. Have wall cores been solidly grouted at jambs?				
G. Have details of nonstandard construction been provided, e.g., bond beam intersections at different levels?				
H. Are locations of intermediate bond beams shown on sections and wall elevations?				
I. Has steel angle lintel schedule been used?				
J. Are shelf angels required for brick? Properly located and anchored?				
K. Are anchors for floor/roof joists, beams, etc., properly located and detailed?				
L. Are control joints placed beyond lintel bearings to allow for arching?				

Project: Project Manager: Reviewer:

Project No.:   Engineer: Date:

Item	✔ Yes	✔ No	✔ N/A	Comment
XII. Structural Steel				
A. Are materials required clearly shown or called for in general notes?				
1. Steel—different for beams and columns?				
2. Bolt size, number, type?				
3. Anchor bolts?				
B. Are structural steel connections to concrete or masonry shown?				
C. Are anchor bolt lengths shown?				
D. Are stud connectors for concrete slab connections to steel beams shown?				
E. Are member forces, axial loads, and end reactions shown for all connections to be designed by fabricator?				
F. Are gusset plate thicknesses given? Are all welds shown by AWS symbols?				
G. Are stress diagrams given for trusses that are not shown with detailed connections?				
H. Are purlin and grit connections shown?				
I. Do the purlin and grit connections prevent purlin overturning on sloped roofs and sidewalls?				
J. Are openings trammed to carry wind loads?				
K. Columns—are the following shown?				
1. Elevations, bottom of baseplate				
2. Number, size, length, and orientation of anchor bolts				
3. Baseplate size, orientation, *and* connection to column				

Project: Project Manager: Reviewer:

Project No.:   Engineer: Date:

Item	✔ Yes	✔ No	✔ N/A	Comment
4. Size				
5. Steel grade				
6. Milled surfaces				
7. Column cap detail				
8. Splice details				
L. Beams—are the following shown?				
1. Elevation to top of beam				
2. Size				
3. Steel grade				
4. Connection				
5. Stud size, length after welding, spacing				
6. Camber (if any)				
7. Brick plates (if any)				
8. Are spandrel beams subject to corrosion?				
9. Splice details				
M. Steel connections—are the following shown?				
1. All weld sizes, lengths, and types				
2. Electrode type must be shown				
3. Bolts				
Size				
Grade				
Friction				
Bearing				
Threads in shear plane				
4. Wrench clearance				
XIII. Timber Construction				
A. Are grades of timber shown in notes?				
B. Is nailing schedule shown or called for by notes or reference to code or applicable criteria?				

Project: Project Manager: Reviewer:

Project No.:   Engineer: Date:

Item	✔ Yes	✔ No	✔ N/A	Comment
C. Are bolt sizes and types clearly indicated and large washers required to avoid crushing of wood?				
D. Are adequate details shown; or if not shown, is design by contractor required to meet National Design Specifications for Stress Grade Lumber and Its Fastenings?				
E. Are required lateral bracing blocking and bridging details called for on drawings?				
F. Are beams blocked at bearings to prevent warping?				
G. Are contractor-furnished trusses required to comply with requirements of Design Specification for Light Metal Plate Connected Wood Trusses, published by Truss Plate Institute?				
H. Are loads shown or specified for trusses to be contractor-designed?				
I. Have plywood grades been clearly identified and the usage specified?				
J. Are wood framing connectors shown?				
XIV. Steel Decking				
A. Are gages and depths of metal decking shown on plans?				
B. Continuous over three spans? If not, check single spans and two-span design. (Note on drawing if three spans required.)				
C. Are required structural properties of floor and roof decking provided and coordinated with project specifications?				
D. Is attachment pattern specified? Side laps, end laps/standard?				

TABLE 1.3 Council of American Structural Engineers Drawing Review Checklist (*Continued*)

Project: Project Manager: Reviewer:

Project No.:   Engineer: Date:

Item	✔ Yes	✔ No	✔ N/A	Comment
E. Is decking supported at columns?				
F. Is continuous edge angle provided at perimeter of metal roof deck?				
G. Is deck finish indicated?				
H. Are sheet-metal pour stops shown?				
I. Support provided for deck openings?				
Staggered?				
Splices required?				
Dowels—size, quantity, length and embedment length into pier—shown?				
XV. Open-Web Steel Joist				
A. Is alignment of panel points called out in notes?				
B. Ceiling extension (bottom chord) required?				
C. Depth of bearing end shown?				
D. Size and spacing shown?				
E. Type of bridging and spacing?				
F. Special connection required when joist frames into column flange or web?				
G. Is bracing for continuous beams at bottom flange required by extending bottom chord angles?				

Project: Project Manager: Reviewer:

Project No.:   Engineer: Date:

Item	✔ Yes	✔ No	✔ N/A	Comment
I. General				
A. Is general contractor's review stamp present and signed on all sheets?				
B. Have all sheets been entered into submittal log?				
C. Have all sheets been reviewed for general completeness immediately upon receipt?				
D. Have dimensions given on structural drawings been verified on submittals?				
E. Have any unusual or questionable conditions been reviewed by a senior engineer?				
F. Have all submittals required by contract documents been provided?				
G. Do general notes on shop drawings agree with structural drawings and specifications?				
H. Have submittals been reviewed/returned within firm's general policy time period?				
II. Concrete Formwork (if Required)				
A. Has dimensional layout of elements been reviewed?				
B. Have shoring/reshoring requirements been submitted for information purposes?				
III. Mild Reinforcing				
A. Have size, quantity, spacing, and layout been reviewed?				
B. Has steel grade(s) been reviewed?				
C. Have lap lengths, stagger, and locations been reviewed?				
D. Have reinforcing lengths been spot-checked?				

TABLE 1.4 Council of American Structural Engineers Submittal Review Checklist (*Continued*)

Project: Project Manager: Reviewer:

Project No.:   Engineer: Date:

Item	✔ Yes	✔ No	✔ N/A	Comment
E. Have configurations (hooks, offset bends, ties, stirrups) been reviewed?				
F. Have chair heights and cover been reviewed?				
G. Have shop drawing details been confirmed with appropriate (structural/architectural) drawing details?				
H. Have epoxy coatings and galvanizing requirements been confirmed for reinforcement and accessories?				
IV. Posttensioning				
A. Have loss calculations been reviewed prior to shop drawing review?				
B. Has tendon layout been confirmed based on actual tendon forces?				
C. Is tendon-stressing sequence appropriate?				
D. Are certified mill reports provided?				
E. Has construction joint layout been reviewed?				
F. Are all tendons accessible for stressing?				
G. Are tendon profiles and chair heights correct?				
H. Have chair heights and cover been reviewed?				
I. Have shop drawing details been confirmed with all structural drawing details?				
J. Have epoxy coatings and galvanizing requirements been confirmed for reinforcement and accessories?				
K. Are placing sequences appropriate?				
V. Precast Concrete				
A. Are all loadings correct?				

TABLE 1.4 Council of American Structural Engineers Submittal Review Checklist (*Continued*)

Project: Project Manager: Reviewer:

Project No.: Engineer: Date:

Item	Yes ✔	No ✔	N/A ✔	Comment
B. Are element depths and sizes correct?				
C. Is fire rating correct?				
D. Is general layout correct?				
E. Are connections to primary structural frame appropriate?				
F. Do plank details allow for necessary diaphragm action?				
G. Do details allow for adequate load transfer to supporting elements?				
H. Are drawings certified by a registered P.E. in project's jurisdiction?				
I. Have certified calculations been reviewed?				
J. Have unusual loadings been included (partitions and equipment pads)?				
K. Are steel coatings (epoxy and galvanizing) correct?				
L. Are embeds in correct locations?				
M. Have opening and notch sizes and locations been verified with architectural, mechanical, and electrical drawings?				
VI. Structural Steel				
A. Have certified calculations and connection drawings been submitted if required by contract documents?				
B. Are steel grades correct for each element?				
C. Are shear stud sizes, type, length, quantity, and layout correct?				
D. Are baseplate elevations, column top elevations, and top of beam elevations correct?				
E. Is camber correct for each beam?				

Project: Project Manager: Reviewer:

Project No.:   Engineer: Date:

Item	✔ Yes	✔ No	✔ N/A	Comment
F. Are connections capable of supporting design loadings including:				
1. Anchor bolt quantity, type, size, and spacing?				
2. High-strength bolt type, quantity, size, and spacing?				
3. Welding material, size and type of welds, location, and sequence?				
4. Connection angles and plate sizes?				
5. Primary connecting element capacity?				
G. Is the correct number of elements framed into each particular connection?				
H. Are all primary elements shown on erection drawings the correct size, elevation, and orientation?				
I. Are all connections consistent with specific details shown on structural drawings?				
J. Is surface preparation (bare steel, shop primer, galvanizing) correct?				
K. Are all elements that are shown on erection drawings present in individual component fabrication drawings?				
L. Have element lengths been spot-checked?				
M. Are all seismic connections and elements in conformance with structural drawings?				
N. Are welder certificates current (last 24 months) and appropriate for type of welding?				
VII. Open-Web Joists				
A. Are joist sizes and spacing correct?				

Project: Project Manager: Reviewer:

Project No.:   Engineer: Date:

Item	✔ Yes	✔ No	✔ N/A	Comment
B. Have critical lengths been spot-checked?				
C. Are bridging types, sizes, and spacing correct?				
D. Are details consistent with structural drawings?				
E. Are ceiling extensions provided, if required?				
F. Are bearing depths and elevations consistent with structural drawings?				
G. Are weld sizes and lengths at bearing details adequate?				
H. Are sizes consistent with any fire assembly rating requirements?				
I. Is surface preparation correct?				
J. If calculations have been provided, are they consistent with shop drawings?				
K. Are cambers in accordance with structural drawings?				
L. If required by contract documents, are joists supplied by a member of SJI?				
M. If "special design" joists are supplied, are fabricator's design loadings consistent with structural drawings?				
N. If concentrated loads are supported off joists, are they located at panel points?				
O. If concentrated loads are not located at panel points, are adequate diagonal elements provided?				
VII. Steel Deck				
A. Are deck gages correct?				
B. Are depths, span direction, and type correct?				

Project: Project Manager: Reviewer:

Project No.:   Engineer: Date:

Item	✔ Yes	✔ No	✔ N/A	Comment
C. Are steel grades correct?				
D. Are span conditions (1, 2, or 3 spans) correct?				
E. Is deck finish correct?				
F. Are deck supports and side lap welds and fasteners correct?				
G. Are pour stop gages, type, and dimensions correct?				
H. Are all details consistent with structural drawings?				
I. If deck shoring is required, is it shown?				
J. Is required reinforcing shown at openings?				
K. If required by contract documents, is deck supplier a member of SDI?				
L. Are all overhang conditions adequate or otherwise in conformance with structural drawings?				
M. Are necessary accessories (closures, ridge/valley plates, clips, and straps) indicated?				
N. Are all opening requirements indicated and coordinated with architectural, mechanical, and electrical drawings?				
IX. Timber				
A. Glulam lumber				
1. Are sizes and configurations correct?				
2. Are lumber grades and grading method consistent with structural drawings?				
3. Are pressure treatments correct?				
4. Are cambers correct?				
5. Are connections consistent with structural drawings?				

Project: Project Manager: Reviewer:

Project No.:   Engineer: Date:

Item	✔ Yes	✔ No	✔ N/A	Comment
6. Have lengths been spot-checked?				
7. Are elevations correct?				
8. If required, are certified calculations consistent with shop drawings?				
9. If required, are certified shop drawings provided?				
10. If required, is an AITC certificate present on drawings?				
B. Wood Trusses				
1. Are sizes, spacings, and configuration correct?				
2. Are accompanying calculations using the proper loadings on top and bottom chords?				
3. Do shop drawings indicate proper loadings?				
4. Have concentrated loads been verified with all drawings (architectural, mechanical, electrical)?				
5. Have lengths been spot-checked?				
6. Are all shop drawing general notes consistent with contract documents?				
7. Are connector plate sizes indicated?				
8. Is end bearing condition detailed?				
9. Is bracing shown and detailed?				
10. Are wood species and treatment as specified?				
11. Are submittals sealed and certified by licensed engineer in appropriate state?				

TABLE 1.5 Consultant's Shop Drawings Log

SHOP DRAWING REVIEW ACTION

A	No exceptions taken
B	Make corrections noted
C	Amend and resubmit
D	Rejected, see Remarks
E	Reviewed only for loads imposed on the structure

PROJECT:

PROJECT#:

TRADE: \qquad DETAILER:

DWG. #	Title	1st Submission			2nd Submission			3rd Submission		
		Date Rcvd.	Action	Date Retd.	Date Rcvd.	Action	Date Retd.	Date Rcvd.	Action	Date Retd.

TABLE 1.6 Daily Work Report Certification

Description of work_____
Location_____ Date(s) work performed_____
Performed by_____ Subcontractor's work ticket #(s)_____

Labor

Trade of employee	# of workers	Hour per	Total hours	Rate of pay	Amount

Material, supplies, and/or equipment

Material	Per	Quantity	Cost per	Amount

Complete description of work done this date	Total

IF APPLICABLE, THE FOLLOWING SUBCONTRACTOR SHALL BE BACKCHARGED:

THE INFORMATION CONTAINED ABOVE IS CORRECT. ALL WORK SUBJECT TO TERMS OF SUBCONTRACT AND PRIME CONTRACT.

SUBCONTRACTOR   OWNER'S OR (ARCH'T) REP.

(NAME)   (COMPANY)

BY _____   BY _____   BY _____

TITLE _____   TITLE _____   TITLE _____

TABLE 1.7 Daily Report

	JOB No.	SHEET ___ OF ___
	JOB NAME	WEATHER
	SUPT. NAME	TEMP. A.M. ___ P.M. ___

	CLASS	EMPLOYEE'S NAME	HOURS	COST CODE	EXPLANATION	TOTAL HOURS	RATE	AMOUNT
1								
2								
3								
4								
5								
6								
7								
8								
9								
10								
11								
12								
13								
14								
15								

SUBCONTRACTOR OPERATIONS

SUB'S NAME & WORKFORCE	WORK PERFORMED

REMARKS

MATERIAL RECEIVED	VISITORS

DATE_____ 19_____ DAY_____

PROJ. MGR. REPORT
INITIAL ____ No._____ SUPT. SIGNATURE_____
OVER W

TABLE 1.8 Construction Permit

Project name:

No.	Permit no.	Description	Location
.			

Contractor	Issued	Expires	Comment

TABLE 1.9   Insurance Log

INSURANCE REQUIREMENTS	SPECIFIED AMOUNT	BASE CONTRACTORS			
EMPLOYER'S LIABILITY + WORKERS' COMP.					
Statutory Limits					
Each Accident					
Disease–Policy Limit					
Disease–Each Employee					
Effective					
Expires					
GENERAL LIABILITY					
General Aggregate					
Products-Comp/OP Agg					
Personal & Adv Injury					
Each Occurrence					
Fire Damage (Ea.)					
Med. Exp. (Ea.)					
Effective					
Expires					
EXCESS UMBRELLA LIABILITY					
Each Occurrence					
Aggregate					
Effective					
Expires					
AUTOMOBILE LIABILITY					
Combined Single Limit					
Effective					
Expires					
ADDITIONAL INSUREDS					
COMMENTS					

GENERAL CONDITION CONTRACTORS

TABLE 1.10   Contract Award and Contract Tracking Log

1	2	3	4	5	6	7	8	9

1: Contractor   2: Contract amount
3: Trade   4: Request owner's approval to award
5: Obtain owner's approval   6: Award date
7: Letter of intent   8: Contract prepared on
9: Contract to owner for review

10	11	12	13	14	15	16

10: Owner comments or approval obtained   11: Contract to contractor
12: Return of executed contract   13: Contract to owner for execution
14: Return of executed contracts from owner   15: Distribute fully executed contracts
16: Remarks

TABLE 1.11 Submittal Log

1	2	3	4	5	6	7	8	9	10	11	12	13	14	15

1: Package number   2: Item number   7: CM to arch/eng   8: Days held
3: Contractor   4: Dwg # – item   9: Arch/eng to CM   10: Days held
5: Description   6: Contractor to CM   11: CM to contractor   12: Days held
                                           13: Total days held   14: Status
NET = No exceptions taken   AAN = Approved as noted   15: Comments
R+R = Revise and resubmit   REJ = Rejected

1.68

TABLE 1.12 Concrete Cylinder Reports

Project name _____   Date _____

Cyl. set #	Date poured	Level/area	Spec'd psi	7 Days' break	Lab. result	%	28 Days' break	Lab. result	%	Remarks

TABLE 1.13   Warranty/Guarantee/Attic Stock Log

Section	Specification	Contractor	Date work accepted	Period specified for guarantee/ warranty
02200	Exc. grading & filling			
02520	Concrete sidewalks			
02810	Irrigation performance			
02850	Wood sitework			
02860	Metal sitework			
02900	Landscape development			
02950	Site furnishings			
03300	Cast-in-place (foundations)			
03310	Cast/place conc. superstr.			
04200	Unit masonry			
04405	Ext. standing stonework			
05500	Metal fabrications			
05700	Ornamental metalwork			
05710	Ornamental railings			
05720	Exterior canopy			
06100	Rough carpentry			
06200	Finish carpentry			
07120	Mech rm waterproofing			
07125	Waterproof parking deck			
07140	Metallic waterproofing			
07160	Bitumin. dampproofing			
07200	Miscellaneous insulation			
07270	Firestopping			
07500	Roofing and sheet metal			
07920	Caulking and sealants			
08100	Hollow metal work			
08210	Wood doors			
08330	Rolling service doors			
08400	Ent. doors and storefront			
08520	Alum. windows & doors			
08700	Hardware			
08800	Glass and glazing			
09250	Gypsum wallboard			
09270	Gyp. brd. shaft wall sys.			
09300	Ceramic tile			
09510	Acoustic ceiling			
09550	Wood flooring			
09650	Resilient flooring & base			
09900	Painting			
09680	Carpet			
09950	Wall coverings			
10162	Toilet partitions			
10550	Postal specialties			
10800	Toilet specialties			
11172	Waste compactors			
11175	Chutes			
11900	Kitchen equipment			
12391	Kitchen cabinets			
14210	Passenger elevators			
14220	Wheelchair lifts			
15575	Boiler flue			
15000	HVAC			
15300	Fire sprinkler			
15400	Plumbing			
16000	Electrical			

Received	Date in effect	Date expires	Attic stock/ other	Received	Sent to owner	Signed by (owner's reps)

CHAPTER 2
DESIGN CODES AND STANDARDS

John F. Duntemann, P.E., S.E.

Code and standard requirements can be important elements in a forensic evaluation after a failure. Therefore, the forensic structural engineer has to be familiar with the provisions as well as the intent, and in some cases the history, of the governing code or standard. Since forensic investigators often deal with old structures, familiarity with and access to old codes are also valuable.

CODES AND STANDARDS IN THE UNITED STATES

The development of laws, rules, and regulations to provide for the safety and serviceability of buildings and structures in the United States is somewhat unique. In most countries, the national government oversees the regulatory development and enforcement process, which results in a single national code. In the United States, however, the development of building codes and standards has become a private-sector enterprise involving federal, state, and local government participation but with only minimal influence or control from these groups except as "users" in local enforcement.

Local building codes in the United States are patterned after the model building codes, which include the *National Building Code* by the Building Officials and Code Administrators (BOCA),[1] the *Uniform Building Code* by the International Conference of Building Officials (ICBO),[2] and the *Southern Standard Building Code* by the Southern Building Code Congress (SBCC).[3] A study conducted by the Council of American Building Officials (CABO) indicated that approximately 85 percent of all state and local governments have either directly adopted one of the three model codes or have patterned their regulations on the provisions of these documents.[4] The geographic region of influence of each of the model codes is illustrated in Fig. 2.1.

The promulgation of codes by the three model authorities is based on a consensus process. Any individual or industry organization may participate in the development of these codes and related deliberations. Industry tends to be heavily involved as code provisions have an obvious impact on the marketplace. The oft-

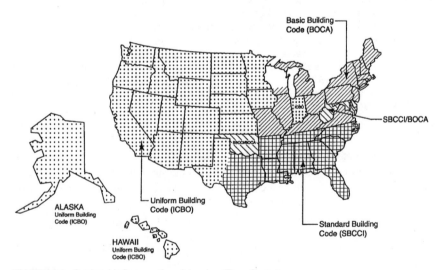

FIGURE 2.1 Regional influence of model codes. (From Perry.)

stated challenge is to develop provisions that provide an acceptable level of risk with respect to potential hazards and at the same time safeguard the economy.

The provisions set forth in the model building codes are only representations of possible regulations and do not become law until enacted by the authority having jurisdiction (state, county, city, etc.). Thus, these documents are usually modified to satisfy local laws and ordinances and to reflect local building practices. For example, the preface to the BOCA *National Building Code* states the following:

> Use of the *BOCA National Building Code* or any of the other *BOCA National Codes* within a government jurisdiction is intended to be accomplished only through adoption by reference in a proceeding of the jurisdiction's board, council, or other authoritative governing body. Additionally, jurisdictions may amend or modify *BOCA National Code* provisions to accomplish desired local requirements, although use of the codes in substantially original and standardized form is encouraged by the BOCA organization.

It is also noteworthy that most building codes use as standard references the code provisions or specifications published by the technical trade associations for each basic structural building material. As these provisions or specifications are not inherently legal documents, they require adoption by legislative bodies. Therefore, the model codes tend to lag behind the state of the art.

DESIGN STANDARDS AND THEIR RELATIONSHIP TO STRUCTURAL PERFORMANCE

If a failure occurs, a comparison of the structure, as it was actually built, with the requirements of applicable building code usually will be required. However, the adherence or nonadherence to building code requirements may or may not have a significant bearing on the assessment of the actual performance of the structure. Factors of safety, load factors, and assumptions regarding interaction between structural components used by designers may or may not reflect *actual* structural performance, but rather may reflect *intended* performance. A fundamental understanding of these engineering principles is a necessary prerequisite to any forensic investigation. The interaction of structural elements as they existed, rather than as they were conceived, must be considered. The properties of materials as they existed, rather than as they were assumed to exist in design, must be determined.

Structural Safety

There are three main reasons that some sort of safety factors, such as load and resistance factors, are necessary in structural design:

Variability in resistance. The actual strengths (*resistances*) of structural elements will almost always differ from their estimated values. The main causes of these differences are the variability of the material strengths; differences between the as-built and as-designed dimensions; and the effects of simplifying assumptions made in deriving the member resistance.

Variability in loading. All loads are variable, especially live loads and environmental loads due to snow, wind, or earthquakes. In addition to actual variations in the loads themselves, the assumptions and approximations made during the course of analysis may result in differences between the actual and estimated forces and moments. Due to the variabilities of resistance and load effects, there is a definite chance that a weaker-than-average structure may be subjected to a higher-than-average load. In extreme cases, failure may occur.

Consequences of failure. A number of factors must be considered in determining an acceptable level of safety for a particular class of structure. These considerations include such things as potential loss of life; lost time, lost revenue, or indirect loss of life or property due to a failure; type of failure, warning of failure, and/or existence of alternative load paths.

For example, the factor of safety for a public auditorium should be greater than the factor of safety for a storage building. Similarly, if the failure of a member is preceded by excessive deflections, as in the case of a flexural failure of a beam, then the persons endangered by the impending collapse will be warned and will have a chance to leave the building before failure. This may not be possible if a member fails suddenly without warning, as may be the case with reinforced concrete column. Thus, the required margin of safety may not need to be as high for a beam as for a column. In some structures, the yielding or failure of one member causes a redistribution of load to adjacent members; in other structures, the failure of one member causes complete collapse. If no redistribution is possible, a higher margin of safety is required.

Probabilistic Calculation of Safety Factors

Structural design should provide for adequate safety no matter what philosophy of design is used. Provision must be made for both *overload* and *understrength.* The study of what constitutes the proper formulation of structural safety has evolved over the past 30 years.[5] The main thrust has been to examine by various probabilistic methods the chances of failure, or limit, states to develop. *Limit states* are generally defined as those conditions of a structure at which it ceases to fulfill its intended function, and can be divided into two categories, *strength* and *serviceability.* Strength (i.e., safety) limit states are such behavioral phenomena as the onset of yielding, formation of a plastic hinge, overall frame or member instability, lateral-torsional buckling, local buckling, tensile fracture, and development of fatigue cracks. Serviceability limit states include unacceptable elastic deflections and drift, unacceptable vibrations, and permanent deformations. Design criteria should ensure that a limit state is violated only with an acceptably small probability, by selecting the load and resistance factors and nominal load and resistance values that will never be exceeded under the design assumptions.

Both the acting loads and the resistance (strength) of the structure to loads are variables that must be considered. In general, a thorough analysis of all uncertainties that might influence achieving a *limit state* is not practical, or perhaps even possible. The current approach to a simplified method using a probability-based assessment of structural safety uses first-order second-moment reliability methods.[6] Such methods assume that the load Q and the resistance R are random variables. Typical frequency distributions of such random variables are shown in Fig. 2.2. When the resistance R exceeds the load Q, there will be a margin of safety. Unless R exceeds Q by a large amount, there will be some probability that R may be less than Q, shown by the shaded portion where the R and Q curves overlap.

Structural failure (achievement of a limit state) may then be defined by comparing R with Q, or in logarithmic form by comparing $\ln(R/Q)$, as shown in Fig. 2.3. Failure corresponds to the crosshatched region on both figures. The distance between the failure line and the mean value of the function $[\ln(R/Q)]$ is defined as a multiple ß of the standard deviation σ of the function. The multiplier ß is called the *reliability index*. The larger ß, the greater the margin of safety.

As summarized by Pinkham,[7] the reliability index ß is useful in several ways:

1. It can indicate the consistency of safety for various components and systems using traditional design methods.

2. It can be used to establish new methods that will have consistent margins of safety.

3. It can be used to vary in a rational manner the margins of safety for those components and systems having a greater or lesser need for safety than that used in ordinary situations.

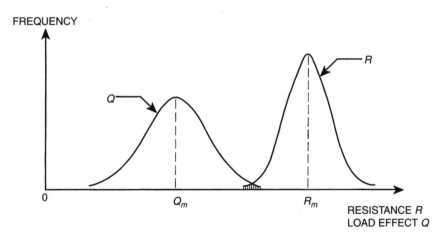

FREQUENCY

Q_m

R_m

RESISTANCE R
LOAD EFFECT Q

FIGURE 2.2 Frequency distribution of load effect Q and resistance R. (From AISC.)

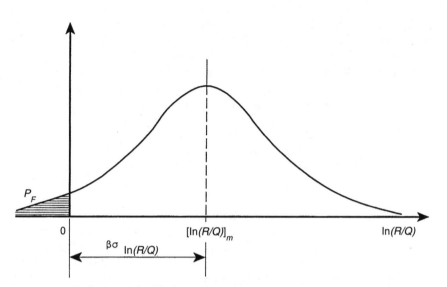

FIGURE 2.3   Definition of reliability index. (From AISC.)

ASD versus LRFD and USD

The *allowable stress design* (ASD) method can be represented by the inequality

$$\Sigma Q_i \leq \frac{R_n}{FS}$$

where ΣQ_i = the *required strength,* which is the summation of the *load effects Q_i* (i.e., forces or moments), and R_n/FS = the *design strength,* which is the *nominal strength or resistance R_n,* divided by a *factor of safety.* When divided by the appropriate section property (i.e., area or section modulus), the two sides of the inequality become the actual stress and allowable stress, respectively.

The greatest attribute of allowable stress design has been its simplicity, since the variable risks and the probability of failure need not be considered in the design process. In most design situations, this method can be used to produce reasonably safe and usable structures. However, the allowable stress design method assumes that the ultimate limit states will automatically be satisfied by the use of allowable stresses. Depending on the variability of the materials and loads, this assumption may not always be valid.

Commonly cited shortcomings of allowable stress design include the inability to properly account for the variability of the resistances and loads; lack of knowledge of the level of safety; and the inability to deal with groups of loads where one load increases at a different rate than the others. The latter condition is especially serious when a relatively constant load such as dead load counteracts the effects of a highly variable load such as wind.

The *load and resistance factor design* (LRFD) and *ultimate strength design* (USD) methods may be summarized by

$$\Sigma\gamma_i Q_i \leq \phi R_n$$

where $\Sigma\gamma_i Q_i$ = the *required strength* corresponding to the summation of the various *load effects* Q_i, multiplied by their respective load factors γ_i, and ϕR_n = the *design strength* corresponding to the *nominal strength* or *resistance* R_n, multiplied by a *resistance factor* ϕ in LRFD and strength reduction factor ϕ in USD. Values of ϕ and R_n are provided by the specific LRFD and USD specification.

The left side of this equation represents the required resistance, which is computed by structural analysis based upon assumed loads, and the right side represents a limited structural capacity provided by the selected members. In LRFD and USD, the designer compares the effect of factored loads to the strength actually provided. The term *design strength* refers to the resistance or strength ϕR_n that must be provided by the selected member. The load factor γ and the resistance factor ϕ reflect the fact that loads, load effects (the computed forces and moments in the structural elements), and resistances can be determined only to imperfect degrees of accuracy. The resistance factor ϕ is equal to or less than 1.0 because there is always a chance for the actual resistance to be less than the nominal value R_n. Similarly, the load factor γ reflects the fact that the actual load effects may deviate from the nominal values of Q_i computed from the specified nominal loads. These factors account for unavoidable inaccuracies in the theory, variations in the material properties and dimensions, and uncertainties in the determination of loads.

It has been noted by Ellingwood et al.[6] that the main advantages of load and resistance factor design are as follows:

1. More consistent reliability is attained for different design situations because the different variabilities of various strengths and loads are considered explicitly and independently.

2. The reliability level can be chosen to reflect the consequences of failure.

3. The designer has a better understanding of the fundamental structural requirements and of the behavior of the structure in meeting those requirements.

4. The design process is simplified by encouraging the same design philosophy and procedures to be adopted for all materials of construction.

5. It is a tool for exercising judgment in nonroutine situations.

6. It provides a tool for updating standards in a rational manner.

EVOLUTION OF DESIGN STANDARDS AND MODEL BUILDING CODES

ASCE 7 (Formerly ANSI A58.1)

A report of the Department of Commerce Building Code Committee, entitled "Minimum Live Loads Allowable for Use in Design of Buildings," was published by the National Bureau of Standards in 1924. The recommendations contained in that document were widely used in revision of local building codes.

These recommendations, based upon the engineering data available at that time, represented the collective experience and judgment of the committee members responsible for drafting this document.

The ASA Committee on Building Code Requirements for Minimum Design Loads in Buildings subsequently issued a report in 1945 that represented a continuation of work in this field. This committee took into consideration the work of the previous committee, and expanded on it to reflect current knowledge and experience. The end result was the *American Standard Building Code Requirements for Minimum Design Loads in Buildings and Other Structures,* A58.1-1945.[8]

The A58.1 standard has been revised five times since 1945, the latest revision[9] corresponding to ASCE 7-95, *Minimum Design Loads for Buildings and Other Structures.** Subsequent to the 1982 edition of ANSI A58.1, the American National Standards Institute (ANSI) and the ASCE Board of Direction approved ASCE rules for the standards committee to govern the writing and maintenance of the ANSI A58.1 standard. The current document prescribes load combinations, dead loads, live loads, soil and hydrostatic pressures, wind loads, snow loads, rain loads, and earthquake loads. Like earlier editions of the ANSI standard, ASCE 7 has significantly influenced the development and revision of other building codes.

Wind Loads.   Because of the complexity involved in defining both the dynamic wind load and the behavior of an indeterminate structure when subjected to wind loads, the design criteria adopted by ASCE 7 are based on the application of an equivalent static wind pressure. This equivalent static *design wind pressure p* is defined in a general sense by

$$p = qGC_p$$

where q = *velocity pressure*, lb/ft^2
  G = *gust response factor* to account for fluctuations in wind speed
  C_p = *pressure coefficient* or *shape factor* that reflects influence of wind
    on various parts of a structure

Velocity pressure is computed from

$$q = K_z(IV)^2$$

where K_z = *velocity exposure coefficient* that accounts for variation of velocity
    with height and ground roughness
  I = *importance factor* associated with type of occupancy
  V = *basic wind speed*, mi/h

The 1982 ANSI standard was a major revision of the 1972 version of that standard. A new wind speed map for annual, extreme, fastest-mile wind, based on an

---

*ASCE 7-99 was being balloted at the time this handbook was published.

annual probability of exceedance of 0.02 (50-year mean recurrence interval), was introduced with 70 mi/h as the minimum design basic wind speed. This one map replaced maps for 25-, 50-, or 100-year mean recurrence intervals that were used as a measure of the importance of the facility (anticipated use, life, hazard to personnel, acceptable risk, and other judgment factors). The importance coefficient I was introduced in 1982 to account, in a more consistent manner than by selecting from three different maps, for the 25-year and 100-year winds by using a multiplier for the wind speed provided on the one map.

There were several new items added in the ASCE 7-95 wind load provisions, including a topography factor, alternate pressure coefficients for main wind-force resisting systems of low-rise buildings, pressure coefficients for additional roof geometries, and provisions for full and partial loading of high-rise buildings. The most significant change in ASCE 7-95 was the use of a 3-s gust speed instead of fastest-mile wind speeds. This change necessitated revision of terrain and height factors, gust effect factors, and pressure coefficients for components and cladding.

Snow Loads. In ASCE 7, the *design roof snow load* is determined from

$$P_f = 0.7C_eC_tIp_g$$

where C_e = *wind exposure factor*
C_t = *thermal effects factor*
I = *importance factor* for end use
p_g = *maximum ground snow load* in a 50-year mean recurrence period (2% probability of being exceeded in any year)

In 1965, the *National Building Code of Canada*[10] first published comprehensive provisions for loads due to snow drifting, together with a commentary, based on prior research; these provisions were reaffirmed in the 1970 edition of the *National Building Code of Canada*; and were adopted by the American National Standards Institute in 1972, in ANSI A58.1-1972[11] and by the BOCA Code in 1975.[12] The drift provisions were again revised in ANSI A58.1-82 and the 1987 BOCA code.

The 1982 ANSI criteria are based on a statistical analysis of snowdrifts with height of drift less than the height of the upper roof.[13] The criteria used an empirical equation to determine the height of snowdrift and provide an empirical relationship between ground snow load and the density of snow in the drift. When the elevation of the top of the drift, as calculated by the empirical equation, is higher than the elevation of the upper roof, the drift height is adjusted so that the top of the drift is at the same elevation as the upper roof. The formula recognizes that the greater the length of the upwind higher roof, the greater is the available snow that can be picked up by the wind and then deposited downstream in the drift at the lower adjoining roof.[14,15]

Earthquake Loads. The history of seismic design codes in the United States is fairly brief. During the 1960s, research was conducted to demonstrate that ductile moment-resisting concrete frames could be designed and constructed in seismic zones. This effort was in response to the Structural Engineers Association of California (SEAOC) requirement that buildings greater than 170 ft in height have a complete moment-resisting space frame. *Design of Multi-Story Reinforced Concrete Buildings for Earthquake Motions* was published in 1961 and provided initial material for the SEAOC Seismology Committee to develop ductile reinforced-concrete provisions.[16] The SEAOC committee subsequently published requirements for reinforced-concrete ductile moment-resisting frames and reinforced-concrete shear walls in the 1966 revision to the SEAOC Bluebook.[17]

In 1974, a cooperative effort was undertaken by the Applied Technology Council (ATC) to develop nationally applicable seismic design provisions for buildings. The project, known as ATC-3, was part of the Cooperative Federal Program in Building Practices for Disaster Mitigation initiated in 1972. The primary basis of the provisions was to protect life safety and to ensure continued functioning of essential facilities needed during and after a catastrophe. Primary consideration was given to the main structural framing system(s) and to energy-absorbing/dissipating effects of interior partitions, exterior cladding, different types of materials, damping, and drift.

After their publication in 1978, the ATC-3 provisions were subjected to an extensive several-year evaluation process by the Building Seismic Safety Council (BSSC) under contract to the Federal Emergency Management Agency (FEMA).[18] The ATC-3 provisions were then modified to better apply to all regions of the United States. The process culminated in 1985 with publications by BSSC of *NEHRP Recommended Provisions for the Development of Seismic Regulations for Buildings,* 1985 edition.[19] NEHRP stands for the National Earthquake Hazard Reduction Program, which is managed by FEMA.

The 1982 edition of ANSI A58.1 and the 1988 edition of ASCE 7 contained seismic provisions based upon those in the *1985 Uniform Building Code.* The *UBC* provisions for seismic safety were based upon recommendations of SEAOC and predecessor organizations. The 1955 and 1972 editions of A58.1 contained seismic provisions based upon much earlier versions of SEAOC and UBC recommendations.

In 1993, the ASCE 7 seismic provisions were substantially changed from prior editions. The 1993 provisions are adopted from the NEHRP *Recommended Provisions for the Development of Seismic Regulations for New Buildings.* These provisions are a direct descendant of the *Tentative Provisions for the Development of Seismic Regulations for Buildings,* developed by ATC under sponsorship of the National Science Foundation and the National Bureau of Standards (now the National Institute for Standards and Technology).

The two most significant differences between the 1993 edition and prior editions are that (1) the 1993 edition is based upon a strength level limit state rather than an equivalent loading for use with allowable stress design, and (2) the 1993 edition contains a much larger set of provisions that are not direct statements of loading. The intent is to provide a more reliable and consistent level of seismic safety in new building construction. Further background and commentary on these provisions can be found in the following publications:

Part 2, Commentary, of the *NEHRP Recommended Provisions for the Development of Seismic Regulations for New Buildings,* Building Seismic Safety Council, Federal Emergency Management Agency, 1991 edition.

Recommended Lateral Force Requirements and Commentary, Seismology Committee, Structural Engineers Association of California, 1990.

The NEHRP provisions have been selected by the federal government as a benchmark for the design of federal buildings. The 1991 NEHRP provisions were modified and adopted as a supplement to the *National Building Code* by the Building Officials Congress of America, and by the Southern Building Code Conference International as an amendment to the *Standard Building Code* in the fall of 1991. The 1991 UBC was judged by the federal government to be equivalent in seismic safety to the 1991 NEHRP provisions. These three codes, although used in separate regions of the United States, currently serve as the principal seismic design codes in the United States.

Model Codes

Uniform Building Code.   The *Uniform Building Code* was first enacted by the International Conference of Building Officials in 1927. Revised editions of this code have been published since that time at approximate 3-year intervals. New editions incorporate changes approved since the last edition. The *Uniform Building Code* is designed to be compatible with related publications to provide a complete set of documents for regulatory use.

The provisions of the 1994 edition of the *Uniform Building Code* were reformatted into the common code format established by the Council of American Building Officials. The new format establishes a common format of chapter designations for the three model building codes published in the United States. Apart from those changes approved by the conference membership, this reformatting has not changed the technical content of the code.

Provisions of the *Uniform Building Code* and the *UBC Standards* have been divided into a three-volume set. Volume 1 contains administrative, fire- and life-safety, and field inspection provisions. Chapters 1 through 15 and Chaps. 24 through 35 are printed in volume 1 in their entirety. Any appendix chapters associated with these chapters are printed in their entirety at the end of volume 1. Excerpts of certain chapters from volume 2 are reprinted in volume 1 to provide greater usability.

Volume 2 contains structural engineering design provisions, and specifically contains Chaps. 16 through 23, printed in their entirety. Included in this volume are design standards previously published in *UBC Standards.* Design standards have been added to their respective chapters as divisions of the chapters. Any appendix chapters associated with these chapters are printed in their entirety at the end of volume 2. Excerpts of certain chapters from volume 1 are reprinted in volume 2 to provide greater usability.

Volume 3 contains material, testing, and installation standards.

The *Uniform Building Code* was metricated in 1994. The metric conversions are provided in parentheses following the English units. Where industry has made metric conversions available, the conversions conform to current industry standards.

National Building Code.   The *BOCA National Building Code* was first adopted by the Building Officials and Code Administrators (BOCA) International, Inc., in 1950. Like the *Uniform Building Code,* revised editions of this code have been published since that time at approximate 3-year intervals. Change proposals to the *BOCA National Codes* are either accepted or rejected by vote of the organization's active members, who are practicing regulatory code officials.

The 1993 edition of the *BOCA National Building Code* was the first model code to implement the common building code format that was cooperatively developed by the three model code groups, the American Institute of Architects, and the Society of Fire Protection Engineers under the auspices of the council of American Building Officials. The new format consists of 11 basic subject matter groups: administration and terms, building planning, fire protection, occupant needs, building envelope, structural systems, structural materials, nonstructural materials, building services, special devices and conditions, and reference standards. Structural systems are subdivided into three chapters corresponding to structural loads, structural tests and inspections, and foundations and retaining walls. A brief summary of revisions to some of the environmental load provisions is tabulated in Table 2.1.[20] Structural materials include chapters on concrete, lightweight metals, masonry steel, and wood. *Building Code Requirements for Reinforced Concrete* (ACI 318), *Building Code Requirements for Masonry Structures* (ACI 530), the AISC *Specification for Structural Steel Buildings, Allowable Stress Design and Plastic Design,* the AISC *Load and Resistance Factor Design Specification for Structural Steel Buildings,* the *National Design Specification for Wood Construction,* and related standards are adopted by reference. Chapter 33 includes requirements for site work, demolition, and construction.

Standard Building Code.   The first edition of the *Southern Standard Building Code* appeared in 1946. The code was developed by M. L. Clement between 1940 and 1945 in Birmingham, Alabama, and was first adopted by the city of Clearwater, Florida. Like the other model codes, the *Southern Standard Building Code* has been periodically revised and, more recently, published at approximate 3-year intervals. In 1974, the Southern Building Code Congress became the Southern Building Code Congress International, Inc., and in early 1975 the word *Southern* was dropped from the titles of all *Standard Codes.*

TABLE 2.1 Revisions to BOCA National Building Code, 1975–1993

Code edition year	Snow	Wind	Earthquake
1975	Section 711.0: • Based on ANSI A58.1-1972 • Recurrence interval 25 to 100 years as a function of building use • Snow drift provisions	Sections 712.0–716.0: no change from 1975	Section 718.0: based on ANSI A58.1-1972 • Detailed design criteria • Seismic map of zones based on past earthquakes
1978	Section 711.0: no change from 1975	Sections 712.0–715.0: • Based on ANSI A58.1-1972 • 50-year mean recurrence wind velocity	Section 718.0: no change from 1975
1981	Section 911.0: no change from 1978	Sections 912.0–915.0: no change from 1978	Section 916.0: moved from an appendix to code body, but no technical changes from 1978
1984	Section 911.0: no change from 1981	Sections 912.0–915.0: no change from 1981	Section 916.0: no change from 1981
1987	Section 1111.0: requirements updated to ANSI A58.1-1982 with modifications by the wood and steel industry	Section 1112.0: requirements updated to ANSI A58.1-1982	Section 1113.0: requirements updated to ANSI A58.1-1982 with modifications by the concrete industry
1990	Section 1111.0: no change from 1987	Section 1112.0: no change from 1987	Section 1113.0: changed seismic map from the zone map to zone/ground acceleration map per NEHRP 1988
1993	Section 1610.0: no change from 1990	Section 1611.0: • Updated to reflect ASCE 7-1988 requirements • Added design methods for components and cladding	Section 1612.0: complete rewrite; updated to reflect NEHRP Provisions for new buildings (1991) • Seismic map revised to delete zones and show only ground acceleration • Ultimate structural design method

Source: From McCluer.

Recent editions of the code, including the 1997 edition, have also adopted the common building code format, and the contents are organized in a manner similar to that of *UBC* and BOCA. The *Standard Building Code* incorporates, by reference, nationally recognized consensus standards for use in judging the performance of materials and systems.

Design Codes and Specifications

The model codes adopt many of the national design standards developed by organizations such as the American Concrete Institute (ACI),[21] the American Institute of Steel Construction (AISC),[22] and the National Forest Products Association (NFPA).[23] The model codes also adopt by reference many of the American Society for Testing and Materials (ASTM) Standards as the recognized test procedures to ensure construction quality. ASTM *Standards in Building Codes* is a compilation of these standards.[24]

Like the model codes, many of these standards are developed and written in a form that allows them to be adopted by reference in a general building code. For example, the introduction of ACI 318-95 notes the following:

> The code has no legal status unless it is adopted by government bodies having the police power to regulate building design and construction. Where the code has not been adopted, it may serve as a reference to good practice even though it has no legal status.

Similarly, the AISC *Code of Standard Practice*[25] states that

> The practices defined herein have been adopted by the AISC as the commonly accepted standards of the structural steel fabricating industry. In the absence of other instructions in the contract documents, the trade practices defined in this *Code of Standard Practice,* as revised to date, govern the fabrication and erection of structural steel.

ACI Building Code Requirements for Structural Concrete. From the early 1900s until the early 1960s, the principal method of design for reinforced concrete was *working stress design.* Since publication of the 1963 edition of the ACI *Code,* there has been a rapid transition to *ultimate strength design.* The 1963 ACI *Code* (ACI 318-63) treated the working stress and the ultimate strength methods on an equal basis. However, a major portion of the working stress method was modified to reflect ultimate strength behavior. The working stress provisions of the 1963 *Code,* relating to bond, shear, and diagonal tension, and combined axial compression and bending, had their basis in ultimate strength.

In 1971, ACI 318-71 was based entirely on the strength approach for proportioning reinforced-concrete members, except for a small section devoted to what was called an *alternate design method.* Even in that section, the service load capacities (except for flexure) were prescribed as various percentages of the ultimate strength capacities of other parts of the *Code*. The transition to ultimate strength theories for reinforced-concrete design was essentially complete in the 1971 ACI *Code*.

In ACI 318-77, the alternate design method was moved to an appendix. The appendix location served to separate and clarify the two methods of design, with the main body of the *Code* devoted exclusively to the strength design method. The alternate design method was retained in App. B of ACI 318-83, and has been retained in App. A of ACI 318-89 and ACI 318-95. Since an appendix location is sometimes not considered to be an official part of a legal document (unless specifically adopted), specific reference is made in the main body of the *Code* (section 8.1.2) to make App. A a legal part of the *Code*. Regardless of whether the strength design method of the *Code* or the alternate design method of App. A is used in proportioning for strength, the general serviceability requirements of the *Code,* such as the provisions for deflection control and crack control, must always be satisfied.

According to ACI 318, the required strength provided to resist dead load D and live load L must be at least equal to

$$U = 1.4D + 1.7L$$

If a wind load W must be considered, the following combinations of D, L, and W should be investigated:

$$U = 0.75(1.4D + 1.7L + 1.7W)$$
$$U = 0.9D + 1.3W)$$

The second equation must be checked for two cases: (1) the live load L, equal to its full value and (2) $L = 0$. In any case, the strength of the member or structure must not be less than required by the first equation. Resistance to earthquake loads E can be investigated by substituting $1.1E$ for W.

The design strength provided by a member, its connections to other members, and its cross sections, in terms of flexure, axial load, shear, and torsion, is equal to the nominal strength calculated in accordance with the provisions and assumptions stipulated in ACI 318, multiplied by a strength reduction factor ϕ which is less than unity. The ϕ factors prescribed by ACI are identified in Table 2.2.

The purpose of the *strength reduction factor* ϕ is to define a design strength level that is somewhat lower than would be expected if all dimensions and material properties were those used in computations; to reflect the degree of ductility, toughness, and reliability of the member under the load effects being considered; and to reflect the importance of the member. For example, a lower ϕ is used for columns than for beams because columns generally have less ductility, are more sensitive to variations in concrete strength, and carry larger loaded areas than beams, and their failure precipitates greater damage.

AISC Manual of Steel Construction. The AISC *Manual for Steel Construction* has evolved through numerous versions from the first edition, published in 1923. AISC

TABLE 2.2   ACI 318-95 Capacity Reduction Factors ϕ

Type of stress	ϕ
Axial tension, and bending with or without axial tension	0.90
Axial compression with or without bending:	
Members with spiral reinforcement	0.75*
Other reinforced members	0.70*
Shear and torsion	0.85
Bearing on concrete	0.70
Bending in plain concrete	0.65

*May be increased linearly to 0.90 as P_u decreases from $0.10 f_c' A_g$ or P_u, whichever is smaller, to zero.

currently publishes design specifications for structural steel with two different design approaches: *Specification for Structural Steel Buildings Allowable Stress Design (ASD)*[22] and *Plastic Design and Load and Resistance Factor Design (LRFD) Specification for Structural Steel Buildings.*[26] Building codes either incorporate both of these approaches or adopt them by reference.

The first edition of the LRFD specification was published in 1986. The LRFD specification requires that factors be applied to both service loads and the nominal resistance (strength) of members and connections. The load factors and load combinations prescribed by AISC were developed to be used with the recommended minimum loads given in ANSI A58.1 *Minimum Design Loads for Buildings and Other Structures.*[27] The load factors and load combinations are developed in Ref. 6 and are as follows:

$$1.4D$$

$$1.2D + 1.6L + 0.5(L_r \text{ or } S \text{ or } R)$$

$$1.2D + 1.6(L_r \text{ or } S \text{ or } R) + (0.5L \text{ or } 0.8W)$$

$$1.2D + 1.3W + 0.5L + 0.5(L_r \text{ or } S \text{ or } R)$$

$$1.2D + 1.5E + (0.5L \text{ or } 0.2S)$$

$$0.9D - (1.3W \text{ or } 1.5E)$$

where D = *dead load* (gravity load from weight of structural elements and permanent attachments)
  L = *live load* (gravity occupancy and movable equipment load)
  L_r = *roof live load*
  W = *wind load*
  S = *snow load*

$E = $ *earthquake load*

$R = $ *rain or ice load*

The load factors and load combinations recognize that when several loads act in combination with the dead load, e.g., dead plus live plus wind loads, then only one of these takes on its maximum lifetime value, while the other load is at its *arbitrary point-in-time value*, i.e., at a value which can be expected to be on the structure at any time. For example, under dead, live, and wind loads, the following combinations are appropriate:

$$\gamma_D D + \gamma L$$

$$\gamma_D D\gamma + \gamma L_\alpha + \gamma_W W$$

$$\gamma_D D + \gamma_L L + \gamma_{W\alpha} W_\alpha$$

where γ is the appropriate load factor as designated by the subscript symbol. Subscript α refers to an arbitrary point-in-time value.

National Design Specification for Wood Construction. The first edition of the *National Design Specification for Stress-Grade Lumber and Its Fastenings* was published by the National Lumber Manufacturers Association in 1944.[28] The specification included allowable unit stresses for stress-graded lumber, design formulas, and design loads and provisions for timber connector, bolted, lag screw, nail, and wood screw joints. Also included were guidelines for the design of glued laminated structural members.

The 1944 edition of the specification was revised five times between 1948 and 1953, and 11 new editions were published between 1957 and 1997. The 1968 edition was the first published under the association's new name, the National Forest Products Association (NFPA). In 1993, NFPA merged with the American Paper Institute to form the American Forest & Paper Association (AFPA).

An *LRFD Specification for Engineered Wood Construction* was developed by the joint NFPA/ASCE Design of Engineered Wood Construction Standards Committee and adopted by the American Wood Council in 1996.[29] The LRFD *Specification* provides an alternative design methodology to allowable stress design procedures specified in prior editions of the *National Design Specification for Wood Construction* (NDS). There are two primary differences between ASD and LRFD procedures for the design of wood structures. In ASD, safety adjustments are applied to strength properties only, and in LRFD, safety adjustments are applied to loads and strength properties. Load duration factors are used in ASD, and time effect factors are used in LRFD.

The *load duration effect*, or the ability of wood to support greater magnitudes of load for short time durations, has been an essential part of the ASD guidelines since the first edition of the NLMA design specification. The load duration effect is incorporated in ASD procedures by publishing allowable strength properties (design values) based on a 10-year *normal* cumulative load duration and providing load duration adjustment factors ($C_D > 1.0$) for shorter load durations. Probabilistic analyses of load histories, load durations, and load combinations, coupled with stochastic analyses of material properties, led to the development of LRFD strength properties (resistance values) based on short-term (5- to 10-min) load duration, and time effect factors ($\lambda < 1.0$) for longer load durations.[30] The following is a comparison of ASD load duration factors with LRFD time effect factors:

Design load	Load duration factors (ASD) C_D	Time effect factors (LRFD) λ
Permanent (dead) load D	0.9	0.6
Storage live load L_S	1.0	0.7
Occupancy live load L	1.0	0.8
Snow load S	1.15	0.8
Roof live load L_R	1.25	0.8
Wind load W	1.6	1.0
Seismic load E	1.6	1.0
Impact load	2.0	1.25

Building Code Requirements for Masonry Structures. In the early 1960s, masonry industry associations began development of a technological database of masonry materials and performance through research and testing programs. The result of this effort culminated in design standards such as the Brick Institute of America's (BIA) *Recommended Practice For Engineered Brick Masonry*[31] in 1966 and the National Concrete Masonry Association's (NCMA) *Specifications for Loadbearing Concrete Masonry* in 1970.[32] Each document addressed only selected masonry materials. In 1970, American Concrete Institute Committee 531 published a report entitled, "Concrete Masonry Structures—Design and Construction,"[33] and in 1976 it published *Specifications for Concrete Masonry Construction* (ACI 531.1-76).[34] Both of these documents served as the basis for *Building Code Requirements for Concrete Masonry Structures* (ACI 531-79), which addressed only concrete masonry.[35]

The American Society of Civil Engineers (ASCE) and the American Concrete Institute undertook the development of a national design code in the late 1970s. An agreement resulted in the ACI/ASCE 530 Masonry Structures Joint Committee, formed in 1978, to develop a consensus standard for masonry design. A design code and construction specifications were drafted for committee ballot by 1984. Final adoption of code, specifications, and commentaries by ASCE and ACI occurred in October 1988.

The ACI *530 Building Code Requirements for Masonry Structures* is primarily directed to the designer and code enforcement officials,[36] while *ACI 530.1 Specifications for Masonry Structures* is primarily directed to the contractor and inspector.[37] Significant aspects related to these documents are that brick, block, and combination of brick and block are covered in a single document; and design is based on the premise that all work will be inspected.

AASHTO Standard Specifications for Highway Bridges. Compilation of the AASHTO *Standard Specifications for Highway Bridges* began in 1921 with the organization of the Committee on Bridges and Structures of the American Association of State Highway Officials. The first edition of the *Standard Specifications* was published in 1931, and it quickly became the de facto national standard. It has been reissued in consecutive editions at approximate 4-year intervals ever since as *Standard Specifications for Highway Bridges,* with the 16th edition appearing in 1996.[38]

The AASHTO *Standard Specifications for Highway Bridges* serves as a standard or guide for the preparation of state specifications and for reference by bridge engineers. The specifications prescribe minimum requirements that are consistent with current practice as well as certain modifications necessary to suit local conditions. They apply to ordinary highway bridges, and supplemental specifications may be required for unusual types and for bridges with spans longer than 500 ft. Specifications of the American Society for Testing and Materials, the American Welding Society, the American Wood Preservers Association, and the National Forest Products Association are referenced. Interim specifications are usually published in the middle of the calendar year.

In 1986, the Subcommittee on Bridges and Structures submitted a request to the AASHTO Standing Committee on Research to undertake an assessment of U.S. bridge design specifications, review foreign design specifications and codes, consider design philosophies alternative to those underlying the *Standard Specifications,* and to develop recommendations based on these investigations. The principal recommendation of the subcommittee was the development of an entirely new LRFD bridge design standard. Bridge engineers now have a choice of two design standards: the long-standing AASHTO *Standard Specifications for Highway Bridges* and the alternative AASHTO *LRFD Bridge Design Specifications*[39] and companion AASHTO *LRFD Bridge Construction Specifications.*[40]

Codes and Standards for the Design of Temporary Structures

The American Society of Civil Engineers (ASCE) and the Federal Highway Administration (FHWA) recently developed new guide standards with respect to design loads during construction and the design of temporary works used in construction. The ASCE effort corresponds to the development of an ANSI/ASCE *Standard for Design Loads in Structures during Construction.*[41] The FHWA document is a guide design specification for use by state agencies to update their existing standard specifications for falsework, formwork, and related temporary construction.[42]

ASCE Standard for Design Loads on Structures during Construction. At the time of this writing, ASCE is completing development of the ANSI/ASCE *Standard for*

Design Loads on Structures during Construction.[43] The objective of the new standard is to establish performance criteria, design loads, load combinations, and safety factors to be used in the analysis and design of structures during their transient stages of construction as well as temporary structures used in construction operations. The standard is composed of six sections corresponding to a general introduction identifying the purpose and scope of the document, loads and load combinations, dead and live loads, construction loads, lateral earth pressures, and environmental loads.

The construction loads, load combinations, and load factors were developed to account for the relatively short duration of load, variability of loading, variation in material strength, and the recognition that many elements of the completed structure that are relied upon implicitly to provide strength, stiffness, stability or continuity are not present during construction. The load factors are based on a combination of probabilistic analysis and expert opinion.[44] The concept of using maximum and arbitrary point-in-time (APT) loads and corresponding load factors is adopted to be consistent with ASCE 7.

The basic reference for the computation of environmental loads is also ASCE 7. However, modification factors have been adopted to account for reduced exposure periods. Furthermore, certain loads may be disregarded due to the relatively short reference period associated with typical construction projects, and certain loads in combinations may effectively be ignored because of the practice of shutting down job sites during these events, e.g., excessive snow and wind.

FHWA/AASHTO Guide Design Specification for Bridge Temporary Works. Following the collapse of the Route 198 bridge over the Baltimore Washington Parkway in 1989, FHWA determined that there was a need to reassess, on a national level, the specifications used to design, construct, and inspect falsework for highway bridge structures. Toward that end, FHWA sponsored a study to identify the existing information on this subject and to develop a guide specification for use by state agencies to update their existing standard specifications for falsework, formwork, and related temporary construction.[45]

As part of the FHWA study, a questionnaire was sent to the 50 U.S. highway departments. Information relating to design and administrative policies for falsework and formwork construction and the bridge construction activity for each state was requested. Virtually every state was found to have general requirements and guidelines for the construction and removal of falsework and formwork. However, only about one-half of the states specified design criteria. Similarly, only 22 states had accompanying design or construction manuals that included specific design information. States which are more active in constructing cast-in-place concrete highway bridges generally were found to have more comprehensive specifications and guidelines.

Besides identifying the content of state specifications, the survey provided some insight into each state's administrative policies concerning falsework and formwork. About two-thirds of the states require the submittal of plans and calculations, sealed by a registered professional engineer, for any significant falsework construction. The survey showed that most states also conduct their own reviews and inspections, subject to availability of staff, complexity of design, and so forth.

In 1993, the Federal Highway Administration produced a new guide specification for the design and construction of falsework, formwork, and temporary retaining structures used to construct highway bridge structures.[42] The new guide specification was developed for use by state agencies to update their existing standard specifications. This specification was subsequently adopted by AASHTO in 1995.

REFERENCES

1. *The BOCA National Building Code/1996,* Building Officials and Code Administrators International, Inc., Country Clubs Hills, IL, 1996.

2. *Uniform Building Code,* 1997 ed., International Conference of Building Officials, Whittier, CA, 1997.

3. *Standard Building Code,* Southern Building Code Congress International, Inc., Birmingham, AL, 1997.

4. Dale C. Perry, "Building Codes in the United States—An Overview," *Proceedings of the WERC/NSF Wind Engineering Symposium,* Kansas City, MO, 1987.

5. ASCE Task Committee on Structural Safety of the Administrative Committee on Analysis and Design of the Structural Division, "Structural Safety—A Literature Review," *Journal of the Structural Division, ASCE,* vol. 98, no. ST4, April 1972, pp. 845–884.

6. Bruce Ellingwood, Theodore V. Galambos, James G. MacGregor, and C. Allin Cornell, *Development of a Probability Based Load Criterion for American National Standard A58,* NBS Special Publication 577, Department of Commerce, National Bureau of Standards, Washington, June 1980.

7. Clarkson W. Pinkham, "Design Philosophies," chap. 3, in *Building Structural Design Handbook,* Richard N. White and Charles G. Salmon, eds., Wiley, New York, 1987, pp. 44–54.

8. *American Standard Building Code Requirements for Minimum Design Loads in Buildings and Other Structures,* ASA A58.1-1945, American Standard Association, New York, 1945.

9. *Minimum Design Loads for Buildings and Other Structures* (ASCE 7-95), American Society of Civil Engineers, Reston, VA, 1995.

10. *National Building Code of Canada,* National Research Council, Ottawa, 1965.

11. *American Standard Building Code Requirements for Minimum Design Loads in Buildings and Other Structures,* ASA A58.1-1972, American Standard Association, New York, 1972.

12. *The BOCA National Building Code,* 1975 ed., Building Officials and Code Administrators International, Inc., Country Club Hills, IL, 1975.

13. M. O'Rourke, W. Tobiasson, and E. Wood, "Proposed Code Provisions for Drifted Snow Loads," *Journal of Structural Engineering, ASCE,* vol. 112, no. 9, September 1986, pp. 2080–2092.

14. J. T. Templin and W. R. Schriever, "Loads Due to Drifted Snow," *Journal of the Structural Division, ASCE,* vol. 108, no. ST8, 1982, pp. 1916–1925.

15. M. J. O'Rourke, R. S. Speck, Jr., and U. Stiefel, "Drift Snow Loads on Multilevel Roofs," *J. of Struct. Engineering, ASCE,* vol. 111, no. 2, 1985, pp. 290–306.

16. J. A. Blume, N. M. Newmark, and L. Corning, *Design of Multistory Reinforced Concrete Buildings for Earthquake Motions,* Portland Cement Association, Chicago, 1961.

17. "Recommended Lateral Force Requirements and Commentary," Seismology Committee, Structural Engineers Association of California, San Francisco, 1966.

18. "Tentative Provisions for the Development of Seismic Regulations for Buildings (ATC-3-06)," report for National Bureau of Standards and National Science Foundation by ATC, Palo Alto, CA, 1978.

19. Building Seismic Safety Council, *NEHRP Recommended Provisions for the Development of Seismic Regulations for New Buildings, 1991 Edition,* Federal Emergency Management Agency, Washington, 1992.

20. Private correspondence with Robert McCluer, manager of Codes, Building Officials and Code Administrations International, May 1999.

21. ACI Committee 318, *Building Code Requirements for Reinforced Concrete* (ACI 318-95) *and Commentary* (ACI 318R-95), American Concrete Institute, Detroit, MI, 1995.

22. *Manual of Steel Construction—Allowable Stress Design,* 9th ed., American Institute of Steel Construction, Chicago, 1989.

23. *National Design Specification for Wood Construction,* 1997 ed., National Forest Products Association, Washington, 1997.

24. *ASTM Standards in Building Codes,* American Society for Testing and Materials, 1916 Race St., Philadelphia, PA 19103.

25. *Code of Standard Practice,* 9th ed., American Institute of Steel Construction, Chicago, 1989.

26. *Manual of Steel Construction, Load and Resistance Factor Design Specification for Structural Steel Buildings,* American Institute of Steel Construction, Chicago, 1989.

27. *Minimum Design Loads for Buildings and Other Structures,* ANSI A58.1-1982, American National Standards Institute, New York, 1982.

28. National Lumber Manufacturers Association, *National Design Specification for Stress-Grade Lumber and Its Fastenings,* NFPA, Washington, 1944.

29. National Forest Products Association/American Society of Civil Engineers, *Load and Resistance Factor Specification for Engineered Wood Construction,* NFPA, Washington, 1996.

30. D. V. Rosowsky and B. R. Ellingwood, "Stochastic Damage Accumulation and Probabilistic Codified Design for Wood," Johns Hopkins University Civil Engineering Report 1990-02-02, Baltimore, MD, August 1990.

31. *Recommended Practice for Engineered Brick Masonry,* Brick Institute of America, McLean, VA, 1969.

32. *Specification for the Design and Construction of Load-Bearing Concrete Masonry,* National Concrete Masonry Association, Herndon, VA, 1970.

33. *Concrete Masonry Structures—Design and Construction,* American Concrete Institute, Detroit, MI, 1970.

34. *Specifications for Concrete Masonry Construction (ACI 531.1-76),* American Concrete Institute, Detroit, MI, 1976.

35. *Building Code Requirements for Concrete Masonry Structures (ACI 531-79),* American Concrete Institute, Detroit, MI, 1979.

36. *Building Code Requirements for Masonry Structures (ACI 530),* American Concrete Institute, Detroit, MI, 1988.

37. *Specifications for Masonry Structures,* American Concrete Institute, Detroit, MI, 1988.

38. *Standard Specifications for Highway Bridges,* 16th ed., American Association of State Highway and Transportation Officials, Washington, 1996.

39. *AASHTO LRFD Bridge Design Specifications,* 2d ed., American Association of State Highway and Transportation Officials, Washington, 1998.

40. *AASHTO LRFD Bridge Construction Specifications,* American Association of State Highway and Transportation Officials, Washington, 1998.

41. R. T. Ratay, "Standards for Design Loads during Construction: An ASCE Effort," *Proceedings of the ASCE Structures Congress '89,* San Francisco, 1989, pp. 870–875.

42. J. F. Duntemann, L. E. Dunn, S. Gill, R. G. Lukas, and M. K. Kaler, *Guide Design Specification for Bridge Temporary Works,* FHWA Report no. FHWA-RD-93-032, Federal Highway Administration, Washington, November 1993.

43. *Design Loads on Structures During Construction* (Draft 2/99), American Society of Civil Engineers, Reston, VA, 1999.

44. D. V. Rosowsky, "Load Combinations and Load Factors for Construction," *Journal of Performance of Constructed Facilities,* vol. 10, no. 4, November 1996, pp. 175–181.

45. J. F. Duntemann, N. S. Anderson, and A. Longinow, *Synthesis of Falsework, Formwork, and Scaffolding for Highway Bridge Structures,* Report no. FHWA-RD-91-062, FHWA, U.S. Department of Transportation, November 1991.

CHAPTER 3

CONSTRUCTION SAFETY CODES, STANDARDS, AND REGULATIONS

Mohammad Ayub, P.E., S.E.

INTRODUCTION

The forensic structural engineer's work is often related to construction because most structural failures occur during construction. Therefore, he or she needs to be familiar with the codes, standards, regulations, and practices that must be followed in the construction of the structures. The purpose of this chapter is to introduce the forensic engineer to the construction safety standards and practices commonly followed in the industry.

Construction of all structures is governed by one or more safety standards. Most notable among them are the standards promulgated by the Occupational Safety and Health Administration (OSHA), U.S. Department of Labor, and the standards adopted by the American National Standards Institute (ANSI). In addition, there are a number of recommended safe practices, guides, and manuals published by trade associations, manufacturers, engineering associations, and other government agencies. These safety standards and recommendations have been developed after years of experience and in the light of lessons learned from the incidents.

Incidents at construction sites occur through either construction errors or design deficiencies. The incidents due to design deficiencies are few and far between, but nevertheless do occur. A majority of incidents, however, are due to disregard of safety regulations, absence of engineering oversight, poor planning, and lack of training on the part of workers. Another major cause is inappropriate shortcuts taken in haste to meet completion dates. Construction personnel often fail to determine when engineering assistance must be sought to address construction problems relating to the means and methods of construction. Consequently, solutions to these problems are left to construction personnel who generally lack the engineering skills to evaluate the potential problem thoroughly. Among all the factors enumerated above, engineering investigations reveal that the disregard of safety regulations emerges as the prime single cause of incidents at construction sites. The forensic engineer must therefore be familiar with the safety standards generally followed in the industry.

INJURIES AND FATALITIES IN U.S. CONSTRUCTION INDUSTRY

Construction is among the most hazardous trades in the United States. Approximately 1000 construction workers die annually. Based upon the data compiled by the Bureau of Labor Statistics (BLS), U.S. Department of Labor, there are about 14 fatalities per 100,000 construction workers compared to about 5 fatalities per 100,000 workers in all occupations combined. Figures 3.1 and 3.2 show the number of fatalities and the rate of fatalities in the construction industry and in all occupations combined. Figure 3.3 indicates the magnitude of employment in the construction industry compared with overall employment. The rate of nonfatal injuries and illnesses of construction workers is compared with that of other selected industries and is shown in Fig. 3.4. While the rate of fatalities in construction is rather constant, the nonfatal injuries and illnesses are steadily declining. From a high of 12.9 injuries and illnesses per 100 full-time construction workers in 1992, the rate has decreased to 9.5 in 1997. Information compiled by OSHA is similar, although the numbers vary due to information collection methods and statutory limitations.

The construction fatality rates, in a limited study conducted by OSHA,[1] were comparable to those in other countries. (See Fig. 3.5.) These rates were based on the number of hours worked and the number of fatalities and/or incidents that occurred in selected countries. Climatic and cultural factors influence the number of hours workers work each year in different countries.

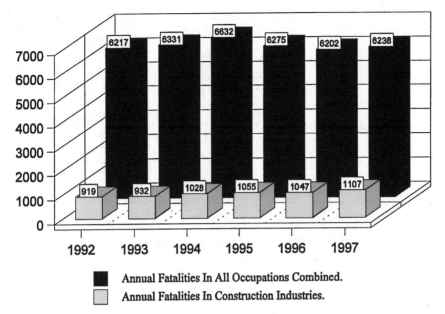

FIGURE 3.1   Number of fatalities.

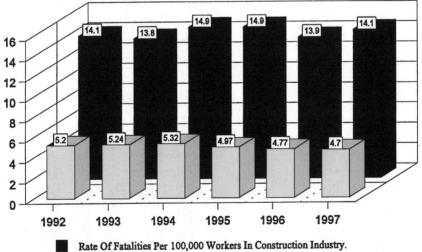

FIGURE 3.2   Rate of fatalities.

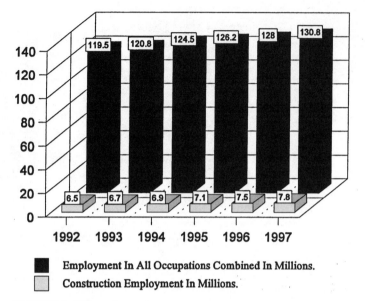

Employment In All Occupations Combined In Millions.
Construction Employment In Millions.

FIGURE 3.3 U.S. employment.

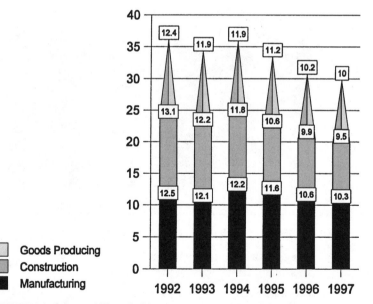

☐ Goods Producing
◼ Construction
■ Manufacturing

FIGURE 3.4 Injury and illness incidence rates per 100 full-time workers.

YEAR	United States	Ontario, Canada	Sweden	France	Japan	Germany
1980	29.8	16.2	16.5	29.0	25.1	26.1
1981	30.3	24.8	15.8	29.3	21.5	23.8
1982	28.0	18.9	18.2	27.4	20.5	24.9
1983	26.3	19.2	22.0	31.3	20.4	23.0
1984	22.8	22.7	16.4	26.4	20.6	23.5
1985	30.8	19.0	12.4	27.8	18.1	19.6
1986	20.3	24.5	16.0	23.1	17.4	17.3
1987	25.0	23.3	19.0	22.8	18.4	19.3
1988	24.5	20.0	12.1	30.8	19.8	16.9
1989	22.4	16.3	13.1	27.0	17.6	17.3
1990	20.6	19.4	16.3	30.2	18.3	15.5
1991	16.6	12.9	13.8	--	17.3	11.3
1992	--	--	10.0		16.0	

FIGURE 3.5 Fatalities per 100,000 foreign full-time workers.

An attempt was made by OSHA[2] to determine the leading causes of fatalities in the construction industry by analyzing the data compiled (by OSHA) for the years 1985 to 1989. Four major categories emerged as responsible for most of the fatalities: *falls, struck by, caught in between,* and *electric shock.* Figure 3.6 indicates the proportions of different categories for the fatalities from 1985 to 1989. A comparison was made with other selected countries, and it was determined that the causes of fatalities were similar; see Fig. 3.7.

Based on the analysis of the years from 1985 to 1989,[2] it was concluded that 50 percent of the fatalities due to falls occurred from heights of 11 to 30 ft and 42 percent of the fatalities from falls occurred due to falls from a height of greater than 30 ft. (See Fig.3.8.) In the struck-by category, most of the fatalities occurred when the workers were hit by a machine, material, or others. Figure 3.9 indicates the percentage of fatalities in the struck-by category. Figure 3.10 shows the fatalities in the category of caught in between. The majority of fatalities from electric shock were from voltage exceeding 480 V, as shown in Fig. 3.11. It is interesting to note that about 80 percent of the fatalities in the struck-by and caught-in-between categories occurred in trenches less than 14 ft deep. (See Fig. 3.12.) The day of the week had little effect on the magnitude of fatalities. The percentage of fatalities on different days of the week is shown in Fig. 3.13.

Construction fatalities based on the OSHA data among iron workers were also examined for the years from 1985 to 1989.[3] The number of iron worker fatalities for these 5 years varied from a high of 91 to 66. An overwhelming percentage of

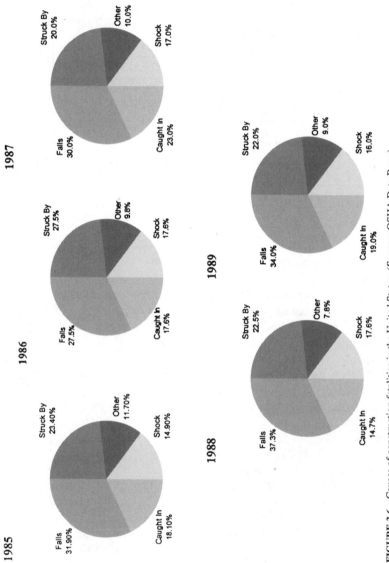

FIGURE 3.6 Causes of construction fatalities in the United States. (*Source:* OSHA Data Base.)

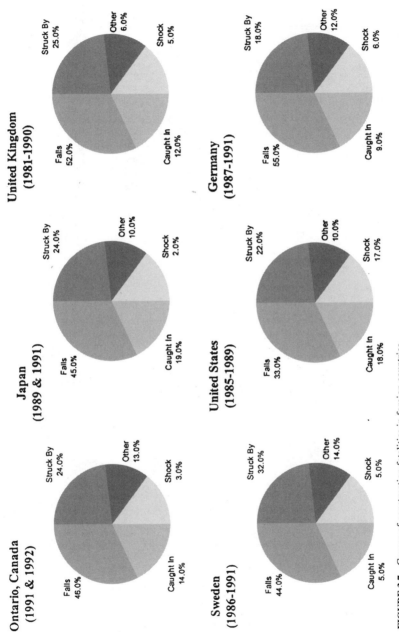

FIGURE 3.7 Causes of construction fatalities in foreign countries.

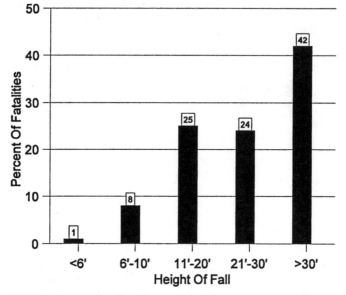

FIGURE 3.8   Analysis of fatalities caused by falls.

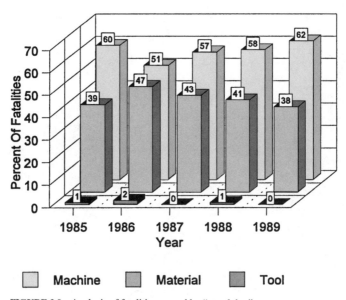

FIGURE 3.9   Analysis of fatalities caused by "struck by."

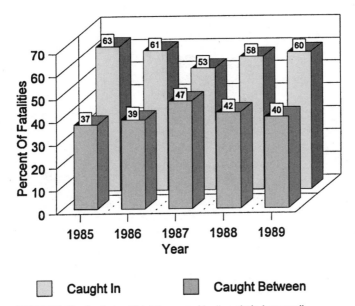

FIGURE 3.10   Analysis of fatalities caused by "caught in-between."

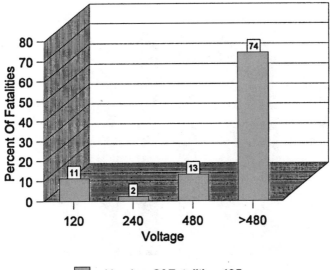

FIGURE 3.11   Analysis of fatalities caused by shock.

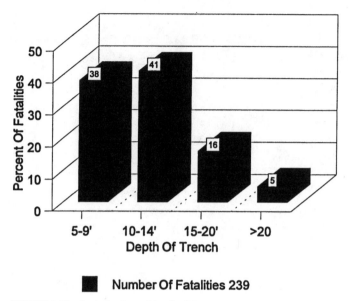

FIGURE 3.12 Analysis of trenching fatalities.

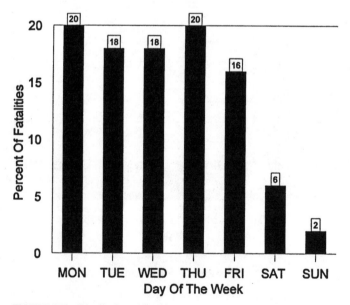

FIGURE 3.13 Distribution of fatalities.

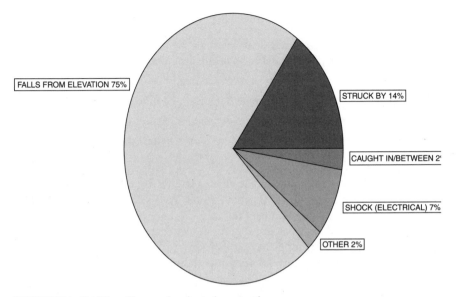

FALLS FROM ELEVATION 75%

STRUCK BY 14%

CAUGHT IN/BETWEEN 2%

SHOCK (ELECTRICAL) 7%

OTHER 2%

FIGURE 3.14   Fatalities of iron workers in steel construction.

fatalities of iron workers was due to falls (75 percent), followed by struck-by (14 percent) and electric shock (7 percent). (See Fig. 3.14.)

THE OCCUPATIONAL SAFETY AND HEALTH ADMINISTRATION AND ITS STANDARDS

Background and History

The U.S. Congress enacted the *Occupational Safety and Health Act* (*OSH Act,* Public Law 91-596 as amended by P.L. 101-552) of 1970 in consideration of the increasing toll of employment-related injuries and fatalities. The costs of lost production, earnings, and disabilities resulting from employment-related incidents were enormous; therefore, the Occupational Safety and Health Administration under the U.S. Department of Labor was established to promulgate safety and health standards and to monitor safety and health conditions at the nation's workplaces. Before the act was enacted, there was no nationwide uniform provision to safeguard the safety and health of the workforce.

Section 5 of the act states:

(a)(1) Each employer shall furnish to each of his employees employment and a place of employment which are free from recognized hazards that are causing or are likely to cause death or serious physical harm to his employees;

(2) Each employer shall comply with occupational safety and health standards promulgated under this Act.

The general objectives of establishing OSHA were, among other things, to

1. Reduce workplace injuries and fatalities by encouraging employers and employees to implement safety and health programs
2. Promulgate safety and health standards and enforce them
3. Keep records of employment-related injuries and illnesses
4. Provide training to occupational safety and health personnel
5. Provide for research in developing newer ways to deal with workplace hazards

The act has a provision to encourage states to develop their own safety and health plans, which are required to be at least as effective as the federal program. Federal OSHA provides up to 50 percent of the states' operating costs to implement the approved state programs. Presently, 23 states have approved state OSH programs. Federal OSHA has jurisdiction in the remaining states. Table 3.1 is a list of the states and territories having their own job safety and health programs and those states where the federal program is enforced.

With the exception of self-employed persons and farms with immediate relatives as employees, the OSH Act covers practically all sectors of employment. Coverage is provided by the federal OSHA or through the federal OSHA-approved state safety and health plans. If other federal agencies are regulating safety and health conditions in a particular industry, then the OSHA standards are not applied. OSHA standards are also generally not applicable to the state and local governments in their role as employers.

OSHA Standards

OSHA standards are applied to a breadth of industries—agriculture, general, maritime, and construction. At the inception of OSHA for a period of 2 years, standards were derived from the then-available resources. OSHA adopted some of the already existing federal laws which were in effect in 1970. In addition, OSHA adopted standards developed by experts in various industries, called proprietary standards. These proprietary standards were written by professional societies and associations. Further, OSHA incorporated a number of standards of the American National Standards Institute (ANSI) and National Fire Protection Association (NFPA) which were developed by consensus throughout industry, labor, and government agencies.

Many of the present OSHA standards continue to be the same as those adopted during 1970 to 1972. The new standards setting procedures for OSHA are, however, tedious and involve a number of steps, which prolong to many years the total time from inception to final rule.

OSHA may initiate the need for new standards based upon complaints from industry, recommendation from the National Institute of Occupational Safety and Health, public petitions, referral from federal agencies, or its own assessment of

TABLE 3.1 List of States under Federal OSHA Program and States under State Safety and Health Plans

States and territories with OSHA-approved state safety and health programs	States and territories with federal OSHA programs
Alaska	Alabama
Arizona	Arkansas
California	Colorado
Connecticut	Delaware
Hawaii	Florida
Indiana	Georgia
Iowa	Guam
Kentucky	Idaho
Maryland	Illinois
Michigan	Kansas
Minnesota	Louisiana
Nevada	Maine
New Mexico	Massachusetts
New York	Mississippi
North Carolina	Missouri
Oregon	Montana
Puerto Rico	Nebraska
South Carolina	New Jersey
Tennessee	New Hampshire
Utah	North Dakota
Vermont	Ohio
Virgin Islands	Oklahoma
Virginia	Pennsylvania
Washington	Rhode Island
Wyoming	South Dakota
	Texas
	Washington, DC
	West Virginia
	Wisconsin

the hazards in a particular industry. In any event, before proposing any rules, OSHA must demonstrate that, in fact, a potential hazard exists which endangers the lives of workers and that the proposed rule making will significantly improve the safety of workers. In addition, OSHA must choose the most effective and economical way to remedy the situation. OSHA prepares a preamble and background information for the proposed rules and may issue an Advance Notice of Proposed Rule Making which is published in the *Federal Register*. Public comments are invited from all groups directly or indirectly affected by the proposed rules. The period of public comments could be from 2 to 6 months. The comments are then studied and evaluated by OSHA, which may then choose to modify or alter some of the proposed rules. Then the notice of proposed rule making is again published in the *Federal Register,* inviting public, industry, labor, and academia to comment. The period of written comments is generally limited to 2 to 4 months. Following this period, a public hearing is generally held, sometimes at a number of locations, presided over by an administrative law judge. Businesses, labor unions, and experts clarify their points of view either in favor of or in opposition to the proposed rules. After the public hearing, OSHA reevaluates all the comments, reexamines the issues, and weighs all the suggestions and recommendations. Then the task of the final rule making begins. The final rule is then developed and adopted following a series of internal reviews by the U.S. Office of Management and Budget, Department of Labor's Solicitors Office, and the Secretary of Labor's Office. The final rule is then published in the *Federal Register:* giving its effective date.

In addition to the permanent standards discussed above, OSHA has the authority to promulgate temporary emergency regulations to address the immediate needs of certain industries where life-threatening hazards exist. These temporary standards remain in effect until permanent standards are adopted.

Recently, OSHA has embarked on the *negotiated rule-making* process whereby representatives of the industry, employers, labor unions, contractors, academia, and OSHA sit together and discuss the potential hazards of a particular industry. Through a series of meetings, a consensus document is developed with the approval of all groups having an interest in the industry. A recent example is the new, proposed steel erection standard which was developed through the negotiated rule-making process.

A study was undertaken by OSHA to list the 100 most frequently cited OSHA construction standards from 1987 to 1991.[3] Table 3.2 indicates the 100 most frequently cited OSHA construction standards related to physical hazards in 1991.[4] It includes violations pertaining to training, recordkeeping, hazard communication requirements, etc. Table 3.3 indicates the 100 most cited construction standards and their relative ranking to 1991.[4]

OSHA PROCEDURES AND PRACTICES

Construction Inspections

Construction sites are inspected by OSHA under the broad categories of programmed and unprogrammed inspections. The programmed inspections are based on randomly selected construction sites, while the unprogrammed inspections result from reported incidents at the construction sites, complaints received by OSHA from employees, referrals made to OSHA, cases of imminent danger, etc.

Federal OSHA believes that the prime time to inspect a construction site occurs when it is between 30 and 60 percent complete. This is the stage at which the construction is most intense and the number of employees and contractors at the site is maximum. Federal OSHA targets the construction sites under the programmed

TABLE 3.2 List of 100 Most Frequently Cited OSHA Construction Standards Related to Physical Hazards in 1991

Rank	Description of standard		Standard (1926. ___)
1	Fall protection	Guarding open-sided floors/platforms	500(d)(1)
2	PPE	Head protection from impact, falling, or flying objects	100(a)
3	Electrical	Ground fault protection	404(b)(1)(i)
4	Electrical	Path to ground missing or discontinuous	404(f)(6)
5	Trench/excavation	Protective systems for trenching/excavating	652(a)(1)
6	Scaffolding	Guardrail specifications for tubular welded-frame scaffolds	451(d)(10)
7	PPE	Appropriate PPE used for specific operation	28(a)
8	Ladders/stairways	Stair rails required @ 30-in change of elevation or four risers	1052(c)(1)
9	Fire protection	Approved containers or tanks for storing or handling flammable or combustible liquids	152(a)(1)
10	General provisions	General housekeeping	25(a)
11	Trenching/excavation	Daily inspection of physical components of trench and protection systems	651(k)(1)
12	Scaffolds	Safe access for all types of scaffolds	451(a)(13)
13	Electrical	Ground fault circuit interrupters (GFCIs)	404(b)(1)(ii)
14	Concrete/masonry	Guarding protruding steel rebars	701(b)
15	Scaffolds	General requirements for guarding	451(a)(4)
16	Trench/excavation	Spoil pile protection	651(j)(2)
17	Welding/cutting	Securing compressed-gas cylinders	350(a)(9)
18	Welding/cutting	Additional rules for welding per ANSI Z49.1-1967	350(j)

TABLE 3.2 List of 100 Most Frequently Cited OSHA Construction Standards Related to Physical Hazards in 1991 (*Continued*)

Rank	Description of standard		Standard (1926. ___)
19	PPE	Eye/face protection for operations which create exposure	102(a)(1)
20	Fall protection	Guarding floor openings	500(b)(1)
21	Ladder/stairway	Ladder extended 3 ft above landings	1053(b)(1)
22	Trench/excavation	Access/egress from trench/excavation	651(c)(2)
23	Electrical	Listed, labeled, or certified equipment used in manner prescribed	403(b)(2)
24	Electrical	Flexible cords designed for hard or extra-hard usage	405(a)(2)(ii)(j)
25	Electrical	Strain relief for cords	405(g)(2)(iv)
26	Woodworking tools	Additional rules for woodworking tools per ANSI 0.1.1-1967	304(f)
27	Fall protection	Safety nets above 25 ft when no other means of fall protection is practical	105(a)
28	Tools	Guarding moving parts of machinery	300(b)(2)
29	Electrical	Protection and grounding for temporary lamps	405(a)(2)(ii)(e)
30	Electrical	Controlled access to installations operating at more than 600 V	403(i)(2)(i)
31	Fall protection	Guarding wall openings	500(c)(1)
32	Scaffolding	Guarding specifications for mobile scaffolds	451(e)(10)
33	Scaffolding	Bracing tubular welded-frame scaffolds	451(d)(3)
34	General duty	Serious hazard not covered by specific standard	5(a)(1)
35	Electrical	Specific types of equipment or operations where grounding is required	404(f)(7)(iv)(c)
36	Health	Emergency phone numbers posted	50(f)

37	Ladder/stairway	Access by means of ladder/stairway when no other means provided and change in elevation > 19 in	1051(a)
38	Electrical	Covering provided for pull boxes, junction boxes, outlets, etc.	405(b)(2)
39	Electrical	Worn or frayed electric cords	416(e)(1)
40	Scaffolding	Sound, rigid, and load capable footings or anchorages for all types of scaffolds	451(a)(2)
41	Electrical	Unused opening in boxes must be closed and conductors entering boxes must be protected from abrasion	405(b)(1)
42	Cranes/derricks	All crawler, truck, or locomotive cranes meet ANSI B30.5-1968	550(b)(2)
43	Scaffolding	Tightly planked mobile scaffolds	451(e)(4)
44	Electrical	Reverse polarity of conductors	404(a)(2)
45	Ladders/stairways	Defective portable ladders tagged and taken out of service	1053(b)(16)
46	Electrical	Protecting flexible cords and cables from damage	405(a)(2)(ii)(i)
47	Material-handling equipment	Horns provided on bidirectional equipment	602(a)(9)(i)
48	Health	Certified first-aid trained personnel when treatment is not readily available	50(c)
49	Fall protection	Components of a fall protection system for low-pitched roof work	500(g)(1)
50	Fall protection	Guarding floor holes	500(b)(8)
51	Scaffolding	Specifications for extension of planking beyond supports	451(a)(14)
52	Fire	Provide for firefighting equipment and a fire protection program	150(a)(1)
53	Electrical	Splicing and tapping electric cords less than no. 12	405(g)(2)(iii)
54	Fall protection	Bodybelt and lanyard while working from aerial lift	556(b)(2)(v)
55	Scaffolding	Plumb and sound base for mobile scaffold—casters locked	451(e)(8)

TABLE 3.2 List of 100 Most Frequently Cited OSHA Construction Standards Related to Physical Hazards in 1991 (*Continued*)

Rank	Description of standard		Standard (1926. ___)
56	Health	Accessible first-aid supplies approved by consulting physician	50(d)(1)
57	Electrical	Electric equipment is free of hazards as determined by specifications	403(b)(1)
58	Fall protection	Guarding runways	500(d)(2)
59	Scaffolding	Ladder/stairway affixed or built in to mobile scaffold for access/egress	451(e)(5)
60	Material-handling equipment	Backup alarm or signalman provided when operating in reverse	602(a)(9)(ii)
61	Fire	Fire extinguisher for every 3000 ft² of protected building area and 100 ft of travel	150(c)(1)(i)
62	Electrical	Branch circuit specifications	405(a)(2)(ii)(b)
63	Ladders/stairways	Ladders extended 3 ft above landing	450(a)(9)
64	Electrical	Assured equipment grounding conductor program	404(b)(1)(iii)
65	Ladders/stairways	Stair rail and handrail specifications	500(e)(1)(iv)
66	Ladders/stairways	No travel on stairways with empty pans	1052(b)(1)
67	Ladders/stairways	Securing portable ladders	450(a)(10)
68	Tools	Power-operated tool guards	300(b)(1)
69	Welding/cutting	Valve protection caps in place and secure	350(a)(1)
70	Electrical	Guarding provided for temporary wiring operating over 600 V	405(a)(2)(iii)
71	Scaffolding	Competent person supervision during erection, dismantling, etc.	451(a)(3)
72	Electrical	Temporary lights suspended from electric conductor cords	405(a)(2)(ii)(f)

73	Material-handling equipment	Seat belts for all earthmoving equipment	602(a)(2)(i)
74	Ladders/stairways	Guarding stairway edges and landings	1052(c)(12)
75	Ladders/stairways	Siting and securing ladders	1053(b)(8)
76	Scaffolding	Scaffold-grade planking or equivalent	451(a)(10)
77	Scaffolding	Foundation specifications for tubular welded-frame scaffold legs	451(d)(4)
78	Cranes/derricks	Annual inspection of cranes/derricks	550(a)(6)
79	Cranes/derricks	Barricading the swing radius of cranes/derricks	550(a)(9)
80	Fire	Specifications for fire extinguisher on each floor of multistory structure	150(c)(1)(iv)
81	Ladders/stairways	Stair rail specifications	500(e)(1)(iii)
82	Scaffolding	Tie specifications for tubular welded-frame scaffolds	451(d)(7)
83	Fire	Inspection of fire extinguisher in accordance with NFPA 10A-1970	150(c)(1)(viii)
84	Electrical	Deenergizing or guarding electric circuits which are in proximity of employees	416(a)(1)
85	Scaffolding	Immediate replacement or repair of any damaged or defective components of scaffolding systems	451(a)(8)
86	Trenching/excavating	High-visibility garments when exposed to vehicular traffic	651(d)
87	Health	Common drinking cup	51(a)(4)
88	Fire	"No Smoking" signs posted in service and refueling areas	152(g)(9)
89	Fire	Fire extinguisher for cranes/derricks	550(a)(14)(i)
90	Ladders/stairways	Swing radius specifications for doors/gates which open onto a stairway or landing	1052(a)(4)
91	Scaffolding	Lifeline support on suspension scaffolds	451(i)(8)

TABLE 3.2 List of 100 Most Frequently Cited OSHA Construction Standards Related to Physical Hazards in 1991 (*Continued*)

Rank	Description of standard	Standard (1926.___)
92	Scaffolding	451(u)(3)
93	Material-handling equipment	602(c)(1)(vi)
94	Motor vehicles	601(b)(4)
95	Fire	150(c)(1)(vi)
96	Welding/cutting	350(h)
97	Cranes/derricks	550(a)(5)
98	Fire	150(a)(4)
99	Fire	153(j)
100	Scaffolding	451(d)(6)

Descriptions:
- 92 — Specifications for catch platform for steep-slope roofs
- 93 — Industrial trucks (forklifts) meet ANSI B56.1-1969
- 94 — Specifications for using vehicles with obstructed views to rear
- 95 — Fire extinguisher specifications for locations near flammable/combustible materials
- 96 — Regulators/gauges kept in proper working order
- 97 — Competent person to inspect crane to identify defects prior to use
- 98 — Periodic inspection of firefighting equipment
- 99 — Storing liquefied petroleum gases in buildings
- 100 — Locking or pinning legs to prevent uplift

Note: The Standard (1926.___) sections quoted are these of the then-prevailing standard.
Source: Ref. 3.

3.20

TABLE 3.3 100 Most Cited Construction Standards and Their Relative Ranking to 1991

Standards [1926 unless noted]	Description	Relative ranking to 1991 Years				
		1991	1990	1989	1988	1987
59(e)(1)	Written haz. comm. program	1	1	1	(1)	
59(h)	Employee training—haz. comm.	2	2	2	(1)	
59(g)(1)	MSDS for haz. chemicals	3	3	3	(1)	
1903.2(a)(1)	OSHA poster	4	4	4	1	2
59(g)(8)	Accessible copies of MSDS	5	5	12	(1)	
21(b)(2)	Safety training/recognition of unsafe conditions	6	7	10	3	6
500(d)(1)	Guarding open-sided floors	7	8	8	5	4
100(a)	Head protection	8	10	7	6	5
404(b)(1)(i)	Ground fault protection	9	6	5	2	1
404(f)(6)	Electrical grounding	10	9	6	4	3
20(b)(1)	Accident prevention program	11	11	9	7	7
652(a)(1)	Protective systems for trench./excav.	12	15	(2)		
451(d)(10)	Guardrail spec. for tubular welded scaffolds	13	13	13	9	11
1904.2(a)	OSHA 200 log	14	12	11	8	9
28(a)	PPE used for specific operation	15	14	14	10	8
1052(c)(1)	Stair rail required @ 30 in	16	(3)			

TABLE 3.3 100 Most Cited Construction Standards and Their Relative Ranking to 1991 (*Continued*)

Standards [1926 unless noted]	Description	Relative ranking to 1991 Years				
		1991	1990	1989	1988	1987
152(a)(1)	Storing and handling flamm. or comb. liquids	17	17	15	12	14
25(a)	General housekeeping	18	18	16	11	10
20(b)(2)	Accident prevention inspections	19	15	17	20	49
651(k)(1)	Inspection of physical components of trench/protect. system	20	22	(2)		
59(f)(5)(ii)	Label spec.—haz. comm.	44	50	65	(1)	
405(a)(2)(ii)(e)	Protection temporary lighting	45	48	38	26	34
500(c)(1)	Guarding wall opening	46	58	57	44	41
403(i)(2)(i)	Access to install. over 600 V	47	45	49	37	36
451(e)(10)	Guarding spec. for mobile scaffolds	48	46	41	34	37
451(d)(3)	Bracing of tubular welded scaffold	49	55	56	48	54
(5)(a)(1)	General duty clause	50	30	54	65	73
404(f)(7)(iv)(c)	Grounding specific types of equipment	51	53	32	30	31
50(e)(4)	Accessibility of written haz. communication program	52	54	(1)		
50(f)	Emergency numbers posted	53	36	26	15	13
1051(a)	Access by ladder/stairway @ change in elevation > 19 in	54	(3)			
405(b)(2)	Covers for pull boxes, junction boxes, outlets, etc.	55	61	58	54	47

No.	Code	Description				
56	416(e)(1)	Worn and frayed electric cords	57	62	55	81
57	451(a)(2)	Load design for scaffolds	60	66	59	61
58	405(b)(1)	Unused opening in boxes	70	74	64	64
59	550(b)(2)	Cranes—ANSI B30.5-1968	65	63	50	52
60	451(e)(4)	Tightly planked mobile scaffold	51	47	42	45
61	404(a)(2)	Reverse polarity of conductors	59	61	45	39
62	1053(b)(16)	Defective portable ladder	(3)			
63	405(a)(2)(ii)(i)	Protection of flexible cords and cables	44	37	28	25
64	1060(a)	Training program for ladders	(3)			
65	602(a)(9)(i)	Horns on bidirectional equipment	78	83	57	53
66	500(g)(1)	Fall protection for low-pitched roofs	76	85	78	79
67	50(c)	Certified first-aid personnel	80	84	73	93
68	500(b)(8)	Guarding floor holes	79	73	60	58
69	451(a)(14)	Extension of planking—scaffold	67	93	69	94
70	405(g)(2)(iii)	Electric cords less than no. 12	81	78	70	67
71	556(b)(2)(v)	Belt/lanyard—aerial lifts	73	80	74	77
72	150(a)(1)	Fire protection programs	87	69	46	32
73	451(e)(8)	Plumb/sound base for mobile scaffolds	68	79	72	68
74	50(d)(1)	Accessible first-aid supplies	66	52	36	30
75	59(e)(1)(ii)	Nonroutine inform.—writing haz. comm	(1)			
76	403(b)(1)	Elect. equip. free of hazards	85			
77	500(d)(2)	Guarding runway	84	72	64	

TABLE 3.3 100 Most Cited Construction Standards and Their Relative Ranking to 1991 (*Continued*)

Standards [1926 unless noted]	Description	Relative ranking to 1991 Years				
		1991	1990	1989	1988	1987
451(e)(5)	Ladder/stairway for access/egress	78	(3)	99	96	99
602(a)(9)(ii)	Backup alarm provided	79	74	82	56	46
150(c)(1)(i)	Fire extinguisher every 300 ft² or 100-ft travel	80	49	44	39	38
405(a)(2)(ii)(b)	Branch circuit specifications	81	92	94	76	75
450(a)(9)	Timber members of scaffold framing	82	24	23	18	18
59(f)(5)	Labeling haz. chemicals	83	56	70	(1)	
50(h)(1)	Employee information	84	88	71	(1)	
404(b)(1)(iii)	Assured equip. grounding conductor program	85	*(5)	*(5)	81	83
500(e)(1)(iv)	Railing on stairway	86(6)	29	28	21	22
1052(b)(1)	Stairway travel with empty pans	87				
450(a)(10)	Securing portable ladders	88(6)	20	21	14	15
451(a)(13)	Safe access for scaffolds	21	25	25	27	33
404(b)(1)(ii)	Ground fault circuit interrupter	22	19	18	13	12
701(b)	Guarding protruding steel rebars	23	40	77	(4)	
59(e)(1)(i)	List of haz. chemicals	24	31	50	(1)	
451(a)(4)	Scaffold guarding specs.	25	21	19	17	19

Code	Description					
651(j)(2)	Spoil pile protection	26	37	[2]		27
350(j)	Welding per ANSI Z49.1-1967	27	28	27	25	20
350(a)(9)	Securing compressed-gas cylinders	28	27	24	19	96
1910.20(g)(2)	Copy of 1910.20 Std. available	29	35	20	40	28
102(a)(1)	Eye/face protection	30	26	29	29	
1910.20(g)(1)(i)	Informing of medical access	31	62	40	[5]	16
1053(b)(1)	Ladder extended 3 ft above landing	32	[3]			
500(b)(1)	Guarding floor opening	33	23	22	16	
651(c)(2)	Access/egress from trench./excav.	34	32	[2]		
1910.20(g)(1)(iii)	Right of access to medical records	35	63	43	[5]	78
403(b)(2)	Listed, labeled, or cert. equip.	36	34	59	68	21
405(a)(2)(ii)(j)	Flexible cords designed for hard or extra-hard usage	37	33	33	22	
1910.20(g)(1)(ii)	Person(s) responsible for medical access	38	69	46	[5]	51
405(g)(2)(iv)	Strain relief for cords	39	38	42	38	
59(f)(5)(i)	Label spec.—haz. chemical(s)	40	39	45	[1]	17
304(f)	Woodworking tools per ANSI 01-1.1967	41	43	34	23	59
105(a)	Safety nets above 25 ft	42	52	48	43	29
300(b)(2)	Machine guarding—moving parts	43	42	39	35	
300(b)(1)	Power-operated tool guards	89	91	81	67	65
350(a)(1)	Valve protection caps	90	75	68	61	66
405(a)(2)(iii)	Guarding protecting temp. wiring over 600 V	91	[5]	[5]	[5]	[5]
405(a)(2)(ii)(f)	Temp. lights from electric cords	92	97		98	72

TABLE 3.3 100 Most Cited Construction Standards and Their Relative Ranking to 1991 (*Continued*)

Standards [1926 unless noted]	Description	Relative ranking to 1991 Years				
		1991	1990	1989	1988	1987
451(a)(3)	Supervision during erection, etc.	93	(5)	(5)	(5)	(5)
602(a)(2)(i)	Seat belts for earthmoving equipment	94	(5)	(5)	95	91
1052(c)(12)	Guarding for stairway edges	95	(5)	(5)	(5)	(5)
1053(b)(8)	Securing ladders	96	(3)			
59(e)(2)	Multiemployer(s) workplaces—written haz. comm. provision	97	83	(1)		
451(d)(4)	Foundation spec. for tubular welded scaffold legs	98	98	95	(5)	(5)
451(a)(10)	Scaffold-grade planking	99	95	(5)	(5)	(5)
550(a)(6)	Annual inspection of cranes	100	93	88	79	76

[1] Full enforcement of Hazard Communication Standard began in March 1989.
[2] Trenching/Excavation Standard became effective on March 5, 1990.
[3] Ladder/Stairway Standard became effective in January 1991.
[4] Standard first included in Concrete/Masonry Standard effective August 15, 1988.
[5] Particular standard was not one of the 100 most frequently cited in the reference year.
[6] Standard was part of old Ladder & Stairway Standards and was effectively discontinued in January 1991.
Note: The Standard sections quoted are those of the then-prevailing standards.
Source: Ref. 3.

inspections by a targeting system operated by the University of Tennessee's Construction Resource Analysis (CRA) Group using the information generated by F.W. Dodge Inc. in regard to all types of construction projects over $50,000, including new construction, additions, and alterations. Sites are selected from a broad range of construction projects—commercial, residential (excluding single-family homes), manufacturing, transportation, industrial, leisure, and public buildings including heavy construction such as nuclear power plants and cogeneration. The CRA then randomly selects on a statistical basis sites which are between 30 and 60 percent completed, and the CRA provides the names to the OSHA area offices for inspection. The selection by CRA is done blindly, i.e., without knowing the names of project owners or the names of the contractors.

For states under federal jurisdiction, about 18,000 construction inspections were made in fiscal year 1996. These inspections resulted in 28,000 violations of OSHA standards. The total penalty imposed upon the employers was about $31 million. Of the total violations, 76 percent were classified as serious, 3 percent as repeat, 1 percent as willful, and the rest as other than serious. State OSHA agencies conducted approximately 23,000 construction inspections. The combined construction inspections (federal and state OSHA) in the fiscal year 1997 totaled approximately 41,000. The nature and type of inspections are noted below:

Safety inspections	38,367
Health inspections	3,088
Total inspections in construction in fiscal year 1997	41,455
Unprogrammed inspections	14,888
Programmed inspections	26,567

Out of the total inspections conducted in fiscal year 1997, 1638 resulted from incidents at construction sites.

OSHA inspections consist of three stages:

1. Opening conference with the employer
2. Site inspection including interviews with employees and employers
3. Closing conference with the employer

Opening Conference

In the opening conference, the OSHA inspector, known as the compliance safety and health officer (CSHO), will discuss the purpose of the visit after presenting her or his credentials. The CSHO will describe whether the inspection is a result of programmed selection of the site, which is always done on an unbiased and neutral basis. If it is an unprogrammed inspection, the CSHO will explain whether it is a result of complaints or any reported incident at the site. If the complaint was received by OSHA from an employee, the OSH Act forbids employers to take retribution against the employee making the complaint. The inspectors will also discuss routine administrative matters and inform the employer about the OSH Act and where the standards could be obtained.

Site Inspection

Depending on the area of interest to the inspector, the site conditions will be observed, noted, and photographed by the compliance officer. Videotapes will also be recorded which can be used later to develop the case in the event that any violations of OSHA standards have occurred. The inspector will generally request documents pertaining to the area of suspected violation. In case of a structural failure, a number of documents are requested. Copies of construction drawings and project specifications including architectural, structural, plumbing, electrical, and HVAC drawings will be requested by the CSHO. Copies of shop drawings prepared by fabricators and erection drawings, if any, will be asked for. Also contract papers between general contractors and subcontractors will be requested in order for the CSHO to review the work of each contractor. The copies of the drawings will be returned to the employer after the investigation. If any trade secret is involved, the CSHO should be informed immediately and the documents should be clearly marked. The CSHO will conduct the inspection in a manner which will present the least disturbance to the ongoing work at the site.

The CSHO might review other documents at the site, e.g., hazard communication plan, safety and health plans, and medical records. Following the documents review, the inspector will schedule interviews with employees and management. During the OSHA interview, management personnel are generally assisted by their attorney. As regards nonsupervisory employees, OSHA can interview them in private without an employer representative. The inspector can interview as many employees as he or she deems fit to establish possible violations of OSHA standards. The interview can be recorded or hand-written, and the employee can be asked to sign the statements after carefully reviewing the contents of the interview.

Closing Conference

The conclusion of the inspection is marked by a closing conference which is conducted informally. The inspector will discuss the alleged violations and can indicate where citations could be issued and penalties imposed. The employer can provide additional information in defense of his or her position and may request reconsideration of any potential citation and penalties.

Citations

If the OSHA area office determines that the OSHA standards have been violated by the employer based upon the facts of the inspection by the CSHO, then citations and accompanying penalties are issued to the employer. Violations of OSHA standards are classified as willful, serious, other than serious, and repeated.

Willful violation: A willful violation is one which is committed intentionally and knowingly. Despite the knowledge that a hazardous condition exists at the site, the employer makes no reasonable effort to correct the situation. The penalty ranges from $5000 to $70,000 for each willful violation.

Serious violation: A serious violation exists where there is a substantial probability that death or serious physical harm could occur and the employer knew or should have known about the danger involved. The range of penalty is $1500 to $7000. However, in the absence of previous violations and given the good standing of the employer, the penalty could be reduced by the area director.

Other-than-serious violation: An other-than-serious violation has a direct relationship to job safety and health but would not result in death or physical harm. A maximum penalty of $7000 for each violation can be imposed. The area office may decide to issue a citation without any penalty.

Repeated violation: A repeated violation is one in which a similar violation is found upon reinspection; it can result in a fine of $70,000 for each violation.

Appeals Process

The employer who wishes to contest the citations must appeal, within 15 days of receipt, the citation and the proposed penalty to the area director in a written form, generally known as a Notice of Contest. If written objection to the citation is not received by the area director, the citation and the proposed penalty become final. The employer, instead of filing a formal notice of contest, can choose to discuss the case informally with the area director to present her or his arguments against the citations. The area director may choose to settle the case by reducing the penalties or downgrading the type of violation in the interest of quick hazard abatement. Upon receiving the notice of contest, the area director forwards the case to the Occupational Safety and Health Review Commission (OSHRC), which then assigns the case to an administrative law judge. The OSHRC is an independent body not associated with the Department of Labor. The administrative law judge will hold hearings at a place near the employer's workplace and will provide ruling in due course. The ruling by the administrative law judge can be appealed by either party to the OSHRC for a review by the OSHRC commissioners. The commission ruling can be further appealed to the U.S. Court of Appeals.

REPORTING AND INVESTIGATING CONSTRUCTION ACCIDENTS

OSHA standard 1904.8 states that the death of any employee from a work-related incident or hospitalization of three or more employees due to work-related injuries must be reported to the nearest OSHA area office either verbally by telephone or in person within 8 hours. The report must include the establishment name, location of incident, number of fatalities or hospitalized employees, contact person, phone number, and a brief description of the incident.

OSHA directive CPL 2.113 directs the area directors to "thoroughly" investigate the event to

- Determine the cause
- Determine whether any OSHA standard has been violated related to the incident
- Determine the effect that a violation of the standard had on the incident

The directive further directs the area director that the incident shall be investigated by appropriately trained and experienced compliance officers as soon as possible. However, during any rescue operation, OSHA has no authority to direct rescue activities; these are the responsibility of local authorities. OSHA does have the authority to monitor the working conditions of the workers engaged in the rescue operation.

Note that there are numerous construction incidents which do not necessarily result in any injuries or deaths. OSHA area directors have the authority to investigate even those incidents to determine the cause of the incident and to determine whether any OSHA standard has been violated. In case of construction incidents of a complex nature, the compliance officers are assisted by the engineers from the OSHA national office, who help determine the cause or probable cause of the incident. In the event of a violation of any OSHA standard or general industry practice under the general duty clause, citations are issued by the OSHA area office director to the employers. See the above discussion on different classes of violations. Section 17(e) of the act provides that if an employer has willfully violated OSHA standards or rules which caused the death of an employee, the case can be referred to the regional solicitor for possible criminal review.

OSHA CONSTRUCTION SAFETY STANDARDS

The Safety and Health Regulations for Construction, Part 1926,[5] has 26 subparts:

Subpart A: General
Subpart B: General Interpretations
Subpart C: General Safety and Health Provisions
Subpart D: Occupational Health and Environmental Controls
Subpart E: Personal Protective and Life Saving Equipment
Subpart F: Fire Protection and Prevention
Subpart G: Signs, Signals, and Barricades
Subpart H: Materials Handling, Storage, Use, and Disposal

Subpart I	Tools—Hand and Power
Subpart J	Welding and Cutting
Subpart K	Electrical
Subpart L	Scaffolds
Subpart M	Fall Protection
Subpart N	Cranes, Derricks, Hoists, Elevators, and Conveyors
Subpart O	Motor Vehicles, Mechanized Equipment, and Marine Operations
Subpart P	Excavations
Subpart Q	Concrete and Masonry Construction
Subpart R	Steel Construction
Subpart S	Underground Construction, Caissons, Cofferdams, and Compressed Air
Subpart T	Demolition
Subpart U	Blasting and the Use of Explosives
Subpart V	Power Transmission and Distribution
Subpart W	Rollover Protective Structures; Overhead Protection
Subpart X	Stairways and Ladders
Subpart Y	Diving
Subpart Z	Toxic and Hazardous Substances

The thrust and substance of these subparts are highlighted in the following.

Subparts A and B: General and General Interpretation

Subparts A and B deal with general provisions concerning scope, general policy, and variances, etc.

Subpart C: General Safety and Health Provisions

This subpart deals with the general safety and health provisions. Instructions about the work areas of employment to be free from unsanitary and hazardous conditions are given. Employers were given the responsibilities to initiate and maintain accident prevention programs. Frequent and regular inspections of the job sites and materials by competent persons are required. Machines and tools are to be used by only trained and competent personnel. OSHA is asked to establish and supervise training and education of the employers and employees in the recognition, avoidance, and prevention of unsafe conditions in the employment. The OSHA Technical Institute, located in Des Plaines, Illinois, provides training and education in safety and health for public- and private-sector employers and employees.

OSHA also provides funds to nonprofit organizations toward training and education in those areas where there is a lack of workplace training. This subpart deals with first aid and medical attention, fire protection, housekeeping, illumination and sanitation, means of egress, etc., at workplaces.

Subpart D: Occupational Health and Environmental Controls

This subpart gives detailed provisions for providing first aid and medical services at the workplaces.

1926.51. Sanitation is emphasized with the requirements on the following:

- Potable water
- Nonpotable water
- Toilets at construction sites
- Food handling
- Temporary sleeping quarters
- Washing facilities including toilets and shower facilities
- Eating and drinking areas
- Vermin control
- Change rooms

1926.52. This section deals with occupational noise exposure with permissible limits identified.

1926.53. When the use of radioactive materials or X-rays is involved at construction sites, the requirements of this section are applicable.

1926.54. This section deals with the installation, use, and operation of laser equipments at the sites.

1926.55. Gases, vapors, fumes, dusts, and mists are dealt with in this section. Threshold limit values of airborne contaminants for construction are given.

1926.56. All construction areas, corridors, offices, storage, etc. shall be lighted according to the minimum illumination intensities given in a table.

1926.57. At construction sites, if dusts, fumes, gases, mists, and vapors are produced, proper ventilation is required and threshold limits are indicated. It deals with the following:

- Local exhaust ventilation
- Design and operation of exhaust system

- Duration of operations of the exhaust system
- Disposal of exhaust materials
- Requirements of abrasive blasting
- Requirements of grinding, polishing, and buffing operations
- Requirements of spray finishing operations

1926.60. If there is a presence of methylenedianiline at the construction sites, the requirements of this section are enforced.

1926.62. If construction workers are exposed to lead, the requirements of this section are enforced. It deals with lead contamination, removal, exposure limits, protection of employees, monitoring of lead at the site, respiratory protection of employees, housekeeping including showers and hygiene facilities, etc.

1926.64. Requirements for preventing or minimizing the consequences of catastrophic releases of toxic, reactive, flammable, and explosive chemicals are provided.

1926.65. Safety precautions and other requirements related to hazardous waste operations and emergency response are provided.

Subpart E: Personal Protective and Life Saving Equipment

This subpart deals with personal protective and lifesaving equipment.

1926.95. Criteria for personal protection equipment for eyes, face, head and extremities, protective clothing, etc. are given. Instructions for maintenance and sanitation of such equipment are provided.

1926.96. It deals with safety toe footwear for employees.

1926.100. This section deals with the requirements of head protection.

1926.101. Provisions of hearing protection are given.

1926.102. Provisions of eye and face protection of employees when faced with potential eye or face injury from physical, chemical, or radiation agents are provided.

1926.103. Requirements of respiratory protection are given.

1926.104. This section deals with safety belts, lifelines, and lanyards. The requirements of minimum breaking strength of lifeline, lanyards, and minimum tensile loading of safety belts and lanyard hardware are provided.

1926.105. Safety net requirements are given.

1926.106. Requirements for employees working over or near water are provided.

Subpart F: Fire Protection and Prevention

This subpart deals with fire protection and fire prevention.

1926.150. The employer's responsibility for development of a fire protection program to be followed throughout all phases of work has been detailed. Water supply, portable and fixed firefighting equipment, fire alarm devices, and fire cutoff requirements are provided.

1926.151. This section deals with the means to prevent fire. It lays down requirements to deal with ignition hazards. It provides the criteria for the storage of combustible materials in open and indoor storage.

1926.152. This section deals with flammable and combustible liquids. It lays down requirements for the storage of flammable liquids in approved containers while storing them indoors and outside the buildings. It also provides provisions for fire control for flammable or combustible liquid storage and handling liquids at the point of final use. Further, it has detailed requirements of design and fabrication of storage tanks, atmospheric tanks, low-pressure tanks, pressure vessels, etc. There are provisions for installation of aboveground tanks, normal venting, emergency relief venting, etc.

1926.153. This section deals with liquefied petroleum gas (LP-Gas). Requirements are detailed for approval of equipment and systems, safety devices, etc.

Subpart G: Signs, Signals, and Barricades

1926.200. Requirements of signs and symbols are given. Specific requirements in regard to danger signs, caution signs, exit signs, safety instruction signs, directional signs, traffic signs, accident prevention tags, etc., are provided.

1926.201. Requirements of flagman are provided in the event that signs, signals, and barricades do not provide necessary protection.

Subpart H: Materials Handling, Storage, Use, and Disposal

1926.250. This section deals with materials storage and housekeeping and provides detailed provisions for all aspects of materials storage.

1926.251. Requirements for rigging equipments are given. It deals with safe working loads, special custom-design riggings, inspections, alloy steel chains, hooks, links, wire ropes, slings, etc. Tables of rated capacities of slings, links, manila rope slings, nylon rope slings, polyester rope slings, and polypropylene slings and safe working loads for shackles are given.

1926.252. Requirements for disposing of waste materials are provided.

Subpart I: Tools—Hand and Power

This subpart deals with the requirements of all hand and power tools and similar equipment.

1926.300. Safety requirements of tools, guarding, types of guarding, exposure of blades, anchoring of fixed machinery, guarding of abrasive wheel machinery, bench and floor stands, cylindrical girders, personal protective equipment, and switches are provided.

1926.301. Safety requirements of hand tools are given.

1926.302. Safety requirements of electric power-operated, pneumatic power, hydraulic power, and power-actuated tools are provided.

1926.303. Safety requirements of abrasive wheels and tools are given. Safety guards of grinding machines, guard design, and use of abrasive wheels are discussed.

1926.304. Safety requirements of woodworking tools are given. Disconnect switches, speeds, self-feed, guarding, personal protective equipment, radial saws, hand-fed cross-cut table saw, hand-fed rip saws, etc., are covered.

1926.305. Operation and maintenance, blocking, and general requirements of lever, ratchet, screw, and hydraulic jacks are covered.

1926.307. This section covers most of the types and shapes of power transmission belts.

Subpart J: Welding and Cutting

This subpart deals with the safety requirements of welding and cutting.

1926.350. This section lists the safety requirements of gas welding and cutting. Provision for transporting, moving, and storing compressed-gas cylinders; treatment of cylinders; use of fuel gas and oxygen manifolds, hoses, torches, regulators, and gauges; and oil and grease hazards are given.

1926.351. This section lists the requirements of arc welding and cutting. Provisions of manual electrode holders, welding cables and connectors, ground returns and machine grounding, operating instructions, and shielding are provided.

1926.352. This section deals with fire prevention during welding and cutting.

1926.353. This section deals with ventilation and protection in welding, cutting, and heating. Provisions with regard to mechanical ventilation, welding, cutting and heating in confined spaces, lifelines, welding, cutting or heating of metals of toxic significance, inert-gas metal-arc welding and general welding, cutting, and heating are covered.

1926.354. This section deals with welding, cutting, and heating on any surface covered by preservative coatings.

Subpart K: Electrical

This subpart deals with safety requirements of electrical work in construction. The requirements are divided into four major categories.

Installation Safety Requirements
1926.402. This defines where the standards could be applied.

1926.403. This section deals with general requirements. It has provisions for approval, examination, installation, and use of equipment; interrupting ratings; mounting and cooling of equipment; splices; arcing parts; marking; identification of disconnecting means; and circuits greater and less than 600 V.

1926.404. This section deals with wiring design and protection. It has provision for use and identification of grounded and grounding conductors, branch circuits, outside conductors and lamps, services, overcurrent protection, grounding, etc.

1926.405. This section deals with wiring, methods, components, and equipment for general use. Provisions are given for wiring methods, cabinets, boxes and fittings, knife switches, switchboards and panel boards, enclosure for damp or wet locations, conductors for general wiring, flexible cords and cables, portable cables over 600 V, fixture wires, and equipment for general use.

1926.406. This section deals with specific-purpose equipment and installation. It has provisions for cranes and hoists, elevators, escalators and moving walks, electric welders, and X-ray equipment.

1926.407. This section deals with hazardous (classified) locations.

1926.408. It deals with special systems, greater than 600 V; class 1, class 2, and class 3 remote control, signaling, and power-limited circuits; communication systems.

Safety-Related Work Practices
1926.416. Provisions are given for protecting employees, passageways and open spaces, load ratings, fuses, and cords and cables.

1926.417.   This section has general requirements for lockout and tagging of circuits. It deals with controls, equipment, and tags.

Safety-Related Maintenance and Environmental Considerations
1926.431.   Provisions for maintenance of equipment are given.

1926.432.   This section deals with environmental deterioration of equipment.

Safety Requirements for Special Equipment
1926.441.   It deals with batteries and battery charging.

Subpart L: Scaffolds

This subpart deals with all types of scaffolds except crane- or derrick-suspended personnel platforms.

1926.451.   The requirements of the capacity of the scaffold and its components are provided. This section also provides general requirements for scaffold platform construction. In addition, it provides criteria for supported and suspended scaffolds. This section deals with access to the scaffold for all employees during its use at the site. Criteria for the use of the scaffold at the site are also given. Lastly, the issue of fall protection is addressed for employees using the scaffold. Some of the highlights related to the capacity of the scaffold are as follows:

- The scaffold and its components (including the connections) must be able to support its dead load and 4 times the intended live load, based upon its ultimate strength. In other words, load factors of 1.0 and 4.0 should be applied to the dead and live loads in the strength design method.

- The suspension rope including connecting hardware must have a factor of safety of 6 to 1 support the intended load.

1926.452.   This section provides additional requirements for specific types of scaffolds, e.g.,

- Pole scaffolds, tube and coupler scaffolds
- Fabricated frame scaffolds
- Plasterers', decorators', and large-area scaffolds
- Bricklayers' square scaffolds
- Horse scaffolds
- Form scaffolds and carpenters' bracket scaffolds
- Roof bracket scaffolds
- Outrigger scaffolds
- Pump jack scaffolds

- Ladder jack scaffolds
- Window jack scaffolds
- Crawling boards (chicken ladders)
- Step, platform, and trestle ladder scaffolds
- Single-point, adjustable suspension scaffolds
- Two-point adjustable suspension scaffolds (swing stages)
- Multipoint adjustable suspension scaffolds, stonesetters' multipoint adjustable suspension scaffolds, and masons' multipoint adjustable suspension scaffolds
- Catenary scaffolds
- Float (ship) scaffolds
- Interior hung scaffolds
- Needle beam scaffolds
- Multilevel suspension scaffolds
- Mobile scaffolds
- Repair bracket scaffolds
- Stilts

1926.453. The requirements of aerial lifts have been provided in this section, which covers the following vehicle-mounted devices:

- Extensible boom platform
- Articulating boom platforms
- Aerial ladders
- Vertical towers
- A combination of any such devices

The requirements are provided for powered or manually operated aerial lifts. Specific requirements have been provided for different devices.

Subpart M: Fall Protection

1926.500. This subpart provides fall protection requirements in construction workplaces. However, certain workplaces are excluded for which requirements are stated in other subparts. The excluded workplaces are

- Employees working on scaffolds—see subpart L
- Employees working on certain cranes and derricks—see subpart N
- Employees working on steel erection—see subpart R
- Employees working on tunneling operation—see subpart S

- Employees working on electric transmission and distribution lines—see subpart V
- Employees working on stairways and ladders—see subpart X

1926.501.   The requirements of the general duty of the employers to provide fall protection for the employees have been provided. The employers must provide one of the three fall protection systems against fall due to unprotected sides and edges for employees working 6 ft (1.8 m) or more above a lower level. The three systems are the guardrail systems, safety net systems, and personal fall arrest systems. Employees working in a hoist area, near holes, near formwork and reinforcing steel, ramps and runways and other walkways, excavations, dangerous equipment, overhead bricklaying and related work, roofing work on low-slope or steep roofs, precast concrete erection, wall openings, etc., must be provided with necessary fall protection. In addition, requirements necessary for protection from falling objects have been provided.

1926.502.   The criteria for each of the three fall protection systems are given. The guardrail system's requirements have been provided, e.g., height of the top and middle rails, screens, intermediate vertical members, and required load-carrying capacity of the guardrails. The safety net system criteria have been given in regard to the location, projection beyond the work surfaces, impact load-resisting capacity, etc. Criteria for personal fall arrest systems are enumerated. Minimum strength of D-rings, snap hooks, lanyards and vertical lifelines, and self-retracting lifelines are given. The minimum strength of anchorage used for attachment of personal fall arrest systems and maximum arresting force on an employee with a bodybelt or body harness are provided.

The criteria for use of positioning device systems have been provided. The maximum free fall, minimum capacity of anchorages of positioning devices, and minimum strength of connecting assemblies, D-rings, and snap hooks, etc., have been stated. Criteria for the warning line systems; controlled-access zones; safety monitoring systems; covers over holes in floors, roofs, and other walking/working surfaces; protection for falling objects; and fall protection plans have been given.

Subpart N: Cranes, Derricks, Hoists, Elevators, and Conveyors

1926.550.   The general requirements for cranes and derricks are given. Provisions of rated loads and inspection of all components are provided, among other criteria. Specific requirements for crawler, locomotive, and truck cranes are provided. Requirements for hammerhead tower cranes, overhead and gantry cranes, derricks, and floating cranes and derricks have been given. Criteria for personnel platforms suspended from crane or derrick are provided.

1926.551.   Requirements for the helicopter cranes are provided.

1926.552.   Requirements for material hoists, personnel hoists, and elevators at construction sites are given.

1926.553.   Base-mounted drum hoist requirements are provided.

1926.554.   The provisions of overhead hoists are given.

1926.555.   This section deals with conveyors.

Subpart O: Motor Vehicles, Mechanized Equipment, and Marine Operations

1926.600.   General requirements of the equipment are given. The provisions for use of heavy machinery and equipment suspended by use of hoists, slings, or jacks are given. The use, care, and charging of batteries are dealt with.

1926.601.   This subsection covers motor vehicles used at construction sites not open to public traffic. Provisions for general requirements of the use of motor vehicles are given.

1926.602.   The requirements of earthmoving equipment are provided in this subsection. Seat belts, access roadways and grades, brakes, fenders, rollover protective structures, rollover protective structures for off-highway trucks, audible alarms, scissor points, etc., are dealt with. Requirements for excavating and lifting and hauling equipment are also provided.

1926.603.   All requirements of pile-driving equipment from land and from barges and floats are provided.

1926.604.   Provisions for site clearing are provided.

1926.605.   This subsection deals with material-handling operations, access to barges, working surfaces of barges, and commercial diving operations, including first aid and lifesaving equipment.

Subpart P: Excavations

This subpart deals with all open excavations including trenches.

1926.650.   This subsection deals with definitions of critical words and the scope of applicability of excavation standards.

1926.651.   Specific excavation requirements are given with regard to surface encumbrances, underground installations, access and egress, exposure to vehicular traffic, exposure to falling loads, warning systems for mobile equipment, hazardous atmospheres, protection from hazards associated with water accumulations, stability of adjacent structures, protection of employees from loose rock or soil, and inspections.

1926.652. This subsection deals with the requirements for protective systems. Provisions are provided for protection of employees in excavations; design of sloping and benching systems; design of support systems, shield systems, and other protective systems; materials and equipment; installation and removal of supports; sloping and benching systems; and shield systems.

Appendix A to subpart P describes a method of classifying soil and rock deposits including definitions. Appendix B deals with the specifications of sloping and benching. Appendix C contains information in regard to timber shoring of trenches. Tables are given for timber trench shoring for different soil types and for varying depths of excavations. Appendix D deals with aluminum hydraulic shoring for trenches. Tables are provided for aluminum hydraulic shoring for different types of soil and for varying depths of excavation. Appendix E provides sketches of alternatives to timber shoring. Appendix F provides a graphic summary of the excavation requirements.

Subpart Q: Concrete and Masonry Construction

1926.700. This subsection gives the definitions and scope of the standard.

1926.701. General requirements are specified in regard to applying construction loads to concrete structures, protruding reinforcing steel bars, posttensioning operations, provisions against riding concrete buckets, working under loads, and personal protective equipment during pneumatic application.

1926.702. This subsection gives requirements for equipment and tools. Provisions are provided for bulk cement storage, concrete mixers, power concrete trowels, concrete buggies, concrete pumping systems, concrete buckets, tremies, bull floats, masonry saws, and lockout/tagout procedures.

1926.703. This subsection provides requirements for cast-in-place concrete. Provisions are given for the design, fabrication, and installation of concrete formwork; shoring and reshoring; vertical slip forms; integrity of reinforcing of reinforcing steel; and removal of formwork.

1926.704. Requirements are given for the support of precast concrete wall units and tilt-up wall units and their lifting inserts, etc.

1926.705. This subsection deals with the requirements of the lift-slab construction. Design, planning, jacking, and lifting provisions are provided.

1926.706. Requirements for masonry construction are provided with regard to limited-access zone and bracing of masonry walls during construction. All masonry walls more than 8 ft high are required to be braced against overturning and collapse. *No maximum wind speed is designated.*

Subpart R: Steel Construction

Presently a new standard for steel erection has been proposed by OSHA as a result of a negotiated rule-making process, with labor and employers and industry representatives participating in the process. Currently, comments have been invited on the proposed standard. The standard is expected to be adopted in the near future. Provisions of the current standard are as follows.

1926.750. Provisions are given for permanent flooring of multistory buildings as the erection of structural steel continues. In addition, requirements of number of floors of unfinished bolting above the base or permanent floor are provided. Provisions for temporary flooring in tiered buildings are dealt with. Also requirements of safety railing, safety nets, etc. are given.

1926.751. During steel erection, the minimum number of bolts is given for structural members at each end before the crane releases the load. The need to provide lateral stability to columns in two directions is discussed. The requirements of bridging the long-span joists and trusses are given.

1926.752. Provisions for carrying and storing bolts, drift pins, etc. are given. The uses of pneumatic hand tools, airline hoses, and eye protection are specified. Locking devices of impact wrenches are also dealt with. Requirements of equipment needed to plumb structural steel frames are provided.

Subpart S: Underground Construction, Caissons, Cofferdams and Compressed Air

1926.800. Access and egress to underground construction, check-in and check-out procedures, safety instructions, and communications are dealt with. Emergency provisions are given that deal with hoisting capability, self-rescuers, the need to designate a person aboveground, emergency lighting, rescue teams, etc. The conditions under which underground construction could be classified as potentially gassy are given. In addition, conditions under which potentially gassy operations could be declassified are addressed. Additional requirements of gassy operations have been given. Provisions of air quality and monitoring have been delineated. In the event of potentially gassy and gassy operations, additional requirements are provided. Provisions for providing fresh air in underground construction are given. Illumination requirements for underground construction and fire prevention and control are provided. Requirements of welding, cutting, and other hot work are addressed. The safety requirements of guarding portal areas are provided. Ground stability and inspection of underground structures are discussed. Safety requirements of shaft, blasting, drilling, haulage equipment, hoisting unique to underground construction, hoists, and personal hoists are given. The requirements of caissons and work and safety for employees working in and around caissons are given. Provisions for cofferdams are made. The rules and regulations of using compressed air are enumerated.

Subpart T: Demolition

This subpart deals with demolition of existing structures. All preparatory operations are discussed. The requirements of conducting an engineering survey before demolition begins are given. Safety requirements of stairs, passageways and ladders, chutes, etc., are provided. Removal of walls, masonry sections, chimneys, and materials through floor openings is given. Safety requirements during manual removal of floors, removal of walls and floors, and materials with equipment are provided. Storage of waste material and debris is discussed. Provisions of removal of steel construction, mechanical demolition, and selective demolition by explosives are given.

Subpart U: Blasting and the Use of Explosives

Safety requirements of blasting and the use of explosives are provided. Minimum qualifications for blasters are given. Provision for surface transportation of explosives including underground transportation is stated. Requirements of storage of explosives and blasting agents, loading of explosives of blasting agents, initiation of explosive charges, and use of safety fuse and detonating cord are given. Additional provisions for firing the blast and inspection following blasting, misfires, and underwater blasting are given. Blasting in excavations under compressed air is also discussed.

Subpart V: Power Transmission and Distribution

1926.950.   Safety provisions during construction of electric transmission and distribution lines are stated. Specific provisions are given for initial inspections, tests or determinations, clearances, deenergizing lines and equipment, emergency procedures and first-aid, night work, work near and over water, sanitation facilities, hydraulic fluids, etc.

1926.951.   This section deals with protective equipment, personal climbing equipment, ladders, live-line tools, measuring tapes or measuring ropes, and hand tools.

1926.952.   Safety requirements of mechanical equipment including aerial lifts, derrick trucks, cranes, and other lifting equipment are addressed.

1926.953.   Provisions are made for unloading, pole hauling, storage, tag line, oil-filled equipment, framing, and attaching the load.

1926.954.   Safety requirements for grounding for protection of employees are given. Specific instructions for new construction, communication conductors, means of attaching grounds, testing without grounds, grounding electrodes, grounding to tower, ground lead, etc., are given.

1926.955. Safety provisions when working near overhead lines are enumerated. Specific requirements for working near metal tower construction, stringing or removing deenergized conductors, stringing adjacent to energized lines, live-line bare-hand work, etc., are provided.

1926.956. This subsection deals with underground lines. Guarding and ventilating street openings used for access to underground lines or equipment, working in manholes, trenching, and excavating are discussed.

1926.957. Provisions for working near energized equipment facilities are given. Requirements for deenergized equipment or lines, barricades and barriers, control panels, mechanized equipment, storage, substation fences, footing excavation, etc., are given.

1926.958. Requirements during operations using a rotorcraft are given.

1926.959. Requirements for lineman's bodybelts, safety straps, and lanyards are given.

Subpart W: Rollover Protective Structures; Overhead Protection

1926.1000. This section provides the safety requirements of different types of material-handling equipment with regard to rollover protection. It applies to rubber-tire scrapers, loaders, dozers, agricultural and industrial tractors, crawler tractors, etc.

1926.1001. This section gives the minimum performance criteria for rollover protective structures for designated scrapers, loaders, dozers, graders, and crawler tractors. Laboratory test procedures and performance requirements to determine the adequacy of structures to protect the operators are provided.

1926.1002. Safety requirements of protective frames are given for wheel-type agricultural and industrial tractors used in construction.

1926.1003. This section deals with overhead protection for operators of agricultural and industrial tractors.

Subpart X: Stairways and Ladders

This subpart provides safety requirements of ladders and stairways used in construction, alteration, and demolition work.

Subpart Y: Diving

This subpart provides requirements for diving during construction activities including scuba diving.

Subpart Z: Toxic and Hazardous Substances

The safety requirements of toxic and hazardous substances are provided.

AMERICAN NATIONAL STANDARDS

The American National Standards Institute is a voluntary nonprofit organization engaged in promoting consensus voluntary standards for the industry. The American National Standards Institute does not develop standards. It rather helps other associations, societies, and interested bodies to develop standards to fulfill the demands of the industry. After the standard has been developed, the American National Standards Institute simply adopts it, provided the criteria for the development of standards have been met. As a condition for adoption by ANSI, the standard developer must demonstrate that during the development phase, "consensus, due process and openness" have been adhered to. Consensus does not necessarily mean unanimity among members but implies that all objections, comments, reservations, and negative votes have been properly discussed and addressed, and all stakeholders who are affected by the activity were able to review the standard and an open environment was provided during its development. Once ANSI adopts a standard, it becomes an industry standard. Currently, ANSI has 21 standards relating to construction, and 14 standards are in the development stage for construction.

The A10 Committee of the American National Standards Institute on safety in construction and demolition operations has produced the following safety standards:

A10.3-1995 Powder-Actuated Fastening Systems.   Safety requirements for a "powder-actuated fastening system that propels a stud, pin, fastener or other object for the purpose of affixing it by penetration to hard structural surface" are given.

A10.4-1990 Personnel Hoists and Employee Elevators.   Safety requirements are given for the design, construction, operation, inspection, and maintenance of hoists and elevators that are not part of building but are installed for use during construction and are used to transport employees.

A10.5-1992 Material Hoists

A10.6-1990 Demolition.   Safety requirements for demolition of structures are provided. The details of the engineering survey before commencement of demolition are given. Provisions for general protection, catch platforms, scaffolds, and warning devices are dealt with. Requirements of fire protection and control are given. Removal of structural elements, tank, vessel, machinery, and use of flame cutting are discussed.

A10.7-1991 Commercial Explosives and Blasting Agents—Safety Requirements for Transportation, Storage, Handling, and Use.   The standard deals with the minimum standard set forth for the construction industry for the transportation, storage, handling, and use of commercial explosive materials; firing the blast and procedures after blasting are given.

A10.8-1988 Scaffolding.   Provisions for the construction, erection, operation, maintenance, and use of scaffolds in the construction, demolition, and maintenance of buildings are given. Requirements for platform units and 17 types of scaffolds are provided.

A10.9-1989 Concrete Construction and Masonry Work.   Provisions are given for in-site construction of concrete and masonry work including prestressing by post- and pretensioning, lift slab, tilt-up construction, and slipform.

A10.10-1990 Temporary and Portable Space Heating Devices and Equipment Used in the Construction Industry.   Provisions for the installation, operation, and maintenance of space heating devices and equipment (temporary and portable designs) are given. Requirements for solid-fuel heaters, liquid-fuel heaters, natural gas heaters, and liquefied petroleum gas heaters are provided.

A10.11-1989 Safety Nets Used during Construction, Repair and Demolition Operations. Safety requirements for the selection, installation, and use of personnel and debris nets during construction are provided. The standard deals with the conditions where nets are required, materials and design of nets, and factors affecting net life.

A10.12-1998 Excavation.   (Under development)

A10.13-1989 Steel Erection.   The standard deals with the safety requirements for handling, erecting, fitting, fastening, and dismantling structural steel at a construction site. Requirements for welding and cutting, scaffolding, and safety nets are given. It deals with temporary floors, bolting, and fitting of structural members. Provisions for material handling and work over water are also given.

A10.14-1991 Safety Belts, Harnesses, Lanyards, and Lifelines.   The standard deals with the requirements of safety belts, harnesses, lanyards, and lifelines during construction and demolition. It provides performance requirements of materials and hardware. Rope grabs and shock absorbers are discussed. Test methods to determine compliance with the applicable performance requirements are provided.

A10.15-1987 Dredging. The standard applies to "operations, inspections and maintenance of any vessel fitted with machinery for the purpose of removing or relocating materials from or in a body of water." It deals with general requirements for floating plant and marine equipment.

A10.16-1988 Tunnels, Shafts, and Caissons. The standard deals with the safety requirements in regard to the construction of tunnels, shafts, and caissons. It deals with environmental control, related facilities, fire prevention, hoisting, haulage and electrical, drilling and blasting, and compressed-air works.

A10.17-1975 Asphalt Pavement Construction. The standard provides operational safety and health guidelines to workers engaged in pavement construction, resurfacing, and general maintenance.

A10.18-1983 Temporary Floor and Wall Openings, Flat Roofs, Stairs, Railings, and Toeboards. The standard deals with the hazards arising out of or associated with temporary floors, wall openings, flat roofs, stairs, railings, and toeboards.

A10.19 Pile Driving. (Under development)

A10.20-1988 Ceramic Tile, Terrazzo, and Marble Work. This standard deals with the safety requirements during handling and installing of ceramic tiles, terrazzo, and marble.

A10.22-1990 Rope-Guided and Non-Guided Workmen's Hoists. The standard deals with the safety requirements for the transportation of workers to and from working elevations during construction and demolition; and it is applicable to work in chimneys, chimney linings, silos, towers, stacks, shafts, etc. It is also applicable when hoisting or lowering a person in a boatswain's chair. The standard applies to transportation of materials nonconcurrently with personnel.

A10.24 Roofing. (Under development)

A10.27 Asphalt Mixing Plants for Construction Projects. (Under development)

A10.28-1990 Work Platforms Suspended from Cranes or Derricks. The standard provides safety requirements for "platforms suspended from lifting cranes or derricks in order to (1) perform work at elevations that cannot normally be reached by other types of scaffolds or aerial work platforms or (2) transport personnel to elevations where other means of access are unsafe or impractical because of design or worksite conditions."

A10.30 Drilled Caissons. (Under development)

A10.31-1995 Digger Derricks.

A10.32 Fall Prevention Systems.   (Under development)

A10.33-1992 Safety and Health Program Requirements for Multi-Employee Projects.
This standard provides safety and health program requirements and defines duties
and responsibilities of construction employers working on a construction project.

A10.34 Public Protection.   (Under development)

A10.35 High Pressure Hydro Blasting.   (Under development)

A10.36 Dry Diamond Saws.   (Under development)

A10.37 Debris Nets.   (Under development)

A10.38-1991 Special Safety Programs.   (Under development)

A10.39-1996 Safety Audits.   (Proposed)

*A10.40 Duties and Qualifications of Individuals Assigned Construction Safety and
Health Responsibilities.*   (Under development)

A10.41 Qualifications and Responsibilities for Equipment Operators and Supervisors.
(Under development)

A10.42 Qualifications for Riggings and Signalmen.   (Under development)

OTHER CONSTRUCTION INDUSTRY STANDARDS

There are other industry standards, guides, recommendations, and manuals pertaining to construction which a forensic engineer should be familiar with. Some
are listed below.

- American Institute of Steel Construction (AISC)
  Code of Standard Practice for Steel Buildings and Bridges
  Erection Bracing of Low Rise Structural Steel Frames
- American Concrete Institute (ACI)
  Guide to Formwork for Concrete
- American Society of Civil Engineers (ASCE)
  Crane Safety on Construction Sites
- Steel Joist Institute (SJI)
  Handling and Erection of Steel Joists & Joist Girders
- Scaffolding, Shoring & Forming Institute, Inc.
  *Code of Safe Practices for Frame Scaffolds, Tube and Clamp Scaffolds, and
  Rolling Scaffolds*

Recommended Steel Frame Shoring Erection Procedures
Guide to Scaffolding Erection and Dismantling Procedures
Guide to Safety Procedures for Vertical Concrete Framework

- National Association of Demolition Contractors
  Demolition Safety Manual

- The Tilt-Up Concrete Association
  Temporary Wind Bracing of Tilt-Up Concrete Panels during Construction

- Precast Concrete Institute
  Erectors Manual (Standards and Guidelines for the Erection of Precast Concrete Products)

- National Concrete Masonry Association
  TEK Manual for Concrete Masonry Design and Construction

- American Institute of Timber Construction
  Timber Construction Manual
  Structural Glued Laminated Timber

- U.S. Army Corps of Engineers
  Safety and Health Requirements Manual

- Department of the Navy
  Naval Facilities Engineering Command's various publications

- Departments of the Army and the Air Force
  Various publications

- Metal Building Manufacturer's Association
  Low Rise Building Systems Manual

- Truss Plate Institute
  Commentary and Recommendations for Handling, Installing and Bracing Metal Plate Connected Wood Trusses

- American Association of State Highway and Transportation Officials
  Standard Specification for Highway Bridges

- Masonry Contractors Association of America
  Bracing Masonry Walls under Construction

OSHA versus ANSI and Other Industry Standards

If there is a specific OSHA standard with regard to a certain construction activity, then the employer is obligated to follow the OSHA standard as a minimum. However, if a certain OSHA standard incorporates by reference an industry consensus standard, e.g., an ANSI standard, then the employer is required to follow not only the OSHA provisions but also the ANSI standard.

In the event there is no OSHA standard addressing the hazard in question, OSHA often refers to consensus standards to demonstrate that the hazard is recognized and that there is a duty to provide protection under OSHA's General Duty Clause.

REFERENCES

1. S. Jin, and C. G. Culver, "OSHA Examines Construction Fatalities," *Safety and Health,* June 1994.

2. C. G. Culver, G. Florczak, R. Castell Jr., C. Connolly, and G. Pelton, *Analysis of Construction Fatalities—The OSHA Data Base 1985–1989,* Occupational Safety and Health Administration, 1990.

3. M. M. Marshall and C. Hardesty, *The 100 Most Frequently Cited OSHA Construction Standards in 1991,* Occupational Safety and Health Administration, 1993.

4. C. Hardesty, C. Culver, and F. Anderson, *Ironworker Fatalities in Construction,* Occupational Safety and Health Administration, 1993.

5. *Code of Federal Regulations,* Title 29, Part 1926, published by the Office of the Federal Register, National Archives and Record Administration.

CHAPTER 4
THE FIRST STEPS AFTER A FAILURE

David B. Peraza, P.E. and Daniel A. Cuoco, P.E.

INTRODUCTION

The first steps following a collapse are critical. They will blaze the trail for subsequent investigations, and they may prevent further damage or loss of life.

The activities immediately following a collapse profoundly influence the success of subsequent technical investigations. So much of the evidence associated with a collapse is of a perishable nature—and some of it highly perishable—that swift action is needed to preserve as much as possible. Snow will melt, fracture surfaces will corrode, the debris will be removed, and memories will fade.

The forensic engineer who is called in following a collapse plays a crucial role in determining what those first steps should be. He or she is the most qualified to recognize perishable evidence and its potential value. The forensic engineer can recommend action, and may be in a position to persuade those who are in control of the site. The decisions made will directly affect the abundance—or scarcity—of evidence, upon which investigations will depend. Sparse evidence leads to tentative conclusions; robust information provides the basis for a persuasive argument.

A successful investigation can be defined as one that satisfies its stated goals in the most efficient manner possible. Although investigations may justifiably have other goals, for the purposes of this chapter, it is assumed that the goal is to determine, within a reasonable degree of engineering certainty, the most probable cause(s) of the failure.

This chapter deals with issues that a forensic engineer may be faced with when she or he first steps onto a collapse site, and in the ensuing days. It includes issues such as safety, preserving perishable evidence, reserving samples, documentation, interviews, document gathering, and preliminary evaluation. With most of these issues, speed and accuracy are of the essence.

SAFETY

The forensic engineer called to a collapse may be requested to assess the safety and stability of the structure for a variety of possible reasons:

- To assist in identifying the safest routes through the debris, or identifying areas that must be avoided until stabilized. These routes may be needed by rescue personnel to reach victims, by safety officials who need to reach utility shutoff valves, or by workers attempting to stabilize the structure. In search-and-rescue situations, the forensic engineer may also be able to assist in identifying "pockets" within the debris where victims might be sheltered.

- To assist in identifying components that are in imminent danger of further collapse.

- To evaluate methods of stabilizing the structure, such as by adding shoring, bracing, or tiebacks.

- To assist in determining whether it is advisable to provide protection for the public, or whether to restrict public access. Protection may include safety netting, sidewalk bridges, and other barriers.

- To assist in evaluating alternative demolition or dismantling sequences. The load paths after a collapse may differ significantly from the intended load paths, and may not be readily apparent. It is important to try to identify stressed components, or potentially stressed components. If a stressed component is cut or removed, it may release its load in a sudden and uncontrolled manner, possibly causing injury or disturbing other components. If it is necessary to remove a potentially stressed component, consideration should be given to first relieving its load (possibly using cables with come-alongs), next removing the member, and then slowly releasing the temporary load in a controlled manner. For complex collapses, the active load paths may become apparent only as demolition proceeds, so it is important that the process be constantly monitored. Removal of posttensioned elements requires special attention to prevent unexpected releases of load.

(a)

FIGURE 4.1 Manhattan's Times Square was immediately closed to the public after portions of this scaffolding and hoist at Four Times Square collapsed on July 21, 1998. Extensive protective measures and stabilization had to be installed before dismantling of the crippled scaffolding could even begin. Engineers from the authors' firm worked closely with contractors throughout the sensitive dismantling operation. (*a*) Protective netting being installed to help contain debris.

PRESERVE PERISHABLE EVIDENCE

After a collapse, the as-built construction, its position, its condition, and other circumstances on the site become evidence. This evidence will play a crucial role in determining the most likely cause of the failure and contributing factors. Some of this evidence is durable and will remain reasonably intact over a period of time, possibly even if left exposed to the elements. Certain evidence, however, is of a perishable nature and therefore must be quickly documented or otherwise preserved.

(b)

FIGURE 4.1   (*Continued*) (*b*) Eerily empty Times Square.

Collapse Configuration

The collapse configuration can provide valuable information about possible collapse mechanisms and the origin of the failure, and may also serve to eliminate some mechanisms from further consideration. Due to various pressures, it is likely that the collapse scene will need to be disturbed—or even altogether removed—within a short time. It is therefore important that the configuration of the collapse be "captured" as quickly as possible.

It is extremely valuable to establish—and to apply—a nomenclature for labeling key components prior to their removal. Wherever possible, it is desirable to use any predefined nomenclature, such as column grid lines, supplementing it as required. In some cases, it is necessary to develop the entire nomenclature. This would be necessary if drawings were not available, or if the structure were composed of interchangeable elements, such as a scaffold system.

If labeling of key components cannot be done prior to their removal, as might be the case when a rescue operation is under way or if access is hazardous, the components will have to be labeled as they are removed. This requires closely monitoring the removal operation, tracking components as they are removed, and labeling them as soon as they reach an accessible location. This operation will usually require a team of two or three people for every crew that is removing items. Cooperation from the contractor performing the removal will greatly facilitate the process.

(c)

FIGURE 4.1 (*Continued*) (*c*) Temporary outriggers cantilever out from the building to help prop up the scaffolding until it can be dismantled.

There are several types of labeling systems. Three of the most commonly used are the following:

1. *Identity piece-mark system.* If the identity of a piece is known, it can be labeled with an identity piece mark that is keyed to a drawing. If the original orientation of the element is known from its context in the debris, but may not otherwise be readily apparent, it should be marked on the piece, for example, "north flange" or "bottom end."

2. *Serial piece-mark system.* In some cases, the identity of a piece may not be known with certainty. Such a piece should still be labeled, but in this case with an arbitrary—but unique—piece mark. This piece mark is arbitrary in the sense that it conveys no information about the identity of the piece; it serves solely as a label to distinguish this piece from other pieces. The assigned piece mark must be unique over the entire project. If multiple persons are simultaneously assigning the piece marks, incorporating the person's initials in the piece mark, such as "JFK-23," will help in ensuring uniqueness. Obviously any information that may assist in later determining the identity of the piece, such as where it was found, should be recorded, either directly on the piece or in field notes.

3. *Match-mark system.* Match marking of mating segments can greatly facilitate later reconstruction. It can be used on members that are severed, members that

FIGURE 4.2 Collapse of this suspended cement plaster ceiling in a rail station during rush hour resulted in two deaths and many injuries to commuters. This PATH station in Jersey City, NJ, was closed for nearly 2 weeks to allow for the inspection of all ceilings, the installation of protective scaffolding in areas of similar construction, and engineers from the authors' firm to conduct field investigations.

are cut, or members that are disconnected. Match marking consists of marking both sides of mating segments with an identical label. If necessary, a *match point* can also be indicated on the mating ends so that they can be reconstructed with the proper relative orientation. When used in conjunction with a piece-mark system, the match-mark pairs need only be unique to that piece. For example, "Match 1" may suffice if both segments are already marked with the same piece mark. If used as a stand-alone notation, each pair of match marks must be unique over the entire project, so the marks will necessarily be more complex.

A combination of nomenclature systems is often used on a given project.

High-quality field notes, photographs, and possibly video are invaluable for documenting the collapse configuration and the removal process.

Aerial photographs can provide a valuable overall view of the site. Consideration should be given to both vertical and oblique photographs. Vertical photographs most clearly show the position of features and components in plan. The intended use of the photographs should be considered in selecting the person or firm to take the pho-

FIGURE 4.3 Portions of this brick facade rained down on the sidewalk and adjacent buildings, forcing officials to immediately close Madison Avenue. A temporary bridge was erected across Madison Avenue to shield the public before it could be reopened to traffic. In this photograph, additional unstable areas of brick have been removed, and other stabilization has been added.

tographs. If the photographs will be used for general information purposes, then high-quality handheld photographs may suffice. If photogrammetric techniques will be used to precisely determine the location of features, or if the photographs need to be viewed stereoscopically, then specialized aerial photography equipment will be necessary. Oblique photographs are useful for capturing the relative heights of elements and provide a more natural, three-dimensional view. Oblique photographs should preferably be taken from all four sides.

FIGURE 4.4 Bracing and shoring were installed to prevent further collapse of this parking deck in Queens, NY.

(a)

FIGURE 4.5 (a) The 1978 collapse of Connecticut's Hartford Civic Center, shortly after a well-attended basketball game, miraculously resulted in no deaths or injuries.

(a)

FIGURE 4.5 (*Continued*) (*b*) Detailed markings on the debris helped preserve information about the collapse configuration, which assisted the authors' firm in determining the cause of the collapse.

For large sites, it may be desirable that professional surveyors lay out baselines or grid lines for reference. The position of collapsed elements can then be measured in relation to these reference lines.

Steel Fracture Surfaces

Features of fractured steel surfaces, if preserved, can provide crucial information regarding the failure. Examination of failure surfaces can assist in determining whether fatigue played a role, the order of magnitude of the cycles experienced, the relative magnitude and suddenness of the applied load, the ductility of the failure, whether the fracture originated at a preexisting crack, and other information. Some of these telltale features exist at the microscopic level and thus are fragile. They can be obscured—or even destroyed—by light corrosion. Corrosion of freshly exposed steel can occur rapidly, especially in humid or seaside environments.

Fracture surfaces can be readily protected against corrosion by spraying with acrylic paint. Use of a pigmented coating will help provide visual confirmation that a surface has not been overlooked. The coating can be easily removed in the laboratory with a solvent. See Fig. 4.9.

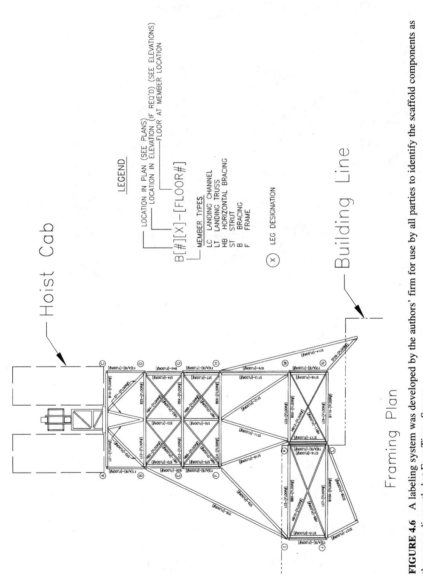

FIGURE 4.6 A labeling system was developed by the authors' firm for use by all parties to identify the scaffold components as they were dismantled at Four Times Square.

FIGURE 4.6   (*Continued*).

Curing Concrete Test Cylinders

If the structure is under construction, curing concrete test cylinders may be on the site. Some concrete cylinders may have already been transported to the testing laboratory. A concerted effort should be made to locate all curing concrete cylinders immediately. These cylinders can provide invaluable information, especially for cases where premature formwork removal may be an issue. If there is any possibility that the cylinders may be damaged or otherwise compromised at their found location, they should be carefully moved to a safe location. Care should be exercised during the move to minimize disturbing the set of the concrete. See Fig. 4.10.

Whether the cylinders are on or off the site, a decision must be made quickly concerning the disposition of curing cylinders. One option is to test the cylinders, using the same protocol called for in the project specifications and using the same testing laboratory. However, consideration should be given to altering the protocol, depending on the nature of the case and the number of cylinders available. For example, it may be advisable to test certain cylinders immediately, to determine the concrete strength on the day of the collapse. Or it may be advisable to send some or all of the cylinders to an independent laboratory. It may also be prudent for the investigating engineer to witness the testing of the cylinders.

Testing laboratories normally dispose of cylinders shortly after testing them. However, consideration should be given to retaining the tested cylinders, either for their own evidentiary sake or for additional testing, such as petrographic examination.

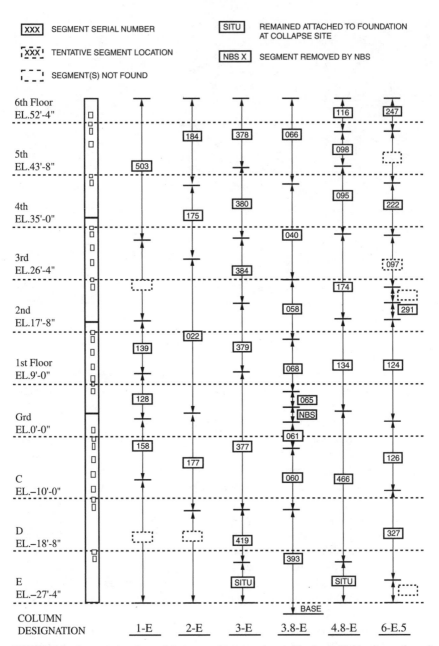

FIGURE 4.7 A comprehensive serial piece-mark system, in combination with identity marks and match marks, by the authors' firm allowed almost complete reconstruction of the columns, leading to a persuasive determination of the collapse cause and the retraction of OSHA's theory.

FIGURE 4.8 Aerial photography, combined with land surveying techniques, is often used to document large-scale collapses, such as that of the Schoharie Bridge (1987), which was investigated by the authors' firm.

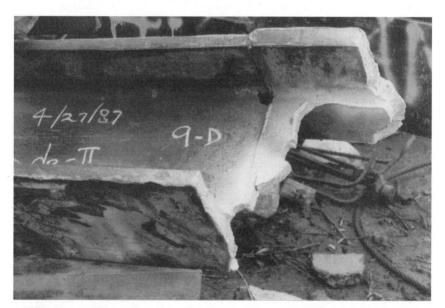

FIGURE 4.9 Application of protective coatings to steel fracture surfaces such as these helps preserve delicate telltale features.

FIGURE 4.10   These curing concrete cylinders were found at the L'Ambiance Plaza site and were instrumental in ruling out substandard concrete strength as a possible cause of the collapse.

Snow and Ice Accumulation

The weight of snow actually on a roof at the time of its collapse is an extremely valuable piece of information. When compared against the code-prescribed design loads for the structure and the design criteria, it can provide an indication of whether the failure was due to an error in design or construction, or due to an unforeseeable overload.

Depending on climactic conditions, the amount of snow and ice may change dramatically in the days—or even hours—following a collapse. Additional precipitation may increase the weight, winds may sweep off snow or add to drifted areas, or melting may reduce the weight. To obtain the most reliable measurement, it is important that the snow weight be measured as quickly as possible.

For several reasons, however, it may be difficult or impossible to accurately measure the snow weight. Measurements of snow weight in collapsed areas may not be representative of conditions present prior to the collapse, since the depth of snow may have been radically altered by the collapse itself. Measurements in adjacent noncollapsed areas of the same roof are potentially the most meaningful, if the thermal characteristics of the roof and the temperature below it match those of the collapse area. Care must be taken that the configuration of adjacent roofs and other obstructions does not materially affect the expected drift heights or accumulations due to sliding snow. Safety of the personnel measuring the snow weight should always be a concern. Metal roofs may be extremely slippery, even those with mild slopes, and the stability of the remaining structure may be questionable.

If it is not possible to measure the snow weight on the roof itself, the next-best alternative is to measure it on nearby roofs with similar wind exposures. The geometric conditions of these roofs should be carefully documented, especially with regard to conditions that simulate or differ from the subject roof.

The physical measurement of the snow weight needs to be made carefully. One way is to use the inverted-container method:

1. Press the inverted container down into the snow until the roof is firmly contacted.
2. Remove the snow and ice on all sides of the container.
3. If it is found that the ice has prevented the container from reaching the roof, carefully remove the ice around the perimeter of the container. If ribs prevent uniform contact with the roof, such as on metal panel roofs, notch the container to fit over the ribs. Another alternative for ribbed roofs is to use a container that fits between the ribs, and to locate it appropriately.
4. Slide a thin sheet, possibly metal, under the container to help in retaining the contents while the container is flipped to its normal position.
5. Weigh the contents, and measure the opening of the container used. The results can then be reported in terms of pounds per square foot.

Depending on the consistency of the snow, it may be possible to remove the inverted container and leave the snow standing. Measurements of the thickness of snow and ice strata could then be made before placing the material in the container for weighing.

If possible, several samples should be taken from each selected location to minimize random measurement errors. It is also recommended that the measurement process be videotaped, or at least extensively photographed. See Fig. 4.11.

RESERVING SAMPLES

Except for the smallest of failures, it is usually impractical and unnecessary to reserve the entire structure. The forensic engineer will usually have to make decisions regarding what portions of the structure should be set aside for future use. It is important that the forensic engineer be present during demolition, so she or he has the opportunity to identify additional components as they are uncovered.

Both failed and unfailed components are of interest to the forensic engineer. For all samples, it is important that a chain of custody be maintained in the event that the matter eventually goes to trial.

Failed Components

Failed components are obvious candidates for preserving. Most important are failed items that are suspected of being associated with the initiation or propagation of the

FIGURE 4.11 Measurements of the snow weight on this preengineered refrigerated warehouse shortly after the roof collapse indicated a snow load nearly double the code value. This photograph was taken after much of the snow had melted.

failure, as opposed to items that failed due to consequential impact. However, in the early stages of an investigation it is not always possible to distinguish initiation damage from consequential damage with any degree of certainty, so it may be prudent to retain all damaged elements. See Fig. 4.12.

Unfailed Components

Unfailed components can be useful for several purposes:

- To use in a testing program. Care must be taken to ensure that the selected sample was not materially damaged in the collapse, if the results are to be used as a basis for estimating the strength of similar failed components.
- To study their construction.
- To study differences between them and companion failed components.
- To exemplify to audiences, particularly nontechnical persons, what a typical unfailed component looks like or how it functions.
- To conclusively show that a certain component did not fail.

DOCUMENTATION OF CONDITIONS

High-quality documentation of the existing conditions is invaluable for developing hypotheses—as well as for ruling them out—and for ensuring that collapse theories are consistent with the physical evidence.

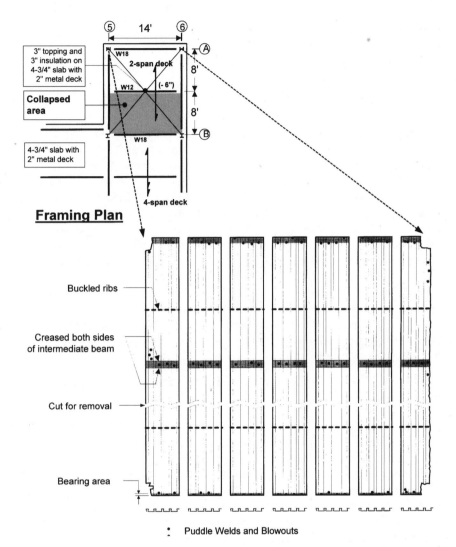

FIGURE 4.12 Judicious retention of key components by early investigators allowed the authors' firm to observe firsthand the as-built conditions of this metal deck that collapsed while concrete was being placed, and to observe the failure mode.

Various methods can be used to document conditions, including field notes, photographs, and video.

Field Notes

Field notes are the backbone of a solid documentation program. They may include

- A log of crucial activities

- Sketches
- Measurements
- Reference to photographs, highlighting what is depicted or indicating the location
- Notes of persons met and information thus gained
- A record of instructions given

Field notes should be made with the mentality that they are an irreplaceable record of firsthand observations, and that other persons may need to understand them, possibly many years in the future, without the benefit of explanation. As such, every effort must be made to make them self-explanatory, legible, and accurate and to keep them well organized. Legends and explanatory notes about what is depicted will assist tremendously in this regard. Dedicated bound field books can be useful for keeping notes organized. Field notes, whether bound or loose, should be dated, pages numbered, and the preparer identified. Permanence is better ensured if the field notes are made in ink, rather than pencil or marker.

Redundant record keeping by different observers is a useful technique for cross-checking the accuracy of the information collected.

Care should be taken that the observer's notes remain factual in nature and refrain from stating preliminary conclusions, since at some point they may have to be turned over to attorneys for other parties.

Photographs

Photographs are, of course, vital to a forensic investigation. They provide a visual record that can assist in determining the cause of the failure, and they are persuasive in reports and presentations.

To ensure the lasting value of photographs, it is important to take and file them in an organized manner. This is especially important where there are numerous photographs taken by multiple individuals. Nothing is more frustrating than not being able to determine who took a photograph or exactly what the photograph depicts. Seldom can a photograph stand on its own. Information that should be kept with each roll includes a roll identifier, a description of what is depicted, the photographer's name, when they were taken, and activities under way at the time of the photograph. A more detailed description of what the individual frames depict, if it is not self-evident, is also valuable.

Some techniques that will assist in making photographs self-explanatory:

- Begin a series of photographs with an overall photograph, and then take close-up photographs of each item of interest within the overall frame. The overall photograph then can serve as a "key plan" for the close-up photographs.
- Use a camera with a properly set date-stamp feature.

- Assign each photographer identifiers for his or her rolls of film. A simple method is to use the person's initials with a sequential suffix, for example, roll JFK-1, JFK-2, etc.

- When a new roll is started, first photograph the roll identifier, handwritten on a card. This will provide a permanent record, on the negatives, of the roll's identifier.

- Label components before photographing them, and make sure that the label is visible within the frame. If it is not possible to label the actual component, or if the label cannot be visible within the frame, an alternative is to write a label on a card and to place the card within the scene.

The use of digital cameras in forensic engineering is currently limited, but will undoubtedly increase rapidly as the technology becomes more affordable and more secure, and as image quality increases. Coupled with computers and appropriate software, digital cameras provide "instant" photographs, without the need for film processing. This is especially useful for distributing the images electronically, via e-mail or Web sites, since the image quality is generally as good as the resolution of conventional monitors. Currently, the resolution of digital photographs is largely unsuitable for reproduction in print articles or for examining fine detail in the image. But image compression technology and the capacity of digital storage media are advancing rapidly. Another hurdle to be overcome is the concern for authenticity—that the image may have been electronically manipulated and altered such that it no longer accurately represents the conditions observed. This concern will probably be allayed as encryption technology and "digital signatures" find their way into the mainstream.

Video

Video can also be a valuable documentation tool. It is best suited for the following:

- An activity or process. Examples include removing and weighing a snow sample, demolition operations, and other events that cannot be adequately captured with a series of still photographs.

- Providing a "walk-through tour."

- Low-light conditions. In situations where the items of interest are so far from the photographer that a camera flash is ineffective, a video camera may be better able to capture the conditions.

- In conditions where note taking is not practical, the camcorder can be used as a Dictaphone.

However, video is not suitable for all tasks, and considerable skill is needed to make a high-quality tape. Amateur videos often suffer from excessive shaking, disorientation due to panning too quickly, leaving the subject too soon, and distracting background noise. A prime disadvantage is the need for special equipment to view the tape.

For most situations, video photography is not necessarily better than still photography. If the situation truly warrants the use of video, consideration should be given to having it done professionally.

INTERVIEWS

Eyewitnesses, and other persons with relevant project knowledge, can provide the forensic engineer with information that is essential to a successful investigation. The accounts can be invaluable in formulating hypotheses, focusing the investigation, and finally arriving at the most probable cause of the failure.

The interviews should be conducted as soon as possible for several reasons:

- To capture the recollection while it is fresh
- To minimize the possibility of accounts being influenced by what other people saw or believe happened
- To facilitate identifying and locating witnesses
- To assist in formulating hypotheses for investigation

In some cases, the forensic engineer may be able to obtain interview transcripts in a timely manner from other parties, such as from government agencies that are investigating the incident.

In other cases, it may be necessary to obtain interviews directly, or to retain a party solely for this purpose. The principal advantage to retaining a professional interviewer is that it allows the forensic engineer to focus on the technical investigation. This is especially useful if there are a large number of potential witnesses, or if they are not easily identified or located. Interviewing is an art, and a professional interviewer will use questioning techniques that elicit candid responses and encourage volunteered information.

If an independent interviewer is retained, he or she will need to work closely with the forensic engineer. The forensic engineer will need to thoroughly brief the interviewer and suggest lines of questioning. The forensic engineer can also assist by identifying types of persons to focus on. The forensic engineer and the interviewer will need to be in constant communication, so that the forensic engineer can make use of the statements and so that the interviewer's lines of questioning can be updated. In some instances, the forensic engineer may suggest follow-up questions for a particular individual, or may feel that he or she should attend a follow-up interview.

Information Sought

Although the specific information that is sought from interviewees will depend on the particular project, certain lines of questioning are common to nearly all types of failures:

1. *Status of construction at time of collapse.* If the collapse involves a structure being constructed, the forensic engineer will probably need to determine the status of the construction. Was the bracing in place yet? Which connections were complete or incomplete? Which slabs were in place? Which had been reshored? What was the status of the underpinning work? Bearing in mind that the interviewee may have incomplete knowledge about the construction, responses should be compared against other accounts and against physical evidence.

2. *Sequence of collapse.* Knowing which element, or which area of the structure, was the first to fail could help to quickly focus the investigation. However, an individual's perception of the sequence will depend on many factors, such as the speed of the collapse, where the individual was and what he or she was doing, what drew her or his attention to it, etc. It is rare that a single individual's perception of the sequence will be fully accurate or provide the complete picture. In all likelihood, it will be necessary to piece together the various accounts into a coherent sequence, weighing the reliability of each account. Wherever possible, physical evidence should be sought to confirm or deny accounts.

3. *Possible triggering events.* Most collapses have a triggering event associated with them, and identifying it may speed the investigation. Sometimes the trigger is conspicuous, such as an errant barge striking a bridge pier; at other times it is subtle, such as one more thermal cycle in a fatigue-critical member.

   a. *Activities under way at the time of collapse.* In the case of a structure under construction or being renovated, it will be important to identify exactly what was being done at the time of the collapse. Was a bracing member being temporarily disconnected? Was concrete being placed and, if so, exactly where? Were workers in the process of plumbing the structure? Persons associated with the project will be the most useful in this regard.

   b. *Unusual loading on structure.* Was there a collision or other unexpected impact? Was the structure overloaded by material's storage? Was the occupancy loading unusually high? Eyewitnesses will often be able to offer some insight into these questions.

   c. *Environmental factors.* These are also possible triggering events, such as high winds, snowfall, and other unusual weather-related patterns. Persons present at the site should be able to provide a sense of the role that environmental factors may have played, which can be quantified through the use of climatological data.

Table 4.1 includes typical questions, as well as information that should be included with each typed transcript or summary. The list should be tailored to suit a specific project. It may also be useful to develop different lines of questioning for different types of interviewees. For example, in interviewing employees of a concrete subcontractor, it would be appropriate to include a line of questioning regarding reshoring practices, which would not be appropriate for a passerby eyewitness.

TABLE 4.1 Typical Interview Questions and Information

Time, date, place, and duration of interview.
Name of person(s) interviewing and others present.
Indicate whether the interview was tape-recorded.
Date that transcript was typed and by whom.

1. What is your name, who is your employer, what is your position/title, what are your responsibilities?
2. What is your experience and education?
3. Where were you at the time of collapse?
4. What were your doing?
5. What was the first indication that something was wrong?
   a. If it was a sound, describe it. Where did it appear to come from? How long did it last? What else was going on?
   b. If it was a sensation, describe it.
   c. If it was visual, describe it.
   d. If you were alerted by someone else, describe. By whom, where was that person, what did he/she say?
6. What happened next?
7. How much time elapsed from the first indication until collapse?
8. Who else was with you?
9. Did you have any concerns previously?
10. Any rumors?
11. What activities were underway at time of collapse?
12. What was the status of construction at the time of the collapse?
13. What was the weather?
14. Any idea what may have triggered failure?
15. Do you mind if I contact you again if necessary?
16. Will you let me know if you think of anything else that may be helpful?

Add questions that are tailored to the project and to the type of knowledge that the interviewee may have.

Who Should Be Interviewed

There are several types of people who may be able to provide useful information.

Passerby eyewitnesses may be able to provide some information about the sequence of the collapse. These witnesses normally will not be familiar with construction terminology and so may not be able to express their observations in the interviewer's terms. They also may be difficult to identify, since they have no association with the project. Project eyewitnesses are persons associated with the project who saw the collapse. Due to their familiarity with construction, these persons will generally be able to give a more sophisticated account than a passerby eyewitness.

Project personnel are persons associated with the project, but who may not have seen the collapse. These persons may have knowledge about the status of construction, activities that were under way, the design or construction of the structure, or other useful background information. Examples include project managers, design professionals, and foremen.

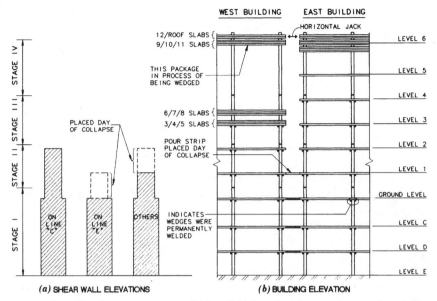

FIGURE 4.13 Eyewitness accounts, examination of debris, and project records were all needed by the authors' firm to establish the status of construction at the time of collapse of L'Ambiance Plaza.

FIGURE 4.14 There was no doubt what triggered this collapse. This tractor-trailer truck, heavily loaded with the gypsum board, ventured into a light-duty area of this structure. Engineers from the authors' firm assisted the contractors in devising a scheme to safely extract the truck.

FIGURE 4.15   The collapse of this roof structure into the occupied hotel room below was virtually "triggerless." Corrosion of the slab reinforcement had been ongoing over many years, until finally the strength of the slab was reduced to the point that it collapsed. Workers are in the process of installing new structural framing.

COOPERATION WITH OTHER FORENSIC ENGINEERS

In the initial stages of an investigation, there are often areas of interest that are common to all parties. These provide opportunities to pool resources, to avoid duplication of effort, and to establish a common knowledge base. Potential areas of common interest include the following:

• *Identification of debris.* Establishing a common identification system from the start will tremendously facilitate later discussion and debate. In addition, sharing of this raw information will minimize the possibility of misidentifying components, which could lead to patently false theories.

A potential consequence of not promptly exchanging this type of information is illustrated by the 1987 collapse of L'Ambiance Plaza. In its investigation OSHA (Occupational Health and Safety Administration) misidentified a key component and subsequently developed a collapse scenario that was dependent on this misidentified component. Despite repeated attempts by the authors' firm to alert OSHA to the misidentification, this scenario was widely disseminated to the public. OSHA eventually retracted the scenario years later in a technical journal, after court settlements were complete.* This unfortunate situation, which obscured the cause of the collapse, could have been avoided if a climate of cooperation had been fostered in the beginning, allowing exchange of this fundamental information.

In contrast, on the 1998 scaffold collapse at Four Times Square, key forensic firms worked together to mark components as they were dismantled and to organize them off the site, using a common identification system developed by the authors' firm. This cooperative effort established a common body of information from which the independent investigations could spring.

- *Destructive testing.* Often there will be certain components that multiple parties would like to perform destructive testing on. One solution is for those parties to agree on the testing to be performed, and on a firm to conduct it, and then to share in the costs and results. This is most feasible for fundamental standardized tests, such as concrete strength tests and tensile tests, and in fact this was the approach taken in the investigation of the scaffold collapse at Four Times Square. More specialized tests will usually have to be undertaken by individual parties.

Sharing of basic information will be greatly facilitated if the leading investigator has neutral interests and fosters a climate of cooperation. Naturally, in cases where there is a possibility of litigation, the forensic engineer should consult with the client or the client's attorney to be sure that he or she does not inadvertently compromise the client's interests.

INITIAL DOCUMENT GATHERING

Gathering of project documents is a top priority. Some documents may be readily obtainable, and others will require perseverance. Types of documents that are typically sought include

- Design drawings
- Specifications
- Boring logs
- Calculations by the engineer of record and by specialty engineers
- Erection drawings, shop drawings (Fig. 4.16), and other contractor submittals
- Submittal logs
- Inspection reports
- Daily reports

---

*C. F. Scribner and C. G. Culver. "Investigation of the Collapse of L'Ambiance Plaza," *J. Perf. Constr. Fac., ASCE,* 2(2): 58–79, 1988. D. A. Cuoco, T. Z. Scarangello, and D. B. Peraza. "Investigation of L'Ambiance Plaza Building Collapse." *J. Perf. Constr. Fac., ASCE,* 6(4): 211–231, 1992. C. G. Culver and R. D. Marshall, discussion of Cuoco et al. (1992), *J. Perf. Constr. Fac., ASCE,* 8(2): 160–161, 1994.

(a)

FIGURE 4.16 (*a*) An unreinforced concrete corbel snapped off, causing a partial collapse.

- Test reports
- Correspondence

The most reliable information is usually obtained from the original creators of the documents, whether they are engineers, architects, contractors, or inspectors. These persons are more likely to have the latest issue of their own documents in an organized fashion. Other potential sources include the owner of the facility and local building officials. Documents filed with local building officials may not reflect the as-built condition if changes were made subsequent to the initial filing.

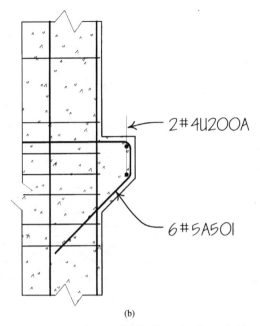

2#4U200A

6#5A501

(b)

FIGURE 4.16 (*Continued*) (*b*) Shop drawings clearly showed reinforcement in the wall corbels, which helped to quickly focus the investigation of this collapse.

Besides project-specific documents, it may be helpful to obtain additional documents, such as

- Climatological data (Fig. 4.17)
- Relevant codes
- Industry standards of practice

PRELIMINARY EVALUATION

After the initial information has been gathered, a preliminary evaluation of the data should be conducted.

- Develop failure scenarios and mechanisms. Every effort should be made to identify as many possible causes and potential contributing factors as possible. At this point the emphasis should be on *including* theories, however unlikely they may seem. The input of all consultants and staff members should be considered. Later phases of the investigation will be directed toward excluding possibilities.

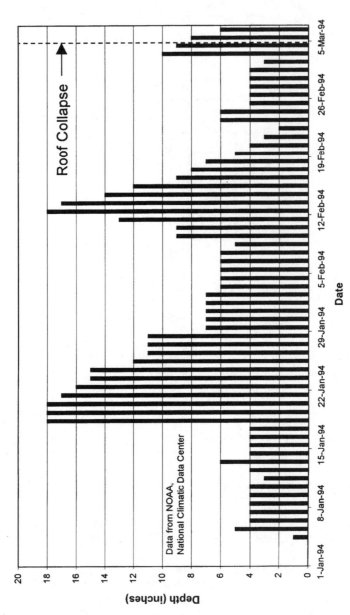

FIGURE 4.17 Climatological data can assist in evaluating the role played by unusual weather conditions.

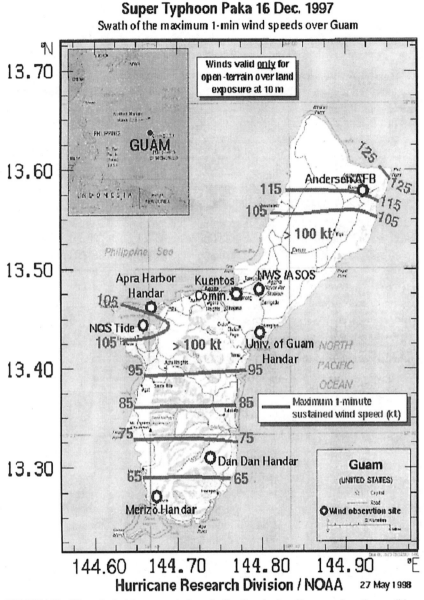

Super Typhoon Paka 16 Dec. 1997
Swath of the maximum 1-min wind speeds over Guam

FIGURE 4.17 Climatological data can assist in evaluating the role played by unusual weather conditions.

- Perform preliminary structural analyses. The purpose of initial analyses is often to test the viability of existing hypotheses, or to identify additional potential failure mechanisms. Preliminary structural analyses are often directed toward studying the sensitivity of the structure to various forces and/or variations in construction.

- Develop a testing program. Some testing may be performed in the early stages of the investigation. This might include tests to confirm or determine basic material properties. Planning for later testing of special assemblies will often be done in this period. The pros and cons of testing project assemblies versus newly fabricated assemblies intended should be weighed. New components may be difficult to fabricate such that they are representative of the as-built project components. Project assemblies may have been damaged during the collapse, or may be difficult to obtain. Testing programs of assemblies often begin as parametric studies, attempting to bound the strength of the structure.

- Identify areas of additional expertise required. Seldom will the forensic engineer have the expertise and resources necessary to investigate all aspects of a particular collapse. Often additional resources will be needed. Depending on the project, it may be necessary to retain a metallurgist, a certain type of testing laboratory, a petrographer, specialty engineers, a meteorologist, and others. Needed fields of expertise should be identified quickly so that qualified persons can join the team and help guide the investigation.

- Identify missing project documents.

- Identify additional field investigation and additional samples needed.

- Identify additional persons to interview, and develop follow-up questions for previous interviewees.

CLOSURE

The first steps after a collapse lay the foundation for subsequent technical investigations, helping ensure that the most probable cause of the collapse and contributing factors are identified to a reasonable degree of engineering certainty.

But while a sound foundation is of course essential, it does not in any way guarantee the integrity of the structure to be laid upon it. Skill, care, and ingenuity will continue to be needed to successfully complete the investigation and, if necessary, to assist in preparation for litigation.

CHAPTER 5
LEGAL CONCERNS AFTER A FAILURE

Michael C. Loulakis, Esq.

INTRODUCTION

Few things can be more frightening to someone involved in a construction project than to hear the words *structural failure* associated with that project. Neither the construction industry nor the general public forgets the major catastrophes caused by construction defects, as can be demonstrated by the continuing industry discussion about such incidents as

- Hartford Civic Center (1978). The roof of this facility collapsed hours after the completion of a college basketball game attended by more than 5000 people.
- Hyatt Regency Hotel, Kansas City (1981). Two suspended walkways collapsed during a dance at the hotel, killing 114 and injuring many others.
- Mianus Bridge, Connecticut (1983). A 100-ft span on one of the most heavily traveled highways in the northeast collapsed, killing three and interrupting traffic for months.
- L'Ambiance Plaza, Bridgeport, Connecticut (1987). Twenty-eight workers were killed in a collapse during construction of this high-rise apartment complex.

Recent failures, such as the Four Times Square high-rise hoist collapse on July 21, 1998, which killed an 85-year-old woman,[1] and the collapse of a six-story office building in Times Square on December 30, 1997, during the excavation of an adjacent building,[2] have also generated significant press coverage and discussion. These projects are remembered not only because of the human and economic losses associated with them, but also because the projects provide valuable lessons in what can go wrong on a project and what responses should be made in these situations.[3]

These high-visibility cases were characterized by structural defects and dramatic collapses, mostly on completed facilities. Construction owners, design professionals, contractors, and other service providers must be aware, however, that most construction failures do not involve the loss of life or issues that command national attention. Instead, they occur when a constructed facility fails to function as intended.[4] These failures can include

- The sudden failure of a gas turbine, which causes a power generation facility to shut down
- Parking decks that have concrete spalling or signs of fatigue
- Substantial postoccupancy deflection in the concrete slabs of an office building
- Retaining walls that appear to be failing

Some functional failures have the same practical impact as structural failures—requiring immediate attention in a "crisis management" mode due to the high potential for impact on life safety. However, most functional failures involve economic losses that, while not posing an imminent threat to public health and welfare, can create major financial exposure to those affected.

Regardless of whether a failure is structural or functional, there are significant legal issues that need to be carefully considered by all parties involved with the failed element of the project. The purpose of this chapter is to highlight some of the most critical legal issues in failure analysis and investigation.[5] As the reader reviews this chapter, she or he should keep in mind that there is no "bright line" distinction between the legal issues associated with a failure and those issues that are technical and forensic—particularly with respect to crisis management. In fact, the most effective response to a failure will be one that considers legal, technical, business, and moral issues together, as part of a cohesive plan to deal with the overall problem.

OVERVIEW OF THE LEGAL INTERESTS

The legal principles and interests associated with construction failures are largely dependent upon the (1) nature of the failure, (2) factual reasons for the failure, and (3) the role of the interested party in the failure. Although each issue is important, the strategy for effectively representing the party's legal interests should be based primarily on the facts surrounding the failure. These facts, which can be determined through documentation, witness recollections, and public records, represent the baseline from which any legal analysis begins. This is just one of the many reasons that the legal and technical teams must be interwoven from the outset of any investigation.

While the methods for performing a legal analysis may differ from those used in the technical and business analyses, the ultimate goals of the studies are identical:

- Determine any immediate steps that should be taken to avoid causing further harm, in order to help mitigate losses and exposure.
- Determine the cause of the failure.
- Determine legal accountability for the failure.

Accomplishing each of these goals requires a methodical evaluation of the problem and a team approach, combining legal, forensic, and in some instances public relations expertise.[6]

Although the goals are interdependent, one may be more important than the others at a specific point in the investigation. For example, determinations of the cause of and legal accountability for the failure are not typically time-sensitive issues. Consequently, they can be developed with some deliberate consideration. On the other hand, if remediation is necessary to contain damages or protect the public welfare, decisions have to be made quickly. These decisions can have a later impact on accountability. Moreover, all three of these legal goals can be impacted by the need to deal immediately with the public and the press. Because of the publicity that often surrounds construction failures, the views of the media can shape the public's view of the situation and impact the legal position of a potentially liable party.

The legal concerns surrounding a construction failure vary with the roles of the parties. For example:

- A potentially responsible party, such as a design professional or subcontractor, will be primarily concerned with determining her or his legal exposure to injured parties.
- An injured party will be primarily concerned with preserving his or her rights against any potentially responsible party.

- The project owner will be interested not only in preserving rights against potentially responsible parties, but also in having the project remedied and put back into use.

Notwithstanding these differing interests, there are several actions which all interested parties must perform in the process of responding to a failure. These steps include assembling an investigative team, developing an action plan, establishing a plan to protect confidentiality, cooperating and dealing with public agencies, and working with the media.

ASSEMBLING THE INVESTIGATIVE AND LEGAL RESPONSE TEAM

Each party with a significant interest in the failure should assemble an investigative team as part of its legal strategy for dealing with the failure. Although the size and complexity of the failure will play a major role in determining the composition of the team, all investigative teams should consist of a mix of both internal and external members. Suggestions for developing the teams are set forth below.

Internal Team

The internal component of the investigative team should be led by a strong, senior-level individual who is intimately familiar with the internal operations of the organization, trusted by the organization's hierarchy, and capable of obtaining full and complete support for the investigative effort. This person must be capable of rendering objective opinions and dealing with the potentially negative news that may surface as the investigation proceeds. The need for objectivity is particularly important if the proposed internal leader also has personal knowledge of the project failure or of the specifics of the overall project prior to the failure. In fact, because one who is involved directly in the project may have preconceived thoughts about the legitimacy of the problem or the causation behind the failure, it may not be appropriate for the internal team to be led by someone with direct knowledge of the facts associated with the failure.

Depending upon the nature of the failure, it is typically beneficial to have the internal team include individuals who can (1) think ahead of the immediate crisis, (2) anticipate future ramifications and play the devil's advocate, and (3) deal with the press and public. Ideally, these functions will be performed by the internal team leader. In some cases, however, it may be preferable to assign these responsibilities to different people. This not only will give the team leader some "political protection" about the public actions of the party, but also may enable the team leader to channel his or her energies and attention to those issues that are most pressing at a particular time.

External Team

Independently retained consultants who can analyze the issues associated with the failure should supplement the internal team. These consultants, together called the *external team,* should include an experienced forensic consultant capable of analyzing the factual and technical details of the failure. Depending upon the complexity of the issues, more than one consultant may be necessary. Additionally, because the legal strategy often "drives" the response to structural and functional failures, the external team should include an attorney capable of determining the viability of legal claims or defenses. Finally, it is critical to determine the location of individuals who have personal knowledge of the work associated with the failure so they can be included in the team. The roles of these external team members are discussed in greater detail below.

Role and Qualifications of the Lawyer.   In most cases, the external team should be led by the attorney responsible for the overall legal strategy—whether the counsel is in house or from an outside firm retained specifically to deal with the failure. Lead counsel should be actively involved in the selection of forensic experts and, as facts are gathered and analyzed by such experts, in determining how such facts affect the position of the client. If the lawyer is representing injured parties, she or he must be able to identify all potentially responsible parties and determine the theories of recovery the client may have against such parties. It is important to remember that the skills needed by the lawyer heading the investigative team are different from those necessary to handle the litigation arising out of the failure. To effectively take the lead during the investigation, the lawyer must have a strong understanding of both the technical issues and the legal tactics associated with the failure, including substantive knowledge of

- The construction process and project delivery systems
- Design and construction contracts—these contracts will have a large bearing on the potential liability to the client.
- The technical issues giving rise to the failure—if the problem involves a geotechnical failure, counsel should have a strong command of geotechnical terminology and technology.
- Applicable insurance coverage and how to deal with carriers.

Once the issues have been analyzed and forensic evidence becomes more clearly defined, the lead counsel should be a strong and compelling advocate, experienced in the trial of complex construction industry disputes.

Two additional points should be made about the role and qualifications of counsel. First, it is critical for counsel to have a strong and clear understanding of the overall goal of the client. For example, if the long-term business objectives of the client will be seriously impacted by the negative publicity associated with a failure, it may benefit the client to quickly "step up to the plate" and resolve the matter without engaging in a protracted discussion about causation. Counsel must be able to recognize these objectives and use them to determine the appropriate legal course of action, rather than simply take the most beneficial legal position.

Second, the counsel representing a party in an investigation must be objective and open-minded about the client's exposure. Parties are not well served when counsel takes a strong advocacy position at the beginning of an investigation. Hasty judgments can suppress the exchange of information and the development of facts, which mask a true assessment of the potential liability exposure to the client.

Role and Qualifications of the Forensic Consultant.   After the general nature of the failure is determined, the parties should select a forensic consultant who is capable of analyzing the failure and rendering an opinion as to causation and responsibility. Some experts may be chosen simply to obtain the best solution to a problem, while others may be chosen because of their ability to testify effectively. The internal team leader and primary legal counsel must determine exactly what is expected of the forensic expert and whether the expert will be expected to provide both advice and testimony.

Generally speaking, a forensic expert should have strong educational and practical experience in the areas of the failure being investigated. Although the consultant's background is important, other factors are helpful in selecting the best expert, including the consultant's willingness to be a good working member of the team and ability to relate well to a trier of fact. These qualifications have been identified[7] as "the seven C's."

- *Capability* to deal with the problem at hand
- Level of *competence* and skill
- Actual or potential *conflicts* of interest
- Ability and willingness to *coordinate* his or her efforts with other members of the team
- *Commitment* of time to the project
- Ability to *communicate* effectively, both orally and in writing
- *Cost* of services

Additionally, because there is always a chance that the case may go to trial, the parties must be aware of any biases or positions that the forensic consultant has on record that could impact the case or her or his testimony.

Making the Key Fact Witnesses Part of the Team.   Key information for the legal and forensic analysis will be obtained from the individuals who were directly involved with the project at the time it was being designed and constructed. Given the amount of time that can elapse between project completion and a failure, it may be difficult to locate these individuals and obtain their cooperation. Efforts should be made early in the investigation to identify and locate critical witnesses and to make them part of the investigative team. If possible, this should be done before any litigation is filed.

DEVELOPING AN ACTION PLAN

After the general nature of the failure is determined and the response team is assembled, an investigation action plan should be developed. Recommended elements of this action plan include the following.

Litigation Assessment Report

Counsel should prepare a report that outlines the primary legal and factual issues that appear to be involved in the case and recommendations on how to proceed. This type of report often includes a plan for (1) conducting legal research, (2) identifying responsible parties, (3) interviewing witnesses, (4) reviewing project records, (5) obtaining expert reports and opinions, and (6) determining whether there are any statutes of limitation or other legal issues that materially affect the ability to proceed. The litigation assessment report should include strategies on moving forward with the investigation of the case. These will entail

- *Site visits.* Counsel and the team should conduct site visits shortly after the team has been assembled.
- *Strategy conferences.* Counsel should establish a schedule for strategy conferences needed to respond to the failure and associated litigation.
- *Timetables for action.* Counsel should ensure that the investigation is proceeding on a specific timetable and that all key members adhere to the schedule.

The litigation assessment report is intended to be a dynamic tool that may be modified as facts are developed, other interested parties are discovered, and litigation is initiated.

A Plan to Obtain and Preserve the Evidence

A key element of the action plan lies in determining what evidence is available relative to the failure and ensuring that the evidence is unaltered and preserved in the state in which it existed at the time the failure occurred. Witnesses, site investigations, and documents are all sources for obtaining evidence about the failure.

The list of potential witnesses should include not only those who were eyewitnesses to the failure, but also those individuals who participated in the design or construction of the failed facility. In the case of a structural collapse, it is best if the information is collected as soon as possible from both types of potential witness (but particularly the eyewitnesses) while memories are still fresh. Specific details are easily forgotten with the passage of time.

When site investigations are conducted, both photographic and video accounts should be made, as they are useful for keeping an accurate record of the conditions at the site. It is wise to develop technical records during site investigations. These should be undertaken and maintained by the principal forensic consultant retained for the problem. Any removal of debris or materials from the site for safety purposes or for purposes of evaluating the failure should be carefully documented, with such debris or materials being securely stored. Any other alterations of the site that occur for the purposes of safety or other reasons should be noted.

Several types of documents should be collected and organized during the investigation. Written communications between the parties should be collected, including communications occurring before, during, and after the construction of the facility. Among these documents will be (1) the contract design drawings and specifications; (2) contractual agreements between the parties; (3) as-built project drawings; (4) any testing, inspection, or consultant reports relating to the facility; (5) project schedules; (6) any design analysis which may have been completed; (7) maintenance and modification records; and (8) building department permits. These will help provide a road map of the activities that took place relating to construction of the facility and an accurate record of the events leading up to the failure.

Ideally, the evidence should be analyzed as it is gathered. Timely analysis is helpful in giving direction to the investigation and in quickly determining who is accountable for the failure. For some failures, the initial analysis methodology may be to simply review the information gathered about the failure and other documentation and/or reports about the facility. For other failures, the initial analysis may require using programs to test materials or structural loads or building models for testing.[8] In some situations, it is effective to use these two approaches in conjunction with each other.

A Plan to Determine Causation

The evidence that is gathered will likely point to one of three primary reasons for the construction failure: technical errors, procedural errors, or events beyond the reasonable control of any party.[9] Categorizing the facts into one of these areas will help in developing the legal theories of prosecution or defense and will focus the search for forensic experts to testify on behalf of the affected party.

The most common event triggering a structural or functional failure is a technical error that occurs during the design or construction processes. Technical errors include errors in calculation, judgment, and application of codes. Parties should be aware of technical errors which may occur in the following high-risk disciplines:

- *Geotechnical.* Because foundation design is critical to the integrity of a structure, geotechnical errors can create major structural and functional failures, such as excessive settlement and earth movement, unanticipated static and dynamic loading, water flow problems, uplift caused by hydrostatic pressures, and unanticipated vibrations on the foundation.

- *Structural.* As with geotechnical investigation and design errors, structural engineering defects can create highly visible problems with the project. These defects can affect both the envelope of a building (as with watertightness) and the structural systems within the building (as with slab deflection and rebar corrosion).

- *Mechanical and electrical control systems.* As facilities become "smarter," there are increasing opportunities for technical mistakes to create problems in the computerized controls that monitor the mechanical and electrical systems within the facility.

The investigation should also consider whether the failure arose from technical errors in a different discipline. For example, excessive settlement could be the result of calculation errors by the structural engineer with regard to the loading requirements which then led to improper assumptions by the geotechnical engineer.

Failures also commonly occur as a result of procedural errors that generally result from breakdowns of communication or review during the administration of the contract. These breakdowns include the failure to (1) properly review shop drawings and contract deviations, (2) conform to OSHA requirements, (3) undertake peer reviews of critical design components, and (4) understand and detail owner expectations regarding the functionality of the facility.

ESTABLISHING A PLAN TO PROTECT CONFIDENTIALITY

One of the most important steps that the legal team can take when a failure occurs is to establish a system for keeping confidential the information obtained during the investigation of the failure. Confidentiality of information, while important at all times, is particularly critical at the beginning of an investigation, when it is virtually impossible to determine what information may or may not be relevant or prejudicial at a later time.

Confidentiality guidelines help parties to properly respond to the media and to decide what information will be disclosed to other parties working on the investigation. To the extent feasible, all individuals involved in the investigation should be carefully instructed not only about the importance of confidentiality, but also about what should and should not be discussed with those outside the investigative team. As noted earlier, one key person should be selected to contact and respond to the media.

Legal Protections to Confidentiality

The litigation discovery process requires the disclosure of all nonprivileged information to any parties requesting such information. Because counsel involved in a failure analysis needs to ask experts and fact witnesses for candid assessments of what went wrong on the project, the discovery of such information by an adversary could present major problems and stifle the manner in which a party prepares its case.

To avoid this problem, certain legal principles have evolved that allow parties to withhold information obtained during the course of an investigation and in preparation of litigation. The *attorney-client privilege* and the *work product doctrine* are the two most common legal mechanisms that protect confidentiality. Although federal and state common law addressing these legal protections has various nuances, the basic principles underlying these concepts are fairly consistent from jurisdiction to jurisdiction.

Attorney-Client Privilege.   As its name suggests, the attorney-client privilege is intended to enable lawyers and clients to communicate candidly, without worrying that they will be legally required to share the communications with other parties. To effectively assert the attorney-client privilege, a party must prove the following elements[10] of the communications:

1. It is indeed a communication.
2. It is made between an attorney and his or her client.
3. It is made in confidence.
4. It is made for the purpose of seeking, obtaining, or providing legal assistance to the client.

Although this privilege provides substantial protection to parties involved in the process of examining construction failures, it must be carefully implemented. Some of the areas that can create problems include these:

• *Protected parties.* "Clients" generally do not include former employees of the client. Therefore, to the extent that such employees are relevant to the investigation, one must assume that anything said to them will be discoverable (unless covered by the work product privilege).

• *In-house counsel.* Because some in-house counsel function as both business adviser and legal adviser, there are often questions as to whether communications with such individuals will be protected. To avoid potential problems, there is a strong benefit in retaining an outside law firm quickly after the failure occurs.

• *Preserving confidences.* Even if a privilege exists, the privilege can be waived if its contents are communicated to third parties who are not clients.

The last point is especially critical, since many businesspersons are accustomed to having the freedom to discuss issues as they see fit with whomever they see fit. As a result, most counsel will make a practice of stamping documents that they generate, or memoranda that are developed for them, as covered by the attorney-client privilege. Likewise, care needs to be taken as to what is said in front of whom. A client who tells a third party what his or her lawyer said can defeat the attorney-client privilege, since the communication will no longer be deemed to be one said in confidence.

Work Product Doctrine. Just as it is critical for attorneys and clients to be able to communicate freely without fear that an adversary will learn of the communications, it is equally critical for those working for an attorney in anticipation of litigation to be able to communicate in confidence. This *work product* privilege protects material collected by counsel in the course of preparation for possible litigation.[11] As stated by one commentator,[12] "The lawyer's thinking—theories, analysis, mental impressions, beliefs, and so on—is at the heart of the adversary system, and privacy is essential for the lawyer's thinking; thus, the protection is greatest, if not absolute, for materials that would reveal that part of the work product." These general principles of protection under the work product doctrine are codified in the Federal Rules of Civil Procedure[13] and the Federal Rules of Criminal Procedure.[14]

As with the attorney-client privilege, the scope of the work product doctrine has some limitations. The most difficult question lies in determining what documents were developed in "contemplation of litigation." For example, does the work product exception cover reports that outline potential problems discovered during quality control—reports that were written during the course of the project? If these reports were prepared under the direction of counsel, after the owner threatened to bring legal action if a problem materialized, there would be a compelling argument that they were covered by the doctrine. On the other hand, if they were simply prepared by a project manager based on his or her observations, with no counsel directly involved, the documents would probably have to be produced to the adversary.

Procedural Method for Protecting Confidentiality

Preserving the attorney-client and work product privileges is a critical component of a failure analysis strategy. Observing several precautions may assist the parties in maintaining the confidentiality provided by these privileges:

- Whenever possible, attorneys should be used to obtain facts or conduct investigations. If an attorney is unavailable, all materials should be gathered under the written instruction of an attorney and should be delivered to the attorney.
- All written communications should be identified with a "confidential/legal" heading. All files and other information from the investigative team should be kept in a separate and segregated location with restricted and limited access. Copying of these materials should be avoided.

- All files created during the initial investigation should be filed under a heading indicating that the documentation was created in anticipation of litigation.

Finally, it is important for all members of the investigative team to understand how the different privileges work and what the team has to do to preserve the privilege. This includes having all forensic consultants recognize those with whom they can freely communicate and those with whom communications should be avoided.

Joint Defense Agreements

Joint defense agreements are another way to protect confidentiality. They are generally entered into by parties who are actual or potential defendants to a case and who have an interest in jointly defending the case. These agreements are often used by owners and design professionals, where the owner must rely heavily on the factual recollections of the design professional's personnel and records. Joint defense agreements are generally written and will enable the parties to the agreement to communicate with one another with a large degree of confidence that such communications will be held in confidence.

COOPERATING AND DEALING WITH PUBLIC AGENCIES

A structural construction failure will typically trigger an investigation by federal, state, and local public agencies. Two federal authorities that may become involved after a failure occurs are

- *OSHA (Occupational Safety and Health Administration).* This agency has the authority to inspect the accident scene and impose civil and criminal fines if there is a violation of OSHA regulations.
- *FEMA (Federal Emergency Management Agency).* This agency has the authority to become involved only if the state governor, finding a situation of such severity and magnitude that an effective response is beyond the capabilities of the state, makes a request to the President of the United States.

Representatives of state and local agencies—including building inspectors and fire marshals—also actively investigate construction activities and failures.

The legal and forensic investigation plan should identify all potentially interested government authorities, the rules or regulations that may have been violated, and a plan for responding to and cooperating with authorities. Legal counsel should tour the site with the authorities and attempt to determine who may be the target of their investigations. Counsel must also convey to the authorities the client's plans to remediate the failure and otherwise address the situation.

DEALING WITH THE MEDIA

All parties potentially affected by the failure are interested in managing the information that is released to the media. This is not only a significant business strategy relative to the failure, but also part of the legal strategy. As noted earlier, it is advisable for a party to establish, upon learning of the failure, a single source for dissemination of information. Ideally, such an individual is chosen prior to any failure and should be prepared with potential initial statements. Using a single spokesperson for the situation is important for a number of reasons. It allows the party to maintain confidentiality of certain information and to provide consistent information to the media, without contradictions and confusion.

SPECIAL CONSIDERATIONS OF INTERESTED PARTIES

As addressed in the preceding sections of this chapter, most of the parties who have an interest in the failure will have some common issues regarding the legal and forensic approach taken relative to the failure. However, depending upon the party's interests, several special considerations must be contemplated when the overall legal strategy is defined. Some of the most important are set forth below.

Property Owner

The property owner is in a special and unique position if a structural or functional failure to the project occurs. The owner is generally among the first to learn of the failure and to face the immediate public relations, regulatory, and economic consequences arising from it. Moreover, unlike other parties, the owner (1) has a long-term interest in the project and faces the greatest financial exposure if there is a failure and (2) is generally the only interested party who has control of the site.

Not all owners will have the same interests in a failure or will adopt the same approach to developing a legal and investigative plan. The identity of the owner, the circumstances of the failure, and the type of project will all dictate what approach should be taken. For example:

- If the owner is a public agency, such as a state department of transportation, its role in a structural failure (such as a bridge collapse) will largely revolve on protecting the life safety interests of the public and avoiding public inconvenience. Because a large number of individuals can be affected by such a failure, a typical legal strategy will be to quickly begin remediation efforts and then to determine accountability.

- If the owner is a public agency dealing with a functional failure, as might be the case with a municipality faced with a sewage treatment plant that is incapable of treating effluent as required, the general public may not be aware of or even directly impacted by the problem. In this case, economic recovery strategies will be the first order of business in developing the legal plan.

- If the owner is a private entity that is directly using the facility, such as the owner/operator of a power plant confronted with an explosion, remediation will be driven by life safety and economic concerns. While the private owner will have the same interest as the public owner in getting people out of harm's way, the speed of the remediation efforts will be affected by both the impact of the failure on the owner's business and the owner's ability to find the responsible parties to fund the correction.

It is critical for the internal investigative team to quickly determine the long-term and short-term objectives of the owner. These will then dictate the legal strategy undertaken. The sections below outline several aspects of the property owner's legal strategy that should be considered.

Remediating the Problem. Unless the owner intends to abandon the project as a result of the failure, the legal team must assist in developing a plan for diagnosing the problem, establishing a remedy, and determining who will pay for the remedy.[15] As noted in the preceding section, the benefit of putting effort and money into a temporary remediation rather than a full and permanent remediation will depend upon the urgency of the failure and what other damages and injuries may occur if the failure is not remedied immediately.

Note, however, that any owner who experiences a structural failure must remember that the legal process will expect the owner to give primary and immediate attention to the public health, safety, and welfare. At a minimum, this will require prompt stabilization of the areas around the failure to avoid further damage or injuries. Owners should not let the economic costs of the immediate-term and short-term safety remediation stand in the way of meeting these commitments.

Insurance Coverage. Another early legal task that should be undertaken by a project owner is to determine whether insurance covers the failure.[16] Property and commercial general liability policies typically cover many of the costs arising out of a failure, including business interruption, personnel injuries, and any damage to third parties. The most controversial issue may be whether insurance will cover the cost of remedying the failure. Note that if the failure occurs before completion of the project, the replacement costs are generally recovered only if there is an applicable builder's risk policy. Even then, however, depending upon the amount and type of coverage defined by the policy, there may be limited coverage for the problem.

As it conducts an insurance analysis, the legal team should look at not only the underlying policies, but also some of the project construction and design contracts. Troublesome issues often include (1) applicable exclusions, including XCU (explosion, collapse, and underground) hazards; (2) the amount of the policy deductible; (3) waivers of subrogation against contractors or design professionals; and (4) notice provisions within the policy.[17]

This last issue is perhaps the most important. Some insurance carriers are not hesitant to rely upon technical defenses in the policy to deny coverage. As a result, the property owner needs to take immediate steps to determine when and how the policy specifies that the carrier be informed of the problem. Every effort should be made to document the notice to the carrier, have claims adjusters visit the project site, and enlist the technical support of the carrier in determining the remedial plan. It is also worth remembering that a good insurance professional can be a valuable member of the investigation team by providing important insight into how to address the failure and enlist cooperation from the carriers.

Notifying the Authorities.   Because the owner has control over the failure site, generally the owner has the initial responsibility to notify any local and state authorities who have an interest in the construction failure. The owner's legal team must understand which agencies have such an interest and must take immediate steps to comply with the obligations required by applicable rules and regulations. It is particularly important to note that if the construction failure causes environmental hazards, several federal and state statutes requiring reporting will be triggered.

Determining Accountability and Providing Notice.   The owner has a particular interest in identifying those responsible for the failure, since contributions from these parties will be a source of funds for the remediation of the problem. The owner will likely seek recourse against some of the parties who provided design and construction services on the project. The owner's legal team will, as a result, be responsible for carefully analyzing the contract documents and project records to determine whether there are any impediments to proceeding against such parties, including limitations of liability and indemnity clauses within these contracts.

To determine accountability, the owner must have a strong understanding of what, if anything, the owner may have done to contribute to the failure. For example, if the failure was caused by a design defect in a product specified by the owner, the owner may have no recourse against the designer or contractor. Likewise, if the owner had knowledge that the design was unproven or risky, the designer could argue that the owner assumed the risk of any functional failures associated with using such a design.[18]

Once the owner has determined that the owner may have recourse against another party, it is vital for the legal team to provide prompt notice of such claim to that party. This gives the potentially responsible party ample opportunity to investigate the facts and to prepare a defense. If the owner is not certain who is responsible for the failure, it is wise to notify anyone who could arguably have potential responsibility. On a major project, this could include providing notification to and getting the involvement of construction managers, design professionals, contractors, subcontractors, and suppliers. Note, however, that a "shotgun" strategy should not be used simply to gain contributions from parties who have absolutely nothing to do with the failure.

Another question that owners need to address in developing their legal strategy is whether to provide potentially responsible parties with an opportunity to observe and/or perform the remedial work. Contracts between owners and contractors often require this process before the owner can undertake self-help. If the contract is silent, the owner may be in a better legal position as a result of providing the potentially responsible party with notice and attempting to enlist that party's involvement.

Consider, for example, a functional failure involving the spalling of a concrete parking slab allegedly caused by improperly placed rebar. By asking the contractor to come to the site and perform the correction, the owner may avoid legal defenses by the contractor that (1) the contractor was unaware of the problem and was prejudiced in investigating the problem or taking steps to protect itself by notifying third parties (such as its insurance carrier or bonding company) of the possible claim, (2) the corrective work was not performed properly, and (3) the owner, by using another contractor to perform the fix, failed to mitigate damages. On the other hand, the legal team needs to balance the owner's interest in preparing the best case for litigation with the owner's interest in having the failure remedied competently and expeditiously.

Injured Third Parties

The legal concerns of third parties injured by the failure will be different from those of the project owner. Injured third parties—including workers, adjacent property owners, and individuals using the project—will primarily be interested in pursuing relief against the potentially liable parties and recovering damages for injuries. Consequently, the legal strategy of such individuals will largely revolve on (1) obtaining information about the failure, (2) determining who may be potential defendants, and (3) pursuing recovery against such defendants.

Given this strategy, prompt and timely notification to the potentially liable parties is crucial for preserving the injured third party's rights against such parties. This notice is so important because it may help to avoid such legal defenses as

- The expiration of statutes of limitation
- Waiver of rights to obtain contributions from insurance coverage
- Prejudice to the potentially liable party for not timely knowing that it was a defendant

The legal strategy of injured third parties should also include determining whether their injuries are covered by insurance and giving their insurance carriers the opportunity to pursue recovery.

Potentially Liable Parties

Many parties could be theoretically responsible for a failure on a specific project. The most likely are those who provided services to the owner during the design and construction of the project, such as design professionals, contractors, and suppliers. Other parties that could face liability include inspection and testing agencies, government agencies, and the property owner.

Although the next section reviews the legal theories on which liability is based, several principles should generally be noted. First, the liability of those who are under contract to the owner will generally be established by the scope of the duties assumed under such contract. For example, if an engineer agreed to have someone on the site full-time to inspect the contractor's work and failed to find the flaw that created the failure, then the engineer will face a professional negligence claim from the owner and injured third parties. Whether the claim is successful will be dependent upon whether the engineer breached the standard of care for the inspection of such work. That is, would a reasonable engineer similarly situated have found the defect during an inspection? Note that, absent a contract to the contrary, design professionals are not required to be perfect in the performance of their work.

Liability against the construction team, including contractors and suppliers, does not generally follow standard-of-care principles. Instead, the contractor is strictly accountable to the owner to perform work in accordance with the contract documents, regardless of applicable industry standards. This does not mean that the general contractor warrants that the design professional's design, when executed, is sufficient to meet the owner's needs. The owner, as the party who contracts with the design professional and contractor, is held to impliedly warrant the sufficiency of the plans and specifications to the contractor. As a result, the contractor may be able to defend itself by claiming that its workmanship was acceptable and that the design caused the problem.

Once a party recognizes that it may be named as a potential defendant in a claim for a construction failure, it is important to begin the process of obtaining information about the nature of the failure and to preserve relevant evidence. As discussed above, competent consulting teams should be involved in the process of gathering information. The other major responsibility of the potentially liable party is to notify (1) other parties who worked on the project (such as contractors and/or subcontractors) of their potential liability and (2) insurance carriers of the potential claim.

Unlike the property owner and injured third party, the potentially liable party is confronted with the important issue of getting its insurance company to defend such party for the damages associated with the failure. Although this duty to defend is required by most policies and broadly enforced by the courts, many carriers will undertake such duty only after reserving their rights to contest payment for the underlying claim at a later date. As a result, it is critical for the insured to have a meaningful dialogue with the carrier as to

- The extent of the reservation of rights
- Counsel who will be representing both the insured and the carrier
- The insured's role in the defense and settlement of the case
- The resolution of any disputes between the carrier and insured

Because the key to answering these questions lies in the comfort level that both parties have with defense counsel, it is important for the insured to actively participate in counsel selection. The insured should not simply rubber-stamp the defense counsel selected by the carrier.

UNDERSTANDING THE LEGAL FRAMEWORK OF THE FAILURE

As noted at the outset of this chapter, the legal concerns associated with a failure are integrally related to the facts. Once the facts and positions of the parties are understood, an investigation should be made into the legal framework of the failure. This includes understanding (1) the theories of liability associated with the failure, (2) contractual limitations of liability, and (3) applicable statutes of limitations and statutes of repose.

Theories of Liability

Several theories of liability can be used to sue and find a potentially liable party responsible for a construction failure.[19] The three most common theories are

   Contract-based liability

   Tort-based liability

   Strict liability

Contract-Based Liability.   A contract identifies the roles, responsibilities, and duties between two parties. A construction project involves a variety of contracts, including contracts between (1) the owner and the owner's design professionals and contractors, (2) the lead design professional and his or her subconsultants, and (3) the lead contractor and her or his subcontractors and suppliers. If a construction failure occurs, each of these contracts and subcontracts may be used to form the basis of a claim by one party to a contract against another.

For example, an owner could use a contract with the general contractor as a vehicle for the contract-based claims of

- Failure to properly supervise the work
- Failure to properly develop, monitor, and enforce a safety program

- Breach of warranty that the work will be free of defects in materials and work-manship and that the work will be performed in accordance with the contract documents
- Failure to indemnify the owner for claims of personal injury and property damage

When confronted with this claim from the owner, the general contractor will likely file similar breach-of-contract claims against the subcontractors responsible for performing the relevant work involved in the failure.

Tort-Based Liability.   In addition to legal rights arising out of a contractual relationship, certain obligations exist between parties as a matter of law. When a party breaches one of these obligations, the party can be subject to a claim in tort. The tort theory that is most commonly used in construction failure analysis is *negligence*—a concept that is based on (1) a duty of care owed by one person to another, (2) the breach of that duty of care, and (3) damages which flow from the breach. Other tort theories include fraud and misrepresentation, both of which involve actions by a party reasonably intended to mislead another party to the second party's detriment. As a result, tort theories can be used not only by parties in privity of contract with a potential defendant (with certain exceptions for states enforcing the economic loss doctrine), but also by third parties harmed by the conduct of the defendant.

Tort theories are highly dependent upon the standards of care owed by one party to another. The most basic standard of care, which is a fundamental component to the negligence theory of liability, is the duty to act in the same manner as would another person similarly situated. Central to determining what duty of care is owed is the contractual responsibility of the potential defendant. For example, a design professional who had no contractual or actual role in construction administration would be unlikely to owe any duty of care to investigate what was happening at the project site in the implementation of the professional's design. This responsibility would flow to other parties, such as the owner, construction manager, and general contractor.

Strict Liability.   Some activities are so hazardous that the law imposes liability regardless of the standard of care. This theory, known as *strict liability,* focuses on defendants who perform the hazardous work. Note that strict liability is a theory that has developed over the years to provide injured consumers with a means of recovering against a seller of a product without having to prove negligence or fault on the part of the seller. Sometimes referred to as *liability without fault,* this concept arose in the context of manufacturers that sold products that were "defective" and "unreasonably dangerous to the user or consumer." Importantly, the doctrine as developed does not provide redress for those with whom the seller has a direct contractual relationship, but instead is meant to help those for whom there is no privity of contract.

Strict liability often arises in such construction activities as hazardous waste remediation, and blasting and support of excavation—although the strict liability standard is usually used against the property owner engaged in such activities and not against those providing services to the owner. However, note that some have argued that the strict liability doctrine should apply to the design-builder and its team members in the event of a job site injury or property damage. They argue that the design-builder has substantial control over the "product," i.e., the completed construction project, and is in the best position to bear the risk of defects, just as is the manufacturer of a product.

Although some courts have found that the design-builder is providing a "product," most courts disagree, finding that construction is a "service" industry. There is a line of cases, however, that routinely has found the design-builder to be a "seller" of a "product" for strict liability purposes. Most of these cases involved the design and sale of residences by a mass-home builder.

Indemnity. As noted above, contracts frequently contain specific clauses that establish indemnity requirements for one or both of the parties. Indemnification provisions are standard tools for distributing the risk of loss on a contract. Sometimes referred to as *hold-harmless* provisions, these clauses define a party's obligations to reimburse another party for the losses incurred or the damages for which it may be held liable. These provisions have a long history of use in the construction industry and are designed to transfer risks to a party who may be factually more culpable or who has the ability to insure for such a risk. Claims for breaches of the indemnity clause fall under the category of breach-of-contract claims. There are three basic types of general indemnity arrangements: broad form, intermediate form, and limited form. Each of these is discussed below.

A broad-form indemnity clause results in the indemnitor assuming any and all liability associated with the event, regardless of fault, and even if the damage is due to the indemnitee's sole negligence. Consider, for example, the following:

> To the fullest extent permitted by law, Contractor shall defend, indemnify and hold harmless the Owner and its agents and employees ("Indemnitees") from and against any and all claims, losses, damages, causes of action and liabilities of any kind, arising out of or in connection with the work performed by Contractor. It is the express intention of both Contractor and Indemnitees that Contractor's obligations hereunder shall apply to claims, losses, damages, causes of action and liabilities caused by the sole negligence of any Indemnitee.

In essence, the indemnitor under this clause becomes the insurance carrier for risk of loss to the owner on the project. Because of the severe nature of this risk transference, numerous jurisdictions have adopted statutory provisions which prohibit the indemnification of a party for its sole negligence or intentional misconduct.

Under an intermediate form of indemnity, the indemnitor is responsible only if it has caused some of the damage or loss. Consider the following clause:

> To the fullest extent permitted by law, Contractor shall defend, indemnify and hold harmless the Owner and its agents and employees ("Indemnitees") from and against any and all claims, losses, damages, causes of action and liabilities of any kind, arising out of or in connection with the work performed by Contractor, provided that any such claim, loss, damage, cause of action or liability is caused in whole or in part by any negligent act or omission of the Contractor.

As a result of this clause, the indemnitor assumes any and all liability if it is partially negligent—even if such partial negligence is as little as 1 percent. However, unlike the broad form of indemnity, it is not required to indemnify the owner who did not do anything wrong.

The limited form of indemnity limits one's indemnity obligations to the extent of one's own negligence. A typical clause might read as follows:

> To the fullest extent permitted by law, Contractor shall defend, indemnify and hold harmless the Owner and its agents and employees ("Indemnitees") from and against any and all claims, losses, damages, causes of action and liabilities of any kind, arising out of or in connection with the work performed by Contractor, but only to the extent that any such claim, loss, damage, cause of action or liability is caused or contributed to by the negligent act or omission of the Contractor.

This will create a comparative liability situation, in which the court would be required to determine how much each party had caused the problem and each party's proportionate share of liability.

Subject to considerations of public policy or statutory restrictions, courts routinely uphold and enforce indemnity clauses in a variety of contexts. It is critical for the legal team to determine whether an indemnity clause is applicable with respect to the particular failure and to take the steps to trigger coverage under the clause.

Liability Limitations

Contract clauses which limit the overall liability of a party to a contract are commonly used in the construction industry, particularly when the risks are so great as to place an organization's capital structure in significant jeopardy. These clauses are generally enforceable if they are agreed upon between parties of relatively equal bargaining positions, are reasonable in amount, and clearly define the liability being limited. Note, however, that some states have found that these clauses are against public policy when they attempt to disclaim liability for a party's negligence and are thus void.[20]

Limitation-of-liability clauses play a critical role in the assessment of liability for failures. For example, if the contract between an owner and an engineer limits the total liability of the engineer to "$50,000 or the engineer's fee, whichever is greater," the owner will be assuming the risk of any functional failures caused by the engineer which cause damages exceeding such an amount. Note, however, that the engineer's exposure to liability from third parties, such as injured workers or users of the facility, will not be limited by any such limitation-of-liability clause.

Statutes of Limitation and of Repose

Statutes of limitation and statutes of repose have a major impact on the legal environment associated with the prosecution and defense of claims arising out of construction failures. Each statute is very different in purpose and in content and should be fully understood by the legal investigatory team.

Statutes of limitation establish a cutoff on the amount of time to file suit from the date the cause of action giving rise to the claim accrues. This time limitation is established for the purpose of requiring diligent prosecution of known claims—since a party's ability to respond to a claim can be affected by the passage of time. State statutes have unique time periods for statutes of limitation and are dependent upon the specific type of claim involved. In general, contract actions have a longer statute of limitations than tort actions.[21]

In some states, the accrual of a cause of action for statute-of-limitations purposes is based on the date that the work was performed, such as the rendering of plans or the completion of construction. In other states, however, it is based on the date the claim was first discovered, which often coincides with the date that the injury occurred. In these discovery-trigger states, parties can be liable for a substantial period of time after their work is completed.

In response to complaints from architects, engineers, and contractors that the never-ending potential liability exposure was unfair, many state legislatures enacted statutes of repose. These statutes create an absolute bar to suits brought after a certain period of time has passed since the project was completed—regardless of when the injury was discovered. Statutes of repose generally cover from 5 to 20 years and are an important part of an overall risk management program for those providing construction services.

The importance of statutes of limitation and statutes of repose to the overall legal strategy of a construction failure mandates that the legal investigative team conduct early preliminary research into the relevant statutes and case law governing the problem. This is important not only for assessing whether the client has any quick legal defenses, but also for determining when a suit must be brought against potentially responsible parties. If a statute of limitations is close to expiring, the potential plaintiff should explore the prospects of obtaining a tolling agreement with potential defendants. This agreement will stop the further running of the statute of limitations and will enable the parties to attempt to investigate the failure and perhaps work on settling the dispute without resorting to litigation.

OTHER STRATEGIC LEGAL ISSUES

Several other strategic legal issues need to be considered by the parties involved in a failure analysis. Some of these have been addressed above, including the participation in joint defense agreements and the correction of the problem. Other issues, which relate to how the case will be presented and resolved, are discussed below.

Alternative Dispute Resolution

The construction industry has found great benefits in attempting to resolve disputes through *alternative dispute resolution* (ADR) processes. These processes, which include advisory arbitration panels, mediation, and dispute review boards, involve the use of third-party neutrals to assist the parties in understanding the facts related to the failure and in determining an appropriate way of resolving the accountability of the parties. ADR can be used by any parties in dispute. It may also be required by the contract between the parties. The legal team should provide clear direction to the client in determining whether to use ADR and, if so, when to seek its use and which method may be the most effective to resolve the dispute. ADR is discussed more fully in Chap. 2.

Partial Settlements

It is possible that some of the parties to the dispute may be able to resolve their differences before trial and before the entire case has been resolved among all the parties. These partial settlements can be very appropriate in simplifying the litigation, as well as in enabling an injured party (such as the owner) to obtain interim relief, including financial support and correction of the problem.[22]

CLOSURE

As noted at the outset of this chapter, development of a legal strategy is closely related to the factual, political, management, and legal issues associated with the failure. Remember that the process is dynamic and that what is important at one point in time, such as early involvement with the media and public, will ultimately become overshadowed by the need to collect evidence about the failure and to determine who is responsible for the damages.

REFERENCES AND ENDNOTES

1. "Causes Probed as Crippled Hoist Comes Slowly Down," *Engineering News Record,* August 10, 1998, pp. 10–15.

2. "Times Square's Troubles Probed," *Engineering News Record,* August 24, 1998, pp. 12–14.

3. See George Derbalian, "Engineering Methodology and Approach for Structural Failure Analysis," chap. 7, *Construction Failures,* Wiley, New York, 1989.

4. For the purposes of this chapter, the term *structural failure* typically refers to cases of collapse, explosion, fire, or other events that have life safety implications. *Functional failure* refers to the failure of a project to work as intended, with the damages largely being economic in nature.

5. Readers interested in a more comprehensive discussion of some of the legal issues associated with construction failures may wish to refer to *Construction Failures,* Wiley, New York, 1989. The reader is also invited to refer to an excellent publication on some of the forensic issues associated with failure, entitled *Guidelines for Failure Investigations,* Task Committee on Guidelines for Failure Investigation, American Society of Civil Engineers, New York, 1989. Specific reference to this book is made in this chapter where appropriate.

6. See Frank A. Shepherd and Stuart J. McGregor, "What to Do When the Phone Rings: How to Survive the Construction Failure," chap. 5, *Construction Failures,* Wiley, New York, 1989.

7. Robert L. Meyers, III and Michael F. Albers, "The Use of Experts in Investigating a Construction Failure," chap. 8, *Construction Failures,* Wiley, New York, 1989.

8. See *Guidelines for Failure Investigations,* Task Committee on Guidelines for Failure Investigation, American Society of Civil Engineers, New York, 1989, pp. 107–108.

9. See *Guidelines for Failure Investigations,* Task Committee on Guidelines for Failure Investigation, American Society of Civil Engineers, New York, 1989, pp. 52–56.

10. Edna Selan Epstein, *The Attorney-Client Privilege and the Work-Product Doctrine* 35 (3d ed. 1997) *citing,* Restatement, The Law Governing Lawyers §118 (Tentative Draft No. 1, 1988), Business Law Section, American Bar Association. For a full discussion of these elements, see Edna Selan Epstein, *The Attorney-Client Privilege and the Work-Product Doctrine* 35-158 (3d ed. 1997), Section of Litigation, American Bar Association.

11. See *Hickman v. Taylor,* 329 U.S. 495 (1947).

12. Edna Selan Epstein, *The Attorney-Client Privilege and the Work-Product Doctrine* 291 (3d ed. 1997), Section of Litigation, American Bar Association.

13. F.R. Civ. P. 26(b)(3).

14. F.R. CIM. P. 16(b)(2).

15. See, generally, Donald G. Gavin, Robert J. Smith, and Daniel E. Toomey, "The Project That Doesn't Work: The Functional Failure and Who Is Responsible," chap. 11, *Construction Failures,* Wiley, New York, 1989.

16. See Stanley A. Martin and James J. Myers, "Getting the Insurance Company on Board," chap. 9, *Construction Failures,* Wiley, New York, 1989.

17. See Owen J. Shean and Douglas L. Patin, "Builder's Risk Coverage," chap. 7, *Construction Insurance: Coverages and Disputes,* The Michie Company, Charlottesville, VA, 1994.

18. Assumption of the risk and contributory negligence are two defenses that can be asserted against an owner's claims for defects. For a discussion of each of these theories in the context of construction failures, see Donald G. Gavin, Robert J. Smith, and Daniel E. Toomey, "The Project That Doesn't Work: The Functional Failure and Who Is Responsible," chap. 11, *Construction Failures,* Wiley, New York, 1989.

19. See, generally, Donald G. Gavin, Robert J. Smith, and Daniel E. Toomey, "The Project That Doesn't Work: The Functional Failure and Who Is Responsible," chap. 11, *Construction Failures,* Wiley, New York, 1989.

20. See, e.g., *City of Dillingham v. CH2M Hill Northwest, Inc.,* 873 P.2d 1271 (Alaska 1994).

21. For example, in Virginia the statute of limitations on written contracts is 5 years, while for personal injury and wrongful death the statute is 2 years.

22. For a discussion about settling disputes on construction failures, see, generally, William J. Postner, Robert A. Rubin, and Lisa A. Banick, "Fixing the Failure and Settling the Dispute," chap. 14, *Construction Failures,* Wiley, New York, 1989.

CHAPTER 6
ENGINEERING INVESTIGATION OF STRUCTURAL FAILURES

Glenn R. Bell, P.E.

INTRODUCTION

The goal of this chapter is to give a broad overview of the *process* involved in conducting an investigation of a structural failure, with emphasis on the author's particular experience in the logic involved. The depth and complexity of investigations described here are appropriate for the most involved of investigations. In many cases, less complexity will suffice.

Purposes of Structural Failure Investigations

Investigations of structural failures are conducted for a variety of purposes. Most commonly, when a structure collapses, there is litigation involved, and the forensic engineer may be retained by a party who represents a plaintiff's or defendant's interest to determine what went wrong and who is responsible. A particular challenge for the forensic engineer in this role is not to succumb to pressure to compromise his or her objectivity and impartiality when answering to a client with a particular bias. For failures less catastrophic than collapse, the forensic engineer may be retained by the owner or manager of a building or an insurance company to diagnose structural malperformance and prescribe a remedy; litigation may not be anticipated at all. Occasionally, an investigation may be commissioned simply to tell the general public or a government agency what went wrong. The National Institute of Science and Technology (NIST), formerly the National Bureau of Standards (NBS), has been called upon by government groups in this role: the U.S. Senate and the mayor of Kansas City asked the NBS to investigate the 1981 walkways collapse at the Hyatt Regency in Kansas City, so that the public would have an explanation for this disaster.[1] OSHA (Occupational Safety and Health Administration) retained the NBS to determine the cause of failure of a cooling tower[2] at Willow Island, West Virginia, in 1977 and of the catastrophic collapse at L'Ambiance Plaza[3] in Bridgeport, Connecticut, in 1987. The purpose of these investigations was to assist OSHA in assessing fines.

While generally the structural engineering profession has no direct means of authorizing investigations to determine what lessons may be learned from failures, many individuals and groups have been active in gleaning the lessons learned from investigations conducted for other purposes, and disseminating those lessons to the profession. Most noteworthy are the efforts of the American Society of Civil Engineers' (ASCE) Technical Council on Forensic Engineering (TCFE).

With a breadth of purposes come a range of client types. Table 6.1 lists some types of individuals and organizations requiring structural investigations.

Technical versus Procedural Causes of Failure

Forensic engineers may be called upon to determine two types of causes of failure: technical and procedural. Technical causes are the actual physical proximate causes of failure. (The hanger-rod-box-beam connection at line U2 ruptured. The roof collapsed due to a 150 percent overload due to drifting snow. The timber truss failed by buckling of the fourth compression diagonal.) Often compounding problems lead to failure, and to determine the relative contributions from various structural defects is challenging. Sometimes compound defects are so debilitating that the challenge is to determine not why the structure fell down, but rather why it stood for as long as it did.

Procedural causes are the human errors, communication problems, or shortcomings in design, construction, or maintenance that were responsible for the flaws that led to the technical cause. (The welding of the hanger-rod-box-beam connections did not meet the design requirements. The structural engineer neglected the effects of drifting snow in the design. The carpenters omitted critical bracing for the truss diagonals.)

Often, determining the procedural causes is the more difficult but important aspect of an investigation, particularly for determining the lessons to be learned. It has been estimated that 90 percent of failures are due not to technical shortcomings, but to procedural errors.[4]

Scope of This Chapter

Several available guides for conducting investigations describe particular techniques.[5–12] There are guidelines and standards for material-specific or test-specific methods, concrete petrography, for example, that are details beyond the scope of this chapter.

The term *forensic* is often misunderstood, as it has two meanings in our profession. In the most literal sense, it relates to court or other public disputes. More

TABLE 6.1 Common Clients of the Forensic Investigator

Owners	Tenants
Developers	Attorneys
Public and government agencies	Insurance companies
Plaintiffs in litigation (injured parties)	Materials manufacturers
Defendants in litigation (parties involved with the design, construction, maintenance, or operation)	Designers
	Contractors

generally, and as used by the ASCE's TCFE, it means all the activities involved with investigating the causes of failure or malperformance. Indeed, typically only a small fraction of the forensic engineer's work is involved in litigation and other dispute resolution activities. The author subscribes to this latter, broader definition.

PROJECT INITIATION

Project initiation requires establishing at least a preliminary objective and scope of work, checking on conflicts on interest, executing a contract agreement, and establishing an investigative plan.

Project Objective and Scope

As with any consulting assignment, the project usually begins with a meeting or phone call during which the potential client describes her or his needs and objectives for the investigation. Always check that you and your organization do not have a conflict of interest in undertaking the assignment. Until you have made such a check, you should caution the potential client not to reveal confidential information to you that could jeopardize the client's position (such as his theory for attacking the litigation), should you have to decline the engagement due to conflict of interest. Otherwise, the potential client could have grounds for your being completely disqualified from the case. See *Recommended Practice for Design Professionals Engaged as Experts in the Resolution of Construction Disputes.*[13]

Beware of "takeout moves," wherein the client agrees to engage you, forwards an executed contract, possibly with a small retainer, and then doesn't extend you any work. The purpose is to inexpensively exclude you from working on behalf of others. It happens.

Inquire as to the client's motives and the degree to which you will be free to perform an objective investigation in order to form opinions with a reasonable degree of engineering certainty (see recommendation 12 of Ref. 13). Obtain authorization for proper scope now, or refuse the engagement.

Carefully examine the potential client's objectives. If the client declares an intention to use you to support a certain point of view as an expert in trial, and you think it is unlikely that you will be able to support that point of view, let the client know at the beginning. It is always better to be honest up front, even if it means losing the assignment.

Conflicts of Interest

The *Recommended Practice*[13] states:

> Regardless of the expert's objectivity, the expert's opinion may be discounted if
> it is found that the expert has or had a relationship with another party which con-

sciously or even subconsciously could have biased the expert's services or opinions. To avoid this situation, experts should identify the organizations and individuals involved in the matter at issue, and determine if they or any of their associates have or ever had a relationship with any of the organizations or individuals involved. Experts should reveal any such relationships to their clients and/or client's attorneys to permit them to determine whether or not the relationships could be construed as creating or giving the appearance of creating conflicts of interest.

Conflict avoidance in large organizations is difficult. In the author's firm, a computer database of current and past projects is maintained to try to identify such conflicts.

Agreements

Many of the standard-form agreements used by architects and engineers in the construction industry are not well suited for forensic work. Most are intended for new constructed works or renovations, and include provisions that do not apply; but, perhaps more importantly, they may not include provisions that are critical on forensic assignments. Such relevant provisions may include the right of entry at the site, disposition of samples, standard of care, and conflicts of interest. Standard provisions for forensic assignments may be developed with assistance of your attorney and professional liability carrier.

Unlike in many design projects, it is often impossible at the outset of an investigative assignment to define the scope and cost of the work with any precision. Yet, it is a risky business practice to proceed without an agreement with your client on the scope, time, and expenditures. In such circumstances it is useful to proceed with your client in phases, in which the scope of estimated cost of subsequent phases is established and agreed to at the end of each phase, as the work unfolds and the direction of the investigation becomes clear.

Establishing the Investigative Plan

To determine the technical causes of failure, the goals of the investigation are to establish (1) the mode and sequence of the failure, (2) the demands (loads) acting on the structure at the time of the failure, and (3) the capacity of the structure at the time of the failure.

The process usually involves developing hypotheses regarding the causes of failure and then analyzing and testing those hypotheses. With effort, certain failure theories are eliminated; and, we hope, in the end, the facts will support one theory. If the investigation reveals that the demand on a certain part of the structure exceeded its capacity for one and only one failure mechanism and that the mechanism is consistent with evidence of the mode and sequence of the failure, you've got it. Sometimes, as will be described below, the results are not so straightforward.

From the outset, the forensic engineer creates an investigative plan, the common steps of which are shown in Table 6.2. A general flowchart of the process is given in Fig. 6.1. However, not all investigations employ all steps, and the investigative plan is continuously revised to account for new information and evolving theories. Some investigators have developed elaborate flowcharts for the investigative process, such as those shown by Blockley[12] and by Kaminetzky.[14]

ESTABLISHING THE INVESTIGATIVE TEAM

Just as determining the proper objective and scope is critical to success, so is engaging the proper individuals and organizations on the project team.

Qualifications of the Investigator

By education, structural engineers are trained generally for the design and construction of new works. To the author's knowledge, no universities offer programs in forensic engineering, although a few offer courses in causes of failure.

Structural design and structural investigations require very different approaches: The first is a process of synthesis; the second is one of analysis. *Design* requires, among other things, an ability to create a cost-efficient load-bearing scheme in accordance with a set of "rules" prescribed by building codes, for minimal design cost. Simplicity and optimization are paramount. *Investigation* requires a structured approach of data collection as well as the development and scrutiny of failure hypotheses. Advanced analyses, precision, and great detail and patience are

TABLE 6.2   Common Steps in the Investigative Process

Commission of forensic engineer by client
Definition of objective of investigation
Collection of background information
Preliminary document review
Initial reconnaissance site visit
Eyewitness interviews
Formulation of investigative plan
Formation of project team
Comprehensive collection of documents
Document review
Site investigation
Sample collection
Theoretical analyses
Laboratory analyses
Development of failure hypotheses, analysis of data, synthesis of information, and formation of conclusions
Determination of procedural responsibilities for failures
Report writing

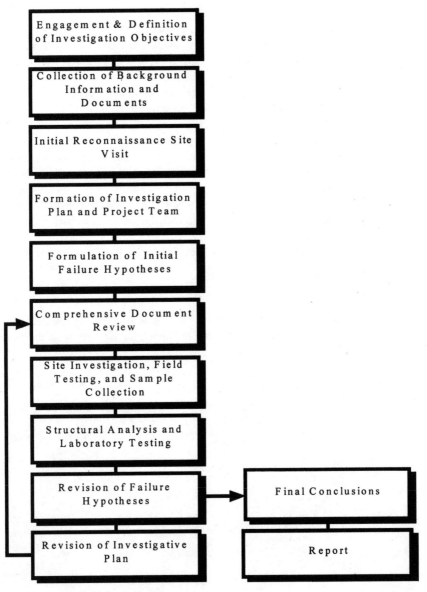

FIGURE 6.1 The investigative process.

key. For this reason, good structural designers are not necessarily good investigators, and vice versa.

The key to proficiency in either discipline is experience, and so the author would recommend to any individual with an interest in structural failure investigations a thorough review of the available literature, as described in the sections below. Review of this literature not only provides insight into investigative processes and techniques, but also exposes the common ways in which structures fail. A veteran investigator of thousands of failures once remarked that "structures nearly always fail by buckling or where loads must turn a corner" (Figs. 6.2 and 6.3). Although it is quite a generalization, this is not far off the mark. It is this real-world understanding of why buildings stand and why they actually fail that, in part, differentiates a good investigator and a good designer.

In addition to technical skills, the forensic engineer requires credentials that give credibility to the individual's opinions, ability to convey often complex issues simply and convincingly to laypeople, absolute honesty and ability to work impartially under pressure from individuals with partial interests, stamina and constitution to sustain the stress of litigation proceedings, ability to remain composed under sometimes hostile examination, and when called upon to convey opinions regarding procedural causes of failures, a knowledge of the standard of care of practitioners in the industry.

Expert consultants and witnesses are discussed further in Chap. 9 of this book.

Available Guides

The process of investigating failures will never follow standard procedures; each investigation is different and requires a tailored approach. Nevertheless, there are

FIGURE 6.2 "Structures nearly always fail by buckling or where loads must turn a corner." (*Jack Janney*).

FIGURE 6.3　"Structures nearly always fail by buckling or where loads must turn a corner." (*Jack Janney*).

some useful guidelines for conducting investigations. The most noteworthy are found in Refs. 5 to 7, 9, 12, 14, and 15.

Sources of Failure Information

For anyone interested in the study of failure investigations, the author strongly recommends the ASCE *Journal of Performance of Constructed Facilities.* Published quarterly, this journal contains case studies of individual failure investigations as well as articles on particular failure issues. Failure books and articles are often published in other industry literature. Examples are Refs. 16 through 30.

Some of the most thorough and well-documented reports of failure investigations are those of the former National Bureau of Standards, now the National Institute of Science and Technology. Among others, the NBS/NIST has investigated the 1981 Hyatt Regency, Kansas City, walkways failure,[1] the 1981 collapse of the Harbour Cay Condominium in Cocoa Beach, Florida,[31] and the 1988 collapse of L'Ambiance Plaza in Bridgeport, Connecticut.[3]

Team Organization

In large, complex investigations it is rare for the principal investigator (PI) to possess all the requisite technical skills, and she or he may rely on specialty consultants in such areas as materials behavior, testing and instrumentation, special load effects (e.g., wind), and special analysis techniques.

A comprehensive list of the many specialists on which the PI may rely is given in Table 6.3. The qualities required of these specialists are generally as mentioned above. The forensic engineer should have preestablished relationships with such specialty consultants, in order to call them on short notice when the need arises.

When large, complex cases are involved, strong project management involving the establishment of clear lines of communication and responsibility is essential. Periodic updates of the investigative plan must be conveyed to the entire team. Continuous quality control/assurance over in-house staff and external consultants must be exercised.

TABLE 6.3   Specialist Consultants

Aerodynamics	Mathematics
Aluminum	Measurement technology
Architecture	Meteorology
Blasting vibrations	Nondestructive testing
Climatology	Ocean engineering
Cold-weather construction	Offshore construction
Composite materials	Painting
Computer design	Parking engineering
Concrete materials	Pavements
Construction equipment and methods	Petrography
Corrosion	Photoelasticity
Cost estimating	Photogrammetry
Data systems	Pile driving
Dynamics and vibration	Pipelines
Elasticity	Pipes
Electronics	Plasticity
Engineering mechanics	Plastic materials
Environmental engineering	Prestressed concrete
Fabrication	Probability theory
Fatigue	Protective coatings
Field testing	Railroads
Fracture	Shoring
Geology	Stability
Geotechnical engineering/foundations	Statistical analysis
Glass	Steel
Groundwater	Surveying
Hydraulics	Waterproofing
Hydrodynamics	Welding
Impact	Wind
Masonry	Wood

Cooperative Efforts with Other Investigators

Investigations can be expensive, and available debris for testing and examination limited. For this reason, investigators answering to parties of different interests sometimes cooperate in the data collection and testing phases of an investigation. This was the case, for example, in the Hyatt Regency walkways collapse, where there were numerous experts representing a number of parties. Critical structural components from the debris needed to be tested destructively. The interested parties assembled and agreed that the NBS would perform the necessary laboratory analysis and testing, using procedures agreed to by all experts. All experts were allowed to witness the testing, and data were shared. Sometimes a "protocol" document is developed, agreed to, and followed by the experts of all parties in the handling and testing of evidence.

GENERAL INVESTIGATIVE PROCESS

This section discusses general considerations in developing the investigative process. Specific activities are reviewed in subsequent sections.

Analysis versus Synthesis

When investigating a structural failure, one cannot think as a designer. Whereas in the design process one has the freedom to arrange the structure to behave as one wants it to, after a structural failure one has no such control; the structure has already behaved as it wanted to.

Code methods that we use as designers are assumed to be conservative, but they don't always describe structural behavior well. For example, even though a structural steel beam may be loaded to its theoretical yield stress, it cannot be assumed that the beam will collapse. The beam has postyield capacity; it can strain-harden; there may be redundancy and alternate load paths; the actual yield strength is likely to be higher than the minimum specified. The more redundant and ductile the structure, the more likely it will yield, redistribute load, and display impressive load-bearing ability. The investigator must take all these factors into account.

Simple and conservative techniques, the hallmark of good design, are not appropriate for investigations. Greater precision is required; advanced analysis is often called for; all facts must be verified; unconfirmed assumptions may lead to critical errors in conclusions.

Development and Analysis of Failure Hypotheses

The most common mistake made by novice and experienced investigators alike is failure to consider all possible failure hypotheses. This is a pitfall for both the inexperienced investigator, who may miss a key action, and the experienced investigator, who may jump to a conclusion, thinking he's seen it before. No stone can be left unturned. All probable hypotheses must be developed and systematically analyzed until they can be either proved or disproved. Key in developing failure hypotheses is to study carefully the configuration of the debris after the failure, and then to imagine all the different failure sequences that the structure could have undergone in order to arrive at its final configuration. These steps are explored more fully below.

Establishing the Loads on the Structure

Dead loads are verified by cataloging observations from field investigations. Sometimes it is necessary to weigh existing components, material samples, or assemblies. Often dead loads are less than the allowances made during design, but they may be greater. Long-term maintenance and modification can lead to increased dead loads in the form of additional roofing membranes, ceilings, or mechanical equipment. Leaky roofs and walls saturate components. In cast-in-place concrete construction, structural deflections due to "ponding" of wet concrete have led to slabs thicker than required by design.

Live loads, of course, take many forms and often are difficult to verify. Snow, ponded water, furniture and equipment, wind, earthquake, and human occupancy are the common forms of live load (Fig. 6.4). Cataloging, sampling and weighing, and eyewitness accounts are all available forms of determining live loads. The increasing use of video security surveillance cameras affords often invaluable sources of information regarding loads and sequences of failures. Special or unusual load effects cannot be overlooked. They may include temperature, shrinkage and creep, wind and earthquake, vehicular impact, vibrations from equipment, and foundation settlements, to name a few (Fig. 6.5).

Live load behavior may vary from simplified assumptions. For example, some materials, such as masonry, will tend to arch over relatively flexible structural components.

Extensive discussion of the nature, magnitudes, and consequences of loads is given in Chap. 10 of this book.

Establishing the Capacity of the Structure

Usually the first step in determining the capacity of the structure is to review the structural drawings for the project. While drawings can be a great time-saver in establishing the overall structural configuration, they can lead one down an erroneous path if they are relied upon without field verification. Dimensions and member sizes must be confirmed. Material strengths must be verified. Structures often are modified over time (Fig. 6.6). The amount of verification required to reach

FIGURE 6.4   Failure of reinforced concrete column from overload during a typhoon.

conclusions with a reasonable degree of engineering certainty may be enormous; occasionally it is practically impossible.

Structures may deteriorate from the as-built condition due to a number of effects, such as water intrusion and other corrosive effects, fatigue, damage from nearby blasting, traffic vibrations, adjacent construction, and, in concrete, material degradation from chloride attack, alkali-silica reaction, or delayed ettringite reaction.

Following documentation of the as-built condition, determination of actual strength may come from load testing, from calculations, or from both. These techniques are described in subsequent sections of this chapter as well as in the other, material-specific, chapters of this book.

FIGURE 6.5 Failure of column in parking garage: The structural designer neglected the effects of axial shortening in the girders due to posttensioning.

Nonstructural elements, most notably exterior walls and interior partitions, may play an unintentional role in the behavior of the structure by interacting with the structural frame.

Advancement of Failure Hypotheses

Over the course of the investigation, failure hypotheses are continuously tested against the facts collected from field investigation, documents, testing, and analysis. Some hypotheses may be disproved and dropped, while new ones may be advanced. It is generally advisable to assemble the investigative team shortly after the initial site investigation for a brainstorming session on failure hypotheses.

FIGURE 6.6   Collapse of Hotel Vendome in Boston during a fire: An ill-planned structural modification to bearing wall created a critical flaw.

DOCUMENT REVIEW

Project documents are key to understanding not only how the structure was built but also how it was maintained and modified over time; without such documents the job is almost impossible for a complex project. Whenever possible, the investigator should obtain and review at least the most fundamental design documents prior to the initial site investigation. Project documents are also key when the forensic engineer is called upon to opine on the procedural causes of the failure in that the documents provide insight into the actions of those responsible for the design, construction, and operation of the facility.

Common sources of project documents are given in Table 6.4.

TABLE 6.4 Sources of Project Documents

Architects and engineers involved in original design, modification, or repair of facility
Past and present owners
Past and present building managers
General contractor and/or construction manager for original construction, modification, or repair of facility
Subcontractors involved in original construction, modification, or repair of facility
Developer of facility
Construction mortgagee of facility
Materials or systems suppliers for original construction, modification, or repair of facility
Previous or other current investigators
Building department
Testing agency involved in original construction, modification, or repair of facility

---

TABLE 6.5 Project-Specific Documents Used in Investigation

Contract drawings (including all revision issues thereof)
    Structural (including progress prints)
    Architectural (including progress prints)
    Mechanical (HVAC)*
    Electrical*
    Plumbing*
    Lighting*
Contract specifications
    Technical sections of interest
    General conditions
    Supplementary general conditions
    Special conditions
Contracts
    Owner/architect
    Architect/structural engineer
Contract revisions
    Addenda
    Bulletins
    Field directives
    Change orders
    Any correspondence authorizing change to structure from contract requirements
Shop drawings and other submissions
    Structural steel (detail drawings and erection drawings)
    Bar joists and prefabricated trusses
    Metal decking
    Reinforcing bar
    Product data

TABLE 6.5   Project-Specific Documents Used in Investigation (*Continued*)

As-built drawings
Field and shop reports (including construction photos)
  Structural steel inspection laboratory (including weld and bolt inspection)
  Concrete inspection laboratory (reinforcing steel, formwork, concrete)
  Concrete mix designs
  Clerk of the works
  Structural engineer
  Architect
  Construction supervisor's daily log
  Local building inspector
  Owner's or developer's field inspectors

Material strength reports or certification
  Concrete compressive strength
  Masonry prism strength
  Steel mill certificates
  Welding procedures (e.g., type of electrodes, required preheat)
  Fastener certification
  Results of special load tests

Project correspondence†
  Owner/consultant
  Intraconsultant
  Owner/contractor
  Consultant/contractor
  Transmittal/records
  In-house memoranda
  Records of meeting notes
  Records of telephone conversations

Consultant reports
  Feasibility studies
  Progress reports
  Soils consultant reports (including boring logs)

Calculations
  Primary structural engineer
  Reviewing structural engineer
  Specific subcontractor's engineers (where required by contract)

Maintenance and modification records

---

*Assist principally in establishing dead loads.
†The scope will vary depending on the investigator's assignment.

Table 6.5 contains a comprehensive list of documents that may be useful for failure investigations. Documents of the nonstructural trades—architectural, mechanical/electrical, etc.—are often useful for determining the dead loads on the structure. In addition, nonstructural elements may play an unintentional role, in the structure's load-bearing capacity, either supplementing the structural frame or debilitating it. Don't underestimate the importance of documents produced subsequent to the issuance of the design documents—addenda, shop drawings, bulletins, and field inspection reports often provide critical information about the departure of the structure from the structural drawings. In the author's experience, as-built drawings are rarely accurate.

FIELD INVESTIGATION

Field investigation may involve making observations and measurements on several scales, documenting existing conditions, removing samples, interviewing eyewitnesses, and performing in-field tests.

Access to and Control of the Site

Particularly following a large, catastrophic failure, the investigator must verify his or her rights and limitations regarding access to the site and to the activities there. (Often disaster sites are controlled by local or state police or the national guard.) Who has authority over site access and who is authorized to admit investigators to the site? Are there limitations on where the investigator may go and what she or he may do? Does the investigator have authority to alter evidence by moving debris or collecting samples?

Site Safety

Collapse scenes can be dangerous places (Fig. 6.7). Once, during an investigation of the collapse of an earth-covered garage, a second section of the garage collapsed.[32] Thus, the leading concern of every team member must be his or her own safety and that of other team members and others at the site. There are other hazards in addition to direct falling objects that are of concern: Sometimes failures lead to the release of environmental hazards; also, investigators may be entrapped in confined spaces. Many OSHA regulations define procedures for construction site safety, training, and certification that are relevant to field investigations.

When rescue operations are ongoing during field investigations, such operations must take precedence over the investigator's interest in data collection. If the investigator arrives on site shortly after the failure while rescue operations are under way, the investigator may find it necessary to suspend investigative efforts to lend her or his special expertise to the rescue effort.

Samples

The principal investigator establishes the overall project protocol for identifying, cataloging, removing, shipping, and storing samples. The author likes to mark

FIGURE 6.7   Failure sites can be dangerous places.

each sample with a permanent marker and then photograph it before removal (Fig. 6.8). Note any existing damage or distinguishing characteristic before removal from the structure. Samples that may deteriorate quickly after removal may have to be environmentally protected. Fracture surfaces may be sprayed with a clear acrylic coating, for example. Moisture-sensitive materials may be placed in sealed bags or other containers, sometimes with desiccants.

It is important to maintain a traceable chain of custody of samples, so that later the sample's origin and handling can be verified without question.

The sampling program should be based, in scope and content, on presumed failure hypotheses. The number and location of samples should be carefully planned and will depend on a number of factors, such as variation from sample to sample, degree of reliability required in results, whether there are any explainable trends in test results (e.g., differing batches of concrete), and size of structure. In straightforward cases, the number of samples may be established from statistical principles such as those set forth in Ref. 33 or in ASTM E105[34] and ASTM E141.[35] Material-specific recommendations are also available in ASTM and other standards.

Field Observations and Documentation

The principal investigator establishes the overall grid or identification system for the structure. The PI also determines the procedures for sample cataloging, photograph identification, observations, openings, and other documentation categories.

FIGURE 6.8 Label and photograph each sample before removal.

The PI should visit the site early in the process, to gain general familiarity with the site. It is important to establish, to the extent possible, the degree to which the debris may have been modified by others prior to the PI's arrival. Other members of the team should similarly obtain a general overview of the site prior to detailed examination. Each investigator should have a kit of basic tools as well as standard safety gear (e.g., hardhats and steel-toe shoes); a suggested list is given in Table 6.6.

A variety of specialists may be needed for the field investigation. A partial list of field support specialists is given in Table 6.7.

Investigators use a number of techniques for recording field observations and activities. Some keep separate logs of samples, sketches, discussions, and general observations. The author prefers that each team member keep a running diary of all field activities in a spiral-bound notebook. Thus later there can be no question as to who was responsible for what observation and at what time the observation was made. It is often important to know at what stage or in what context various activities took place. Also, it is much less likely that notes will be misplaced. Common field activities that require recording are given in Table 6.8. Individual logs or summaries of observations of activities of many investigators can later be constructed from these individual diaries. Sketches and photographs are better than lengthy verbal descriptions (either in writing or tape recording), as they can record more information in a shorter space and are less likely to be misinterpreted.

Speed of observation and data collection may be important in an ever-changing site where rescue operations are ongoing and evidence is being destroyed. This is

TABLE 6.6   Small Tools and Equipment for Field Investigation

Measurement	Stationery
10-in dial caliper	White lined paper
12-in steel ruler	Calculation pad
20-ft tape	Architect scale
100-ft tape	Pencil and leads
Optical comparator	Eraser
Tape-on crack monitors	Field notebooks
Tools	Triangles
Hammer	Felt-tip markers
Screwdrivers	Clipboard
Prybar	Lumber crayons
Pocket knife	Books
Flashlight	AISC manual
Photographic	ACI code
Film	Other applicable failure guides
Camera	Other
Lenses	Calculator
Flash	Stick-on labels
Batteries	Wire-on labels
Lens papers	Plastic sample bags
Clothing	Duct tape
Hardhat	Job file
Coveralls	Spray paint
Steel-toe workboots	Dictation recorder and tapes
Gloves	

TABLE 6.7   Field Support Specialists

Surveyors
Concrete coring or sawing technicians (for sample removal)
Welders (for sample removal)
Photographers
Crane operators
Shoring specialists
Field and laboratory testing technicians
Measurement technicians
Witness interrogators

where the experienced investigator is invaluable in quickly assessing the probable failure hypotheses and targeting the field work accordingly.

Field observations are made and recorded on three scales:

1. *Overall configuration.* How did the structure fail? Note movements from initial position and relative positions of components. What is the relationship of

TABLE 6.8 Records of Field Activities

Sketches of overall failed configuration
Observation of behavior of adjacent construction during and subsequent to failure
Detailed sketches of critical members and connections
Inventory of construction materials to establish dead loads
Observation of deterioration
Records of detailed as-built conditions, including plan and detail dimensions
Description of fracture surfaces
Records of samples removed
Procedures and results of field tests
Indications of environmental conditions acting on facility at time of failure
Log of photographs
Records of conversations with others

---

damaged and undamaged components? Examine and describe the interfaces of damaged and undamaged components.

2. *Member and connection configuration.* How are members bent and fractured? Describe fracture surfaces.

3. *Materials.* Is there degradation (corrosion, spalling, cracking, rot)? Are there signs of distress (e.g., flaking paint)?

Photography is an essential recording medium, and although some investigators prefer to use professional photographers, the author prefers to take his own shots. Since you know what you want the photograph to show, there is no substitute for doing it yourself. The investment in good 35-mm equipment and in the time needed for developing photographic skills is worth it. Videos are useful to convey action, but the author's experience is that for still recording, video is more cumbersome to use.

Early in the investigation, good overall aerial shots are invaluable to establish the overall failed configuration and conditions at the site. Such shots may be obtained from an adjacent building, from an aerial lift, or from aircraft.

Field Tests

Field testing generally falls into two types: load tests and material tests.

Load tests are useful when an undamaged portion of the structure remains that is representative of the section that has failed. They are particularly useful when the structure is severely deteriorated. Load tests can also be expensive, particularly when several tests are required to obtain statistical significance. A number of loading methods are available, including hydraulic jacks, mechanical jacks, water or other weights, and air bags. Redundancy in instrumentation is helpful to ensure reliability in results. If possible, calibrate equipment before and after testing.

Safety is critical. Have a safeguard, such as shoring or immediate load relief, in the event that the structure begins to fail catastrophically. In cases involving many parties in a litigation, it is often appropriate or even required to offer to other parties the opportunity to witness tests. The portion of the structure being tested must be isolated from structural and nonstructural elements that are not part of the test. Some form of backup or verification of the test results is advisable, in the form of either corroborating calculations or another type of test.

ASTM Publication STP 702, *Full-Scale Load Testing of Structures,*[36] provides additional information on this subject. There are also a number of ASTM standards on material or assembly-specific tests (for example, Refs. 37 through 43).

In-field materials tests are numerous and are set forth in many documents. Two comprehensive guides are Refs. 8 and 44.

Eyewitness Accounts

The author's experience with eyewitness accounts is that they are rarely fully reliable. This is not because people are intentionally dishonest, but because most lay observers are not trained in structural engineering, and the experience of witnessing a traumatic collapse can leave memories distorted. Nevertheless, eyewitness accounts can be useful for obtaining clues and for corroborating other evidence. Useful guidelines for eyewitness accounts are provided in Ref. 6.

LABORATORY ANALYSIS

Laboratory tests may be performed on materials or on structural components.

Materials Testing

Testing of samples of materials removed from the structure may take many forms, and a comprehensive treatment of this subject is beyond the scope of this chapter. However, some of the more common laboratory techniques for different materials are mentioned in Table 6.9.

Testing is also discussed in the material-specific chapters of this book.

Component Testing

Load testing may be performed on components removed from the field or on mockups made in a laboratory (Fig. 6.10). It is too easy to take the results of component testing as gospel. However, component testing is subject to many sources of error, just as calculations are. In particular, the modeling of the test boundary conditions is critical to obtain realistic results. Follow established procedures,

FIGURE 6.9   Scanning electron micrograph of a fracture surface.

such as ASTM standards, wherever possible. If you must deviate from accepted standards, do so while understanding fully the consequences, and be prepared to defend your reasons. An individual who is prepared to testify to the authenticity of the test procedures and results must witness the tests. Maintain all test equipment in good working order and properly calibrated. Use redundant checks on the test results by corroborating calculations or alternative tests. The number of tests must be consistent with your objectives for a satisfactory level of confidence.

STRUCTURAL ANALYSIS

Calculations are almost always required to determine the loads acting on the structure, and to determine the structure's resistance. In many cases, simple hand calculations suffice, and the author advocates these over complex computer analyses wherever possible. Often, however, it is necessary to resort to computer methods, such as finite-element or finite-difference techniques.

Methods

Structural failures, of course, often result in material and geometrically nonlinear behavior, which can be handled directly or indirectly by many finite-element techniques. In many cases, however, nonlinear behavior can be sufficiently described by hand methods.

TABLE 6.9   Common Laboratory Techniques

Metals	
Basic mechanical properties	Yield and tensile strength, elongation, reduction of area, modulus of elasticity, fatigue properties
Fractography	Failure analysis of fracture surface, usually with optical or scanning electron microscope (Fig. 6.9)
Fracture toughness	Charpy V-notch, fracture toughness, nil-ductility transition temperature
Welding	Radiography, visual, dye penetrant, ultrasonic, magnetic particle, eddy current, metallography
Hardness tests	Brinell, Rockwell, Vickers, and Knoop
Metallurgy and quantitative analysis	Chemical composition, grain analysis, phase type, flaw detection
Metallurgy	
Basic mechanical properties	Compressive strength, tensile strength, shear strength, modulus of elasticity; density, bond strength, fatigue strength, abrasion resistance
Dimensional stability	Creep and shrinkage, coefficient of thermal expansion
Petrographic analysis	Quantitative analysis, air content, degree of hydration and carbonation, alkali-carbonate reaction, alkali-silica reaction, cement aggregate reaction, cement content, soundness, water/cement ratio, sulfate attack
Corrosion and durability	Permeability, half-cell potential
Wood	
Basic mechanical properties	Tensile, shear, compressive, and bearing strength; modulus of elasticity; density
Dimensional stability	Creep and shrinkage, moisture content
Presence of decay	Microscopic inspection

Great care is required in complex computer analysis. Programs should be prequalified and their limitations understood; models must capture all important structural actions; input must be verified; the mathematical "goodness" of the solution verified; and results scrutinized. Computer analysis should be checked approximately by hand calculations. Secondary effects of temperature, creep, foundation settlement, stresses induced by construction sequence, and eccentricities are often

FIGURE 6.10 Full-scale load testing of bar joist.

neglected but may be quite significant. In reviewing structural designs, do not get hung up in exhaustive documentation of simple code violations that have no causal relationship to the failure.[45]

Scrutinize all the parameters in the resistance relationships to see whether the values you are using accurately represent the state of the structure at the time of failure.

Precision and Sensitivity Analysis

Sometimes one or more structural parameters affecting the strength are not known with precision. In such cases, it is common to perform sensitivity tests, wherein multiple analyses are performed with uncertain parameters input with their probable high and low extreme values.

DETERMINING THE CAUSE OF FAILURE

Failure theories are often developed based on prior experience with similar failures, although the team members should always be open-minded as to causes or combinations of causes never before experienced.

Analysis of Competing Failure Theories

As the investigation advances, facts are collected and failure hypotheses are either substantiated or disproved and dropped. New hypotheses may emerge. In a straightforward investigation, all hypotheses will be eliminated but one (i.e., in only one circumstance do the actions on the structure meet or exceed its predicted capacity). Often, however, the results are not so straightforward, and the investigation concludes that different causes are more or less probable. There may be multiple causes leading to a critical combination of load and capacity (Fig. 6.11).

If the estimated loads acting on the structure at the time of failure greatly exceed the predicted capacity, this may be a sign that something is wrong with the analysis.

Closing the Loop

After the potential causes of failure are narrowed down to one or a few, reexamine all the evidence to determine whether it does or does not support the presumed

FIGURE 6.11 Collapse of 2000 Commonwealth Avenue in Boston during construction. Misplaced reinforcement and understrength concrete caused the failure.

cause(s). In particular, the evidence regarding the initiation and sequence of the failure should agree with the load-and-resistance analysis.

REPORTS

The final report is usually the culmination of all the investigative efforts. It may be the final and only work product that the client sees. If it is used as part of a litigation process, it is the basis for the expert's testimony. Well prepared, it may help the client avoid litigation altogether by setting forth the client's engineering case so convincingly that the opposition is compelled to settle. Poorly written, it is a source of unending difficulty for the expert witness.

A properly structured report will set forth the factual bases for the analysis as well as present the facts on which the conclusions will be based. In this respect, the process of writing the report serves as a type of quality check on the investigation, because all facts and opinions must be supported and argued in the text.

For these reasons it is advisable to devote a large fraction of the investigative effort to the report. Examples of excellently prepared reports are those of the NBS, previously mentioned.[1–3,31]

Reports should be organized so that proven facts from a variety of sources are laid out first. Hearsay normally should not be relied upon in forming opinions. Where it is necessary to do so owing to lack of factual information or another reason, such qualification should be clearly stated.

Table 6.10 provides a general outline for reporting structural investigations that has stood the test of time at the author's firm. Sections 1 and 2 of the report contain introductory information useful for orienting the reader, describing the scope and objective of the investigation, and setting forth the sources of information relied upon. Sections 3, 4, and 5 set forth factual information obtained from the field program, from laboratory testing, and from calculations. In the testing and calculations sections, the standards employed must be stated clearly.

All facts collected are reviewed in the discussion section, including statements of failure hypotheses explored and an analysis of which hypotheses were proved and disproved and why. The discussion is the first point at which nonfactual information is presented. All discussion must be supported by facts in the previous sections. Conclusions and recommendations should flow logically from and be supported entirely by the discussion.

Some investigators use an Executive Summary section at the beginning of the report, giving a very brief statement of the project, summary, and conclusions.

The entire report must present a convincing and logical argument based on facts from discussion to conclusion. The causal relationship between identified deficiencies in design, construction, and maintenance must be shown.

TABLE 6.10   General Report Outline

Letter of transmittal

Abstract

Table of contents

1. Introduction
   1.1 Objective
   1.2 Scope
   1.3 Background
   1.4 Responsible design and construction agencies
   1.5 Construction documents

2. Description of structure (or project)

3. Field investigation

4. Laboratory tests

5. Results of calculations

6. Discussion of field investigation, laboratory tests, and results of calculations

7. Conclusions

8. Recommendations

CLOSURE

Investigations of structural failures serve many purposes in our society, most notably to help settle disputes between parties, to diagnose problems so that the building owner may make repairs, and to help our profession learn from its failures.

The activities of the forensic engineer offer, on one hand, enormous professional challenge—there are few things more difficult than sorting through the wreckage of a structural collapse and pinpointing the cause of failure. On the other hand, the forensic engineer's work can be disheartening and stressful. No one likes to witness failures of major constructed works, especially when human casualties occur, and the legal process can be fatiguing and hostile.

Forensic engineers are not prepared for their trade by academic training, and they must learn from their own experience and that of others. The synthesis required in structural design is very different from the analysis of structural investigations. Few engineers are both good designers and good investigators.

A thorough review of case studies of structural failures is invaluable to develop the forensic engineer's expertise and ability to readily form failure hypotheses.

Structural investigations cannot be reduced to prescribed standards. Each investigation must be tailored to the task at hand. However, there are certain logical methods common to all investigations that help to guide the process.

Failure investigations involve an iterative process of data collection, formation of failure hypotheses, testing and analyses, and testing of hypotheses. The goal is to establish the loads and other environmental factors acting on the structure at the time of failure, to establish the resistances of the various critical structural components, and, through a process of confirmation or elimination, find the failure cause(s) that is (are) consistent with evidence regarding the collapse sequence.

Communication, both verbal and written, of the findings of the investigation is the ultimate product of the work and should receive a substantial fraction of the effort of the investigation.

REFERENCES

1. National Bureau of Standards (NBS). *Investigation of the Kansas City Hyatt Regency Walkways Collapse,* NBS-BSS 143. Washington: U.S. Department of Commerce. May 1982.

2. NBS. *Investigation of Construction Failure of Reinforced Concrete Cooling Tower at Willow Island, WV,* NBS-BSS 148. Washington: U.S. Department of Commerce. September 1982.

3. NBS. *Investigation of L'Ambiance Plaza Building Collapse in Bridgeport, Connecticut,* NBSIR 87-3640. Washington: U.S. Department of Commerce. September 1987.

4. S. P. Gatje. The Role of the Federal Government in the Investigation of Structural Failures. *WISE Internship Report to ASCE.* Unpublished, 1984.

5. Task Committee on Guidelines for Failure Investigation of the Technical Council on Forensic Engineering. *Guidelines for Failure Investigation.* New York: ASCE. 1989.

6. J. R. Janney. *Guide to Investigation of Structural Failures.* New York: ASCE. 1986.

7. L. Addleson. *Building Failures—A Guide to Diagnosis, Remedy and Prevention.* London: Architectural Press. 1982.

8. American Society of Civil Engineers (ASCE). *Guideline for Structural Condition Assessment of Existing Buildings,* ASCE 11-90. New York: ASCE. 1991.

9. R. Crist and J. Stockbridge. Investigating Building Failures. *Consulting Engineer* (New York). June 1985.

10. R. Roberts and A. Pense. Basics in Failure Analysis of Large Structures. *Civil Engineering* (ASCE), vol. 50, no. 5. May 1980.

11. G. F. Sowers. Investigating Failure. *Civil Engineering* (ASCE), vol. 57, no. 5. May 1987.

12. D. I. Blockley. Logical Analysis of Structural Failure. *Journal of the Engineering Mechanics Division* (ASCE), vol. 107, no. EM2. April 1981.

13. *Recommended Practices: For Design Professionals Engaged as Experts in the Resolution of Construction Industry Disputes.* American Society of Forensic Engineers, Silver Spring, MD, 1988.

14. D. Kaminetzky. Failure Investigations, Who? Why? When? What? and How? *Proceedings—Construction Failures: Legal and Engineering Perspectives,* American Bar Association, Houston, TX. October 1983.

15. *Building Pathology: A State-of-the-Art Report.* Publication 155. CIB Report. Delft, The Netherlands. June 1993.

16. American Society of Civil Engineers (ASCE), Research Council on Performance of Structures. *Structural Failures: Modes, Causes, Responsibilities.* New York: ASCE. 1973.

17. G. R. Bell and J. C. Parker. Roof Collapse, Magic Mart Store, Bolivar, Tennessee. *Journal of Performance of Constructed Facilities* (ASCE), vol. 1, no. 2. May 1987.

18. V. Fairweather. Bailey's Crossroads: A/E Liability Test. *Civil Engineering* (ASCE), vol. 45, no. 11. November 1975.

19. J. Feld and K. L. Carper. *Construction Failure,* 2d ed. New York: Wiley. 1997.

20. B. B. LePatner and S. M. Johnson. *Structural and Foundation Failures: A Casebook for Architects, Engineers, and Lawyers.* New York: McGraw-Hill. 1982.

21. R. S. Loomis, R. H. Loomis, R. W. Loomis, and R. W. Loomis. Torsional Buckling Study of Hartford Coliseum. *Journal of the Structural Division* (Proceedings of ASCE), vol. 106, no. STI, Proc. Paper 15124. January 1980.

22. J. Loss and E. Kennett. *Identification of Performance Failures in Large Scale Structures and Buildings,* NSF Project No. ECE 8608145. College Park: University of Maryland. 1987.

23. E. O. Pfrang and R. Marshall. Collapse of the Kansas City Hyatt Regency Walkways. *Civil Engineering* (ASCE), vol. 52, no. 7. July 1982.

24. J. C. Ropke. *Concrete Problems: Causes and Cures.* New York: McGraw-Hill. 1982.

25. S. S. Ross. *Construction Disasters: Design Failures, Causes, and Prevention.* New York: McGraw-Hill. 1984.

26. I. Schousboe. Bailey's Crossroads Collapse Reviewed. *Journal of Construction Division* (Proceedings of ASCE), vol. 102, no. C02, Proc. Paper 12186. June 1976.

27. E. A. Smith and H. I. Epstein. Hartford Coliseum Roof Collapse: Structural Collapse Sequence and Lessons Learned. *Civil Engineering* (ASCE), vol. 50, no. 4. April 1, 1980.

28. J. G. Stockbridge. Cladding Failures—Lack of a Professional Interface. *Journal of the Technical Councils,* Proceedings of ASCE, vol. 43, no. 1, Proc. Paper 15085. January 1973.

29. C. H. Thornton. Lessons Learned from Recent Long Span Roof Failures. *Notes from ACI Seminar on Lessons from Failures of Concrete Buildings.* Boston: American Concrete Institute. April 1982.

30. D. W. Vannoy. 20/20 Hindsight—Overview of Failures. *Proceedings—Construction Failures: Legal and Engineering Perspectives,* American Bar Association, Houston, TX. October 1983.

31. National Bureau of Standards (NBS). *Investigation of Construction Failure of Harbour Cay Condominium in Cocoa Beach, Florida,* NBS-BSS 145. Washington: Department of Commerce. August 1982.

32. D. Kaminetzky. Structural Failures and How to Prevent Them. *Civil Engineering* (ASCE), vol. 46, no. 8, August 1976.

33. A. H. S. Ang and W. H. Tang. *Probability Concepts in Engineering Planning and Design.* New York: Wiley. 1975.

34. Standard Practice for Probability Sampling of Materials (E 105-58). *1996 Annual Book of ASTM Standards: General Test Methods, Nonmetal; Laboratory Apparatus; Statistical Methods; Forensic Sciences,* vol. 14.02. Philadelphia, PA: American Society for Testing and Materials. 1996.

35. Standard Practice for Acceptance of Evidence Based on the Results of Probability Sampling (E 141-91). *1996 Annual Book of ASTM Standards: General Test Methods, Nonmetal; Laboratory Apparatus; Statistical Methods; Forensic Sciences,* vol. 14.02. Philadelphia, PA: American Society for Testing and Materials. 1996.

36. W. R. Schreiver. *Full-Scale Load Testing of Structures,* ASTM STP 702. Philadelphia, PA: American Society for Testing and Materials. 1980.

37. Standard Practice for Static Load Testing of Truss Assemblies (E 73-83). *1996 Annual Book of ASTM Standards: Building Seals and Sealants; Fire Standards; Building Constructions; Dimension Stone,* vol. 04.07. Philadelphia, PA: American Society for Testing and Materials. 1996.

38. Standard Practice for Gravity Load Testing of Floors and Flat Roofs (E 196-95). *1996 Annual Book of ASTM Standards: Building Seals and Sealants; Fire Standards; Building Constructions; Dimension Stone,* vol. 04.07. Philadelphia, PA: American Society for Testing and Materials. 1996.

39. Standard Guide for Conducting Flexural Tests on Beams and Girders for Building Construction (E 529-94). *1996 Annual Book of ASTM Standards: Building Seals and Sealants; Fire Standards; Building Constructions; Dimension Stone,* vol. 04.07. Philadelphia, PA: American Society for Testing and Materials. 1996.

40. Standard Practice for Reporting Data from Structural Tests of Building Constructions, Elements, Connections, and Assemblies (E 575-83). *1996 Annual Book of ASTM Standards: Building Seals and Sealants; Fire Standards; Building Constructions; Dimension Stone,* vol. 04.07. Philadelphia, PA: American Society for Testing and Materials. 1996.

41. Standard Method of Measuring Relative Resistance of Wall, Floor, and Roof Construction to Impact Loading (E 695-79). *1996 Annual Book of ASTM Standards: Building Seals and Sealants; Fire Standards; Building Constructions; Dimension Stone,* vol. 04.07. Philadelphia, PA: American Society for Testing and Materials. 1996.

42. Standard Test Method for Structural Performance of Glass in Exterior Windows, Curtain Walls, and Doors Under the Influence of Uniform Static Loads by Destructive Methods (E 997-84). *1996 Annual Book of ASTM Standards: Building Seals and Sealants; Fire Standards; Building Constructions; Dimension Stone,* vol. 04.07. Philadelphia, PA: American Society for Testing and Materials. 1996.

43. Standard Test Method for Structural Performance of Glass in Windows, Curtain Walls, and Doors Under the Influence of Uniform Static Loads by Nondestructive Method (E 998-84). *1996 Annual Book of ASTM Standards: Building Seals and Sealants; Fire Standards; Building Constructions; Dimension Stone,* vol. 04.07. Philadelphia, PA: American Society for Testing and Materials. 1996.

44. *Appraisal of Existing Structures,* London: The Institution of Structural Engineers. July 1980.

45. J. R. Janney. Fixing a Failure. *Proceedings—Construction Failures: Legal and Engineering Perspectives,* American Bar Association, Houston, TX. October 1983.

FURTHER READING

American Society of Civil Engineers (ASCE), Research Council on Performance of Structures. *ASCE Official Register 1997.* New York: ASCE. 1997.

Bendat, J. S., and A. G. Piersol. *Random Data: Analysis and Measurement Proceedings.* New York: Wiley. 1971.

Colloms, M. *Computer Controlled Testing and Instrumentation.* New York: Wiley. 1983.

Ellingwood, B. Design and Construction Error Effects on Structural Reliability. *Journal of Structural Engineering* (ASCE), vol. 113, no. 2. February 1987.

Gibble, K., ed. *Management Lessons from Engineering Failures.* New York: American Society of Civil Engineers. October 1986.

Jones, L., and A. F. Chin. *Electronic Instruments and Measurements.* New York: Wiley. 1983.

Smith, D. L. *Test and Measurement Techniques Using Personal Computers.* Madison, NJ: American Institute for Professional Education. 1985.

Whitehurst, E. A. *Evaluation of Concrete Properties from Sonic Tests.* Detroit, MI: American Concrete Institute. 1966.

CHAPTER 7

STANDARD OF CARE

Joshua B. Kardon, S.E.

INTRODUCTION

Often in the course of the investigation or resolution of disputes involving construction defects or failures of structures, the performance of a structural engineer is called into question. The question may be one of performance under the contract for the engineer's services, or for any number of torts. The engineer could be accused of professional negligence, which is generally defined as the failure of the engineer to possess and use the skill of a normally competent practitioner. If that is the question, there is a need for expert testimony in order to do two things: define what is the skill possessed by normally competent practitioners and come to an opinion as to whether the defendant structural engineer conformed to that level. These are "standard of care" questions. Why are structural engineers compared with such a standard? What is *care*? How does the forensic structural engineer know what it is?

This brief chapter introduces the concept of the standard of care of structural engineers. At the end of the chapter are several examples of situations in which questions arose regarding structural engineers' performance relative to the standard of care.

SOURCE OF THE DUTY OF CARE

Society requires us to behave civilly toward one another despite our varying needs and our different points of view. Laws are established by society to define acceptable and unacceptable behavior, and criminal penalties can be imposed if our actions are so detestable or egregious that they are contrary to those laws. In addition to criminal laws, other laws, such as those dealing with contracts, are established to spell out the rules for how we get along. Tort laws address circumstances in which one person's behavior injures another regardless of whether that behavior is subject to criminal law penalties, such as when mistakes are made or accidents happen. These laws require us to behave reasonably as individuals and, as structural engineers, to exercise an adequate degree of care.

Laws have also been established defining liability, or responsibility to pay for damages. Liability is not a recent concept. During his reign from 1792 to 1750 B.C. in the golden age of the first Babylonian dynasty, the great King Hammurabi assembled, revised, and expanded on the old Akkadian and Sumerian laws which his society inherited; and he wrote one of the first codes of law in human history, including laws concerning liability. The Code of Hammurabi defined acceptable behavior among Babylonians in their personal and business interactions, addressing such issues as family law, military service, land dealings, business regulations, wages, prices, taxes, and debts. Fairness was the main principle of the Code of Hammurabi; it institutionalized a social order based on the rights of the individual and based on the assertion that "the strong shall not injure the weak."[1]

A portion of the Code of Hammurabi defines statutory liability for construction failures. It states[2]:

> If a builder builds a house for a man and does not make its construction firm and the house which he has built collapses and causes the death of the owner of the house, that builder shall be put to death.
>
> If it causes the death of the son of the owner of the house, they shall put to death a son of that builder.
>
> If it causes the death of a slave of the owner of the house, he shall give to the owner of the house a slave of equal value.

If it destroys property, he shall restore whatever it destroyed, and because he did make the house which he built firm and it collapsed, he shall rebuild the house which collapsed at his own expense.

If a builder builds a house for a man, and does not make its construction meet the requirements and a wall falls in, that builder shall strengthen the wall at his own expense.

Liability laws have changed in the intervening four millennia, some would say for the better. This fact illustrates an important characteristic of liability: The definition of liability is not rigid, but varies with the cultural and societal environment, both in time and from place to place. However, the Code of Hammurabi also dramatically presents a basic element of liability which still applies today: Someone who causes injury to another could be held responsible for the injuries and for paying the injured party restitution for the injury.

Hammurabi's statutory liability for construction failures includes the idea of negligence in the wording "If a builder builds a house for a man *and does not make its construction firm* and the house which he has built collapses...." A question of fact—that is, Was the construction firm?—must have been answered in each case heard in the Babylonian court. It may have been that the fact of a collapse was enough to pin responsibility on the builder, in the manner of strict liability. In that case, Hammurabi's court would need no testimony as to whether the house was built in accordance with standards of the time, or whether the builder was any less competent than other builders.

Today, engineers have a duty to provide their services in a manner consistent with the standard of care of their professions. A good working definition of the standard of care of a professional is *that level or quality of service ordinarily provided by other normally competent practitioners of good standing in that field, contemporaneously providing similar services in the same locality and under the same circumstances.*[3] An engineer's service need not be perfect. Since the engineer, when providing professional services, is exercising judgment gained from experience and learning, and is usually providing those services in situations where certain unknown or uncontrollable factors are common, some level of error in those services is allowed.[4] When you hire an engineer, you "purchase service, not insurance," so you are not justified in expecting perfection or infallibility, only "reasonable care and competence."[5]

The fact that an engineer makes a mistake, and that mistake causes injury or damage, is not sufficient to lead to professional liability on the part of the engineer. In order for there to be professional liability, it must be proved that the services were professionally negligent, i.e., that they fell beneath the standard of care of the profession. When you hire an engineer, you are accepting the risk, and the liability, of that professional's making a mistake similar to mistakes that any other normally competent engineer makes.

The standard of care is not what an engineer *should have done* in a particular instance, it is not what others say an engineer *would* do or what they *would have done*. It is just what competent engineers actually *did* in similar circumstances.

Ordinary liability, as opposed to professional liability, is the failure to use reasonable care which any reasonable, nonprofessional, person would. In cases where a structural engineer is accused of ordinary negligence, the testimony of an expert structural engineer is not required. The people sitting on the jury don't need help identifying that kind of negligence.

Other sources of liability which a structural engineer may face include warranties and negligence per se. The concept of strict liability may also apply to a structural engineer.

Warranties

Professional liability is different from liability arising from a warranty. A warranty is a stipulation that a fact in relation to the subject of a contract is as it is stated or promised to be in the contract. The warranty may be express, in which case it is written or stated as such in the contract; or it may be implied. Implied warranties of fitness for purpose, merchantability, and warranty of title are recognized in the *Uniform Commercial Code.* A warranty of fitness for purpose is implied in contracts for construction based on case law.[6,7]

Implied warranties of fitness for intended purpose have been applied to professional design service contracts, but courts have not been consistent in their rulings.[8] Some have ruled that the only warranty implied is the warranty that the services are provided without professional negligence. (To be clear as to warranties, contracts for professional design services should spell out precisely what the designer warrants. A prudent engineer will place in the contract for engineering services a statement to the effect that the only express or implied warranty in the contract is that the services will be provided within the standard of care of the profession. To warrant otherwise may expose the designer to uninsurable risks.)

An engineer is not liable under theories of implied warranty and strict liability to purchasers of a building for alleged defects in the design and construction of the building. Absent privity between parties, real property purchasers cannot recover on warranty claim against the original owner/developer of property. A nonsuit on implied warranty claim is proper where there is no connection of privity between parties.[9]

An implied warranty of fitness for purpose may apply to a construction contract where four specific conditions exist: (1) The contractor professes to be competent to perform the contracted work; (2) the owner has no particular expertise in the kind of work contemplated; (3) the owner furnishes no plans, designs, specifications, details, or blueprints; and (4) the owner indicates a reliance on the experience and skill of the contractor, after making known to the contractor the specific purposes for which the building is intended.[7,10]

An example of where this decision was applied involved a contractor who designed and installed an electrical system in a building which later was damaged by a fire caused by the electrical system. The court applied the *Dobler* rule and found that an implied warranty of fitness for purpose existed in the design-install contract.[11] Other cases touch on the applicability of the implied warranty of fitness in contracts for design services,[6,12–14] but courts have generally not been eager to apply that theory, especially when a claim of breach of contract or negligence would be just as effective.[15,16]

Strict Liability

A more stringent definition of liability applies for manufacturers. In the case of manufactured products, current law imposes on the manufacturer strict liability for any injury caused by the product. Strict liability exists if there is an injury; there does not have to have been negligence for strict liability to arise. It is presumed the manufacturer had a duty not to introduce in the marketplace products which injure people who are using the product as it was intended to be used. This duty is owed by the manufacturer to the ultimate consumer, even though the consumer bought the product from someone other than the manufacturer. Case law has applied strict liability to contractors or developers who build multiunit housing developments,[12] and there have been attempts to apply the strict liability standard to professional design services.[4]

Strict liability also applies to those engaged in ultrahazardous activity. This applies to an activity that by its nature is especially hazardous, yet is deemed to have some value for society. The activity will be "tolerated by the law,"[17] but any injury caused by the ultrahazardous activity is the responsibility of the one engaged in it, without there having to be negligence. In other words, if the activity is so hazardous that even exercising reasonable care does not eliminate the risk, then there will be liability for injury regardless of the use of reasonable care.

Negligence per se

Negligence of the engineer is presumed if the engineer violated a statute, the violation caused injury that the statute intended to prevent, and the injured party was one of the class of people for whose protection the statute was adopted.[9] Violation of a statute setting forth a standard of conduct is negligence as a matter of law, or negligence per se. Expert testimony is not required to establish negligence per se.

In a case involving a staircase built contrary to the building code tread width and height requirements, resulting in costs for rebuilding the staircase to be in compliance with the building code, the plaintiff's claim of negligence per se was denied. The reason was that the building code tread width and height requirements were designed to ensure safety in the use of the staircase, and were not designed to prevent owners from incurring costs associated with correction of code violations.[18]

ROLE OF THE STRUCTURAL ENGINEER

Structural engineering is a profession. In his book[19] *The Ethics of Science,* David B. Resnick characterizes a "profession" as being distinguished from other societal organizations or institutions in several ways: Professions allow the achievement of socially desired goals; incompetence or unethical behavior on the part of the professional can result in harm to the public; professions have standards of conduct and levels of competence which practitioners are expected to maintain, and standards of professional competency or conduct are maintained by governing bodies; members of the profession must be educated and trained; society places responsibilities on professionals and grants professionals certain privileges.

Structural engineering satisfies Resnick's requirements for a profession. Structural engineering makes possible the safe and efficient presence of buildings, bridges, and other components of our technological civilization. Structures that fail to achieve their desired utility can result in waste and financial losses. Those that fail to achieve their desired safety can injure or kill people. Many organizations of structural engineers have codes of ethics or practice guidelines, and engineers can have their licenses or registrations revoked if they are found to have been incompetent or unethical. To qualify to take structural engineering license examinations, an applicant must have a certain amount of experience and education; and to become registered or licensed, a structural engineer must demonstrate competency by passing an examination. Some states are requiring continuing education of registrants to document the practitioners' maintenance of a level of competency.

One of the responsibilities of the structural engineer is to achieve and maintain a level of competency consistent with public safety. A privilege granted structural engineers, because they are professionals, is the acceptance by society of a certain amount of the engineers' error.

Structural Engineering Design

What in fact is structural engineering? It certainly involves the knowledge and application of materials science, physics, and mathematics, and as such it is often thought of as an objective, "hard" science in its own right. However, structural engineering is an activity based on education, experience, and judgment, one characterized by collaboration among several parties, often with contrasting or contradictory goals and world views. It is a design profession, a human activity involving iteration and selection of a preferred solution among several alternate possibilities. Despite this fact about the "soft" side of structural engineering, and because of its foundation in the real world of materials, forces, construction, budgets, and schedules, structural engineering is likely to always have a positivist, rational perspective. The fact is, however, that the best structural engineering seems to be done by practitioners who use both sides of their brains—both the intuitive and the rational.

Forensic Structural Engineering

Forensic structural engineers are asked to help when construction projects result in disputes or failures. The forensic structural engineer can help to determine the cause of a structural failure, or the presence of construction that fails to meet the letter or intent of building codes; and can assist in designing efficient and effective repairs for failed or defective construction. The forensic structural engineer is also asked to express opinions concerning the performance of a structural engineer.

To offer an opinion as to whether a structural engineer met the standard of care, the forensic expert must first determine what level of skill, judgment, and diligence was possessed by normally competent structural engineers practicing in similar circumstances. Society has determined that "normal competence" of a structural engineer includes a certain amount of error. This is because the competent structural engineer applies judgment gained from variable training and experience, while dealing with materials, forces, and procedures which are fraught with uncertainty.

When forensic structural engineers testify in deposition or at trial, they are asked for their expert opinion to assist the trier of fact in the decision. The trier of fact (a judge or a jury) determines whether a particular engineer has or has not met the standard of care of the defendant engineer's particular practice discipline. In determining that fact, the opinions of expert witnesses qualified in that discipline may be considered. Expert opinions can be taken by the jury as facts to be considered in deliberations.

The admissibility of expert opinion as fact, rather than its rejection as hearsay, originated in English common law in 1782, in the case of *Folkes, Bart v. Chadd et al.*[20] Folkes owned a dike protecting low-lying pastures near the harbor at Wells, a town on the east coast of England. Chadd et al. were trustees of the harbor who had obtained an injunction against Folkes, requiring him to remove the dike because it was causing silting in the harbor. Folkes sued Chadd to have the injunction set aside, and during the trial, Folkes put on the stand John Smeaton, an engineer knowledgeable in the fields of dikes and harbor silting. Smeaton testified his opinion was that the dike had nothing to do with the silting. Chadd's attorney objected on the grounds of hearsay, but the court ruled that "Of this [matter], such men as Mr. Smeaton alone can judge. Therefore we are of the opinion that his judgment, formed on facts, was very proper evidence."

STANDARD OF CARE

Uncertainty

One reason why structural engineers' services contain errors is that the services are provided in circumstances of uncertainty or variability. There is uncertainty in the natural world of loads, materials, and the environment, and there is uncertainty in the human-made world. The structural engineer practicing under these uncertain conditions has as a goal a finished structure that satisfies all its intended purposes over its intended service life. To accomplish this goal, the structural engineer anticipates the levels of uncertainty and builds into the structure appropriate strength, stiffness, stability, redundancy, and robustness. Building codes and standards are drawn up with an acknowledgment of the variability and uncertainty in loads and materials; allowable stresses and deflections, safety factors, load and resistance factors, and other limits on materials, elements, and assemblies less than their theoretical maxima attest to this appreciation.

Building codes, however, cannot stand in for the structural engineer's professional judgment regarding the variability in the loads, materials, and human factors which will act upon the structure over its expected life. Lev Zetlin[21] has said, "Engineers should be slightly paranoiac during the design stage. They should consider and imagine that the *impossible could* happen. They should not be complacent and secure in the mere realization that if all the requirements of the design handbooks and manuals have been satisfied, the structure will be safe and sound."

Error

The role of error and failure in structural engineering design is amply described in the books of Henry Petroski, among others. This chapter does not delve into that most important topic. The reader is encouraged to refer to Professor Petroski's many excellent volumes on the subject.

Error can be broadly defined as the failure to achieve an intended outcome. An error can be categorized as accidental or systematic, or as a blunder, a slip, a lapse, a mistake, or a violation.

Accidental error is also referred to as *random error.* Accidental error can be seen in a target on a rifle range. A shooter aiming at the bull's-eye is likely to not hit the exact center every time. The bullet holes in the target will be randomly clustered around a central area. The source of this scatter is the random variability of each shot. The size of the cluster is a display of the precision of the shots. A shooter who is very precise will have a target with a closely packed cluster of holes; a less precise shooter will have a wider cluster. Random error can be reduced, or precision enhanced, by controlling the randomly varying influences on each shot. Note that a tight cluster and a wide cluster can both be accurate. That is, they can both be centered on the bull's-eye. The accuracy of the cluster of shots is the distance between the bull's-eye and the average shot, or the central point of the cluster. Both the tight cluster and the wide cluster can have the same average, in which case they would be equally accurate.

Systematic error can be illustrated using the same target on a rifle range. If the bullet holes in the target are clustered around a spot other than the bull's-eye at which the shooter was aiming, then the distance between the center of the cluster and the bull's-eye discloses the systematic error. This error might be a characteristic of the rifle if the sights are not correctly aligned, or of the shooter if the rifle is consistently jerked to one side at every shot.

This kind of error can be corrected by adjusting the rifle to eliminate the misalignment, by aiming away from the bull's-eye to compensate for the misalignment, or by learning how to fire without jerking the rifle. Note that the cluster of shots can be very precise, or tightly packed, yet they can still be off target, or far from accurate.

Again looking at the target at the rifle range, we see that a blunder, or a slip, a lapse, a mistake, or a violation, can be analogous to the single stray shot that goes wide of the main grouping of shots. There might be many reasons for such an error, including (but certainly not limited to) inattention, distraction, fatigue, mechanical or material defect, organizational deficiency or human frailty, venality, and avarice.

To tie this discussion to structural engineering practice, rather than riflery, an example of random error might be the variation between the design floor live load and the actual load on any particular part of a floor in a building. There is no need to precisely forecast the exact load on each square foot of the floor if the design live load is appropriately selected. The accuracy of the design floor live load is adequate if the structure performs as intended without being "overengineered." The building codes that specify minimum design floor live loads intend to guide engineers to this result. Those minimum loads were selected by the engineers who wrote the codes, with an appreciation of the random error inherent in defining the load.

A systematic error in structural engineering can be seen in the use of small coupons of wood in determining allowable stresses in wood. Since the small coupons are less likely to have the full range of defects that a full-size member has, the allowable stresses derived from small coupons will be higher than those derived from full-size members. This systematic error has in fact resulted in failures of some older wood structures, and a subsequent revision downward of allowable stresses.

Blunders, slips, lapses, and mistakes in structural engineering practice occur all the time to varying degrees and with varying consequences. A mislocated decimal point, a mathematical error, a column from an upper floor neglected down below, and the omission of a portion of a building's mass in estimating the seismic load are probably all too familiar errors to most practicing structural engineers. Careful checking of the work, adherence to verified design procedures, and a clear understanding of what "feels right" despite what the calculations say, are ways to keep these types or errors small and reasonable.

Identifying Error

A trier of fact (judge or jury) has to determine the standard of care and whether an engineer has failed to achieve that level of performance. The trier does so by hearing expert testimony. People who are qualified as experts express opinions as to the standard of care and as to the defendant engineer's performance relative to that standard. (This is one of the few instances when opinion can be entered as factual evidence.) The trier of fact weighs the testimony from all sides and decides in each case what the standard of care was and whether the defendant met it.

Jury instructions have been standardized. In the *Book of Approved Jury Instruction,* BAJI 6.37, "Duty of a Professional"[22] reads:

> In performing professional services for a client, a [structural engineer] has the duty to have that degree of learning and skill ordinarily possessed by reputable [structural engineers], practicing in the same or similar locality and under similar circumstances.
>
> It is [the structural engineer's] further duty to use the care and skill ordinarily used in like cases by reputable members of [the structural engineering] profession practicing in the same or similar locality under similar circumstances, and to use reasonable diligence and [the defendant structural engineer's] best judgement in the exercise of professional skill and in the application of learning, in an effort to accomplish the purpose for which [the structural engineer] was employed.
>
> A failure to fulfill any such duty is negligence.

Four key items in this instruction can serve as the definition of the standard of care of structural engineers:

1. Have learning and skill ordinarily possessed by reputable structural engineers, practicing in the same or similar locality and under similar circumstances

2. Use care and skill ordinarily used in like cases by reputable members of the structural engineering profession practicing in the same or similar locality under similar circumstances

3. Use reasonable diligence and one's best judgment in the exercise of professional skill and in the application of learning

4. Accomplish the purpose for which the structural engineer was employed

A forensic structural engineer asked to opine as to the performance of a structural engineer relative to the standard of care will have to understand the error that allegedly led to the claim. If the error is within the realm of errors made by normally competent structural engineers using judgment, care, skill, diligence, and reasonable care, then the error is not necessarily an instance of professional negligence. The forensic structural engineer providing expert testimony should identify the error of the defendant and place it in the context of error in general. Was the source of the error the engineer's failure to use diligence or reasonable care? Did the defendant structural engineer have, and use, the learning and skill ordinarily possessed by reputable members of the profession practicing in similar circumstances? Did the defendant fulfill the purpose of that job?

This last question must take into account the requirements of a professional: The structural engineer is not just working for the client; there is also a professional obligation on the part of the structural engineer to the general public.

Testifying to the Standard of Care

Many structural engineers believe expert testimony is the hardest work they do. Nowhere else is their work subject to as intense examination and criticism. In the litigation arena, there is usually a "loser" and a "winner." As such, forensics is different from design or consulting services.

The design process is an iterative one involving interaction with other members of the project team to arrive at a solution to a problem, or a response to a need. Team members have different points of view and are concerned with different, sometimes conflicting, goals; therefore, the design solution is usually not the optimal one for each design discipline. Collaborative design is not an optimizing process, it is a "satisficing" one: It is a solution which best satisfies all the participants' programs while dissatisfying the fewest. Since there is this inherent suboptimization, a dissatisfied party looking for recompense is apt to find someone to blame. It is important for forensic structural engineers, asked to help resolve disputes arising from these exercises, to be able to distinguish between professionally negligent errors and the normal suboptimization inherent in structural engineering design.

Some structural engineers refuse to provide forensic services, because they feel the practice is inherently unethical or unfair. Good engineers are problem solvers, who correctly see the engineering process as one wherein an acceptable solution is devised under conditions of limitations and restraints. In forensic engineering, some see too much advocacy for a particular position as opposed to the achievement of a mutually satisfactory solution. Additionally, the goal of the litigation process is seen to be the domination of one position over another, which some think is antithetical to the collaborative, creative process in which engineers participate otherwise.

There are some structural engineers whose practice consists primarily of expert testimony. This may pose a problem if the expert can be challenged for lack of experience in the design discipline about which the testimony is given. Admissibility of expert testimony can be challenged on the basis of its validity or reliability, and the judgment of the expert concerning the subject at issue can be discounted if the witness does not have experience in that subject other than testifying about it.

The practice of forensic structural engineering itself is subject to the standard-of-care test. A forensic structural engineer can be held to the same type of standard as any other engineer. The question can be asked, Have the forensic services been provided at a level of diligence, skill, and care consistent with similar services provided by normally competent forensic engineers?

Contractor's "Standard of Care"

General contractors are held to a different standard than structural engineers are. Whereas the structural engineer is held to a professional negligence standard, which admits a certain level of error, the general contractor is bound by the express and implied warranties of the construction contract. A general contractor's negligence is more likely to be measured against the "reasonable person" rather than the "competent practitioner."

CASE STUDIES

The question of a structural engineer's performance relative to the standard of care arises when errors occur, or when there is a failure of a constructed facility to achieve its intended safety, durability, serviceability, or utility. The standard of care is not a fixed "standard" in the way other standards are, such as the ACI standard method of taking concrete samples. The standard of care of structural engineers varies with time, locale, and circumstances and depends on the specific practice being examined. It is informative to review instances in the past where a structural engineer's performance relative to the standard of care was in question. Some of these examples come from the published record, and others are from the author's experience.

Steel-Frame Design. A two-story, mixed-use, wood-frame building on a corner lot incorporated two full-height moment frames, one on each of two adjacent sides facing the streets, in order to accommodate storefronts and office windows. The location was in seismic zone 4, close to a known, active fault. The engineer of record produced a set of calculations for the frames. One frame was designed based on five lines of calculations; the other frame was designed based on one line of calculations, which read, "Similar." The calculations did not include any treatment of the vertical loads which the frame had to support, or any evaluation of earthquake-induced drift. A thorough and detailed computer-aided analysis performed during an investigation of the building showed that the frame as originally designed was adequate in terms of stiffness and strength for Code-required loads. In fact, the analysis showed the frames were a very efficient and economical design.

The calculations were not adequate to describe the design intent of the structural engineer. They did not include the evaluation of the performance of the frames under Code-required dead and live loads, or any required combinations of loads. The stresses and deflections induced by required or anticipated loads were not compared with allowable values.

Was the structural engineer negligent in his design of the steel frame? Calculations are not in themselves engineering. However, they do convey the thought process and the design intent of the engineer. The quality of the calculations, their clarity, thoroughness, and accuracy, can be considered an indication of the level of care and diligence exercised by the structural engineer. However, even the best calculations only substantiate, but do not substitute for, the judgment of the structural engineer. The structural engineer of this example designed the steel frames without exhaustive calculations, but as a detailed analysis indicated, not without apparently a clear understanding of good structural engineering design.

The in-plane lateral load-resisting design of the steel frames of this example was not, in this author's opinion, beneath the standard of care. There certainly was an absence of complete documentation substantiating the in-plane lateral design of the frame. However, the frame design—the actual size, configuration, and details of the beams and columns—was not in error. The engineer may have proportioned the frame members correctly by intuition, but it was not an erroneous design.

Retaining Wall Design. A structural engineer provided design services to a subcontractor who was building a retaining wall for a developer. The subcontractor had selected a proprietary retaining wall system utilizing precast, prestressed concrete modules to be assembled into a crib wall and reinforced-earth type of retaining structure. The structural engineer had never designed such a wall before. The retaining wall system vendor provided sample calculations to the structural engineer as an example of how to design the wall, but the method included errors. The structural engineer used the calculation method provided. After the wall was completed, during heavy rains, a portion of the wall failed.

During the meetings and depositions that ensued, an experienced expert forensic engineer who had designed and analyzed "thousands of these walls," and who had developed his own calculation method, described the structural engineer as negligent.

The use of "canned" calculations and design approaches without understanding their application and limitations can be beneath the standard of care and can be an instance of professional negligence. However, the practice of the experienced expert, far exceeding that of a normally competent engineer, is not the standard of care. The question was not, How did the defendant engineer's performance compare with the expert's? It was more appropriately, Did the defendant engineer utilize reasonable diligence and his or her best judgment given the fact that he had not designed such a retaining wall before?

The answer to that second question, in this author's opinion, was no. Reasonable diligence would have resulted in the error in the canned calculations becoming apparent to the structural engineer. The structural engineer's best judgment would have resulted in his or her reverting to first principles, as described in readily accessible soils engineering texts on retaining wall design. The failure may or may not have happened anyway, given the intensity and duration of the rain; but the actions of the design engineer would have been defensible under a standard-of-care defense.

Foundation Design. A large condominium project was built in six phases, spread out over several years. For phases 1 through 3 the soils engineer recommended the foundation be a drilled pier type, and that the piers be 4 ft deep. When construction of phase 4 started, he recommended 6-ft-deep piers. Later, during construction of phases 5 and 6, the structural engineer went back to 4-ft piers. All the buildings in all six phases were of the same design, based on the same soils report. The soils were similar in all phases. Was the structural engineer negligent in not carrying forward the soils engineer's phase 4 recommendations?

Management and control of information are part of diligent engineering practice. It was argued that the structural engineer's failure to carry forward the revised soils engineering parameters represented an error inconsistent with the standard of care.

Unreinforced Masonry Wall Collapse. Engineering design drawings and specifications for the seismic strengthening of a circa 1888 unreinforced brick masonry building included the requirement for the general contractor to produce shoring and bracing plans and submit them to the structural engineer of record (SER) for review. Construction started without the knowledge of the SER, and work was done without those plans. The SER was excluded from the construction process, including the review of shoring and bracing plans, by the owner and the contractor. Due to the absence of shoring and bracing, a brick wall collapsed during construction, killing the contractor's foreman. The SER was sued for professional negligence and wrongful death. Two years after the "accident" and after a 6-week trial, the jury found the SER not negligent and not liable. The jury found against the owner and, through an indemnity clause in the construction contract with the contractor; and the jury awarded the widow and stepdaughters more than $1 million in damages.

Low bidders and "can-do" types kill people. Construction is dangerous, and builders sometimes take undue risks in order to save time or money. The engineer may be forced to accept the consequences of that risk under the worst circumstances. In this case, the jury decided that the general contractor and the owner actively prevented the SER from fulfilling his obligation to exercise care and diligence. The jury found the actions of the SER were not beneath the standard of care, and the jury placed responsibility where it belonged.

Tacoma Narrows Bridge Collapse. In 1940, wind-induced oscillations destroyed the brand new Tacoma Narrows suspension bridge. One hundred years earlier, the dangerous dynamic effects of the wind were known, and suspension bridge design of that era included measures to counter those effects. The engineer for the Tacoma Narrows Bridge superstructure, described as "among the highest authorities in suspension bridge design,"[23] was not thought by many at the time to be negligent. This was in spite of the fact that normal competence of suspension bridge designers of a century earlier included avoidance of this kind of failure.

Diane Vaughan[24] wrote about the *Challenger* explosion. She describes the actions of the engineers and managers of the space shuttle program as succumbing to the "normalization of deviance," the gradual acceptance of sequential minor errors and failures, accumulating and culminating in a major catastrophe. The Tacoma Narrows failure may have been an example of this phenomenon.

The advancement of the state of the art is not always forward. It is important to know the history of the technology you are working with. Contrary to Henry Ford's opinion, history is not bunk.

Hyatt Regency Kansas City Walkway Collapse. A minor, "nonstructural" feature of a hotel—a walkway suspended from the roof and spanning a central atrium—collapsed suddenly, killing and injuring a great number of people. The detail of the connection of the walkway beam to the suspender was not carried out as drawn, but was changed by the contractor for constructibility reasons.

The structural engineer who reviewed and approved the change was found to be negligent. Several important lessons can be learned from this tragedy: (1) Attention to the constructibility of a detail is essential to good design. (2) Communication of field changes to the designer is essential. (3) Shop drawing and change order review is important, and should not be performed without the participation of an experienced practitioner. (4) The smallest detail can cause a major problem. (5) In practice, the consequences of an error can have a bearing on the evaluation of negligence.

CitiCorp Building, New York. To accommodate a smaller building on the site, the high-rise CitiCorp tower was designed and constructed with its main columns at the middle of each side, rather than at the corners. The New York City code, and high-rise structural engineering practices, required the building frame to be analyzed and designed to resist winds acting perpendicular to each face. Well after the building was completed and occupied, the design engineer reviewed the frame for adequacy against "cross-corner" winds. He found that based on that loading assumption, the building had a small but unacceptable probability of collapse. Work to strengthen the building was carried out. It was widely agreed that the structural engineer's performance was not beneath the standard of care. That is, the structural engineer exercised an acceptable degree of care and diligence, and therefore, the error was not due to professional negligence.

This situation illustrates the importance of a rapid response to the discovery of error, and the fact that even nonnegligent errors can be dangerous and very expensive to correct.

Lighting Tower Collapse. Competent engineering practice includes timely communication of information. A recent tragic construction failure resulted in significant liability on the part of an engineer.[25] The SER for the Olympic Stadium in Atlanta, Georgia, discovered an error in his design of a portion of a steel light tower to be built as part of the stadium. He notified his client, the architect for the stadium, and designed a repair for the error. The SER was not aware of the progress of construction, and did not consider the error and the repair an emergency. Unbeknownst to the SER, construction had indeed progressed to the point that the light tower was being erected 10 days after the SER informed the architect of the error and the need for repair. The repairs had not been carried out by that time. During erection, the light tower collapsed as a result of the design error, killing one ironworker and injuring another.

The SER's engineering registration was suspended for 3 years by the Georgia Board of Registration for Professional Engineers and Land Surveyors, and the SER has been sued for wrongful death. The professional negligence alleged by the plaintiffs was the SER's failure to "explicitly indicate to the project manager (the architect) that emergency action was required." The error in the design was not negligent, but the lack of urgency in the SER's response to uncovering the error was.

The lack of urgency only became significant because the SER was unaware of the progress of the construction. Coordination or communication which should have occurred in order for the SER to have been aware of the progress of construction was apparently absent. Despite the possibility that the SER may have had nothing to do with this absence of coordination or communication, the SER was on the hook. In this case, the engineer's liability apparently existed at least partially because of the failure of others to keep him informed. This is an important lesson for practicing engineers. Make sure that important information flows in a timely manner to all appropriate parties.

Bridge Collapse and the Duty to Warn.   Another duty of an engineer is the duty to warn. California Attorney General's Opinion Number 85-208 (1985) states that a registered engineer hired to investigate the integrity of a building has a duty to warn the building's occupants if the engineer determines they face an imminent risk of serious injury due to a hazard the engineer observes.[15] This opinion requires the engineer to warn the occupants even though the building owner-client of the engineer requires confidentiality on the part of the engineer.

The extent of the duty to warn varies with location and circumstance, and the standard of care in one locality may not be the standard of care in another. The following case study is an example of this fact.

A 77-year-old county-owned suspension bridge for pedestrian traffic, nicknamed Swinging Bridge, collapsed into the Little Red River in Arkansas in 1989.[26] Forty people were on the bridge at the time, engaged in the apparently popular activity of forcing the bridge to swing from side to side. The bridge collapsed, five people were killed, and dozens were injured.

In 1982, seven years prior to the collapse, an engineering study evaluated and analyzed the bridge, and came to the opinion that the bridge was sound and that it could provide adequate service for as long as an additional century. The engineer recommended further study be carried out, and although the bridge cables were free of rust, he recommended a protective coating be applied. The county did not follow the engineer's recommendations.

The victims and their relatives sued the county, charging it with failure to warn of the hazard presented by the bridge. The court ruled against the plaintiffs, stating, "Mere knowledge of danger to the individual does not create an affirmative duty to protect." The pedestrians caused the collapse, and the county had nothing to do with it. The court apparently decided the defendants did not have to warn anyone, and the plaintiffs had to bear the consequences of their actions themselves.

This finding may not have been the conclusion of a court in a different jurisdiction, one where juries are more sympathetic to plaintiffs. If it were known the bridge could be damaged by being forced to swing back and forth, or if that fact should have been known, and if it were known that pedestrians regularly engaged in such activity, then a more sympathetic court might have found the engineer who evaluated Swinging Bridge negligent in his failure to warn of the dangers. This tragedy could certainly have been prevented.

REFERENCES

1. "Hammurabi," *World Book Encyclopedia, 1989,* World Book, Inc., Chicago.

2. Jacob Feld, *Construction Failure,* Wiley, New York, 1968.

3. *Paxton v. County of Alameda* (1953) 119 C. A. 2d 393, 398, 259 P. 2d 934.

4. *City of Mounds View v. Walijarvi* 263 N. W. 2d 420, 424 (Minn. 1978).

5. *Gagne v. Bertran* 1934 43 C. 2d 481, 275 P. 2d 15.

6. *Markman v. Hoefler* (1960) 252 Iowa 118, 106 N. W. 2d 59.

7. *Robertson Lumber Co. v. Stephan Farmers Cooperative Elevators* (1966) 274 Minn. 17, 143 N. W. 2d 622.

8. Jack D. Bakos, Jr., and Randall J. Hake, "Professional Liability Exposure of Casual Consultants," *Journal of Professional Issues in Engineering,* American Society of Civil Engineers, vol. 113, no. 4, October 1987.

9. *Huang v. Garner* (1984) 157 C. A. 3d 404, 203 C. R.

10. *Dobler v. Malloy* (1973 No. Dakota) 214 N. W. 510.

11. *Air Heaters v. Johnson* 258 N. W. 2d 649 (1977).

12. *Kriegler v. Eichler Homes,* Inc. 269 C. A. 2d 224, 74 C. R. 749 (1969).

13. *Insurance Co. of North America v. Radiant Electric* (1974) 55 Mich. App. 410 222 N.W. 2d 323.

14. *Arkansas Rice Growers Coop v. Alchemy Ind.* 797 F. 2 565 (8th Cir. 1986).

15. James Acret, *Architects and Engineers,* 2d ed., Shepard's/McGraw-Hill, Colorado Springs, CO, 1991.

16. Justin Sweet, *Legal Aspects of Architecture, Engineering and the Construction Process,* 3d ed., West Publishing, St. Paul, MN, 1985.

17. *Goodwin v. Reilley* (1985) 176 C. A 3d 86, 221 C. R. 374.

18. *Morris v. Horton* (1994) 22 C. A. 4th 968, 27 C. R. 585.

19. David B. Resnik, *The Ethics of Science: An Introduction,* Routledge, London, 1998.

20. Neal Fitzsimons, "An Historic Perspective of Failures of Civil Engineering Works," *Forensic Engineering: Learning from Failures,* Kenneth L. Carper, ed., American Society of Civil Engineers, New York, 1986.

21. Henry Petroski, *Design Paradigms: Case Histories of Error and Judgement in Engineering,* Cambridge University Press, 1994.

22. California Jury Instructions, Civil, West Publishing Company, St. Paul, MN, January 1986.

23. T. L. Condron, Supervisory Engineer, 1938. Appendix IV of Section B, "The Failure of the Tacoma Narrows Bridge: A Report to the Honorable John M. Carmody, Administrator, Federal Works Administration, Washington, D.C." by Othmar B. Ammann, Theodore von Karman, and Glen B. Woodruff, Pasadena, California, 1941. Reprinted in the *Bulletin of the Agricultural and Mechanical College of Texas, Texas Engineering Experiment Station,* College Station, Texas, 4th series, vol. 15, no. 1, January 1, 1944.

24. Diane Vaughan, *The Challenger Launch Decision: Risky Technology, Culture, and Deviance at NASA,* University of Chicago Press, 1996.

25. "Suspended Engineer's Lesson: Never Wait Until It Is Too Late," *Engineering News Record,* p. 12, June 24, 1996.

26. "Appeals Panel Finds No Fault in Bridge Collapse," *Civil Engineering News,* p. 15, November 1996.

CHAPTER 8
LITIGATION AND DISPUTE RESOLUTION*

Robert A. Rubin, Esq., P.E., and Dana Wordes, Esq., P.E.

*The authors gratefully acknowledge the extensive and thoughtful assistance of Andrew Meyers in the preparation of this chapter. Meyers, a student at New York University School of Law, is a law clerk at Postner & Rubin.

INTRODUCTION

When a forensic engineer is commissioned to investigate a construction defect or failure, it is expected that the engineer's conclusions will be utilized by the client in two ways: for evaluation of the claim's strength and as an evidentiary tool in subsequent dispute resolution proceedings. A forensic engineer should consider both of these goals at every step of the engineer's investigation and report preparation. Toward this end, the report should accurately reflect the matters under investigation while anticipating possible alternative interpretations of the data. In addition, the investigation should be conducted with an eye to the relevance and admissibility of the report's findings in subsequent proceedings.

Very few disputes in the construction industry actually make their way to a courtroom. Most construction disputes are resolved by settlement or some form of alternative dispute resolution (ADR). Despite the small chance that the dispute will be the subject of sworn testimony, all forensic investigations should be conducted under the assumption that the engineer will be called to offer sworn testimony on the engineer's investigation and conclusions in a court proceeding. A forensic report that will not stand up to cross-examination in a legal proceeding is ineffective in representing the client's interest in or outside of the courtroom.

The construction industry has been innovative in the use and development of dispute resolution methodology. This chapter provides a brief overview of the various proceedings in which a forensic engineer may be asked to participate. The survey provided below is not exhaustive. Because rules of court procedure vary between jurisdictions and due to the flexibility of the various ADR techniques, a forensic engineer must ultimately rely on the client's attorney for specific guidance through the maze of rules. The goal of this chapter is to create the groundwork with which the forensic engineer can participate in the engineer-attorney relationship in service to the client.

TRADITIONAL BINDING DISPUTE RESOLUTION

Basic Litigation Procedures

While the forensic engineer need not be fully knowledgeable in the procedural details of a civil lawsuit, it is desirable that the expert have a basic understanding of the various stages of a case. The procedures in litigation are governed by statute in each jurisdiction. For example, in New York courts, procedure is governed by the *Civil Practice Law and Rules,* and in federal courts by the *Federal Rules of Civil Procedure.* Basically, a lawsuit is divided into two major phases: pretrial and trial.

Pretrial procedures identify the parties to a lawsuit and the issues in dispute, and they permit each party to learn about other party's witnesses and potential evidence.[1]

Summons and Complaint.   Generally, service of a summons gives the defendant notice of the action and an opportunity to defend the action. In many jurisdictions, service of the summons starts the lawsuit. In federal court, the suit is commenced when the summons and complaint are filed with the court, prior to service on the defendant.

The complaint is usually served with the summons. However, in some jurisdictions the complaint need not accompany the summons if the summons notifies the defendant of the nature of the action. The primary purpose of the complaint is to give the court and the parties notice of the transactions and/or occurrences that the plaintiff intends to prove as well as the legal grounds for the plaintiff's suit. The courts liberally construe a complaint and will find it sufficient as long as it states a cause of action. A *cause of action* is a legal term defined as a ground on which an action may be maintained or sustained.[1]

Answer.   The answer is the defendant's response to the plaintiff's complaint. In the first part of the answer, the defendant responds specifically to each allegation in the plaintiff's complaint by either denying or admitting it. In many jurisdictions, failure to respond to any allegation is deemed an admission.

The second part of the answer contains the defendant's affirmative defenses (matters that the defendant, not the plaintiff, is required to prove). Some examples of affirmative defenses include previous arbitration and award, payment, whether there has been a release, or that the statute of limitations has expired.

The third part of the answer includes any counterclaims the defendant may have against the plaintiff. A counterclaim generally need not be related to the transactions or occurrences alleged in the plaintiff's suit. However, if it is unrelated and would confuse the jury, a counterclaim may be severed by the court and tried separately.

Finally, in the case of multiple defendants, one defendant may cross-claim against another codefendant in the answer. Jurisdictions vary on whether the cross-claim must be related to the lawsuit.[1]

Reply.   If the answer contains a counterclaim, the plaintiff must answer it in a reply.[1]

Third-Party Practice.   Third-party practice or impleader is used by the defendant to bring an outside party into the suit who may be liable to the defendant if the defendant is held liable to the plaintiff. For example, a defendant owner could serve a third-party complaint on a project designer stating that if the owner is found liable to the plaintiff, then the designer is liable to the owner to the extent that liability was caused by defective plans.

Discovery Techniques.   Since the complaint need only contain the barest allegations to set forth a cause of action, lawyers use various techniques to reveal the details of the adverse party's claim. This process is called *discovery* or *disclosure.*

Interrogatories are written questions formulated by one party and served upon the other. The recipient answers the questions under oath and returns them. Interrogatories may cover any matter that would tend to prove or disprove the existence of a material fact. In a case involving complex technical issues, forensic engineers may be of assistance in the creation of outgoing interrogatories and the interpretation of incoming responses.

Depositions, also known as *examinations before trial* (EBTs), are in-depth questionings of a party or witness by the lawyers for all the parties involved in the case. A deposition in broad terms resembles a cross-examination except that there is no judge or jury present. The questioning is generally done at a lawyer's office, but may also be done at the court in a room set aside for such purposes. All the parties' attorneys are present at a deposition, as is a court reporter. The deposition is given under oath and is recorded verbatim. The transcript is sent to the deponent, who certifies its accuracy by signature. Depositions take on great importance at the trial. The deposition testimony of a party can be used at trial for any relevant purpose (see discussion on relevancy), even if the party does not personally testify. If the deponent does take the stand, the deposition testimony can be used to discredit (impeach) trial testimony that contradicts the previous testimony.

Discovery and inspection allows a party to inspect an adversary's files. A discovery and inspection is initiated by serving a document demand on the adversary listing specific documents that the party wants to inspect. In a construction case, a document demand might include inspection of daily reports, minutes of job meetings, records of payments, correspondence, photographs, etc.[1]

Motion Practice.   Often attorneys will make formal requests to the court regarding the proceedings. These requests are submitted in the form of motions. Motion practice is regulated by local procedural rules and varies across jurisdictions. Motions are often brought before the court during the pretrial stage of litigation. However, motions may be brought at the trial stage as well.

Common motions include

- Motion for summary judgment that posits that even if the court were to accept all the assertions in the claim as true, the claimant is not entitled to legal relief. For example, summary judgment motions may allege that the claimant has not stated a triable cause of action or that an affirmative defense such as expiration of the statue of limitations applies.

- Motion for a change of venue that asserts that the jurisdiction in which the action has been brought is inappropriate and/or prejudicial.

Trial.   The following is a very brief discussion of the steps of a trial.

First a jury is selected. The procedure for jury selection varies among the jurisdictions. It may be done by the attorneys themselves with or without a judge present, or by a judge, depending on the rules of the particular court.

The trial itself starts with the attorneys from both sides making opening statements that summarize what the attorneys will attempt to prove in the trial. The plaintiff's attorney always goes first, followed by the defendant's attorney.

After the opening statements, the plaintiff's witnesses take the stand, followed by the defendant's witnesses. Each witness is examined in the same manner: direct examination by the proponent's attorney, cross-examination by the adversary's attorney, and redirect by the proponent's attorney.

Next, the attorneys make closing arguments that summarize their cases. In closing, the attorneys state what they have proved and what inferences can be drawn from such proof. Here, the defendant's attorney speaks first, followed by the plaintiff's attorney.

The judge then charges the jury by telling them what law to apply to the facts. The jury is the sole judge of the facts. The jury deliberates. During this phase the jury members can inspect all documents entered into evidence and can have parts of the trial transcript read to them. The final stage of the trial is the verdict rendered by the jury.[1]

Rules of Evidence

The law of evidence is a body of rules that governs the admissibility of evidence in a trial. These rules vary from court to court. In many state courts, the rules of evidence have developed through the common law (judicial opinions), while in the federal courts evidence is governed by the *Federal Rules of Evidence*. In mediation, arbitration, and other alternative methods of dispute resolution, judicial rules of evidence may not apply.

Sometimes evidence which logically should be included in a proceeding may be excluded on technical grounds. As a result, forensic engineers should be sure to consult with the client's attorney to familiarize themselves with the relevant rules of procedure and evidence. The following discussion covers several major topics of the law of evidence that are relevant to expert witnesses, including relevancy, hearsay, opinions of witnesses, and privileged communications.[1]

Relevancy. In the rules of evidence, relevance is given a broad meaning. Relevant evidence is evidence having the tendency to make the existence of a fact that is material to the outcome of the litigation more probable or less probable than it would be without such evidence. In other words, evidence is relevant if it both relates to or bears directly upon the point or fact in issue and proves or has a tendency to prove the proposition alleged. A fact is material if it touches upon a substantial matter in dispute and has a bearing on the decision of the case.

Generally, all relevant evidence is admissible unless its probative value is outweighed by the danger of prejudice through unwarranted conclusions, confusion of issues, misleading of the jury, undue delay, or waste of time, or is barred by some exclusionary rule.[1]

Hearsay Rule.   *Hearsay* is defined as an out-of-court statement offered into evidence to prove the truth of the matter asserted. The out-of-court statement may be oral, written, or even nonverbal conduct (if such conduct was intended by the person to be an assertion). Furthermore, the statement must be offered to prove the truth of the matter asserted.

Hearsay is inadmissible into evidence unless it falls within an established exception. The reason for the hearsay rule is that our court system is an adversarial one in which every party has the right to confront witnesses against it. If hearsay were allowed into evidence, a party would not have the opportunity to cross-examine the declarant and therefore would not be able to test the person's veracity, sincerity, perception, and memory and whether the person was accurately communicating what the person saw.

Some documents are held as inadmissible because they are written hearsay, e.g., testing laboratory or other reports prepared by parties not present in court to testify to the accuracy of statements contained in the reports. In some instances, hearsay testimony will be admissible under an exception to the rule (see below). Additionally, an attorney may call witnesses familiar with a document in order to have it admitted. Experts can take steps to ensure that documents are not held inadmissible as hearsay. Steps include visiting the testing laboratory so that the experts are familiar with the procedures used in testing and personally checking the work of their employees.[1]

Exceptions to Hearsay.   There are many exceptions to the hearsay rule that have developed through the common law and through statutes. The forensic engineer as expert witness should have some knowledge of the more common exceptions to this rule.

An *admission* is a statement or act made by a party to the litigation which is inconsistent with the party's position at trial. A third party who heard the admission will be allowed to testify as to what was heard. A party admission is an exception to the hearsay rule. It is deemed reliable since a party would not normally make a damaging statement unless it were true.

An admission also includes a statement by the party's agent (also known as a *vicarious admission*). Courts differ as to what type of agency is needed to fall within this exception. Many courts that use a common law of evidence hold that the agent must be in a high managerial position in order to use the agent's admission at trial (e.g., president of a corporation, managing agent). The federal courts, under the *Federal Rules of Evidence*, hold that an admission can be used at trial if the agent made the statement concerning a matter which was within the scope of the agent's employment and was made during the existence of the relationship. This is a more liberal rule than that used in many state courts.

An admission may be implied from *silence,* if it can be shown that an ordinary reasonable person under such circumstances would have denied the statement. Before silence will be admitted into evidence, a foundation must be laid. It must be proved that the person heard the statement, knew what the statement was about, and had an opportunity to respond. For example, if engineer A said to contractor B, "You failed to use air-entrained concrete!" and contractor B failed to respond, the silence would be admissible providing the above requirements were met.

A *declaration against interest* is defined as a statement which, at the time it was made, was so contrary to the speaker's pecuniary or proprietary interest, or tended to subject the speaker to civil or criminal liability, or to render invalid a claim by the speaker against another, that a reasonable person in this position would not have made the statement unless the person believed it to be true. It is different from the party admission exception in that the speaker need not be a party to the lawsuit and the statement must be against the speaker's interest when it was made. In contrast, a party's admission must be against the position the party takes at trial.

The reason for the declaration against interest exception to the hearsay rule is that it is unlikely that a person would say something disserving unless it were true. This makes the statement reliable and an adequate substitute for cross-examination at trial.

Former testimony introduced into evidence at another hearing that was sufficiently similar in issues and parties to the present case may be admissible as an exception to the hearsay rule. Former testimony is excepted from the hearsay exclusion only if the speaker (former witness) is unavailable to testify, and the party against whom the former testimony is being admitted had the opportunity to cross-examine the witness in the former trial.

A *spontaneous declaration* is a statement relating to a startling event made while the speaker was subject to stress or excitement caused by the event. A spontaneous declaration is presumed reliable and therefore a legitimate exception to hearsay because of its unpremeditated and instinctual nature.

Any writing made in the regular course of business may be admissible under the *business records* exception if it meets the following requirements:

- The record must have been maintained in conjunction with a business activity.
- The person making the record must have a business duty to make the record.
- The record must consist of matters within the personal knowledge of the entrant or within the personal knowledge of someone with a business duty to report to the entrant.
- The entry must have been made at or near the time of the actual transaction.

The entrant need not be unavailable at the time of trial. A foundation is laid by having the custodian of the records or another qualified witness testify to the identity of the record and the method used in its preparation. Examples of business records include resident engineers' daily reports, pile-driving records, job meeting minutes, requisitions, and change orders.[1]

Opinion Testimony.   A basic rule of our legal system is that witnesses must testify to facts of which they have firsthand knowledge and the jury should draw inferences from those facts. However, there are exceptions for both the lay and expert witnesses.

A lay witness is generally not allowed to give conclusions or opinions. However, a lay witness's opinions are admissible in particular situations, such as the general appearance or condition of a person (that a person was old, weak, strong, etc.), the speed of a car, and the emotional state of a person (the person was angry).

Opinion testimony of an expert witness is treated differently from that of a lay witness. Before an expert may give opinion testimony at a trial, several requirements must be met. First, the subject matter must be appropriate for expert testimony. Jurisdictions vary as to what is considered appropriate. Many courts that follow the common law of evidence hold that the expert opinion must be necessary to enable the jury to draw an inference (i.e., the subject matter is beyond the understanding of the average juror). The federal courts only require that the expert testimony assist the jury in understanding the subject matter—a more liberal standard. Second, the witness must be qualified as an expert. To qualify, the witness must have special knowledge, skill, experience, or education on the subject to which the testimony relates. If the court does not grant the witness expert status, the witness's opinion testimony will be limited to the bounds of lay witness opinion testimony as described above.

A witness's qualification as an expert is presented at the onset of direct examination by the client's counsel. Qualification entails establishing the witness's credentials of expertise in the areas relevant to the issues on which the expert will be giving opinion testimony. The client's attorney will ask questions to illustrate the witness's educational and professional history and the relationship of the testimony to the disputed issues at trial. Courts consider other factors in their determination of expert status including prior testimony in similar matters, teaching experience, and publications.

As part of the qualification process, the opposing attorney is permitted to request a *voir dire*—a preliminary examination by which a witness's qualifications may be questioned.

The third requirement is that the expert's opinion be supported by a proper factual basis. There are three possible sources of information: the expert's personal observation, facts made known to the expert at the trial by use of hypothetical questions, or facts made known to the expert outside the court that the expert did not personally observe. The third source is applied restrictively and is admissible only if the facts are the type generally and reasonably relied on by experts in the particular field.

The general rule is that an expert cannot give an opinion regarding the ultimate issue of the case. For example, an expert cannot state that the defendant engineering firm was negligent. However, in a growing number of jurisdictions, including the federal courts, an opinion is not made inadmissible because it touches upon the ultimate issue in the case.[1]

Privileged Communications. There are several categories of communications that are deemed privileged and therefore are protected from admission at trial. These include communications between attorney and client, husband and wife, physician and patient, and clergy and penitent. These privileges permit a person to refuse to disclose, and to prohibit others from disclosing, information communicated. In addition, certain attorney work product is considered privileged.

Materials or documents prepared by an attorney that contain legal opinions, strategies, or analysis are known as *attorney work product.* These materials are absolutely privileged and are not subject to disclosure.

Material prepared in contemplation of litigation, such as reports provided by an expert witness to a client's attorney, are also privileged. However, unlike attorney work product, a report prepared in contemplation of litigation is not absolutely privileged. This means that if the adversary can show substantial need and if the information is not available elsewhere, then the court may require disclosure.

Factual information contained in a nontestifying expert's report is discoverable. Only the nontestifying expert's opinion and conclusions are potentially privileged.[1]

Claims against the Government

The doctrine of sovereign immunity holds that an entity that makes the laws cannot be sued under those laws. This ancient Anglo-Saxon principle is still, strictly speaking, in effect. The right to sue a federal or state government entity is granted only by way of that body's consent. Governments enact statutes setting the ground rules providing how and for what the governments may be sued. The federal government has consented to suits on federal construction projects pursuant to the Contract Disputes Resolution Act of 1978. Most states have enacted similar provisions for dispute resolution. Municipalities and agencies within many states are not protected by the doctrine of sovereign immunity. Nevertheless, many local governments require compliance with their dispute resolution system as a condition of contracting.[2]

Contract Disputes Resolution Act. Construction claims on projects with the federal government are subject to resolution under procedures outlined in the Contract Disputes Resolution Act of 1978.[3] Standard federal dispute resolution provisions are found in the Federal Acquisition Regulations (FAR) which are inserted into all federal procurement contracts.[4] These provisions have the same legal effect as a binding arbitration clause. The FAR provisions differ from voluntary private contract dispute resolution clauses in two important aspects. First, adherence is mandatory; second, a contractor may be obliged to continue the work on the disputed contract pending final resolution of any claim arising under or relating to the claim.

The federal claim process requires that the contractor submit a claim and documents of certification to the appropriate government personnel (contracting officer). The contracting officer then reviews the claim and renders a decision. A decision must be rendered within a specified time frame, and failure of the officer to issue a timely answer is deemed to be a denial of the contractor's claim.

If the contractor's claim is denied, the claimant may appeal the decision to either the appropriate board of contract appeals (BCA) or the U.S. Court of Federal Claims. Once a claimant elects the BCA, the claimant is bound by that decision and further appeal is limited to the court of appeals for the Federal Circuit. Judicial decisions of the Court of Federal Claims are subject to review only by the U.S. Supreme Court, and such review is rarely granted. Judicial review of a BCA decision is usually limited to matters of law. In other words, the Federal Circuit court generally cannot review the BCA's determination on the facts of a case, only the board's application of the law. As a result, evidence and testimony are not heard during appeal of a BCA decision.

Each federal agency whose caseload justifies three full-time members has its own contract appeals board. The boards are comprised of officials with at least 5 years of experience in public contract law and special knowledge of construction and disputes. These officials are appointed by the agencies whose cases they oversee.

Procedures at BCA hearings are similar to those of a court. BCAs may authorize depositions, administer oaths, and subpoena related witnesses and records. Failure to comply with an order or subpoena from a BCA may result in a citation for contempt from the federal district court.

State Contract Dispute Resolution.   While the Federal Acquisition Rules provide a single orderly method for dispute resolution, the 50 individual states have developed many different approaches. In most cases, the first step in a state construction dispute parallels the FAR procedures, with an initial claim directed to the state's contracting administrator. States have instituted various methods for appeal of these administrative decisions. These methods include appeal to the state comptrollers, administrative boards patterned after federal BCAs, review boards, and direct appeal to a state court of claims. It is essential that claimants, their representatives, and their witnesses be familiar with the procedural rules of the state.

Local Municipal Government Rules.   Absent a specific waiver, there is no right to trial by jury in a claim against the federal or state governments. Generally, this protection does apply to claims against local governments. However, the right to bring suit against a local municipality may be waived by stipulation of the contract. Many municipalities require adherence to specific local rules for dispute resolution as a precondition to contract.

BINDING ALTERNATIVE DISPUTE RESOLUTION

Our legal system is based on the premise that all individuals and corporate entities should have recourse to the courts for resolution of disputes. Our court system has developed an intricate set of procedures to protect litigants from broken promises and other harms. Our system also recognizes the right of persons to agree by contract to settle their disputes through alternative means. Theoretically two parties could agree to bind themselves to dispute resolution through a game of chance. The most common method of private binding alternative dispute resolution (ADR) utilized in the construction industry is arbitration.

Arbitration

Arbitration is an adjudicative procedure in which a neutral person or panel renders a decision based on application of the facts to law and, in some cases, to industry standards. The decision of an arbitrator is legally enforceable if the disputants have agreed to bind themselves beforehand or if, in the case of court-mandated arbitration, they stipulate their satisfaction with the decision after the fact.

Arbitration is the oldest and most familiar of the alternatives to judicial adjudication. The rules of procedure and scope of subject matter can vary widely from case to case. Some arbitrations are quick and informal; others can last as long as, if not longer than, court trials. All arbitrations share one characteristic of a court trial: A decision is rendered by an adjudicative body after the disputants have presented their own versions of the facts.

Consent to Arbitration. In the majority of arbitration cases, the disputants have elected to participate. Disputants may elect to arbitrate at the time of dispute, or more frequently they may provide for arbitration before the dispute arises through an arbitration provision in the contract. Arbitration provisions are very common in construction and professional service contracts for the reasons discussed below.

An election to arbitrate is not synonymous with voluntary participation. Frequently, a participant who believed arbitration was a good idea when signing a contract thinks differently when problems arise. There has been a great deal of litigation over the enforceability of arbitration clauses agreed to at a project's inception but challenged by disputants who would prefer their day in court after problems have surfaced. In general, courts look with favor on arbitration agreements, upholding them even after a contract has been completed or terminated.

The Federal Arbitration Act (9 U.S.C. § 1 *et seq.*) governs the enforceability of arbitration agreements for matters under federal jurisdiction. Similar statutes for enforcement of arbitration agreements have been adopted by many states.

Consensual arbitration awards are binding, but they are not self-enforcing. If a party to an arbitration refuses to comply with the arbitrator's award, the aggrieved party must seek an enforcement order from a court.

Court-Mandated or Compulsory Arbitration. In some jurisdictions, a court may order mandatory arbitration. Because resolution of a claim through arbitration bypasses the disputants' constitutional right to a day in court, participants in a court-mandated arbitration have recourse to a trial *de novo* (as if the arbitration had never taken place). The particular rules for compulsory arbitration vary across state and between federal jurisdictions.

In an effort to facilitate more efficient adjudication of civil cases, the federal Civil Justice Reform Act of 1990 (CJRA) created wide guidelines for the implementation of discretionary arbitration programs in all the federal districts. Since the act's implementation, various districts have initiated some form of arbitration rules including mandatory arbitration. Under the CJRA each district may create its own "delay reduction" plan including voluntary and mandatory arbitration in specific classes of disputes including construction and design defect claims. The Eastern District of New York's local arbitration rule providing for compulsory arbitration in cases of less than $100,000 is typical.[5]

State Compulsory Arbitration. Some states require mandatory arbitration of claims not exceeding a threshold amount.

Why Arbitrate? Given the risk of trying a case before a decision-making body with the almost omnipotent power of an arbitrator, why would anyone agree to arbitration? In some instances the choice to sign a contract with an arbitration provision is not an entirely voluntary election. The standard construction documents of the American Institute of Architects (AIA) mandate arbitration for the resolution of disputes. Arbitration provisions can be included by the owners of large, competitively bid projects on a "take it or leave it" basis. In these cases, the lure of a profitable job is enticing enough that the contractor feels it has no choice but to accept the provision. While this type of decision may not be commonly understood as voluntary, the courts recognize it as a voluntary election.

There are also several reasons why a contracting party might willingly choose arbitration both before and after problems arise. Generally the disputants are attracted to the cost and time savings that can sometimes be achieved by arbitration's less formal rules and procedures. In disputes affecting an ongoing construction project, expedient resolution of a dispute that may impede project completion is in the interest of all parties. In addition, disputants may prefer arbitration because it allows them to select an adjudicator from a pool of arbitrators familiar with the intricacies of their industry.

Procedures for Arbitration. Parties who consent to arbitration may tailor the proceedings to suit their particular needs. The variations are limitless. Parties can choose to require formal discovery of evidence, testimony under oath, and formal transcription of all proceedings. Alternatively, they may provide for specialized rules of procedure and a strictly limited scope of subject matter. The rules of procedure are normally left to the discretion of the arbitrator. Many construction contracts such as those of the AIA provide for arbitration by reference to the American Arbitration Association's (AAA) *Construction Industry Arbitration Rules.* The AAA's Construction ADR Task Force has developed a three-tier structure of arbitration procedures comprised of the standard or "regular track" and two variations.[6]

Under the AAA's *regular track* procedures, the party initiating the arbitration (claimant) may start the process by (1) giving written notice to the other party (respondent) and (2) filing the notice with the AAA. Upon notice to its offices, the AAA becomes the arbitration administrator. The AAA then officially notifies the respondent, who must file an answer and any counterclaim to the AAA and the claimant within 10 days. An arbitral claim or counterclaim may be amended at will any time prior to the appointment of the arbitrator.[6]

After filing the preliminary claims and counterclaims, disputants may be required to participate in a series of administrative conferences and preliminary hearings to expedite the actual arbitration proceedings. As in traditional litigation, many arbitration cases settle before the formal proceedings begin. Settlement can be achieved through private negotiations or negotiations facilitated by the AAA.

The arbitration may proceed as an open hearing or through transmission of the disputants' evidence and position papers to the arbitrator(s). The determination of an arbitrator results in a binding award. According to AAA rules, an award will be announced no later than 30 days after the close of hearings.

The arbitrator's procedural rulings and final award are subject to judicial review only in very rare instances that are spelled out in the jurisdiction's arbitration statue. Generally an arbitrator's rulings are not subject to review for errors of fact or law. The arbitrator's award will be reversed only if an abuse of discretion or gross error can be shown. This policy is in contrast to the constitutional protections of the court system wherein a litigant may petition for appeal of a court's determination and decisions can be overruled on procedural grounds.

Courts rarely vacate an arbitrator's award, but it does happen. Examples of grounds for setting aside an arbitrator's award include a miscalculation of figures, abuse of discretion, a decision from an improperly selected arbitrator, and arbitrator bias. However, courts will not review or reverse arbitration awards on the grounds of arbitrator error. This means that an award from a binding arbitration is valid regardless of a misinterpretation of the facts or misapplication of the relevant law.

In the absence of the formalized rules of evidence and procedure or any provisions to the contrary in the disputants' arbitration agreement, the arbitrator(s) have free reign to determine when and how proceedings will be conducted. Due to the less stringent rules regarding evidence in arbitration, a forensic engineer may be asked to provide evidence, testimony, or opinion that might not be admissible at a trial. An arbitrator can allow or preclude witness testimony, and in most jurisdictions an arbitrator's subpoenas may be enforced by court order. At an arbitrator's discretion a witness may be cross-examined.

As a result of the wide discretion granted to arbitrators, a fair selection process is crucial. The selection of an arbitrator may be effected by administrative appointment or by disputant preference. Administrative appointment entails selection of an individual or panel of neutrals by a court or an administrative body empowered by the disputants such as the AAA. Alternatively the disputants may select their own arbitrator(s). The disputing parties may simply agree to an arbitrator appointed by the administrative agency. Alternatively, parties can choose candidates by striking off unacceptable candidates from a common list provided by the administrative agency. Another method of arbitrator selection requires each party to select an "advocate" arbitrator. The advocate arbitrators in turn elect a neutral arbitrator to complete their three-member panel.

The AAA has also promulgated *fast-track* procedures to expedite smaller and less complex cases. The fast track is intended for multiparty cases when no party's claim or counterclaim exceeds $50,000 (excluding costs and interest) or by agreement of the parties. However, fast-track procedures are available for all two-party disputes regardless of the claim amount.[6]

Under fast track, the arbitrator appointment process is streamlined by limiting the time period by which disputants may object to an AAA roster candidate. In addition, the hearing is scheduled within 30 days of the arbitrator's appointment, and the award is rendered not later than 7 days after the hearing.

Along with provisions limiting extensions on filing and changes of claims or counterclaims, the fast-track option does not allow for discovery other than the exchange of exhibits prior to the hearing.

Recognizing the need to provide more sophisticated procedures and expertise for the growing caseload of large multiparty arbitrations, the AAA developed the *Large, Complex Case Program* (LCCP). If no party objects, cases in which any party's claim or counterclaim totals $1 million or more (excluding costs and interest) are administered under the LCCP. The two main features of this process are expanded management provisions and a roster of elite neutrals trained specifically in the resolution of large, complex cases. As with all arbitration, the rules of an LCCP proceeding are subject to the arbitrator's discretion. However, the structure allows for greater latitude on discovery and scheduling.[6]

NONBINDING ALTERNATIVE DISPUTE RESOLUTION

Nonbinding ADR techniques are efficient alternatives to adjudicative proceedings, saving parties to a dispute both time and money. The techniques can be used at the job site, after project completion, or even after the start of adjudicative proceedings, although their greatest advantages come with prompt use. The interim nature of nonbinding ADR makes it appealing because the participants retain the option of a judicial solution if the ADR process is concluded without success. Typical nonadjudicative techniques include private negotiations, dispute review boards, mediation, and minitrials.

Negotiation without Third-Party Intervention

Many construction disputes are resolved by disputants without third-party intervention. The parties may consider some of these disputes so insignificant relative to the job as a whole that an accommodation is easily forthcoming. But other disputes, of greater significance, settle without any outside adjudicative or facilitative assistance.

In some instances, long-term financial considerations induce parties to accept an apparently unfavorable settlement in the hope of maintaining a beneficial relationship. Similarly, political considerations can create incentives for settlement.

Arguably, it is the disputants' assessment of the relative strength of their claims that is the most common reason for settlement. A rational party who perceives its case is weak will avoid incurring the expense of outside dispute resolution services. Of course, this description of a rational player does not account for the strategic and face-saving rationale behind many business decisions. Nonetheless, it is fair to assume that a disputant's election to settle is strongly influenced by an understanding of the merits on both sides.

In assessing the strength of their positions, disputants turn to legal and technical experts for evaluation of their claims and defenses. Technical experts should prepare expert evaluations for informal dispute resolution with the same degree of care as they would use for a trial or arbitration.

Very often negotiation without third-party intervention occurs at the earlier stages of a dispute when the parties may be unaware of the nature and strength of their claims. At this stage the forensic engineer's role is to conduct an investigation and impart a neutral evaluation to the client's attorney. In short, a forensic engineer should work in tandem with the client's attorney in preparation for negotiation.

A forensic engineer does not serve the client's interests by reporting only favorable facts and opinions. Probable alternative theories must be presented to facilitate efficient and informed negotiation. It is essential that the forensic engineer inform the client and client's attorney of any possible weaknesses in the opinions or facts of the expert's findings. Almost without exception, the opposing party will have its own expert conducting a similar investigation, and a client's attorney who is not properly prepared to address potential challenges to the client's position will be greatly handicapped.

When negotiations begin, the client's attorney may request that the investigating forensic expert attend some of the meetings and negotiations. It is important that an expert's presence at a negotiation not impair the expert's usefulness as a witness in a subsequent proceeding if the disputants fail to settle. To this end, an expert present at a negotiation should look to the client's attorney to avoid tainting the effectiveness or admissibility of any future testimony. The expert witness should also avoid saying anything in a settlement negotiation that can be used later to controvert the expert's testimony in court and thereby impeach the expert's credibility.

In addition, an expert witness present at a negotiation should avoid acting as an advocate or displaying any partisan behavior. A posture of overt advocacy may compromise the legitimacy of an expert's findings in the eyes of an opposing party. The power of expert opinion at the negotiating stage is only as strong as its admissibility and perceived neutrality and legitimacy.

Finally, and perhaps most important, an expert witness participating in negotiations should present the appearance of a well-informed and credible witness. This is essential at the negotiating stage as the opponent's willingness to settle is often influenced by its perception of the court presence of an expert witness. If an opposing attorney believes that an expert witness will be credible to a fact-finding body, the attorney will be more likely to consider settlement.

Dispute Review Board

One effective way to resolve construction disputes as they arise is to establish a dispute review board (DRB) to meet regularly over the duration of a project to address project claims. By providing a forum for the exchange of grievances and independent evaluations, DRBs provide a means for the settlement of claims and controversies. Through the participation of a DRB, issues such as the interpretation of contract documents, delays, scheduling, differing site conditions, design changes, and extra work orders can often be resolved without recourse to litigation.[7,8]

DRBs are usually instituted at the onset of a project pursuant to a three-party agreement among the owner, contractor, and DRB members. The role of the DRB is that of a neutral observer following the job's progress and developing the requisite familiarity to facilitate efficient and accurate recommendations for resolution of disputes as they arise. A DRB meets periodically during the project. Board members review progress reports and meet with key personnel on the job. The guidelines for DRB meetings as well as procedures for submittal of claims are normally established by the board itself unless they are specified in the three-party agreement. Ideal guidelines balance the need for expedient processes with the flexibility necessary for the evolving circumstances of a complex work site.

When conflicts arise on the job site that are not amenable to negotiation, disputants may appeal to the DRB for recommended solutions. Disputants submit "claims" that are addressed by the board at its meetings. The contractor and owner present evidence supporting their positions. Each party presents in turn, and there may be provisions for one or more rebuttals. DRB members may interrupt these proceedings with questions. While the board's meetings may hint at its eventual "recommendations," the meetings are not hearings. Normally attorneys are not present, and there is a complete exchange of material before the meetings to avoid surprises. If one or both parties should desire the presence of technical experts, approval of the board and notice to all participants are usually required.

After private consideration by board members, the DRB issues a recommendation. The content and format of the board's recommendations are discretionary. Recommendations may address the merits of a claim as well as suggested quantum. The board's findings are not binding; instead the recommendations are intended to assist the parties in their own negotiations. After a specified time period, each party responds with an acceptance or rejection of the board's recommendations.

As with all nonbinding resolution methods, if the dispute remains unresolved, the parties retain the right to resort to arbitration or litigation. While the recommendations of a DRB are not binding, its decision and any supporting records are admissible in subsequent actions if so provided in the three-party agreement or the contract documents.

Mediation

Negotiation is usually the most flexible, inexpensive, and therefore efficient method of dispute resolution. Regardless of the merits of a negotiated solution, construction disputes are not always amenable to resolution by the participants. Both negotiation and DRBs presuppose a certain willingness to cooperate. In some instances, however, poor communication, inefficient exchange of information, and the personal intransigence of negotiators result in an apparently immovable impasse. In addition, otherwise cooperative disputants may wish to guard their positions in anticipation of possible subsequent legal actions. In these cases mediation may be appropriate.[9]

Mediation is the process of dispute settlement through the facilitation of a neutral third party. Mediations are usually convened through a series of conferences. Unlike DRBs, which meet with all parties simultaneously and render recommendations on the issues before them, mediators meet privately with the individuals involved in the dispute (*ex parte caucuses*) and gather necessary information to promote settlement without presenting decisions. The particular procedural mechanics of a mediation are at the discretion of the participants and their mediator. The basic format is as follows: (1) The parties meet jointly with the mediator to exchange facts and briefly summarize their positions. If desired, witnesses can appear at this time. (2) The mediator caucuses privately with each party, and proceeds to shuttle back and forth between the parties, discussing each party's concerns, presenting offers and counteroffers as authorized. (3) If a settlement is reached, the parties are brought together again to confirm its terms and sign an agreement or a memorandum of understanding.

Central to the role of the mediator is the concept of neutrality and an understanding that the final decision rests with the participants. A mediator is not a judge, and the parties' understanding of this limitation of the mediator's authority is essential to process success. Because a mediator is not a decision maker, and because all discussions are kept confidential, a party is more likely to disclose information that it might otherwise keep hidden regarding its position and the facts surrounding the dispute. In the mediator's role as negotiator, a mediator may offer his or her interpretation of a party's legal or factual position in order to give an objective and accurate assessment of the party's claim.

The confidentiality inherent in mediation is one of its chief advantages. Unlike the recommendations of DRBs, the materials from a mediation are not automatically admissible in subsequent legal proceedings. The AAA's *Construction Industry Mediation Rules* ensure that "confidential information disclosed to a mediator by the parties or witnesses in the course of the mediation shall not be divulged by the mediator...nor shall the mediator be compelled to divulge such records or to testify in regard to the mediation in any adversary proceeding or judicial forum."[10]

Parties to a typical mediation agreement are similarly prohibited from introducing into evidence, either directly or indirectly, views, proposals, or admissions made during the mediation. This assures all participants that they will not be prejudiced by their candor if they choose to stop mediation and return to the status quo. In addition, several states have enacted specific legislation to preserve the confidentiality and nondiscoverability of mediation proceedings.

Minitrial

There is an ongoing debate among mediation practitioners and theorists about the relative efficacy of an evaluative versus a strictly facilitative approach to mediation. Evaluative mediators give their personal opinions of the merits of each party's position. Facilitative mediators act as conduits for the parties' views, without interjecting their own opinions. Mediation purists argue that evaluation jeopardizes the mediator's neutral status and can unduly influence willingness to settle among disputants. In construction disputes, disputants themselves often desire guidance as to the relative merits of their positions. The increasing use of minitrials in construction and design disputes emphasizes the evaluative role of the neutral.

The minitrial is in effect a structured mediation proceeding, usually set in motion by a submission agreement between the parties. As with other private dispute resolution agreements, stipulations to minitrials establish their own particular procedural ground rules. Like mediation, a minitrial is a private and nonbinding settlement procedure. Like arbitration, a minitrial gives disputants the psychological satisfaction of having their "day in court" before an adjudicative neutral. The end product of a minitrial is a nonbinding settlement recommendation.

Generally the minitrial process can be divided into three phases: preparation for the hearing, conduct of the hearing, and negotiation among management representatives with settlement authority.

The preparatory phase is usually brief, with only limited discovery permitted and voluntary exchange of documents. Prior to the hearing, the parties can prepare 10- to 15-page position papers for simultaneous exchange. It is recommended that the minitrial hearing not contain any surprise evidence.

The second phase of a minitrial, the hearing, is also known as the *information exchange*. Here management representatives can interact, unfettered by the structure imposed by a typical court. Presentations are made to the minitrial panel, which consists of key executives from each party with full authority to settle and, in most cases, a mutually agreed upon neutral adviser. The neutral adviser's role in this phase is to moderate the proceedings. The presentations, which generally last two to three hours, proceed uninterrupted, thereby giving each party a view of the merits of the other side's position. Direct witness testimony is rarely utilized during the information exchange, but the disputant's position papers may reflect expert and fact witness accounts. Members of the panel may ask questions for clarification, and at the end of each presentation a short rebuttal period is generally allowed.

The minitrial information exchange typically lasts one or two days and is immediately followed by the third phase: a meeting of the key executives to negotiate the dispute. If the executives are unable to reach a settlement agreement, the neutral adviser may then attempt to mediate the negotiation and ultimately may write an opinion outlining the probable outcome of adjudication. If an impasse still exists, a cooling-off period is recommended prior to the initiation of legal proceedings. This often affords the parties an opportunity to digest the information gathered at the hearing and make a less impassioned decision.[11]

SUMMARY

The forensic engineer must be aware of many legal aspects in order to render effective services to the client. These include the steps in a civil litigation and the expert's role and interface in each; the rules of evidence that apply to the expert's investigation and work product; and the various facets of alternative dispute resolution and the expert's role and interface in these as well. Because the forensic engineer enters an arena for which she or he may not have specific training, the legal arena, the expert needs to know how the game is played and the rules governing conduct in that arena. Otherwise, the expert runs the risk of prejudicing rather than aiding the client, having the fruits of his or her efforts barred from receipt into evidence; and impairing the expert's own credibility and professional standing.

REFERENCES

1. Sayward Mazur, William J. Postner, Robert A. Rubin, and Joseph S. Ward, *The Engineer as an Expert Witness,* Elizabeth A. McGahan, ed., American Society of Civil Engineers, New York, 1985.
2. Robert A. Rubin, Virginia Fairweather, Sammie D. Guy, and Alfred C. Maevis, *Construction Claims: Prevention and Resolution,* 2d ed. van Nostrand Reinhold, New York, 1992, pp. 196–202.
3. 41 U.S.C. § 601 *et seq.,* 1987 & Supp. 1998.
4. 48 C.F.R. § 52, 1997.
5. Civil Justice Reform Act of 1990, Pub. L. 101-650.
6. American Arbitration Association, *Construction ADR Task Force Report,* New York, 1995.

7. Postner & Rubin, Catherine Kettle Brown, *New York Construction Law Manual* § 16.06, 1992.

8. Robert M. Matyas, A. A. Mathews, Robert J. Smith, and P. E. Sperry, *Construction Dispute Review Board Manual,* McGraw-Hill, New York, 1996.

9. Dana Wordes, "The Art of Construction Mediation," in *Handling Construction Risks,* K. Cushman, ed., Practicing Law Institute, New York, 1998, pp. 139–165.

10. American Arbitration Association, *Construction Industry Mediation Rules,* New York, January 1, 1992, p. 12.

11. CPR Institute for Dispute Resolution, *Construction Industry ADR: CPR Model ADR Procedures and Practices,* C. Cronin-Harris, ed., New York, 1994, pp. I106–I112.

CHAPTER 9
THE EXPERT CONSULTANT AND WITNESS

David E. Thompson, P.E. and Howard W. Ashcraft, Jr., Esq.

ROLE OF THE EXPERT WITNESS

Who Is an Expert?

Lay witnesses cannot generally testify concerning their opinions. Opinion testimony is the province of experts. Experts are persons who have special knowledge and training that laypersons do not have. But as a practical matter, a person is not an expert witness until a court of law or some other dispute resolution forum formally recognizes the person as such. To become an expert witness, the expert must testify concerning his or her qualifications and must be offered to the court. The opposing attorney may request a *voir dire* of the witness, which is basically a cross-examination of the witness's credentials with the hope of disqualifying that person as an expert. After this qualification process, the court decides whether the witness may testify as an expert.

The expert witness plays a pivotal role in our legal system. The expert explains complicated technical issues and provides expert opinions and conclusions to aid an arbitrator, judge, or jury in rendering decisions. In this regard, the testimony of the expert witness is the key event in every technical case. This is especially true when a professional has been sued for malpractice. Given this critical role, it is vital that experts be both technically qualified and unbiased.

The Ethical Challenge

In theory, the expert witness's testimony should be unaffected by who has retained her or him. The role of the expert witness is to be a truthful witness, obliged to testify as clearly and honestly as possible. The expert is not an advocate. Although there are differences in the opinions of expert witnesses, these differences should arise from differing technical opinions, not advocacy.

In practice, expert witnesses are generally retained by legal counsel who are obligated to be zealous advocates for their client and to present their client's case in the best possible light. It is inevitable that the expert witness should be swept up by the strong currents of advocacy and soon adopt partisan opinions and testimony. Some experts are so entranced by advocacy that they become more zealous than their attorney client!

In these authors' experience, this conflict has produced major problems in fairly resolving professional negligence disputes in our legal system. In many cases, expert witnesses become professional advocates and will adopt almost any position in support of their client's case. Our industry has its share of "hired guns" who make a living as professional expert witness advocates. In this environment, it is difficult for the trier of fact to sort through complex technical issues and arrive at a fair determination of fault.

ROLES OF THE FORENSIC ENGINEER/EXPERT

Forensic engineering, forensic architecture, and similar terms are used to connote the full spectrum of services provided by expert witnesses in their respective fields. These services can be engaged early in a dispute, even before a dispute materializes, such as when a failure occurs and a project participant retains an expert to investigate immediately, while facts and memories are still fresh. Services might include evaluation of proportional fault; calculation of damages; consultation with clients and attorneys to develop strategies; and creation or conceptualization of graphics, models, demonstrations, or animations to better communicate technical concepts to laypersons.

As much as 95 percent or more of the work performed by experts engaged in forensic services occurs outside of formal dispute resolution forums. Even when a court appearance is required, the time involved typically is less than one-tenth that associated with research and other pretrial activities. And the vast majority of all cases never reach trial. Most cases are settled, often as a result of experts' findings and the desire to avoid the enormous cost of trial as well as the uncertainty of its outcome.

Forensic engineers serve different roles in different circumstances. From confidential consultant to testifying expert, the role that the engineer plays will dramatically alter the approach used to complete the forensic engineering task. In many instances, a given assignment will combine several of these roles. But it is important to understand the role to be performed and to ensure that one has the skills and temperament to perform the tasks.

Common roles for forensic engineers include the following:

Confidential Consultant

The confidential consultant is an adviser to the retaining attorney and is considered an extension of the attorney's staff. The confidential consultant's thoughts, opinions, and work papers are protected by the attorney's work product privilege. Except in rare circumstances, nothing the confidential consultant does or says can be discovered by the opposing parties.

The confidential relationship gives great freedom to communications between the attorney and the engineer. Together, they can openly explore weaknesses in the client's position and may even—as an aid to preparation—try to assemble the best case *against* the client. This approach can be used to evaluate the client's case or to prepare the attorney—or even another expert—to anticipate the opposing party's questions. The confidential consultant often teaches the attorney the technical principles involved in the case and provides important background information concerning the industry and its personalities. The confidential consultant serves an invaluable role by frankly assessing the technical merits of the client's case and the attorney's arguments.

Because the confidential consultant's work product is solely for the attorney's use, the relationship is informal and open. The consultant rarely needs to extensively document opinions or maintain precise logs of evidence and information. Many engineers prefer this role because it is intellectually stimulating, but avoids the rigors of testifying and cross-examination.

Detective

Technical mysteries abound in complex engineering cases. Who did it? and How was it done? are riddles the forensic engineer must solve. The detective role requires the engineer to assume the work habits of a prosecutor and an archaeologist. Information must be carefully screened, preserved, and recorded. Data must be unearthed from records, files, and tests. Hypotheses must be formulated, tested, modified, and refined. Finally, the engineer must assemble the information in a concise, persuasive package.

The best "detective-engineers" combine an inquisitive intellect with meticulous work habits. They often lead a team of researchers who pour over project files and records to glean the relevant facts. Like archaeologists, they assemble these facts into a reconstruction of the events leading to the claim. Since this reconstruction must meet evidentiary standards, they must carefully preserve key evidence and record the methodology used for the reconstruction. The detective-engineer works closely with the retaining attorney to ensure that the final work product can withstand legal critique.

Although it is intellectually challenging, some engineers do not like the tedious aspects of detective work and may not have the time—or the staff—necessary to correctly perform this role.

Teacher

In some instances, education is the forensic engineer's primary goal. Attorneys, arbitrators, judges, and lay juries often have the sketchiest understanding of relevant technical principles or of the standards used in an industry. The "teacher-engineer" fills this gap by giving miniseminars to judge and jury. Persuasion is an after-effect of enhanced knowledge.

The teacher-engineer is not an advocate. In fact, advocacy undermines the teacher-engineer's role. A good teacher-engineer focuses on clearly presenting complex information and allowing the listener to deduce the answer.

Few are capable of teaching well. The teacher-engineer must simplify complex issues without distorting them. This role requires superior communication skills and an ability to simultaneously view a problem from the perspectives of expert and novice.

Because a court's time and attention span are limited, the teacher-engineer must be able to quickly communicate the essential points. Modern multimedia techniques are extremely helpful, and the teacher-engineer must be able to use these tools effectively.

Technician

Materials are often tested and analyzed during a construction case. To directly introduce the evidence, someone must testify concerning the gathering, preserving, and testing of the materials. A responsible engineer at the materials testing laboratory provides this testimony. It is usually straightforward, although care must be given to preserving samples and maintaining records that can accurately track the samples from collection to report.

Judge

An engineering malpractice action turns on a critical opinion: Did the engineer breach the standard of care? In most instances, this is determined from the testimony of experts as to the standard and whether it was breached.

The standard of care is the legal measure of professional negligence. An engineer is negligent if he or she does not use the care and skill employed by other competent engineers performing similar services under similar circumstances during the same time period in which the services were performed. In some instances, the standard of care is also tied to the locality where the services were performed.

The standard of care is not a static concept. It evolves as knowledge permeates through the engineering community. Events such as the Northridge earthquake in southern California change our view of acceptable practices. Advances in technology and computer modeling also affect how engineers should perform their work. The standard-of-care expert must determine what the standard was when the work was performed, not what it is today.

The standard of care is not an individual concept, but is based on engineering consensus. At any time, there are engineers whose work exceeds the standard just as there are those whose work falls below it. The standard-of-care expert must judge whether the defendant's services were acceptable to the majority of competent engineers—regardless of how the expert would have performed the services personally.

The standard-of-care focus leads the expert to look at the work of other engineers as much as the work of the defendant. Standards need to be researched, other projects reviewed, and interviews conducted with other engineers who performed similar services in the past. Once the standard is clear, the engineer must judge whether the standard was met. As with any judge, the engineer should be honest, careful, and fair.

Advocate

Persuasion is often the goal of investigation, analysis, and testimony. A persuasive expert skillfully blends investigation, analysis, and presentation. The persuasive expert also critically analyzes opposing views and spots inconsistencies and errors of logic. Persuasion is not arguing. It is an effort to convince the judge, jury, or opponent that your explanation best fits the known facts.

Unfortunately, some engineers become overly invested in their positions and argue beyond any reasonable interpretation of the facts. This is not persuasive, for people are rarely fooled by extreme arguments. This approach undermines the expert's credibility and devalues the expert's opinions.

Hybrids

Many assignments blend aspects of each role. The detective may need to become the teacher to provide sufficient background to explain the significance of the findings. The findings may be the basis for judging the standard of care. But because each role requires different skills, one should consider what roles one will perform before taking on an assignment. Too often, experts begin an interesting project only to later discover that they do not like—or are not well suited for—a later phase of the work.

ENGAGEMENT OF THE FORENSIC ENGINEER/EXPERT

The Initial Call

Your first experience as an expert will probably begin with a phone call. Either a client or the client's attorneys will ask whether you would be willing to testify on the client's behalf. They will undoubtedly ask you about your experience and your rates, and they may want your "gut reaction" to the case. But what information do you need from them?

First, who are the clients and what do you know about them? Can you trust these clients? Do they share your views about honesty and integrity? Would you be proud to tell colleagues that you worked for these clients? If you don't know these clients, you should ask for references just as they should ask you for references. Being an expert is a significant business and professional assignment and should be undertaken with the same care you would use for other projects.

You should also determine who is responsible for payment and whether payment is dependent upon receipt of funds from a third party, such as an insurance company. Many law firms will not guarantee prompt payment and only act as a conduit of funds from other sources. The funding source may pay slowly and may disallow some of or all your fees. If you are dependent upon payment from an unknown third party, you may not have any remedy for nonpayment. If you are unsure of payment, you should consider requiring a retainer or a guarantee of payment directly from the client.

Second, determine who else is involved in the case. You need the names of parties, attorneys, and other experts, if known. You should identify and disclose your firm's relationships with any of these people, even if you feel they are insignificant. Attorneys are governed by strict conflict-of-interest standards and will be upset if you haven't disclosed a relationship that they would be forced to disclose. You need to determine whether you could give unbiased testimony concerning the parties and issues involved.

Third, determine what role you will serve. Are you an undisclosed consultant or a testifying expert? Are you being asked to head a broad investigation or to provide specific testimony on a single issue, such as the standard of care? Are you competent to address the substantive issue?

Fourth, what are the client's expectations concerning scope of work and budget? Is it sufficient to allow you to develop your opinions? Is the client intending to limit your research to information provided by the client? Will you need to develop tests or other data? What is the schedule for your work? Is it sufficient for the tasks involved? When will you likely testify? Do you have scheduling conflicts? If you have planned vacations or other obligations, you should advise the client during the initial interviews.

In many instances, these questions cannot be completely answered during the initial discussions. If this is the case, you should schedule a follow-up meeting to develop answers to the issues of scope, conflicts, payment, and schedule. If you aren't comfortable with the client's apparent honesty and integrity, you should immediately decline the engagement.

The Chicken and the Egg   Most attorneys will be very interested to determine the opinion of an expert witness at the earliest possible opportunity, sometimes during the initial telephone conversation. However, the expert in most cases needs to review at least a minimal set of facts, conduct limited analyses, and perform some tasks to arrive at an opinion.

The most reasonable way to resolve the dilemma is for the expert to be charged with the examination of the most significant readily available facts and, for a nominal fee, provision of a preliminary verbal opinion as to his or her position on this issue. Based on the expert's preliminary opinion, the attorney may choose to continue to develop the case with the expert or look elsewhere for expert services.

Expert-Shopping

Experts can be critical to a client's case, and good attorneys often identify and retain experts well before any work is needed. They want to "lock in" a good expert before she or he has been retained by another party. They will also interview several experts to identify the one best suited to their case. This is good legal practice.

But some attorneys interview a variety of experts for a different purpose. The attorneys want to contact as many experts as possible, to create a conflict-of-interest issue if one is later retained by another party. If you suspect this may occur, you should advise the attorney—preferably in writing—not to disclose confidential information to you until you are actually retained; that you remain willing to discuss your qualifications, but you reserve the right to be employed by another party should the attorney or client decide not to retain you.

Contracts

The initial discussions concerning scope of work, payment, schedule, and budget should be summarized in a brief written agreement. This can be based on your standard consulting agreement or can be a contract specifically drafted for expert work. Issues to be addressed in the agreement include these:

What is the scope of your assignment? Are there any specific budget or schedule limitations?

Who is responsible for your payment?

When is payment due?

Can you stop work if you are not paid in timely fashion?

Are there different rates for testifying and for office engineering?

Who is authorized to request additional work? If authorization must be in writing, will your written confirmation suffice?

How will disputes be handled? Will they be arbitrated, mediated, or litigated?

What are the requirements for confidentiality?

Who stores samples or other data? Who pays for long-term storage, and when can the samples and data be discarded?

Some firms include indemnification and limitation-of-liability provisions in their contract. These provisions may force the client to defend the engineer in a suit or may limit the client's remedies against the engineer for errors in the expert assignment. But many attorneys object to these provisions in a consulting agreement. To some, these provisions imply that the engineer's objectivity has been "bought" by the agreement to indemnify. But it is just as true that the clauses permit the engineer to act independently of any liability concerns. Engineers should generally try to get these provisions in their expert agreements.

Contingent-fee arrangements, however, should not be accepted. The expert's neutrality is compromised by any interest in the outcome.

If the consultant is identified as a testifying expert, the contract will be subject to discovery. Knowing this, many attorneys deliberately draft vague work scopes and budgets. This avoids later questions concerning why specific tasks were abandoned and whether an opinion is premature if not all tasks have been completed. Although this is a reasonable approach from the attorney's view, you should make sure that you, and your client, have a clear understanding about the scope of your work, the cost, and the schedule.

Fees and Budgets   Expert fees are highly variable. They depend upon the nature of the assignment, the sophistication of the issues, competition, and similar issues. Expert fees often exceed normal engineering hourly rates. First, expert work is often very personal. If you are going to be cross-examined concerning your opinions, you should have done the majority of the work yourself. Otherwise, you will not appear knowledgeable. This means that you are not providing significant amounts of work for junior personnel, and do not have the leverage you would have in a conventional engineering assignment. Second, expert work is often erratic. Months may pass without any work being performed, and suddenly everything needs to be done by next week. Orderly scheduling is difficult. Third, testifying interrupts your normal workday. You may be required to stand by for substantial periods while other persons testify or the court is involved in other issues. Fourth, repeat work is a rarity. The clients hope they do not need your services again. The time you spend developing a relationship with the client and attorney may have no future benefit. Finally, many engineers don't like to be cross-examined. Thus, they request "combat pay" for testifying assignments.

Clients need budgets to evaluate their options. The cost of the expert investigation is one factor in determining whether a case should be settled and at what amount. Clients also need realistic budgets to anticipate cash flow demands.

Budgets also benefit engineers by avoiding "sticker shock" and consequent payment delays.

Expert budgets are difficult to prepare. In most instances, the scope of work develops over time. When first contacted, the expert may have little idea of the scope of document review, whether physical investigation or testing is required, or the extent of other significant items.

Although it is difficult to prepare a comprehensive initial budget, a phased budget is practical. In a phased budget, the expert is given a limited, and often arbitrary, budget to perform a preliminary investigation. This investigation typically includes limited review of documents, review of key reference materials, and interviews with a few key project personnel. At the conclusion of this phase, the expert provides a verbal initial impression, a work scope and schedule for developing the opinion, and a budget for this work. With a good understanding of the problem and the nature and quality of available information, the expert should be able to develop an accurate estimate of costs.

Marketing

Good experts are hard to find. A testifying engineer with a reputation for honesty, technical competence, and good presentation skills will be very busy. But how do you get the first assignment?

Networking is the best method of marketing. If you know attorneys who regularly retain engineers, you should contact the attorneys and express your interest in serving as an expert. They can often suggest others who may be interested, or they may be contacted by other attorneys seeking experts. Your professional liability insurer may also be a good source of referrals. Your insurance broker can introduce you to the claims supervisors for your area. The attorneys that brokers retain often ask them to recommend experts, and brokers prefer to recommend qualified experts who are also their insureds.

Local bar associations may maintain lists of technical experts. Experts also advertise in state bar and similar periodicals. These may lead to assignments from attorneys with little experience in construction, but sophisticated construction counsel rarely use these lists. To make contact with these attorneys, you should become involved as an affiliate to their professional organizations, such as the American Bar Association's Forum on the Construction Industry.

Brochures have some utility, but mailings on technical subjects are more likely to catch an attorney's eye. Most construction attorneys keep files of information from experts. When attorneys need an expert, they will review these files for possible leads. A well-written article can lead to referrals.

Once you have an assignment, execute it well. Keep the attorney and client informed, promptly notify them of unexpected (or unpleasant) developments, be responsive, and stay within budget. Experts who heed these recommendations will be busy indeed.

RECOMMENDED PRACTICES FOR FORENSIC ENGINEERS AND EXPERT WITNESSES*

Genesis of the Recommendations

Once they have been qualified as experts, forensic engineers may testify in most states with little fear of repercussion. Exceptions do exist, however. In Missouri, e.g., the state's supreme court allowed a contractor to pursue a $4 million claim against an expert it had retained. The expert was negligent in preparing and presenting testimony before an arbitrator, the contractor alleged, resulting in a $1 million award when $5 million actually was justified. The expert—an engineer—argued that a ruling in the contractor's favor would result in experts taking extreme positions to help ensure their clients were victorious. The court responded, in part, that "Imposing liability would encourage experts to be careful and accurate. They are liable if they perform their services negligently. Certainly these professional individuals are subject to liability in any of their other work if they fail to comply with the degree of care, skill and proficiency commonly exercised by ordinary skillful, careful, and prudent professionals and if their failure to do so causes injury to their client. The fact that this particular service may be related to litigation should not bar their clients this protection."†

Missouri is not alone in its position. Other states that do not extend immunity to experts include California, Texas, and New Jersey. In many other states, however, the courts generally bend over backward to help ensure that experts are able to render their testimony without fear of reprisal. Does this apply to experts before they are qualified as such, i.e., when they are serving as forensic consultants? For example, if a case moved forward due to a false premise created by a forensic consultant's careless work, such as sloppy calculations, would plaintiffs have standing to sue on the ground that the forensic consultant was negligent? It is an interesting question and one that apparently has not been addressed. If such liability does exist, however, it might go a long way toward reining in some of the excesses of hired-gun experts, i.e., individuals who adopt attitudes, positions, and opinions not because of their education, training, or experience, but rather for the purposes of advocacy.

ASFE: Professional Firms Practicing in the Geosciences was the first organization to take on the hired guns. It developed recommended procedures for experts' testimony and then sought to have most of the nation's design professional organizations endorse the procedures, in order to create a quasi-standard.

ASFE took its concept to the Interprofessional Council on Environmental Design (ICED), an organization comprising organizations such as the American

---

*From: *EXPERT—A Guide to Services as a Forensic Professional and Expert Witness,* published by ASFE: *Professional Firms Practicing in the Geosciences,* Silver Spring, MD, 1998.

†31 USCA §§3279-3731. Some states, and even some cities, have their own versions of false-claims acts—generally modeled on the federal act. See, California Government Code §12650, *et seq.*; 740 Ill. Stat. Ann. 175 (Smith-Hurd); Fla. Stat. Ann. §68.081-.092 (West) for examples of state false-claims acts.

Society of Civil Engineers, the American Institute of Architects, and the American Consulting Engineers Council, among several others. Together, these organizations created a document entitled *Recommended Practices for Design Professionals Engaged as Experts in the Resolution of Construction Industry Disputes.* Endorsement of the document began in 1987. Today, more than 30 national, international, and regional organizations have become endorsers, and the list continues to grow.

Recommended Practices comprise 13 separate recommendations. These are based on generally accepted standards of professional practice as enunciated by a wide range of engineers, architects, and attorneys.

The issues addressed by *Recommended Practices* go far beyond testifying about the standard of care (recommendation 7).

Note that *Recommended Practices for Design Professionals Engaged as Experts in the Resolution of Construction Industry Disputes* does much more than provide basic guidance to forensic engineers. Attorneys should use it as a tool to help them impeach those who do not do the type of work really required to enlighten a trier of fact. In this latter regard, the attorneys who retain you need to recognize that *you* could be impeached if you are not permitted to provide the appropriate quality. For example, a number of attorneys wait until the very last moment to retain experts, and then ask them to perform in an extremely short time span and/or for a tiny fee. An opinion given based on this kind of work will be fraught with uncertainty and thus far more likely to mislead than to enlighten. For this reason, many highly respected forensic engineers will not accept engagements for which they cannot perform the services required to provide an informed opinion. Experts who take a different approach could easily have their opinions impeached by an attorney who refers to recommendation 5 or 12.

The following section repeats the thirteen recommendations and commentaries given in *Recommended Practices for Design Professionals Engaged as Experts in the Resolution of Construction Industry Disputes,* as published by ASFE (8811 Colesville Road, Suite G106, Silver Spring, MD) and endorsed by more than 30 professional organizations.

The Recommendations

These recommendations have been developed from the belief that adherence to them will help experts provide to triers of fact substantial professional opinions unbiased by the adversarial nature of most dispute resolution proceedings. The organizations which endorse these recommendations do not require any individual to follow them.

It is the obligation of an expert to perform in a professional manner and serve without bias. Toward these ends:

1. The expert should avoid conflicts of interest and the appearance of conflicts of interest.

Commentary

Regardless of the expert's objectivity, the expert's opinion may be discounted if it is found that the expert has or had a relationship with another party which consciously or even subconsciously could have biased the expert's services or opinions. To avoid this situation, experts should identify the organizations and individuals involved in the matter at issue, and should determine if they or any of their associates have ever had a relationship with any of the organizations or the individuals involved. Experts should reveal any such relationships to their clients and/or clients' attorneys to permit them to determine whether the relationships could be construed as creating or giving the appearance of creating conflicts of interest.

2. The expert should undertake an engagement only when qualified to do so and should rely upon other qualified parties for assistance in matters which are beyond the expert's area of expertise.

Commentary

Experts should know their limitations and should report their need for qualified assistance when the matters at issue call for expertise or experience they do not possess. In such instances, it is appropriate for experts to identify others who possess the required expertise and to work with them. Should an expert be asked to exceed his or her limitations and thereafter be denied access to other professionals, and should the expert be requested to continue association with the case, the expert should establish which matters she or he will and will not pursue; failing that, the expert should terminate the engagement.

3. The expert should consider other practitioners' opinions relative to the principles associated with the matter at issue.

Commentary

In forming their opinions, experts should consider relevant literature in the field and the opinions of other professionals when such are available. Experts who disagree with the opinions of other professionals should be prepared to explain to the trier of fact the differences which exist and why a particular opinion should prevail.

4. The expert should obtain available information relative to the events in question in order to minimize reliance on assumptions, and she or he should be prepared to explain any assumptions to the trier of fact.

Commentary

The expert should review those documents, such as tenders and agreements, which identify the services in question and any restrictions or limitations which may have applied. Other significant information may include codes, standards, and regulations affecting the matters in dispute, as well as information obtained through discovery procedures. If pertinent to the assignment, the expert should also visit the site of the event involved and consider information obtained from witnesses. Whenever an expert relies on assumptions, each assumption should be identified and evaluated. When an assumption is selected to the exclusion of others, the expert should be able to explain the basis for the selection.

5. The expert should evaluate reasonable explanations of causes and effects.

Commentary

As necessary, experts should study and evaluate different explanations of causes and effects. Experts should not limit their inquiry for the purpose of proving the contentions advanced by those who have retained them.

6. The expert should strive to ensure the integrity of the tests and investigations conducted as part of the expert's services.

Commentary

Experts should conduct tests and investigations personally, or should direct their performance through qualified individuals who should be capable of serving as expert or factual witnesses with regard to the work performed.

7. The expert witness should testify about professional standards of care only with knowledge of those standards which prevailed at the time in question, based upon reasonable inquiry.

Commentary

When a design professional is accused of negligence, the trier of fact must determine whether the professional breached the applicable standard of care. A determination of the standard of care prevailing at the time in question may be made through investigation, such as the review of reports, records, or opinions of other professionals performing the same or similar services at the time in question. Expert witnesses should identify standards of care independently of their own preferences and should not apply present standards to past events.

8. The expert witness should use only those illustrative devices or presentations which simplify or clarify an issue.

Commentary

The attorney who will call the expert as a witness wants to review and approve illustrative devices or presentations before they are offered during testimony. All illustrative devices or presentations developed by or for an expert should demonstrate relevant principles without bias.

9. The expert should maintain custody and control over whatever materials are entrusted to the expert's care.

Commentary

The preservation of evidence and the documentation of its custody and care may be necessary for its admissibility in dispute resolution proceedings. Appropriate precautions in some cases may include provision of environmentally controlled storage.

10. The expert should respect confidentiality about an assignment.

Commentary

All matters discussed by and between experts, their clients and/or clients' attorneys should be regarded as privileged and confidential. The contents of such discussions should not be disclosed voluntarily by an expert to any other party, except with the consent of the party who retained the expert.

11. The expert should refuse or terminate involvement in an engagement when fee is used in an attempt to compromise the expert's judgment.

Commentary

Experts are employed to clarify technical issues with objectivity and integrity. Experts should either refuse or terminate service when they know or have reason to believe they will be rewarded for compromising their objectivity or integrity.

12. The expert should refuse or terminate involvement in an engagement when the expert is not permitted to perform the investigation which the expert believes is necessary to render an opinion with a reasonable degree of certainty.

Commentary

It is the responsibility of experts to inform their clients and/or their clients' attorneys about the scope and nature of the investigation required to reach opinions with a reasonable degree of certainty, and the effect which any time, budgetary, or other limitations may have. Experts should not accept or continue an engagement if limitations will prevent them from testifying with a reasonable degree of certainty.

13. The expert witness should strive to maintain a professional demeanor and be dispassionate at all times.

Commentary

Particularly when rendering testimony or during cross-examination, expert witnesses should refrain from conducting themselves as though their service were a contest between themselves and some other party.

Discussion of the Recommendations

The foregoing recommendations have been endorsed by an impressive list of professional organizations. In addition, most professional organizations have codes of ethics that apply to forensic engineering and expert-witness activities. Professionals should review these standards before embarking on an expert-witness assignment.

The following additional points and reinforcements are offered with respect to some of the recommendations:

Qualifications. Never offer expert opinions outside of your area of expertise. Engineers can be tempted to do so when a good client requests their services. If you develop a reputation as a persuasive expert witness, attorneys may want to engage you even if the subject area is not closely related to your area of expertise. Before you undertake an assignment, ask yourself two questions: Is this the type of work you routinely do? If you were the client, would you hire yourself to do this work or would you hire someone with more experience? If you can't answer both questions affirmatively, do not undertake the assignment.

You also have a duty to tell your client the limitations of your expertise. If you have limited experience with part of the proposed assignment, you should disclose this fact and propose teaming up with another engineer or expert, or should decline the assignment.

Your qualifications are an issue of credibility and integrity. If you overstate your qualifications, you will undermine the effectiveness of your testimony on other issues. Being honest with your client and yourself is central to your integrity. Without credibility and integrity, you cannot function successfully as an expert.

Consider the Options.   Few litigated issues have only one conclusion. In most instances, there are several competing theories to explain an occurrence or loss. A good expert does not rule out other experts' opinions without carefully considering their assumptions and validity. At the very least, this exercise provides the basis for differentiating your opinion from other proposed theories and for explaining the advantages of your approach.

Limit or Clearly State Assumptions.   Expert opinions can be based on assumed facts. This is done explicitly through hypothetical questions whereby the expert is asked to render an opinion assuming that certain facts are true. But assumptions can be implicit as well. An opinion may be supported by an expert's suppositions or inferences based on records or other evidence.

These basic facts may be subject to debate. Experts have crumbled under skilled cross-examinations when forced to admit their opinion is based on unstated assumptions. If the opposing party can prove these assumptions were false, the expert's credibility and opinions are destroyed. If the assumptions are limited or clearly stated, however, debate over basic facts is less damaging. At worst, the debate becomes a difference of opinion rather than an attempt by the expert to deceive the judge or jury.

Level of Inquiry.   In a design assignment, the client and engineer develop a scope of work that is appropriate for the client's needs. A hospital client may require rigorously developed plans and specifications. A design-build warehouse contractor may prefer diagrammatic information. Each level of work is acceptable in its context.

Expert testimony is different. It is a representation to the judge or jury of what is true. It follows that you should not accept a testifying assignment unless you are satisfied that the level of inquiry is sufficient to support a strongly stated opinion. Thus, there is a zone of acceptable intensity where the client's preferences and budget should not be a factor in defining the level of inquiry. You must determine the lower boundary of that zone and must stay above it.

Integrity.   An expert offers two attributes: technical competence and integrity. If either is lacking, the expert's opinion is worthless.

Integrity is the sum of several issues discussed in this chapter. It is more than honesty. It includes ensuring an adequate level of inquiry, testifying only where competent, fairly considering opposing opinions, and avoiding even the appearance of impropriety. As an expert, you are asking to be trusted. You must do everything in your power to respect that trust.

Standard of Care. Engineers are liable in professional malpractice actions if their services fall below the standard of care. Although there are slight differences in phraseology between jurisdictions, the essential elements of the standard of care are that services must be consistent with the level of care and skill ordinarily exercised by members of the profession practicing in the same locality under similar conditions at the same time. Some services are locality-specific, such as structural design in a seismically active zone. Other services are more general and are governed by regional or even national standards. The standard of care does not require perfection, for perfection is beyond human capability. The standard simply requires the design professional to exhibit the normal care exercised by the average professional in the field.

A design professional is liable when a breach of the standard of care causes damage. Because the trier of fact (judge, jury, or arbitrator) does not know the standard of care and may not be able to analyze the technical issues involved with causation, most courts require expert testimony on these issues. Breach of the standard of care is ordinarily proved by testimony of experts who are conversant with the applicable standard. There are three problems with this approach.

First, being human, experts tend to apply personal standards. Thus, their personal practices color their perception of the standard of care. Since experts are often chosen for their high technical competence, they risk raising the standard of care by relying on their personal experience and practices.

Second, litigation is retrospective. Often one must prove what the standard of care was in the past, not what it is at present. Unless the expert practiced during the time period in question, he or she may not know what the past standards were. Also, if there were competing practices in the past, knowledge of which practice became the accepted standard tends to devalue the other competing practices— even if they were well accepted at the time.

Third, there are unique services for which no standard exists.

Experts retained to discuss the standard of care must consciously attempt to solve these problems. This requires using a protocol for defining the standard of care. Although no protocol will fit every circumstance, the following steps will assist an expert in defining the standard of care.

- Determine the time period involved. If there is reason to believe the standard is locality-specific, determine the applicable geographic region.
- Determine the circumstances that relate to the services. Review the engineer's contract or any other documents that define the engineer's scope of work and any limitations on the engineer's services.

- Perform a literature search to determine if the standard was documented in publications, regulations, or codes that should be known to competent engineers. Arcane academic publications may be useless in defining the standard of care because they are not read by any significant percentage of practicing engineers.
- Interview a spectrum of practitioners to determine a consensus standard of care. When you are dealing with a past standard, reviewing building department files for projects constructed during the applicable time period can be useful.*
- Compare the consensus standard, as modified by contract, circumstances, or other justifications, with the questioned decision or design.

It is possible to research the standard of care and testify solely based on your research. But you will be easily impeached if you do not have personal experience with the type of work being reviewed. As a general rule, do not testify about the standard of care unless you have performed similar work under similar circumstances.

Confidentiality.   An expert consultant is an extension of the retaining attorney. Until the consultant has been designated as a testifying expert, any information provided to the consultant and any of the consultant's thoughts, opinions, and work documents are confidential. They cannot be disclosed without the express permission of the retaining attorney and the client.

When a consultant is listed as a testifying expert, the privilege protecting thoughts, opinions, communications, and files vanishes. Common sense and good manners should still cause you to show discretion in discussing anything related to your assignment, but you will now be subject to discovery (i.e., producing documents and being deposed). As discussed below, your work files should be well organized and free from inappropriate comments and half-considered opinions. As a general rule, work papers should contain observations, not opinions, until you have done sufficient work to reach a definite conclusion.

Record Keeping.   If you testify, other parties will obtain copies of your work papers. As noted above, ensure that your work papers are neat, organized, and free of inappropriate comments and half-considered opinions.

You may want to organize your work papers to enable you to respond to anticipated questions. If you can quickly find supporting documentation, your credibility will be enhanced.

---

*This is also a useful way to avoid the "do as I say, not as I do" problem. ASFE: Professional Firms Practicing in the Geosciences performed a survey of its members to define the standard of care for preliminary site assessments. Later, ASFE audited a group of representative phase 1 files from the surveyed firms. They discovered that the surveyed firms reported that the standard of care required completing more tasks than the firms actually performed. Audits of project files or reports, therefore, may be a better indicator of the standard of care. If possible, interview the engineer to determine the reason for the decision you are reviewing. If this is not possible—and in most litigation a direct interview cannot be done—review any available explanatory material, such as depositions, other expert reports, or similar documents that might justify the questioned decision or design.

Whether you prepare a report or not will vary between assignments. Reports are commonly prepared and submitted in arbitrations. They are also submitted during mediations or initial presentation of a claim. But they are less commonly prepared during litigation. Under normal evidentiary rules, an expert report may not be admissible in a legal action—the expert needs to testify concerning the opinion. Thus, the report can be used by the opposition to focus its cross-examination, but cannot be used as evidence of your opinions. You should discuss this issue with the retaining attorney before preparing any report or any documents that summarize your opinions.

Personal Involvement. Nothing is less impressive than testimony that only summarizes the work of others. Your credibility will suffer unless you are personally involved in all phases of the work. At a minimum, you should spot-check the work of subordinates before accepting their results. Better yet, you should personally perform as much work as possible.

FORENSIC SERVICES

Research

Many technical issues require extensive research of existing records, construction documentation, applicable codes and design criteria, and the technical literature. This type of research can be an end, in and of itself; or it can form the basis for further analysis.

Nontestifying consultants often perform research on behalf of the retaining attorney. Most engineers are better suited than the attorney's staff to perform literature searches or to identify relevant codes and standards. The consultant organizes and summarizes the material (or highlights significant excerpts) and explains how these materials bear on the technical issues. This focuses the attorney's efforts and assists in evaluating the claim.

Site Visit

When a site or facility is the focal point of the issue, it is essential that the forensic engineer visit the site or facility and observe, firsthand, the conditions in the area as soon as possible after the incident or claim. A videotape recorder and a digital or 35mm camera are important to document conditions and details that may not be noted visually and will probably be subject to disturbance at a later date. It is important to record the date, time, and exact location of all photographic documentation. If scale or dimensions are important, the photograph should include a visible steel tape or identifiable objects of known size. This allows the viewer to infer approximate size.

A pocket tape recorder can be helpful in recording observations, thoughts, and notes in a rapid and complete manner in the field. If the site inspection is being conducted with multiple parties, be careful not to dictate when you can be overheard.

Field sketches using a site plan or structural drawings for reference should be prepared as required to document significant conditions, physical measurements, and the location and orientation of photographs.

Analyses

Analyses of possible failure mechanisms should be conducted using standard analytical procedures, generally accepted in the industry. Loads and forces should be based on code-recommended values or logical interpretation of conditions existing at the time of failure. To the fullest extent possible, all analyses should be conducted by the forensic expert directly, or at least under the direction of the expert, using analyses and assumptions determined and reviewed by her or him.

If computer analyses are used, the results should be randomly checked by hand calculations or other quality control procedures to ensure the accuracy of the programming. You must be able to explain and validate the software used. If you cannot explain the algorithms used by the software or its accuracy and limitations, the results may be excluded and your credibility will certainly suffer.

Inspection and Testing

Before undertaking inspection and testing, the forensic expert should consider how the information will be used. Do samples need to be maintained for an opposing party's examination? Should the inspections or testing be videotaped for later display to a judge or jury? Are written records sufficient? What evidentiary standards apply to the tests? These issues should be discussed with the retaining attorney at the inception of your work.

All testing should be performed in strict accordance with recognized standard procedures such as those of the American Society for Testing and Materials (ASTM). To the fullest extent possible, the forensic expert should oversee the testing unless the individual actually performing the tests is qualified to testify as an expert regarding the test procedures. The test results should be checked, and all tests should be reported. Outlying data should not be excluded unless exclusions are statistically valid.

Models and Simulations

Models have long been used to physically demonstrate principles or to test hypotheses. More recently, computer-generated simulations have assumed a similar role. But models and simulations must be carefully prepared or must risk being excluded from evidence. Before undertaking these tasks, you should carefully discuss these issues with the retaining attorney to ensure that the completed work is admissible.

As a practical matter, most courts will allow the opposing party to view the model or simulation, review the underlying data, and have access to the algorithms used to transform the underlying data into the visual display. You should assume the opposing party will object to admitting the model or simulation into evidence. Common objections include these:

The model or simulation is based on unproven underlying facts for assumptions (garbage in, garbage out).

The model or simulation overly emphasizes (or deemphasizes) facts and is, therefore, more deceptive than useful.

The model or simulation is not based on widely accepted scientific principles.

The proponent of the model or simulation cannot prove that the computer program accurately transforms the data. (This is a significant problem where the consultant uses a program without any real understanding of how it works. This is less of a problem where the program is regularly used in engineering, as opposed to a custom program created to generate simulations for legal purposes.)

Despite these difficulties, models and simulations are extremely important. There is no better tool for rapidly explaining complex facts to judge and jury. Seeing may not be believing, but it stimulates understanding, which enables persuasion. The power of multimedia is quickly transforming simulations from an expensive toy to an indispensable tool.

Claim Evaluation

Claim evaluation is a complex task that blends factual research, technical investigation, engineering and construction practices, accounting, and legal analysis. Because of the breadth of skills required, claims analysis is often performed by teams of experts. Some firms specializing in claims evaluation employ individuals with the requisite expertise and offer a "one-stop shopping" approach to claims evaluation. This approach is convenient, but the firms may not have the best-qualified individuals for the specific project.

If a claims team is comprised of individuals from different firms, someone must be designated as the team leader and must be responsible for overall strategy and coordination. If the claims evaluation is being prepared for a legal proceeding, the client's attorney will need to have this leadership and coordination role. During prelegal negotiations, however, the coordinator may be the client or the principal claims consultant. The exact structure will depend upon the issues and the persons involved—but someone must have the leadership coordination role.

Claims evaluation typically breaks into three separate analyses: entitlement, quantum, and allocation. The entitlement analysis determines whether the claimant can recover under the applicable facts, law, and contract provisions. If entitlement exists, the evaluation next determines the amount of additional compensation or time extension allowed, i.e., the quantum of recovery. Finally, a determination is made concerning how the damages should be allocated among the culpable parties. In many instances, it takes as long, or longer, to determine allocation as it does to determine entitlement and quantum.

Claimants often conclude claims evaluation by preparing a report summarizing the investigation and conclusion. The report must be carefully prepared because it becomes the claimant's "Bible" during negotiations. Later deviations from the claims analysis significantly undermine the claimant's credibility. It will also be difficult to add significant new claims and assertions. This may lead claimants to overinclude arguments and claims. This, too, has dangers. For instance, an unsupportable claim made to the federal government (or some state and local governments) may violate False Claims Act* provisions and subject the claimant to significant penalties and criminal sanctions.

Delay and impact analysis is a thorny problem in claim evaluation. It is often easy to determine whether an event could delay the project. But to determine whether it actually delayed the project, how that delay interacted with other delays, and what effect the combined delay and events had on a contractor's productivity is an infinitely more complex task. There are many methodologies, and each claims analyst has favorite approaches for analyzing delay and impact claims. No method is foolproof, however. All have subjective bases and require thoughtful application and adjustment.

Insensitive (or devious) manipulation of claims methodologies can erroneously magnify (or diminish) claims. Be wary of simplistic, "objective" calculations.

Avoid testifying about delay and impact claims unless you have significant experience in analyzing and quantifying these claims.

Discovery

American litigation permits discovery of information from opposing parties or third parties. Discovery is intended to allow each party to fully understand the opposing party's position prior to trial and to have an opportunity to view the evidence on which the position is based. Discovery should reduce surprise, increase the likelihood of settlement, avoid unfairness, and shorten the trial. But experience with modern discovery also shows that full-fledged discovery is very expensive and time-consuming. In complex construction cases, the discovery phase can be the most expensive portion of the process.

There are four basic discovery tools: written interrogatories, requests for admissions, production of documents, and depositions.

Written interrogatories are questions that can be sent to other parties in litigation who must reply within a specified time, often 30 days. They are a good way to generate specific data, such as the addresses of witnesses, but are poor ways to discover complex information. Unfortunately, responses to interrogatories are sometimes drafted to provide as little information as possible.

---

*31 USCA §§3279-3731. Some states, and even some cities, have their own versions of false-claims acts—generally modeled on the federal act. See, California Government Code §12650, *et seq.*; 740 Ill. Stat. Ann. 175 (Smith-Hurd); Fla. Stat. Ann. §68.081-.092 (West) for examples of state false-claims acts.

Requests for admissions are similar to interrogatories, except the respondent is asked to admit the truth of a fact or the genuineness of a document. As with interrogatories, requests for admissions are best suited to simple, discrete facts.

Document productions are extremely valuable tools. Unlike interrogatories and requests for admissions, document productions can be addressed to persons and organizations that are not parties to the litigation. The assembly and reviewing of all the relevant documents are the basis for most litigation fact finding. Contemporaneous records are especially persuasive.

Depositions are also very important—but very expensive. In a deposition, the person being deposed answers questions under oath. The deponent only has to answer the exact question asked, and witnesses are counseled to keep their answers short and direct. Thus, the amount of useful information developed will depend upon the skill and thoroughness of the questioning attorney. In the worst situations, this becomes a game between the witness and attorney and substantially lengthens the process. Thousands of dollars in time can be spent trying to develop small amounts of information. But because this is the only opportunity the parties have to hear the testimony of the witnesses before trial, depositions are taken in most cases.

The amount of discovery permitted in arbitration varies depending upon the arbitration rules being used and the agreement of the parties. For instance, the standard construction arbitration rules of the American Arbitration Association do not permit prearbitration discovery without the agreement of the parties.

Experts have several tasks regarding discovery. First, they aid the attorneys in defining the questions to be asked and the documents to be obtained. The expert may propose interrogatories or deposition questions to be asked by his or her retaining attorney. In some instances, experts may attend depositions, providing the questioning attorney with immediate analysis of the witness's testimony and suggestions for specific areas of inquiry. Second, they analyze the information obtained through discovery. Experts will carefully read the deposition transcripts and review the produced documents to assemble the information relevant to the claim. Third, experts will be deposed by opposing attorneys concerning the opinions they have developed.

Storage of Evidence

Opposing parties generally have the right to inspect evidence that will be used against them. If you have gathered evidence, you need to carefully document, record, and preserve it until it is no longer needed. You should document where the evidence came from, who collected the evidence, and, if relevant, where and how it was stored. The person collecting physical evidence should mark the sample so that she or he can testify that the sample being introduced in evidence is the actual sample collected or tested.

Since construction litigation can continue for years, include a provision in your contract regarding charges for preserving evidence and procedures for disposing of evidence after your work has finished. Generally, your contract should state that you will return the evidence to your client, but may discard it if the client will not accept the evidence or pay for its storage.

Presentation Development

Construction disputes present experts with a daunting task: How do you quickly present complex technical information to an audience which has limited technical knowledge and is indifferent to the issues? Multimedia presentations are one answer. They allow the expert to organize information into easily remembered units of knowledge and to quickly link and contrast data from many different sources.

Multimedia presentations can be carefully scripted three-dimensional simulations combined with video clips, testimony, and documentary evidence delivered through a high-definition laser disk player or simple PowerPoint presentations. In either event, well-designed presentations can be devastatingly effective. Sadly, many are not.

If you are going to rely on multimedia presentations, you need to learn the basics of multimedia design. The mechanics of preparing a presentation are simple. Most slide-based programs, like PowerPoint, are easily learned. But to be effective, you need to understand how a presentation should be organized and how information is best displayed.*

Claims consultants know the value of multimedia. Many can prepare complex presentations and will do so for their own subject area, or for the testimony of others. If you have never prepared a complete presentation, you should work with a presentation expert before developing your own.

TESTIMONY IN COURT AND AT DEPOSITION

The investigation, research, and analysis come together when the expert testifies. An expert who can testify well is very effective—and rarely short of work! This section summarizes observations about good testifying experts.

Preparation

The good expert is prepared and never surprised. The expert should be conversant with all the key data, should know the references cited, and should be able to discuss the weaknesses of his or her opinion as well as its strengths.

---

*The many skills necessary for good multimedia presentations are not described in any single text. However, Professor Edward Tufte's books *The Visual Display of Quantitative Information* and *Envisioning Information* are invaluable sources. Both are available from Graphic Press.

Preparation should include the substance and mechanics of testimony. Before you testify, practice what you are going to say when directly examined and how you will respond to likely cross-examination. By practicing direct and cross-examination you will be comfortable when testifying and will be perceived as a credible witness. If you are nervous and stumble during testimony, the judge and jury may doubt your ability and conviction.

Presentations should also be practiced before an audience—preferably of persons who do not know the case. You should ask them what was unclear, what they had trouble understanding, and what they did not believe. You should use their criticisms to fine-tune the presentation until your audience understands what your opinion is and why you believe that opinion is correct.

Demeanor

Be yourself. Even professional actors have difficulty portraying people greatly different from themselves—amateurs should not even try. If a judge or jury members do not believe in you as a person, they will not believe your opinions as an expert.

There are, however, a few basic rules regarding demeanor.

First, don't be argumentative. An expert is supposed to be independent (even if paid by a party) and should appear neutral while testifying. The substance of your testimony should be the key feature, not the volume.

Second, don't be demeaning or condescending. Many experts have the apparent attitude that they know more than any other expert does and much more than the judge and jury. Even if this is true, it is poor strategy to insult the persons controlling the ultimate outcome.

Third, be frank. There is very little time available during a trial. The judge and jury don't want you to waste their time. If you have an opinion, don't hide it in caveats and obfuscations. Just say it.

Fourth, be helpful. Try to see the issue from the judge and jury's point of view. Try to see where they may be confused and put extra effort into that portion of the presentation.

Fifth, be respectful. If you treat the judge and jury with respect, the respect will be returned.

Dress   Your dress should be appropriate for the occasion. In court, you should wear a good business suit, or at least a sport coat and tie. For mediations and arbitrations, you can be less formal although your dress should still be conservative and in good taste.

You do not want your dress to detract from your opinions. The author recalls a well-qualified expert who wore his hair in an unusual style. Weeks after his presentation, no one could remember the details of his opinions, but everyone remembered his hair. If you have any questions concerning the appropriateness of your dress, discuss them with the retaining attorney or someone you trust to give frank advice.

Speech

Speak plainly. Technical jargon is a convenient way for experts to exchange information quickly. But it assumes a common understanding of the technical terms. To the uninitiated, technical jargon confuses and builds a wall between the expert and the audience. If the expert wanted the audience to understand, the audience reasons, he or she would have expressed the opinion in nontechnical terms. In extreme cases, the audience may infer that the expert is using technical jargon to deliberately hide weaknesses in an argument. When practicing a presentation, ask your audience what terms they did not understand and rephrase that portion of your presentation.

Speak clearly. When people get excited, they speak quickly and in higher tones. Both impair listening. When speaking publicly, speak at a pace that seems excessively slow—and then pause often for emphasis. Not only will your testimony be easily heard, but also the slower pace will give you time to phrase your thoughts more clearly.

Direct Examination

Direct examination is your opportunity to tell your story in your own way. The questioning attorney will ask open-ended questions (what, why, how, etc.) that will prompt you to explain your opinions. If you have prepared properly, you should know what questions will be asked and should have carefully considered your responses. Because you can control direct examination, it is the best time to integrate multimedia aids.

Cross-Examination

The objective of cross-examinations is quite different. Skillful cross-examination tries to obtain your agreement to key facts supporting the opponent's view of the case, or to suggest, by the questions themselves, the opposing party's principal arguments. The cross-examiner can use "leading" questions that state the answer and only seek your agreement. Commonly leading questions follow a form such as "Isn't it true that..." or "Wouldn't you agree that..." In a properly crafted leading question, the only proper answer is yes or no. But if you believe your answer needs explanation, give one. For example, stating "No, but may I explain?" will usually force the attorney to allow you to place your answer in context. If he or she does not, the jury will conclude that the attorney is more interested in playing games than in uncovering the truth.

Because the opposing attorney often seems bent on picking apart an opinion, many experts become quite aggressive in arguing back. This is usually an error. An expert who argues loses the appearance of neutrality and undermines his or her opinion. To achieve this may have been the primary objective of the cross-examination.

CLOSURE

Expert consultants and witnesses have a tremendous responsibility to oversee the quality of services provided by our profession to the public. This responsibility must be taken very seriously and executed with fairness and objectivity and in the highest ethical manner. The manner with which we fulfill our responsibilities in this regard will determine how our profession is perceived by our clients and by the public in general.

CHAPTER 10

LOADS AND HAZARDS: THEIR NATURE, MAGNITUDE, AND CONSEQUENCES

Donald O. Dusenberry, P.E.

INTRODUCTION

Every engineer knows that there are "two sides to the equation." One side repre-sents the resistance characteristics of a structure, and the other side represents the applied loads. In the evaluation of a nonperformance or failure, a thorough investigation must reveal the facts concerning both sides so that the investigator can weigh the merits of competing failure theories. Ultimately, the investigator must be sufficiently convinced to rule out improbable causes and to develop defensible opinions about the true reasons for a failure. Then the investigator must be able to convince a body of skeptics under aggressive challenge by parties who feel harmed by those opinions. This effort necessarily involves critical analyses of the loading history for a failed structure.

The investigator should start with loads on the structure at the time of the failure. These loads, which can be generated by gravity, wind, seismic events, and several other causes, are the most obvious potential contributors to a failure. However, often an investigator must assess whether loads other than those on the structure at the time of failure are relevant to the investigation. Sometimes a structure's prior load history contains events or circumstances that affect the ability of the structure to survive a subsequent extreme event. Cyclic loads can cause fatigue damage. A single overload can weaken a connection or cause other inconspicuous damage without leading to obvious or immediate failure. When such damage occurs, it might lead to a later failure that otherwise would not have occurred.

Often it is a challenge to determine the loads on a structure at the moment of failure. Building components and contents can be in disarray in a debris pile. Wind storms and earthquakes obviously have passed by the time investigators arrive at a site. Even snow loads often are hard to assess, since they can vary widely even over relatively small roofs. Furthermore, snow and ice often melt and rain dissipates before investigators can collect important data.

When the loads on a structure cannot be measured directly, the investigator often needs to conduct substantial research, interrogation, and analyses to estimate—sometimes from circumstantial evidence—the loads that most probably affected the structure at the critical times. In addition to being theoreticians, investigators are detectives: They must be observant and resourceful as they analyze the debris for clues about the failed structure's loading history.

The purpose of this chapter is to present some issues that an investigator should consider when evaluating loads on structures that have failed. Some guidance is given to assist the investigator during calculations of loads. For detailed analytical procedures, the investigator should refer to the references listed at the end of this chapter and to other authoritative references on loads and load effects.

GRAVITY LOADS

Nature and Consequences of Gravity Loads

Gravity loads result from the weights of structures and their contents. Normally such loads are classified as dead (fixed weight of the structure), live (variable loads resulting from the use of the structure), snow, ice, or rain. In addition, live loads, sliding snow or ice, bulk materials handling, and any other moving load have the potential to impose impact loads that can magnify the load effect on the structure.

While gravity loads normally create no net horizontal loads on a structure, they can generate horizontal forces in individual members and at the foundation level. An example is a rigid-frame structure that experiences balanced horizontal thrusts at opposite footings as it resists vertical loads on its horizontal or inclined members. Gravity loads also can generate horizontal loads when sliding snow strikes a surface with significant horizontal velocity. In this case, the horizontal load is a transient that imparts momentum that must be arrested by the structure for it to survive.

Gravity loads can cause overstresses and instabilities in structural elements and connections (Fig. 10.1), overall structural instability, and foundation settlement.

Determination of Gravity Loads

The best way to obtain reliable information about gravity loads on a structure is through direct measurement. When possible and practical for an investigation, objects on a structure at the time of a failure should be extracted and weighed.

FIGURE 10.1 Collapse of L'Ambiance Plaza, Bridgeport, Connecticut, 1987. (*Credit: D. Dusenberry, Simpson Gumpertz & Heger Inc.*)

Then, to the extent that their locations on the structure can be determined after the failure, the influence of measured weights can be calculated with high reliability.

When it is not practical or possible to weight loads directly, their magnitudes must be estimated from geometric data collected at the site, or from circumstantial evidence that may be used to infer the loads that may have been present.

In some cases, the weights on a structure can be estimated with sufficient accuracy by measuring or estimating the volume of each material in the area of interest and relying on standard tables[1,2] of unit weights to calculate the weights of each component and the total weight on a structure. This approach may be appropriate for rough estimates of weights for early evaluation of the significance of gravity loads to the causes of a failure.

Dead Loads.   The first place to look for estimates of the weight of the structure itself is the construction documents used to construct the building. When you use this resource, be certain to assess conditions that may have changed during construction and those changes that might have been made after the building was finished. It is common for building alterations to change the weights. Over the life of a building, its roof may be replaced several times. Since different roofing systems have different unit weights, such common alterations can increase or decrease weight. Sometimes curtain wall systems change, or new flooring materials are added. Each of these changes can affect loads on a building frame.

Even when it can be established that the original construction was not altered, often it is insufficient to rely on construction documents to estimate volumes of structural materials in a building. Standards of practice for installation of construction materials acknowledge that variations in material quantities are unavoidable, and allow for deviations from specified design dimensions. For instance, a concrete slab designed to be 4 in thick and built within tolerance can be $4^3/_8$ in thick.[3] With this acceptable variation from the intended dimensions, the deadweight of a slab can be more than 9 percent higher than is normally used for design. Further, deviations exceeding those allowed by normal standards of care should be investigated whenever gravity loads are suspected to have contributed to a failure. Through variations in care during concrete placement or due to structural deformations that occur during installation of wet concrete, it is not uncommon for concrete floor slabs to vary from the specified thickness by 20 percent or more in local areas—particularly near the middle of slabs cast on potentially flexible structural elements such as open-web joists.

When appropriate for forensic analyses, samples of each material or building component should be taken to determine the actual unit weight. Then, with precise measurements of volume, accurate estimates of total weight are possible. When the greatest accuracy is required, all materials associated with a failure should be collected and weighed, if such effort is feasible. Care must be given to include all materials, and only those materials, affecting the structure at the time of the collapse. Further, to the extent possible, the location of all materials at the time of the failure should be established and recorded for analysis.

Live Loads.   Loads that are derived from the use of the building normally vary with time. As such, it is difficult to conduct anything but the most rudimentary estimates of the live load on a structure at any particular time without an on-site survey. Usually live loads must be established through a thorough inventory of the debris.

For loads that are derived from solid materials, accurate inventories often are possible. However, after a major failure it is difficult usually to relate objects to specific locations in the building. The substantial disruption that a major failure causes obscures much reliable evidence about the arrangement of building contents. This problem often is complicated further by rescue operations, which justifiably are not directed toward preservation of evidence for investigations.

Sometimes the most reliable information about live loads is established by interviewing persons familiar with the use of the building. The recollections of witnesses, while often imperfect, should be considered a useful resource.

Snow, Rain, and Ice Loads.   The weights of snow, rain, and ice (and other fluids) often are difficult to assess. Melting, dissipation, evaporation, and additional precipitation after a failure can obscure the amount of fluids supported by a structure at the time of failure.

It is important always to search for records of precipitation in the vicinity of the failure site. Such data often can be obtained in the United States from the National Climatic Data Center.[4] In addition, local airports, television and radio stations, colleges and universities, municipal public safety agencies, departments of public works, and hobbyists sometimes accumulate data on precipitation. The National Climatic Data Center and some other data-recording entities sometimes maintain continuous records of ground snow accumulation, which often is more important than the amount of precipitation that fell during a single storm immediately before a failure. In all cases, the accuracy and applicability of data accumulated off site and by entities that are not universally acknowledged as reliable should be accepted only with consideration and evaluation of the potential of error.

Data that are collected off site often must be adjusted to account for differences in conditions at the location of data acquisition compared to those at the site of the failure. Storms often deposit precipitation that varies significantly, even within small local regions. In addition, a building's proximity to hills, trees, wooded areas, and other buildings can affect snow and ice accumulation. If wind is channeled by terrain or nearby construction, the resulting locally high wind speed might sweep snow from its path. Likewise, a sudden decrease in wind speed and associated turbulence, such as might occur at the edge of a roof, can cause drifting on lower surfaces (Figs. 10.2 and 10.3). Snow accumulation on a roof often is less than that on the adjacent ground because heat from within a building can melt snow as it falls. As long as the melt water is able to flow from the roof, the effective weight of snow on a heated roof generally will be less than that on an unheated surface (Fig. 10.4).

Sometimes snow and ice can be weighed accurately if measurements are made soon after a failure and before significant melting has occurred. A relatively simple way to determine the weight of snow is to extract a measured volume of a column of snow from the structure and weigh it as snow, or later as water after it has melted. A 6- or 8-in-diameter stovepipe driven into the snow effectively isolates a sample for weighing. Care should be taken to obtain a sample of the full depth of the snow, since compaction, melting (sometimes from the bottom up on heated structures), or accumulation at different times can cause the density of snow to vary with depth from the snow surface.

Often snow on a failed structure is too disrupted to be weighed reliably. In these cases, it might be possible to measure snow on an adjacent surviving portion of the structure, or on the ground near the structure. Frequently, a scarp remains on snow at the edge of a collapse. Depth measurements and samples can be extracted at such locations. However, before any measurements made away from the actual failure location can be used with confidence, the investigator must assess whether differences in exposure, drifting characteristics, heating and melting, or other factors affect the reliability of such measurements.

Ice weight is best evaluated by determining the surface area over which ice accumulated and estimating the surface load by one of two means: (1) measuring the ice thickness at several locations and (2) weighing an ice-covered object before and after the ice melts.

FIGURE 10.2 Roof failure due to drifting snow, Seaboard Building, Danvers, Massachusetts. (*Credit: C. Russo, Simpson Gumpertz & Heger Inc.*)

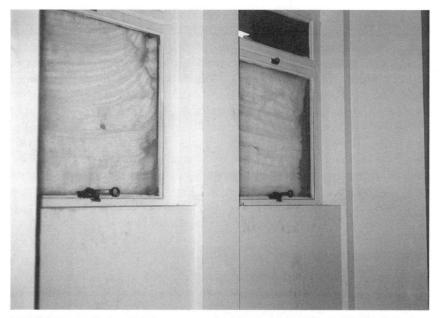

FIGURE 10.3 Drifting and sliding snow accumulation outside windows. (*Credit: N. Vigener, Simpson Gumpertz & Heger Inc.*)

FIGURE 10.4 Roof failure of unheated skating rink, Durham, New Hampshire. (*Credit: D. Dusenberry, Simpson Gumpertz & Heger Inc.*)

Usually, rain load is transient, with a duration similar to the length of a storm. As such, the determination of the weight of rain frequently requires hydraulic flow rate calculations based on the rate of precipitation and rate of draining from surfaces. Consideration should be given to the possibility that drains were obstructed or, especially in the case of rain on snow, that flow to drains was inhibited during a storm. Furthermore, on relatively flat roofs with flexible structural systems, the potential for ponding should be evaluated.

Liquids in containers, granular solids, and other bulk materials that are handled or conveyed in structures require special analyses. Handling loads and membrane stresses in bins, containers, and tanks are functions of the methods for handling, filling, and emptying and of the bulk properties of the material. Impact and vibratory loads commonly result from handling. For fluids, it is possible that rapid drawdown of a tank can cause negative pressure inside the tank. Volatile materials and materials subject to heating and cooling can cause pressure changes in closed vessels.

WIND LOADS

Nature and Consequences of Wind Loads

In general, wind pressures are derived from the effects of a moving stream of air passing an object. Wind pressures generally originate either from the inertial effects caused by the impediment that an object in the stream creates to the flow of air or as Bernoulli pressures caused by the flow of a fluid over a surface. Depending on the orientation of the loaded surface to the direction of the wind, the pressures are characterized as either drag forces that cause loads parallel to the direction of the wind or lift forces that cause loads transverse to the direction of the wind. In all cases, wind loads act essentially perpendicular to the surface on which pressures are exerted.

Lift forces can be either vertical or horizontal, depending on whether the surface exposed to wind pressures is horizontal or vertical. In general, lift forces on the exterior surface are suction, acting outward, due to reductions in pressure that are associated with the moving mass of air. As such, the general field of walls and other surfaces that face the oncoming wind is subjected to inward, positive pressures due to inertial forces, whereas walls that are oriented parallel to the direction of wind, low-sloped roofs, and the leeward walls of buildings experience outward, suction pressures. With increasing roof slope, and in walls that are oblique to the direction of the wind, positive, inward pressures occur as well.

The total load due to wind on an object is the net of the forces due to pressures on all surfaces. Therefore, a component of a building's exterior cladding will respond to pressure differentials between its inside surface and its outside surface, whereas a building in its entirety will respond to pressure differentials that exist between windward and leeward faces, and between opposite wall surfaces that are oriented parallel to the direction of wind.

The most common form of wind damage in buildings is failure of components of the building envelope and collateral damage that results from intrusion of rain that often accompanies wind storms.[5-7] Envelope damage often takes the form of glazing or roofing failures (Figs. 10.5 and 10.6) or failure or damage to cladding systems. Roofing failures are common when ballast or mechanical fasteners that restrain roofing materials are insufficient to resist suction loads caused by wind moving over horizontal or inclined roofs. It is most common for building envelope components to fail first near building and roof edges (Figs. 10.7 and 10.8). Turbulence and vortices caused by building edges increase pressures locally. In addition, the wind speed at edges usually exceeds that of the approaching wind because air accelerates as it takes a longer path to move around the building.

Except in extreme cases, glass usually has sufficient strength to resist the direct pressures that are caused by wind. Glazing failures are most common near grade level where airborne debris lifted by severe winds can become missiles (Fig. 10.9) that impact brittle and relatively weak glass.

Another form of collateral damage due to failure of glazing or other components of the building envelope occurs as wind pressure differentials change. During a wind storm, the interior of an enclosed building will be pressurized at a level that is dependent on the relative air permeability of the various surfaces

FIGURE 10.5 Roof damage to metal-framed building, Dickingen bei Stuttgart, Germany. (*Credit: Kaiser Aluminum/Prussag Aluminum.*)

FIGURE 10.6   Roof damage to wood-framed building, Hurricane Andrew. (*Credit: L. Morse-Fortier, Simpson Gumpertz & Heger Inc.*)

exposed to wind pressures. For instance, if there are relatively few openings and other incidental paths for air exchange through the windward face compared to the other surfaces of the building, then the interior of a building will be at negative pressure relative to the ambient pressure. This occurs because suction caused by air moving past openings—large and small—on sidewalls and leeward walls will reduce the pressure inside the building.

Since the net effect on a building component is the difference between pressures on opposite surfaces, negative pressure inside a building will increase the total demand on windward surfaces. On these surfaces, interior and exterior pressures

FIGURE 10.7   Wall cladding failure near corner of wood-framed building. (*Credit: Department of Civil Engineering, Clemson University.*)

FIGURE 10.8   Roofing failure near edge of building, Kodiak, Alaska. (*Credit: R. Schroter, Simpson Gumpertz & Heger Inc.*)

FIGURE 10.9 Airborne missile damage to siding, Hurricane Andrew. (*Credit: R. Schroter, Simpson Gumpertz & Heger Inc.*)

are additive. Interior negative pressures generally diminish demand on all other surfaces where outside pressures usually are negative. The condition changes when windows or curtain walls on the windward face are damaged by airborne debris. Normally such damage will substantially increase the size and influence of openings on the positively pressurized windward face relative to openings on building surfaces with negative pressures. Consequently, the interior of the building will be raised to net positive pressure relative to ambient pressure. Then interior and exterior pressures become additive on the leeward wall, sidewalls, and the roof, adding to the potential that components of these surfaces will be damaged.

It is rare that engineered buildings experience severe damage or collapse of the main wind-resisting systems that support the building against lateral loads. Several factors contribute to the relative success that these systems enjoy compared to component systems. First, design procedures that are associated with design standards normally contain conservative simplifying assumptions that allow designers to deal with the very complicated and uncertain wind environment and pressures which normally occur on buildings. This adds a measure of reserve to the strength of buildings that are designed conventionally. Second, designers normally ignore the substantial, but uncertain, wind-resisting strengths that are offered by building frames and components that are not part of the designed lateral load systems. In particular, frames that are not braced or designed as moment frames, and frames that are in buildings with shear walls that are assumed to resist lateral loads, have substantial strengths that designers usually ignore. Also, incidental building components, such as exterior curtain walls and interior partitions, have resistances that are disregarded in conventional design. To the extent that these circumstantial strengths are not considered during design, they become strength reserves that help the designed force-resisting systems respond in extreme wind events. Finally, it is often the building envelope system that fails first (Fig. 10.10). As this happens and surfaces that receive wind pressures are removed from a building, the overall forces on the building diminish and the demand on the main force-resisting system is reduced.

When main force-resisting systems of engineered buildings do fail, often it is the result of structural modifications or deterioration that occurs over time. Obviously, if important components of the main force-resisting system are compromised, the potential for failure under extreme loadings is significant. Main force-resisting systems also fail in tornadoes, usually because conventional design of common buildings that are not shelters usually acknowledges that the probability that a tornado will strike a particular building is very low. Consequently, designers usually disregard wind velocities and rapid pressure changes associated with tornadoes. At wind speeds typically between 150 mi/h (67 m/s) and 250 mi/h (112 m/s) and with rapid changes in air pressures, tornadoes can cause pressures on components and structures to exceed normal design pressures by severalfold (Fig. 10.11).

Occasionally, high winds cause main force-resisting systems to fail in buildings that are not specifically designed for lateral loads. For instance, wind pressures can

FIGURE 10.10   Metal roof removed by Hurricane Andrew. (*Credit: R. Schroter, Simpson Gumpertz & Heger Inc.*)

FIGURE 10.11   Tornado damage to school, Lancaster, Texas. (*Credit: J. Ceruti, Simpson Gumpertz & Heger Inc.*)

exceed resistances of conventionally framed wood buildings (Fig. 10.12), especially when the buildings are constructed with minimal connections. Even with inadequate main force-resisting systems, such buildings usually fail first by components, because these individual elements also have insufficient strength to resist applied pressures.

Building systems can respond dynamically to wind loads. Certainly, if frequencies in the wind speed spectrum excite structural frequencies, dynamic amplification can occur. Additional dynamic responses, called *aeroelastic phenomena,* also are possible for flexible structures. These phenomena are divided into three major categories: galloping, vortex-shedding excitation, and flutter.

Galloping instability occurs when the aerodynamic damping of an asymmetric body is negative and exceeds, in absolute magnitude, the mechanical damping of a structural system. Power transmission lines sometimes oscillate transverse to the wind due to this phenomenon if they have an asymmetric accumulation of ice (cylindrical bodies cannot gallop). Vortex-shedding excitation is transverse oscillation that occurs when slender bodies, such as chimneys, alternately shed vortices of wind from opposite surfaces at a frequency that is near to a natural frequency of the structure. In these case, the frequency of the pressure changes that are associated with the turbulence of the vortices "locks in" with the frequency of the structure, and the structure is forced in a transverse direction at its natural frequency. Flutter normally occurs when two degrees of body motion, such as rota-

FIGURE 10.12   Collapse of wood-framed building, Hurricane Andrew. (*Credit: L. Morse-Fortier, Simpson Gumpertz & Heger Inc.*)

tion and transverse movement, couple in the wind stream. Flutter is the phenomenon that causes street signs on single, torsionally flexible posts to twist violently in strong winds. Flutter also causes flags (and sometimes fabric structures) to wave in the wind.

Determination of Wind Forces

Wind forces on structures can be determined by analytical and experimental procedures. However, before reliable calculations can be made, it is necessary to establish the wind environment at the site of an investigation. Relevant information includes wind speed and direction, "gustiness," and storm duration. Most major airports maintain reliable anemometers. Also research facilities, such as colleges and universities, and public safety and disaster response facilities sometimes maintain anemometers and record useful data. In general, facilities that record and report data to the National Climatic Data Center should be consulted first about conditions during a particular storm.

Often, reliable data at a particular site are not available readily. The nearest reliable anemometers often are far from a site of interest. Furthermore, the wind environment in a storm often is highly variable, with gustiness and local wind cells that cause speeds to differ over relatively short distances. This may be particularly true in thunderstorms which can be very severe, but highly localized. It is possible for winds during a thunderstorm to be extreme at a site when, a short distance away, official records indicate nothing unusual.

Sometimes, circumstantial evidence, such as the general extent of damage to trees and structures in the vicinity of a site under investigation and at the location where data were recorded, will help to assess what appear to be major discrepancies between recorded data and observed conditions. The Beaufort scale (Table 10.1) (adapted from Ref. 8) is helpful for estimating site wind speeds based on nearby physical damage and eyewitness accounts.

Care must be taken when interpreting data from any source. The standard currently used for design of structures is based on a particular storm return period (usually 50 years) for the maximum 3-s gust wind speed measured at 32.8 ft (10 m) above grade. Other time-averaging wind speeds, including the fastest mile, the 60-s gust, and the mean hourly wind speed, sometimes are recorded at wind monitoring stations. The fastest-mile wind speed is determined essentially by measuring the time necessary for a column of air 1 mi long to pass a recording station. The 60-s gust wind speed is the average speed of the wind during a 1-min interval. Averaged over 1 min, a wind with a speed of 60 mi/h (26.8 m/s) will have the same fastest-mile and 60-s gust speeds. The mean hourly wind speed is the average wind speed recorded over a period of 1 h.

TABLE 10.1   The Beaufort Scale

No.	Beaufort description	Speed mi/h	Speed m/s	Land effect
0	Calm	Under 1	Under 0.4	Smoke rises straight up
1	Light air	1–3		Direction shown by smoke drift
2	Light breeze	4–7	1.8–3.1	Wind felt on face: leaves rustle
3	Gentle breeze	8–12	3.6–5.4	Leaves in constant motion; wind extends light flag
4	Moderate breeze	13–18	5.8–8.0	Raises dust and loose paper; small branches move
5	Fresh breeze	19–24	8.5–11	Small trees in leaf begin to sway
6	Strong breeze	25–31	11–14	Large branches in motion, whistling of telegraph wires
7	Moderate gale	32–38	14–17	Whole tree in motion; difficulty in walking
8	Fresh gale	39–46	17–21	Breaks twigs off trees
9	Strong gale	47–54	21–24	Some damage to vegetation and structures
10	Whole gale	55–63	25–28	Trees uprooted; considerable damage
11	Storm	64–75	29–34	Widespread damage
12	Hurricane	Over 75	Over 34	

Source: Adapted from Ref. 8.

Typically, the 3-s gust wind speed will be higher than the fastest-mile, 60-s gust, and mean hourly wind speeds measured in the same wind. Shorter time-averaging periods are more likely to represent the highest pressures associated with the gustiness of extreme winds. Based on the statistics of the wind environment, there are relatively constant relationships among the wind speeds recorded by these methods. The theoretical ratios of the probable maximum wind speeds for various averaging periods to the probable maximum wind speed averaged over 1 h are plotted in Fig. 10.13. This figure may be used to convert among the different wind speed–recording methods. However, since the adjustment to convert among different averaging periods often is complicated by the nature of the storm and other factors, sometimes it is prudent to consult with wind engineers or meteorologists. For instance, note that the probable wind speed ratios at shorter recording intervals compared to longer intervals are higher for hurricanes than for nonhurricane storms. This follows from high gustiness normally associated with hurricanes.

Adjustments also need to be made for the height that the recording anemometer is mounted above the ground. If the anemometer is not at the standard height of 32.8 ft (10 m), the data should be calibrated to standard conditions. Calibrations are performed using the ratio of the height of interest to the

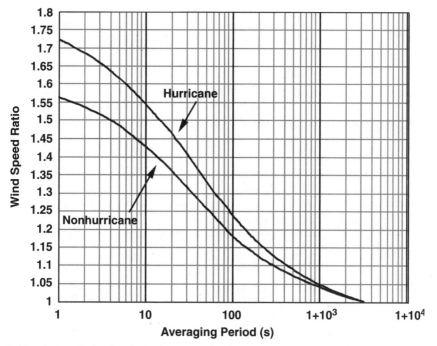

FIGURE 10.13   Ratio of probable maximum speed averaged over t seconds to hourly mean speed. (*Credit: Adapted from Ref. 1.*)

"gradient height," normally 700 ft (213 m) to 1500 ft (457 m) above ground,[1,9] above which wind speed is assumed to be constant with height. The value of an exponent that is applied to this ratio is a function of the terrain for 0.5 to 1 mi (0.8 to 1.61 km) upwind from the point of interest.

The 3-s gust wind speed over open land, where the "surface roughness" is small, normally is taken to vary with height above ground according to the height ratio raised to the power of 1/9.5.[1,9] Over water, which offers very little surface roughness, speed normally is assumed to vary with an exponent of 1/11.5 on the height ratio.[1,9] Therefore, wind approaching over a large body of water will create higher wind speeds near ground than will wind that approaches over land. Of course, the nearer to ground that one wishes to approximate the wind speed, the less accurate will be any conversion or extrapolation.

When there is little surface roughness, uniform wind speed is achieved relatively near to the ground. Therefore, over open terrain and water, the gradient height is nearer to the lower end of the height range. The gradient height may be taken as approximately 700 ft (213 m) over water and 900 ft (274 m) over open land.[1,9]

Severe local terrain and the built environment near a particular site will have a significant impact on wind speeds near the ground. The wooded environment and suburban community development effectively slow the near-ground wind speed for most building heights. For these conditions, the exponent for the height ratio normally is taken in the range of 1/7,[1,9] and the gradient height, at 1200 ft (366 m), is near to the high end of the range. For the most developed urban environments, the exponent can be as large as 1/5, and the gradient height can be at 1500 ft (457 m).[1,9]

In cities with tall buildings, conditions near ground are influenced not only by the general surface roughness of the suburban areas, urban areas, or water that surrounds the city, but also by the extensive cityscape of the area itself. The urban development effectively increases the nearby surface roughness, which tends to decrease wind speeds near to the ground. However, the arrangement of buildings in cities, with streets and squares that connect and tend to align, often will channel winds into streams that pass along ground level at speeds that exceed the average speed of the approaching wind. In addition, in cities with tall buildings and other broad and tall features, there can be shielding offered by upwind structures, or buffeting by vortices shed by such structures.

As such, individual buildings in city centers can feel reduced or magnified wind pressures, depending on the cityscape for up to 1 mi (1.61 km) in any direction, and depending on the direction of the approaching wind. Needless to say, it is very difficult to estimate actual wind speeds adjacent to buildings in city centers. Investigators dealing with very hilly terrain face similar difficulties.

Analytical Approaches

Wind Speed Adjustment. The analytical approach for calculation of wind pressures during a storm usually starts with the calculation of the basic wind pressure that corresponds to the 3-s gust wind speed at the standard height of 32.8 ft (10 m) above ground. Wind speed data averaged over time intervals other than 3 s should be converted before subsequent calculations are performed. When the speed is measured at nonstandard height, or when the terrain upwind of the measurement location differs from that upwind of the site of interest, wind speed should be adjusted for these differences.

Figure 10.13 can be used to adjust wind speed averaging effects. To account for height and exposure, the wind speed at the measured height, together with the proper gradient height and exponent on the height ratio determined for the recording site, should be used to calculate the wind speed at the gradient height. The wind speed thus calculated at the gradient height then can be used with the gradient height and exponent appropriate for the environment at the investigation site, to calculate the wind speeds at various heights on a structure.

This basic wind pressure is then determined[1,10] by the formula

$$q_z = 0.00256 \, V_z^2 \text{ lb/ft}^2 \qquad (q_z = 0.613 \, V_z^2 \text{ N/m}^2)$$

where V_z is the calculated wind speed, as a function of height, in miles per hour (meters per second) at the site. The coefficient in this formula is based on the mass density of air under standard conditions of temperature and pressure. For conditions that differ significantly from standard conditions—69°F (15°C) at 29.92 in of mercury (101.325 kPa)—the coefficient should be adjusted by the ratio of the mass density of air at the site to that of air at standard conditions.

When more accurate data are not available, wind speeds below approximately 15 ft (4.5 m) should be taken as constant and equal to the wind speed at 15 ft (4.5 m).

For structures or wind data recording sites that are located near the tops of hills or escarpments, wind pressures should be adjusted for wind speed-up that occurs over the windward slope, and which diminishes down the leeward slope and with distance beyond an escarpment. These topological features act, in a sense, as airfoils in moving air masses. Winds that approach an incline must accelerate to pass up and over the crest. In so doing, wind speeds near the crest exceed speeds at similar heights above level ground.

One approach for adjusting wind pressures for hills and escarpments is found in ASCE 7-98.[1] [Older references on wind loads (Ref. 11 and its predecessors) generally referenced the fastest-mile wind speed. Investigators must not use wind pressure coefficients that do not correlate with reference wind speeds.] This method gives coefficients, calculated based on the geometry and size of the topological feature, that are applied to the pressures calculated as above from wind velocities. According to this procedure, wind pressure adjustments are needed for structures located above the midheight of "steep" hills or escarpments when the topological feature exceeds certain heights, ranging from 15 ft (4.5 m) near open water to 60 ft (18 m) for urban areas. A "steep" feature is one with the ratio of the horizontal dimension to vertical dimension of the upper half of the windward slope of less than 5.

It should be obvious that significant inaccuracies and uncertainties will result whenever the wind speed at a specific site is estimated from wind speeds recorded elsewhere. Each adjustment factor used in the process includes some uncertainty. When several are applied in the calculation, the uncertainty increases. Furthermore, some of the adjustment factors are applied to wind speed, a term that is squared for the calculation of wind pressure.

To address these uncertainties, the investigator should obtain and analyze wind speed data from as many nearby reliable sources as reasonably possible. With multiple, independent paths to the determination of basic wind pressures at a site, the investigator will improve confidence in the values to be used to calculate surface pressures on a structure.

Pressure Calculations. ASCE 7-98[1] contains an authoritative procedure for using the basic wind pressure calculated for the local wind speed to calculate the wind pressures on various surfaces of a building. The procedure involves the application of coefficients to the basic wind pressures to estimate actual pressures at all locations on a structure. The procedure has been developed to provide engineers with guidance on wind pressures that may be used for the design of structures. As such, there are elements of conservatism in the approach as well as significant simplifications of the complicated phenomena of airflow around objects. Furthermore, pressure coefficients used in common design procedures generally represent the worst-case "enveloped" pressure distributions, considering that wind can approach a structure from any direction. Therefore, any set of pressure coefficients intended to be used for design likely includes coefficients that do not, in any way, represent the pressure distributions on some surfaces for specific storms with wind that approaches from specific directions. Investigators need to evaluate carefully how best to employ coefficients intended for design, considering these potential shortcomings in the applicability of these coefficients for the investigation of specific wind-related problems.

In analytical approaches, loads on the overall building systems that resist lateral loads (e.g., braced frames, moment frames, or shear walls) are calculated using coefficients that are applied to the basic wind pressures to determine wind pressures on windward and leeward faces of a structure. When buildings have sloped roofs, horizontal components of the wind forces of these elements need to be considered.

It is important to consider the possibility that nonsymmetric buildings, particularly those with curved surfaces, will have unbalanced transverse wind loads. A curved exterior wall can act as an airfoil during a storm, thereby generating larger suction pressures than flat surfaces will. In these cases, there can be a net transverse force on the building as a whole due to wind.

Wind pressures on components of buildings can be calculated based on tabulated factors as well. For these elements, effective pressures usually are larger than those for the overall building system because components respond to shorter-duration, higher-intensity gusts than do complete buildings. Also, spatial averaging of time-varying pressures over the relatively small areas of components as compared to entire structures results in higher effective pressures for components.

Components need to be evaluated for net pressures, considering both internal and external pressures. Depending on the relative air permeability of the several layers of a particular roof or the wythes of a wall, one layer or wythe may support essentially all the differential pressure, or several layers or wythes may share load. One layer might support most of the load if it is relatively airtight and the other layers of the system are permeable. In this case, pressure in internal voids in the system will tend to equalize pressure on the opposite side of the wall surface that is permeable, causing essentially all the net pressure difference to be supported by the impermeable layer. If both layers are relatively impermeable, the air pressure in interior voids will be relatively unaffected by rapid pressure changes on either exterior surface. As such, the air in the void will tend to transmit movement of one layer to the other, and both impermeable layers will share the total differential pressure.

Structural components near edges of buildings have higher wind pressure factors than do components located in the field of a building surface to account for wind speed-up, wind separation, and vortices that develop as wind passes over the sudden geometric changes of a building edge.

Special consideration needs to be given to buildings that have a disproportionate open area on one wall. These buildings have unusual interior pressurization, because wind on an open windward wall can cause positive stagnation pressures inside the building. Conversely, a disproportionate area of openings on a sidewall or leeward wall can increase negative interior pressures. Canopies, overhangs, and alcoves have similar wind load characteristics.

Frames that are fully open, signs, chimneys, and other linear structures must be evaluated on an element-by-element basis. Loads can be calculated from drag factors that have been determined theoretically or by testing.[1,12–15] In linear structures with relatively dense and repeating patterns of elements (e.g., laced members), allowance should be made for shielding that windward elements provide for leeward elements.[12,14] For shielding to occur, there must be regularity of the member patterns and the along-wind distance between planes of similar geometry must be relatively short. However, care must be used when evaluating the potential that shielding reduces the total load on a structure. Small angles of attack between the wind and the normal to the structural plane can eliminate the potential for one plane to shield another. In these cases, wind loads often can be calculated as the sum of the loads on all members subjected to wind.

Analyses of aeroelastic phenomena usually should follow detailed review of available literature. Useful approaches and thorough bibliographies are contained in Refs. 10 and 16.

Wind Tunnel Studies.   Without question, the best way to estimate surface pressures and wind speed distributions in the vicinity of structures, particularly in urban environments and with irregularly shaped structures, is through wind tunnel studies. Wind tunnel studies, if properly designed and executed, can account accurately for the effects of general surface roughness over the fetch and specific buildings upwind and immediately adjacent to a site. In addition, wind tunnel studies perhaps are the only way currently available to estimate the dynamic response of low-frequency (less than 1-Hz primary frequency) structures that are not of the simplest prismatic shapes.

Properly designed and executed wind tunnel studies can model irregular building shapes that are difficult to analyze otherwise for local pressures on walls and roofs, and buffeting by vortices shed by upwind features, channeling of winds, across-wind effects, periodic loads due to vortex shedding from the structure of interest, flutter and galloping instabilities, and complicated torsional loads.

Properly designed and executed wind tunnel studies can be substantially more reliable than analytical approaches.

To be suitable for such studies, boundary-layer wind tunnels and their models should be constructed and operated to properly represent the atmospheric boundary-layer wind profile with height, and the modeled building and surrounding structures and features must be represented in relative detail and to scale. The macro and micro length scales of the atmospheric turbulence must be modeled to approximately the same scale as the physical model; and the longitudinal pressure gradient that exists in the tunnel, but not necessarily in the actual wind environment, must be considered when collecting and analyzing data. It is best to minimize the Reynolds number effects on pressures and forces. Also, the response characteristics of the pressure-sensing instruments must be matched properly to the recording requirements.[1]

Tunnels that are suitable for modeling wind response typically have apertures 6 to 12 ft (2 to 4 m) wide and 6 to 10 ft (2 to 3 m) high. Wind normally is drawn at 25 to 100 mi/h (10 to 45 m/s) over a length of 50 to 100 ft (15 to 30 m) before reaching the model. Suitable wind tunnels may be either open-circuit or recirculating.

Several types of models can be constructed, depending on the nature of the data that need to be acquired. A rigid pressure model is the simplest, and it can be used to measure local peak pressures for analysis of cladding and mean pressures for overall mean loads. A rigid high-frequency base balance model can be used to measure overall fluctuations of loads for analysis of dynamic response. Aeroelastic models are necessary to investigate the potential for structural motions themselves to affect wind loading on the structure of interest. Aeroelastic models require accurate, scaled representations of the flexibility of the modeled structure.[1]

EARTHQUAKE LOADS

Nature and Consequences of Earthquake Loads

Earthquake loads on structures originate not from externally applied forces or pressures, but from dynamic structural distortions that occur as the ground below a structure is displaced. In the beginning moments of a seismic event, ground movements induce foundation motions. Immediately, structural stiffnesses from shear walls, braced frames, moment frames, or incidental structural and architectural elements develop shear forces which are transmitted from one building level to another. Almost immediately, the entire building sways dynamically in response to the ongoing ground movements. It is the interplay among structural masses at each level and interstory stiffness and relative distortions that generate the member forces that must be supported by the structure.

Ground movements are both horizontal and vertical. However, most commonly it is the horizontal movements that cause the greatest distress in buildings. Often, the accelerations and motion amplitudes are larger in the horizontal direction than in the vertical direction. Also, horizontal ground motions tend to cause forces that are more difficult for conventional structures to support. Substantial frame strength or shear wall strength is needed to prevent lateral failures during severe earthquakes. However, the inherent strength designed into structures to support gravity loads usually has sufficient reserve to support loads from vertical components of seismic ground motions. When axial loads induce compression failures in columns, the sources of those vertical loads usually are overturning moments caused by horizontal excitation.

Clearly, vertical excitations cannot be ignored entirely. The 1994 Northridge earthquake demonstrated that significant vertical excitation can cause damage in structures.

For most common structures in regions of severe earthquake activity, there are few practical ways to design lateral load systems to remain elastic during seismic events. The interstory forces that would develop during elastic response exceed capacities that can be provided practically and economically. Therefore, conventional design philosophy accepts that building frames will deform inelastically. The inelastic distortion effectively dissipates the kinetic energy that is imparted to the structure by ground motions, and "softens" the response of the structure to the excitation.

It follows that structures that perform as designed during severe earthquakes will sustain damage. This anticipated damage can include large permanent deformations; serious cracking of walls, columns, and beams; and partial disintegration of joints (Fig. 10.14)—particularly in concrete structures. Sometimes the expected damage is difficult or impossible to repair economically. However, it is this expected damage that saves the building from collapse.

In general, the lowest levels of buildings can receive the most serious damage during an earthquake. Depending on the dynamic characteristics of a building and the frequency content of the earthquake, the stiffness of the lowest levels of the building may be low enough that the mass on the upper levels is not easily excited by the higher-frequency components of ground motions. While this can promote the survivability of the upper levels, it can be disastrous for the lowest levels. If the lowest levels of the building are not designed to withstand the large differential

FIGURE 10.14 Northridge Earthquake damage to tilt-up building, Chatsworth, California. (*Credit: M. Celebi, U.S. Geological Survey.*) (*Source: Geologic Hazards Photos, a compilation by the National Geophysical Data Center of the U.S. Department of Commerce, National Oceanic and Atmospheric Administration.*)

movements that occur as the ground moves and the upper levels remain relatively stationary, serious failures can occur (Fig. 10.15). In the most dramatic instances, failure at the lowest levels can cause total collapse (Fig. 10.16).

Unfortunately, buildings often do not respond as the designers envisioned. While a designer might plan a system to support lateral loads, and might provide adequate strength and detailing in that system, in fact, buildings respond according to their mass and stiffness distributions, and not necessarily according to the design. Building components "attract" loads roughly in proportion to their relative stiffnesses

FIGURE 10.15 Earthquake damage to second level of Santa Monica Hospital, Northridge Earthquake. (*Credit: J. Dewey, U.S. Geological Survey.*) (*Source: Geologic Hazards Photos, a compilation by the National Geophysical Data Center of the U.S. Department of Commerce, National Oceanic and Atmospheric Administration.*)

FIGURE 10.16 Collapse of garage level below apartments, Reseda, California. (*Credit: J. Dewey, U.S. Geological Survey.*) (*Source: Geologic Hazards Photos, a compilation by the National Geophysical Data Center of the U.S. Department of Commerce, National Oceanic and Atmospheric Administration.*)

compared to the stiffnesses of other elements that act in parallel. Seismic response involves large, inelastic deformations. Therefore, by design (and necessity), stiff elements that are not part of the "intended" load path for seismic forces will be subjected to the large deformations allowed by the anticipated response of the elements designed to support seismic loads. As such, elements that are not part of the lateral load system may sustain serious damage, if they are not properly detailed.

It is very common for brittle architectural components and nonstructural infill elements to be damaged by earthquakes. These building components often are not designed to accommodate the interstory deformations that are imparted by the building motion. Such elements can fail due to frame motions in their plane; or if they are lightly reinforced or inadequately supported, they can fail out of plane from the forces generated by their own inertias. In older, unreinforced masonry structures, collapses of walls (Fig. 10.17), parapets (Figs. 10.18 and 10.19), and other components are common in seismic events. When the support of the entire structure is compromised by these local failures, total collapse often follows.

Buildings in close proximity to adjacent structures can pound against each other. Large-amplitude, out-of-phase sway of adjacent buildings can close gaps between buildings that are directly next to each other, particularly at upper levels. When contact is severe enough to damage columns or bearing walls, partial or total collapse of one or both buildings is possible.

Large-amplitude sway also leads to P-delta response that must be evaluated. As a building deforms laterally, the weights of each floor are displaced relative to the floor below. The resulting eccentricities between vertical loads and their supporting elements tend to amplify overturning moments. Building response to seismic loads, with large inelastic distortions an inherent characteristic, normally involves greater potential for significant P-delta response than does elastic building response to wind loads. The amplification of moments can be unstable when the inelastic frame stiffnesses and strengths cannot resist the amplified movements and forces.

Structures with insufficient internal ties can fail when structural distortions exceed movement capacities of supports. Beams sometimes drop from their supports because connections have insufficient strength to resist forces due to differential movements at opposite beam ends, and the length of bearing is insufficient to accommodate the resulting movements.

Differential foundation movements also damage buildings during earthquakes. Consolidation and liquefaction sometimes cause foundations to displace vertically. Foundation elements that are not adequately tied together may separate during an earthquake. Certainly, structures that span a fault will experience severe differential foundation displacements during an earthquake.

Determination of Earthquake Loads

The assumption of inelastic behavior complicates the seismic analysis of structures. First, it is not necessarily valid to assume that loads can be superimposed

FIGURE 10.17 Loma Prieta damage to upper-level of Clay Building, Oakland, California. (*Credit: C. Stover, U.S. Geological Survey.*) (*Source: Geologic Hazards Photos, a compilation by the National Geophysical Data Center of the U.S. Department of Commerce, National Oceanic and Atmospheric Administration.*)

linearly. For instance, generally it is not adequate to treat gravity loads separately from seismic loads in accurate analyses. It is important to know which structural elements are taken beyond elastic limits by the combination of applied forces, because effective stiffnesses change when this happens. Analyses that do not consider the impact of nonseismic loads may overlook building response characteristics that are important to a structure's survival.

The assumption of inelastic behavior also complicates analyses because accurate analyses for such conditions are nonlinear. Furthermore, our understanding of

FIGURE 10.18 Northridge Earthquake damage to St. Monica's Church, Santa Monica, California. (*Credit: C. Searls, Simpson Gumpertz & Heger Inc.*)

FIGURE 10.19 Loma Prieta Earthquake damage, Westonville, California. (*Credit: C. Stover, U.S. Geological Survey.*) (*Source: Geologic Hazards Photos, a compilation by the National Geophysical Data Center of the U.S. Department of Commerce, National Oceanic and Atmospheric Administration.*)

postelastic, cyclic response of building elements generally is not as developed as that for elastic response. Most conventional seismic design approaches dictate construction detailing that is intended to ensure a level of ductility in the completed structure that allows engineers to apply simplifying assumptions in analytical procedures. For these reasons, investigators face a dilemma when they must analyze structures that are not detailed in conformance with prescribed standards, and when analyses must be performed with high accuracy.

Earthquake Data.   The earthquake data needed for an investigation of a seismic event normally come from monitoring stations in the vicinity of a site of interest. Most seismically active regions are monitored for earthquake activity. Seismographs at various sites in and around earthquake zones are poised to collect data on ground motions during all serious events. Records acquired at these sites normally will contain data necessary to perform any of the common calculations for estimating earthquake response: time-history analyses, empirical calculations, and modal analyses.

It is common to base seismic analyses on a response spectrum that is calculated from earthquake records using 5 percent damping to be representative of typical building response.[17] To the extent that the characteristics of a structure under investigation are not represented by these parameters, adjustment is needed.

Ground motions are site-specific. Not only do seismic motions attenuate and change character with distance from the epicenter, but also there may be soil conditions at any particular site that will amplify motions. Therefore, to use data collected off-site, conditions should be evaluated at both sites to judge whether data must be adjusted.

If the structure of interest is much closer to the ground motion recording site than to the fault that generated the earthquake, it sometimes is possible to use motion records without adjustment for attenuation. However, consideration should always be given to seismic ground motion attenuation models that can be used to improve the applicability of seismic ground motion data to the site of interest. In general, published attenuation models[18–23] are based on regional geology and seismicity and therefore are of limited applicability outside the study region.

Subsurface materials normally are assigned to one of six classifications for seismic response evaluations, based on the conditions in the top 100 ft (30 m) of the layer:

A   Hard rock, with an average shear wave velocity v_s greater than 5000 ft/s (1500 m/s)

B   Rock, with v_s greater than 2500 ft/s (760 m/s) and less than or equal to 5000 ft/s (1500 m/s)

C   Very dense soil and soft rock with v_s greater than 1200 ft/s (360 m/s) and less than or equal to 2500 ft/s (760 m/s)

D   Stiff soil with v_s greater than 600 ft/s (180 m/s) and less than or equal to 1200 ft/s (360 m/s)

E   A soil profile with v_s less than or equal to 600 ft/s (180 m/s), or average field standard penetration test results less than 1000 lb/in^2, or soft clay

F   Soils that are vulnerable to failure or collapse (liquefiable, quick and highly sensitive, weakly cemented), peat and organic clays, very high-plasticity clays, and very thick soft/medium stiff clays.

The NEHRP Recommended Provisions for Seismic Regulations for New Buildings and Other Structures[24] contains a procedure to determine the effective soil classification when more than one of these materials are present in the top 100 ft (30 m). Further, NEHRP contains tables of factors that can be used to modify response spectra to represent different excitation characteristics for each soil condition. Therefore, by using these factors, spectra developed for records at one site can be modified for soil conditions to estimate response spectra for another nearby site.

Conversions between sites should reference motions at bedrock. Spectra at the recording site should be normalized to bedrock using factors appropriate for the soil conditions at that site, and then site-specific spectra can be generated for the site of interest. NEHRP provides two factors for different frequency ranges of interest. Therefore, judgment is needed when using these factors to adjust ground motion data. In most cases, appropriate consultants with expertise in the extrapolation of seismic motion data should be consulted.

Analysis Procedures

Time-History Analyses.   Perhaps the most accurate analyses that can be performed are nonlinear, time-history analyses. These studies require actual time histories of ground motion at the site of interest, or representative artificial time histories generated from response spectra. The nonlinear response characteristics of the lateral load-resisting system of the building must be established accurately. Finally, the analysis needs to be performed in piecewise fashion, accounting for the formation of plastic hinges, element failures when appropriate, and *P*-delta behavior.

Empirical Analyses.   Simplified approaches are available in several resources.[1,24] Specifically, NEHRP allows an analytical approach that approximates earthquake response by a series of static lateral loads applied at the floor levels of the structure. This approach can be used accurately for structures that are relatively regular in configuration and that are up to 240 ft (70 m) tall, and for structures that have plan or vertical irregularities and are less than 65 ft (20 m) tall. Plan irregularities include shapes that are likely to induce significant torsion, diaphragm discontinuities, and nonparallel elements in the lateral force-resisting system, among others. Vertical irregularities include soft stories, nonuniform weight distributions, and discontinuities in the vertical lateral force-resisting system, among others.

With this empirical approach, *P*-delta effects are neglected if the stability coefficient Θ is less than 0.10:

$$\Theta = \frac{P_x \Delta}{V_x h_{sx} C_d}$$

where P_x = building weight above building level of interest
Δ = calculated story drift
V_x = calculated seismic shear at level of interest
h_{sx} = story height below level of interest
C_d = a deflection amplification factor that is a function of type of seismic force-resisting system

If this limit is not satisfied, rational analysis must be used to evaluate P-delta effects.

Modal Analyses. Also available in NEHRP and other reference standards are modal analysis approaches. The basic NEHRP modal analysis approach uses elastic properties (calculated for cracked concrete, and with panel zone deformations accounted for in steel moment frames) and assumes that the building base is fixed. By using appropriate spectral response curves, the modal shears, moments, and drifts are calculated for a sufficient number of modes to accurately represent the participation of at least 90 percent of the actual mass in each orthogonal direction. Overall responses are calculated by combining the modal participations by the square root of the sum of the squares method.

In separate procedures, the effects of soil-structure interaction and P-delta amplifications can be estimated. However, empirical approaches are used in both cases, with the caution that inclusion of soil-structure interaction effects will decrease the calculated shears and moments, but increase the calculated drifts.

FLOOD LOADS

Nature and Consequences of Flood Loads

Flood loads can be classified as hydrostatic loads and hydrodynamic loads. Hydrostatic loads result from the static pressure of a head of water acting against a surface. For bodies that are completely surrounded by water at a constant depth, the net hydrostatic load on the body as a whole equals zero. Hydrostatic forces are important if the water depth is not the same all around a body. This occurs in floods when building components, such as walls, retain floodwaters, or if water depths on opposite sides of a building are not the same.

Hydrodynamic loads have two primary forms: loads that originate from flowing water and loads due to waves. In both cases, pressures on buildings result from the inertial effects, or drag, caused when the flow of the water is diverted by the object in its path. Flowing water most often influences loads on buildings in floodplains near river channels. Wave action and flowing water both are important at coasts.

Flood loads can cause collapse of walls that tend to restrain water and, in very severe conditions, displacement of entire buildings that are in strong storm surge and wave action during a coastal storm, or in the strong current of a flooding river. Collapse can occur when structural elements are overloaded by water pressures (flood loads easily can exceed pressures due to wind by severalfold, even when water depths are only a few feet) or by toppling structural elements that have sufficient foundations to support overturning forces. Floods also can induce impact loads on structures if heavy debris is being carried by river flow. Strong currents can induce collateral damage, by undermining foundations by scour or by inducing movements of earth slopes and scarps. To the extent that these soil movements affect foundations for buildings and bridges, the effects of floods can be severe when water pressures are small.

Floods also can cause uplift on structures if the structures prevent water from finding a level inside that matches the level outside. Uplift also is possible if flowing water is able to pass under a structure, in contact with the underside of the lowest floor. This is particularly true if the water flow becomes constrained as it passes under the structure. In this case, inertial forces can pressurize the water slightly, and induce upward forces.

Determination of Flood Loads

Hydrostatic loads can be determined relatively easily once the flood level is known. These important data often can be determined from records on flood levels kept by public safety agencies. In addition, reliable information at specific sites often can be determined by establishing the high-water mark through examination of stains or debris left on the structures or in its immediate vicinity. Once the water elevation is known, hydrostatic pressures on surfaces can be calculated easily, using the density of water and the water elevation.

Hydrodynamic loads due to water flow must be calculated based on estimates of the velocity and direction of water flowing by the structure. This information is best obtained from local, state, or federal government agencies that record such data, or through consultation with engineers specializing in hydrology or hydraulics.

A simple way to account for water flow loads is to add a calculated equivalent head to the hydrostatic head for the water elevation. The following formula[1] can be used to calculate the equivalent head to represent flowing water:

$$h = \frac{DV^2}{2g}$$

where h is the equivalent head, V is the velocity of the flowing water, g is acceleration due to gravity, and D is the drag coefficient for the shape of the object in the flow stream. For complicated wave action, more refined approaches are necessary.

Normally, it is sufficient to apply the equivalent head to the upstream face of the structure only, where the inertial effects of the flowing water on the building are most severe. Sidewalls and the walls in the tailwater usually experience pressures similar to those associated with the hydrostatic head.

Analysis for wave action must consider the effects of breaking waves, wave run-up, and drag due to water flow.[25,26]

BLAST LOADS

Nature and Consequences of Blast Loads

Blast loads arise from accidental and intentional detonations of explosives and other volatile substances in or near structures. Such explosions generate hot gases, air pressurization, and shock waves that radiate away from the detonation point. Shock waves that strike rigid surfaces are reflected and proceed onward to the next surface. Shock waves diffract around corners. Pressurized gases expand into confined spaces. Explosion-generated "winds" pass by structures, causing negative pressures on sidewalls and roofs. For severe explosions, a negative pressure phase often follows the initial positive pressure phase, as overexpanded gases contract and air movement reverses back toward the detonation point.

Structures near to explosions receive a complex sequence of positive and negative pressurizations that typically occur in a fraction of a second. A roof first will be pushed down by a shock wave that passes a building and then will be drawn upward by the rebound and the negative pressure caused by moving air. The magnitude of the pressure can be orders of magnitude larger than the pressures associated with environmental loads derived from wind and gravity. The duration is very short: Often the entire loading sequence is complete in a few tenths of a second. Often the loading sequence is so short that massive objects do not receive enough momentum to respond significantly. However, relatively light objects, and structures with little ductility, can be devastated by relatively minor explosions.

Large explosions inside closed structures, such as occur when natural gas leaks into an enclosed building, can literally blow the structure apart. Simply put, the energy released during the explosion often far exceeds the energy-absorbing capability of the building elements, and there is insufficient venting to allow the energy to be dissipated into the atmosphere.

The forces of a blast often remove nearby partitions and exterior walls that are not specifically designed for the effects of blast. Severe blasts also can remove important structural elements, such as columns, leading to progressive collapse. It is unusual for blasts outside buildings to impart enough energy to a building to cause structural elements (i.e., columns and beams) other than those very near to the blast to fail. Progressive failure is the most common reason why buildings collapse when there is an exterior blast.

Explosions often cause fires. Typically, fires start at the periphery of the area of blast damage, where the heat generated by the explosion is substantial, but beyond the region where the available oxygen is consumed by the blast itself. The collateral damage caused by fire can exceed the damage of the blast itself.

The most common damage from blasts is the devastation of weak and nonductile architectural features, such as windows, light curtain walls (Fig. 10.20), partitions, and unreinforced masonry walls. These elements often have insufficient ability to absorb energy to resist the momentum imparted by the explosion.

Blast Environment

In all explosions, there are two primary sources of pressure forces that can affect buildings: shock fronts and expansion of hot gases. The detonation of explosives creates a shock front that radiates away from the center of the explosion at supersonic speeds. It is generated by the initial detonation of the explosive. Following the shock front is a pressure wave that is generated by the expanding, hot gases from the rapid consumption of the explosive fuel. It is, in effect, a wind created by the movement of the air. The shock front "shell" usually is quite thin: Pressures increase to a maximum as a step function, and they diminish rapidly. The air movement that follows the shock front has associated with it the momentum of the air mass: After the outward velocity peaks and diminishes, there is often a period

FIGURE 10.20 Curtain wall blast damage, Hong Kong and Shanghai Office Tower, London. (*Credit: R. Massa, Lorron Corporation.*)

of rebound when air movement reverses direction, and negative pressures are induced on surfaces facing the explosion site.

The importance of these sources of pressure on a building depends on whether the explosion is located outside or inside the building, how far the explosion is from the surface on which pressures act, the effective yield of the explosive, and the nature of the explosive itself.

In general, the very short duration of very high blast loading (usually on the order of several milliseconds) imparts an impact load on buildings and structural elements with relatively low vibrational frequencies. To survive, structural elements must have sufficient strength and energy-absorbing ability to arrest the resulting motion before being destroyed. However, the impulse function is dependent on the magnitude of the blast, the efficiency of the explosive, and the distance between the detonation point and the receiving structure. With smaller charges, lower efficiency, and larger distance, the effective pressures diminish, but the durations lengthen. Progressively, the nature of the load changes from impulse to dynamic to quasistatic in the limit, depending on element's natural frequency.

Exterior Blasts.   Exterior blasts can be classified into three groups: free air explosions, air explosions, and ground explosions. Free air explosions are those that occur in the atmosphere, remote to objects that might affect the expansion of shock fronts and hot gases. While such explosions might not be very interesting for the design of blast-resistant structures, their character is the basis for the description of blasts of other types.

Free Air Explosions.   In a free air explosion, the shock front advances away from the detonation point in a spherical pattern at a speed approximated by[27]

$$V = \frac{\sqrt{6p_s + 7p_0}}{7p_0} \, v$$

where p_0 is the ambient air pressure, p_s is the static overpressure created by the explosion, and v is the speed of sound in air at the ambient pressure. For most explosives, the static overpressure initially is many times the ambient air pressure.

Close to the detonation point, when the static overpressure exceeds approximately 1 MPa, the static overpressure can be approximated by the formula[28]

$$p_s = \frac{0.67}{z^3} + 0.1 \quad \text{MPa}$$

where $z = R/W^{1/3}$, R is the radius from the center of the detonation, and W is the TNT equivalent mass of the charge. As such, the strength of the advancing shock front initially diminishes rapidly with the inverse of the cube of the radius. At greater distances (and for smaller charges) the rate of pressure decrease is somewhat slower, following a relationship of the form[28]

$$p_s = \frac{0.098}{z} + \frac{0.15}{z^2} + \frac{0.59}{z^3} - 0.002$$

At the same time, the blast creates the maximum dynamic overpressure at the leading surface of the shock front, due to moving air, according to the formula[27]

$$q_s = \frac{5p_s^2}{2(p_s + 7p_0)}$$

In all cases, the duration of the overpressure is very short, and the pressure magnitude and, therefore, the potential influence that an explosion might have on an object such as a building diminish rapidly with distance.

Air Explosions. Air explosions are those that occur in the air, but closer to the ground than to objects such as buildings that might be affected by the blast. Typically, detonations are characterized as air explosions if the horizontal distance between ground zero (a point on the ground vertically below the detonation point) and the object is at least 3 times the height of blast above the ground. In blasts of this type, the strength of the advancing shock front can be substantially higher than that for free air explosions. As the incident shock front radiates in a spherical pattern away from the detonation point, it reaches and is reflected off the ground surface before it reaches the object. The reflected front, which continues away from the point of reflection, can combine with the advancing incident front to create a "mach front" of greater magnitude than the incident front. In addition, the combination of these fronts creates a front pattern that radiates away from ground zero with a vertical cylindrical shape. The pressure of this front is nearly uniform with height. As with free air explosions, the magnitude of the shock diminishes rapidly with distance.

Surface Explosions. Surface explosions probably are of greatest relevance for most designs and investigations, because the most frequent explosions affecting buildings occur near the ground. Explosives that are detonated on the ground create hemispherical shock fronts that radiate upward and outward from the detonation point. This form is the result of the instantaneous reflection of the initial blast from the ground. Theoretically, the reflective surface at the location of the detonation can cause the magnitude of the pressure to double. In fact, the ground is not a perfect reflector (some energy is absorbed by the creation of a crater and seismic waves). Therefore, the shock is seldom amplified by more than approximately 80 percent.

Interior Blasts. Interior blasts also are of three types: fully confined explosions, partially vented explosions, and fully vented explosions.

Fully Confined Explosions. Fully confined explosions occur in enclosed spaces. To survive, the structure that surrounds such explosions must be able to contain and absorb all the energy released by the explosion, including the shock front, expanding gases, and heat.

Partially Vented Explosions. Partially vented explosions occur in confined spaces that have perhaps 5 to 10 percent of their exterior surfaces open to the atmosphere. In explosions of this type, very complex patterns of reflections of the shock from the surfaces of the volume amplify the effective impulse exerted on the structure, and pressures can build substantially as the expanding gas is released relatively slowly to the atmosphere through constricted openings.

Fully Vented Explosions.   Fully vented explosions are characterized by many reflective surfaces near to the detonation point, but with much of the perimeter surface open to the atmosphere. An explosive detonated in a building with one wall totally open to the atmosphere is an example of a fully vented explosion. In these explosions, there will be significant amplification of shock through many reflections from surfaces, but gas pressure buildup usually is not more significant than for exterior explosions.

In buildings subjected to forces due to explosions, most exterior blasts are surface explosions and most interior blasts are partially vented explosions.

Determination of Blast Loads

To determine the magnitude of blast effects, it is important to know the size of the explosive charge, the nature of the explosive, and the location of the explosion relative to the receiving object. With the size and nature of the explosive, the blast characteristics can be determined and an equivalent TNT charge weight can be estimated. This equivalent TNT charge weight is essential for the use of most blast effects formulas.

Alternatively, the size and efficiency of the charge can be estimated from the physical evidence at the site. Distances to which debris is thrown can indicate the magnitude of a blast. The depth of the blast crater can be correlated with the position of the explosive device and the amount of explosive.[29]

Once the magnitude of the explosion has been estimated, the nature of the influence on a structure can be assessed. First, the pressures and loading durations must be estimated.

When the distance between the detonation point and the nearest face of a building exceeds approximately twice the larger dimension of that face of the building, the incident pressures reaching the near surface of the building are relatively uniform. However, when the incident shock reaches the rigid wall surface, the moving air is further compressed as it is reflected from the surface of the building. This causes an amplification of the pressure on the near face of the building, following the theoretical relationship that is approximated by the following formula[30] for a 90° angle of incidence:

$$p_r = 2p_s \left(\frac{7p_0 + 4p_s}{7p_0 + p_s} \right)$$

According to this relationship, surfaces that are close to large charges ($p_s \gg p_0$) can experience effective pressure that is as much as 8 times the incident pressure. In fact, pressures up to 20 times the incident pressure have been measured when incident pressures are orders of magnitude larger than atmospheric pressure.[30]

At oblique angles of incidences, the magnification of pressure through reflection diminishes with angle. Reductions generally are relatively small until the angle between the incident shock front and the normal to the surface are approximately 40° (Ref. 30). At larger angles, the magnification diminishes rapidly.

As the pressure front passes the near surface of the building, the building begins to become engulfed by compressive forces that act on all surfaces. First the near face experiences a step increase in pressure that is the sum of the incident and reflected fronts. Then the shock front passes the near face and momentarily engulfs the roof and sides of the building. Pressure fronts passing the sidewalls and roof normally are not amplified by reflection, but these surfaces do experience first pressure variations due to compression of the air and then potentially reversing pressures due to the explosion "winds" and vortices created by building edges. As the front progresses along the depth of the building, the pressure on the front face drops because the reflected front leaves this surface and travels back toward the detonation point. In a fraction of a second, the pressurized gas has reached the far face of the building, and that wall experiences compressive forces as diffraction of pressure fronts around corners contributes to the development of significant pressures on all surfaces.

Following a time decay function of the form[30]

$$p(t) = p_s \left(1 - \frac{t}{T_s}\right) \exp\left(-\frac{bt}{T_s}\right)$$

where T_s is the time to zero pressure (normally reported in hundredths of seconds) and b is the waveform parameter, significant pressurization of building surfaces ends. The entire loading cycle is completed in tenths of seconds.

At this point, the building and its components have been set in motion by the pressure impulses that they experienced, and their ability to survive depends on their ability to absorb and dissipate the acquired kinetic energy. The analysis of the response of the structure rarely can be treated as a static or quasistatic phenomenon. Consideration must be given to the dynamic response of the structure to the very short-duration loading cycle, and to the inelastic response necessary for building components to absorb the imparted energy.

For explosives that are detonated close to buildings, there can be very significant variations of pressure on near surfaces [e.g., variations in effective pressures on the near wall of the Murrah Building in Oklahoma City exceeded 10,000 lb/in^2 (70 MPa) at ground level near to the detonation point, and diminished to less than approximately 10 lb/in^2 (0.3 MPa) at the more remote portions at the top of the near face of the building].[31] This occurs primarily because the radial distances to different portions of the near surface are substantially different. Also, as the shock front progresses up and away on a building face, the incident and reflected fronts can combine and magnify effective pressures much as they do in air explosions.

In urban environments with many closely spaced buildings, blast effects can be further magnified. First, many complex reflections can occur when an explosive is detonated between buildings that line often narrow city streets. Then, when large explosives are detonated between tall buildings on very narrow streets, the expansion of gases is not entirely free. Through reflection and diffraction, the significant effects of major explosions can be felt around corners and on streets adjacent to explosion sites.

Buildings with overhangs, recesses, and reentrant corners can experience disproportionate damage. These features, which allow the shock front and expanding gases to pass into a partially confined space, can substantially magnify the pressures exerted on a building's facade through reflection of the blast pressures and confinement of expanding gases.

Structural elements also receive shock loads that can destroy elements before their structural strength can be mobilized. When the shock from a blast strikes the near surface of a hard object, the shock sets in motion a compressive wave that travels through the material. When this wave reaches the far surface of the object, some of its energy is transmitted out of the object (to the air) and some energy is reflected from the back surface through the object again. The reflected wave in the object now is a tension wave. Concrete and other materials that are strong in compression and weak in tension might be able to sustain the first compressive wave to travel though the object, but for significant explosions it is possible that the reflected tension wave will have high enough stress to progressively and explosively shed spalls from the far face of the object. In effect, the concrete can be stripped away from the back side of structural elements.

A comprehensive reference[32] to calculate the effects of blast loads on structural elements is "Structures to Resist the Effects of Accidental Explosions."

FIRE LOADS

Nature and Consequences of Fire Loads

In general, fires affect structures directly in two ways: High temperatures reduce the strength and stiffness of structural materials, and thermally induced expansion damages structural and nonstructural components. However, collateral damage from falling debris and other causes can be high as well.

Effects of Fire on Materials

Extensive research and testing have been performed to determine the effects of heat on materials of construction. These studies have shown that all common building materials are affected by fire temperatures, which often exceed 1700°F (900°C).

Structural steel is, perhaps, the building material that is most susceptible to damage during fires. When steel is exposed to heat, its temperature increases rapidly. At approximately 575°F (300°C), steel begins to lose strength and stiffness.[33] Above this temperature, permanent deformations can occur, stability begins to be compromised, and factors of safety diminish. When a simply supported steel beam reaches 900°F (550°C), its strength can be reduced by approximately 30 percent,[33] which places it at risk of failure if it is at the same time loaded to its design capacity. This, of course, is why external fire protection is needed for structural steel members.

The strength of concrete is first affected at approximately 575°F (300°C).[34,35] However, most reinforced-concrete members can be exposed to temperatures far in excess of this level without failure. Compared to steel, concrete is relatively slow to increase in temperature when heated. The strength of most reinforced-concrete members is governed by the strength of the reinforcing steel, which is insulated from heat by the concrete.[36] In general, reinforced-concrete members do not fail due to direct exposure to heat until the concrete cover over the steel has spalled, exposing the reinforcing steel to heat.

Prestressed concrete is, in general, more prone to failure than reinforced concrete when exposed to heat. Tendons lose strength rapidly above approximately 575°F (300°C).[37] Members with unbonded tendons can be particularly susceptible to damage, depending on the tendon patterns and the amount of mild steel, because they can lose strength over their entire length (both positive and negative moment regions) when any one section of the member has been heated enough to soften the tendons.

Thermal Expansion from Fires

The coefficient of expansion of many building materials is temperature-dependent. For instance, the coefficient of expansion for structural steel is[38] $\epsilon = (6.1 + 0.0019t)10^{-6}$ /°F [$\epsilon = (6.16 + 0.0034t)10^{-6}$ /°C], where t is the temperature. At fire temperatures, the rate of expansion is at least 30 percent higher than at room temperature.

At fire temperatures, steel and concrete can expand by 1 to 1.5 percent. For a 26-ft (8-m) span, this expansion corresponds to approximately 3 in (8 cm) to 5 in (13 cm) of movement. Few building systems can accommodate this movement even for one bay, much less the cumulative effects caused by expansion over several bays.

Normally in floor systems, this full expansion in the horizontal plane never occurs. Beams often are protected against heat, fire durations are short enough that members do not achieve the fire temperature, or the supporting members sag as strength and stiffness reduce. Sometimes, if restraint of expansion is sufficient, the floor system buckles before the full horizontal movement can occur.

However, structural slabs and certain other structural elements can undergo horizontal expansions on the order of 1 percent when conditions permit. For example, when a structural slab is supported on beams and subjected to a fire above, it can heat without failure out of plane because the supporting members are shielded from the fire and retain their strength and stiffness. The resulting movement of the slab can cause severe damage in structural elements that are outside the fire zone[39] (Fig. 10.21). Another common form of damage is cracks that radiate from the center of the fire zone in regions of slabs adjacent to, but outside, the fire zone.

In fires, expanding floor systems often cause severe damage to rigid bearing walls and infill walls and to curtain walls and cladding. Rarely are these elements designed with sufficient strength to withstand the very high expansion forces, which can be orders of magnitude greater than lateral forces due to normal environmental loads.

The forces due to thermal expansion can have damaging effects on structural systems, even in areas relatively remote to the fire location. If a structural steel member could be fully restrained axially, heating it from room temperature to a mere 250°F (121°C) would cause it to yield. Although in building structures members are not fully restrained, the effects of expansion and restraint of expansion are significant.

The effects of thermal expansion are not all detrimental. The benefits of thermal expansion to the survival of restrained structural beams during fires has been studied and documented.[40] When beams are heated from below, the compressive stresses that develop in the expanding lower flange reduce tension due to external loads. This reduction of stress partially offsets the concurrent reduction in tensile strength due to heating.

Columns, which may be restrained from free vertical growth in multistory

FIGURE 10.21 Thermal expansion damage due to fire on floor above, Amherst College, Massachusetts. (*Credit: D. Dusenberry, Simpson Gumpertz & Heger Inc.*)

buildings, can experience increased compressive loads at the same time that the strength of the member is reduced by heat if the expansion occurs at a rate that exceeds the rate of reduction of the modulus of elasticity of the material. Columns also can fail in shear due to expansion of the floor system, particularly in multibay fires and with relatively short columns.

Explosive Overpressures

When buildings that are on fire are not vented, fumes composed of partially consumed combustion products can build in interior spaces. Under proper combinations of heat and oxygen content, these explosive gases can ignite suddenly during the fire, causing an explosion that can damage windows and walls, and spread the fire rapidly. This phenomenon sometimes is referred to as "flash-over." Flash-over can damage rooms and building components outside the areas of active combustion.

Catenary Beam Action

Eventually, when the temperature of a beam during a fire increases enough to generate significant expansion and to affect the material's stiffness, the beam will begin to sag. This deformation results from the reduction of modulus at elevated temperature, creep (particularly in concrete beams), buckling if the restraint against expansion is rigid, and reduction in material strength.

Steel members are likely to sag due to yielding of the flanges at approximately 900°F (550°C). At similar temperatures, concrete beams also will sag if the cover over the bottom steel has spalled, exposing the steel to fire heat.

For simple span beams without axial end restraint, yielding of the beam at midspan usually results in collapse. As the deflection of the beam increases to approximately 10 to 20 percent of the span length, the ends of the beam can overstress their connections or lose bearing.

For beams with restraint for axial loads, failure can be delayed as the beams sag. (Of course, continuous beams with negative moment capacity also have reserve strength after a hinge forms at midspan.) First, as beams undergo this inelastic deflection, they elongate. This reduces fire-induced compression. Eventually, member tension develops if suitable end-restraint details exist and the beam sags enough. This tension allows catenary action to develop in deflected beams. This alternate load-carrying mechanism can support weights on beams heated to temperatures far in excess of those which causes the initial hinge to form.

For steel beams proportioned for deflections on the order of L/360, where L is the span length, the maximum tensile stress in beams supporting loads by catenary action is on the order of 10 to 15 percent of the room-temperature yield strength of the steel. The horizontal component of this force, pulling inward on supports, is much less than the heat-induced outward force that usually precedes it in the fire, but often is significantly more than axial forces assumed during the design of connections. If the connections can support the force, the collapse of the beam will be delayed.

As a fire continues after catenary action has been initiated, beam temperatures and deformations continue to increase. Eventually, the strength of the heated steel may be insufficient to support catenary forces (steel yield stress is only approximately 15 percent of room-temperature yield strength when it is heated to 1500 to 1700°F (800 to 900°C).[33]

Stability of Vertical Members

Maintenance of stiffness is critical to the survival of vertical members during fires. When stiffness is reduced or floors that provide lateral support for columns fail, total structural stability is placed at risk. At approximately 950 to 1300°F (500 to 700°C), steel members lose 50 percent of their stiffness. Depending upon the composition of and the load on a concrete member during heating, concrete can lose 50 percent of its stiffness at approximately 1100°F (600°C). At these temperatures, slender columns at their design load may be at risk of failure due to buckling.

For columns and walls that are heated on one side only during a fire, the rates of temperature increase in the members are lower than when they are heated from all sides. However, nonsymmetric heating results in deformations that can affect the overall stability of the member. Due to expansion of the heated side, vertical members tend to bow toward the fire. This creates force eccentricities, distorts connections, and increases the compressive stress near the midheight of the column or wall. Fortunately, the stress increase occurs on the "cool" side where the material strength is relatively unaffected by heat. However, with sufficient deformation, yielding of steel, crushing of concrete, or member buckling is probable.

Increased Gravity Loads

Failure of a single floor can effectively double the weight on the floor below when debris falls from one level to the next. This added weight alone can be sufficient to exceed the factor of safety designed for that floor. Successive failures can cause progressive collapse.

With impact, such as by the dropping of one floor onto the other, short-term loads will be higher than twice the added static load. Properly designed and detailed bending members can be resilient enough to absorb the shock of a load failing from a short distance (if the members are not themselves damaged by high temperatures). However, if the falling weight lands near to the support of a beam, shear failure and progressive failure of successive floor elements are possible.

Firefighting water also adds weight to burning structures. Modern firefighting equipment is capable of delivering huge volumes of water to buildings. If this water is retained in the structure, it adds to the weight already on floors and columns.

Determination of Fire Loads

Fire loads can be estimated by computing the amount of combustible material in a structure at the time of the fire. These data, together with an assessment of the extent of ventilation during a fire and witness accounts of the fire intensity and duration, can be used to estimate maximum fire temperatures. The estimated fire temperatures, in turn, can be used to estimate the effects that a fire had on material strength, material stiffness, and thermal deformations and associated stresses.

Useful information about fire temperatures can be acquired by assessing the condition of building materials found in the fire debris. Different materials burn or melt at different temperatures. When samples of various materials found in the fire debris can be related to locations of fire damage, the conditions of those materials can be indicators of the maximum fire temperatures nearby. Reference 39 contains a useful list of the melting points of materials commonly found in buildings.

Information about fire temperatures also can be revealed through metallurgical analysis of metallic materials and petrographic analysis of cementitious materials. Petrographic analyses can reveal changes in material characteristics, and the depth that heat penetrated members.

Once ambient fire temperatures are known, analyses must be performed to estimate the temperatures reached in building components. These calculations require assessment of the exposure of the component to ambient temperature and direct radiation, the influence of insulation that remained on the component during the fire, and the characteristics of heat flow into the component. For calculation of the overall effect of a fire on a structure, it is important as well to understand and account for the progress of the fire through the building. It is possible that the first area to burn began to cool as another area of the building became fully involved in a conflagration. Analysis of fire effects, therefore, sometimes includes a "time history" approach similar to that sometimes used to analyze other random processes.

SELF-STRAINING LOADS

Nature and Consequences of Self-Straining Loads

Self-straining loads arise primarily from volumetric changes in building materials. These volumetric changes, which are due to environmental changes or in some cases aging effects, cause strains that lead to structural movements. If these strains and movements are constrained in any way, then stresses build in structural components. It is these stresses due to constrained movements that can cause damage in structures. Since these stresses arise not from any externally applied loads, but instead from changes within the building materials themselves, loads from these causes usually are classified as self-straining loads.

The most common environmental conditions that cause volumetric changes and self-straining loads in building materials are changes in temperature and moisture.

All common building materials expand and contract with changes in temperature. The amount of expansion and contraction depends on the temperature change and the coefficient of expansion for the building material. In addition, some building materials such as concrete and masonry shrink or swell with changes in moisture.

In most cases, if the temperature or moisture content of an isotropic object changes uniformly, the object experiences no stress change when it comes to equilibrium if it is not otherwise constrained externally. Uniform growth or contraction of a body that has no external restraints creates no internal stresses of consequence to the performance of normal building elements. In structures, conditions that can cause detrimental stresses are external restraint of building movement, internal restraint of movements of portions of structures, strain gradients in constrained elements, and temperature or moisture changes in elements of dissimilar materials that act compositely.

While damage is possible in almost any structure, usually movements induce damage in rigid elements that in some way anchor the movement of relatively long portions of structures that are subjected to volume changes. An example is a structure with rigid masonry walls that infill opposite ends of a multibay steel frame that is erected in a northern climate in the winter. If the frame is cold when it is erected and then is allowed to heat when the building is enclosed, the frame will expand. If insufficient relief is provided for this expansion, masonry walls built into the frame will receive very large forces as they tend to restrain the growth of the frame. Rigid nonstructural elements, such as precast curtain wall panels, also are susceptible to damage if not properly isolated from the movements due to volume changes of the supporting structures. These elements, which usually are designed for self-weight and tributary pressure loads, often are of insufficient strength to withstand the very large forces induced on them by the movement of their supporting frame elements.

Damage due to expansion or contraction of a frame is most likely to occur at the lowest levels of buildings. At these locations, the lateral restraint created by the foundation system can inhibit movement of the frame, thereby creating stresses that are less likely to occur at higher levels where the frame is not restrained by the foundation system.

The most common forms of the damage due to self-straining forces are cracking and spalling of structural and nonstructural components. Cracking occurs due to tensile stresses usually caused by direct tension, shear, or bending. Spalling results from high compressive stresses. Often, spalling occurs at joints and connections where high local contact stresses can exceed by several fold the average stress in an element.

Loads due to Temperature Changes

One source of thermal loads in a structure is the dimensional changes that occur between the time a structure is erected and the time that it is put into service. In northern regions of the country, structural frames sometimes are erected in sub-freezing weather. Assuming that the framing elements of a steel structure are bolted together at a temperature of 32°F (0°C), and the structure is then raised to an operating temperature of 70°F (21°C), the compressive strain in elements that are fully locked against movement (if these could be achieved) would be 38°F × 0.0000065 in (in/°F) = 0.00025 in/in, or approximately 20 percent of the yield strain and stress of ASTM A36 steel. Similarly, over a 60-ft (18.3-m) length of expansion, this temperature change would cause free expansion (if this could be achieved) of approximately $3/16$ in (4.8 cm). In practice, full restraint and free expansion both are impossible. Typically, the actual stresses and the amounts of movement in the frame will be less than these limits.

Structural analyses are necessary to assess stresses and the amounts of movements. Accurate estimates must be made to model relative flexibilities of the elements assumed to change temperature and the elements restraining movement. Consideration needs to be given to any slippage of connections, local flexibilities in connections or members, and deformed shapes attributable to other loads on a structure at the time of a temperature change.

All these conditions, which normally are neglected in design for loads that are not self-straining, can have significant impact on stresses due to self-straining loads. For instance, for the example of temperature change from construction to service given above, cumulative deformations and connection slippage of $3/16$ in (4.8 cm) over the length of 60 ft (18.3 m) will entirely relieve thermal stresses. Consider that this condition of temperature change might exist in a frame with three bays of W16 × 36 ASTM A36 steel beams, each spanning 20 ft (6.1 m). Fully restrained, these beams would generate tensile stress of approximately 7.2 ksi (0.05 MPa), or approximately 76 kips (338 kN) axial load for the beam area of 10.6 in^2 (68.4 cm^2). However, if the beams in this example were supported by single-plate shear connectors to the walls of tube columns, at each of six locations (three bays, one connection at each end of each beam), the wall of the tube column would need to deform by only $1/32$ in under the action of the axial load in the beam to relieve the stress. In fact, if the column walls deform, the axial load that develops in the beams cannot achieve the theoretical 76 kips (338 kN), and equilibrium is reached at a lower load.

To the extent that strain due to temperature changes occurs over a long time in materials such as concrete that are subject to creep and shrinkage distortions, the stresses that develop from self-strain in building materials may be mitigated by these other self-straining phenomena.

In most enclosed and temperature-controlled buildings, thermal strains during service conditions are not significant. Heated and air-conditioned buildings commonly experience interior temperature excursions that rarely exceed 10 to 20°F (6 to 11°C). Normally this range of temperature change is insufficient to damage structural elements as long as connections have sufficient capacity to support the resulting loads in restrained members.

Unusual building uses and structures that are not temperature-controlled can experience large service temperature excursions. For example, open parking structures in some northern regions of the United States experience ambient annual air temperature excursions of 100°F (55°C) or more. Restrained structures that respond fully to temperature ranges on this order should be expected to experience damage.

Thermal gradients are important considerations for designs of structures. These gradients arise from transient conditions when structural elements are responding to changes in ambient temperatures, in structural components with surfaces that are subjected to different steady-state temperatures, and in structural components that are subjected to solar and other thermal radiation. The top level of an unshaded parking garage in a southern climate easily could experience a gradient through the slab thickness of 35°F (20°C) or more.

Thermal stresses can build in structures when dissimilar materials or systems with dissimilar exposures are locked together against thermal movement. Curtain walls experience fluctuations in ambient temperatures and solar radiation, whereas the frames that support them are insulated against this environment. If these two elements are connected rigidly, the differences in thermal strains in the two elements will generate stresses in both. Conversely, if connections are flexible, sufficient movement joints must be provided to allow freedom from constraint.

Data on ambient thermal variations can be obtained from the National Climatic Data Center[4] and local news agencies. In addition, local airports often maintain accurate records of temperature. These data must be adjusted for the variations possible within a reporting region. For instance, temperatures often are warmer in city centers than in nearby suburbs. Large bodies of water often mitigate daily and seasonal temperature fluctuations. Also, radiational cooling during the night is influenced by objects, such as trees, over or around structures. Wind can affect the rate at which heated objects change temperature by accelerating heat loss (wind chill).

Loads due to Moisture Changes

Perhaps the two most common types of structural damage due to moisture changes are (1) movements and cracking due to shrinkage of moist construction materials that tend to contract when drying and (2) spalling and distortions of masonry construction as it absorbs moisture and tends to expand in service.

The phenomena of shrinkage cracking and movement in concrete are well documented.[41] In general, common types of damage include cracking of long and broad elements such as walls and slabs, cracking of beams, curling of slabs (elevated and on grade), and differential movements between concrete elements and elements of other materials, such as steel, that are not subject to shrinkage.

The amount of shrinkage that a concrete element experiences is influenced by the concrete mix design, the method of placement, the amount and type of curing that are applied during the days and weeks after placement, and the environment while in service.[42]

Swelling by clay masonry units upon takeup of moisture can be a serious problem in large masonry structures. Clay masonry units, such as brick, are manufactured by kiln drying. The moisture content of brick when it is first manufactured is significantly less than the moisture content later when the brick is in service. Expansion can be on the order of 0.03 to 0.05 percent.

Large exterior applications of brick usually require careful detailing to allow the brick to expand without causing distress. Midrise and high-rise buildings without horizontal relief joints can develop severe distress in brick facades as the brick expands vertically while the frame remains at constant height. Differential movements can damage connections to the backup structure, shelf angles, lintels, and other interconnected elements. If adjacent segments of interlocked brick are supported at different levels (such as when a segment that rests on supported shelf angles is interlocked with a segment that extends to the foundation), vertical and step cracks can form near the interface. It is possible for structures with concrete frames to have more acute potential for damage than do structures with steel frames because differential movements can be greater if the concrete frame shortens due to creep and shrinkage.

Horizontal expansion of clay masonry will cause damage if the spacing and size of vertical expansion joints are inadequate. Common forms of damage are cracking and outward displacement at building corners, as perpendicular faces of brick move relative to each other.

Wood-frame structures also can experience damage due to moisture changes. New lumber often is intentionally dried before being sold for construction. However, at a maximum moisture content of 19 percent as specified by the National Forest Products Association[43] for wood at installation, further drying is possible over time. When wood dries, it contracts, especially in directions perpendicular to the grain of the lumber. Construction details that include stacking wood elements across the grain can lead to dimensional shortening. Accumulations over multiple details with this potential can cause damaging distortions.

SETTLEMENT

Nature and Consequences of Settlement

Structural settlement normally occurs when the foundation is inadequate to support the loads applied to a structure. Settlement can occur if a foundation is inadequately designed or installed, or if conditions unforeseen during design affect the structure during its life. Certainly, settlement can occur if, due to changes in use, loads on a foundation exceed those envisioned by the designer. However, excavations near existing foundations can cause settlement as well. Changes in groundwater elevation can cause consolidation that can affect foundations. Bridge piers in rivers can be undermined by scour of foundation materials below footings. Decay of organic materials below footings can cause volume changes in the foundation materials. In most cases, the reasons for settlement are best determined by a thorough geotechnical investigation and assessment.

Settlement causes distortions that affect the function of a structure, stresses that can damage structural members and their connections, cracking of structural elements, overloads in structural elements that acquire extra load due to distortions of indeterminate structural systems, and damage to architectural components. Usually when settlement is severe enough to cause significant distress in conventional buildings, its manifestation is readily visible.

Determination of Settlement Loads

As with self-straining loads, loads due to settlement are the result of internal restraint of movement, rather than from an externally applied load. Structures that are fully pinned theoretically can be subjected to settlement without developing stresses. However, since few practical structures are without restraint, structures generally become stressed when settlement occurs.

The analysis of settlement effects is best begun with a survey of the building to measure its distortion. Care must be taken to obtain accurate data on relevant structural elements.

Data points must be selected to be representative of the movements of the structure. Normal deformations due to beam flexure, for instance, must be excluded from settlement deformation analyses. Data collected on architectural features that are not locked fully with the structural system, such as wood trim or column boxing, may not reflect structural movements accurately.

Useful places to acquire data are the tops of column baseplates, because these elements usually are installed at elevations close to those specified. Differences in elevations of the tops of structural steel at various places on any level of the building usually are reliable indications of settlement amounts. When the floor system is concrete slab, analysis of the patterns of elevation differences, as measured on the top of slabs next to columns over several floor levels, can reveal settlement amounts.

The investigation must establish whether the original, as-built positions can be determined with sufficient certainty. Normal construction tolerances allow floor surfaces, for instance, to vary from specified elevations. Data should be assessed with consideration to the possibility that data points were not precisely at specified elevations, but within tolerances. Furthermore, it is common for buildings to be erected out of level or out of plumb.

If an as-built survey was performed at the time of construction, it can be used to compare to the data collected during the investigation. The investigator must assess the precision with which field surveys are performed so that measurement errors do not unduly affect judgment about settlement. When high precision is required, such as when movements are to be monitored over time, special survey instruments and procedures are needed to achieve the required precision.

Sometimes useful information can be obtained by observing the architectural and structural features of the building. For instance, mortar joints in masonry construction usually are constructed relatively straight and level.

Once the amount of settlement is known, the load effects on the structure must be determined by analysis. Reliable models must represent the behavior of the structure as it is deformed. Using these reliable models, forces in structural elements can be evaluated by imposing the measured support movements. Care must be taken to ensure that the model adequately represents connection stiffness and the potential for bearing points or connections to slip under load. Furthermore, if structural materials are susceptible to stress relaxation, these effects must be considered when determining the residual forces in members.

REFERENCES

1. American Society of Civil Engineers, *Minimum Design Loads for Buildings and Other Structures,* ASCE 7-98, New York.

2. American Institute of Steel Construction, Inc., *Manual of Steel Construction, Load & Resistance Factor Design,* 2d ed., AISC, 1994.

3. American Concrete Institute, *Standard Specifications for Tolerances for Concrete Construction and Materials* (ACI 117-90), American Concrete Institute Committee 117, November 1989.

4. "Local Climatological Data Daily Summary," National Climatic Data Center, Asheville, NC.

5. T. A. Reinhold, ed., "Wind Tunnel Modeling for Civil Engineering Applications," *Proceedings of the International Workshop on Wind Tunnel Modeling Criteria and Techniques in Civil Engineering Applications,* Gaithersburg, MD, Cambridge University Press, 1982.

6. N. Stubbs and D. C. Perry, "Engineering of the Building Envelope," *Proceedings,* ASCE Conference on Hurricanes of 1992, Miami, 1993.

7. D. Surry, R. B. Kitchen, and A. G. Davenport, "Design Effectiveness of Wind Tunnel Studies for Buildings of Intermediate Height," *Canadian J. Civ., Engrg.,* 4(1): 96–116 (1977).

8. P. C. Sachs, *Wind Forces in Engineering,* vol. 3, Pergamon Press, New York, 1972.

9. N. Cook, *The Designer's Guide to Wind Loading of Building Structures,* Part I, Butterworth, London, 1985.

10. E. Simiu and R. H. Scanlan, *Wind Effects on Structures,* 3d ed., Wiley, New York, 1996.

11. American Society of Civil Engineers, *Minimum Design Loads for Buildings and Other Structures,* ASCE 7-93, New York.

12. D. W. Boggs and J. A. Peterka, "Wind Speeds for Design of Temporary Structures," *Proceedings of the ASCE Tenth Structures Congress,* San Antonio, TX, April 13–15, 1992, pp. 800–803.

13. H. I. Shapiro, J. P. Shapiro, and L. K. Shapiro, *Crane and Derricks,* 2d ed., McGraw-Hill, New York, 1991.

14. H. D. Nix, C. P. Bridges, and M. G. Powers, *Wind Loading on Falsework, Part I,* Caltrans Publication, Sacramento, CA, June 1975.

15. B. J. Vickery, P. N. Georgiou, and R. Church, "Wind Loading on Open-Framed Structures," *Third Canadian Workshop on Wind Engineering,* Vancouver and Toronto, Canada, 1981.

16. Robert D. Blevins, *Flow-Induced Vibration,* 2d ed., Krieger, Malabar, FL, 1994.

17. Federal Emergency Management Agency, *NEHRP Recommended Provisions for Seismic Regulations for New Buildings and Other Structures,* 1997 edition, Part 2— Commentary, FEMA 303, February 1998.

18. R. K. McGuire, G. R. Toro, and W. J. Silva, "Engineering Model of Earthquake Ground Motion for Eastern North American," Report NP-6074, Electric Power Research Institute, Palo Alto, CA, October 1988.

19. Weston Geophysical Corporation, "Seismic Design Recommendation, Massachusetts Water Resources Authority, Deer Island Secondary Treatment Facility," Weston Geophysical Report prepared for Metcalf & Eddy, Inc., Wakefield, MA, 1989.

20. G. M. Kinson and D. M. Boore, "Ground Motion Relations for Eastern North America," *Bull. Seism. Soc. Am.,* 85: 17–30 (1995).

21. G. R. Martin and R. Dobry, "Earthquake Site Response and Seismic Code Provisions," *NCEER Bulletin,* 8: 1–6 (1994).

22. D. Sadigh, C. Y. Chang, N. A. Abrahamson, S. J. Chiou, and M. S. Power, "Specifications of Long Period Ground Motions; Updated Attenuation Relationships for Rock Site Conditions and Adjustment Factors for Near-Fault Effects," *Proceedings, Seminar on Seismic Isolation, Passive Energy Dissipation and Active Control,* Report No. ATC-17-1, Applied Technology Council, Redwood City, CA, 1993.

23. *Seismological Research Letters,* 68(1) (1997), Seismological Society of America.

24. Federal Emergency Management Agency, *NEHRP Recommended Provisions for Seismic Regulations for New Buildings and Other Structures,* 1997 ed., Part 1— Provisions, FEMA 302, February 1998.

25. American Society of Civil Engineers, *Ocean Wave Measurement and Analysis,* vols. 1 and 2, *Proceedings* 3rd International Symposium, Waves, 1997.

26. American Society of Civil Engineers, "Wave Forces on Inclined and Vertical Wall Structures," Committee on Waves and Wave Forces of the Waterway, Port, Coastal and Ocean Engineering Division, 1995.

27. H. W. Liepmann and A. Roshko, *Elements of Gas Dynamics,* Wiley, New York, 1957.

28. H. L. Brode, "Numerical Solution of Spherical Blast Waves," *J. App. Phys.,* no. 6, June 1955.

29. M. Y. H. Bangash, *Impact and Explosion Analysis and Design,* CRC Press, Boca Raton, FL, 1993.

30. G. C. Mays and P. D. Smith, "Blast Effects on Buildings," *Design of Buildings to Optimize Resistance to Blast Loading,* Thomas Telford Publications, London, 1995.

31. American Society of Civil Engineers, *The Oklahoma City Bombing: Improving Building Performance Through Multi-Hazard Mitigation,* Federal Emergency Management Agency, FEMA 277, August 1996.

32. Joint Departments of the Army, the Navy, and the Air Force, "Structures to Resist the Effects of Accidental Explosions," Revision 1, TM 5-1300/NAVFAC P-397/AFR 88-22, November 1990.

33. American Iron and Steel Institute, *Fire-Resistant Steel-Frame Construction,* Washington, 1974.

34. Report of a Joint Committee of The Institution of Structural Engineers and The Concrete Society, *Fire Resistance of Concrete Structures,* The Institution of Structural Engineers, London, 1975.

35. Report of a Concrete Society Working Party, *Assessment of Fire-Damaged Concrete Structures and Repair by Gunite,* Concrete Society Technical Report No. 15, London, 1978.

36. *Fire Engineering for Building Structures and Safety,* The Institution of Engineers, BArton, ACT, Australia, 1989.

37. M. Holmes, R. D. Anchor, G. M. E. Cook, and R. N. Crook, R.N., "The Effects of Elevated Temperatures on the Strength Properties of Reinforcing and Prestressing Steels," *The Structural Engineer,* 60B(1) (March 1982).

38. American Institute of Steel Construction, Inc., *Manual of Steel Construction, Load & Resistance Factor Design,* 1st ed., AISC, Chicago, 1986.

39. D. O. Dusenberry, "Evaluation and Repair of Fire Damage to Amhearst College Gymnasium," *International Symposium Re-evaluation of Concrete Structures,* Lyngby, Denmark, 1988.

40. E. Salse and T. D. Lin, "Structural Fire Resistance of Concrete," *Journal of the Structural Division,* ASCE, 102(ST1) (January 1976).

41. *Control of Cracking in Concrete Structures,* ACI 224R-90, American Concrete Institute, Farmington Hills, MI 1990.

42. *Prediction of Creep, Shrinkage, and Temperature Effects in Concrete Structures,* ACI 209R-92, American Concrete Institute, Farmington Hills, MI, 1992.

43. American Forest & Paper Association, *National Design Specification for Wood Construction,* 1997 ed., ANSI/AF & PA NDS-1997, American National Standard, August 7, 1997.

CHAPTER 11
STEEL STRUCTURES

John W. Fisher, Ph.D., P.E., and Alan W. Pense, Ph.D.

INTRODUCTION

The discussion of engineering properties of structural materials in this chapter assumes some familiarity with both the properties of standard structural steels and alloys and the basic behavior of steels as found in a variety of handbooks and textbooks. For example, the mechanical properties of structural and other steels are found in current editions of the *Metals Handbook,* desk edition (ASM International, Materials Park, OH 44073) or within the current American Society for Testing Materials (ASTM) Specifications, the most relevant being found in volume 01.04, *Steel-Structural Reinforcing, Pressure Vessel, and Railway* (American Society for Testing and Materials, 100 Bar Harbor Drive, West Conshohocken, PA 19428).

A review of the compositions and properties of the structural steels indicates that, in spite of the variety of specifications, most structural steels share the same basic composition: carbon contents of 0.10 to 0.30 percent, manganese contents of 0.5 to 1.3 percent, silicon contents up to 0.4 percent, and phosphorus and sulfur contents up to 0.05 percent (as residuals from the steelmaking process). For grades which require greater corrosion resistance, or for which greater strength or toughness is desired, alloy additions of copper, nickel, chromium, and molybdenum up to 0.7 percent may be employed.

The vast majority of these materials are not heat-treated, but rather their microstructure and properties reflect the hot rolling and air cooling cycles that result from the production of plates and shapes. Their metallurgical microstructure is coarser in the heavier sections, resulting in lower strength, and this is often compensated for by increasing the carbon and alloy content as the section thickness increases. This is reflected in some ASTM specifications.

From the late 1960s until the present, structural steels with higher strength, toughness, or corrosion resistance are increasingly being used. Some of these steels require heat treatment to achieve their properties, typically quenching and tempering, and they usually have higher alloy content.

The typical strength of structural steels, as measured by the normal tension test (to be discussed later), has also gradually increased over the last 40 years. The typical yield strength of the earlier steels was 35 to 40 ksi (240 to 275 MPa), while tensile strengths were 60 to 70 ksi (415 to 485 MPa). Old structural materials had a yield strength close to 30 ksi (210 MPa). Currently, many structures utilize steels with yield strengths of 50 ksi (345 MPa), and tensile strengths of over 65 ksi (450 MPa), with some having yield strengths of 100 ksi (690 MPa) and tensile strengths greater than 115 ksi (795 MPa).

Toughness requirements for structures, typified by the use of Charpy impact test specifications, have also grown steadily in the last 40 years. Most structures built prior to 1945 were designed without any toughness requirements. Analysis of the brittle fracture of ships in World War II led to the development of the Charpy impact test and to toughness requirements for some ship hull steels. In the 1950s and 1960s, toughness requirements were extended to pressure vessels and in the 1970s, to bridges. The 1960s and 1970s were also the period during which new and more sophisticated methods of analysis of brittle fractures, primarily using the concepts of fracture toughness, were developed for aerospace structures, and are now widely applied for other structures.

The results of these efforts have been an increasing expectation that structural steels will be both strong and tough. It should be remembered during forensic analysis of older structures that toughness requirements were typically not a part of the design, materials selection, or construction process, and are still not a part of the design or materials selection process for most buildings. In forensic analysis, however, understanding of the toughness properties of the steels involved in a failure may be the key to explaining the sequence of events, whether or not the properties were part of design consideration.

In the presentation of failures related to design problems in this chapter, a basic knowledge of allowable stress design (ASD) is assumed. Until recent time, in one form or another, this design philosophy was the principal one used in structures. The use of ASD is widely discussed in basic textbooks such as *Structural Steel Design, ASD Method* by Jack C. McCormick (4th ed., HarperCollins, 1992). The pre-1986 versions of the American Institute of Steel Construction Codes employ ASD.

In this chapter, however, the analysis of structures by load and resistance factor design (LRFD) is recommended when forensic analysis is undertaken. It is recognized that many existing structures were designed on the basis of ASD concepts, and it may be, and probably will be, necessary to use ASD to determine that a failed structure was originally designed in an acceptable manner. In a post-failure analysis, however, the question to be answered is a broader one—not how it was designed, but why it failed. There is substantial support for the use of LRFD analysis to determine the true capacity of structures, and for this reason, analysis on the basis of LRFD is emphasized in this chapter. A basic text on LRFD concepts is *LRFD Steel Design* by William T. Sequi (PWS Publishing Company, 1994). A text comparing ASD and LRFD is *Design of Steel Structures* by E. H. Gaylord, Charles N. Gaylord, and James E. Stallmeyer (3d ed., McGraw-Hill, 1992). This latter text will also be useful to those who do not have a working familiarity with tension, fatigue, and impact testing. The basics of these tests, which are discussed in the next section, are found in *Design of Steel Structures.*

ENGINEERING PROPERTIES OF STRUCTURAL MATERIALS

Strength and Strength-Related Properties

The most common measure of the resistance of structural steel materials to failure is the *strength* of the members. The normal methodology for determining these properties is typically through yield and tensile strength, but the ductility characteristics of the steels, total elongation, and reduction of area also play a role. These properties are defined by ASTM[1] Specifications such as E8 and A370. The significance of these properties to failure is discussed later in this chapter; but, in general, since design against failure requires a knowledge of the maximum load which any part of a structure must be able to bear without either excessive local or general yielding or separation of members through ductile fracture, they are critical properties.

The significance of the ductility-based parameters, total elongation and reduction of area, is not that designers normally plan to directly utilize these properties; i.e., they design structures to undergo general yielding, but rather to demonstrate that the materials are being used in the ductile rather than in the brittle regime. Since all structures, especially welded structures, have local "hot spot" stresses that can be at the yield point of the material, the ability to plastically deform to relax or redistribute these local stresses is essential to the practical utilization of the measured yield and tensile strength. Normal design practice is based on utilizing only some fraction of the yield and tensile strengths of the materials, typically on the order of 70 percent of the yield strength and/or 50 percent of the tensile strength, thus leaving a reserve "safety factor" beyond that which may result from typically conservative sizing of members.

However, potential problems exist when the tensile or other mechanical properties of steels are determined according to the requirements of ASTM Specification A6 or A20, which is the normal practice. These two specifications, for materials for general construction and for pressure vessel materials, respectively, also define the manner in which tension and other kinds of tests shall be made, where tests to measure these properties will be taken, and how many tests shall be run. In attempting to use these measurements to determine what the mechanical properties of a structural material are at a potential or actual failure location, it is important to realize that the metallurgical structure and therefore strength, ductility, and toughness of a steel will vary with material thickness, location within a specific member, and even location within the original ingot (if ingot cast) from which it was produced. These variations are not usually revealed when performing standard tests taken from standard locations with specimens in standard orientations, and thus it may be essential to perform tests at the locations and in the orientations which, as much as possible, match those of the actual or potential failure in service. Deviations from standard test values determined from such nonstandard tests should not be taken as a failure of the material to meet "specifications" unless modified test procedures were requested and agreed to by the material supplier; but the deviations can reveal why a failure occurred or could occur even though it would otherwise seem unlikely.

Toughness and Fracture Toughness

Toughness testing, when performed for structural steels, is usually confined to the Charpy impact test as defined by ASTM Specification E23. The locations of test pieces and testing specimen sizes are also designated in ASTM Specification A673 for structural steels (where toughness tests are frequently only a supplemental requirement) and ASTM Specification A20 for pressure vessel steels. The reality is that, with the exception of some bridge member specifications [covered in ASTM Specification A709, AWS (American Welding Society) code[2] D1.51, and AASHTO[3] (American Association of State Highway and Turnpike Officials)] and pressure vessel toughness requirements, which are covered in the ASME (American Society for Mechanical Engineers[4]) Boiler and Pressure Vessel Code, many structures are built without any toughness specification being applied to the steels utilized, and thus the potential for brittle fracture is always present.

The fact that more brittle fractures do not occur in structures is attributable to a number of factors. First, the materials codes allowed to be used in many applications have evolved over time to the point where steels with really unsatisfactory toughness are no longer employed, even when toughness is not explicitly measured. Second, in applications where high levels of toughness are truly required, codes and specifications have been created that make toughness testing mandatory. Third, the toughness of structural steels is strain-rate sensitive. Because of their size, and therefore inherent inertia, large structures have service loading rates that are rarely as great as the material experiences in the Charpy impact test. Thus, there is an inherent, often unrecognized, safety factor built into these steels which engineers can utilize; i.e., they are tougher in service than the Charpy test predicts. The AASHTO bridge code recognizes and utilizes this factor explicitly. Fourth, stresses in some structures are sufficiently low to preclude brittle fractures. And fifth, modern steelmaking practice has evolved in the direction of lower carbon contents and more sophisticated processing for structural steels, both of which improve toughness performance.

For some, but not many, structural applications, fracture toughness characterizations using linear elastic or elastic-plastic fracture toughness testing are required. These tests are typically governed by ASTM Specifications, such as E813, E1152, and E1290. These types of tests can provide substantially more information about fracture potential in structures, but require a more sophisticated testing capability to perform and a more sophisticated analysis of the data to ascertain how the results can be applied to a given structure.

When a postfailure fracture evaluation is being performed in which the size of the initiating flaw can be determined, a fracture mechanics analysis is very useful because it enables the investigator to relate the size of the initiating flaw a, the stress of the flaw σ, and the critical stress intensity for fracture of the material K_c.

These factors are related, in a simplified way, as follows:

$$K_c = C\sigma \sqrt{\frac{\pi a}{Q}} \tag{11.1}$$

Here C and Q are factors that depend on the geometry and location or the flaw a in the structure. For thick materials in which the flaw is transverse to the stress, K_c decreases to a minimum for the material at a given temperature, and is referred to as K_{IC}, the plane strain fracture toughness. The units of a are inches (millimeters), the stress units are ksi (MPa), and the K_c units are ksi $\sqrt{\text{in}}$ (MPa $\sqrt{\text{m}}$).

If the stress on the flaw and the material fracture toughness can be determined through testing or calculation, then the critical flaw size in other parts of the structure or similar structures can be determined. This knowledge allows for creation of an inspection plan to seek additional flaws that may be subcritical but growing, and to assess factors of safety. If the calculated critical flaw is too small to be readily detected, the potential for fractures is high. The methods for the determination of critical flaw sizes in structures are found in Ref. 5.

Since formal fracture mechanics toughness tests are more difficult and expensive to perform than Charpy impact tests, many investigators use empirical correlations between Charpy impact tests and more formal fracture mechanics tests to establish approximate values of fracture toughness to use in calculations of critical flaw sizes in structures. This methodology also has its complications since it is necessary to compensate for strain rate effects and constraint effects related to thickness, but it is an invaluable tool for assessing fracture conditions when only Charpy toughness data are available. This methodology is also well described in Ref. 5.

Fatigue and Fatigue-Crack Growth Properties

Historic fatigue failure analysis utilizes rotating (bending) or axial (tension) smooth bar specimens to establish stress versus number of cycles to failure curves (*S/N* curves) to predict the fatigue life of structures. This type of analysis assumes that the structure or component, like the test specimen, is flaw-free, and failure results from initiation and then growth of fatigue cracks. The specimens are sometimes modified to incorporate notches or grooves to simulate the configuration of service components. The "smooth" bar tests for steels usually show a plateau in the *S/N* curve below which no failure will occur for millions of cycles, and design stresses below this level are assumed to preclude fatigue failure. Axial fatigue tests of this type are covered by ASTM Specification E466.

For complex structures, however, these tests are not particularly helpful because (1) structures are rarely flaw-free since fabrication operations often create small but significant flaws and (2) if welding processes are used, welding creates both high local residual stress levels and microscopic flaws at the welds. The effect of these conditions is to eliminate the crack initiation portion of this classical *S/N* curve so that only the crack growth portion of the curve applies. This renders the classical *S/N* curve a poor predictor of the fatigue behavior of structures.

An alternate procedure for predicting fatigue life in structures using fracture mechanics characterizations provides a more effective approach to both failure analysis and failure avoidance. This procedure relates the service stress range $\Delta\sigma$ in the structure to the stress intensity range ΔK in the vicinity of the flaws or discontinuities and allows prediction of the rate of flaw growth at any point in the life of the structure. With this information and a knowledge of the material K_{IC}, the time at which the growing flaw becomes or will become critical to the integrity of the structure can be predicted. Knowledge of the fracture mechanics crack growth properties of the material, as well as its K_{IC}, can be a powerful tool in both failure analysis and failure prevention for live loaded structures. The methodology used in these calculations is also found in Ref. 5.

It is based on the relationship

$$\frac{da}{dN} = A(\Delta K)^m \tag{11.2}$$

where a is crack length, N is the number of cycles, ΔK is the stress intensity factor fluctuation, and A and m are constants. The units of a and ΔK are as indicated above.

An application of the fracture mechanics approach to bridges is found in the AASHTO bridge code, where the stress ranges applied to typical design details are correlated to fatigue lives, assuming the structure is welded and the fabrication and inspection procedures have eliminated all macroscopic flaws. This approach has proved to be accurate in prediction of failure in a large number of live loaded structures but appears not be widely recognized outside the bridge field.

Corrosion and Deterioration

Of all the material properties that relate to service behavior and failure, perhaps the most difficult to characterize and predict is corrosion resistance. This is primarily due to the fact that corrosion processes are complex chemical reactions that are sensitive to small changes in the service environment, the chemical composition of the material, stress, electric currents, the combinations of materials present, material strength, geometric configuration, and other factors. Thus, it is not surprising that there are myriad ASTM specifications covering general corrosion, stress corrosion, electrochemical corrosion measurements, seawater corrosion, and intergranular corrosion, to name but a few.

Failure analysis of corrosion controlled or assisted failures is a complex engineering science which usually necessitates familiarity with, or experience in, corrosion engineering. A good general reference in this field is Ref. 6.

STRUCTURAL STEEL CODES AND STANDARDS

Since most structures are intended to be in compliance with some industry- or government-endorsed code or specification, structural failure analysis will inevitably involve a determination of whether the materials involved were or were not in compliance with the relevant specification, and whether the structure was designed and fabricated in compliance with the relevant code. In fact, many of these codes, standards, and specifications are interlocked by cross-references, creating a complex legal and engineering puzzle when a failure of structural integrity analysis is required. For example, materials and their properties are often referenced to ASTM Specifications. The ASTM Specifications usually include both the chemical composition of the material and its mechanical properties. Occasionally they also specify a heat treatment by which its properties are to be achieved. However, materials may also be referenced to an American Iron and Steel Institute (AISI)[7] standard or a similar standard created by another metals industry (aluminum, copper, etc.). These standards usually only specify composition, with properties being dependent on heat treatment (which may or may not be part of the specification). Sometimes ASTM Specifications also reference AISI Standards or SAE[8] (Society of Automotive Engineers) specifications.

Structural design and fabrication codes, such as those of the AISC (American Institute for Steel Construction),[9] the AASHTO, the AREMA (American Railway

Engineering and Maintenance-of-Way Association),[10] and the API (American Petroleum Institute), specify materials, sometimes by reference to ASTM, but also specify design rules and fabrication procedures, such as bolting or welding requirements. When the latter are specified, it is normal to invoke the AWS *Structural Welding Code,* D1.1, which specifies welding materials, procedures, and procedure qualifications. On the other hand, some industries, such as the pressure vessel industry, rely on the ASME *Boiler and Pressure Vessel Code,* a comprehensive code that specifies design rules, materials and their properties, welding and other fabrication procedures, and inspection methodology. Even this code cross-references ASTM, AISI, and AWS codes and standards.

As a result, when assessing the integrity of a structure, it is often necessary to follow an extended trail of information and certification to determine what codes and standards are or were applicable to the structure *when it was constructed.* Since these codes and standards change over time, it is often necessary to pursue the trail through historic standards, not current ones. This process may lead to the conclusion that the structure in question meets the standards of the time of its construction but not those of today. Such a finding may be particularly important if the structure is to be retrofitted or repaired so it can be returned to service. It may have to be retrofitted extensively if it is to be upgraded to current standards.

METHODS OF ANALYSIS

Many structures and their components can be evaluated by using simple equilibrium models and basic principles of mechanics to determine stress resultants acting on the member. Loads and load combinations are specified in the AISC LRFD specifications for structural steel buildings with the recommended minimum loads given in Ref. 11 (ASCE 7, *Minimum Design Loads for Buildings and Other Structures*). These loads are sometimes modified by the applicable building code (i.e., Ref. 12).

The availability of a larger number of structural analysis and design computer programs provide tools that are readily available to model and analyze the structure under a variety of loading conditions. Where there is no evidence of significant plasticity, an elastic analysis will provide reasonable estimates of the failure load.

Where obvious plasticity has occurred such that large deformations are apparent, a nonlinear analysis can be carried out. Many programs have the capability to account for nonlinear characteristics of the material and the structural system.

Where the complexity of the system warrants it, finite element analysis can be carried out to evaluate stress concentrations as well as nonlinear behavior.

Design Codes: Loads and Resistance Factor Design

Increasingly, design codes are moving toward load and resistance factor design (LRFD).[13,14] The basic limit states are strength and serviceability. For structural steel buildings the AISC LRFD Specification provides a sound means of assessing the strength of structural members and connections.

Similarly, the AASHTO Specification provides a sound basis for assessing the strength and performance of highway bridges. The serviceability limit state of fatigue and fracture often is the cause of cracking under the random variable live loads that the structure is subjected to. The HS15 *fatigue truck* represents the root mean cube load that is characteristic of the variable load spectrum that highway bridges will be subjected to. It is based on the linear damage hypothesis attributed to Miner. The load cycles from vehicle passage produce stress range cycles that can be related to life in the exponential model given in Eq. (11.6). The specification uses an impact factor for fatigue equal to 0.15 which is based on experimental observations of in-service bridges.

Steel railroad bridges are designed by American Railway Engineering and Maintenance-of-Way Association (AREMA) Specifications. These remain an allowable stress design for strength.

Other Major Codes

Several other codes are used to design and assess steel structures. Some are relied upon by several of the design codes for specific issues. For example, the American Society for Testing and Materials provides standardization of materials and methods of testing which are relied upon by the AISC, AASHTO, and AREMA Specifications for designing building and bridge structures. Likewise, the American Welding Society (AWS) Specifications are utilized to identify welding electrodes and fluxes, to qualify welders and weld processes, and to provide quality assurance.

Steel railroad bridges are designed and rated by Committee 15 of the AREMA Specifications. These remain in the allowable stress design format. Serviceability limits for fatigue and fracture use a design reference load for new construction. Actual traffic is used to rate and assess existing bridges.

Other codes such as the AISI *Load and Resistance Factor Design Specification for Cold-Formed Steel Members* deals with light structural building components such as purlins, columns, joists; metal deck provides a means of assessing light-gauge components and systems. The ASME Pressure Vessel Code and the API Code may be useful for special structures.

CRITICAL CHARACTERISTICS OF STEEL STRUCTURES

The basic limit states that govern the design of steel structures provide the basis for understanding why a steel member, an assemblage of members, or the entire structure experiences distress or fails.[15,16] These limit states are the following:

- *Yielding* is a common failure mode for many components as the elastic limit is exceeded. This can result in visible deformation as members are stretched or bent.

- *Ductile tearing and fracture* occur when the tensile strength of the steel has been exceeded. Often this is at a connection where the section is reduced by holes or geometric change; large deformations and necking of the material are often apparent.

- *Buckling* of members and components is an indication that the buckling capacity has been exceeded. This may be the result of inadequate bracing and lateral support, higher-than-anticipated load, or other factors that were not anticipated in the design.

- *Fatigue cracking* can result from cyclic loads that exceed the fatigue strength of a given detail. Another possibility is that unusual defects or geometric cracklike conditions exist that are susceptible to crack growth from cyclic loads. Generally, fatigue cracks do not exhibit yielding. Fracture can result when the material (base metal and/or weld metal) is relatively brittle or a large crack already existed. A preexisting crack or defect may first enlarge from fatigue, and then fracture or fabrication defects and brittle welds may cause a fracture. There is often no significant evidence of yielding indicating that the material's fracture resistance is low.

Connections are the most common source of failures both during construction and in service. Welds may be defective because of lack-of-fusion (LOF) cracks, slag, or geometric cracklike fusion planes that are perpendicular to the stress field. High-strength bolts may be improperly installed. Connections are the critical links that permit transfer of the forces in a member. Hence, one or more critical conditions may exist in a connector or in the connection because of the primary cause of failure.

Most structures have a degree of redundancy. This can provide alternate load paths should a local failure occur. In these cases, the damage is limited, and the local failure does not result in collapse. In many cases the redundancy of the system is enhanced by contributions that are not even accounted for in the design model. For example, roof decking may act compositely with the supporting members due to friction, tack welds, and other minor contributions.

Design Parameters

Members such as beams, columns, and their connections are prepositioned to resist design loads. The applicable design limit states must be satisfied to ensure that the component is capable of resisting the applied loads.

Beams, e.g., must satisfy the applicable limit state for flexure which may be yielding, lateral buckling, local buckling of its flange or web, or web crippling if concentrated loads are applied to the web such as at support points. Lateral buckling is dependent on the type and spacing of lateral supports provided to the beam compression flange.

Columns are designed for axial loads if they serve primarily as compression members. Often they also resist bending as a beam-column. Lateral support and bracing of the compression member govern its design capacity and are essential to its performance.[17]

Often beams and columns are assembled into frames for buildings. Their connections are critical to the frames' performance. Rigid frames utilize moment-resisting connections that resist sway and deformation of the frame. Depending on the structure and loads, secondary effects may need to be considered. Braced frames rely on truss-type bracing to resist lateral loads and deformations. They may use simple, partial, or full moment-resisting connections.

Bridges make extensive use of beams and girders to support the roadway. Girders are supported by piers and abutments and may have transverse members or diaphragms between the girders. These provide lateral support to the compression flanges during construction and before the roadway is installed. The roadway may act compositely with the beams and the girders after construction. The transverse diaphragms or floor beams play a minor role, providing lateral support to the top compression flange once the slab has been completed.

Connection Design

Connections are typically designed to transfer the joint forces to which they are subjected. Generally simple equilibrium models are used to proportion the mechanical or welded connectors and the plate or beam elements used in the connection.[18–20] Design criteria and procedures are fully explained in these references.

The connectors generally used for steel structures are either high-strength bolts or welds.

Bolts are designed based on their nominal shank area A_b for both tension and shear. For tension, the nominal strength is provided by

$$F_n = C_t F_u \tag{11.3}$$

where F_u is the minimum specified tensile strength and $C_t = 0.75$, which is the ratio of the stress area to the nominal shank area.

For shear, the nominal strength of a single bolt is provided by

$$F_v = C_s F_u \tag{11.4}$$

The coefficient $C_s = 0.62$ for a single bolt when the threads are excluded from the shear plane. This coefficient is reduced to $C_s = 0.5$ to account for connection lengths up to 50 in parallel to the line of force. When threads are not excluded from the shear plane, the coefficient C_s is reduced by 20 percent to $C_s = 0.496$ and 0.4, respectively.

Bolts transfer forces from one component into another by bearing and shear of the fastener. This can result in net section failure of the connected member. Another failure mode is block shear, which combines the tension and shear resistance of the connected elements. An example of a combination of two of these failure modes can be seen in Fig. 11.1. This shows four angles of a tension chord member framing into a gusset plate. Two angles have caused the connecting bolts to fail in double shear. The other two angles show failure on the net section. This indicates that all elements were at their design load capacity.

The commonly used weld connectors are either groove welds or fillet welds. Groove welds are designed for the same basic capacity as the connected base metal. Fillet welds, on the other hand, are designed for the weld throat area, which is the effective cross-sectional area of the weld. The nominal strength of a linear weld group loaded in-plane through the center of gravity is[18,21]

$$F_w = 0.6F_{EXX}(1.0 + 0.5 \sin^{1.5} \theta) \tag{11.5}$$

where F_{EXX} is the electrode classification number (minimum specified strength in pounds per square inch) and θ is the angle of loading measured from the longitudinal axis in degrees. Hence, when the load is parallel to the weld, the capacity is $0.6F_{EXX}$, and when it is perpendicular to the longitudinal axis, it increases to $0.9F_{EXX}$.

Discontinuities such as porosity and slag seldom cause a significant loss of static strength. On the other hand, lack of fusion or cracks can have a major impact on strength and can result in joint failure at loads below the design load. This will depend on the size of the discontinuity or defect and its orientation to the applied loads.

Fatigue and Fracture Design

Fatigue and fracture are often closely related phenomena as both involve cracking. Fracture control involves material fracture toughness, controlling crack extension usually by considering fatigue strength, quality control to prevent undesirable defects and discontinuities that are susceptible to crack extension and premature failure, and in-service inspection when cyclic loading is a design consideration.

Fatigue resistance is governed by the stress range to which a given structural detail is subjected. The residual tension stresses that exist at all as-welded details are a primary reason that the dead load stress or mean stress has a negligible impact on fatigue strength.

Figure 11.2 shows the fatigue crack surface of a welded cover plate detail where the crack has formed at the weld toe in the heat-affected zone and has propagated into the flange plate as a semielliptical surface crack until it extended through the plate thickness. Beachmarklike features can be seen on the smooth crack surface. Once the crack became an edge crack, the rate of crack growth increased; this is apparent in the rough surface features as the crack extended toward the beam web.

FIGURE 11.1   Tension member failure showing net section fracture and bolt shear failure.

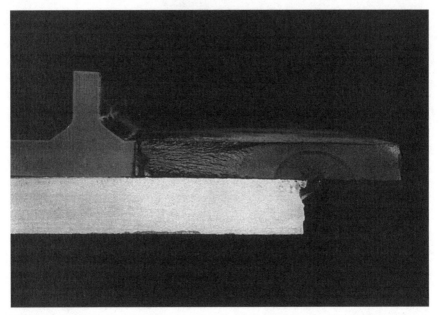

FIGURE 11.2 Fatigue crack forming at the end of a longitudinal weld attaching a coverplate to a flange.

Fatigue resistance does not depend on the type of steel or on its tensile properties. For a given type of detail, the fatigue strength is uniformly described by an exponential model[22,23] that relates life, N cycles, to the nominal stress range S_r

$$N = C_f S_r^{-3} \tag{11.6}$$

where C_f is a coefficient that defines the various categories of details. Coefficient C_f is defined in the AASHTO LRFD Specification and will appear in the 1999 AISC LRFD Specifications.

The stress range S_r is the nominal stress range in the base metal at the welded detail. It does not include the stress concentration from the weld geometry, as that is incorporated in the type detail classification and its coefficient C_f.

The fatigue limit for each category is an estimate of the stress range below which no cracking develops. The fatigue limit varies with the detail category. For category A it occurs at about 2×10^6 cycles and increases in life for all other categories reaching about 2×10^7 cycles for category E'.

Most structural systems are subjected to random variable loads that result in a skewed stress range spectrum. Laboratory studies on variable loaded details have demonstrated that fatigue cracks will develop when as few as 0.05 percent of the variable cycles exceed the category fatigue limit (CAFL). Miners effective stress range S_{re} is defined as

$$S_{re} = (\Sigma \alpha_i S_{ri}^3)^{1/3} \tag{11.7}$$

where α_i is the frequency of occurrence of stress range level S_{ri}. The effective stress range S_{re} from Eq. (11.7) can be used to define the total variable cycles N_v when substituted into Eq. (11.6), N_v replacing N, and S_{re} replacing S_r.

The greatest uncertainty in fatigue damage estimates lies in the actual service load history of the structural system. The resistance estimates provided by Eq. (11.4) are better defined than the service loads to which most systems are subjected.

Fracture toughness for structural steels is most often defined by the Charpy V-notch test for absorbed energy.[5] Generally members subjected to cyclic loading have mandatory values of absorbed Charpy V-notch energy (CVN) to ensure that fatigue cracking does not result in premature fracture. This requirement serves to screen out the use of steels that have a higher risk of brittle fracture because of notch sensitivity. Fracture toughness is highly desirable in weld metals as they are far more likely to have defects such as lack of fusion, slag, and gas pockets, and cracklike discontinuities when backing bars are used. Weld toughness played a major role in beam-column connection failures during the Northridge earthquake.

Design for Corrosion Control

Corrosion often develops in steel members when dirt and debris are allowed to accumulate and cause active corrosion cells due to wetting and lack of water control and the presence of other contributors to electrochemical cell activity, such as salts, bird guano, and other contaminants. Failure to keep exposed structural elements clean has been a problem with bridges, garages, stadiums, and many other structural systems.

Atmospheric corrosion can also lead to deterioration, but this depends on the corrosivity of the atmosphere at a specific location. Environmental protection laws have resulted in significant changes in atmospheric conditions at many locations. For example, the atmospheric conditions in the Bethlehem, Pennsylvania, area were observed to be about the same as those in a rural environment in the late 1980s rather than an industrial environment cited in the 1960s,[24,25] even though an integrated steelmaking facility remained in operation throughout that period.

Weathering steel has generally performed well when the environment was not a severe marine or industrial atmosphere and water was controlled. A protective oxide coating that acts as a self-healing barrier to further corrosion will form and will prevent significant loss. However, dirt and debris and lack of water control can result in a poultice and active corrosion cell loss.

TESTING OF MATERIALS AND STRUCTURES

The testing of base metals used in structures was discussed earlier in this chapter, where the importance of reference to ASTM Specifications both for testing procedures and for the mechanical properties of products is highlighted. When testing moves from the properties of steels in structural shapes, plates, forgings, rods, bars, etc., to fabricated structures and components, such as weldments, bolted connections, subassemblies, and even complete structures, then there are fewer standard methods of test, and the existing tests may not provide the needed information.

This is well illustrated in tests for weldability of steels used in structures. Within the AWS D1.1 *Structural Welding Code,* welding consumables, process parameters (preheat, postheat, weld heat input, etc.), and inspection criteria for welded quality for structural joints are mandated. The AWS D1.1 code also lists approved standard weld joint designs and procedures by which alternate joint designs may be approved.

Many welded structures rely on AWS "prequalified" welded joints to reduce the qualification tests that need to be run, or use qualification tests that are permitted to cover a range of plate thicknesses or are made under ideal conditions that do not represent the conditions under which the welds are actually made. Thus, these tests may not fully ensure that weldment discontinuities such as cracking will not occur. Another problem with these kinds of tests is that they do not usually separate *fabrication* weldability, which is an indication of whether the joint can be fabricated using the proposed procedure free of impermissible discontinuities, from *service weldability,* which is an indication of the performance of the weldment in service.

There are, in addition, a large number of weldability tests not in any code or specification which, although developed for research purposes, are used to evaluate weldments. Without attempting to describe these tests, we stress that they may measure either or both characteristics of weldments, and they may or may not represent the service weldments. Thus to use the results of "weldability" testing in a failure analysis is a complex and often confusing process.

Another complicating factor in weldment tests is the fact that weldments are a composite of both microstructures and materials. Weld metals, for a number of reasons, rarely have the same chemical composition or microstructure as the plates they join, and their composition and properties are also influenced by the consumables (flux, gas covering) used. In addition, the heat of welding creates a zone between the unaffected base plate and the weld metal, called the *heat-affected zone,* a region heated in some locations close to the melting point of the base plate and in others, only a little above room temperature. This means that the microstructure and properties of weldments cover a range that is difficult to sample in one test. Based on experience, current thinking is that sampling of the base metal, the weld metal, and the zone in the base metal just adjacent to the weld metal (the *coarse-grained* heat-affected zone) provides the relevant information on properties, especially toughness, of the weldment. The heat-affected zone is generally too narrow for tension testing; however, Charpy V-notch testing or fracture toughness testing can be done by careful (sometimes tedious) notching or precracking in the heat-affected zone.

During forensic analysis it is often necessary to examine failed weldments in much greater detail than they were initially examined, and tests in the weld metal and the heat-affected zone may provide critical information relating to fracture characteristics of the weldment. Sometimes it is necessary to duplicate welds similar to those in the structure in modified joint designs that have straight fusion lines perpendicular to the plate surface so that a straight and flat heat-affected zone results. This allows Charpy impact or fracture toughness specimens to be produced that have heat-affected zones that can be more accurately sampled. Since production weldments do not often have weld joint configurations that meet this criterion, even these idealized tests may yield data of uncertain value.

Almost no code or specification requires testing at the component or whole-structure level, with the notable exception of proof testing of pressure vessels and storage tanks. The pressure vessel procedure typically overpressurizes the vessel by 10 percent; and, in addition to providing some assurance of integrity, if performed at a temperature high enough to ensure that the vessel plates and weldments are in ductile range of toughness, it will blunt any cracks or other discontinuities that may be present. Proof tests of this type performed *below* the ductile-to-brittle transition temperature are potentially quite dangerous, especially in vessels made of steels of marginal quality. No such proof tests are normally employed in bridge or building codes (although some load tests have been done on bridges). For bridges, erection procedures sometimes inadvertently perform the same function.

Occasionally, both in forensic analysis and when new designs are contemplated, large-scale component or whole-structure tests are undertaken. It is essential (and may seem obvious) that they be carefully planned to duplicate the structure being studied, they be instrumented to provide the critical information required, and that the conditions of loading (and thus, the resulting fracture mode, if a full failure test is contemplated) be compatible with those known to be present in the structure. Because large-scale and full-structure tests are expensive and often provide only a single test result (success or failure), careful analysis of the structure prior to testing, installing good instrumentation, and gathering as much data as possible are a better investment than posttesting explanations. Despite the difficulties in performing them, in postfailure investigations, in demonstrating the viability of new designs, and in certifying the success of retrofitting procedures to prevent failures, full-size or large-component tests are sometimes the only way to provide information on how a complex structure will behave.

TYPES AND CAUSES OF NONPERFORMANCE AND FAILURE

Design Deficiencies

Gross design deficiencies may occasionally occur when a design assumption is not valid. An example was the nodal point supports of the Hartford Coliseum space frame. The top chord bracing did not provide support for the assumed column length. As illustrated in Fig. 11.3, the diagonal elements were connected to flexible gusset plates that were unable to prevent lateral displacement. Hence, the effective column length was nearly twice as great as assumed in the design.[26, 27] As a result, many members were highly overloaded and deformed, which redistributed load and resulted in total collapse of the structure, as illustrated in Fig. 11.4.

Another example is the creation of cracklike details where a lack-of-fusion plane results that is normal to cyclic stresses. This can result in unanticipated crack growth and premature failure. Figure 11.5 shows a crack that originated at the tip of a plate girder flange that was inserted through a box girder web. In this case the groove weld had significant lack of fusion because of the difficulty of making a full-penetration weld in such a short distance.[28] Similar conditions have been observed when *seal welds* were used, as illustrated in Fig. 11.6. Cracks were found to develop quickly, as illustrated in Fig. 11.7.

Details and connections are the most frequent source of failure or poor performance in structural systems. Both the connected material and the connectors (bolts or welds) may play a role in the failure. This is clear from the experience with heavy W shapes used in tension.[29] Fracture of the bottom chord adjacent to a groove welded splice can be seen in Fig. 11.8. Low toughness of the web-flange core region of the W14X370 section resulted in cracks forming in the flame-cut copes that were made to permit the web and flange groove welds as a result of the residual tensile stresses from weld shrinkage. Figure 11.9 shows the initial crack at the web cope that developed because of the low-toughness core material and the yield point stresses introduced by weld shrinkage. This preexisting crack subsequently was the source of the fracture that occurred as the structure was being built and dead loads were introduced into the tension chord. An examination of the cope

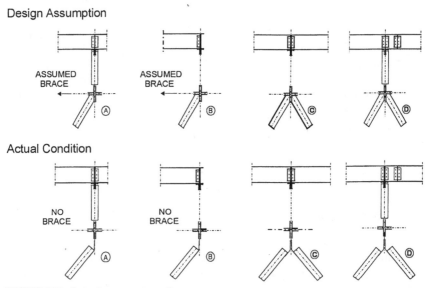

FIGURE 11.3   Lateral support connections.

FIGURE 11.4   Collapsed roof.

on the other side of the welded flange demonstrated that a crack had formed in that section as well (see Fig. 11.12a).

The experience with heavy shapes demonstrated the need to have improved toughness in the web-flange core of the base metal and improved finish and geometry of the weld access copes when such members are used in tension applications. Charpy V-notch tests of the core material demonstrated that the impact energy was between 3 and 10 ft·lb (4 and 14J) over a wide test temperature range [0 to 130°F (−18 to 55°C)]. Static fracture toughness tests were found to provide about 45 ksi $\sqrt{\text{in}}$ fracture resistance K_c over common service temperatures between 50 and 90°F (10 and 32°C). This low toughness is not critical for W sections used in columns and other compression members. When used in tension, the desirability of having better notch tough material has resulted in the AISC Specifications requiring supplemental CVN notch toughness in the core region of group 4 and 5 shapes and for plates thicker than 2 in (50 mm) when they are to be weld-spliced and used in tension applications. It also demonstrates the need to examine the fracture properties of the material when there is no evidence of yielding in the steel at the connection.

Brittle fractures of welded steel moment frame (WSMF) connections during the Northridge earthquake in 1994 are a related problem where low-toughness material, in this case the groove weld metal, became the principal reason for essentially elastic fractures of the connections.[30,31] In this case the discontinuities were the steel backing bars that were used at the column face and provided an unfused edge lack-of-fusion condition perpendicular to the bending stresses in the beam

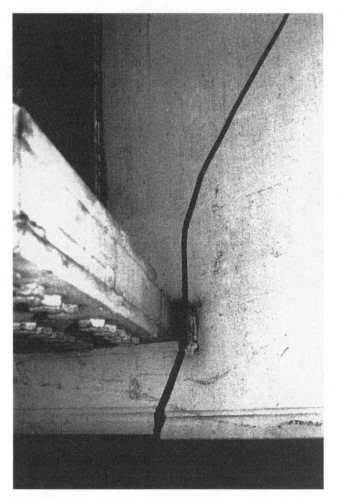

FIGURE 11.5   Crack that formed at box pier cap.

flanges, as illustrated in Fig. 11.10. This initial geometric condition provides an edge crack equal to the backing bar thickness and any lack of fusion (LOF) at the weld root. The stress intensity for this condition can be estimated as

$$K_{max} \cong 1.12\sigma \sqrt{\pi a} \qquad (11.8)$$

where $a = b_b$ + LOF (backing bar thickness + LOF), and σ is the sum of the dead load stress, residual tensile stress, and live load stress in the beam flange. The available test data have demonstrated that brittle weld metal is likely when E70T-4 flux core welds exist. The resistance to fracture for the groove weld shown in Fig. 11.10 is not much different from the base metal in the core of heavy W shapes that do not satisfy the supplemental CVN notch toughness in the core region. When low-toughness base metal or weld metal is used, careful attention will be required to assess notch conditions (flame-cut edges), cracklike geometric details and lack of fusion, and the role that residual stresses from the welding process and sequence play in the failure. Only notch tough material will be capable of ductile failure in the presence of severe notches and defects.

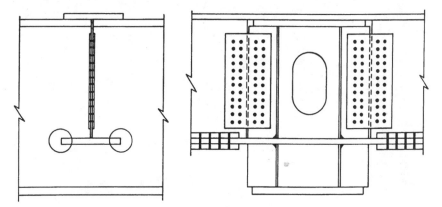

FIGURE 11.6   Seal welds between box girder web plates and inserted flange plate.

FIGURE 11.7   Crack detected at flange tip of plate girder flange in box web.

FIGURE 11.8 Fracture of jumbo section tension chord adjacent to groove weld at weld access hole.

FIGURE 11.9 Initial crack in web-flange core at web access hole.

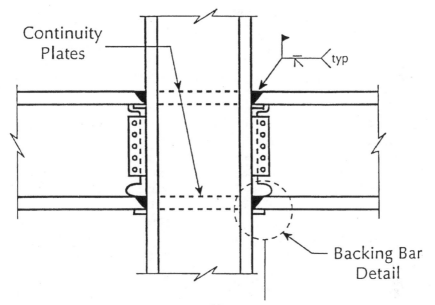

Continuity Plates

typ

Backing Bar Detail

(a)

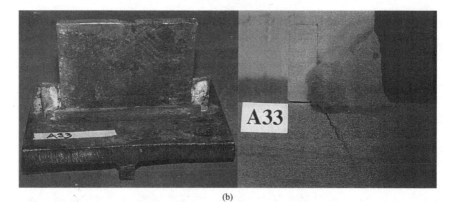

A33

(b)

FIGURE 11.10   Crack at bottom groove weld connection.

Fabrication and Erection Errors

For most structures, the connections of structural components to each other are frequently the places where discontinuities are most common, stresses are the highest, and, therefore, the structure is most failure-prone. It is in implicit recognition of this fact that most construction codes place more emphasis on these fabrication details and their inspection than on other places in the structure. In spite of this attention, failures occur most at connections of various types.

Failures of welded connections result most often because the welds contain discontinuities of such a type and size that fatigue and/or brittle fractures can occur rather than because of metallurgical deficiencies in the joint. Experience indicates that many common weldment discontinuities, such as porosity or inclusions, do not result in failure by brittle fracture or fatigue because they are rounded and do not serve as crack initiation or propagation sites.

The discontinuities in welds that do result in brittle fracture or fatigue failures are cracks, lack of penetration, and lack of fusion. The most common type of cracking experienced in structural weldments is hydrogen-induced *underbead* or *cold* cracks. These cracks are a result of residual stresses, the presence of hydrogen, and a base metal composition that results in a hard heat-affected zone microstructure. These cracks often form hours, possibly days, after welding and are located in the base plate heat-affected zone (under the weld bead) such that they cannot be easily seen. The most commonly employed preventive measure to avoid these cracks is to make sure the joint is free of moisture and grease and to use adequate preheat prior to welding. The International Institute of Welding (IIW)[32] has developed a predictive equation that indicates the susceptibility of a given steel to hydrogen-induced cracking.

$$C_{eq} = C + \frac{Mn}{6} + \frac{Cr + Mo + V}{5} + \frac{Ni + Cu}{15} \tag{11.9}$$

where C_{eq} is the carbon equivalent and C, Mn, Cr, etc. are the percentages of the alloy elements in the steel. A steel with a carbon equivalent of 0.45 percent or more is typically susceptible to hydrogen-induced cracking, and some preheat prior to welding is indicated. This typically starts at 150°F (65°C) but may exceed 300°F (150°C) for steels with carbon equivalents of 0.70 percent or more. The AWS D1.1 code lists recommended *minimum* preheats for structural steels. Typically, many fabricators apply some preheat to all joints to ensure that the joints are at least dry prior to welding.

Another important factor in preventing hydrogen-induced cracking is proper care of welding electrodes and other consumables, i.e., using low-hydrogen electrodes and fluxes and making sure the manufacturers' recommendations about keeping them moisture-free to ensure their low-hydrogen characteristics are followed. Low-hydrogen consumables are only low-hydrogen if they are properly maintained.

Another possible cause of fatigue and brittle fracture in weldments is lack of fusion in the joint. This usually results from either poor welding procedures or poor execution, and typically it leaves a cracklike unfused plane in the joint. Poor weld joint design can also lead to a cracklike defect, i.e., design that requires a weld to penetrate more deeply in a joint than can be expected with the weld parameters specified. Experience indicates that one of the common causes of lack of fusion (and other defects that can lead to fractures) is the use of backing bars to form the root of the weld bead in joints welded from one side, especially if they are not subsequently removed and the root repaired. Backing bars left in place are a common initiator of both fatigue and brittle fracture because they contain both lack-of-fusion discontinuities and cracks. Weld designs using backup bars are permitted in many welding codes but are much harder to execute successfully than most weld designers realize.

Welded design can create potential causes of fatigue and fracture even if the joint is "defect-free" because, unless ground smooth, they are a geometric discontinuity that promotes the growth of fatigue cracks and sometimes subsequent brittle fracture. Design codes, especially the AASHTO *Bridge Design Code,* includes provisions for assigning specific fatigue lives for various types of welded details. These life expectancy estimations include the effects of both the gross detail geometry and the effect of the unavoidable residual-stress patterns and microscopic weld toe discontinuities that are usually present. It is surprising that there are large segments of the structural community who design and operate live loaded structures, but are unaware of the provisions, and more important, the engineering data that form the basis for this code. Experience indicates that one of the more common causes of the fatigue failure of bridges, transportation vehicles, power transmission equipment, and many other structures subjected to cyclical loading is inadequate design of welded details, not inadequate welding. Of course, inadequate welding may also be a cause, so careful evaluation of welded joints experiencing fatigue cracking is necessary to identify the true cause.

Mechanical connections may be a cause of structural failure, but brittle fractures from this source are rare. Bolted or riveted joint failures are usually associated with inadequate design, but bolt failures due to fatigue cracking at thread roots or bolt-holes does occur in long-life service. Unless the materials joined are relatively low in toughness, or no inspection is made of the structure in service, these cracks can usually be identified before significant fractures occur. High-strength bolts, ASTM A490 types, e.g., are susceptible to stress corrosion cracking if their yield strength or hardness is too high. Cracking of these types of bolts under adverse environmental conditions can lead to significant structural failure. The ASTM specifications for high-strength bolts limit bolt hardness to avoid just such failures.

While structures are designed for service, they must usually go through an erection process during which they experience types of loading that they will not see in service. Failure during erection is most often due to inadequate care in the calculation of stresses on the members erected or the supports used in the process. Many failures are due to poorly designed temporary welds, lifting lugs, and restraining members. Too often lifting structures are not so much designed as simply built with the most cursory design in the expectation that their apparent size will render them adequate. The materials used in these structures are often of unknown origin or properties. Experience shows that erection failures can result from such an approach. Proper design for erection and proper attention to welding or bolting of these "temporary" structures as well as control of their composition and properties are mandatory for failure prevention.

A somewhat more general problem that can lead to structural failures is lack of proper review of shop drawings and erection or assembly plans. For a variety of reasons, the design of the structure may be changed between the time drawings are submitted to the fabricator and the structural components are actually built. These changes are usually, but not always, reflected in shop drawings; therefore a careful review of the sequence of design drawings, shop drawings, erection plans, and the as-built structure is sometimes necessary to trace why a structure has failed. At least one major structural failure, the Hyatt-Regency Skywalk in Kansas City, has been attributed to failure of a connection, the design of which was changed during shop fabrication. These drawings and plans should also be checked for tolerances and interferences. In one nuclear power facility, the seismic pipe restraints on the cooling water main for the reactor were placed in locations not as shown in the original design because of interference with equipment not shown on the drawings. The misplacement of these restraints invalidated the computer analysis of earthquake resistance of the facility, forcing a multimillion-dollar reanalysis and retrofit.

Service and Repair Errors

Repair of structures already in place, while sometimes necessary, is another potential source of structural failures. There is apparently a perception on the part of many engineers that repairs to correct corrosion problems or in-service cracking, or modifications to improve access, or to install new capacity, are of such a minor nature that no special care is required. Like temporary welds used to assist in erection, they are often not subjected to any particular design process, are placed in the wrong location, are executed carelessly, or are of inadequate strength. In some cases, the materials employed are not similar to, or compatible with, the materials and processes used in the original fabrication. For older structures made of steels having low weldability, welded repairs or additions are particularly troublesome.

Examples of this type are hangers for pipes or cables added to bridge members, welds made to steels of poor weldability to replace corrosion-damaged members, weld plugging of misdrilled or punched holes, and replacement bolts not properly tightened. In many of these cases, fatigue cracking from the stress concentrations not considered in the design process and/or cracking from an erroneous welding process occurs. Weld cracking also occurs because the repair weld is made in a now fairly rigid structure, which requires greater care and skill in welding and higher welding preheat than the original shop weld. When the repair is made in the field, neither of these requirements is likely to be met. Indeed, repair welding is often made without a well-thought-out weld procedure even though the weld configuration of the repair is seldom anything like a common or standard one and often nothing like the original one in the structure.

One of the most serious errors that is made as a result of such modifications, and which sometimes occurs even without modification, is to use a structure in a type of service which the original designer never intended. Examples of such modifications are reinforcement by welding of storage tanks to take higher loads than originally contemplated, increasing live loading in a structure without verification of fatigue life, or changing the density or height of a fluid in a storage tank without recalculation of resulting stress increases. All these types of errors have been documented to result in fractures in structures, some of them disastrous.

Deterioration Failure

Loss of section and in some cases fatigue cracking and fracture are examples of corrosion-induced deterioration that can ultimately damage or destroy structures. Fortunately, since deterioration is common, few instances of corrosion have caused loss of life, but the collapse a decade ago of a major span in the Mianus River Bridge due to corrosion processes is one example that did. During the past 25 years, corrosion conditions have also developed in a number of other bridge structures that have resulted in loss of service, costly repairs, and concern about the safety of these structures. Corrosion by itself may lead to failure conditions, but it can also promote, through section loss or pitting and grooving, fatigue crack initiation and growth that can cause failures.

Because most corrosion conditions are time-dependent, this is one failure mode that can usually be controlled by inspection and correction as it occurs. However, good inspection of structures requires that there be access to critical locations, that these locations be known, and that inspections be performed at appropriate intervals.

Since corrosion is an electrochemical process of a complex nature, it is difficult to describe briefly all the possible causes of corrosion in structures. However, the major types of corrosion can be highlighted, and some potentially critical situations are identified in the following paragraph.

For many structures, the primary corrosion mode is general atmospheric corrosion, and for steel products this occurs by rusting. Rust is the product of reactions of iron and steel with oxygen and moisture, and typically rust proceeds relatively slowly unless additional chemical continuants, such as ions from sodium chloride or other salts, are present to accelerate the process. The classical solution to this type of corrosion in structures is to create a barrier layer between the corroding solution and the steel surface, usually by painting. When the paint layer fails or is otherwise removed, corrosion occurs. Since the integrity of this barrier layer can usually be assessed by visual inspection, it is a situation that can be monitored and controlled.

There are some conditions under which corrosion in structures cannot be as easily assessed, typically where corrosion occurs in crevices and less accessible locations. Areas with crevices, under debris and dirt, and in confined spaces can also undergo accelerated and more aggressive corrosion processes. These locations are often kept moist, and electrochemical cells form which change the water chemistry and promote corrosion. For some years, this fact was not understood by users of "weathering" (ASTM A588) steels that were used in the unpainted condition with the expectation that normal atmospheric corrosion processes would lead to the formation of a protective dark patina which would preclude further significant corrosion. The formation of the patina is dependent on wet and dry cycles of service. In the presence of dirt and debris, or in confined spaces, the surfaces of these steels do not dry, and thus the effectiveness of the corrosion protection system is greatly reduced. The same principles also apply to painted structures if the paint is allowed to deteriorate. Sometimes corrosion products that form in these confined spaces can fill the space and can exert considerable mechanical force, separating members, cracking fasteners, and inducing mechanical failures. The latter was the case in the Mianus River Bridge failure.

Another form of corrosion that occurs in structures is stress corrosion, and it is characterized by cracking phenomena rather than by general or even localized section loss. This type of corrosion usually occurs in higher-strength alloy steels, typically with yield strengths greater than 100 ksi (690 MPa), but it can also occur in stainless steels at much lower strength levels. This has been a special concern in the chemical process industries where a number of types of stainless steels are used in aggressive solution service. Some large pressure vessel failures have been attributed to this cause. Since this process is controlled by the composition of the steel, the level of stress, and the solution contained, welded structures with high residual stresses are particularly sensitive. In some cases, these steels cannot be thermal-stress-relieved after welding due to adverse metallurgical effects in the weld and heat-affected zone by the heat of stress relief; thus careful selection of appropriate alloys for various types of service is essential.

In at least one case, inappropriate use of common 18 chromium, 8 nickel (sometimes referred to as "18-8") stainless steel led to a significant structural failure. It was used in a concrete ceiling slab hanger system in a swimming pool in Switzerland in which the hangers were exposed to chloride-containing moist air as a result of the action of a ventilation system. This resulted in progressive failure of the hangers over time and in the ultimate collapse of the ceiling with loss of life. The use of the same material in roof hangers for ceiling slabs in highway tunnels has also resulted in hanger cracking at tunnel ends, where salt spray from vehicle tires during winter has been pulled across the hangers by the ventilation system. The intended philosophy was to provide a material that would resist general corrosion as a tunnel hanger; however, the material selected was stress-corrosion-sensitive in chloride environments, creating dangerous potential for cracking.

Stress corrosion cracking has also been observed in high-strength steel fasteners and other products that have exceeded specified hardness levels for atmospheric corrosion or corrosion in other more aggressive environments. Indeed, the failure of the Silver Bridge in West Virginia in 1969 with substantial loss of life was, in part, attributed to stress corrosion cracking in a material of very low fracture toughness.

Stress corrosion has also been identified as one of the causes of cracking of wires in suspension bridge main cables which have experienced long-time service. The wires were generally processed to a high strength level through mechanical deformation [greater than 200 ksi (1380 MPa) yield strength], and some, but not all, were galvanized. The general deterioration of the galvanized coating through water intrusion in the cables has apparently created electrochemical processes that lead to pitting corrosion, general corrosion, and stress corrosion of the wires.

A system of corrosion protection widely employed in some structures is *sacrificial* protection. In the former, a more reactive metal, such as zinc or magnesium, is attached to, or more commonly in civil engineering structures, *coated* on the steel. The more reactive metal corrodes in preference to the steel, creating microscopic electric currents that protect the steel surface underlying or adjacent to it. Galvanizing of steel structures or consumer products is the most well-known example of this protection system. Attachment of metal anodes to ship hulls or pipelines is another system of corrosion protection. A similar protection system using impressed current imposes a voltage differential between the structure and surrounding environment to prevent corrosion. This system is sometimes used for pipelines.

In both cases these systems can fail. The sacrificial system fails when the coating or anode material is consumed and can no longer protect the structure from rusting. The impressed current system can fail when the imposed voltage is not maintained or is at an insufficient level to counteract the corrosion conditions surrounding the structure.

REPAIR OF DAMAGED STRUCTURES

The method of repairing a cracked element will depend on the nature of the damage and geometric change that has resulted from the crack. Other failure modes such as buckling of a member (local or global) may require temporary shoring and bracing to prevent further damage or collapse pending a final repair or removal of the member or structure.

When providing emergency and temporary repairs, care needs to be taken so that useful information from the damaged element is not destroyed. Should a crack develop, it is highly desirable to avoid welding directly to the crack surface. That destroys the surface and may prevent an assessment of the failure origin.

When cracks are found in an element as a result of fatigue, the web or flange may still be carrying load. Often it is desirable to drill holes at the crack tips in order to minimize further crack extension and to avoid the undesirable fracture of the section. In some cases, such as distortion cracking in girder webs where diaphragms are provided for stability during construction, the drilled holes may prevent further crack extension and may serve as a permanent repair. Figure 11.11 shows two holes drilled in a girder web after repeated distortion has caused web gap fatigue cracking. Centering holes at the crack tips will arrest the crack and may prevent reinitiation.

FIGURE 11.11   Crack arrest holes in girder web at diaphragm connection plate web gap.

After holes are drilled, it is desirable to check the hole to ensure that the crack tip has been removed. Otherwise, crack growth will continue and may even accelerate as the structure is subjected to cyclic loading. Holes are often a temporary retrofit pending development of a permanent repair. As is apparent in Fig. 11.11, angles have been bolted into place between the transverse connection plate and the girder flange to minimize the continued out-of-plane movement and to prevent reinitiation of the crack beyond the retrofit holes.

The heavy-section truss members in the structure that developed a fractured bottom chord shown in Fig. 11.8 had numerous cracks similar to the cracked cope shown in Fig. 11.12. A temporary repair was achieved after first making a detailed inspection and identifying cracked copes, as illustrated in Fig. 11.12a, and then grinding out these cracks and the flame-cut copes, as shown in Fig. 11.12b. The removal of the embedded cracks provided assurance that the connection would not prematurely fail prior to the installation of bolted splices to ensure structural integrity. Permanent repairs were achieved by installing bolted web and flange shear splices, as illustrated in Fig. 11.13. The use of high-strength steel plate and A490 high-strength bolts provided a permanent repair of all groove welded heavy W-section tension splices in the roof truss system.

Bolted splices have been commonly used to repair cracked elements and members. They are easy to install in the field and can be made without concern for the loads acting on the member. The hole geometry can be selected to maximize the net area A_n so that the member capacity is not adversely affected.

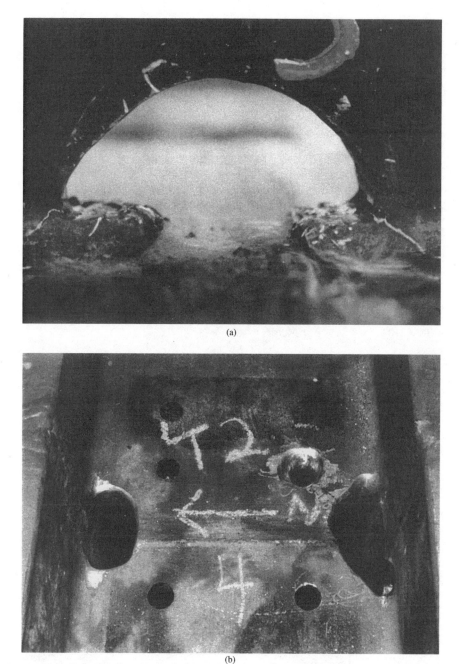

(a)

(b)

FIGURE 11.12 Temporary retrofit to remove crack tips. (*a*) Crack indications at cope in flange-web core. (*b*) Cracks in cope removed by grinding.

FIGURE 11.13   Bolted splices for permanent retrofit.

FIGURE 11.14   Example of emergency repair by welding splice plate that destroyed crack origin.

Care needs to be exercised when making emergency repairs or reinforcement to aid in removal of specimens. Welding directly to a fracture surface, as was done in Fig. 11.14, destroyed the crack origin. Hence, a failure analysis is impeded as evidence is destroyed. In general, fracture surfaces should be protected so that the surface features are not destroyed. Spray coating the crack surfaces with a clear acrylic lacquer, such as Krylon, will minimize development of corrosion product on the surface and will keep the surface features intact for subsequent evaluation.

It is usually desirable to remove part of the crack in order to assist with the investigation of its cause. However, prior to the removal, data need to be acquired on the size, location, and orientation of the crack. This should be accomplished by

1. Detailed sketches showing the crack location and dimensions of the crack and member. These sketches should also indicate the crack widths and the orientation of the crack with regard to the primary stresses in the member.

2. Photographs showing the visible crack conditions and its location relative to the detail at which it formed. The use of 35-mm color slides or prints will aid in the assessment.

After documentation, a portion of the crack can be removed to permit the causes of the cracking to be evaluated where it is not obvious or apparent. There are generally two types of samples that can be removed. If the material characteristics need to be determined, then a large segment can be removed, as illustrated in Fig. 11.10. In this case the beam and column flange and the groove weld with backing were removed. Hence, it was possible to remove both surfaces of the crack in the welded joint and column flange. Often, only one crack surface needs to be removed.

During removal of samples, steps should be taken to ensure that the crack surfaces do not come into contact, as that will damage the surface and destroy important information.

Often much smaller cracks exist, and it is not necessary or possible to remove such a large segment. Core samples can be used to remove all or part of the crack. Figure 11.15 shows the polished surface of a core sample removed from a groove weld. The core was positioned near the end of the crack in order to see if fatigue crack growth had occurred.

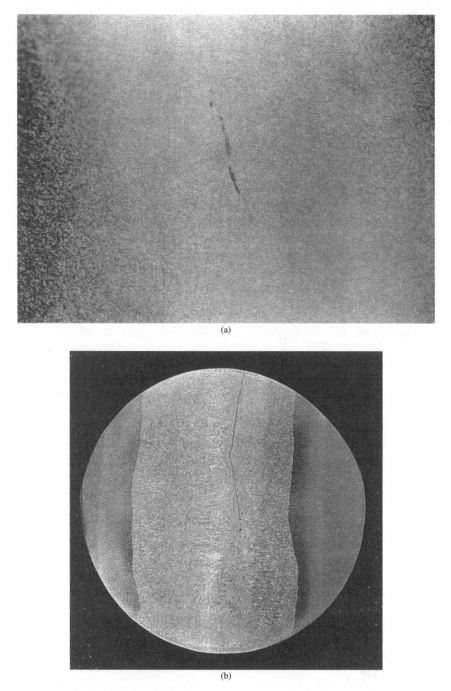

(a)

(b)

FIGURE 11.15 Core sample removed for assessment of crack. (*a*) Crack detected in groove weld. (*b*) Polished and etched surface showing weld crack.

REFERENCES

1. American Society for Testing and Materials (ASTM), 100 Bar Harbor Drive, West Conshohocken, PA 19428.

2. American Welding Society (AWS), 550 NW 42d Avenue, Miami, FL 22126.

3. American Association of State Highway and Transportation Officials (AASHTO), 444 North Capitol Street, NW Suite 225, Washington, DC 20001.

4. American Society of Mechanical Engineers (ASME), Three Park Avenue, New York, NY 10016-5990.

5. John M. Barsom and Stanley T. Rolfe, *Fatigue and Fracture Control in Structures,* 2d ed., Prentice-Hall, Englewood Cliffs, NJ, 1987.

6. Mars G. Fontana, and Norbert D. Greene, *Corrosion Engineering,* 2d ed., McGraw-Hill, New York, 1978.

7. American Iron and Steel Institute (AISI), 1101 17th St., NW, Suite 1300, Washington, DC 20036-4700.

8. Society of Automotive Engineers (SAE), Warrendale, PA 15086.

9. American Institute for Steel Construction (AISC), One East Wacker Drive, Suite 3100, Chicago, IL 60601-2001.

10. American Railway Engineering and Maintenance-of-Way Association (AREMA), 50 F Street, NW, Washington, DC 20001.

11. ANSI/ASCE 7-95, *Minimum Design Loads for Buildings and Other Structures,* American Society of Civil Engineers (ASCE), Fairfax, VA, 1995.

12. *ICBO Uniform Building Code,* International Conference of Building Officials, Whittner, CA, 1997.

13. *AISI Load and Resistance Factor Design Specification for Cold-Formed Steel Members in Cold-Formed Steel Design Manual,* 1996.

14. *Load and Resistance Factor Design Specification for Aluminum Structures in Aluminum Design Manual,* The Aluminum Association, Pittsburgh, PA, 1997.

15. AISC, *Load and Resistance Factor Design Specification for Structural Steel Buildings,* 1999 ed., Chicago (Specification and Commentary).

16. W.F. Chen, ed., *Handbook of Structural Engineering,* CRC Press, New York, 1997.

17. T. V. Galambos, ed., *Guide to Stability Design Criteria for Metal Structures,* 5th ed., Wiley-Interscience, New York, 1998.

18. AISC, *Manual of Steel Construction, LRFD,* vol. 2, *Connections,* Chicago, 1994.

19. J. W. Fisher, T. V. Galambos, G. L. Kulak, and M. K. Ravindra, "Load and Resistance Factor Design Criteria for Connectors," *Journal of Structural Division, ASCE,* vol. 104, no. ST9, September 1978.

20. G. L. Kulak, J. W. Fisher, and J. H. A. Struik, *Guide to Design Criteria for Bolted and Riveted Joints,* 2d ed., Wiley, New York, 1987.

21. D. F. Lesik and D. J. L. Kennedy, "Ultimate Strength of Fillet Welded Connections Loaded In-plane," *Canadian Journal of Civil Engineering,* vol. 17, no. 1, 1990.

22. J. W. Fisher, K. H. Frank, M. A. Hirt, and B. M. McNamee, *Effect of Weldments on the Fatigue Strength of Steel Beams,* National Cooperative Highway Research Program (NCHRP) Report 102, Washington, DC, 1970.

23. P. B. Keating and J. W. Fisher, *Review of Fatigue Tests and Design Criteria on Welded Details,* NCHRP Report 286, Washington, DC, 1986.

24. C. R. Shastry, J. T. Friel, and H. R. Townsend, *Sixteen-Year Atmospheric Corrosion Performance of Weathering Steels in Marine, Rural and Industrial Environments,* ASTM, STP 965, S. W. Dean and T. S. Lee, eds., ASTM, Philadelphia, 1988, pp. 5–15.

25. R. D. Granata, J. C. Wilson, and J. W. Fisher, "Assessing Corrosion on Steel Structures Using Corrosion Coulometer," *Journal of Infrastructure Systems, ASCE,* vol. 2, no. 3, September 1996.

26. Lev Zetlin Associates, Inc., New York, Report of the Engineering Investigation Concerning the Causes of the Collapse of the Hartford Coliseum Space Truss Roof on January 18, 1978.

27. E. A. Smith and H. I. Epstein, "Hartford Coliseum Roof Collapse: Structural Collapse Sequence and Lessons Learned," *Civil Engineering, ASCE,* April 1980.

28. J. W. Fisher, *Fatigue and Fracture in Steel Bridges,* Wiley, New York, 1984.

29. J. W. Fisher and A. W. Pense, "Experience with Use of Heavy W Shapes in Tension," *Engineering Journal, AISC,* vol. 24, no. 2, 1987.

30. E. J. Kaufmann, M. Xue, L. W. Lu, and J. W. Fisher, "Achieving Ductile Behavior of Moment Connections," *Modern Steel Construction,* vol. 36, no. 1; Part II, vol. 36, no. 6, 1996.

31. E. J. Kaufmann, J. W. Fisher, R. M. DiJulio, and J. L. Gross, *Failure Analysis of Welded Steel Moment Frame Damaged in the Northridge Earthquake,* NISTIR 5944, NIST, Gaithersburg, January 1997.

32. The International Institute of Welding, 550 NW Le Jeune Road, Miami, FL 33126.

CHAPTER 12
CONCRETE STRUCTURES

W. Gene Corley, P.E., S.E., Ph.D.

Reinforced concrete is an excellent morphological building material. In its fluid state, concrete can be placed in forms to make virtually any shape. Continuity is easily obtained by continuing reinforcement through beam-to-column connections. Once concrete is in place, creep and shrinkage assist in the redistribution of loads to locations where resistance is provided by reinforcing bars.

When defects and failures occur in a reinforced-concrete structure, careful analysis can determine the causes and point to appropriate remedial measures. Documented forensic investigations are required to demonstrate the cause of poor performance.

ENGINEERING PROPERTIES

Any textbook may be consulted for detailed discussions of the engineering properties of concrete. Only those properties that are most common in creating problems and failures are highlighted in this section.

Deformation Properties

Concrete consists of three basic materials: portland cement and other cementitious materials, aggregate, and water, as shown in Fig. 12.1. When they are mixed together, the portland cement reacts chemically with water to form a hard, inexpensive structural material. The quality of the concrete improves inversely in proportion to the amount of water added. Details of mix design and concrete properties are given in the book *Design and Control of Concrete Mixtures,* published by the Portland Cement Association.[1]

After hardening, concrete resists load by first responding elastically and then continuing to deform or "creep" under sustained compressive or tensile loads. Figure 12.2 shows idealized stress versus strain relationships for concrete as load is applied over a short time. Important properties for use in forensic investigation are the modulus of elasticity E_c and the limiting compressive strain ε_u. For most cases, the value of modulus of elasticity can be taken as the ACI 318[2] value of $w_c^{1.5}(33) \sqrt{f_c'}$ (in pounds per square inch). The value of limiting strains for unconfined concrete is generally assumed to be 0.003. Larger limiting strain may be considered when confinement is present. Reference 3 gives guidance for calculating increased strain capacities.

Time-Dependent Properties

After concrete is hardened and load has been applied, two time-dependent effects begin to be seen. First, concrete shortens in length as a result of continued chemical reaction and drying. The curves in Fig. 12.3 show representative values for drying shrinkage strain in concrete commonly used in structures. The lower curve

FIGURE 12.1 Three basic materials of concrete, aggregate, portland cement, and water. (*Courtesy of Portland Cement Association.*)

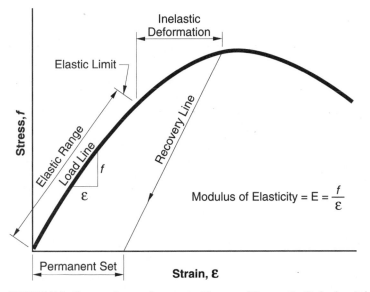

FIGURE 12.2 Stress-strain curve for concrete. (*Courtesy of Construction Technology Laboratories, Inc.*)

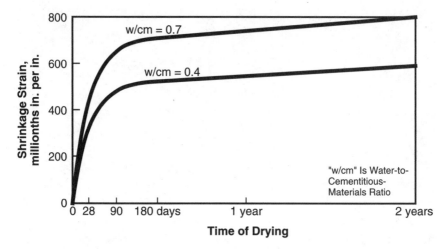

FIGURE 12.3 Representative drying shrinkage for concrete. (*Courtesy of Construction Technology Laboratories, Inc.*)

represents good-quality concrete with a water-to-cementitious-materials ratio *w*/cm of 0.4. The upper curve is representative of concrete commonly used in residential construction. Shrinkage amounts that exceed these values can cause excessive cracking or large deflections. As illustrated, most of the drying shrinkage takes place in the first 12 months. After that time, increases in moisture in the concrete will cause slight swelling while decreases will cause small amounts of additional shrinkage.

Another time-dependent phenomenon is creep. Under load, concrete changes length to relieve load. When in compression, concrete shortens; but when in tension, concrete lengthens. In general, creep is proportional to stress. Excessive creep can cause sag in beams and floors.

In Fig. 12.4, the upper curve shows the combined amounts of instantaneous strain, shrinkage strain, and creep of concrete under compressive load. As can be seen, creep strains can be significantly greater than either shrinkage strains or instantaneous strains. All three contribute to deflections. If creep and shrinkage strains are allowed to be too high, unacceptable deformations may occur. Early loading and use of high water-to-cementitious-materials ratios both increase time-dependent deformations.

Bond Slip

For reinforced concrete to function as designed, force must be transferred between concrete and steel. Deformed bar reinforcement transfers this force primarily through compression on the face of lugs, as illustrated in Fig. 12.5. Methods used in Ref. 2 give a conservative evaluation of bond strength for deformed bars.

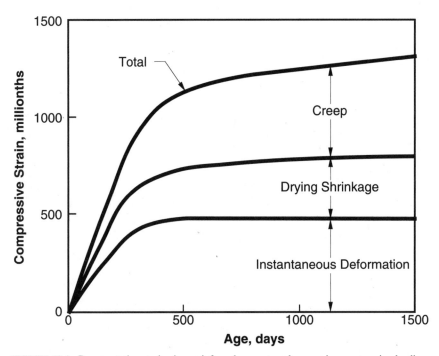

FIGURE 12.4   Representative strains in a reinforced concrete column under compressive loading. (*Courtesy of Construction Technology Laboratories, Inc.*)

Thermal expansion properties of both concrete and steel are similar. Each has a coefficient of thermal expansion of about 6 millionths per degree Fahrenheit. Consequently, thermal changes usually have no influence on bond.

Pretensioned prestressing wires or strands transfer force by a combination of friction and compressive action. When a wire is under tension, it has a smaller diameter than when it is at zero stress. Seven-wire strand is manufactured with its wires twisted around a straight center wire. Under tension, the twist has a greater pitch than at zero stress. After prestressing of a bonded tendon has been released and transferred to the concrete, the tendency for wires to increase in diameter creates a compressive force at the face of the wires. This compressive force transfers stresses from wire to concrete through the friction at the face of the wires.

Bond failures of pretensioned strands can occur if the tendons are lubricated. Accidental application of oil, grease, and debonding agents can cause this phenomenon. Failure of manufacturers to remove lubricants used to assist in strand manufacture can also cause bond failures. One piece of physical evidence suggesting bond failure is the pulling in of strand at the end of a pretensioned member. If the strand has pulled in more than approximately 3/16 in, investigations should be undertaken to determine if there is a potential for bond failure. The

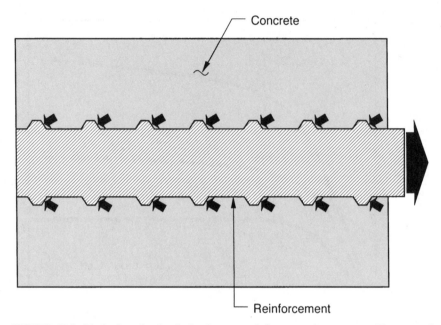

FIGURE 12.5 Mechanism for bond development reinforcement in concrete. (*Courtesy of Construction Technology Laboratories, Inc.*)

investigation should include analysis to determine whether lubricants or other contaminants are present on the surface of the strand.

Other indicators of possible bond failure include splitting of stems and other narrow parts of precast members, excessive deflection at low loads, and open flexural cracks at low loads.

Corrosion Properties

Most deformed bars are hot-rolled and conform to ASTM designation A615 or A706 (Refs. 4 and 5, respectively). Neither of these steels has corrosion resistance when exposed to the open air. However, the alkaline conditions provided by concrete surrounding the bars give excellent corrosion protection for reinforcement.

Corrosion protection can be destroyed in the presence of chloride ions or if natural carbonation that occurs at the surface of concrete works its way to the level of the reinforcing bar. Both conditions cause the loss of an alkaline environment and thereby destroy corrosion protection. Details of this phenomenon are discussed in Ref. 6.

Where cracks occur to the depth of reinforcing bars, both carbonation and attack by chloride ions may accelerate even faster. When corrosion is indicated, investigations should be done to determine the depth of carbonation, amount of chloride ion, and chloride profile with depth.

Several methods are available to protect reinforcement against corrosion. A discussion of these methods is provided in Ref. 7. In general, use of high-quality concrete, epoxy, or galvanized coatings on bars and minimizing the ability for chlorides to get to the level of the reinforcing bars are effective.

Once corrosion has started because of carbonation or the presence of chlorides, several methods are available to minimize its effects. Cathodic protection has been successful in some cases. However, cathodic protection requires continued monitoring of the system to be sure it is working. Surveys have shown that many cathodic protections are ineffective because of lack of maintenance.[8]

Barriers have been used to stop the intrusion of chloride and moisture and to control corrosion. In general, drying of the concrete is most effective inside buildings where humidity can be controlled. Drying in combination with periodic maintenance, which includes chipping out damaged concrete, cleaning off reinforcing bars, coating the bars, and replacing concrete that has been removed, has been proved to extend the life of buildings and bridges substantially.

CODES AND STANDARDS

In North America, most buildings constructed after 1910 have been designed following recommendations of ACI 318, *Building Code Requirements for Reinforced Concrete,*[2] and its predecessors. Concrete bridges have been designed according to the AASHTO *Standard Specifications for Highway Bridges.*[9] Both documents have evolved with similar, though not identical, design requirements.

Historical Perspective. A history of the development of North American design requirements for reinforced-concrete buildings is given in Ref. 10. In that document, it is noted that the first building code for reinforced concrete was adopted in February 1910. The code was 12 pages long and covered reinforced concrete as listed in Table 12.1. A comparison with more recent requirements is shown in the third column of Table 12.1.

Up until the mid-1900s, working stress design was used almost exclusively. The use of low design stresses and low design strengths for concrete generally

Table 12.1 Comparison of ACI 318-10 with Current Requirements

	1910	Current
f_c', psi	2000	18,000
f_c, maximum psi	−650	N/A
f_s, maximum psi	20,000	41,000
f_y, maximum psi	50,000	80,000
Pages	12	300+ w/commentary

created robust structures. Due to lack of sophisticated analytical tools, continuity was often provided but ignored in analysis. Consequently, reinforced-concrete buildings and bridges built prior to World War II usually have reserve flexural and compressive strengths.

During and after the 1940s, designers made significant efforts to reduce the amount of materials used and to take advantage of higher-strength concrete and reinforcement. In 1963, building codes were changed by adding *strength design* procedures to take advantage of newer materials.

Possible Deficiencies. Research that was carried out in the 1950s and 1960s demonstrated that previous requirements for shear and bond provided less safety than previously believed. As a result, shear and bond requirements have been made more restrictive in recent years.

Due to a lack of understanding about the relationship between shear and moment when applied to reinforced concrete, codes prior to 1963 required stirrup spacing that was only partially effective. Also, allowable shear stresses on the concrete sometimes exceeded strengths that are now known to be available.

Bond of deformed reinforcing bars is another issue where older structures may not meet the more restrictive requirements of recent codes and specifications. Although bond designed by current ACI 318 requirements results in much longer lap splices and development lengths, there is no documented evidence of failures attributed directly to bond design requirements of the past.

CRITICAL CHARACTERISTICS OF CONCRETE STRUCTURES

Plain Concrete

Plain concrete is a structural material with high compressive strength and low tensile strength. When loaded to destruction, plain concrete exhibits low amounts of energy dissipation. However, under normal conditions, it is a very durable and economical structural material.

From the point of view of structural performance, plain concrete is defined in Ref. 2 as follows: "Plain concrete—structural concrete with no reinforcement or with less reinforcement than minimum amount specified for reinforced concrete." (Minimum reinforcement for reinforced concrete is specified in Ref. 2.)

In general, minimum reinforcement required for concrete to be considered "reinforced" is that amount necessary to provide a strength after cracking equal to that of the cross-section just before cracking. With the required minimum reinforcement, the structural element will have some ductility after a crack occurs. With amounts of steel less than minimum, the element may collapse as soon as the first crack due to load occurs, as illustrated in Fig. 12.6. Consequently, concrete with less than minimum reinforcement as defined in Ref. 2 is defined as plain concrete and is allowed to be used only in situations in which the element will be supported if a crack occurs. Requirements for design of plain structural concrete are given in chapter 22 of ACI 318 (Ref. 2).

Plain concrete can exhibit cracking from distress due to shrinkage, due to chemical attack, and due to freeze-thaw damage. Control joints are used to concentrate shrinkage cracking along straight lines. When suitably spaced, control joints can be easily maintained and sealed. The cause of damage to concrete resulting from chemical attack or freeze-thaw can generally be determined by microscopic analysis. Details of these procedures are discussed under the heading "Petrography."

Reinforced Concrete

Reinforced concrete is designed on the assumption that concrete can carry no tension. Steel reinforcement is used to carry all tension in concrete cross-sections.

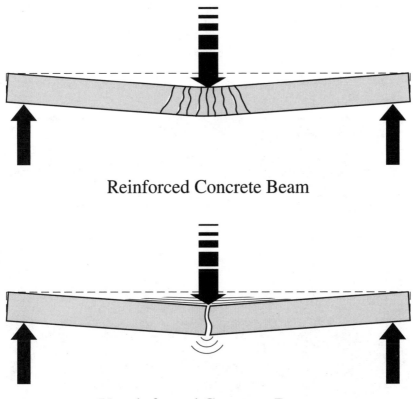

FIGURE 12.6 Behavior of reinforced and unreinforced concrete beams under load. (*Courtesy of Construction Technology Laboratories, Inc.*)

When reinforced concrete is designed for nonearthquake conditions, flexural elements can sustain large amounts of inelastic deformations under overload. However, components that resist forces primarily by shear or compression may exhibit only a modest amount of inelastic behavior.

Flexural damage to a concrete member is generally characterized by large deflections, large cracks parallel to the direction of loading, and eventual crushing of the concrete, as shown in Fig. 12.6.

Shear failures in reinforced concrete may be sudden and explosive and may occur with little warning. Beams that display large cracks inclined at an angle of more than 45° to the vertical may be near failure and should be carefully investigated for the potential of a shear failure. Any evidence that a shear failure may occur should be handled with caution, because such failures can be sudden and catastrophic. Figure 12.7 shows a photograph of a beam with a large diagonal crack that resulted in a shear failure. When shear strength is found to be low, external stirrups or straps can provide an effective repair.

Corrosion of reinforcement caused by the penetration of chlorides and/or carbonation of concrete is one of the most prevalent causes of damage to reinforced-concrete structures. If carbonation reaches the depth of the reinforcement or if chloride ion reaches a concentration exceeding about 0.15 percent by weight of cement, corrosion can occur. In uncracked concrete, penetration of chlorides can take many years. However, if chlorides are present at a crack, they may reach the

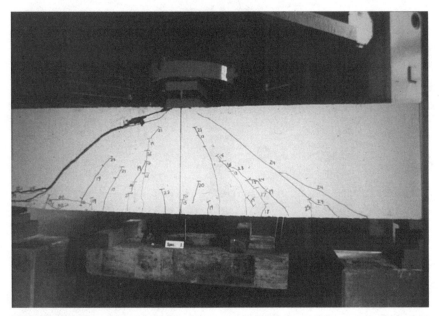

FIGURE 12.7 Shear failure of reinforced concrete beam. (*Courtesy of Construction Technology Laboratories, Inc.*)

depth of the reinforcement virtually immediately after chloride-laden water is applied to the concrete surface.

Remedial actions for corrosion include periodic maintenance that removes damaged concrete, cleans rusty bars, and replaces damaged concrete with new materials. Also, drying the concrete and use of cathodic protection have proved successful. As indicated in Ref. 8, penetrating sealers have also been used to slow the rate at which chlorides enter concrete.

Forensic investigations to determine the cause of corrosion should include determination of the depth of carbonation, the profile of chloride ion concentration, and whether or not sealers have been applied. Where carbonation or high levels of chloride ion have reached the depth of reinforcement, corrosion is expected to continue unless the concrete is dried below the critical humidity, the concrete is replaced, or other corrosion protection is provided.

Prestressed Concrete

Prestressed concrete is a form of reinforced concrete. This mode of construction takes advantage of very low-cost, but high-strength, wire and strand to make an extremely efficient structural element. By applying a permanent precompression to concrete with high-strength wires or strands, very slender members can be constructed. Also, prestressed members can be designed to have little or no cracking under service loads, thereby improving their overall durability and appearance.

Bond and anchorage of prestressed elements are important in prestressed concrete. Contaminated strands in pretensioned concrete can cause loss of bond with a resulting potential for large deformations and possible failure. Although strands can become contaminated in the field, failure to clean strands of lubricants used during manufacturing has been identified as the cause of distress in several jobs.

Elastic and/or time-dependent movements sometimes may cause damage to precast concrete structures. When prestress is applied and continued for more than 2 years thereafter, structural elements shorten. If this movement is not properly considered in the design, damage can be caused to connections, columns, and the prestressed member.

Precast Concrete

Structural elements may be precast either in a remote factory, as shown in Fig. 12.8, or at the job site, as shown in Fig. 12.9. Precast concrete may be either ordinary reinforced or prestressed. In general, structural considerations are the same for precast as they are for cast-in-place concrete.

The major differences between precast and cast-in-place concrete are methods of connecting structural elements together. Most connections of precast concrete have little or no continuity. Connections often are a source of distress in precast buildings. Major items of potential distress include damage caused by unantici-

FIGURE 12.8   Precasting in a plant. (*Courtesy of Portland Cement Association.*)

FIGURE 12.9   Site precast tilt-up construction. (*Courtesy of Portland Cement Association.*)

pated restraint, inadequate bearing because of construction tolerances, and failure to provide a suitable load path.

Transportation and erection of precast concrete often are sources of distress. When precast members are being lifted, inadequate anchorage of lifting embedments can result in pullout of the embedment. Improper lifting of tilt-up and other site-cast elements can cause excessive cracking. Also, impact of precast elements against other parts of a structure can cause spalling of concrete.

Steel-Concrete Composite Deck

In recent years, a popular method of constructing floors in steel-frame buildings has been to use metal deck with a thin concrete topping. Metal deck can be designed either to be composite with the thin topping or to be noncomposite and thereby carry the entire load in the metal deck. According to recommendations of the Steel Deck Institute,[11] a small amount of reinforcement should be placed in the concrete deck. The recommended amount of reinforcement falls below that recommended by ACI 318 to qualify for reinforced concrete. However, the reinforcement called for is often enough to carry full dead load plus live load with some margin of safety even if the metal deck is lost due to corrosion or other damage.

Metal deck supporting reinforced concrete is highly susceptible to corrosion due to the chlorides in concrete. When chlorides are present, corrosion can quickly and severely damage the metal deck. When metal deck is needed as part of the structural system, remedial measures may include addition of reinforcement either below or above the concrete slab. Added reinforcement must be protected against corrosion.

Formwork, Shoring/Reshoring

The location of formwork establishes the bottom location for all cast-in-place concrete. Where deflections may be of concern, the forms may be cambered to offset initial dead load and creep deflections. While sometimes used on beams and one-way slabs, camber is seldom used on two-way slabs. Consequently, it is not uncommon to find large deflections at the centers of cast-in-place concrete slabs.

Removal of formwork prematurely can cause a safety problem as well as a deflection problem. If concrete strengths are not high enough to carry dead load shears, collapse of a structure may result, as shown in Fig. 12.10 and described in Ref. 12.

Early removal of forms and reshoring can also cause serviceability problems by increasing cracking and creep-related deflections. In general, the earlier concrete receives load, the greater the creep will be per unit stress. Similarly, the modulus of elasticity is much lower at an early age than it is at a later age. For these reasons, cracking and deflections are related to the properties of the concrete at the time formwork is removed.[13] Reshoring after removal of forms generally has little effect on reducing deflections started by early removal of forms. However, stay-in-place shores are effective in controlling sag.

FIGURE 12.10   Bailey's Crossroads. (*Reproduced from National Bureau of Standards Report, February 1997.*)

METHODS OF ANALYSIS

Instantaneous Properties

In doing forensic work on an existing reinforced-concrete structure, it is usually necessary to determine the physical properties of the concrete and reinforcement. In relatively new structures, construction records may provide adequate data.

Quality control tests of concrete can often be used to estimate concrete strength. When the increase in strength due to time is taken into account, construction records provide a good starting point.

A more defensible way of determining material properties is to take cores from the concrete, as recommended in ACI 318[2] and ASTM C42.[2,14] Following ASTM procedures, cores can be used to determine the modulus of elasticity as well as the strength of concrete in place. As noted in ACI 318, section 5.6.4, concrete design strength can be taken as the core strength divided by 0.85.

To analyze structures, computer programs available from the Portland Cement Association are useful. Two-way slabs may be checked by the program ADOSS, and flexural members may be checked by the program BEAM.

Time-Dependent Properties

When time-dependent properties are of concern, values for use in analysis may be obtained from tests of cores or may be estimated. Core tests to determine creep and shrinkage properties, following procedures of ASTM C-512 and C-157, provide the most reliable data but are relatively time-consuming and expensive. Analytical methods for determining time-dependent properties are given in reports of ACI Committee 435.[15] A simple direct approach is given in Ref. 16.

Inelastic Properties

Design procedures of ACI 318 limit redistribution of negative moment at a support to a maximum of 20 percent. However, for lightly reinforced flexural members, full redistribution of moments can generally be achieved. Under this condition, capacity of a flexural member can be determined assuming that nominal moments M_N develop at each end and at the location of maximum positive moment. When special confinement reinforcement is placed in beams, a common practice in seismic regions, calculations often show that full redistribution is realized even in heavily reinforced flexural members.

Large amounts of redistribution are also possible in two-way reinforced-concrete slabs. Strength based on yield line analysis may be calculated following the procedures of Ref. 17. In general, calculated capacity based on yield line analysis will significantly exceed capacity indicated by design procedures such as those of ACI 318.[2]

Once capacity has been calculated by yield line analysis, shear strength and torsion capacity must also be checked. In many cases, either shear or torsion may control capacity.

Note that yield line analysis does not consider either deflection or cracking at service loads. When serviceability is the prime consideration, specific calculations of deformations should be done.

METHODS OF TESTING MATERIALS, COMPONENTS, AND ASSEMBLIES

Visual inspection of the structure and review of documents are important first steps in any investigation. Often, this step will indicate likely causes of the distress. However, it is usually necessary to determine physical properties of materials, components, and assemblies in order to arrive at final conclusions.

Field Load Tests

To obtain physical dimensions and material properties for use in an analytical investigation, it may be necessary to take cores of the concrete and obtain representative samples of the reinforcement. In addition, locations of reinforcement within the concrete and dimensions of the structure should be measured. Nondestructive means can be used to determine the size and location of reinforcement.

When questions arise about the in-place strength of an existing structure, strength evaluation is most often done following procedures in chapter 20 of ACI 318. As recommended there, the strength evaluation should start with calculations based on as-built conditions. Analyses should be based on measured dimensions and material properties to the extent feasible.

When sampling concrete, it is desirable, when conditions permit, to obtain three cores for each 10,000 ft^2 of area and for each type of concrete in the structure. Similarly, if a particular portion of the structure is suspected to have deficient concrete, three cores should be obtained from the suspect concrete, if possible.

If deleterious behavior of concrete is suspected, it is essential that samples be obtained. Samples approximately the size of a fist generally will be adequate if cores cannot be obtained.

In cases where litigation may follow, all samples should be tracked with chain-of-custody records. These records should track who has possession and all activities associated with the sample from the time the sample is obtained through the end of any litigation. A sample chain-of-custody sheet is shown in Fig. 12.11.

Where it is not practical to obtain core samples, nondestructive procedures described in this section may be used. If access to the structure is not possible, values given in Table 12.2 can be used to determine sensitivity to expected concrete strengths.

If it is not possible to obtain enough information to do a reliable analytical evaluation of strength, an in-place load test can be used to determine the strength of the structure. Most building codes require that a load test be done if a potential strength deficiency cannot be resolved or if dimensions and material properties cannot be established by measurement.[2] Load tests also can be used to rate old structures that have no construction records and where it is not cost-effective to determine material strengths and reinforcement locations.

CTL **Construction Technology Laboratories, Inc.** 5420 Old Orchard Road, Skokie, IL 60077-1030 (847) 965-7500 FAX (847) 965-6541	**CHAIN OF CUSTODY** **RECORD**			
Project Name:	**CTL Proj. No.:**	**Date:**		**Sheet ___ of ___**
		Sampled by:		
Sample No.:				
Sample Description:	*(Photo or Sketch)*			
Transmitted By	**Transmitted To**	**Time**	**Date**	**Activity**

FIGURE 12.11   Sample chain of custody form. (*Courtesy of Construction Technology Laboratories, Inc.*)

Historically, load tests were intended to be used only where flexural strength was in question. However, application of in-place load tests has been permitted by chapter 20 of ACI 318 since 1995.

In planning a load test, safety is the most important consideration. Any portion of the structure that has heavy loads, or might collapse in the event that the struc-

Table 12.2 Expected Structural Concrete Strengths

Year of Construction	Low	Usual	High
Prior to 1918	800	2,000	2,000
1918 to 1930	1,000	3,000	4,000
1930 to 1950	2,000	3,000	5,000
1950 to 1960	2,000	4,000	6,000
1960 to 1970	2,000	4,000	8,000*
1970 to 1980	3,000	4,000	9,000*
After 1980	3,000	4,000	11,000*

*Strengths over 6,000 psi are not common for cast-in-place concrete outside of large metropolitan areas in the eastern United States.

ture cannot carry the applied load, should be safely shored. The shoring should be provided in such a way that it does not interfere with the load test.

Following the procedures of ACI 318, loads should be arranged to create maximum deflection and stresses in the critical regions of the structure in doubt. In some cases, more than one loading application may be required. Intensity of the load applied should not be less than 85 percent of the quantity $1.4D + 1.7L$, where D is deadwood and L is leveled.

Prior to starting a load test, the owner, engineer, and building official should all agree on a protocol for the load test. Such items as whether to load net area or gross area of a floor and how the load should be arranged should all be agreed to. After load has been applied to the structure for 24 h, measured deflection shall not exceed the span squared divided by 20,000 times the member thickness.[2] Upon removal of applied load, recovery must be at least 75 percent of measured deflection.

Acceptance criteria are spelled out in ACI 318, chapter 20. It is noted that all structures, both reinforced concrete and prestressed concrete, can be reloaded if deflections under the first loading exceed limiting values.

In some cases, loading to destruction may be desirable. This is particularly true when a question arises concerning bond of pretensioned strand. Under most conditions, field load testing to destruction is done with applied deadweight, such as stacks of concrete block. Inability to quickly remove load creates safety hazards and should be done with great caution (Fig. 12.12). A preferred alternative is to transport the structural element to a laboratory and perform the test to destruction with hydraulic equipment that can be safely controlled.

Laboratory Tests of Components

Laboratory testing of components provides a method for determining the causes of distress in the field. In cases where field load testing is impractical (i.e., failure has already occurred), construction and testing of small-scale models in the laboratory provide an alternative strategy for determining field performance.[18]

FIGURE 12.12   Field load test of precast double T-beam. (*Courtesy of Construction Technology Laboratories, Inc.*)

Where precast elements are involved, particularly when there is a question concerning bond of pretensioned strand, full-size component tests to destruction may be conducted in the laboratory. Figure 12.13 shows a test to destruction of a full-size double tee. In conducting a test of this sort, instrumentation of all strands should be provided to determine if there is premature bond slip. Figure 12.14 shows an example of instrumentation on the strand.

Load testing to destruction provides information concerning flexural strength, shear strength, as well as bond slip.

Petrography

One of the most rapid, least expensive methods used to evaluate concrete quality, diagnose causes of deterioration, and determine the extent of internal damage is petrographic (microscopical) examination. Petrography is applicable to aggregates, concrete, mortar, grout, plaster, stucco, terrazzo, and similar portland cement mixtures.

Petrographic methods combine inspection with the unaided eye and microscopic examination using stereo and metallographic microscopes. Interpretation of findings by professional petrographers has provided valuable assistance in development of practical solutions to problems. At least one petrographic examination is desirable on every job involving concrete. When visual examination suggests

FIGURE 12.13 Laboratory test to destruction of precast double T-beam. (*Courtesy of George Pfoertner Photography.*)

FIGURE 12.14 Dial gage used to measure slip of prestressing strand. (*Courtesy of Construction Technology Laboratories, Inc.*)

deleterious behavior of concrete, petrographic examination should be done on each type of concrete and on each apparently different condition.

Information developed during a petrographic examination using guidelines given in ASTM C 856, *Standard Recommended Practice for Petrographic Examination of Hardened Concrete,*[19] includes

- Condition of material
- Causes of inferior quality, distress, or deterioration
- Probable future performance
- Compliance with project specifications
- Description of concrete, providing:

Degree of cement hydration
Estimation of water-cement ratio
Extent of paste carbonation
Presence of fly ash and estimation of amount
Extent of corrosion of reinforcing steel
Identification of evidence of harmful alkali-aggregate reaction, sulfate attack, or other chemical attack
Identification of potentially reactive aggregates
Evidence of improper finishing
Estimation of air content
Evidence of early freezing
Amount of microcracking
Causes of cracking

Examples of several forms of distress are shown in Figs. 12.15 through 12.21.

Although petrographic examination is extremely useful, it can only provide approximate values of the water-to-cementitious-materials ratio and cement content. When more accurate values are needed, chemical analysis, X-ray diffraction analysis, and scanning electron microscopy may be required.

Chemical Analysis

Although petrographic analyses provide information concerning the quality of hardened concrete, it is often necessary to perform chemical analyses to determine causes of damage to the material. Chemical analysis can be used to identify such things as excessive alkalies in cement, cement content, types and amounts of admixtures, presence of fly ash, presence of slag, and chlorides in concrete.

The durability of concrete is often more important than its strength, but ways to measure or predict durability are still being debated. As more and more chlorides have been used as deicers, corrosion of reinforcing has become a serious problem.

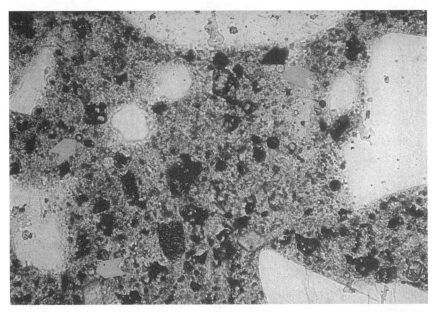

FIGURE 12.15 A 20-µm-thick section of pavement concrete shows dark unhydrated portland cement clinker particles in the paste. Fly ash particles are indicated with arrows. Failure to entrain the proper amount of air resulted in slight scaling observed after one winter's exposure. (L. to R.) is 0.7 mm. (*Courtesy of Construction Technology Laboratories, Inc.*)

FIGURE 12.16 A thin section of concrete damaged by the expansive alkali-silica reaction is shown. Microcracks partially filled with alkali-silica gel (*arrows*) extend away from reactive chert (*upper right*). The reaction produced numerous popouts in a parking garage floor. (*Courtesy of Construction Technology Laboratories, Inc.*)

12.22

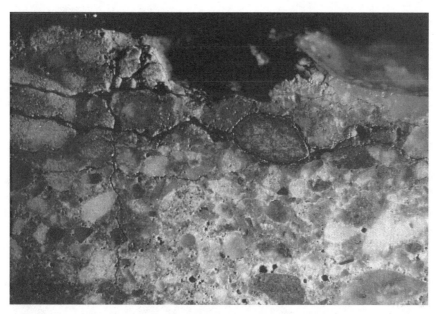

FIGURE 12.17 Microcracks are a result of cyclic freezing and thawing of inadequately air-entrained pavement concrete. Premature finishing and overworking removed most of the entrained air near the top surface. (*Courtesy of Construction Technology Laboratories, Inc.*)

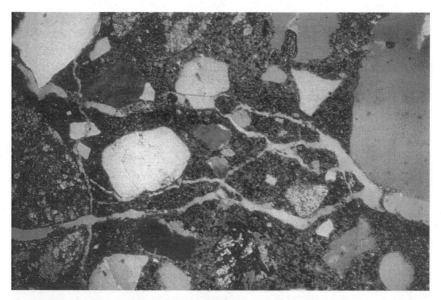

FIGURE 12.18 A photomicrograph of transparent thin section of upper few millimeters of pavement concrete shows cracks resulting from cyclic freezing and thawing. Premature finishing and overworking of the surface removed most of the entrained air, seriously reducing durability. (*Courtesy of Construction Technology Laboratories, Inc.*)

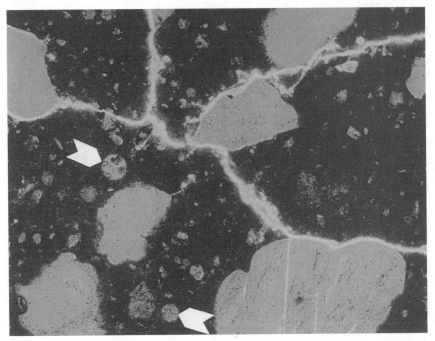

FIGURE 12.19 A thin section of compression-tested 20,000 psi concrete containing fly ash (*arrows*) and a superplasticizer is shown. Paste is dark, due to an abundance of anhydrous portland cement clinker particles. Sample was impregnated with fluorescent epoxy after testing and is viewed with a combination of ordinary and ultraviolet light. (*Courtesy of Construction Technology Laboratories, Inc.*)

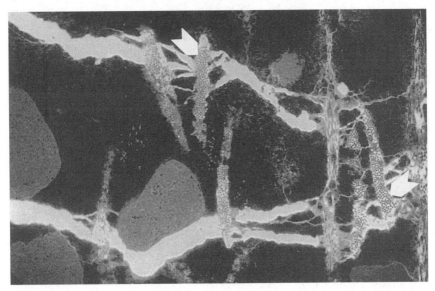

FIGURE 12.20 A thin section (20 μm thick) of glass fiber reinforced concrete is shown after it was subjected to flexural strength testing. Note bundles of glass fibers in which the circular cross sections of glass can be seen (arrows). Sample was impregnated with fluorescent epoxy after strength testing. (*Courtesy of Construction Technology Laboratories, Inc.*)

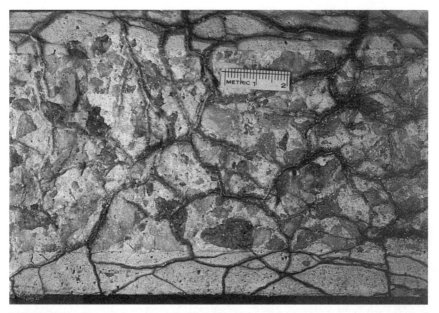

FIGURE 12.21 Open cracks are partially filled with calcium carbonate in a precast capping block of a chimney. Damage from cyclic wetting and drying, heating and cooling, freezing and thawing of non-air-entrained, moderately high water-cement ratio concrete. (*Courtesy of Construction Technology Laboratories, Inc.*)

One important measure of potential durability is the ability of concrete to protect the reinforcing steel from the penetration of chloride ions from deicing salts or seawater.

One useful tool for predicting durability is to determine precise chloride profiles of concretes exposed to salt solutions. These profiles are particularly suited for evaluating high-quality concretes. evaluating new materials or mix designs, and for litigation.

A precise chloride profiling method, shown in Fig. 12.22, affords several advantages over other test methods, including these:

- Either field or laboratory concretes can be tested.
- No artificial transport mechanisms are introduced.
- Core sampling prevents loss or contamination of field powder specimens.
- Large sample size gives representative, repeatable results.
- Suspect data points are easily identified and reanalyzed.
- The results are sensitive enough to distinguish among high-performance concretes.
- The sampling technique can be used for substances other than chlorides.

More traditional methods of evaluating the ability of concrete to resist the penetration of chloride ions are not sensitive enough to make comparisons of

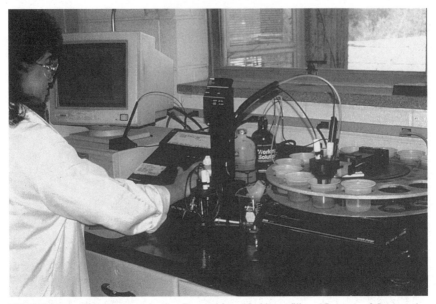

FIGURE 12.22   Chloride determination for precision chloride profiling. (*Courtesy of Construction Technology Laboratories, Inc.*)

high-performance concretes, or to make fine distinctions among concretes. Accelerated test methods, while convenient for quality control purposes, have been the subject of intense debate and may be problematic if introduced as evidence in litigation. Precise chloride profiles can show fine distinctions among concretes and have built-in checks to ensure high-quality data. Thus they provide a high degree of confidence in the results.

Steel reinforcement is normally well protected from corrosion by the surrounding concrete. Because of the high calcium hydroxide and alkali content of cement paste, the pH of the pore water is usually greater than 12.5, high enough to maintain the passive layer of iron oxides and hydroxides on the surface of the steel. This passive layer restricts further corrosion of the steel. The passive layer may be broken down either by reduction of the pH (due to carbonation or to leaching of the calcium hydroxide) or by the ingress of chloride ions. Chloride ions migrate toward the surface of the steel, polarize, and enter the passive layer. The negative chloride ions aid in the dissolution of the ferrous (Fe^{2+}) ions. Additional chloride ions are attracted to the location where the passive layer has been broken. Because the chloride ions act as catalysts in this process, they are not consumed. Consequently, the process of corrosion continues.[27] Generally accepted threshold values range from 0.1 to 0.4 percent by mass of cement.[28] The actual value of chloride ion will depend on the ability of the cement paste to bind the chlorides, the moisture content of the concrete, the ambient temperature, the electrical resistivity of the concrete, the pore solution chemistry, and the availability of oxygen.

Fick's second law is commonly used to describe the transport of chloride ions through concrete. In the following form, the equation is used to calculate the effective diffusion coefficient from chloride profile data using a curve-fitting program.

$$y = C_s\left(1 - \text{erf}\,\frac{x}{2\,\sqrt{D_{ec}t}}\right)$$

where x = distance from surface, m

y = chloride content (% by mass of concrete) at depth x

C_s = notional surface chloride level (constant; set at concentration obtained for outermost layer)

t = time of exposure, s

D_{ec} = effective diffusion coefficient, m²/s

erf = error function/$\text{erf}(x) = 2/\sqrt{\pi} \int_o^x e^{-t^2}\,dt$

Strictly speaking, Fick's law applies only to transport by diffusion in materials that are homogeneous, do not change over time, and do not interact with the diffusing substance. Even though it does not directly apply to chloride ion transport in concrete, Fick's second law does provide a convenient way to compare concretes that have been exposed to ponding under the same conditions for the same length of time. (Note that very different values may be obtained for the same concrete under different exposure conditions.) An apparent diffusion coefficient can be calculated and used for this purpose. Some values[29] obtained for D_{ce} for high-quality concretes ponded with a 3% NaCl solution for 6 months are shown in Table 12.3.

Some practitioners use the effective diffusion coefficient in models that predict the service life of concrete. These models make a series of assumptions about the behavior of the structure. While any one assumption may be reasonable, one must use the results with caution, if at all. For example, one might calculate the service life under a given set of conditions in order to compare the life-cycle costs of several alternate construction methods. Even in this type of application, it would be

Table 12.3 Apparent Diffusion Coefficients for Concretes Ponded with 3% NaCl solution for 6 months[29]

	% Silica Fume	Water-to-Cementitious-Materials Ratio	Apparent Diffusion Coefficient (m²/sec)
Effect of Silica Fume Content	0	0.40	4.11E-12
	6	0.40	1.66E-12
	12	0.40	1.08E-12
Effect of w/cm	6	0.35	0.96E-12
	6	0.40	1.66E-12
	6	0.45	2.47E-12

helpful to calculate the service life based on different assumptions in order to see the sensitivity of the result.

Under field conditions, several transport mechanisms are at work which cannot be described or predicted by Fick's second law. Nevertheless, chloride profiles based on field specimens still provide useful information about the past performance of the concrete. They are also a reasonable basis for comparing different concretes that have been exposed to the same field environment.

Nondestructive Testing

Nondestructive testing on concrete has always been an effective method of gaining information about hardened concrete. Some of the simplest methods can give useful information. A rebound hammer (Schmidt hammer) provides a qualitative measure of the surface condition of concrete. This instrument has a spring-loaded weight that impacts and rebounds from the concrete surface. The amount of rebound, read as a number directly from the instrument, is used as a measure of the quality of concrete. Although not reliable as a measure of strength, this procedure can be used to identify surface damage. By using the rebound hammer method at many locations over a large area, surface damage caused by fire or other attack can be mapped. When calibrated with core tests, rebound hammers can be used to give an approximate value of concrete strength.

Chain drags and surface tapping with a mason's hammer or other metallic device are useful in finding delaminations. When a surface is lightly tapped with a piece of metal, a "ringing sound" will be heard when the concrete is sound. If delaminations are present between the surface and reinforcement, a hollower sound will be heard. Chain drags and hammer tapping can provide reliable methods for identifying the extent of corrosion damage.

Another method of determining the quality of concrete is the Windsor Probe. Although listed as a nondestructive test, the Windsor Probe does cause some damage to the concrete. ASTM C803 provides a standard for use of the Windsor Probe. Concrete strength is determined by measuring the resistance of the concrete to penetration by a steel probe driven into the concrete. Note that the Windsor Probe measures properties only of the concrete at the location where it is used.

As in the case of the rebound hammer, results of tests using the Windsor Probe will vary depending on conditions. Surface conditions, type of aggregate, and other variables will influence results. For best results, the Windsor Probe can be calibrated by testing cores obtained from the concrete being evaluated.

In recent years, many new and powerful techniques have been developed for nondestructive testing. New developments include the following:

Impact echo

Impulse radar

Impulse response

Ultrasonic pulse velocity

Modal analysis

Cover meter

Half-cell potential testing

Among the most useful of these new systems are impulse radar, impact echo, impulse response, and half-cell potential testing.

Impulse Radar. The impulse radar technique, illustrated in Fig. 12.23, employs high-frequency electromagnetic energy for rapidly and continuously assessing a variety of characteristics of concrete structures. The principle of operation is based on reflection of electromagnetic waves from dielectric constant boundaries in the material being probed.

A single contacting transducer (antenna) is used for transmitting and receiving radar signals. High-frequency, short-pulse electromagnetic energy is transmitted into the concrete. The transmitted pulse travels through the material and is partially reflected when it encounters a change in dielectric constant. Reflected pulses are detected by the receiving section of the transducer. The location of the dielectric constant boundary is evaluated by noting the transit time from start to pulse to reception of reflected pulse. Boundary depth is proportional to transit time. Since

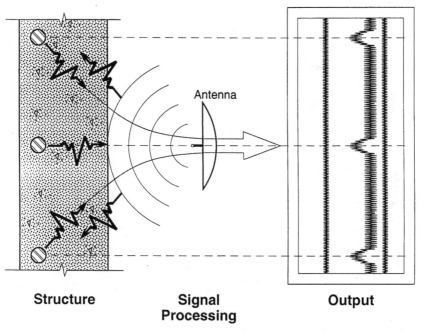

| **Structure** | **Signal Processing** | **Output** |

FIGURE 12.23 Schematic of impulse radar. (*Courtesy of Construction Technology Laboratories, Inc.*)

concrete-to-metal, concrete-to-air, concrete-to-water, and concrete-to-backfill interfaces are electronically detected by the instrument as dielectric constant boundaries, the impulse radar method is capable of assessing a variety of reinforced-concrete and masonry characteristics. The impulse radar technique can be used for the following applications:

- Evaluate presence and location of reinforcing steel, conduits, drain lines, and other embedments in and beneath reinforced-concrete structures.
- Assess thickness of reinforced-concrete structural elements.
- Evaluate presence of voids beneath concrete structural elements.
- Inspect concrete masonry construction for presence of reinforcement and grout in block cavities.

Impact Echo.   The impact-echo technique is one of several nondestructive test methods that specialists use for existing-condition assessment, material property evaluation, and quality assurance testing. The impact-echo method, illustrated in Fig. 12.24, employs transient stress waves and their reflection to rapidly detect, locate, and classify flaws within hardened concrete.

The impact-echo technique can serve as a very effective tool when there is a need to

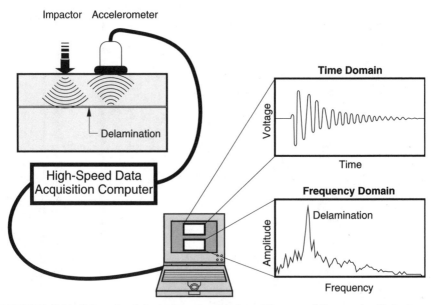

FIGURE 12.24   Schematic of the impact-echo technique. (*Courtesy of Construction Technology Laboratories, Inc.*)

- Evaluate the thickness of a concrete member
- Locate poor consolidation and voiding in reinforced concrete
- Detect areas of delamination in concrete
- Detect debonding of an overlay
- Detect degree of grouting in posttensioning ducts

The impact-echo nondestructive technique employs low-frequency mechanical energy to rapidly detect, locate, and classify discontinuities within hardened concrete; detect voids and delaminations; and measure the thickness of concrete elements. The test method is based on physical laws of elastic stress wave propagation in solids.

A mechanical impactor source and an electromechanical receiving transducer/accelerometer are positioned on the same face of the test object. The impactor generates a broadband stress pulse. Waves of mechanical energy propagating through the concrete are reflected from the opposite boundary of the test object, and the reflected energy is detected by the transducer. The time-voltage responses of the receiving transducer are averaged for two to three impacts with fast Fourier transform (FFT) frequency analysis algorithms by a dynamic signal analyzer. Reflections or "echoes" are indicated by frequency peaks in resultant spectral plots of displacement amplitude versus frequency.

Since amplitude, phase, and direction of mechanical energy are modified by interfaces between materials of different density and stiffness, the location and characterization of internal discontinuities such as defects in concrete are possible. As the wave passes through the interface at a discontinuity, part of the energy is reflected from the interface back to the transducer, and the remainder continues forward to the back boundary of the member where virtually all wave energy is reflected by the air interface. The location of the discontinuity is evaluated by noting the echo frequency peaks. The frequency peak for the intermediate echo is inversely proportional to the depth of the discontinuity in the concrete member. Evaluation of reflected signal strength and shape allows characterization and classification of flaws.

Impulse Response. The impulse response test, illustrated in Fig. 12.25, has several advantages over other nondestructive testing methods, including the robust nature of the apparatus, which can be used to test relatively rough concrete surfaces; its fast output, with a test rate of a point every minute in ideal access conditions; and the repeatability of test results. Structures with very difficult access such as chimneys, silos, tunnels, and dams have been economically tested using the impulse response method as the principal evaluation tool.

The method uses a low-strain impact to send a stress wave through the tested element. The impactor is usually a 1-kg sledgehammer with a built-in load cell in the hammer head. The maximum compressive stress at the impact point in concrete is

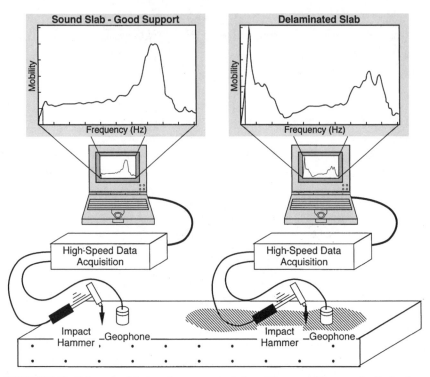

FIGURE 12.25 Schematic of the impulse response technique. (*Courtesy of Construction Technology Laboratories, Inc.*)

directly related to the elastic properties of the hammer tip. Typical stress levels range from 5 MPa for hard rubber tips to more than 50 MPa for aluminum tips. The response to the input stress is normally measured by a velocity transducer (geophone). This receiver is preferred because of its stability at low frequencies and its robust performance in practice. Both the hammer and the geophone are linked to a portable field computer for data acquisition and storage.

Both the time records for the hammer force and the geophone velocity response are processed in the field computer using the FFT algorithm, and the resulting velocity spectrum is divided by the force spectrum to obtain a transfer function, referred to as the *mobility* of the element under test. The test graph of mobility plotted versus frequency from 0 to 1 kHz contains information on the condition and integrity of the concrete in the tested elements, obtained from the following measured parameters:

- *Dynamic stiffness:* The slope of the portion of the mobility plot between 0.1 and 1 kHz defines the compliance or flexibility of the area around the test point for a normalized force input. The inverse of the compliance is the dynamic stiffness of the structural element at the test point. The degree of stiffness is determined by concrete quality, element thickness, and element support conditions.

- *Mobility and damping:* The element's response to the impact-generated elastic wave will be damped by the element's intrinsic rigidity, also known as *body damping.* The mean mobility value over 0.1 to 1 kHz is directly related to the density and thickness of a plate element. A reduction in plate thickness corresponds to an increase in mean mobility. For example, when total debonding of an upper layer is present in a slab, it becomes more mobile. The mean mobility reflects the thickness of the upper, debonded layer. In addition, any cracking or honeycombing in concrete will reduce the damping and hence the stability of the mobility plot over the tested frequency range.

- *Peak/mean mobility ratio:* When debonding or delamination is present within a structural element, or when there is loss of support beneath a concrete slab on grade, the response behavior of the uppermost layer controls the impulse response result. In addition to the increase in mean mobility between 0.1 and 1 kHz, the dynamic stiffness decreases greatly. The peak mobility below 0.1 kHz becomes appreciably higher than the mean mobility from 0.1 to 1 kHz. The ratio of this peak to mean mobility is an indicator of the presence and degree of either debonding within the element or voiding/loss of support beneath a slab on grade.

Half-Cell Potential.   Steel embedded in concrete is normally protected against corrosion by the natural alkalinity of the concrete. Concrete typically has a pH greater than 12.5, and this alkalinity produces a thin passivating film on the embedded steel that protects the steel against corrosion. The passivating film can be compromised by one or more of the following: cement paste carbonation, chloride in the concrete, acidic chemical infiltration, and incomplete consolidation of concrete.

Once a corrosion cell is established, the rate of corrosion depends on the potential difference between the anode and cathode of the cell. This potential difference is affected by variations in chemical concentrations, oxygen availability, moisture content, and·temperature. Corrosion of embedded steel in concrete and associated concrete deterioration can also occur due to stray electric currents and dissimilar metals in contact.

When embedded steel in concrete corrodes, corrosion products (rust) create expansive pressures within the concrete. As corrosion continues, these expansive pressures cause concrete deterioration in the form of cracking, delamination, and spalling.

Half-cell potential testing is a nondestructive test that evaluates the probability of active corrosion in reinforcing steel at the time of testing. Half-cell electrical potentials of reinforcing steel are measured by moving a half-cell probe about on the concrete surface, as shown in Fig. 12.26. Half-cell potential testing can detect the presence of active corrosion when no visible or physical evidence of damage is apparent.

Half-cell measurements can be presented on a topographical plot, showing the probability of corrosion activity by location. A time series of half-cell topographical plots is helpful in evaluating the long-term progression of corrosion in a structure.

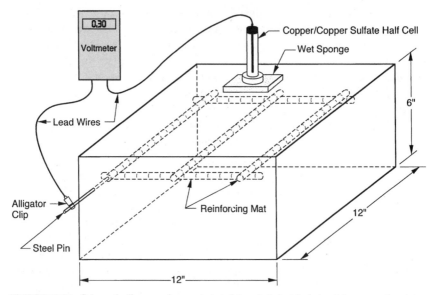

FIGURE 12.26   Schematic diagram of concrete test slab and of electrical circuit for measuring potentials. (*Courtesy of Construction Technology Laboratories, Inc.*)

TYPES AND CAUSES OF COMMON NONPERFORMANCE AND FAILURES

Construction Failures

Many times, the largest loads that ever go on a structure occur during construction. Consequently, collapses and other damage are most frequent during the construction phase. Formwork collapse, removal of formwork prematurely, and failure of formwork support are the most common causes of construction collapse.

Modern building codes are calibrated to provide economical and safe structures. Designs that follow these codes seldom fail either during or after construction under gravity or wind loading. However, seismic loading has caused failures in buildings of all types of materials.

In most cases where there is a structural failure or where concrete buildings perform poorly, the reason can be attributed to misinterpretation of the code or mathematical blunders or faulty construction. An example of such a blunder is failure of the Cocoa Beach, Florida, Apartments during construction. Investigations[20] disclosed that the slabs had not been checked for shear. Consequently, inadequate shear strength was provided, and a collapse occurred.

Overload

In prestressed concrete roof structures, sometimes *ponding* can become a source of overload. For very shallow sections, deflections caused by the weight of rainwater on the roof can cause enough sag that additional water accumulates until failure occurs. Although building codes require that this possibility be checked, it is a condition sometimes missed by inexperienced designers.

Corrosion

One of the most ubiquitous causes of poor performance of concrete structures is corrosion of reinforcement. Chlorides as deicers were not commonly used prior to about the middle of the 20th century. Once they were in common use, corrosion began to occur in parking decks, bridge decks, balconies of buildings, and other places where deicers were used. While complete replacement using the best of current technology for corrosion protection is a solution that will minimize the possibility of future damage, this procedure also is usually the most expensive. Less expensive maintenance programs that include periodic removal of damaged concrete and replacement with good concrete often are more economical alternatives. Use of coatings such as silane has also been proved to slow down the potential for corrosion.

Posttensioning

Posttensioned concrete is a form of prestressed concrete. In posttensioned concrete, unbonded reinforcement is placed through openings in the hardened concrete. After the concrete has gained adequate strength, the unbonded tendons are pulled to a predetermined force and anchored to apply stress to the structure.

One common cause of failure in posttensioned concrete is overload in the anchorage zone. Overload can cause excessive bursting stresses to develop under the anchorage plate. If the bursting stresses exceed the tensile strength of the concrete, failure can occur. For some commonly used prestressing systems, reinforcement is needed to resist bursting stresses when anchorages are placed close together.

Another cause of failure in posttensioned concrete is corrosion of the tendons. In older systems, corrosion inhibitors were sometimes not adequate to protect tendons under highly corrosive conditions. Water that works its way into the tendon duct can cause corrosion that eventually leads to fracture of the tendon. After a tendon fractures, it is often possible to replace the broken strand with a smaller-diameter tendon.

For grouted posttensioning systems, voids in the grout may also lead to corrosion damage. Voids may be caused by air pockets or water pockets left in the posttensioning duct at the time grout is pumped through the opening. Corrosion caused by voids in ducts often will lead to surface cracking prior to the time tendons fracture. Horizontal cracks following the ducts often are the warning that repairs are needed.

Another potential problem is the result of shortening of beams or girders due to posttensioning which induces horizontal forces into already constructed columns. If the columns are very stiff, high diagonal tension shear is created in them which is manifested by diagonal cracking across the column.

Misplaced Reinforcing Steel

Strength of reinforced concrete is highly dependent upon proper placing of reinforcement. In flexural members, the most important dimension is the distance between the centroid of the reinforcement and the extreme fiber of the compression zone of the concrete. Where shear reinforcement is required, excessively wide spacing of stirrup reinforcement can lead to a potential for shear failure.

Where earthquake is not a major consideration in the design of a structure, effective depths of reinforcement greater than that called for in the plans may be acceptable. However, where earthquake design requirements call for special moment frames or intermediate moment frames, effective depth greater than called for may lead to structural members that are critical in shear rather than flexure. Consequently, effective depths that are too great can sometimes require repair.

An effective depth that is significantly smaller than called for must always be evaluated. In doing the evaluation, measurements of cover cannot be relied upon to determine effective depth. Rather, cover measurements must be used in combination with total thickness to determine safety of a structure.

Another common problem that occurs during construction is the misplacement and/or shifting of reinforcing bars that results in inadequate concrete cover. This is especially critical and leads to corrosion, spalling, and cracking when the concrete surface is exposed to weather or earth backfill.

TEMPORARY AND PERMANENT REMEDIAL REPAIRS

There are many ways to repair damaged or failed concrete structures, depending on the type and extent of the problem, accessibility, aesthetics, etc. Only some are mentioned here for illustration.

Shoring

Safety of the public, as well as of workers, is paramount to any investigation. The first course of action after a failure should be to stabilize any structural and nonstructural element with cables and shoring.

Although shoring is a temporary method of repair, supports must be designed to carry all loads that may be put on them. Off-the-shelf shoring of known capacity should be used when possible. Also, foundations for the shoring must be adequate to carry loads that will be applied.

More permanent repairs can be provided after the problem has been identified. Reinforced concrete provides many options for permanent repair. Often, it is economical to simply shore up portions of the structure, remove low-strength or damaged areas, put in additional reinforcement, and recast the concrete.

External Prestressing

Often, structures are already in place, and it is not practical to remove concrete. External prestressing is one method that can be used to strengthen the structure. This is particularly useful where questions arise because of beam-column joint capacity. Figure 12.27 shows external prestressing used to strengthen a structure.

When external posttensioning is used, it is important to attach the tendons to the beams at intervals along the span. If the tendons are not attached, the capacity of the beam will be reduced.

Supplemental Reinforcement

Where space is available, another method of strengthening concrete structures is to provide supplemental bonded overlays. Figure 12.28 shows a reinforcing cage in place, ready to receive concrete. Externally applied reinforcement in concrete, in this case, strengthens both the columns and the beams.

Shear friction may be used to design overlays. In design, attention must be given to the development of shear friction reinforcement and supplemental reinforcement. During construction, surfaces that will receive overlays must be intentionally roughened, free of laitence, and clean prior to application of concrete.

FIGURE 12.27   External prestressing. (*Courtesy of Construction Technology Laboratories, Inc.*)

FIGURE 12.28 Supplemental reinforcement for strengthening of column. (*Courtesy of Construction Technology Laboratories, Inc.*)

CASE STUDIES OF NONPERFORMANCE AND FAILURES

To illustrate forensic techniques in reinforced concrete, the results of three case studies are presented. Each case presents different forensic techniques used to determine the facts.

Case Study of Cracking in Bridge Pier

A bridge pier to support a crossing of a major midwestern river was placed during cool weather. Contractual documents required that the temperature gradient between the center of the pier and the exposed surface be within specified limits. Measurements taken during placement of the concrete indicated that temperature requirements had been violated. As a result, the owners proposed to apply penalties on the contractor. It was the contractor's belief that these penalties were uncalled for.

To develop information concerning the reasonableness of the penalties, a forensic investigation was started by first reviewing plans and specifications for the project. Concrete mix design was used to calculate temperature gradients that could be allowed without causing significant cracking at the surface during construction. These calculations indicated that a much higher temperature than that specified in the contract documents could be accommodated. Consequently, cracking due to thermal gradients should not have been expected to be a problem.

As a next step in the investigation, the pier was visually inspected and crack mapping was carried out. Crack mapping indicated that spacing between cracks was in excess of 50 ft, more than would be expected for the amount of reinforcement and other restraint provided within the pier. Also, crack widths were measured as illustrated in Fig. 12.29. Maximum crack width measured was 0.005 in. Most cracks had a width of 0.001 to 0.003 in. Observed patterns indicated shrinkage was a likely cause of the cracking.

As a final step, cores of the concrete were taken and petrographic analyses done. Cores indicated that the concrete equaled or exceeded the quality called for in the specifications. No deleterious materials were found in the concrete, and strength exceeded the minimum required for the job.

Based on the finding that concrete temperatures measured were below those that would be expected to cause damage to the concrete and that observed cracking was more widely spaced and with narrower widths than would be expected from ordinary drying shrinkage, it was concluded that the higher-than-specified differential temperatures did not damage the concrete.

Case Study of Deficient Parking Structure

Soon after construction was completed, reinforced-concrete decks of a multistory parking garage exhibited extensive cracking with water leakage through the cracks. Results of nondestructive evaluation indicated significant repairs were required to correct flaws before the garage could be opened to traffic. Results of the evaluation repair methods used to restore structural integrity and the techniques to provide long-term durability of the parking facility are described.

The parking garage described here is a four-level structure consisting of one level supported on-grade and three framed levels above grade.[21,22] Ramps located in the middle of the structure connect the four levels. The above-grade parking decks and ramps consist of conventionally reinforced lightweight concrete and are supported by concrete pile foundations. Concern with the integrity and durability of the structure developed shortly after completion of construction when extensive cracking and water leakage through cracks were observed.

FIGURE 12.29   Measuring a 0.002-in-wide crack on mass concrete. (*Courtesy of Construction Technology Laboratories, Inc.*)

At the request of the garage owner, a detailed structural investigation was performed. The objectives of the investigation were to determine the cause(s) of observed cracking and to evaluate the significance of cracking with respect to the integrity and durability of the structure. Investigative work[23] included the following:

1. Design documents and construction records were reviewed.
2. A detailed field investigation including visual inspection, R-meter, impulse radar, and concrete sampling was performed.
3. Use of copper–copper sulfate half-cell tests was considered.
4. Laboratory examinations and tests were performed on concrete samples.
5. A review of the structural design was performed.

The investigation concluded[24] that the cracking was attributed to the following design and construction deficiencies:

1. Amount of cracking in slabs significantly exceeded that to be expected in a conventionally reinforced pan joist framing system. Crack maps for the three framed levels are shown in Fig. 12.30.
2. The majority of cracks extended through the entire slab thickness, thereby allowing leakage through cracks.

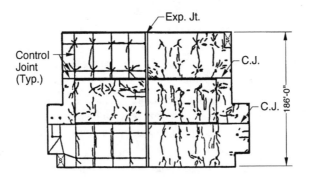

Level 2

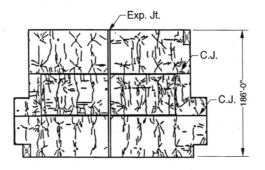

Level 3

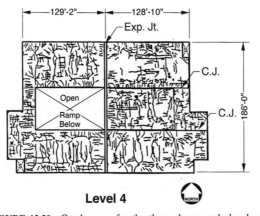

Level 4

FIGURE 12.30 Crack maps for the three above-grade levels of parking structure. (*Courtesy of Construction Technology Laboratories, Inc.*)

3. The majority of cracks were wider than the "tolerable" crack width indicated by the American Concrete Institute[25] for reinforced concrete exposed to deicing salts.

4. Cracking is attributed to restrained volume changes associated with drying shrinkage and temperature changes, and to flexural behavior of the floor system.

5. Significant factors contributing to cracking include less reinforcement in slabs than required by building code, existing built-in restraint, and a relatively high shrinkage potential of the lightweight aggregate concrete used.

6. As-built slabs throughout the majority of the garage contained only one-third of the minimum amount of steel reinforcement required by the American Concrete Institute's *Building Code for Reinforced Concrete* (ACI 381-83).[26]

7. As-built slabs throughout the majority of the garage did not meet structural requirements of the *ACI Building Code for Reinforced Concrete*[26] for the 2000-lb concentrated wheel load required by the prevailing municipal building code.

8. Several beams did not meet strength requirements of the ACI *Building Code for Reinforced Concrete.*[26]

9. Durability of the concrete was compromised due to extensive cracking and leakage through cracks. Experience indicates that corrosion of embedded steel reinforcement and related concrete deterioration would likely occur relatively early in the service life of the garage in the absence of repairs.

The findings indicated that significant repairs were required to ensure structural integrity and provide a durable structure.

The following four alternatives were considered for repair[30] of the garage:

1. Demolish the superstructure and rebuild the garage, using the remaining foundations.

2. Remove and replace slabs and strengthen deficient beams.

3. Install supplemental below-slab framing spanning between joists, and strengthen deficient beams.

4. Place a bonded reinforced-concrete overlay and strengthen deficient beams.

Important criteria in evaluating repair alternatives included cost, construction schedule, construction methods, effect of repairs on the remainder of the garage (structural and operational), and durability. The bonded reinforced overlay alternative was chosen for the following reasons:

1. Estimated cost was lowest of the four options.

2. Repairs could be completed in approximately 4 months.

3. Construction methods were proved, and many contractors have overlay experience.

4. Effect on the remainder of the garage would be minimized because work could be phased to allow portions of the garage to be used prior to completion.

5. New overlay slab would provide a durable wearing surface.

Case Study of Shear Failure in Waffle Slab

Approximately 8 years after construction was completed, a sudden shear failure occurred at two columns around the perimeter of a two-story office building. Figure 12.31 shows the failed slabs after curtain walls had been removed. Figure 12.32 shows a close-up of one of the shear failures. Temporary timber shoring was placed under the column to provide emergency support.

Once the safety of the building had been secured with emergency shoring, an investigation to determine the cause of the failure was begun. Samples of concrete and reinforcement were obtained to determine material properties. Simultaneously, plans for the structure were obtained and verified by field inspection.

Figure 12.33 shows framing at each perimeter column for the building. As can be seen, columns for the second story did not line up with columns for the first story, but were cantilevered outward around the perimeter of the structure. The second-story column was supported by a solid section of the waffle slab spanning from the bottom of the second-story column to the top of the first-story column.

FIGURE 12.31 Shear failures of columns on second story of building. (*Courtesy of Construction Technology Laboratories, Inc.*)

FIGURE 12.32   Closeup of shear failure with temporary shoring in place. (*Courtesy of Construction Technology Laboratories, Inc.*)

To provide deflection control for the long spans used in the interior of the building, the waffle slabs were posttensioned.

Figure 12.34 shows reinforcing details in the vicinity of the cantilever portion of the slab. Because of negative moments over the interior column, posttension-

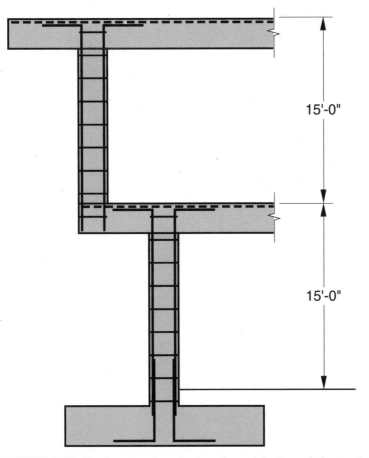

FIGURE 12.33 Framing at each perimeter column. (*Courtesy of Construction Technology Laboratories, Inc.*)

ing was located near the top of the slab. The bottom of the slab had extremely light reinforcement consisting of one no. 4 bar in each stem of the waffle slab. The resulting reinforcement provided less than minimum flexural reinforcement at the bottom of the slab. Consequently, the full depth of the section could not be utilized to carry shear forces. Rather, shear forces were more closely related to an effective depth between the top of the slab and the depth of the posttensioning tendon. This depth resulted in an inadequate strength to carry shear that was applied.

Properties of concrete and steel used in construction were found to be consistent with those specified. Review of the original construction documents disclosed

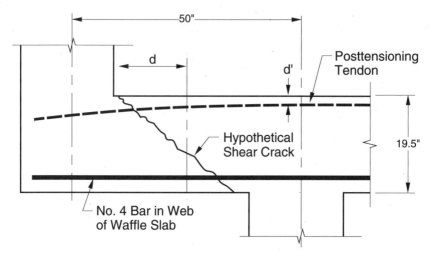

FIGURE 12.34 Reinforcing details in the vicinity of the cantilevered portion of the slab. (*Courtesy of Construction Technology Laboratories, Inc.*)

no indication that shear strength had ever been checked anywhere in the building. Consequently, it was determined that the cause of failure was primarily due to a failure to provide adequate shear strength in the cantilever sections carrying the load from the second-story column to the first-story column.

REFERENCES

1. S. H. Kosmatka and W. C. Panarese, "Design and Control of Concrete Mixtures," 13th ed., Portland Cement Association, Skokie, IL, 1994.

2. ACI 318-95, *Building Code Requirement for Reinforced Concrete*, American Concrete Institute (ACI), Detroit, MI, 1995.

3. A. Azizinamini, W. G. Corley, and L. S. P. Johal, "Effects of Transverse Reinforcement on Seismic Performance of Columns," *ACI Structural Journal*, American Concrete Institute, vol. 89, no. 4, July-August 1992, pp. 442–450.

4. ASTM A 615-94, *Standard Specifications for Deformed and Plain Billet-Steel Bars for Concrete Reinforcement*, annual book of ASTM standards, American Society for Testing and Materials, Philadelphia, PA.

5. ASTM A 706-92b, *Standard Specifications for Low-Alloy Steel Deformed Bars for Concrete Reinforcements*, annual book of ASTM standards, American Society for Testing and Materials, Philadelphia, PA.

6. D. Stark, "Influence of Design and Materials on Corrosion Resistance of Steel in Concrete," Bulletin RD098, Portland Cement Association, Skokie, IL, 1989.

7. W. G. Corley, "Designing Corrosion Resistance into Reinforced Concrete," *Materials Performance*, NACE International, Houston, September 1995.

8. D. Whiting, B. Ost, M. Nagi, and P. D. Cady, *Condition Evaluation of Concrete Bridges Relative to Reinforcement Corrosion,* vol. 5: *Method for Evaluating Effectiveness of Penetrating Sealers,* SHRP-S-327, National Research Council, Washington, 1993.

9. *Standard Specifications for Highway Bridges,* 16th ed., American Association of State Highway and Transportation Officials, Washington, 1996.

10. W. G. Corley, "Protecting the Public from Fools and Rascals—Building Codes for the Millennium," *Concrete International,* vol. 14, no. 9, September 1992, pp. 57–62.

11. *Steel Deck Institute Design Manual for Floor Decks and Roof Decks,* Steel Deck Institute, St. Louis, MO, 1981–1982.

12. "Investigation of the Skyline Plaza Collapse in Fairfax County, Virginia," NBSIR 94, National Bureau of Standards (National Institute of Standards and Technology), U.S. Department of Commerce, Washington, 1977.

13. ACI Committee 301, *Standard Specifications for Structural Concrete (ACI 301-96),* American Concrete Institute, Detroit, MI, 1996.

14. ASTM C42, *Standard Method of Obtaining and Testing Drilled Cores and Sawed Beams of Concrete,* annual book of ASTM standards, American Society for Testing and Materials, Philadelphia, PA.

15. ACI 435R-95, *Control of Reflection in Concrete Structures,* American Concrete Institute, Detroit, MI, 1995.

16. W. G. Corley and M. A. Sozen, "Time-Dependent Deflections of Reinforced Concrete Beams," *Journal of the American Concrete Institute,* March 1966, pp. 373–386.

17. C. W. Yu, and E. Hognestad, "Review of Limit Design for Structural Concrete," *Journal of the Structural Division, Proceedings,* vol. 84, ST8, American Society of Civil Engineers, December 1958.

18. F. A. Noor and L. F. Boswell, *Small Scale Modeling of Concrete Structures,* Elsevier, London, 1991.

19. ASTM C856, *Standard Recommended Practice for Petrographic Examination of Hardened Concrete,* annual book of ASTM standards, American Society for Testing and Materials, Philadelphia, PA.

20. "Investigation of Construction Failure of Harbour Cay Condominium in Cocoa Beach, Florida," NBSIR 81-2374, National Bureau of Standards (National Institute of Standards and Technology), U.S. Department of Commerce, Washington, 1981.

21. W. G. Corley, J. F. Vincent, M. K. Lim, and C. A. Olson, "Nondestructive Evaluation and Repair of an Understrength Building," *Proceedings of Seminario Internacional Evaluacion de Estructuras de Concrete,* Mexico, D.F., May 30–31, 1991.

22. K. A. Michols and J. F. Vincent, "Reinforced Overlay and Shotcrete Restore Integrity to a Multistory Parking Structure," *Concrete International: Design and Construction,* vol. 12, no. 9, September 1990, pp. 55–58.

23. M. K. Lim and C. A. Olson, "Use of Non-Destructive Impulse Radar in Evaluating Civil Engineering Structures," *Proceedings, Nondestructive Evaluation of Civil Structures and Materials,* University of Colorado, Boulder, October 1990, pp. 167–176.

24. ASTM C 876, *Test Method for Half Cell Potential of Reinforcing Steel in Concrete,* American Society for Testing and Materials, Philadelphia, PA, 1987.

25. ACI Committee 224, *Control of Cracking on Concrete Structures (ACI 224R-80, Revised 1984),* American Concrete Institute, Detroit, MI, 1984.

26. ACI Committee 318, *Building Code for Reinforced Concrete (ACI 318-83)*, American Concrete Institute, Detroit, MI, 1983.

26. Anders Nielsen, "Holdbarhed," *Benton-Bogen.* Aalborg Portland, Aalborg, Denmark, 1979 [in Danish].

28. D. A. Whiting, *Origins of Chloride Limits for Reinforced Concrete,* Portland Cement Association, Research and Development Serial no. 2153, Skokie, IL, 1997.

29. D. Whiting and R. Detwiler, *Silica Fume Concrete for Bridge Decks,* National Cooperative Highway Research Program, Report 410, National Academy Press, Washington, 1998.

30. 12.2x ACI Committee 546, *Concrete Repair Guide,* American Concrete Institute, Detroit, MI, 1996.

CHAPTER 13
MASONRY STRUCTURES

Clayford T. Grimm, P.E.

INTRODUCTION

This chapter addresses forensic investigation of stone, clay brick, and conventional concrete masonry. It does not include consideration of chemical resistant, refractory, aerated concrete, or glass block masonry.

Forensic investigation of masonry structures involves failure of masonry to perform adequately. The purpose of such an investigation may be to avoid greater failure, provide a basis for recommended remedial measures, or settle a claim by negotiation, arbitration, or litigation.

Masonry failures may relate to aesthetics, engineering, or economics and may involve any of the following:

Abrasion	Deflection
Adhesion	Demolition
Anchorage	Dimensional tolerance
Building investment analysis	Durability
Cleaning	Expansion joints
Coatings	Fire resistance
Color discrimination (of masonry)	Maintenance
Constructibility	Radiation shielding
Construction cost	Restoration
Construction quality control	Staining
Construction technique	Strength during construction or in service
Control joints	Volume change
Corrosion	Water, heat, or sound transfer or absorption
Cracked, warped, or chipped units	Workmanship

Masonry falls off a building facade somewhere in the United States about every three weeks. In the decade or so prior to 1999, at least 49 such masonry failures killed 30 persons and injured 81 in the United States. The failures occur under normal loading conditions, not during construction, and are not subject to earthquake, hurricane, tornado, fire, blast, collision, or demolition.

It has been the author's experience with hundreds of masonry failures that the primary cause of failure was design error or omission in about 50 percent of cases, construction error or omission in about 25 percent of cases, and inadequate materials in about 15 percent of cases. The owner's failure to mitigate damage by proper maintenance was the primary cause in about 10 percent of cases.

Only an experienced engineer who is supported by a wide array of other experts and laboratory facilities should investigate masonry failures. Site visits are required to define the problem, collect data, and conduct tests. Document discovery, interviews with persons involved with the failure, literature searches, and perhaps chemical and physical research can provide information to supplement that obtained by site visits. Reports to the client can be used as a basis for solving an anticipated problem or settling a claim. When that is not possible, arbitration, mediation, or litigation often results, which may involve depositions, court testimony, and preparation of exhibits by expert.

STRUCTURAL ENGINEERING PROPERTIES

This section discusses the following: Incorrect assumptions about wall weight can result in a multiplicity of design errors involving structure, acoustics, and heating, ventilating, and air conditioning (HVAC) systems. An increase in wall weight can provide increased resistance to fire, sound transmission, and roof uplift as well as reduced air conditioning costs and can contribute to passive solar heating and cooling. The compressive strength of masonry is affected by the strength and size of masonry units, mortar strength, mortar joint thickness, workmanship, moisture content, and exposure to freezing. Compressive strength and modulus of elasticity of masonry are typically much greater than the building code–assumed values. Shear strength increases with compressive stress. As long as mortar remains plastic, an increase in the water-cement ratio increases the bond strength of mortar to masonry units. Very high slump grout can have very high compressive strength, because the water-cement ratio is reduced by absorption of masonry units. A cited reference provides wall section properties for a wide array of masonry walls.

Clay Brick Masonry

Weight of Clay Masonry.   The weight of clay brick masonry can vary by more than 30 percent from the minimum design dead load required by ASCE 7-95.[49] Variations in clay brick masonry weight have implication not only for structural and acoustical design, but also for design of heating, ventilating, and air conditioning systems.

Incorrect assumptions about wall weight can result in excessive or inadequate seismic loads on masonry walls; insufficient resistance to uplift; increased structural framing and foundation costs; reduced factors of safety in shear walls; increased summer air conditioning costs; overestimates of acoustical transmission loss; and inefficiency in passive heating and cooling systems. Designers should be aware that masonry wall weight is variable and should consider that variability where appropriate. The density of brick masonry has a mean value of 116 lb/ft^3 (1858 kg/m^3) with a standard deviation of 12 lb/ft^3 (192 kg/m^3).[33] Brick masonry wall weights are given in Table 13.1.

Clay Brick Masonry in Compression.   The mean expected 28-day compressive strength of masonry f'_m—measured perpendicular to bed joints and built with standard modular clay brick [nominally $2\frac{1}{4}$ in (57 mm) high], inspected workmanship, and ASTM C 270, type S mortar, without air entrainment[62]—is estimated by the author as f'_m (lb/in^2) ≈ 0.283 $(f'_u + 8380)$, where f'_u is the brick compressive strength in pounds per square inch.

That strength is reduced about 29 percent by use of type N mortar, about 27 percent by uninspected workmanship, and about 15 percent by increasing the mortar air content from 5 to 18 percent. Mortars without air entrainment typically have air contents of 5 percent or less. The specification for type N masonry cement (ASTM C 91, *Specifications for Masonry Cement*[62]) permits an air content of 22 percent, which may result in typical mortar air content of 24 percent. Use of type M mortar increases strength about 6 percent. Use of 3^5/$_8$-in (92-mm) high clay

TABLE 13.1 Clay Brick Masonry Wall Weight, lb/ft² (kg/m²)*

Nominal thickness, in (mm)	Actual thickness, in (mm)	Hollow brick ASTM C 652		Face brick ASTM 216 and building brick ASTM 62	
		Class H60V cored more than 40%, at least 40% solid	Class H40V cored more than 25%, at least 60% solid	All grades and types at least 75% solid	All grades and types 100% solid
3.38 (86)	3 (75)	10 -> **12** -> 14 (49 -> **59** -> 68)	15 -> **18** -> 21 (73 -> **88** -> 103)	25 -> **29** -> 33 (122 -> **142** -> 161)	28 - > **33** -> 38 (137 - > **161** -> 186)
4 (100)	3.5 (89)	12 -> **14** -> 17 (59 -> **68** -> 83)	18 -> **22** -> 25 (88 -> **107** -> 122)	29 -> **34** -> 39 (142 -> **166** -> 190)	34 - > **39** -> 44 (166 - > **190** -> 215)
	3.63 (90)	12 -> **15** -> 17 (59 -> **73** -> 83)	19 -> **22** -> 26 (93 -> **107** -> 127)	30 -> **35** -> 40 (146 -> **171** -> 195)	34 - > **40** -> 46 (166 - > **195** -> 225)
6 (150)	5.5 (140)	19 -> **23** -> 26 (93 -> **112** -> 127)	28 -> **34** -> 39 (137 -> **166** -> 190)	46 -> **53** -> 60 (225 -> **259** -> 293)	53 - > **61** -> 69 (259 - > **298** -> 337)
	5.63 (140)	19 -> **23** -> 27 (93 -> **112** -> 132)	29 -> **35** -> 40 (142 -> **171** -> 195)	47 -> **54** -> 61 (47 -> **264** -> 298)	53 - > **62** -> 71 (259 - > **303** -> 347)
8 (200)	7.5 (191)	26 -> **31** -> 36 (127 -> **151** -> 176)	39 -> **46** -> 53 (190 -> **225** -> 259)		
	7.63 (190)	26 -> **31** -> 36 (127 -> **151** -> 176)	39 -> **47** -> 54 (190 -> **229** -> 264)		

*Typical wall weights are shown in bold type. Range in wall weight is shown in regular typeface.

brick with $^3/_8$-in (10-mm) mortar joints rather than a $2^1/_4$-in (57-mm) high clay brick increases strength about 22 percent. Other things being equal, use of high air entrainment and uninspected workmanship combine to reduce the compressive strength of clay brick masonry about 36 percent. Clay brick masonry in compression has a mean cracking strength of 47 percent of its f'_m ultimate strength with a coefficient of variation of 15 percent. Frequent application and withdrawal of load may cause fatigue and strength reduction and therefore may increase cracking probability. The compressive strength of brick masonry is typically significantly greater than the building code–assumed values. The ratio of saturated to air-dry strength of clay brick is reported to be 0.83. One hundred cycles of freezing and thawing reduce the compressive strength of clay brick by an average of 11 percent with a standard deviation of 13 percent.[61]

Elastic Modulus of Clay Brick Masonry. Masonry elastic modulus in compression is rather constant over the stress range from 5 to 33 percent of the masonry's ultimate strength. Within that stress range, the mean chord modulus of elasticity E_m of solid clay brick masonry with a prism aspect ratio of 5 is $464 f'_m$ (lb/in^2) with a standard deviation of $185 f'_m$ (lb/in^2). The modulus E_m is reduced about 24 percent when compressive stress is parallel to bed joints. The modulus of elasticity of masonry is typically significantly greater than the building code–assumed values.

Clay Brick Masonry in Flexure. Flexure cracks in masonry form primarily at the unit-mortar interface. Resistance to such cracks depends on tensile bond strength of the unit-mortar combination. Higher bond strength reduces cracking, leaking, staining, and spalling. Bond strength is a function of (1) initial rate of water absorption, texture, and cleanliness of clay brick; (2) water retentivity, flow, and cement and air content of mortar; and (3) quality of workmanship.

Allowable stress in flexural tension with non-air-entrained portland cement-lime mortars is about twice as great as that with masonry cement or air-entrained portland cement-lime mortar.

The 28-day flexural strength of clay brick masonry walls built with ASTM C 270, *Mortar for Unit Masonry,*[62] type S, portland cement-lime, non-air-entrained mortar, and inspected workmanship, with stress perpendicular to bed joints, has a mean value of 140 lb/in^2 with a standard deviation of 31 lb/in^2, when tested in accordance with ASTM E 72, *Methods of Conducting Strength Tests of Panels for Building Construction.*[62]

Walls with type M mortar are about 10 percent stronger in flexure. Use of type N mortar reduces strength about 23 percent. Increasing air content reduces flexural bond strength. Uninspected workmanship reduces mean strength by about 23 percent. Other things being equal, use of type N mortar with air content of 18 percent and uninspected workmanship typically reduces flexural strength about 60 percent below that attained by type S mortar.

For 4-in (100-mm) wythes of standard modular clay brick, flexural strength is about 3.7 times greater when stress is parallel rather than perpendicular to bed joints.

First crack in clay brick masonry in flexure occurs at about 80 percent of ultimate strength. Out-of-plane cracking occurs at a deflection of about 0.05 percent of wall span with a coefficient of variation of 26 percent.

Clay Brick Masonry in Shear. Modulus of rigidity (shear modulus E_v) is about 40 percent of E_m. In the absence of compressive stress, the ultimate shear strength of clay brick masonry f_{sb} can be approximated as follows with a coefficient of variation of about 30 percent: f_{sb} (lb/in^2) $\approx$ 40 exp $(f'_m/1780)$. Compressive stress increases shear strength.

Concrete Masonry

Concrete Masonry Wall Weight. Weights of concrete masonry walls are given in Table 13.2.

Concrete Masonry in Compression. Compressive strength of concrete masonry is a function of concrete masonry unit (CMU) compressive strength, mortar type, stress direction, and workmanship. For ASTM C 270, *Mortar for Unit Masonry,*[62] type M or S non-air-entrained mortars, stress perpendicular to bed joints, and inspected workmanship, the mean 28-day compressive strength on net area of a standard prism of concrete masonry f'_m can be estimated as f'_m (lb/in^2) $\approx$ 0.635(f_{cu} + 1120), where f_{cu} = compressive strength of concrete masonry units in pounds per square inch.

Strength is reduced about 25 percent for type N mortar, 35 percent for uninspected workmanship, 10 percent by increasing the air content from 5 to 18 percent, and 25 percent for stress parallel to bed joints.

Elastic Modulus of Concrete Masonry. Mean chord modulus of elasticity of ungrouted concrete masonry with a prism height/length ratio of 2 is 615 f'_m with a standard deviation of 365 f'_m.

Concrete Masonry in Flexure. Concrete masonry walls 28 days old constructed with hollow concrete masonry units, non-air-entrained ASTM C 270, *Mortar for Unit Masonry,*[62] type S mortar, inspected workmanship, and stress perpendicular to bed joints have an estimated mean flexural tensile strength of 76 lb/in^2 with a standard deviation of about 12 lb/in^2. Strength is reduced 21 percent by use of type N mortar. High air content associated with use of masonry cement or air-entrained portland cement-lime mortars reduces flexural strength about 50 percent. Strength is increased by 105 percent by use of solid units instead of hollow units for out-of-plane flexure normal to bed joints. Strength is more than doubled when bending stress acts parallel rather than perpendicular to bed joints. Deflection at flexural cracking is about 0.036 percent of wall span.

Concrete Masonry in Shear. Mean shear stress at first crack in concrete masonry is about 64 percent of ultimate compressive strength with a coefficient of variation of 25 percent.

TABLE 13.2 Load-Bearing Concrete Masonry Wall Weight, lb/ft² (kg/m²)

Nominal single wythe wall thicknesses, in (mm)	Typical CMU solidity dimensionless	Concrete density, lb/ft³ (kg/m³)						
		Light weight			Medium weight		Normal weight	
		85 (1362)	95 (1522)	105 (1682)	115 (1842)	125 (2002)	135 (2162)	145 (2323)
4	0.5	13 (63)	14 (68)	16 (78)	17 (83)	19 (93)	20 (98)	22 (107)
4 (100)	1	26 (127)	29 (142)	32 (156)	35 (171)	38 (186)	41 (200)	44 (215)
6 (150)	0.48	19 (93)	21 (103)	24 (117)	26 (127)	28 (137)	30 (146)	33 (161)
6 (150)	1	40 (195)	45 (220)	49 (239)	54 (264)	59 (288)	63 (308)	68 (332)
8 (200)	0.45	24 (117)	27 (132)	30 (146)	33 (161)	36 (176)	39 (190)	41 (200)
8 (200)	1	54 (264)	60 (293)	67 (327)	73 (356)	79 (386)	86 (420)	92 (449)
10 (250)	0.44	30 (146)	34 (166)	37 (181)	41 (200)	44 (215)	48 (234)	51 (249)
10 (250)	1	68 (332)	76 (371)	84 (410)	92 (449)	100 (488)	108 (527)	116 (566)
12 (300)	0.41	34 (166)	38 (0)	42 (0)	46 (0)	50 (0)	54 (0)	58 (0)
12 (300)	1	82 (400)	92 (449)	102 (498)	111 (542)	121 (591)	131 (640)	140 (684)

Grout Compressive Strength

Compressive strength of fine grout f_f (lb/in^2) may be estimated as $f_f = 45.23R^{-1.596}$, where $R = $ volumetric ratio of aggregate to cement, which is dimensionless. The compressive strength of course grout f_c (lb/in^2) may be estimated as $f_c = 54.6R^{-1.425}$. The modulus of elasticity of grout may be assumed to be 500 times the compressive strength of grout.

Stone Properties

Properties of granite, limestone, and sandstone are given in Table 13.3. Properties of marble and slate are given in Table 13.4.

Wall Section Properties

Section properties depend on conformance of materials to specifications. Load-bearing and non-load-bearing masonry units have different dimensional properties, as illustrated in Fig. 13.1.

Reference 37 provides equations and tabular values for the mechanical properties, such as bed area, moment of inertia, and section modulus, for single-wythe walls of clay or concrete masonry in thickness of 4, 6, 8, 10, or 12 in (100, 150, 200, 250, or 300 mm).

A sketch of a composite wall is shown in Fig. 13.2. The mechanical properties of a transformed composite section are functions of each material's modular ratio n. For a given material the modular ratio is the quotient of the elastic modulus of the solid material divided by the elastic modulus of the hollow masonry. Reference 37 gives the wall bed areas, moments of inertia, and section moduli for both sides of composite walls having modular ratios of 0.25, 0.5, 1, 1.5, 2, 2.5, and 3 for walls having a specified 3-in (75-mm) or 4-in (100-mm) solid masonry withe and a 4-, 6-, 8-, 10-, or 12-in (100-, 150-, 200-, 250-, or 300-mm) wythe of hollow masonry.

ARCHITECTURAL ENGINEERING PROPERTIES

This chapter section provides information on sound transmission and absorption, fire resistance, and transmission of heat, air, and vapor.

Acoustical Properties

The sound transmission class (STC) of clay and concrete masonry may be estimated as STC $= 0.18W + 39$, where W is wall weight in pounds per square foot (see Tables 13.1 and 13.2). Table 13.5 provides data on sound absorption of

TABLE 13.3 Physical Properties and Characteristics of Granite, Limestone, and Sandstone

Characteristic	Igneous		Sedimentary					
	Granite	Traprock "black granite"	Limestone			Sandstone	Sandstone	
			Density					
			Low	Medium	High	Sandstone	Quartzitic Sandstone	Quartzitic
Geology	Igneous		Sedimentary					
Mineralogy	Quartz, alkali, feldspar	Pyroxene, hornblend, biotite	Calcite, dolomite			Quartz, feldspar		
Chemistry (Approximate)	$70\% \ SiO_2$ $15\% \ Al_2O_4$		50% to $97\% \ CaCO_4$ 2% to $50\% \ MgCO_4$			$SiO_2NaAlS_2O_4$ $KAlS_2O_4CaAlS_2O_4$		
Geology	MA, NH, VT, RI, CT, NY, NJ, MD, VA, NC, SC, GA, WI, MN, MO, OK, TX, CA, SD, ME, PA		NY to AL, IN to MS, IA, NE, KS, MO, OK, AR, TX, WI, CO, SD, CA, MN, WY			Most states		
Colors	Pink, brown, gray, white, blue, black, green, red	Pink, green, blue, black	White, cream, gray, rust, pink, black, buff, tan, ivory, blue, rose			Brown, gray, rose, cream, buff, ivory, pink, tan, yellow, beige, white, red, gold, purple, blue, rust		
ASTM specification	C 615.		C 568			C 616		
Density, lb/ft², min	160		110	135	160	125	150	160
Water absorption (% by weight), max.	0.4		12	7.5	3	8	3	1
Permanent set, %*	0.02			0.035			0.0235	
Compressive strength, ksi, min (f'_c)	19		1.8	4	8	4	10	20
Modulus of rupture,† ksi, min	1.5		0.4	0.5	1	0.35	1	2
Flexural strength,‡ ksi, min	1.2							

*Thermal expansion/contraction hysteresis.
†Determined by a single midpoint load.
‡Determined by two quarter-point loads.

TABLE 13.4 Physical Properties and Characteristics of Marble and Slate

Characteristic	Marble				Slate building stone	
	Calcite	Dolomite	Serpentine	Travertine	Exterior	Interior
Geology	Metamorphic			Sedimentary	Metamorphic	
Mineralogy	Calcite, dolomite				Quartz, mica	
Chemistry (approximate)	$CaCO_3$, $MgCO_3$				$H_2KAl_3(SiO_4)_3$; $(H,K)_2(Mg, Fe)_2Al_2(SiO_4)_3$	
Geography	NY to AL, IN to MS, NE, KS, MO, OK, AR, TX, CO, SD, WY, CA, MN, WI				MA to GA, CA, AR	
Colors	White, gray, red, pink, buff, rose, gold, green, black, yellow, brown, tan				Blue, green, black, purple, gray	
Size, ft² max.	5 ft × 7 ft					
ASTM Specification	C 503				C 629	
Density, lb/ft², min	162	175	168	144		
Water absorption (% by weight), max.			0.2		0.25	0.45
Permanent set‖			0.045			
Compressive strength, ksi, min			75			
Modulus of rupture,* ksi, min.			1		9, ‡7.2§	
Flexural strength,† ksi, min			1			
Acid resistance, in max.					0.015	0.025

*Determined by a single midpoint load.
†Determined by two quarter-point loads.
‡Crossgrain.
§Along grain.
‖Thermal expansion/contraction hysteresis.

13.11

FIGURE 13.1   Load-bearing and non-load-bearing masonry units have different dimensional properties.

masonry. Figure 13.3 illustrates potential sound leaks. Grimm[26] discusses the acoustical properties of masonry walls.

Fire Resistance

The *Standard Method for Determining Fire Resistance of Concrete and Masonry Construction Assemblies*[58] provides a method for calculating fire resistance. Grimm[30] provides a bibliography on masonry fire resistance with 192 citations. Tables 13.6 through 13.10 provide data on masonry fire resistance. Data in Tables 13.6 and 13.8 are excerpts from Ref. 55.

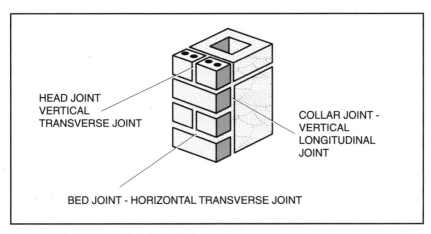

FIGURE 13.2 Mortar joint location definitions.

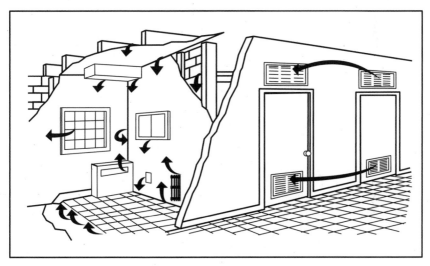

FIGURE 13.3 Acoustical leaks.

Thermal Conductivity

Clay Brick Masonry. The author's estimate for the thermal conductivity of clay brick masonry is $k_b \approx 1.139 W^{0.2321} e^{\omega/76.62}$, where k_b = thermal conductivity, Btu/(h·ft²·°F·in); W = density of brick masonry, lb/ft³; and ω = moisture content, percent. For interior walls $\omega \approx 1$ percent; for exterior walls in winter $\omega \approx 7$ percent, and in summer $\omega \approx 2$ percent or after a few rainy days $\omega \approx 12$ to 20 percent.

Concrete Masonry. Thermal conductivity of solid concrete masonry k_c may be estimated as $k_c \approx 0.082w - 3.84$, where w = concrete density in pounds per cubic foot (see Table 13.2).

TABLE 13.5 Masonry Sound Absorption Coefficients, Sabines lb/ft^2

Material	Type	Thickness, in (mm)	Frequency, Hz						NRC
			125	250	500	1000	2000	4000	
Brick masonry	Unpainted	Any	0.024	0.025	0.031	0.04	0.05	0.07	0.037
Brick masonry	Painted	Any	0.012	0.013	0.01	0.02	0.023	0.025	0.018
CM usual low	Unpainted	Any	0.3	0.45	0.3	0.25	0.4	0.25	0.35
CM usual high	Unpainted	Any	0.35	0.55	0.5	0.35	0.5	0.35	0.48
CM usual low	Painted	Any	0.1	0.08	0.05	0.05	0.1	0.1	0.07
CM usual high	Painted	Any	0.2	0.2	0.15	0.2	0.2	0.2	0.19
CM Soundblox	Unpainted	4 (100)	0.19	0.83	0.41	0.38	0.42	0.4	0.5
CM Soundblox	Painted	4 (100)	0.2	0.88	0.63	0.65	0.52	0.43	0.65
CM Soundblox	Painted	6–12 (150–300)							to 0.85

NRC = noise reduction coefficient.

TABLE 13.6 Required Minimum Equivalent Thickness for Fire Resistance* of Concrete Masonry Walls, in (mm)

Concrete aggregate	Fire resistance rating, h				
	1	1.5	2	3	4
Calcareous or siliceous gravel (other than limestone)	2.8 (71)	3.6 (91)	4.2 (107)	5.3 (135)	6.2 (157)
Limestone, cinders, or air-cooled slag	2.7 (69)	3.4 (86)	4.0 (102)	5.0 (127)	5.9 (150)
Expanded clay, shale, or slate	2.6 (66)	3.3 (84)	3.6 (91)	4.4 (123)	5.1 (130)
Expanded slag or pumice	2.1 (53)	2.7 (69)	3.2 (81)	4.0 (102)	4.7 (119)

*Fire resistance ratings between those listed should be determined by linear interpolation based on the equivalent thickness of the masonry.

Required minimum equivalent thickness corresponding to the fire resistance rating for tests made with a combination of aggregates should be determined by linear interpolation based on the percent by volume of each type of aggregate.

TABLE 13.7 Minimum Equivalent Thickness Required by ASTM C 90 for Load-Bearing Concrete Masonry Units*

Nominal thickness, in (mm)	Specified thickness, in (mm)	Minimum equivalent thickness, in (mm)
4 (100)	3.63 (92)	1.91 (49)
6 (150)	5.63 (143)	2.66 (68)
8 (200)	7.63 (194)	3.41 (87)
10 (250)	9.63 (245)	4.16 (106)
12 (300)	11.63 (295)	4.91 (125)

*Some manufacturers produce concrete masonry units having greater equivalent thicknesses than the minimum requirements of ASTM C 90, *Specification for Loadbearing Concrete Masonry Units.*[62]

Air and Vapor Transmission

Air and vapor transmission is important to structural engineers, because condensation can affect serviceability of structural materials, principally steel corrosion and masonry durability.

Vapor retarders are not necessary in masonry cavity walls in most building types in the 48 contiguous states. However, they are required where average interior relative humidity exceeds 50 percent or where glazed brick is used if the

TABLE 13.8 Required Minimum Equivalent Thickness for Fire Resistance of Clay Masonry Walls, in (mm)*,†,‡

Material type	1 h	2 h	3 h	4 h
Solid clay or shale brick	2.7 (69)	3.8 (97)	4.9 (124)	6.0 (152)
Hollow brick or structural clay tile or clay or shale	2.3 (58)	3.4 (86)	4.3 (109)	5.0 (127)
Hollow brick or structural clay tile of clay or shale solidly grouted or aggregate-filled§	3.0 (76)	4.4 (112)	5.5 (140)	6.6 (168)

*Determine fire resistance ratings between those listed by linear interpolation.

†For units in which the net cross-sectional area of cored brick in any plane parallel to the surface containing the cores should be at least 75 percent of the gross cross-sectional area measured in the same plane.

‡Where combustible members are framed into the wall, the thickness of solid material between the ends of each member and the opposite face of the wall, or between members in from opposite sides, shall be not less than 95% of the thickness shown less ³/8 in.

§Sand, pea gravel, crushed stone, or slag (ASTM C 33, *Specification for Concrete Aggregates*); pumice, scoria, expanded shale, expanded clay, expanded slate, expanded slag, expanded fly ash, or cinders (ASTM C 331, *Specifications for Lightweight Aggregates for Concrete masonry Units*); ASTM C 549, *Specification for Perlite Loose Fill Insulation*; or ASTM C 516, *Specification for Vermiculite Loose Fill Thermal Insulation.*[62]

TABLE 13.9 Minimum Equivalent Thickness Required by ASTM C 652-92 for Clay or Shale Hollow Brick

Nominal thickness, in (mm)	Specified thickness, in (mm)	Equivalent thickness, in (mm)		
		Filled 100% solid	Class H60V 40% solid	Class H40V 60% solid
4 (100)	3.5 (90)	3.5 (90)	1.40 (36)	2.10 (53)
6 (150)	5.5 (140)	5.5 (140)	2.20 (56)	3.30 (84)
8 (200)	7.5 (190)	7.5 (190)	3.00 (76)	4.50 (114)
10 (250)	9.5 (240)	9.5 (240)	3.80 (97)	5.70 (145)
12 (300)	11.5 (290)	11.5 (290)	4.60 (117)	6.90 (175)

TABLE 13.10 Minimum Equivalent Thickness Provided by ASTM C 216, C 62, C 55, and C 73 for Brick

Nominal thickness, in (mm)	Specified thickness, in (mm)	Equivalent thickness, 75% solid, in (mm)	Equivalent thickness, 100% solid, in (mm)
3 (75)	3 (75)	2.35 (60)	3 (75)
4 (100)	3.5 (89)	2.63 (67)	3.5 (89)
4 (100)	3.63 (90)	2.72 (69)	3.63 (90)
6 (150)	5.5 (140)	4.13 (105)	5.5 (140)
6 (150)	5.63 (140)	4.22 (107)	5.63 (140)

weathering index exceeds 50. That index is found in ASTM C 216, *Specifications for Facing Brick (Solid Masonry Units Made from Clay or Shale).*[62]

Examples of building types in which the need for vapor retarders should be investigated include laundries, indoor swimming pools, hockey rinks, and cold storage facilities. When required, a vapor retarder should be placed on that side of the insulation which is warmer for most of the year. Vapor permeance of a nominal 4-in (100-mm) wythe of brick masonry is about 0.8 perm [gr/(h·ft²·inHg)] [46 ng/(Pa·s·m²)].

Vapor permeance of a nominal 8-in (200-mm) wythe of hollow CMU (limestone aggregate) is about 2.4 perm.

Air leakage is usually more important to condensation control than vapor retardation. When an air pressure differential occurs across a wall, air may pass through or around the wall. Wind, fan pressure, or stack effect may cause a pressure differential. In winter when warm air rises in a tall building, a positive pressure is created in upper stories and a negative pressure in lower stories. Air supply by mechanical ventilation may increase air pressure. Exhaust fans may reduce air pressure. A windward facade experiences pressure, and a leeward encounters suction. These phenomena may combine to create a significant pressure differential across a wall.

In winter, if interior pressure is greater, then warm, moist interior air may exfiltrate to a cooler part of the wall where condensation can form. In hot, humid climates during summer, the warm, moist exterior air may infiltrate and cause interstitial condensation. If interior surface material becomes moist, mold may flourish. The smell may make human occupancy intolerable, causing evacuation of rental property. See "Case Study for a Low-Rise Hotel."

An air barrier on the cavity side of the interior wythe would limit air leakage and thus mitigate the problem. Air barriers must be continuous, durable, impermeable, and structurally capable of sustaining the air pressure differential. A perfect air barrier is not attainable in conventional buildings. Complete control of air and vapor flow is not feasible. For that reason and because of permeance of masonry to wind-driven rain, corrosion protection for metal connectors in masonry is an important design consideration.[48]

For additional information on air and vapor retarders see Refs. 1 and 50.

MASONRY STANDARDS

This section provides information on national standards specifications for masonry products and their assembly, methods for sampling and testing, and methods for structural design of masonry.

Materials

In 1998 the American Society for Testing and Materials (ASTM)[62] published 91 standards for masonry, including 6 definitions of terms; 12 specifications for brick; 7 for structural tile; 8 for concrete masonry units; 5 for stone; 13 for mortar; 19 for metal connectors and their coatings; 2 for masonry fill insulation; 2 for masonry assemblages; and 17 for sampling and testing.[62] All those are individually available from ASTM, and many are included in *ASTM Standards on Masonry*.[2]

Design

Structural design of masonry is governed by many building codes by reference to *Building Code Requirements for Masonry Structures*[4] and *Specifications for Masonry Structures*.[56] The documents are typically revised every 3 years.

FAILURE MODES

Masonry does not fail. Brick commits no sin. Mortar does no wrong. People fail. To paraphrase Kipling, there are many reasons for failure, but there is no excuse. The most prevalent people failures with regard to masonry's failure to perform as intended include designer arrogance to compensate for ignorance; salesperson ignorance of product; worker carelessness; and owner negligence. Masonry's ability to take that kind of abuse from all concerned is the secret of its 10,000-year success. Masonry is the most forgiving of building materials.

Performance failure may result from a combination of errors in design, construction, manufacture, and maintenance. For example, a masonry durability failure may result from improper flashing design, unfilled mortar joints, underfired brick, and deteriorated sealant joints.

Structural

Quality Control in Reinforced Masonry. Poor workmanship, characterized by unfilled mortar joints, reduces the compressive strength of air-dry masonry by about one-third. Oversanding of mortar (use of ASTM C 270 type N mortar[62] rather than type S) reduces mortar compressive strength by about 25 percent. The wet/dry compressive strength ratio for clay brick masonry is about 0.83. In concrete masonry, saturated strength loss is about 25 percent. Poor workmanship and a soaking rain can cut the strength of masonry in half. Freeze-thaw cycles produce a further reduction.

The average compressive strength of dry clay brick is 11,300 lb/in². Building codes[5] assume a compressive strength of 3790 lb/in² for inspected masonry built with that average brick laid in C 270 type S mortar.[62] The average tested compressive strength of such masonry is 5370 lb/in². If tested strength is cut in half by poor workmanship and a soaking rain, the masonry strength is less than three-quarters of the assumed strength.

The *Masonry Designers' Guide*[47] is an authoritative treatise of structural masonry. One of the example problems in that text can illustrate the effect of poorly built wet masonry. If the reinforced clay masonry wall in example 11.1-7 were built with poor workmanship and became wet, analysis indicated that the masonry would be overstressed 40 percent. If that wall became wet and the bars were misplaced the $1/2$ in (13 mm) permitted by the code,[4] the masonry would be overstressed 118 percent and steel would be overstressed 17 percent. If, when no one was looking, no. 5 bars were substituted for no. 6 bars but properly placed, steel in an air-dry wall would be overstressed 40 percent. Spliced bars lapped less than 48 in (1219 mm) are deficient.

The average compressive strength of hollow concrete masonry units (CMUs) is about 3000 lb/in^2 on net area. Building codes[4] assume a compressive strength of 2121 lb/in^2 for dry masonry built with that average CMU laid in ASTM C 270 type S mortar.[62] The average tested compressive strength of such masonry is about 2000 lb/in^2. If tested strength is cut in half by poor workmanship and a soaking rain, the concrete masonry strength is less than one-half of the assumed strength.

Another example from the *Masonry Designers' Guide*[47] can illustrate the effect of workmanship on wet concrete masonry. If the reinforced wall in example 11.1-2 were built with poor workmanship and became wet, analysis indicated that the concrete masonry would be overstressed by nearly 50 percent. If the bars were misplaced the $1/2$ in (13 mm) permitted by the code,[4] the masonry would be overstressed 62 percent and steel overstressed 7 percent. If, when no one was looking, no. 5 bars were substituted for no. 6 bars and misplaced $1/2$ in, steel would be overstressed by more than 40 percent.

Cracks.   *Rogmephobia* is the fear of cracks, especially if they are haphazard. A contractor applied epoxy paint over sealant control joints in a concrete masonry wall. As the concrete masonry shrank, the paint cracked, whereupon the owner sued the architect and the contractor for fear that the building was about to collapse.

Although most masonry cracks are benign, all masonry structural failures begin with a crack. Applied force or restraint of volume change may induce excessive stress. Stiffness attracts load. Masonry is stiff but weak in flexure. Placing rigid masonry veneer over flexible steel studs results in cracked masonry.[21,23,24] Cracks beget leaks, corrosion, stains, and spalls. Cracks precede collapse.

Clay masonry has irreversible net expansion, and concrete masonry has irreversible net contraction. Unaccommodated differential movement between juxtaposed materials may cause cracks. Table 13.11 provides data on volume change in masonry materials.

Because concrete masonry has net contraction (shrinkage), control joints in concrete masonry widen. They may, therefore, be filled with mortar or grout but must be free of reinforcement, stiff flashing, and debris. Because clay masonry has net growth, expansion joints in clay masonry must be free of mortar, reinforcement, stiff flashing, and debris.

TABLE 13.11 Estimated Masonry Volume Change Coefficients, 10^{-6} in/

Property	Masonry material	Number of data	Mean	Standard deviation (CV, %)	Median	Mode (most likely)	95% characteristic
Thermal expansion coefficient	Clay products[f] ⊥	75	3.3/°F	1.07/°F (32)	3.14/°F	2.84/°F	5.3/°F
	=	Estimate[a]	4.0/°F	1.31/°F (33)	3.83/°F	3.47/°F	6.51/°F
	Concrete masonry	87	4.13/°F	0.56/°F (14)	4.09/°F	4.02/°F	5.14/°F
	Granite	48	11.22/°F	1.216/°F (11)	11.14/°F	10.97/°F	13.67/°F
	Limestone	22	4.33/°F	1.45/°F (33)	4.11/°F	3.7/°F	7.07/°F
	Marble	10	4.33/°F	0.56/°F (13)	4.29/°F	4.22/°F	5.33/°F
	Sandstone	10	5.45/°F	0.81/°F (15)	5.39/°F	5.28/°F	6.9/°F
	Mortar	12	4.87/°F	0.68/°F (14)	4.82/°F	4.73/°F	6.09/°F
	Glass block	108	5.04/°F	0.06/°F (1)	5.04/°F	5.04/°F	5.13/°F
	Reinforced concrete	Estimate	5.5/°F	0.3/°F (5)	5.49/°F	5.48/°F	6.02/°F
	Structural steel	Estimate	6.5/°F	0.15/°F (23)	6.5/°F	6.5/°F	6.75/°F
Moisture expansion[b]	Clay products	27	200	190 (95)	140	76	540
	Granite	48	39	22 (56)	34	26	81
	Limestone	3	25	9 (36)	24	21	42
	Marble	3	15	9 (60)	13	10	32
	Sandstone	3	223	188 (84)	171	100	581

Freezing expansion	Clay products	68	148	144 (97)	106	55	416
Shrinkage	CMU[d] Type I	94[c]	360	120 (33)	340	310	590
	Type II	Estimate[e]	180	60 (33)	171	154	294
	Mortar	184	1180	680 (58)	1020	760	2500
Masonry	Clay product	31	1.05/psi	0.52/psi (50)	0.94/psi	0.75/psi	1.92/psi
Creep	Concrete masonry	Estimate	2.31/psi	1.27 (55)	2.02	1.53	4.45

[a]Increased 22% for extruded brick parallel to the direction of extrusion, i.e., vertically for extruded brick laid as a stretcher.

[b]Stone moisture expansion is reversible. Clay products have reversible moisture expansion but net long-term growth.

[c]S_1 = total linear drying shrinkage of concrete masonry units determined in accord with ASTM C 426, *Test Method for Drying Shrinkage of Concrete Block*.[62]

[d]Values given are for vertical contraction. Horizontal shrinkage is restrained by attachment on one or more edges to supporting structure. Vertical movement joints should control horizontal shrinkage at appropriate intervals. See section on volume change.

[e]The average reduction in CMU drying shrinkage for "low-shrinkage" units below that of "normal-shrinkage" units is reported to be about 50%.

$f_\perp$ = Perpendicular to the direction of extrusion. ∥ = Parallel to the direction of extrusion.

Figures 13.4 through 13.18 illustrate masonry crack patterns. Grimm[18] discusses masonry design for crack control. Movement joints should be placed at the following locations: at beam soffits, under shelf angles, at wall intersections, at horizontal intervals of about 25 ft (7.62 m), near corners and wall openings, at changes in wall thickness or height, and at pilasters, recesses, chases, or columns.

Crack control depends on properly functioning expansion joints in brick masonry (see Fig. 13.19). Shelf angles supporting masonry should be mitered at corners (see Fig. 13.20). Shelf angle shims should extend to the heal of the angle to prevent angle rotation and cracked masonry, as illustrated in Fig. 13.21. Lintels supporting masonry must have adequate bearing. (See Fig. 13.22.) Two-thirds of a masonry wythe supported on a lintel or shelf angle should bear on the lintel or shelf angle. (See Fig. 13.23.)

Masonry Veneer over Wood Frame.   As wood dries, it shrinks. A significant part of that shrinkage occurs after construction. When expanding masonry veneer is placed over a shrinking wood frame, unaccommodated differential movement may cause distress at wall openings. In single-story buildings, the differential movement is typically so small as to cause no problem. However, in a three-story structure, differential movement can cause distortions at windows and doors. Even when differential movement is significant, very inexpensive construction details can accommodate anticipated dimensional changes.[39]

FIGURE 13.4   Facial separation cracks.

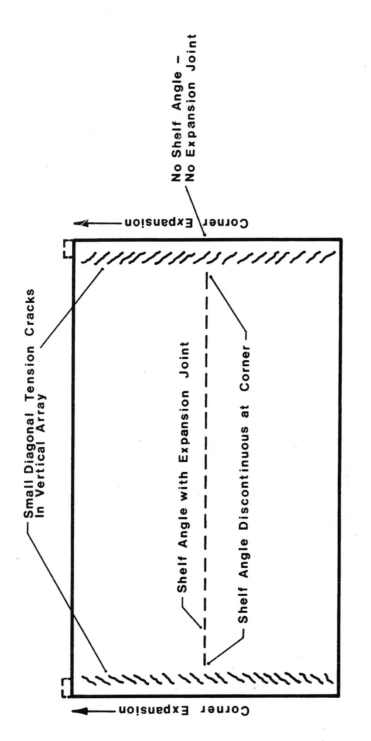

ELEVATION

FIGURE 13.5 Differential vertical movement at corners due to discontinuity of shelf angle. (See Fig. 13.20.)

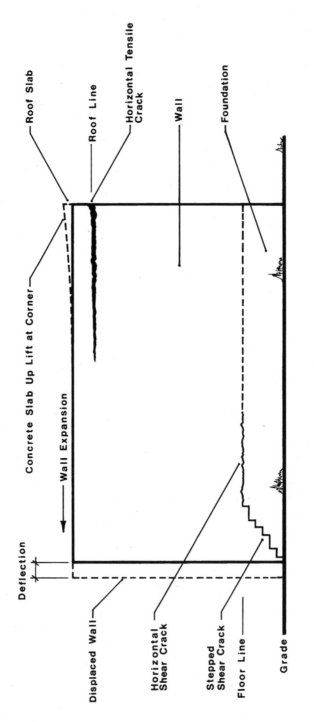

FIGURE 13.6 Slab curl at right; wall expansion at left.

13.24

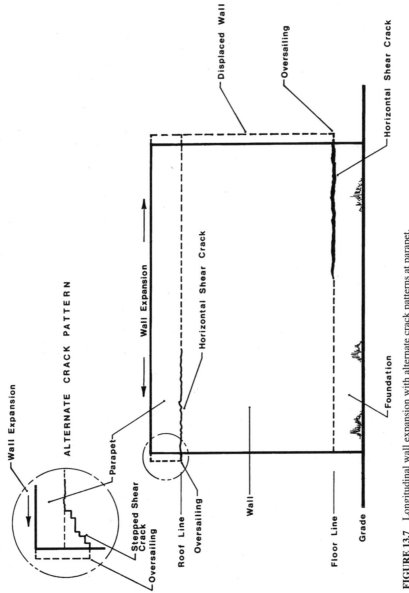

FIGURE 13.7 Longitudinal wall expansion with alternate crack patterns at parapet.

13.25

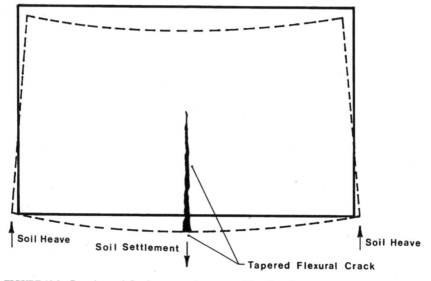

FIGURE 13.8   Deep beam deflection, corner heave, or mid-wall settlement.

Collapse.   Absence of a horizontal expansion joint under a shelf angle supporting brick masonry on a concrete structure has led to collapse of several masonry walls.[16] Masonry is typically supported on shelf angles attached to the concrete frame. Concrete frames contract owing to shrinkage, creep, and elastic deformation. Clay brick masonry expands owing to temperature increase, freezing, and moisture absorption. If masonry is held vicelike between shelf angles, the differential movement induces an eccentric compressive force on the masonry, which can buckle inadequately anchored masonry. (See Fig. 13.24.)

On May 16, 1968, in Ronan Point, England, a gas explosion occurred in a bathroom on the 18th floor of a multistory apartment building. The explosion caused a progressive collapse that drew public attention to the adequacy of buildings to resist accidental damage. Since then, there has been extensive research and discussion about the robustness and stability of buildings. Much of available published information relates to masonry structures, which were thought to be susceptible to such damage. Leyendecker[45] and Lai[44] each provide a review of the literature on the stability of masonry buildings against accidental damage.

Pavement Delamination.   Concrete base slabs and mortar setting beds shrink at different rates. Contraction of a concrete base and cementitious setting bed combines with expansion of clay brick paving units to induce a shear stress between the two materials. The level of that stress typically equals the shear strength. Thus, cracking and delamination are the natural and virtually certain result. Attempts to bond masonry pavements to base slabs with conventional or latex mortars have

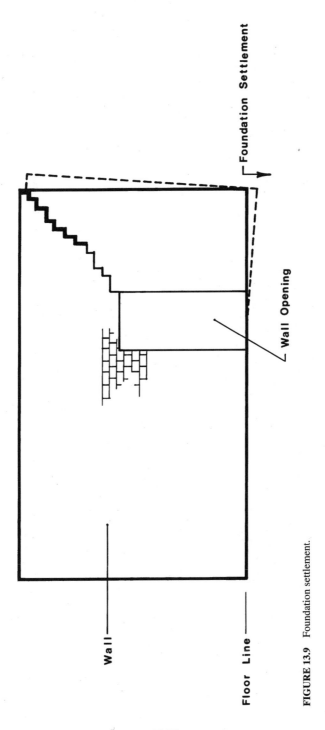

FIGURE 13.9 Foundation settlement.

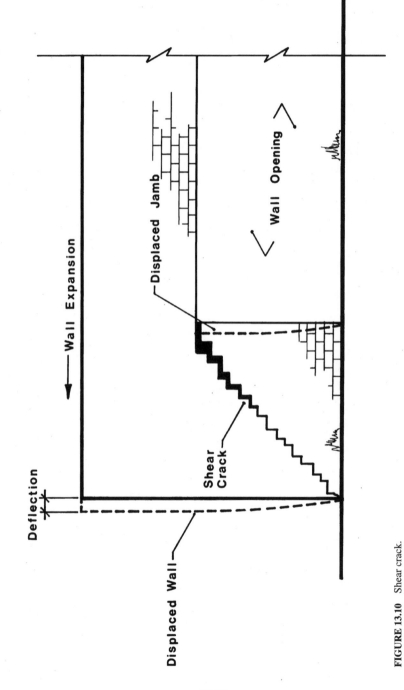

FIGURE 13.10 Shear crack.

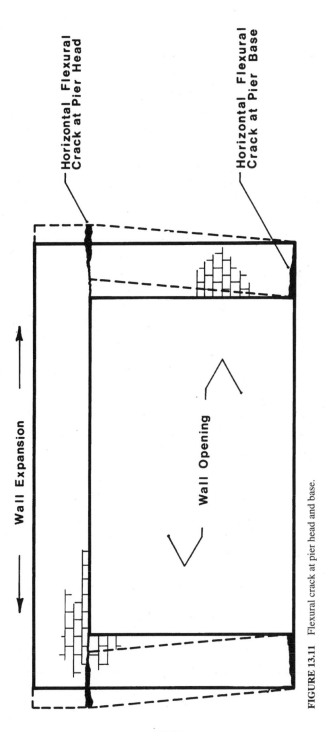

FIGURE 13.11 Flexural crack at pier head and base.

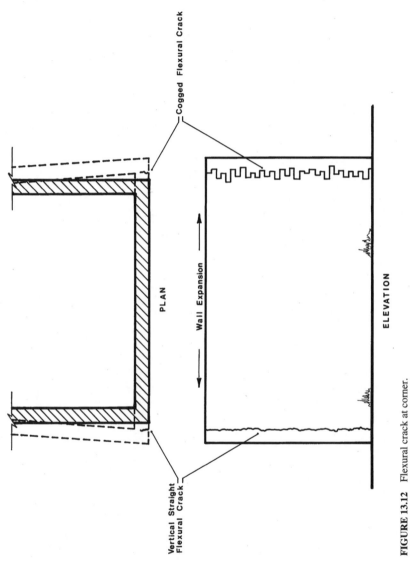

FIGURE 13.12 Flexural crack at corner.

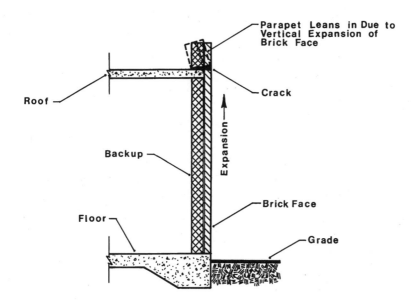

Parapet Leans in Due to
Vertical Expansion of
Brick Face

Roof

Crack

Backup

Expansion

Brick Face

Floor

Grade

SECTION

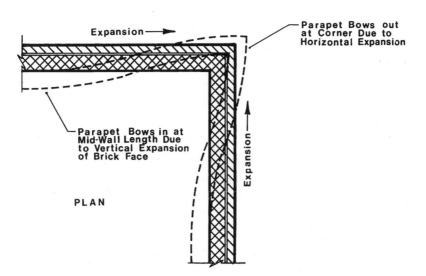

Expansion

Parapet Bows out
at Corner Due to
Horizontal Expansion

Parapet Bows in at
Mid-Wall Length Due
to Vertical Expansion
of Brick Face

Expansion

PLAN

FIGURE 13.13   Leaning parapet.

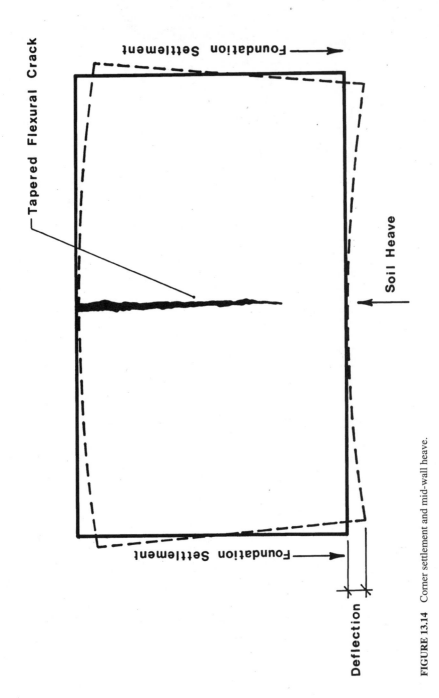

FIGURE 13.14 Corner settlement and mid-wall heave.

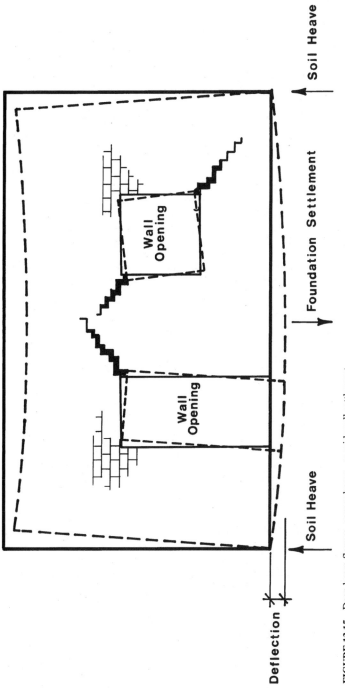

FIGURE 13.15 Deep beam flexure, corner heave, or mid-wall settlement.

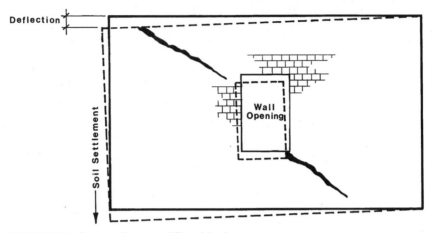

FIGURE 13.16   Corner settlement or differential column movement.

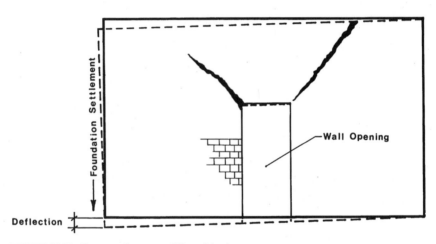

FIGURE 13.17   Corner settlement or differential column movement.

often been unsuccessful, providing annual failure rates of 2.4 percent. Masonry paving units should be set on a sand bed.[27]

Architectural

Water Permeance.   Water permeance is the leading cause of masonry's failure to perform as intended. Water damage may include dimensional change, corrosion, decay, florescence, freeze-thaw spalling or splitting, increased heat transmission, condensation, deterioration of interior finishes and building contents, and tenant inconvenience.

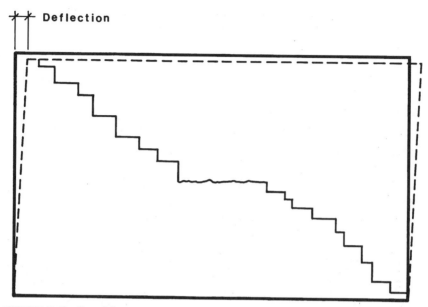

FIGURE 13.18   Shear failure.

FIGURE 13.19   False expansion joint.

FIGURE 13.20 Shelf angles should be mitered at corners.

FIGURE 13.21 Rotated shelf angles cause cracked masonry.

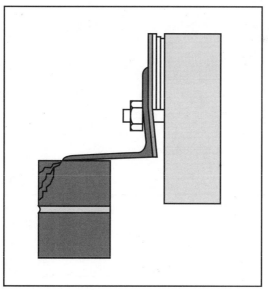

FIGURE 13.21   (*Continued*) Rotated shelf angles cause cracked masonry.

FIGURE 13.22   Lintels supporting masonry must have adequate bearing area.

FIGURE 13.23   Two-thirds of the wythe should be on a lintel or shelf angle.

FIGURE 13.24   Wall anchorage depends on conformance to specifications.

Four inches of unit masonry, no matter how built, by whom, or of what material, never stopped a wind-driven rain. Rain does not permeate through masonry units or mortar in significant quantities. It enters through cracks between units and mortar. Figure 13.2 shows definitions of mortar joint locations. Figure 13.25 shows recommended mortar joint configurations. Unfilled mortar joints and raked mortar joints increase leakage. Grimm describes problems associated with unfilled mortar joints[29] and the importance of mortar materials.[32] Drainage-type walls collect penetrating water and redirect it to the exterior by flashing through weep holes. Weep holes should be provided 24 to 32 in (600 to 813 mm) on center immediately above flashing.

It is virtually impossible for a mason to keep a 1-in (25-mm) airspace clean of mortar droppings, because a trowel cannot be maneuvered in such a narrow space, especially if the mason cannot see the space, as depicted in Fig. 13.26. However, mortar droppings in a 2-in (50-mm) or wider cavity, as shown in Fig. 13.27, can be avoided by beveling rather than furrowing mortar bed joints.

Flashing is typically improperly detailed, specified, and installed. There are at least 106 types of through-wall flashing with costs ranging over one magnitude. Manufacturers guarantee a life expectancy of 5 years for a product that is supposed to protect a wall for 100 years. Figure 13.28 illustrates flashing terminology. Flashing end dams, shown in Fig. 13.29, and corner flashing, shown in Fig. 13.30, are particularly important. Through-wall flashing should extend beyond the face of the wall

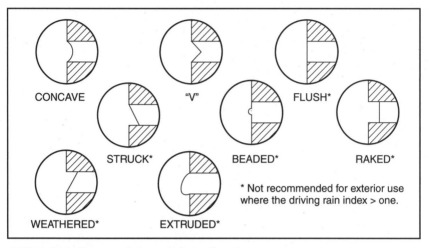

FIGURE 13.25   Recommended mortar joint configurations.

VENEER WALL

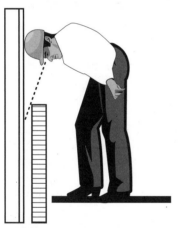

FIGURE 13.26   Mason cannot see cavity.

and turn down to form a drip, as shown in Fig. 13.31. Otherwise, water enters the wall below the flashing. Figure 13.32 shows the consequences of not providing a proper sealant joint and lipped fascia. Flashing should not extend through movement joints and should be provided at the following locations with joints lapped 6 in (150 mm) and sealed: heads of wall openings, wall spandrels and bases, intersections of walls with floor and roofs, under copings and sills, and above lintels and shelf angles.

Grimm[28] provides advice on flashing materials and their limitations, including corrosion protection, recommended construction details, guide specifications, and a flashing bibliography with 59 citations. Grimm[14] provides a review of the literature on water permeance of masonry walls with more than 60 references and a bibliography of 233 entries under nine keywords.

Durability.   Grimm[15] provides a review of the literature on weathering of masonry. Maurenbrecher and Grimm[48] have written on corrosion of metal connectors in masonry.

Stains.   At least 100 types of stains occur on masonry. They may be removed by more than 150 cleaning agents. The problem is to match the most effective agent

FIGURE 13.27   Mortar droppings in cavity.

with a given stain. Objectionable stains may form a small spot in a conspicuous place or may cover an entire facade. Grimm[20] discusses stains on masonry and provides a bibliography of 108 citations.

Florescence is the crystalline residue of an evaporated salt solution. *Cryptoflorescence* is florescence within the pores of a material. *Efflorescence* is florescence on the face of a material. It is a common masonry stain, usually a white powder but sometimes green.

Efflorescence may be aesthetically objectionable but is not physically harmful. However, cryptoflorescence can be damaging. Salt crystal formation results in a large increase in physical volume. If the expansion is restrained within pores, very large pressures can develop, sufficient to cause rupture of masonry materials.

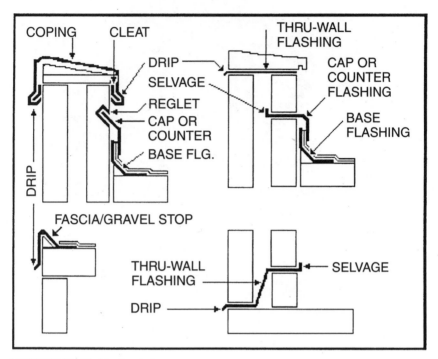

FIGURE 13.28 Flashing terminology.

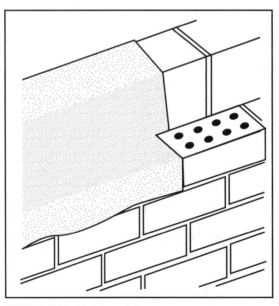

FIGURE 13.29 Flashing end dam.

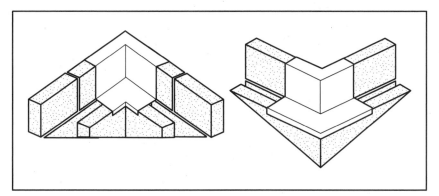

FIGURE 13.30   Corner flashing.

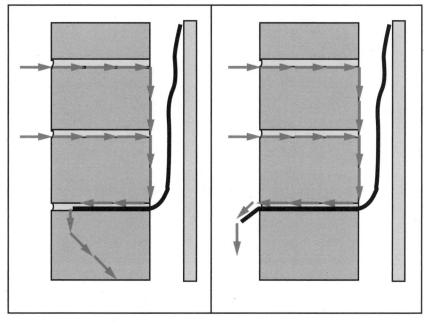

FIGURE 13.31   Flashing should extend beyond wall face.

Fortunately, there is often sufficient void space into which crystals can grow without exerting destructive pressure.

The way to reduce the potential for physical and aesthetic damage of florescence is to minimize salt content and reduce water permeance of masonry.

Masonry may be contaminated by water-soluble salts from external sources, including acid rain, seawater aerosol, groundwater, pavement deicing salts, cleaning

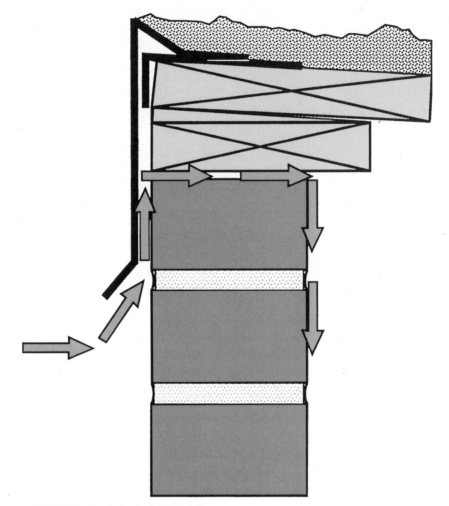

FIGURE 13.32   Fascia lip should be sealed.

compounds, and lawn sprinklers. Water-soluble salts may be found in stone, clay brick, concrete block, cement, sand, water, admixtures, or cleaning compounds. Lime is essentially free of solubles other than calcium hydroxide. The contribution of concrete masonry to efflorescence has been well documented. There are many water-soluble salts, but alkali is the most prevalent. It may or may not be contained in other masonry materials, but alkali is always present in portland cement.

The probability of alkaline efflorescence may be reduced by restrictive selection of materials. Sand can be thoroughly washed. Clay brick may be tested to determine its efflorescence potential (ASTM C 67, *Test Methods of Sampling and Testing Brick and Structural Clay Tile*[62]). Hydrated lime does not generally con-

FIGURE 13.32   (*Continued*) Fascia lip should be sealed.

tribute to efflorescence. Although many authorities have found normal portland cement to be a primary source of efflorescence, portland cement can be specified to conform with the optional chemical requirements for low-alkaline cement of ASTM C150, *Standard Specification for Portland Cement.*[62] Under those provisions, alkali content is limited.

Low-alkali portland cement can be specified for use in a wide array of masonry materials: mortar, grout, concrete brick, concrete block, cast stone, and precast concrete. Because those products are not customarily made with low-alkali cement, manufacturers may resist the imposition of a requirement to use it. Nevertheless, ASTM standard specifications for those products provide for the use of low-alkali cements, which are available in bags or bulk from several cement companies.

The use of low-alkali portland cement per se would not eliminate efflorescence, because alkali in cement cannot be eliminated, and salts from other sources can cause efflorescence. However, use of low-alkali cement reduces the propensity for florescence.

Color Discrimination.   Masonry color can be identified in three ways: by verbal description, by comparison with a sample, or by numerical results of color measurement. Vagaries of language lack the precision required for genteel architectural tastes. Samples submitted to at least one brick manufacturer for matching have included "paint chips, cloth swatches, various sizes and textures of colored paper, pieces of porcelain enamel, and glazed tile chips."

Verbal descriptions of colors to be matched by the same manufacturer have included "a dark blue with reddish cast," "a light pinkish orange, like X brand lipstick," and "a dark gray with brown spots like match heads." Inability to meet such specifications leads to off-color masonry units in the wall. When that happens, stain coatings may be used to solve the problem. Grimm[37] addresses the problem of masonry color selection and specification.

Construction

Workmanship.   Mistakes in masonry construction include the following:

- Unfilled mortar joints weaken walls and increase water permeance.
- Improper mortar batching usually results in cement deficiency and color variation.
- After cracked or chipped brick is placed in the wall, the manufacturer is no longer responsible.
- The absence of flashing, flashing without end dams, and misplaced or unsealed flashing contribute to water leakage.
- Bridged expansion joints cause cracks.
- Improper shimming of shelf angles causes cracks (see Fig. 13.21).
- Discontinuity of shelf angles at external corners causes cracks (see Fig. 13.20).
- Strength of reinforced masonry is reduced and corrosion is promoted by voids in grouted spaces or by substitution of concrete for grout.
- Juxtaposition of stainless steel and mild steel may cause corrosion.
- Misplaced or missing reinforcement weakens masonry.
- Mortar droppings in cavities 2 in (50 mm) and wider can cause walls to leak and can be avoided. Mortar droppings in cavities less than 2 in (51 mm) wide can be expected.

Construction Tolerances.   Masonry construction tolerance problems concern three issues: structural integrity, aesthetic tastes, and incompatibility of construction tolerances for masonry supported on structural frames.

It is often difficult but important in establishing fault to determine whether masonry that is now out of position was misplaced or displaced.

Aesthetic construction tolerances involve vertical alignment of head joints, mortar joint thickness variation, and out-of-wall plane alignment of masonry units. Statistical data on such tolerances are available,[19] but there are currently no industry standards. The construction contract should specify such tolerances. If it does not, one must rely on what is customary and ordinary in the trade at that place and time. Figure 13.33 depicts the aesthetic problem.

Construction tolerances for structural frames of steel or concrete are much more liberal than those for masonry. Such difficulties should be recognized dur-

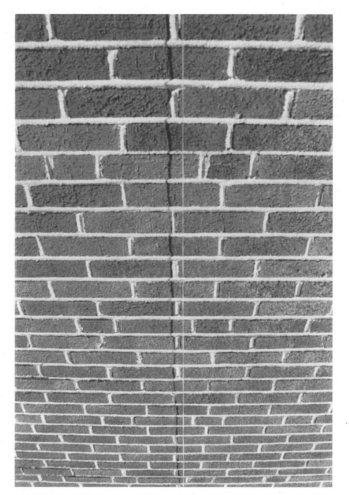

FIGURE 13.33   Head joint thickness variation and misalignment.

ing design where they can be solved much more economically. If not, the contractor should ask for a clarification prior to construction. Advanced theories of architectural tectonics notwithstanding, two solids cannot occupy the same space at the same time.

Mason Productivity.   Brick may be specified by allowance. That is, the contractor includes in the bid a specified unit price for purchase of brick, which is subsequently selected by the architect. The contractor assumes that a local brick of usual characteristics will be selected. Instead, the architect selects a foreign brick of unusual characteristics, which causes an unanticipated reduction in mason productivity. The contractor files a claim. The literature on mason productivity may provide the solution,[12] or productivity research with specific materials may be indicated.

Temporary Bracing.   During a typical month in the United States, falling walls kill 1 building construction worker and injure 12. Occupational Safety and Health Administration (OSHA) regulations for bracing masonry walls during construction are woefully inadequate. The American National Standards Institute (ANSI) requirements for bracing masonry walls during construction are insufficient, inaccurate, and antiquated. Building codes for bracing masonry walls during construction are nonexistent or grossly inadequate. Masonry researchers have not been interested in bracing masonry walls during construction.[34]

Masonry supported by a structural frame or intersecting masonry walls typically does not require temporary bracing during construction to prevent blow-over due to high wind, because such masonry is anchored as it is built. However, tall, thin walls typical of warehouses do require temporary bracing. Requirements by building codes and the Occupational Safety and Health Administration notwithstanding, such walls are often unbraced for two reasons. First, the requirements for undefined "adequate" bracing are vague. Second, the insurance deductible is typically greater than the cost of repair. Currently there is an attempt to develop a national consensus that would provide requirements that may be more specific.

MASONRY FAILURE INVESTIGATION

This section presents information on investigator qualifications, services offered by investigators, problem statements, site visits, equipment needs, data collection, materials sampling and testing, interviews with potential witnesses, document discovery, literature search, research needs, and reports.

Qualifications of a Masonry Investigator

The forensic engineer should be familiar with the literature on masonry. More than one-half of the ASTM standards relating to masonry are revised, and several are added every 10 years or so. On average, an authoritative paper on some aspect of masonry is published in English everyday. In the 6-year period from 1990 to 1995, there were 59 books on masonry published in the United States. The *Specifications for Masonry Structures*[56] with its referenced standards occupies 293 pages. The *Masonry Designers' Guide*[47] is 862 pages long. The *Building Code Requirements for Masonry Structures*[4] uses nearly 34,000 words. It is revised every 3 years. To keep up with this dynamic process is a full-time effort for an experienced structural engineer.

Nevertheless, there are many so-called masonry experts. They are a mixed bag of former bricklayers, association executives, and manufacturers' representatives;

has-been masonry contractors; born-again architects, sometimes academicians; testing laboratory technicians; ceramists, chemists, and petrographers. Some claim expertise in several materials including masonry. There are at least 136 self-proclaimed masonry "experts" scattered among 34 of the United States. Few are worthy.

Bricklaying experience is certainly helpful, as is previous employment by a building products trade association; but neither prepares one to opine on the cause of displaced masonry. A doctorate in ceramics and experience in refractories do not qualify one to investigate a durability failure of face brick masonry. One may know a lot about chemistry and very little about the effects of corroded steel. Many very talented structural engineers know almost nothing about masonry.

A licensed, experienced structural engineer who is thoroughly familiar with all aspects of masonry materials, design, construction, and maintenance should conduct masonry failure investigations. The masonry forensic engineer should be familiar with building codes, material specifications, test methods, construction and maintenance specifications, contracts, and costs, not only for masonry per se but also for building materials and systems related to masonry directly or indirectly, including anchors, ties, reinforcement, expansion and control joints, insulation, flashing, and supporting structural systems in concrete, steel, or wood. Teaching experience and research experience are very beneficial.

Consulting and Investigating Services

The investigator of masonry failures should be an engineer who has a working relationship with an experienced team of experts in the related disciplines of:

Architecture	Soil mechanics and geotechnology
Structural mechanics and design in concrete, steel, and timber	Pavement design
	Statistical analysis
Petrography	Literature searches
Chemistry	Experiment design in engineering
Electrochemistry of corrosion	Research
Computer science	Engineering secretarial and drafting services
Meteorology and climatology	
Heat transfer	Materials and structural testing in laboratory and in situ on building
Construction management and cost	

It is important that each person in related disciplines have prior work experience with the masonry failure investigator, be familiar with masonry-related problems, and have a record of accomplishment in joint efforts with the forensic engineer. Although several other persons may assist the forensic engineer, that engineer alone should assume sole responsibility for the investigation. On occasion, a client may wish to retain more than one forensic engineer; if they are to cooperate, one should assume primary responsibility.

Engineering services in masonry failure investigations may include the following:

- Client contact, initial problem definition, and agreement on engineering services and fees
- Reconnaissance site visit
- Document discovery
- Interviews with craftsmen, contractors, and designers of the original project
- A second site visit for documentation of existing conditions of masonry and for retrieval of masonry test specimens
- Literature search
- Perhaps a third site visit for in situ testing of masonry
- Research on some aspects of novel problems
- Report preparation for verbal or written presentation to the client or her or his attorney, establishing mode, cause, and responsibility for failure, and recommendations for repair methods and their estimated cost
- Negotiation of claim settlement
- Deposition of the investigation engineer and advice by him or her to client attorneys on preparing complaints, interrogatories, and depositions of adversaries during discovery and cross-examination of adversaries at trial
- Evaluation of opinions and credentials of adversarial witnesses
- Testimony in administrative hearings or courts, including videotape rehearsal, preparation of exhibits, and retention of all investigation records and test specimens subsequent to trial for possible use on appeal

Initial Problem Statement

The initial problem statement provided by the client may be simplistic. For example: The walls blew over during construction. The walls leak. The walls are cracked and bulging. The walls fell off the building. The bricks are spalling. Birds are eating the mortar. The pavement is delaminated and buckled. The red brick turned white. The white brick turned red or green. The gray brick turned purple when laid.

Clients vary greatly in their knowledge of masonry. Some need only brief conversational guidance, providing very generalized solutions to generic problem types. Typically, however, the initial problem statement is erroneous. For example, the masonry walls are not leaking, rather roof flashing is leaking, or perhaps sealant joints are leaking. Very often, the initial problem statement is only symptomatic of a much more serious problem. For instance, red stains may be due to iron oxide in mortar sand, which may only be offensive to finely honed aesthetic sensitivities; or iron oxide may be filtering through the masonry due to severe corrosion of reinforcing steel, which may require wall demolition. On the other hand, the owner's observation may be quite accurate. Birds have been known to eat mortar. (It contained a little cement and a lot of salt leached from brick formerly used in a brewery.)

Site Visits

At least two site visits are usually necessary, one for reconnaissance and one for data collection. A third site visit for field testing may also be necessary. If a suit has been filed and the client is not the building owner, and if the owner is reluctant to grant permission for site visits or specimen removal, then the client's attorney may obtain a court order requiring appropriate discovery of relevant facts. Defendants have a right to information necessary to their defense, as do plaintiffs for their purposes. If the building is under construction and the client is a party to the construction contract or is an agent or representative of one of the parties, then permission for site visits, sample removal, and field testing is usually obtained easily. Potential adversaries may wish to have their experts present during site visits, but experts for adversaries should not communicate regarding any aspect of the investigation without their clients' permission. However, with such permission it is sometimes possible that technical experts could come to an agreement on recommended remedial measures to settle a dispute.

Reconnaissance Site Visit.   Purpose of a reconnaissance site visit is to better define the problem and identify resources (workers, money, materials, and machines) necessary for investigation. Prior to a reconnaissance site visit, construction contract documents should be reviewed. This first site visit may be made with perhaps only an aide and the client. During a reconnaissance site visit, the investigator should note qualitatively many of the items to be observed quantitatively later during a data collection site visit.

Two types of equipment are normally needed for on-site masonry failure investigations. The forensic engineer will usually provide for his or her personal needs, listed below as items 1 to 22. A local masonry contractor will normally provide equipment required for masonry specimen removal, as described in items 23 through 30.

1. Camera: 35-mm camera with minimum 210-mm telephoto, wide-angle, and close-up lenses, $f/3.5$. ASA 100 color slide film and, possibly, infrared film; flash attachment.
2. Photograph record forms.

3. Measuring magnifier with 0.1-mm scale.

4. Compass.

5. Small level.

6. Two-way radios.

7. Flashlight.

8. Tape recorder.

9. Notebook and clipboard with graph paper.

10. Waterproof felt-tip pens (two colors) and yellow and black marking crayon or chalk.

11. Scales: a 12-in (300-mm) rule [0.1-in (2.5-mm) divisions] and a 6-ft (1.829-m) rule.

12. Hard hat, steel-toed shoes with rubber soles, rain suit, gloves, and windbreaker jacket.

13. Specimen collection bags large enough to hold a brick with specimen identification tags.

14. Calculator.

15. Heavy-duty pocketknife.

16. First-aid kit.

17. Extra batteries for all electrically operated equipment.

18. Plumb bob with 100-ft cord.

19. Calipers.

20. Binoculars.

21. Metal detector.

22. Fiber scope.

23. Gasoline-driven, portable, masonry saw with at least three 12-in (300-mm) masonry and steel cutting blades.

24. Respirator dust mask.

25. Three mason's chisels 1 to 4 in (25 to 100 mm) wide.

26. Four-pound mashing hammer.

27. Braided nylon mason's line, 170-lb (77-kg) test, 50-ft (15.24-m) minimum.

28. One 12-ft (3.658-m) long, 2-in (50-mm) square, extruded aluminum pole and one 40-in (1.016-m) aluminum I-beam mason's level, or a telescoping, drywall layout level.

29. Scaffolding needs vary from boatswain's chair through tubular steel sections and cherry-pickers with a two-person bucket, to suspended adjustable (swinging) scaffolds. Scaffold safety is very important.

Guardrails and toe boards are required for all open sides and ends of platforms more than 10 ft (3.048 m) above ground. Two-point, suspended, adjustable scaffolding having a working load of 750 lb (340 kg) is required for three workers without masonry specimens or two workers with masonry specimens. A safety harness attached to an individual lifeline should protect each person on the scaffold.

30. Steel banding equipment.

It is preferable to observe first the exterior of the building briefly by walking around it at ground level, and then from the roof for examination of flashing and the parapet. Very often parapets lean inward at midwall length and outward at corners. Each elevation of the building in turn should then be observed as closely as possible from top down. Where possible, the interior masonry surfaces of exterior walls should be observed for cracks, stains, and mortar joint solidity, especially above ceiling level. Grimm[38] provides a method for measuring mortar joint solidity. All these areas should then be observed a second time in the same order. During the reconnaissance visit, copious photographs should be taken, but thoroughly documented photography is not necessary. The primary purpose of this photography is to brief the investigation team for subsequent work during the data collection site visit.

The type of masonry distress to be qualitatively observed during the reconnaissance site visit may include the extent of stains; weep holes, flashing, coping, masonry units, mortar joints, or sealant joints; water leaks; structural cracks; separation cracks between brick and mortar; displaced or misplaced masonry; and possible locations for future removal of masonry specimens and for observation holes to be cut into masonry during the data collection site visit.

Data Collection Site Visit. After the reconnaissance site visit, a second visit may be necessary to document existing surface conditions, remove laboratory test specimens, and cut observation holes. Everything even remotely connected with the masonry failure should be photographed, and important subjects should be photographed twice.

Observation holes may be cut at shelf angles, copings, heads, and sills of wall openings, roof-wall intersections, and bases of walls. Holes may be cut at wall opening jambs, sealant joints, stains, wall anchors at beams and columns; at floor-wall, roof-wall, and wall-partition intersections; and at random locations to observe flashing, mortar joint solidity, cavity cleanliness; position, size, and condition of metal reinforcement, anchors, and ties; and conformance of masonry with the construction contract documents. Very often field changes are made without benefit of formal change orders and are not noted in construction documents.

Masonry Testing

Masonry units, prisms, wallettes, or entire prefabricated masonry wall panels may be removed from the wall, then packaged, shipped, and laboratory-tested. Mortar samples may be examined for volumetric proportions of ingredients by chemical analysis and petrographic examination, as well as for air content and for evidence of having been frozen while plastic. Stained specimens may be tested for chemical composition, although that is usually unproductive. Cutting coupons of steel reinforcement or shelf angles may be necessary for metallurgical analysis. It is very important that, where available, standard test methods be used. Continuous care and custody of test specimens is crucial since a trial may be delayed for several years. Two independent laboratories may conduct critical tests. Fattal and Cattaneo[8] provide an interesting report on the evaluation of structural properties of masonry in existing buildings.

The purpose of materials testing is to formulate generalizations about characteristics of those materials. To determine absolutely the mean strength of a large quantity of material, it would be necessary to test all the material, which may be impractical, virtually impossible, or even self-defeating. Accordingly, only some of the material may be tested, from which inferences may be drawn about the strength of all the material. Valid tests of a sample give results, which are certain only for the sample, but those results permit conclusions of varying certitude about the material from which the sample was taken.[17,51]

The material from which a sample is taken is called a *lot*, i.e., a quantity of material which, insofar as is practical, consists of a single type, grade, class, size, finish (texture), and composition produced by a single source by the same process and under practically the same conditions. Size of a lot is sometimes standardized. For example, ASTM C 67, *Method of Sampling and Testing Brick and Structural Clay Tile,*[62] establishes 250,000 bricks as a *lot.*

A *specimen* is an individual piece of material from a lot. A *sample* is a number of specimens. Valid conclusions about a lot can be drawn by testing a sample only if the sample is representative of the lot. For that reason the method of selecting specimens must be unbiased. Bias is avoided by selecting a *random sample,* in which every specimen has an equal chance of being selected in every trial. A sample selected haphazardly, without a conscious plan, is not a random sample. It is a haphazard sample. It is virtually impossible to draw a sample at random by exercise of human judgment alone. Proper use of an artificial or mechanical device for selecting a random sample is necessary. Specimens may be selected by assigning a number to each unit or small group of units in the lot and using a table of random numbers or an electronic random number generator to select a number of specimens. For any given set of conditions, there are usually several possible sampling plans, all valid, but differing in speed, simplicity, and cost.

The degree of certitude with which conclusions are drawn from tests increases with the number of randomly selected specimens in the sample. The required number of specimens depends on (1) the variability in characteristic to be tested, (2) the permissible difference between the tested mean value and the mean value of the lot, and (3) the degree of confidence with which one wishes to state what that difference may be. Reference 54 provides a standard practice for establishing sample size.

Consideration of acceptable statistical reliability of results, cost of testing, cost, and accessibility of masonry plays a role in determining the number, size, and location of test specimens. In general, the number of observation holes and test specimens may be 1 for each 5000 ft² (464.52 m²) of each type of masonry; but no less than 5 should be cut for investigation of even small buildings, and more than 30 are necessary under only very unusual circumstances.

Consultants who do not operate their own materials testing laboratory can offer clients the benefit of the best independent third-party testing facilities available. Thus their clients are never in doubt that a conflict of interest may have motivated the prescription for the type or number of tests to be conducted. If the forensic investigation firm operates its own laboratory, it may be appropriate to have tests prescribed by that firm conducted in a third-party laboratory in which the forensic firm has no financial interest. (The situation is analogous to having a physician prescribe a medication on whose sale the physician profits.)

When the number or size of masonry specimens to be removed, packaged, and shipped is large, it is desirable to negotiate a contract for that service. Tall cranes or helicopters may be needed for removing whole, prefabricated, masonry wall panels. Replacing masonry to minimize aesthetic differences may be difficult. Safety and insurance requirements should be given thoughtful consideration. Containers for masonry specimens must ensure that the specimens are not broken during shipment.

Testing Masonry in Situ. Field tests may require a third site visit. Field test data may assist in the determination of the level of in situ stress by comparing strain gage measurements before and after specimen removal with laboratory determination of strength and elasticity. ASTM C 1196, *Test Method for in Situ Compressive Stress Within Solid Unit Masonry Estimated Using Flatjack Measurements,* and C 1197, *Test Method for in Situ Measurement of Masonry Deformability Properties Using the Flatjack Method,*[62] provide procedures for doing so.

Field tests may include water permeance of masonry by an adaptation of ASTM E 514, *Test Method for Water Penetration and Leakage through Masonry.*[62] In-place testing of flexural resistance of masonry walls is occasionally required to prove structural adequacy or effectiveness of proposed remedial measures. A field adaptation of ASTM E 72, *Conducting Strength Tests of Panels for Building Constructions,*[62] is used for this purpose.

Nondestructive test methods for masonry include examination of facial separation cracks, low-frequency ultrasonics, gamma radiography, and pachometrics.[60] Some of these techniques may be very expensive and are frequently unnecessary.

Interviews

After site reconnaissance, the investigating engineer may conduct interviews with the architect, engineer, and general contractor. In cases of structural collapse, interviews with eyewitnesses and survivors may be useful. Meetings may be helpful with crafts-men employed during the original construction of masonry as well as with the masonry contractor and her or his foreman and superintendent. Without demolition or bore scope examination, no one better knows what is in the wall than the person who built it. The client's consent should be obtained for all such interrogations.

If craftsmen are to be interviewed, seek meetings with masonry foremen, work-ing masons, and mortar makers. Ask permission to tape-record the interview. Make written notes of pertinent answers. Be informal in dress, speech, and con-duct. Make small talk. Ask about family, sports. Find something in common. Only one respondent and no more than two interrogators should be present during the interview. The craftsman's employer should not be present. If answers are vague, pause and rephrase a question.

Document Discovery

If litigation is pending, it may be desirable for the forensic engineer to read all dis-covery documents relating in any way to masonry. This may include the following:

All contract documents:

Correspondence between owner and architect, between owner and construction manager, and between owner and builder; subcontracts between the general contractor and the masonry subcontractor, including plans, specifications, gen-eral and special or supplementary conditions, addenda and change orders for construction and maintenance or repair, and auxiliary materials.

Contractor's, job inspector's, project representative's, and construction man-ager's daily job logs involving masonry or its auxiliary materials.

Weather records from the closest weather station for the period from date of construction start to date of failure investigation, including temperature, humidity, precipitation, and velocity and direction of wind. These are available from the National Climatic Data Center, Asheville, NC.

Product literature and correspondence between any of the parties to any of the contracts, materials manufacturers, or suppliers, relating to any masonry mate-rials or auxiliary materials and their design, construction, testing, maintenance, or repair.

Construction progress photographs of masonry acquired directly or indirectly.

News media accounts of design, construction, failure, or repair of masonry.

Shop drawings for masonry and its supporting structure.

Reports, tests results, and photographs by all other engineering investigators.

Project construction schedules, bar charts, and CMP or PERT diagrams involv-ing masonry.

Copies of test report on masonry materials or masonry during construction.

Copies of invoices from masonry materials or auxiliary masonry materials suppliers to contractor or subcontractor.

Building permit and building code in effect at time of design.

Minutes of prebid, preconstruction, and construction progress meetings between contractual parties or their representatives.

Transcripts of depositions referring in any way to masonry.

Transcripts of testimony given by adversary expert witnesses in prior cases.

Review interrogatories to be answered and answers to all interrogatories relating to masonry.

Design calculations, notes, and sketches relating to masonry design.

If the owner of these documents is a party to the suit and is reluctant to provide copies, the client's attorney may obtain a court order to produce them. Review of these documents is an arduous, time-consuming task, but the forensic engineer should do it. It is not in the client's interest to delegate this task to others. The author has spent many boring hours reading material, which he could not assign to others, because he could not tell them exactly what to look for. Only experience can recognize value when it is seen. This process is expensive. If the client cannot afford it, he or she should settle the case for the best deal possible. Kraft[43] says, "Nothing is more damaging after the expert's direct testimony than for the expert to admit, on cross-examination, that he never...read a particular relevant document."

Literature Search

The *Masonry Bibliography*[46] contains 8135 entries. Very useful subject indexes are published by the American Society of Civil Engineers, American Concrete Institute, American Ceramic Society, and British Ceramic Society; but these by no means cover the subject of masonry as thoroughly as the *Masonry Bibliography*. Engineering libraries in many universities and some commercial sources can provide online computer literature searches with databases in many fields related to masonry problems, but none adequately cover the subject of masonry. Trade associations in the masonry industry, such as the National Concrete Masonry Association and the Brick Industry Association, publish very useful indexes to their own periodicals. Proceedings of international conferences and symposia and journals of The Masonry Society (U.S.) and the British Masonry Society can be most helpful. Grimm[31] provides a bibliography and guide to the literature on conventional masonry mortar. Drysdale, Hamid, and Baker[7] created the best single reference on masonry now available.

Research Needs

Special problems may arise for which there is inadequate or no published literature. If the magnitude of the case warrants the cost of research, the research needs should be clearly defined. It may be worth a million dollars to correctly answer one question during a trial. Only the client in consultation with an attorney can place a proper value on research.

Report

Oral reports by the forensic engineer of a masonry failure should precede all written reports. A written report should be prepared only at the client's specific request and only after the client has consulted with an attorney on the necessity for such a written report. Written reports may conform to ASTM E 620, *Practice for Reporting Opinions of Technical Experts.*[62]

Although the forensic engineer should be generally familiar with construction law, her or his written reports should not quote legal precedent or cite law cases. However, the client's attorney may wish to have such pertinent citations given orally. The report may, however, quote from the literature on dispute resolution.

Each description of a masonry condition should be well illustrated with an identified photograph or sketch. The report should contain an abstract, table of contents, and introduction. In addition to opinions and conclusions, the report should state precisely how all data were obtained, by whom, from whom—or what, when, and where. References to the literature should be cited, and author's biographical data should be provided.

REMEDIAL MEASURES

Cracks, voids, leaks, stains, deteriorated mortar joints or masonry units, color variation in joints or units, and collapse are the principal problems requiring remedial work.

Cracks and Voids

Crack repair methods may be classified as those which do not significantly change wall appearance and those which do. Fine cracks less than $1/16$ in (1.5 mm) are not very conspicuous and in brick masonry could be made more unsightly by tuck-pointing. Void mortar joints may be filled by pressure injection of grout.

Surface grouting, tuck-pointing, stucco, or two coats of brush-applied water-cement paint greatly reduce water permeance. The only effective and durable methods of reducing water permeance of brick walls without significantly changing their appearance is by tuck-pointing, grout injection, or surface-grouting mortar joints.[14]

Grout Injection

Proper functional performance of masonry walls requires solidly filled collar and head joints. Seismically damaged masonry walls and those with void mortar joints have been successfully repaired by pressure injection of fine, cement-based grout. Schuller and Grimm[54] provide guide specifications for repair of masonry walls by grout injection. Project specifications for grout injection should include requirements for a preinstallation conference; preinjection evaluation; environmental requirements; grout materials, delivery, storage, handling, proportioning, batching, mixing, and testing; surface repairs; injection holes; grout injection; and cleanup.

Tuck-Pointing

Tuck-pointing of mortar joints is appropriate when joints are severely deteriorated. It is a process of cutting out old mortar to a uniform depth and placing new mortar in the joint. Employ only qualified and experienced tuck-pointing craftsmen. An individual who is an excellent bricklayer may not be a good tuck-pointing craftsman.

A tuck-pointing trial is advisable. In an inconspicuous area cut out 10 linear ft (3.048 m) of cracked mortar joints. Use a power-driven pointer's grinder to cut joints to a uniform depth of $3/4$ in (19 mm). Remove dust and debris from the joint by brushing or blowing with air under high pressure.

Tuck-point with *Specifications for Mortar for Unit Masonry,* C 270, type N[62] mortar in accordance with appendix X3 of that standard. Prehydrate tuck-pointing mortar as follows: Carefully measure and record the amount and origin of each dry ingredient. Thoroughly mix all dry ingredients. Add only enough clean water to the dry mix to produce a damp, workable consistency, which will retain its shape when formed into a ball. Let mortar stand in this dampened condition for 1 to $1^1/2$ h. Dampen cut joints, but leave no standing water in the joint. Add water to prehydrated mortar to bring it to a workable consistency but somewhat drier than conventional mortar. Pack mortar tightly into joints in thin layers of not more than $1/4$ in (6 mm). Allow each layer to become "thumbprint-hard" before applying the next layer. After the last layer of mortar is thumbprint-hard, tool joints to match the profile of the original joints.

Let trial tuck-pointed joints stand for two weeks of dry weather. Compare the color of tuck-pointed joints with that of adjacent original mortar joints. If the color difference is not acceptable to the owner, adjust the mortar dry ingredients and repeat the trial tuck-pointing process until the color difference is acceptable. When acceptance is obtained, use the final trial mix of dry ingredients to tuck-point all cracked mortar joints. They are defined as numerous, short, thin horizontal cracks at the mortar-unit interface.

Surface Grouting

Tooling masonry mortar joints shortly after masonry units are laid closes cracks that would otherwise occur at the face of the wall between mortar and the unit. Improper tooling leaves such cracks. Wind-driven rain can enter a crack wider than 0.1 mm (0.004 in). Surface grouting can satisfactorily fill such cracks.[42] Surface grouting requires about one-seventh of the labor required for tuck-pointing. Because grout remaining in the texture of rough surfaces may affect wall appearance, trial application is suggested to an inconspicuous wall area. Nonproprietary materials and methods for surface grouting are described in the literature.[5,9-11] Proprietary products for this purpose include Manchester Grout (Western Waterproofing Co., St. Louis, MO) and D-J Grouting Mortar (Standard Dry Wall Products, Miami, FL).

Coatings

Clear coatings for masonry typically do not bridge cracks and, therefore, do not prevent water permeance in masonry, although they may temporarily reduce it. This writer does not recommend clear coatings on brick masonry.[25]

Reference 53 discusses paint coatings for masonry. Two coats of water cement paint are inexpensive and effective. Stucco application is described in ACI[40] and ASTM[55] publications. Stain coatings to solve color problems are described by Suprenant[60] and Hooker.[41]

Color Variation

Comparison of masonry in place with a previously approved sample panel built at the job site is the current method of determining color acceptance for brick. Slight deviations in the color of brick may not amount to failure to comply with a contract.[6] "Brick Color Selection and Specification"[37] and "The Color of Structure"[13] address brick color discrimination.

Cleaning

The multiplicity of stains, which occur on the several types of masonry, has generated a bewildering array of cleaning agents and methods. At least 100 types of stains can occur on 14 different masonry materials. There are a dozen cleaning methods using at least 159 cleaning agents containing 105 chemicals made by 87 manufacturers. There are at least 77 cleaning operations using 27 types of equipment. Many cleaning methods, especially sandblasting, can be very damaging to masonry.[22] The cited literature presents specific recommendations for cleaning virtually all types of stains from all types of masonry.[20]

Demolished or Collapsed Masonry

Spurling[57] discusses specifications for demolition. Minor masonry demolition may be necessary to replace defective flashing, in which case three or four courses of masonry are removed immediately above the flashing. Grimm[28] discusses flashing specifications. Collapsed or demolished masonry should be rebuilt to conform to *Building Code Requirements for Masonry Structures*[4] and *Specifications for Masonry Structures.*[56] The *Masonry Designers' Guide*[47] is based on those two standards.

CASE HISTORIES

Masonry failures have a lot in common, but all are different.

A Low-Rise Hotel

Mold and mildew costs the U.S. hotel and motel industry approximately $68 million each year in lost revenues and damage repair.[3] Rooms cannot be rented that smell stale due to odors emitted by mold and mildew. In one case, bathroom exhaust fans removed more air than the air conditioning system supplied, creating a negative air pressure. In the warm, moist climate, air infiltrating through exterior walls condensed behind wall covering, providing an ideal condition for mold growth.

In that case the hotel ordered demolition of all exterior walls and sued everyone involved, including the masonry contractor who, it was alleged, had built a leaky brick masonry veneer over steel studs. Worse yet, bricklayers, it was said, used chloride in the mortar. An engineering firm's report stated that chloride would "...greatly accelerate corrosion of wall ties, resulting in premature failure of the wall." That finding was based on a laboratory report, which stated that three of seven mortar specimens tested contained a level of chloride which exceeded 0.2 percent by weight of cement.

In response, another engineering firm conducted a survey of other buildings in the same city to determine the mortar chloride content. Three mortar specimens were removed from exterior walls of each of 10 other buildings of various ages, providing a sample of 30 mortar specimens. The sample was sent to the same laboratory that had tested the original seven mortar specimens.

Seven of the 10 buildings had average estimated mortar chloride contents of 0.2 percent or more by weight of cement. Sixteen of the 30 mortar specimens had chloride contents of 0.2 percent or more. Based on the lognormal distribution there is better than 50 percent probability that mortar selected at random from buildings in that city would have a chloride content of 0.2 percent or more.

Masonry on the 10 buildings has performed adequately for up to half a century with mortar chloride contents of 0.2 percent or more. The level of chloride in mortar in that case provided no basis for masonry demolition. A contrary view would require that one-half of the exterior brick masonry in the city be demolished.[35]

In addition, the architect's design details were found to have contributed to water permeance of the exterior walls. Stiff brick masonry veneer was placed over flexible steel studs, which resulted in veneer cracks under coastal winds.[21] Incompatible flashing materials were juxtaposed, which resulted in their deterioration. Faulty design of flashing and coping caused leakage of wind-driven rain.[28] Specification for masonry cement mortar resulted in greater water permeance than would have occurred with portland cement-lime mortar.[32]

It was also alleged that bricklayers did not keep the 1-in airspace between the masonry and the stud wall clean of mortar droppings, which caused water leaks. The architect should have known that it is virtually impossible to keep a 1-in (25-mm) airspace clean of mortar droppings.

As often occurs, the case against the masonry contractor was settled out of court under a confidentiality agreement, which keeps the settlement conditions secret.

A High-Rise Hotel

In violation of recommended good practice and the standards of care for the profession, the architects committed serious design errors and omissions, which the architects knew or in the exercise of due care should have known would result in cracked and leaking masonry walls. In violation of law, no provision was made for differential movement of the masonry and its supporting structure. The architect failed to heed well-published warnings about failures in the wall system that he chose to use. His design was improper for base wall flashing and exterior sills. The architect did not require a sufficient number of vertical expansion joints or weep holes. Flashing was improperly designed, and other design errors were committed.

Walls were structurally designed to crack, which cracks admitted wind-driven rain. The brick masonry veneer/steel stud wall system was introduced and promoted without adequate research, and the behavior of the system is not generally well understood. Brick masonry veneer/steel stud construction evolved without either adequate laboratory research or a sufficient period of field-testing. The current usual design procedure does not adequately account for the actual behavior of the wall system. The only structural element holding the masonry on the building is the fine, thin arris of a single thread of an abraded screw, which is periodically bathed in a salt solution. Corrosion of those screws, due to water leakage through cracked masonry and due to interstitial condensation, will ultimately make the wall life-threatening.

A structural analysis was made of exterior walls. Computer printouts of the analysis were provided. The assumption was made that the masonry wythe was free at the top, as it should have been had an expansion joint under the shelf angle been provided in accordance with the building code. Flexural tensile stress in the masonry at design wind load was estimated at 147 lb/in². Mean flexural strength of the masonry was estimated at 140 lb/in² for the type of mortar and workmanship specified. It is probable that more than one-half the masonry would have cracked had the specified mortar been used.

The contractor left holes in mortar joints, did not fill all mortar joints, used insufficient cement in the mortar, used about one-half as many wall ties as required, and did not properly install shelf angles. In addition, the contractor did not provide an adequate expansion joint under all shelf angles, and may have used a mortar admixture in violation of the law. The contractor did not keep the wall cavity clean, frequently bridged expansion joints, and did not properly install some masonry connectors. These violations of the law and breaches of contract caused the walls to crack and to leak.

Sealant joints at windows, expansion joints, and shelf angles were not well maintained, which permitted wind-driven rain to enter the wall.

Extensive repairs were recommended, including immediate repair in some areas to protect the public safety.

REFERENCES

1. *ASHRAE Handbook of Fundamentals,* American Society of Heating, Refrigerating, and Air Conditioning Engineers, Inc., Atlanta, 1989, pp. 20.1–23.2.

2. *ASTM Standards on Masonry,* American Society for Testing and Materials, West Conshohocken, PA, 1997.

3. Theodore Boelens, "Introduction," *Mold and Mildew in Hotel and Motel Guest Rooms in Hot and Humid Climates,* The Hospitality Lodging & Travel Research Foundation, Washington, D.C., 1991.

4. *Building Code Requirements for Masonry Structures,* ACI 530/ASCE 5/TMS 402, The Masonry Society, Boulder, CO.

5. T. I. Coe, "Moisture Penetration of Brick Walls," *The Octagon,* American Institute of Architects, Washington, February 1930.

6. Robert F. Cushman, John D. Carter, and Alan Silverman, *Construction Litigation, Representing the Contractor,* Wiley, New York, 1986, p. 383.

7. Robert G. Drysdale, Ahmad A. Hamid, and Lawrie R. Baker, *Masonry Structures Behavior and Design,* The Masonry Society, Boulder, CO, 1999.

8. S. G. Fattal and L. F. Cattaneo, *Evaluation of Structural Properties of Masonry in Existing Buildings,* BSC 62, National Institute for Standards and Technology, Gaithersburg, MD, 1977.

9. C. C. Fishburn, D. F. Parsons, and P. H. Peterson, *Effect of Outdoor Exposure on the Water Permeability of Masonry Walls,* BMS 76, National Institute for Standards and Technology, Gaithersburg, MD, 1941.

10. C. C. Fishburn and D. F. Parsons, *Tests on Cement-Water Paints and Other Waterproofings for Unit Masonry Walls,* BMS 95, National Institute for Standards and Technology, Gaithersburg, MD, 1943.

11. D. W. Fowler and Clayford T. Grimm, "Effects of Sand Blasting and Face Grouting on Water Permeance of Brick Masonry," *Masonry—Past and Present,* ASTM STP 589, American Society for Testing and Materials, West Conshohocken, PA, 1975, pp. 255–271.

12. Clayford T. Grimm, "Mason Productivity," *Masonry—Past and Present,* ASTM STP 589, American Society for Testing and Materials, West Conshohocken, PA, 1975, pp. 133–139.

13. Clayford T. Grimm, "The Color of Structure," *Journal of the Structural Division,* Proceedings of the American Society of Civil Engineers, Reston, VA, September 1975, p. 1871.

14. Clayford T. Grimm, "Water Permeance of Masonry Walls—A Review of the Literature," *Masonry: Materials, Properties, and Performance,* American Society for Testing and Materials, STP 778, West Conshohocken, PA, 1982, pp. 178–199.

15. Clayford T. Grimm, "Durability of Brick Masonry: A Review of the Literature," *Symposium on Masonry: Research, Application, and Problems,* ASTM STP 871, American Society for Testing and Materials, West Conshohocken, PA, 1985, pp. 202–234.

16. Clayford T. Grimm, "Probabilistic Design of Expansion Joints in Brick Cladding," *Proceedings of the 4th Canadian Masonry Symposium,* University of New Brunswick, Canada, vol. 1, June 1986, pp. 553–568.

17. Clayford T. Grimm, "Statistical Primer for Brick Masonry," *Symposium on Masonry: Materials, Design, Construction, and Maintenance,* ASTM STP 992, American Society for Testing and Materials, West Conshohocken, PA, 1988, pp. 169–192.

18. Clayford T. Grimm, "Masonry Cracks: A Review of The Literature," *Symposium on Masonry: Materials Design, Construction, and Maintenance,* ASTM STP 992, American Society for Testing and Materials, West Conshohocken, PA, 1988, pp. 257–280.

19. Clayford T. Grimm, "Some Brick Masonry Workmanship Statistics," *Journal of Construction Engineering, and Management,* American Society of Civil Engineers, Reston, VA, vol. 114, no. 1, March 1988, pp. 147–149.

20. Clayford T. Grimm, *Cleaning Masonry: A Review of the Literature,* Construction Research Center, University of Texas at Arlington, November 1988.

21. Clayford T. Grimm, "What They Say about Brick Masonry Veneer over Steel Studs," *Construction Specifier,* Construction Specifications Institute, Alexandria, VA, September 1989, pp. 76–77.

22. Clayford T. Grimm, "Don't Sandblast Brick," *The Magazine of Masonry Construction,* March 1990, pp. 115–116.

23. Clayford T. Grimm and R. E. Klingner, "Crack Probability in Brick Masonry Veneer over Steel Studs," *Fifth North American Masonry Conference,* University of Illinois, Urbana-Champaign, June 3–6, 1990, pp. 1323–1334.

24. Clayford T. Grimm, "What Is Wrong with Brick Masonry Veneer over Steel Studs?" *TMS Journal,* vol. 10, no. 2, February 1992, pp. 9–14.

25. Clayford T. Grimm, "Clear Consequences," *The Construction Specifier,* Construction Specifications Institute, Alexandria, VA, May 1993, pp. 143–152.

26. Clayford T. Grimm, "Acoustical Properties of Masonry Walls," *The Construction Specifier,* Alexandria, VA, March 1993, pp. 78–82.

27. Clayford T. Grimm, "Delamination of Masonry Pavements," *TMS Journal,* The Masonry Society, Boulder, CO, vol. 12, no. 2, February 1994, pp. 93–99.

28. Clayford T. Grimm, *The Hidden Flashing Fiasco,* Construction Research Center, University of Texas at Arlington, April 1994.

29. Clayford T. Grimm, "Void Mortar Joints: Bane of Brick Masonry," *Journal of Construction Engineering and Management,* American Society of Civil Engineers, Reston, VA, vol. 120, no. 1, March 1994, pp. 152–161.

30. Clayford T. Grimm, "Masonry Fire Resistance: A Bibliography," *Proceedings of the Seventh North American Masonry Conference,* The Masonry Society, Boulder, CO, June 2–5, 1996, vol. 2, pp. 1019–1024.

31. Clayford T. Grimm, "Conventional Masonry Mortar: A Bibliography and Guide to the Literature," *Proceedings of the Seventh North American Masonry Conference,* The Masonry Society, Boulder, CO, June 2–5, 1996, vol. 2, pp. 745–758.

32. Clayford T. Grimm, "Effect of Mortar Air Content on Masonry," *TMS Journal,* The Masonry Society, Boulder, CO, December 1996, pp. 21–24.

33. Clayford T. Grimm, "Clay Brick Masonry Weight Variation," *Journal of Architectural Engineering,* American Society of Civil Engineers, Reston, VA, December 1996, pp. 135–137.

34. Clayford T. Grimm, "Bracing Systems for Masonry Are Dangerous," *The Magazine of Masonry Construction,* Addison, IL, January 1997, pp. 15–17.

35. Clayford T. Grimm, "Demolish Charleston's Brick Walls Because There Is Chloride in the Mortar?" *Journal of Materials in Civil Engineering,* vol. 9, no. 3, August 1997.

36. Clayford T. Grimm, "Mechanical Properties of Masonry Walls," *TMS Journal,* The Masonry Society, Boulder, CO, June 1998, pp. 69–73.

37. Clayford T. Grimm, "Brick Color Selection and Specification," *TMS Journal,* vol 18, no 1, The Masonry Society, Boulder, CO, Spring 2000.

38. Clayford T. Grimm, "Measuring Brick Masonry Mortar Joint Solidity," 12th International Brick/Block Masonry Conference, June 25-28, 2000, Madrid, Spain.

39. Clayford T. Grimm, "Volume Change in Brick Masonry Veneer over Wood Frame," *Proceedings of the Eighth North American Masonry Conference, June 6–9, 1999,* The Masonry Society, Boulder, CO.

40. "Guide to Portland Cement Plastering," *ACI Materials Journal,* American Concrete Institute, Detroit, MI, section 7.3.3, January-February 1993, pp. 69–93.

41. Kenneth A. Hooker, "Changing the Face of Masonry," *The Magazine of Masonry Construction,* Addison, IL, December 1991, pp. 470–472.

42. Kenneth A. Hooker, "Surface Grouting to Repair Mortar Joints," *The Magazine of Masonry Construction,* Addison, IL, September 1994, pp. 423–425.

43. M. D. Kraft, *Using Experts in Civil Cases,* Practicing Law Institute, New York, 1980.

44. L. F. W. Lai, "A Review of the Literature Currently Available on the Stability of Masonry Buildings Against Accidental Damage," *Proceedings of the 8th International Brick/Block Masonry Conference,* Elsevier Applied Science, Reston, VA, 1988, pp. 1599–1612.

45. Edgar V. Leyendecker, *Abnormal Loading on Buildings and Progressive Collapse: An Annotated Bibliography,* NBS Building Science Series 67, National Institute for Standards and Technology, Gaithersburg, MD, January 1976.

46. *Masonry Bibliography,* International Masonry Institute, Washington, D.C., vol. 1, 1985; vol. 2, 1988; vol. 3, 1993.

47. John H. Matthys, ed., *Masonry Designers' Guide,* The Masonry Society, Boulder, CO, 1993.

48. A. H. P. Maurenbrecher and C. T. Grimm, "Corrosion of Metal Connectors in Masonry Cladding," *The Construction Specifier,* The Construction Specifications Institute, Alexandria, VA, October 1998, pp. 51–64.

49. *Minimum Design Loads for Buildings and Other Structures,* ASCE 7-95, American Society of Civil Engineers, Reston, VA, 1996.

50. "Moisture Resistance of Brick Masonry Walls—Condensation Analysis," *Technical Notes on Brick Construction,* no. 7D, Brick Industry Association, Reston, VA, May 1988.

51. Mary Gibbons Natrella, *Experimental Statistics,* Handbook 91, National Institute for Standards and Technology, Gaithersburg, MD, August 1, 1963, pp. 1-3–1-4.

52. "Painting Brick Masonry," *Technical Notes on Brick Construction,* no. 6, Brick Industry Association, Reston, VA, May 1972.

53. "Recommended Practice for Choice of Sample Size to Estimate the Average Quality of a Lot or Process," ASTM E 122, annual *Book of ASTM Standards,* American Society for Testing and Materials, West Conshohocken, PA, 1990.

54. Michael P. Schuller and Clayford T. Grimm, "Masonry Repair by Grout Injection," *Proceedings of the Seventh North American Masonry Conference,* The Masonry Society, Boulder, CO, June 2–5, 1996, vol. 1, pp. 449–457.

55. *Specification for Installation of Portland Cement-Based Plaster,* ASTM C 926, American Society for Testing and Materials, West Conshohocken, PA, 1995.

56. *Specifications for Masonry Structures,* ACI 530.1-95/ASCE 6-95/TMS 602-95, The Masonry Society, Boulder, CO, 1995.

57. Everett G. Spurling, "Specifying Demolition," *The Construction Specifier,* Alexandria, VA, July 1989, pp. 100–113.

58. *Standard Method for Determining Fire Resistance of Concrete and Masonry Construction Assemblies,* ACI 216.1-97/TMS0216.1-97, The Masonry Society, Boulder, CO, 1997.

59. Bruce A. Suprenant, "Staining Concrete Masonry," *The Magazine of Masonry Construction,* Addison, IL, August 1989, pp. 352–353.

60. Bruce Suprenant and Michael Schuller, *Nondestructive Evaluation & Testing of Masonry Structures,* The Aberdeen Group, Addison, IL, 1994.

61. L. A. Palmer and J. V. Hall, "Some Results of Freezing and Thawing Tests Made with Clay Brick," *ASTM Proceedings,* American Society for Testing and Materials, West Conshohocken, PA, vol. 30, part II, 1930, p. 769.

62. Annual *Book of ASTM Standards,* American Society for Testing and Materials, West Conshohocken, PA.

CHAPTER 14
THE BUILDING ENVELOPE

Kimball J. Beasley, P.E.[a] and David S. Patterson, A.I.A.[b]

---

[a]Kimball J. Beasley—Facades.
[b]David S. Patterson—Windows and Curtain Walls.

INTRODUCTION

The building envelope is usually considered to include facades, windows, and roofs. The first portion of this chapter deals with building walls and facades and the second part with windows and nonmasonry curtain walls. Roofs and roof terraces are not included in this chapter.

Prior to the 20th century, building walls served not only to keep out the weather, but also to support the building's floor and roof loads. Within the last 100 years the function of supporting the structure has usually been relegated to a structural skeleton, with the wall serving only to enclose the building. The building wall's primary role has become that of shedding water and containing occupants, furnishings, heat, etc. The wall also supplies light and vision via windows, and it defines the architectural character of the building. As buildings grow in size and complexity, and as economic pressures lead to thinner, less costly wall systems coupled with greater performance expectations, the potential for building envelope problems and failures increases.

In light of the role of forensic structural engineering, which involves the application of engineering principles to investigate and resolve causes of failure, to provide information for the development of repairs, and to aid in the jurisprudence process, the intent of this chapter is to provide information on principles of investigation and analysis and on common failures associated with various building envelope systems.

CODES AND STANDARDS

Building codes and standards are usually intended to provide the minimum requirements for the design and construction of building elements. In addition to commonly used national building codes such as BOCA, a municipality may develop its own building code. Codes pertaining to the building envelope generally emphasize safety, fire, structural, and some durability issues. Codes do not usually address serviceability issues such as water leakage; however, many such issues are addressed in certain standards for construction materials and systems.

Many entities and organizations are responsible for developing standards for construction and testing of building materials and systems that are applicable to building facades and to window and curtain wall systems. Among these organizations are membership organizations, such as the American Society for Testing and Materials (ASTM), that generate consensus documents through the work of committees and task groups. For example, the task groups of ASTM Subcommittee E6.24, "Building Rehabilitation and Preservation Technology," are developing standards that are specifically applicable to work on existing buildings and structures. These task groups represent different areas of practice and include architects, engineers, conservators, scientists, contractors, and others. The documents published by ASTM include standard test methods, standard practices, and standard guides. While a test method or practice provides recommendations for a definite course of action, a guide may propose a series of options and does not establish a specific course of action.

Other organizations developing standards for the construction industry are specifically devoted to work in one area of the field or in one material. Examples of such organizations include the American Concrete Institute (ACI); Brick Institute of America (BIA), which provides a series of technical notes as well as standards; the Indiana Limestone Institute, which publishes a handbook to guide designers; the National Building Granite Quarriers Association (NBGQA); the National Concrete Masonry Association (NCMA); and the Sheet Metal and Air Conditioning Contractors' National Association (SMACNA), which publishes a notebook of recommended details for sheet metal and flashing; among many others. The American Architectural Manufacturers' Association (AAMA) and National Wood Window and Door Association (NWWDA) publish test procedures and standards specific to windows, doors, and curtain walls, sometimes in conjunction with the American National Standards Institute (ANSI).

The current direction in the development of codes and standards is for the promulgating entities to combine their efforts. For example, there are presently committees working on the development of international building codes, including an international code specifically addressing the preservation of existing structures. This effort may eventually simplify the application of codes and standards, but as this work is in progress, it can add to the complexity of selecting and specifying appropriate codes and standards for a project.

In determining what standard is appropriate for a specific investigative task, the investigator needs to be familiar with the current standards that are applicable. The latest version of appropriate standards should be carefully reviewed, since standards are constantly changing. For example, the newest version of a standard may be either more or less stringent than the previous version.

In addition, for investigation and repair of an existing building or structure, it may be important to review the codes and standards that were in effect at the time of construction. Note that there may not have been codes or standards in place to address specific issues of building construction or performance. In that case, the investigator needs to decide whether existing construction should be, or even can be, held to the requirements of present-day standards.

The requirements of the specific test, material, or repair need to be considered to determine what standard is appropriate and applicable for a given task. In addition, the requirements of that standard may affect the criteria selected for the building element or system. Some specific standards and their applications are discussed in the following sections.

FACADES

Facade Categories

Building walls may be divided into two broad categories: load-bearing and non-load-bearing. Facades may involve either the exposed outer veneer of bearing or non-load-bearing walls, or infill panels spanning the building's perimeter structural frame members. Facade systems must be designed and connected to the structure in a manner to support their own weight and resist any anticipated lateral and planar forces. There is a great deal of flexibility in the choice of materials, appearance, and configuration of building facades. Industrial facilities, e.g., may simply require a utilitarian envelope of light-gauge metal sheets over an economical building frame. First-class commercial office buildings, however, may require a highly stylized envelope combining glass and architectural metal, masonry, or stone veneer panels.

Over the past several decades, building facade design has evolved from traditional unit masonry to contemporary panel or composite veneer wall systems. Each type of facade has distinct benefits and potential problems. Common traditional walls are usually solid barrier or cavity walls constructed of brick or terra cotta, ashlar or dimension stone, precast concrete, cast stone, concrete masonry, stucco, wood, or cementitious shingles. Contemporary facades may be skin barriers or rain screens constructed of precast concrete panels, thin stone veneer, metal plate, composite panels (metal sandwich panels, ceramic veneer on cementitious backer board), and metal and glass curtain wall.

In most cases, the successful facade employs features that are not overly complex with materials, connections, and details that are time-proven. A successful facade system design incorporates connections and details that do not invite construction problems, and it includes a redundant support mechanism and internal wall drainage system. Also, the facade design must include adequate provisions for anticipated planar movements (e.g., thermal or moisture expansion of the facade) and provide support without restraint against accumulated material expansion and contraction.

Facade Failures

Two broad categories of facade failures include stability failures (e.g., complete wall collapse, dislodged portions of the facade, or loose pieces) and serviceability failures (e.g., water leakage, cracks, or aesthetic degradation). According to the *Merriam-Webster Dictionary,* the word *failure* means "...the inability to perform a normal function adequately." A building collapse is an obvious failure; however, a facade that appears to be intact but would not sustain normal wind loads because of missing or corroded anchors behind the wall surface is also a failure. Such "latent failures" can be more troubling because they are difficult to detect and may result in collapse without warning. Loss of function of building facades (e.g., leaking or cracking) is far more common than failures resulting in a catastrophic collapse that claims life and property. Collectively, the economic consequences of such serviceability failures may be far greater than those of collapses.

Facade cracking, bulging, delamination, and leakage usually occur with patterns or features that can offer clues to their causes. Properly recognizing the symptom of failure and pattern of distress is essential to identification of the cause of failure. Facades are subjected to a wide variety of agents that may lead to failure. Deterioration of facade or connection materials undermines their ability to resist normal loads. External forces of a magnitude or orientation not anticipated in design can damage facade and connection elements. Defects introduced during construction may affect the facade's ability to perform as designed.

Since facades are generally considered nonstructural, the responsibility for design may be shared between the project architect and engineer. This fragmenting of responsibility and the resulting lack of coordination are also frequent indirect contributors to failures.

Identifying the source of failures, establishing the means of correcting damages due to the failure, and convincingly demonstrating the cause of failure and appropriateness of the remediation are frequently the charge of the forensic structural engineer.

External and Internal Force-Induced Failures.   While the building's facades do not intentionally carry loads imposed by the building's structure, they must resist a variety of externally and internally imposed forces. External forces may include lateral loads from wind or earthquakes and vertical loads from the facade's own weight (gravity load). The facade also may be subjected to localized internal forces imposed by expanding elements embedded in the wall (e.g., corroding shelf angles or reinforcing steel) or by differential planar movements between the facade element and the wall's substrate or the building's structural frame.

External forces are usually well understood, and the response of the facade to these forces may be predictable. Wind, gravity, and even earthquake loads can be quantified and analyzed. The facade's mechanical properties and connection system can be designed to accommodate such forces with an appropriate factor of safety. However, internal forces are more complex and may vary substantially from structure to structure and within the same structure, depending on the facade materials and configurations employed. Such forces are often overlooked or misunderstood, leading to failures that are difficult to analyze.

Facade system supports and anchors are common areas of force concentration. Considering that anchors may be somewhat flexible and that facade systems may be rigid and brittle (e.g., stone or concrete), unexpected and complex distribution of forces may result from the differences in relative stiffnesses. Anchors may involve point engagement (e.g., dowels, pins, or bolts) or linear engagement (e.g., angles set into kerfs with stone facades).[1] The design relies upon support redundancy and factors of safety to accommodate the unanticipated support and anchor forces. Complex anchor and support behavior may be properly evaluated by modeling and testing, described later in this chapter.

Following are some examples of possible facade failures associated with external and internal forces.

Wind—External Force. Many wall systems involve rigid facade materials that are weak in tension with backup materials that are strong in tension but flexible. The distribution of wind loads in such a composite wall system is a function of the relative stiffness of each wall component. For example, cementitious claddings may resist virtually all the wind load while the light-gauge steel stud frame shares very little. Also, the lateral flexibility of the wall tie or facade anchorage system will affect the proportion of wind load shared with the backup wall. Disproportionate distribution of wind load to the backup system sometimes causes excessive cracking and deflection in this type of wall system.[2]

Unaccommodated Gravity Loads—External Force. Since facades are usually positioned outward beyond the centroid (center of gravity) of the building's perimeter beams and columns, the weight of facade materials often produces an eccentric load on the facade support.[3] The ability of the spandrel system, shelf angle support, or clip angle to resist the resulting load depends on several design factors and as-built features. For example, a shelf angle may be adequately sized; however, excessive shimming of the angle will lead to moments and rotations not anticipated in design. Figure 14.1 shows a sketch of a spandrel assembly rotation caused by eccentric loading from the masonry facade.

Corrosion Jacking—Internal Force. Exposed concrete or masonry wall elements with mild steel reinforcement near the exposed surfaces are vulnerable to spalling (Fig. 14.2). When the steel corrodes, the corrosion scale occupies up to 10 times the volume of the original steel. The expanding scale induces tensile stress in the adjacent masonry or concrete in which it is embedded. Steel corrosion potential may be further exacerbated by soluble chlorides introduced during con-

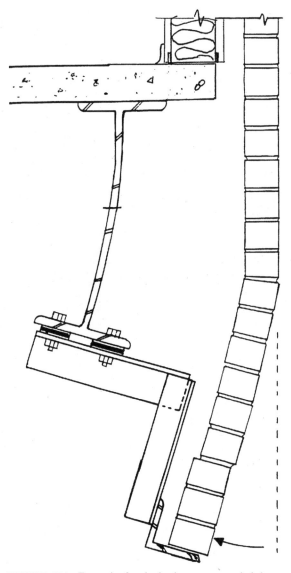

FIGURE 14.1 Eccentric facade load rotates spandrel beam assembly.

struction to accelerate concrete or mortar setting, or from environmental exposure (e.g., a saltwater marine environment). Also, as the concrete or mortar ages, it slowly loses its alkalinity from a chemical reaction with carbon dioxide in the atmosphere. This "carbonation," which starts at the exposed concrete surface and progresses inward, may take several years to reach the embedded steel. Sometimes

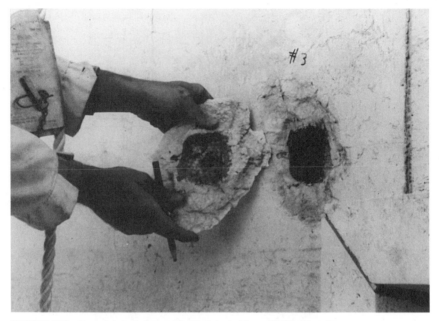

FIGURE 14.2   Corrosion scale from embedded steel plate spalls thin travertine veneer.

this results in a rash of spalling when the carbonation reaches the depth of much of the embedded steel. This may occur several decades after construction.

   Restrained Planar Expansion and Contraction—Internal Force.   Restrained expansion and contraction of the facade material relative to the building's structural frame is a frequent cause of facade stress failures.[4] This type of distress is often related to cyclic thermal facade expansion coupled with resistance from the structural frame. The frame does not expand with the facade because it is sheltered from the weather and relatively free from thermal fluctuations. Load-induced elastic deformation, and shrinkage and creep in concrete construction further increase planar facade forces by shortening the structural frame. Also, with fired-clay masonry products, slow ceramic/moisture expansion of the facade contributes to differential movement and compressive stress. These differential movements accumulate in long or tall walls, creating potential facade stress many times greater than that due to normal gravity or wind loading.

   Facade expansion joints are designed to accommodate differential movement. These joints may be compromised by mortar blockage within the wall cavity or by inadequate joint width.

   The symptoms of high stress in the facades are often readily recognizable. High vertical stress may cause specific bulging or crack patterns. Compression buckling or vertical shear cracks may occur at building corners where there is reduced lateral confinement of the facade (Fig. 14.3). Horizontal facade stress causes step cracking and horizontal displacement owing to masonry's relative weakness in tension. Cracking and displacement, however, are not always caused by such compressive forces. Sometimes deflections, settlement, and other causes may create similar symptoms.

Thin Stone Hysteresis—Internal Force. Certain types of stone commonly experience failure in the form of increased surface moisture absorption, disaggregation (sugaring), bowing, and strength loss when installed as exterior building facades. Although failure due to hysteresis is more commonly seen in thin (2- to 3-cm panels), this phenomenon can also occur with thicker panels in some stones. Stone composed of crystalline calcite grains adhered together with a narrow calcite

FIGURE 14.3 Terra cotta facade buckling from high compression force due to differential vertical expansion.

binder, such as marble, tends to be vulnerable to this failure. The complex grain morphology (tightly interlocked rhombohedral/hexagonal crystals) may lead to intergranular fracturing from cyclic temperature changes.[5] During thermal excursions the grains tend to dislocate and do not return to their original positions, sometimes called *hysteresis*. Disassociation of grains near the exposed surface of certain thinly cut marble panels may lead to uneven expansion of the panel, resulting in bowing. Further, the intergranular fractures cause increased water absorption, leading to increased dissolution of the calcite grain binder and strength loss. Since the calcite is soluble in acidic water, this loss of binder is usually more severe in an urban acid rain environment. Certain types of stone panels that are cut thicker (5 cm or greater) have been found to better resist bowing and deterioration. Figure 14.4 shows severely bowed thin marble facade panels.

Moisture-Related Failures.   Aside from the obvious erosion of mortar joints or soft stone, water may damage facade and wall elements in a variety of ways. Water that enters and is retained in the wall leads to corrosion of embedded metal, which both reduces the strength of the steel support/anchor element and produces corrosion scale that expands and spalls or cracks the facade. When saturated with water and subjected to cyclic freezing temperatures, stone, concrete, mortar, or clay masonry materials deteriorate from freeze-thaw action. This occurs when water fills microscopic voids in the materials and expands upon freezing, rupturing the adjacent materials (Fig. 14.5). Water-soluble materials within the wall (e.g., salts) dissolve when exposed to water and usually migrate to the facade surface due to vapor pressures caused by the thermal gradient. When this water evaporates at the surface, the mineral may recrystallize, creating efflorescence deposits. If recrystallization occurs beneath the surface (subflorescence), exfoliation of the surface material may result. To minimize water-related failures requires proper water management design.[6] This requires an understanding of the mechanism of potential water entry points and migration paths within the wall. Water management means that water penetration through the exposed facade surface or water vapor condensation within the wall is collected and diverted out of the wall by an internal wall drainage system. Water that penetrates the facade must be conveyed via internal cavities to wall flashings that are watertight, continuous, and properly enveloped. Weep holes must be configured to promptly drain water collected on the flashing. Blocked or bridged wall cavities, breached flashings, and blocked or poorly positioned weep holes may each result in water leakage to the interior. Exterior walls built directly over occupied spaces are especially problematic in terms of water leakage because failure of the wall drainage system results in direct water entry to the interior. Water that gets past the base flashing either collects on the adjacent floor or drips into the occupied space below (Fig. 14.6).

Ice Lensing.   Ice lensing refers to the facade bulging or displacement that occurs when water trapped within the wall freezes and expands. Figure 14.7 shows a barrier wall with internal wall flashings installed without a weep hole/drainage

FIGURE 14.4 Severely bowed thin marble panels.

system. Severe bulging of the brick facade occurred when water became trapped in the wall at the flashing level.

Masonry Deterioration from Impermeable Coatings. Deterioration of painted masonry often results from water trapped in the masonry body behind the paint surface. Water may enter the wall from sources other than the facade surface (e.g., copings, roof flashings, joints). Water vapor then migrates to the exposed wall surface and accumulates beneath any impermeable surface coating. Masonry walls with a clear internal drainage system and a well-ventilated cavity will resist paint-related damage better than barrier walls. Some coatings substantially inhibit moisture vapor transmission; however, acrylic coatings and certain clear penetrating sealers commonly have better vapor penetration properties. However, all coatings

FIGURE 14.5   Freeze-thaw action causes cast stone facade panels to disintegrate.

inhibit water vapor transmission to some degree. Therefore, it is always necessary to correct water penetration problems and evaluate the wall's drainage characteristics and potential masonry contamination with chlorides or other deleterious materials prior to considering any coatings.

Skin Barrier Walls.   Thinner wall systems[7] require a radical change in the wall's water leakage resistance design. Traditional masonry barrier walls controlled water leakage either by absorbing the water and slowly expelling it as water vapor or by draining it via an internal cavity and flashing system. The skin barrier wall

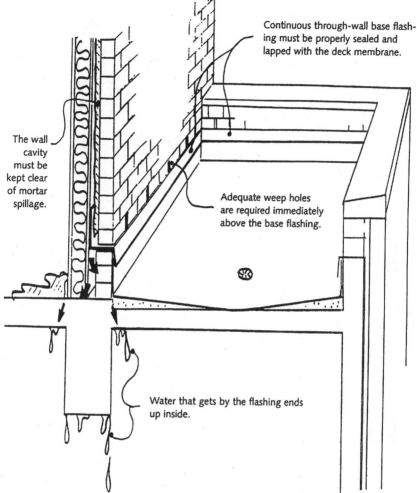

Continuous through-wall base flashing must be properly sealed and lapped with the deck membrane.

The wall cavity must be kept clear of mortar spillage.

Adequate weep holes are required immediately above the base flashing.

Water that gets by the flashing ends up inside.

FIGURE 14.6 Wall directly above interior space is especially vulnerable to water leakage.

system, however, must deflect all water at the wall's surface to avoid leakage (Fig. 14.8). The watertight integrity of the skin material and elastomeric joint sealants is critical to the success of this new wall system. Exterior insulation and finish systems (EIFS), which have become popular new skin-barrier wall systems, involve a thin (about 1/8-in-thick) polymer-based skin material that is trowel-applied to a rigid insulation board. New variations in EIFS design modify the EIFS to a form of cavity wall by providing an internal drainage mat to enhance the wall drainage capabilities (Fig. 14.9), and incorporate a moisture-resistant backer board.

FIGURE 14.7 Bulging brick facade occurs where water became trapped and froze within the wall.

Aesthetic Failures. Facade performance failures are not limited to inadequate functioning. An unsatisfactory facade appearance may also be considered a failure. Staining, cracking, corrosion, displacement, joint drifting (gradual variation in joint width), and nonuniform color are examples of aesthetic failures. Figure 14.10 shows "oil canning" of a light-gauge metal wall system. In this case, physical performance was not an issue; however, the system may be considered an aesthetic failure.

Facade Failure Investigation Methodology

Investigation of failure of any building or component is required for the following reasons:

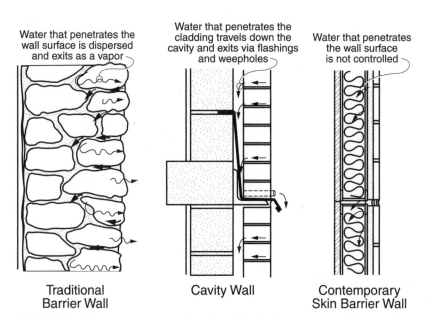

Water that penetrates the
wall surface is dispersed
and exits as a vapor

Water that penetrates the
cladding travels down the
cavity and exits via flashings
and weepholes

Water that penetrates
the wall surface
is not controlled

Traditional
Barrier Wall

Cavity Wall

Contemporary
Skin Barrier Wall

FIGURE 14.8   Water management mechanisms for traditional and contemporary skin barrier wall systems.

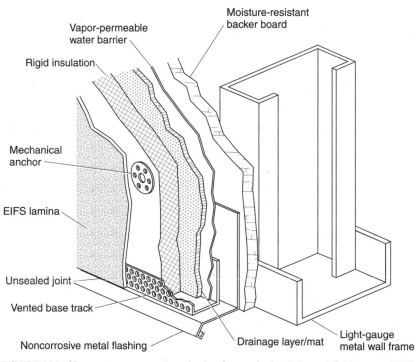

Vapor-permeable
water barrier

Moisture-resistant
backer board

Rigid insulation

Mechanical
anchor

EIFS lamina

Unsealed joint

Vented base track

Noncorrosive metal flashing

Drainage layer/mat

Light-gauge
metal wall frame

FIGURE 14.9   New water management mechanism for exterior insulation and finish system (EIFS).

FIGURE 14.10   Oil canning of thin metal cladding system.

1. To assess and develop appropriate repair procedures
2. To further the body of engineering knowledge to avoid similar failures in the future
3. To establish a factual basis to assign responsibility for any economic loss

While the failure investigation methodology is generally similar for most types of building system failures, the investigation scope depends on the nature, severity, and consequences of the failure.[8] For minor serviceability failures, the entire investigation process may involve a single investigator for only a few hours. For a major collapse the process may take teams of investigators representing several disciplines over many years. Facade failure investigations usually fall somewhere in between these two extremes. The typical forensic investigation involves a systematic, logical approach; it cannot be simplified to a prescriptive series of steps that must be followed without variation. Such "cookbook" investigation methods discourage the free thought, imagination, and flexibility that are essential to the collection and synthesis of data fundamental to the investigation.[9]

Most failure investigations contain four common elements:

1. Acquisition of data
2. Analysis of data
3. Development and evaluation of hypotheses
4. Formulation and communication of opinions

The activities associated with each of these tasks are discussed below.

Initial Site Visit. The goal of the initial site visit varies depending on the nature of the failure being investigated. A wall or facade collapse with associated cleanup effort requires prompt systematic collection of as much reliable information on the existing conditions as possible before the conditions are disturbed. A good-quality still camera and often a video camera can capture the position of remaining facade or collapse debris during or prior to cleanup operations. Digital cameras provide a computer-readable file that can be embedded in report text or transmitted via e-mail. Unstable walls or facades in a state of incipient collapse require prompt assessment and emergency stabilization measures after immediate notification of the governing agencies.

Data Acquisition. Data relevant to the failure may be acquired from numerous sources. These may include original structural and architectural drawings, specifications, shop drawings, prior maintenance or repair records, interviews with witnesses, and field observations. News media coverage may also provide useful information. Newspaper photographs or film footage shortly after a collapse is sometimes the best source of initial collapse information. As the investigation progresses, data from laboratory and field tests, detailed inspections, and condition surveys are also collected.

Condition Survey. A visual condition survey usually involves documenting observations by annotating conditions onto building elevation drawings or by high-resolution photographs. The condition survey objectives are to identify the location and nature of deterioration and distress, identify patterns of deterioration and distress, establish potential scope and locations for repair work, and establish a baseline for subsequent detailed inspections.

Binoculars or telephoto equipment is often used to facilitate observation of fine cracks, bulges, and spalls. The condition survey drawings offer a valuable method of documenting the nature and location of facade distress and visualizing the overall patterns of distress and underlying force paths.

Conditions identified during the survey will usually help to determine the need for and type of additional studies and laboratory tests. The distress patterns provide clues to the underlying cause(s). Conditions often identified during a condition survey include cracks, spalls, displacements, corrosion, delamination, efflorescence, honeycombs, scaling, and staining.

Detailed Inspections. Close-up visual examination of collapsed and damaged facade areas and of adjacent areas that are representative of the undisturbed wall is useful to gain knowledge of as-built construction and the conditions likely to have existed prior to the collapse. Safe access for such close-up examination may be from roof setbacks, balconies, and swing or pipe scaffolding, or even from rappelling. Examination of subsurface wall elements, facade connections, and adjacent construction requires probe openings (removal of surface materials) or inspections via an optical borescope (see "Tools and Equipment"). Special access and contractor assistance are usually required for close-up access and for making and later patching probe openings. Detailed inspections will almost always include various measurements, such as dimensions of typical wall panels, masonry units, joint widths, measurement of displacements, crack widths, etc. In situ strain measurements via strain relief method or during load tests, and measurements of concealed elements (e.g., via metal detector or pulse velocity methods) may also be required.

Detailed sketches of typical connections, anchors, and other relevant wall elements observed at probe locations are usually required. This is important to determine the as-built or existing configuration of wall elements. These sketches are also used to confirm whether the original construction documents accurately represent as-built or existing conditions.

Sample Collection and Custody.   Securing samples of visibly deteriorated or corroded elements and sometimes companion samples of apparently intact elements is required for subsequent laboratory testing. Since the opportunity to collect samples may be limited in the future, taking more samples than needed may be prudent where possible. The quantity, locations, and type of samples taken will be based on the nature of the failure and on the preliminary hypotheses developed. If the samples need to be statistically representative of the entire subject wall, random samples may be required. Since purely random sample selection is seldom possible due to limitations such as restrictions to access or to damaging finishes, sample bias is almost always present. The sample bias may not necessarily affect negatively the test results if the bias is anticipated and fully understood so as to avoid inadvertently skewing the data.

Tools and Equipment.   A wide variety of simple, traditional, and advanced new equipment are available to the facade investigator.

Common tools: The tools and equipment required to investigate facade failures vary with the type of failure being investigated. However, certain tools are common to most investigations. Camera, flashlight, tape measure, binoculars, probe, hammer, knife, magnet, field book, tape recorder, etc., are used in many facade investigations. Tools that are more sophisticated, more accurate, or dedicated to a specific purpose may also be required.

Photographic equipment: A high-quality 35-mm camera and video camera are fundamental tools. Sometimes a professional photographer may be needed under certain conditions. Specialized photographic methods may be used to measure and document a multitude of conditions. Infrared photography can be used in some cases to determine whether delaminations, cracks, spalls, or voids exist within solid walls. Minute variations in the facade's surface temperature correlate with the resulting discontinuity in thermal conductivity within the wall. Photogrammetry, which involves stereoscopic methods, may help to detect nonuniform or displaced wall surfaces.

Borescope: The borescope employs fiber optics or mirrors and lenses to view hidden spaces, such as wall cavities. The borescope's small-diameter (6- or 8-mm) metal tube is inserted through a small hole or joint. The device includes a power supply and light source, as well as an eyepiece and camera mount. Still or video camera may be used with the borescope (Fig. 14.11).

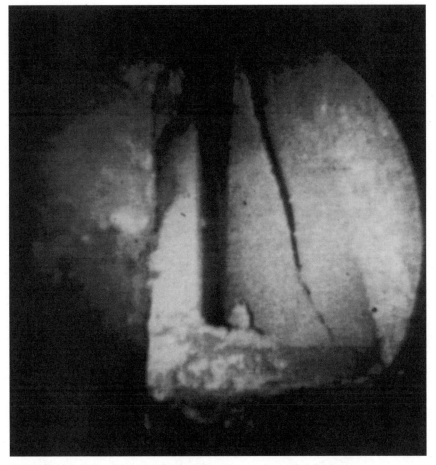

FIGURE 14.11   Defects hidden behind the wall surface are observed via borescope.

Measuring devices: Simple measuring devices include a tape measure, plumb bob, and optical crack comparator. More sophisticated devices such as a theodolite and electronic distance-measuring (EDM) instrument are used to measure precise positions of visible building facade areas relative to a reference point. Current technology allows precise measurement using a variety of methods. High-precision global positioning systems (GPS) and various inclinometers, accelerometers, and other devices can accurately monitor building movements.

Metal detector/pachometer: The location and size of embedded steel reinforcement and steel support or anchor elements within the masonry wall may need to be known to fully evaluate the wall or facade. A metal detector simply detects metals behind the wall surface. The pachometer measures changes in electric inductance to indicate the presence of underlying ferromagnetic metal (Fig. 14.12). An analog meter measures the intensity of electromagnetic signal in order to precisely locate the steel.

Rebound hammer: The principles of the rebound hammer, also called the Swiss or Schmidt hammer, are based upon the rebound of a mass after impacting a concrete or masonry surface. The rebound displacement is indicated on a calibrated scale called the *rebound number.* Generally, the greater the hardness of the test surface, the greater the rebound number. The rebound hammer provides a quick determination of the relative strengths of concrete or masonry. A rebound number that is calibrated with a compressive strength test from a concrete core or masonry prism can be used to extrapolate approximate compres-

FIGURE 14.12   A pachometer is used to detect size and/or depth of underlying steel reinforcement.

sive strength for other areas tested. The rebound hammer is generally used to supplement, but not replace, compressive strength testing of concrete cores or masonry prisms.

Pulse velocity methods: The velocity and waveform of a sonic pulse traveling through concrete or solid masonry approximate the material's relative strengths or identify internal discontinuities. The test is conducted in accordance with ASTM C597, *Standard Test Method for Pulse Velocity through Concrete.* The technique was originally developed for concrete and is still considered experimental for use with masonry. A V-meter uses two transducers. A transmitter introduces an ultrasonic energy pulse into the concrete or masonry (Fig. 14.13), a receiving transducer detects the transmitted signal, and through timing circuits, the elapsed time of transit is displayed. The pulse velocity is determined by dividing the distance between the transducers by the transit time. The velocity of a sonic pulse in an elastic solid is a function of its elastic modulus, density, and Poisson's ratio. The velocity of sonic pulses traveling in concrete or solid masonry corresponds to the material's elastic modulus and strength.

Impact echo: The impact-echo technique involves impacting the wall with a known energy quantity while monitoring reflected pulse waves, using a receiver located near the impact point (Fig. 14.14). The impact-echo method has been reliably used to determine the thickness of concrete members, as well as to detect internal delaminations and voids. This technique was devel-

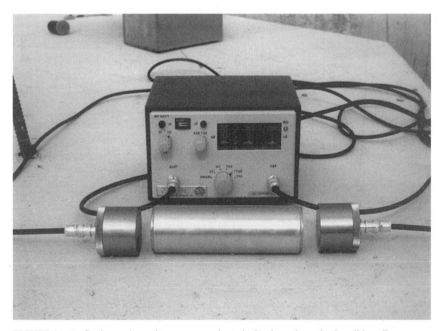

FIGURE 14.13   Soniscope is used to measure pulse velocity through an elastic solid medium.

Impact   Echo

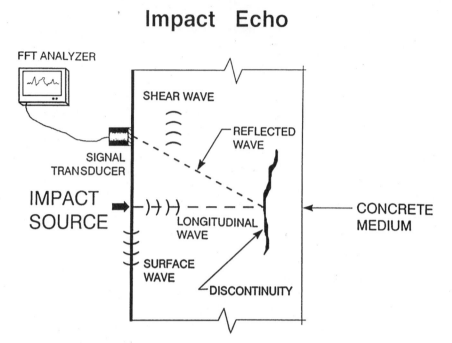

FIGURE 14.14   Principles of impact-echo test method.

oped to find flaws within concrete structures. It has also been applied to solid masonry walls.

Strain relief: Strain relief testing involves application of carbon-filament strain gauges to the surface of the subject wall element, usually brick or terra cotta (Fig. 14.15). The instrumented unit or area is then isolated from the surrounding wall by saw cutting. The strain value before and after saw cutting is measured. Using the modulus of elasticity of the base material, the in situ residual stress is then computed. This technique is particularly useful to determine the potential for compression or buckling failure of masonry facades and for cracking of wall panels.

Field Load Tests.   The behavior of facade or wall elements under controlled load application often helps to establish their strength, deflection characteristics, and mode of failure. A wide variety of devices are available to measure strain and deflections. Computerized data acquisition systems can collect, store, and display data rapidly during the test. A modem may be used to access data from a remote site.

Laboratory Tests—Mockups and Models.   Testing of mockups and models may be a very useful aid to understanding the behavior of complex building facade systems. Service loads can be duplicated while monitoring displacements and strains in a controlled environment. Loads can be increased to test the model to failure.

Tests may focus on connections or facade components of concern. Duplicating an actual failure with a mockup of the as-built elements offers a very convincing verification of a failure hypothesis.

Laboratory Analysis and Tests. Numerous laboratory methods are available to determine the properties of facade materials, the nature of deterioration, and the effectiveness of remedial measures. Following is a list of common material tests.

Petrographic microscopy: Petrography involves a standardized microscopic examination of stone, concrete, brick, or mortar based on the methods outlined in ASTM C856, *Petrographic Examination of Hardened Concrete.*[10] The objectives of a petrographic examination are to identify such conditions as the presence of microscopic defects and visible indicators of deterioration; evidence of

FIGURE 14.15 Strain gauge applied to stone surface.

unsound or reactive aggregate, unhydrated cement, and carbonation of the concrete and mortar. Petrographic examination also is used to determine the cement content, water-cement ratio, percent of entrained air, characteristics of the air void system, and degree of consolidation of concrete or mortar. In general, petrography indicates the overall quality and soundness of the stone, brick, concrete, or mortar.

Chloride content: The chloride ion content and profile (variation in concentration with distance from the surface) in concrete or mortar provide quantitative evidence of the potential for corrosion of embedded steel elements. The chloride content is determined by an acid-digestion, potentiometric titration procedure described in ASTM C1152, *Acid-Soluble Chloride in Mortar and Concrete.*[11]

Mechanical tests: Properties of materials, such as compressive or tensile strength and modulus of elasticity, are used to establish behavior of facade materials. With masonry facades, coupons or prism samples may be saw-cut from the wall and tested to failure in the laboratory. Prism test methods are described in ASTM E447.[12]

Coefficient of thermal and moisture expansion: Linear expansion and contraction of facade materials are measured under controlled thermal variations to determine the coefficient of thermal expansion. Relative-humidity levels with uniform temperature are varied to measure the coefficient of moisture expansion, usually a predictor of shrinkage cracking in cementitious products.

Freeze-thaw testing: Sensitivity of masonry and concrete materials to cyclic freezing and thawing is measured by alternately exposing uniformly sized, critically saturated samples to temperatures above and below freezing. Deterioration is measured by weighing the samples periodically during the test to assess weight loss related to fragmentation. Dynamic modulus methods determine variations in the sample's resonant frequency as an early detection of internal sample degradation.

Structural Analysis.   A mathematical model of an existing structure is developed to determine the theoretical properties of a facade panel, wall segment, or structural element. This includes analyzing its capacity to resist loads or to approximate load deflection characteristics. This analysis can help to determine if the element meets the requirements of design codes and standards. Finite-element computer models are often used in the structural analysis. Physical load tests on the existing structure or on a laboratory mockup are sometimes used to verify analysis results. Calculations must be well documented and organized since the results may be presented in a contentious litigation environment. The computer has become an indispensable tool for such analyses. However, due to the perceived certitude of the computer output, computer analysis methods have a potential for misuse. Accuracy of results is dependent on assumptions and input parameters. Complex analyses may be based on oversimplified or erroneous assumptions. Other inaccuracies result where failures, which usually involve inelastic deformations, are modeled with analytical methods which are based on linear elastic behavior.

Hypotheses Development. Failure hypotheses are developed and systematically rejected according to the data and analyses. Because of the wide variety of possible failure scenarios associated with most failures, *all* viable failure modes must be considered. Many experienced investigators fall into the trap of neglecting prospective failure causes by narrowing their search too early because they have "seen it before." No two failures are identical, and different causes of failure may display the same symptoms. An opinion of the most probable cause of failure is established after the implausible failure scenarios are ruled out.

Organization and Communication of Findings. Depending on the goal of the investigation, the report may take a variety of forms. A highly technical investigation of a major failure may be documented in a multivolume report with relevant data reproduced in appendixes. The client may require an executive summary. Attorney clients may request an oral report to assess the culpability of their client before the information is commemorated in writing.[13] The information in the report usually follows a logical sequence from factual findings to opinions to recommendations: typically introduction and background, observations and factual information, analysis and discussion, opinion/conclusions, and recommendations.

If a preliminary determination and early report are needed based on the initial site visit, all assumptions and limitations due to incomplete data which formed the basis of the report must be described. However, it will be necessary to explain discrepancies if later investigations and evaluation of additional data lead to opinions which differ substantially from the preliminary opinions.

Depending on the client's needs, communication of investigation findings may also include group presentations, video representations, or development of models and court exhibits.

Repair Concepts

Depending on the nature of the nonperformance and/or failure, temporary repairs or permanent repairs (or both) will need to be developed.

Temporary Repairs. Temporary stabilization of facades is usually implemented on an emergency basis. Such repairs may involve netting, strapping, shoring, or anchoring unstable facade elements (Fig. 14.16). Removal of loose masonry or dislodged facade panels may be undertaken as emergency protection measures with little consideration for aesthetic impact. Sometimes sidewalk bridging is erected to protect the public; however, several months or even years may pass before permanent repairs are implemented. If the temporary repairs are to remain for a protracted period, damaged facade areas also need to be protected from the elements.

Permanent Repairs. Long-term repairs may include anchoring or removing and patching loose materials. Replacement of deteriorated or dislodged facade

FIGURE 14.16   Temporary netting protection for unstable terra cotta facades.

materials may involve restoring with similar materials or substitute materials. The decision to use replacement materials rather than to replicate in kind may be driven by economic or scheduling issues. Numerous issues, such as preservation requirements, structural limitations, and fire codes, may restrict the use of replacement materials.

WINDOWS AND CURTAIN WALLS

The investigation and diagnosis of problems with exterior walls are not complete without taking into consideration the window and curtain wall components of the wall. The following portion of this chapter addresses design issues, causes of failure, and methods of investigation, diagnosis, and testing for windows and curtain walls.

Fenestration Types and Materials

Windows may be fixed or operable, and they are often grouped in various combinations of units. Types of operable windows include single- and double-hung, casement, vertically or horizontally pivoted, sliding, and projected. Pivoted, casement, and projecting windows are commonly incorporated into metal-frame curtain wall systems, while hung, sliding units and smaller projecting windows are typically utilized as single units (punched openings), or grouped (ganged) together in horizontal or vertical bands.

Curtain wall systems typically consist of a metal framing system infilled with a combination of vision or spandrel panels (Fig. 14.17). Vision panels can be either fixed or operable, while spandrel panels are typically fixed and opaque and are used to visually obscure the interstitial floor spaces. Spandrel panels can be made of a variety of materials such as glass, metal, stone, and composite.

FIGURE 14.17 Three facade types are illustrated in this photograph. Reflected in the facade of the monolithic glass and aluminum curtain wall is a highly articulated curtain wall with natural stone infill. The traditional stone facade with punched window openings engages the monolithic curtain wall.

While most curtain walls are aluminum-framed, windows may be constructed of wood, steel, bronze, aluminum, or polyvinyl chloride (PVC). Wood windows are available clad in aluminum or vinyl for ease of maintenance. Wood provides good insulation and does not transmit heat or cold as readily as metal. Unprotected wood will decay after repeated wetting and drying, unless protected by coatings. Wood window components will also swell when subjected to moisture or with seasonal volume changes, affecting operability.

Steel windows are primarily found in industrial or other institutional buildings. Steel windows offer fire resistance, superior strength, and thin sight lines. Hollow metal frames are composed of sheet metal formed into frame and sash members, and they permit reduced weight of windows. Disadvantages of steel windows include the following: Metal conducts heat and cold readily, making the frames susceptible to condensation and frost formation; and corrosion of steel frames and sash affects window operation and can also break glass infill and damage surrounding construction (Fig. 14.18). Significant corrosion may become a structural issue, particularly with hollow metal frames.

Aluminum windows offer several advantages over wood and steel. Aluminum is resistant to corrosion, and although the metal has poor thermal characteristics, most aluminum windows manufactured today incorporate thermal breaks. Aluminum has lower strength characteristics than other metals and requires larger frame members than steel windows. Also, aluminum window components must be isolated from dissimilar metals such as steel.

Windows made of polyvinyl chloride or vinyl have only recently come into use, and they are primarily used in residential construction. These windows offer low cost, good thermal performance, and airtightness, but must be composed of relatively thick members. The material deteriorates in ultraviolet light and can warp as a result of environmental stresses. The long-term effects of temperature extremes and sunlight on vinyl windows are still unknown.

A variety of glass types are used in windows and curtain walls, including annealed, heat-strengthened, tempered, insulated, laminated, and other special glass types. Glass may be tinted or coated with reflective or thermal films. Glazing methods range from putties and sealants to rubber, neoprene, silicone, and PVC gaskets.

Common Causes of Failure

The most common problem associated with window and curtain wall systems is water leakage. Even small amounts of water can damage expensive interior finishes or occupant possessions and can render insulating materials within the wall ineffective. Chronic water leakage can also promote mold and mildew growth, creating potential health risks (Fig. 14.19). Structural components can be adversely affected by ongoing water leakage, causing corrosion.

The performance of windows and curtain walls is affected by original design, initial installation, and aging. Shortcomings or deficiencies in the original design

FIGURE 14.18 As seen in this example, one advantage of steel windows is their narrow sight lines. However, the steel components, although strong, are vulnerable to corrosion. This may lead to glass breakage and difficulty of operation.

such as lack of effective flashings or subsills, inadequate drainage from glazing pockets, inadequately engaged anchors, and poor-quality materials can result in significant problems. Problems with curtain walls and windows can also develop when the installation does not accommodate construction tolerances, when inadequate materials are substituted, when poor workmanship is used, when construction time frames are cut short, etc. Finally, the aging process takes its toll on exterior building components and compromises the effectiveness of various components. For example, weathering seals as well as internal seals can fail from

FIGURE 14.19 Finishes can often disguise as well as promote the growth of mold and mildew at locations of chronic water leakage associated with a window or curtain wall system.

exposure or movement, resulting in increased levels of water leakage and air infiltration. Steel components can corrode, expand, and cause distress such as glass breakage or structural inadequacy. Lack of proper maintenance can also affect performance and shorten the service life of a window or curtain wall installation.

Problems associated with glass typically include spontaneous breakage (tempered glass only) (Figs. 14.20 and 14.21), coating failures on spandrel glass, and failure of insulating glass units. Problems with paint coatings include peeling, chalking, and fading. Problems may also occur at structural connections. Exterior weathering gaskets can experience shrinkage, embrittlement from ultraviolet exposure, and softening. Weatherstripping can become torn, matted from debris, and compressed. Internal component failures include internal seal failures and shrinkage of thermal break material. Glazing compounds and sealants may fail through aging, improper installation, or use of a sealant that is not appropriate for the substrates to which it is applied. Distress can occur where inappropriate repairs were implemented in the past. For example, the inadvertent plugging of drainage holes with sealant may potentially result in water leakage (Fig. 14.22).

Design of Fenestration Systems

Before the problems and failures of a window or curtain wall system can be diagnosed, an understanding of the principles of window design is required. The long-term durability of windows and curtain walls depends on the structural adequacy

FIGURE 14.20 Typical example of spontaneous glass breakage. This phenomenon, caused by expansion of nickel sulfide inclusions within the glass, is only experienced in tempered glass.

of the system, its effectiveness in controlling water leakage and moisture migration, and its ability to resist unwanted air infiltration. In addition, the system must be able to accommodate thermal movements, loadings, and special movements such as seismic, interstory drift, and building slab deflections. To properly assess the condition of the window or curtain wall, the installation, components, and coatings must be evaluated, and the feasibility of implementing component repairs must be understood.

Structural Capacity and Selection of Design Pressures

Local wind loadings on windows and curtain walls are determined by calculating the design wind pressures for the building. Design wind pressures depend on wind

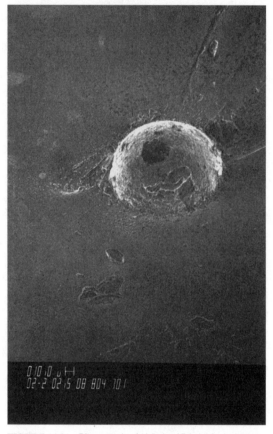

FIGURE 14.21 Photograph of nickel sulfide inclusions magnified 100,000 times by an electron microscope. These inclusions are introduced into the glass during fabrication and can expand when introduced to heat. This expansion can lead to spontaneous breakage in tempered glass.

speed, building type, shape, height, location, and size of the openings. The design wind pressure controls window characteristics such as depth and width of framing members and glass size. In addition, the American Architectural Manufacturers Association (AAMA) publications relate resistance to water penetration and air infiltration to the design pressure of the window and curtain wall system.

The American Society of Civil Engineers (ASCE) has established a standard, *Minimum Design Loads for Buildings and Other Structures,* ASCE 7-95,[14] a nationally recognized consensus standard that defines design wind pressures associated with curtain walls and windows as components of the building's exterior cladding. Design wind load calculations are different for the components and cladding than for the main structural framing system of the building.

FIGURE 14.22   Often poor or misdirected maintenance of window and curtain wall systems, such as the sealing of drainage holes shown here, can adversely affect the performance of the system.

Wind pressures are based upon recorded 50-year mean recurrence intervals. Peak wind gust speeds (3-s duration), from which design pressures are determined, vary for different geographic locations across the United States. The wind load values obtained from ASCE 7-95 define the wind pressures that a window or curtain wall must resist. The ASCE 7-95 standard has been adopted or referenced by many national building codes, such as Building Officials Congress of America (BOCA).[15] The forensic engineer must decide which standard or method of determining the design pressure is appropriate, as local building codes are often considered to be minimum requirements.

Once the design pressure has been determined, other resources can be referenced. The American National Standards Institute (ANSI) and AAMA have developed document ANSI/AAMA 101-93, *Voluntary Specification for Aluminum and Poly Vinyl Chloride (PVC) Prime Windows and Glass Doors.* This document includes primary performance requirements for various window types and grades, based upon calculated design pressures. This standard also references different grades of windows, such as R (residential), C (commercial), HC (heavy commercial), and AW (architectural windows), and performance criteria associated with each of these grades. Similar industry standards for wood windows have been adopted by the National Wood Window and Door Association (NWWDA) and are published in their standard NWWDA I.S.2-93. These reference standards have recently been combined as AAMA/NWWDA 101/I.S.2-97, entitled *Voluntary Specifications for Aluminum, Vinyl (PVC), and Wood Windows and Glass Doors.*[16]

Understanding Performance Criteria

The intended or mandated performance criteria for the window or curtain wall must be clearly identified.

Structural Performance.   Failures due to structural inadequacy of a window or curtain wall system are rare. However, it is important to understand the condition of the existing components of the system and how the window or curtain wall is anchored. For example, where existing or new windows are anchored to an existing window surround, the integrity of the surround must be verified (Fig. 14.23). Also, in areas where the window or curtain wall is a replacement unit, if components of the original system were incorporated in anchorage of a new window system, then the construction of these components must be understood and their structural integrity verified.

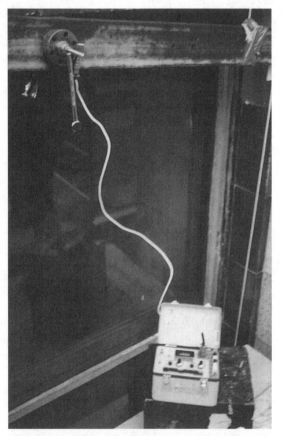

FIGURE 14.23   Structural integrity of the window and curtain wall anchorage can be verified in the field through the use of relatively unsophisticated and inexpensive techniques.

Water Penetration. Water leakage in window and curtain wall systems is often associated with framing joints within the system, or with joints between individual units that are linked together. A flashing or subsill is typically required to capture leakage at these locations and direct it back to the exterior. In some manufacturers' designs, the sill flashing or subsill must be penetrated with an anchor during installation of the window; even if covered with sealant, this fastener penetration is vulnerable to water leakage. End closures, or end dams, of sill members are also common water leakage sources. Mechanically attached end dams (properly sealed) and integral draining condensate gutters help capture water and prevent interior leakage.

Flashings are also commonly associated with water leakage. Typical problems with flashings include anchor penetrations; breaches, tears, or punctures at projecting building components such as anchor bolts; improper terminations; and poorly executed or nonexistent end dams. As flashings are typically not an integral component of the window and curtain wall system, special attention to their design and installation is required to ensure a successful installation. Three general categories of flashing materials include solderable, nonsolderable, and polymeric. Solderable flashing materials, including copper, lead-coated copper, and stainless steel, are durable and enable a watertight seal to be made at the splice joints. Nonsolderable flashing materials include aluminum; however, although aluminum can be welded, special detailing is required to create watertight connections, and aluminum is vulnerable to attack from cementitious products such as mortars. Traditional polymeric flashings include plastic or PVC materials, which are typically unreinforced and become brittle over time. Contemporary polymeric materials include rubberized asphalt sheets and ethylene propylene diene monomer (EPDM), which are flexible and less expensive than metal flashings, but are also less durable, more prone to puncture, and more difficult to form into proper end dams. Flashings need to be designed and installed to promote drainage. The flashing must be installed with a slope to the exterior to drain properly, and it must incorporate properly executed end dams to prevent unwanted water from migrating into adjacent construction. Where flashings are used at window corners and materials are overlapped, there must be an effective seal at the intersection.

AAMA provides recommendations for test pressures below which water leakage should not occur. These test pressures are based on the design pressure of the window and its classification. The designation *architectural* typically designates a higher-performing window. It is important for the designer to define water leakage in the project specification and to select the test pressure suitable for the specific project. Windows that meet a minimum water resistance test pressure of 6 to 8 psf typically do not have water leakage problems in the field if other details, some of which are discussed above, are properly addressed.

Air Infiltration. Occupants of buildings with older windows are often conscious of air infiltration associated with drafts. The air infiltration values obtained from

AAMA tests can be used for comparing window types, window manufacturers, unique features, etc. AAMA/NWWDA 101/I.S.2-97 provides criteria for maximum rates of air infiltration for different window types and classifications. The air infiltration performance of the new windows can differ significantly from that of the original windows, and this can affect heating, ventilation, and air conditioning performance. However, it is rare that windows or curtain walls are repaired or replaced due to poor air infiltration resistance performance alone.

Thermal Performance.   One of the important developments in aluminum window design is the incorporation of improvement features such as thermal breaks into the aluminum window extrusion. A thermal break is a material of lower thermal conductivity that separates the interior and exterior sections of the main framing members in order to minimize heat flow through the metal components. Thermal breaks are not incorporated into wood windows because wood is a much better insulator than metal. Thermal breaks are also typically not found in steel windows. Other types of windows and curtain walls are designated as thermally improved. In lieu of utilizing thermal breaks in their design, these thermally improved systems rely on nonconductive isolators, such as polyvinyl chloride, to separate interior and exterior components. Other thermally improved systems do not use any isolation but rather eliminate as much of the metal material as possible structurally, to minimize transfer of heat and cold.

One criterion used in assessing thermal performance of aluminum windows is the condensation resistance factor (CRF). The CRF is an especially valuable tool for assessing the thermal performance of aluminum windows because aluminum is a good conductor of heat and cold. AAMA 1503.1-98, *Voluntary Test Method for Thermal Transmittance and Condensation Resistance of Windows, Doors and Glazed Wall Sections,*[17] assists the designer in selecting an appropriate CRF number. The CRF compares inside and outside surface temperatures of the window and ambient air temperatures. By using design air temperatures and the dew point temperature, an appropriate CRF number can be identified.

The *U factor* is the overall thermal transmittance of a window, as determined by testing in accordance with AAMA 1503.1-88. As with condensation resistance, the *U* factor is more important for metal windows than for other window materials because of higher conductance values. The *U* values of various window manufacturers and types can be compared to obtain the most effective window type and construction for the particular application. As glass typically represents the greatest area of a window unit, *U* values of the glass infill are an important factor in the overall performance of the assembly.

Sealants

Sealants are an integral part of the window system and create the first line of defense against water infiltration. Important issues in sealant joint design are to recognize the sealant movement capabilities and preferred sealant configurations (Fig. 14.24). Sealant must also have a proper surface with which to bond. To ensure that the sealant can accommodate the required tolerances, existing conditions should be carefully surveyed to determine the size of joints to be sealed. Construction tolerances should be carefully considered to provide proper perimeter joint widths.

The selection of sealants for aluminum windows is dependent on the required bonding capacity and the adjoining substrates. Silicone sealants typically have a better bond to metal than urethanes, and also provide excellent ultraviolet resistance, but may cause staining problems with adjacent substrates. Urethane sealants can have good bond and less tendency to stain, but they are typically less durable than silicones. New products such as "clean" or surface-modified silicone sealant may help to overcome the problem with staining; however, as these are relatively new products, their durability and performance have not been tested by time.

Window and Curtain Wall Investigation Methodology

Document Review. As with other building envelope components, investigation of windows and curtain walls begins with a review of available original drawings and specifications. In addition, manufacturer's literature, shop drawings, and submittals

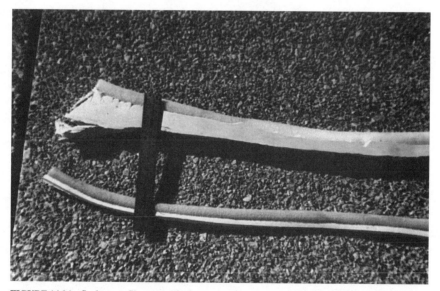

FIGURE 14.24 Sealant profiles are critical to proper long-term performance. These two examples of sealant removed from a building show the difference between properly installed sealant with a consistent profile (bottom) and an improperly installed section of sealant with a disproportionate depth to width ratio (top).

should be reviewed if available. These documents provide information on construction and concealed conditions, although close-up investigation and possibly inspection openings are usually required to confirm existing construction. Repair documents for the building are useful as they indicate the history of problems with the windows or curtain wall over time. The type, time, frequency of occurrence, and location of problems such as water leakage should also be researched through service records and other building maintenance documents.

Visual Condition Survey. An overall visual survey of the building windows and curtain wall should be performed to provide a general assessment of existing conditions, identify potential causes of the reported problems, determine the extent of these conditions, and potentially identify additional unrecorded problems. During these observations, the types and locations of distress should be recorded. An interior visual survey should be performed, as damage to interior finishes is a good indicator of past or ongoing water leakage.

Close-up Examination. Close-up visual examination of windows and curtain wall areas should be performed at selected representative locations. These examinations will typically require the use of a personnel lift, swingstage, or building window washing equipment for proper access. The inspection should determine if the window construction matches the original design documents and should address all window components and finishes. The operability of windows can be checked. Locations of water leakage or damage can be viewed. The type and amount of maintenance or repairs, such as sealant applications, should be documented, and their apparent success noted. Information gathered during the survey of window and curtain wall elements should be reviewed in conjunction with the survey of conditions on other wall and roof elements, to confirm the source of the problems observed.

During these close-up exterior examinations, deglazing or partial disassembly of a window or portion of the curtain wall can be performed, with the assistance of a window contractor or glazier, to reveal concealed conditions. Inspection openings can be performed in areas where the wall has already been damaged by water leakage and will require repair. Disassembly can also expose underlying conditions and reveal how a window system can be taken apart and reassembled to assist in repair design (Fig. 14.25).

A general checklist of items to be addressed in the close-up visual examination follows. This list should be adjusted to meet the requirements of the specific system examined.

Interior Finishes

• Are there signs of previous water leakage, such as damaged gypsum board or plaster, peeling wall treatments (paint, vinyl, or other wall coverings), mold and mildew, or stained or damaged floor and ceiling finishes?

FIGURE 14.25   As part of a close-up examination of a window or curtain wall, disassembly of the system may be required to expose underlying conditions and reveal how the system can be taken apart, repaired, and reassembled.

Exterior Sealants

- Has cohesive failure occurred?
- Has adhesive failure occurred?
- What is the sealant consistency?
  - Is the sealant resilient?
  - Is the sealant hard or nonpliable?
  - Is the sealant gummy or tacky?
  - Is there craze cracking in the sealant?
  - Has migration to adjacent materials occurred?

Window/Curtain Wall System

- What is the condition of the finish?

- Are drainage provisions clear and unblocked?
- How are splice joints detailed and installed (subsill, flashing, receptors, etc.)?
- Are there gaps in metal to metal joinery?

Gaskets

- Are gaskets well set?
- Has shrinkage occurred at gasket corners?
- Are corners sealed with sealant?
- Are corners molded (vulcanized)?
- Do gaps exist at corners?
- Are gaskets resilient?
- Are gaskets brittle or hard?
- Do gaskets have surface cracks?
- Is gasket compression at glass interface exhibiting consistent pressure?

Operable Vents

- Is vent operation smooth or difficult?
- Is the vent out of square or warped?
- What is the condition of the vent weatherstripping?
- What is the condition of the vent hardware: latches, hinges, balances (hung windows)?

Glass/Infill Panels

- What is the surface condition of the infill panel (signs of etching, staining, loss of finish, or other deterioration)?
- What is the condition of the insulated glazing (IG) units? Identify all failed (fogged) units.
- Are there cracked or broken infill panels?

Disassembly

- What is the condition of splices in subsills or sill flashing?
- Are there end dams? What is their condition relative to resisting water leakage?
- Are all fasteners in the subsill or sill flashings properly sealed?
- Has shrinkage occurred in the thermal breaks?
- Are there holes or voids in the system that would be potential sources of water leakage?

Field Testing.   Field testing may be required to fully understand how the curtain wall or window system performs under various conditions. Testing helps to evaluate existing conditions and performance such as fastener and anchor weaknesses and resistance to water leakage and air infiltration. For example, water leakage problems can be studied to determine how widespread the problem is, as well as to identify the significant features that are leading to the leakage. Inspection openings may need to be made from the interior and/or exterior of the building to expose underlying wall elements and potential water leakage paths, and to determine the effects of past leakage.

Structural Testing. Although there are no published standards for structural performance testing of windows and curtain walls in the field, laboratory test methods of ASTM E 330-97e1, *Standard Test Method for Structural Performance of Exterior Windows, Curtain Walls, and Doors by Uniform Static Air Pressure Difference*,[18] can be adapted for field use. This test involves the application of a positive or negative pressure to the interior and exterior of the window and curtain wall system. The test pressure is related to recorded wind speeds of the region where the building is located. The actual performance of the window is determined by measuring temporary and permanent deflections in the window frame during the test. Separate components of the window or curtain wall system such as anchorage can also be tested for structural adequacy in the field.

Water Penetration Testing. Field tests to evaluate water resistance performance include ASTM E 1105-96, *Standard Test Method for Field Determination of Water Penetration of Installed Exterior Windows, Curtain Walls, and Doors by Uniform and Cyclic Static Air Pressure Difference*[19]; AAMA 501.1-94, *Standard Test Method for Exterior Windows, Curtain Walls, and Doors for Water Penetration Using Dynamic Pressure*[20] (Fig. 14.26); AAMA 501.2-94, *Field Check of Metal Storefronts, Curtain Walls, and Sloped Glazing Systems for Water Leakage*[21]; and AAMA 501.3-94, *Field Check of Water and Air Leakage through Installed Exterior Windows, Curtain Walls, and Doors by Uniform Air Pressure Difference.*[22] ASTM E 1105 and AAMA 501.3 are similar and involve the application of a uniform spray of water at the exterior while a static air pressure difference is induced across the test specimen, during which the interior is monitored for water leakage. As part of this test procedure, a chamber must be constructed on either the interior or exterior of the test specimen, so that an air pressure difference can be induced across the plane of the specimen during the test (Figs. 14.27 and 14.28). AAMA 501.2 uses a water spray from a calibrated nozzle to test nonmoving joints within a window, door, or curtain wall assembly while the interior of the test specimen is monitored for water leakage during the test period (Fig. 14.29). The forensic engineer should be well acquainted with these test methods and determine which method is most suitable for the project.

In addition to the standardized test methods outlined above, other test methods may be utilized to determine sources of water penetration where unique conditions or systems are encountered. One such test method is fire hose testing. Using a $1\frac{1}{2}$-in-diameter hose and nozzle connected to a building fire suppression riser, this test method is a very effective tool when faced with difficult curtain wall geometries such as barrel vaults, sloped glazing, and skylights (Fig. 14.30). With this testing,

FIGURE 14.26 Example of water penetration testing using dynamic pressure (supplied by a modified aircraft engine). This test method is typically restricted to laboratory mockup testing.

once water leakage develops, the source can be pinpointed by nozzle testing in accordance with AAMA 501.2.

Materials Testing. The presence of hazardous materials also needs to be taken into consideration during the investigation of windows and curtain walls. For example, older wood and steel windows may incorporate paints containing lead or other toxic metals that require special abatement, handling, and disposal for either repair or replacement. Sealants used with window and curtain wall systems may also contain hazardous materials such as asbestos fibers or polychlorinated biphenyls (PCBs) that require special abatement and disposal. These materials should be tested for the presence of hazardous components prior to implementing a repair or replacement program.

Another special issue is diagnosis of failures related to modern coatings and finishes. In particular, aluminum windows and curtain walls may use anodized, mill finish, or painted coatings. Each finish type has its own durability and repair issues and its own requirements for sealant compatibility. Laboratory analysis of existing coatings may be required to determine the type of coating, evaluate the causes of failure, and make appropriate repair recommendations.

Repairs

The information gathered through investigation and diagnosis is used to assess the existing performance of a window or curtain wall system and to develop the design for

FIGURE 14.27 Example of field water penetration testing (ASTM E 1105 test method).

repair or replacement. In determining whether to repair or replace windows or a curtain wall, performance, cost, and aesthetics need to be evaluated. The use of mockups of proposed systems provides a means to evaluate performance, constructibility, and suitability, as well as aesthetics, and is often invaluable in assisting in the selection of alternative approaches. Special consideration is required if the building is an historic structure. The Secretary of the Interior's *Standards for Rehabilitation,*[23] published by the National Park Service, provides a guide to evaluating repair measures for historic structures. A guiding principle of the standards is that existing historic materials should be retained and repaired, rather than replaced, wherever possible.

The choice of methods to repair or replace can be determined by properly evaluating the myriad solutions with an understanding of the types of problems balanced by the projected costs and the building owner's requirements. Only by fully recognizing the issues can an appropriate, cost-effective decision be reached.

FIGURE 14.28 The ASTM E 1105 test can be performed with an interior or exterior chamber, and the test area can vary in size from small (as shown in the previous figure) to very large (as shown here). The test shown, using an exterior chamber, covered an area 24 ft × 42 ft in size.

FIGURE 14.29 Joints in window and curtain walls can be tested for resistance to water leakage, including the AAMA 501.2 nozzle test method illustrated here.

FIGURE 14.30 Nonstandard test methods, such as fire hose test, can be helpful when evaluating skylights and unique conditions or structures. However, such testing should be followed by recognized standard test methods to verify and pinpoint sources of water leakage.

ACKNOWLEDGMENT

Deborah Slaton and Dennis Johnson, both of Wiss, Janney, Elstner Associates, substantially contributed to preparing and editing this chapter.

REFERENCES

1. Michael D. Lewis, *Modern Stone Cladding,* American Society for Testing and Materials, Philadelphia, 1995.
2. Glenn Bell, "Evaluation of Brick Veneer/Stud Walls, Part 2," *Proceedings of the Third North American Masonry Conference,* Construction Research Center, Civil Engineering Department, University of Texas at Austin, 1985.

3. David H. NiCastro, *Failure Mechanisms,* American Society of Civil Engineers, New York, 1997.

4. Kimball J. Beasley, "Masonry Cladding Stress Failures in Older Buildings," *Journal of Performance of Constructed Facilities,* American Society of Civil Engineers, New York, November 1988.

5. C. Wildhalm, E. Tschegg, and W. Eppensteiner, "Acoustic Emissions and Anisotropic Expansion When Heating Marble," *Journal of Performance of Constructed Facilities,* American Society of Civil Engineers, New York, February 1997.

6. Kimball J. Beasley, "Trouble Prone Architectural Features: Masonry Walls Likely to Leak," *The Construction Specifier,* October 1997.

7. Kimball J. Beasley, "Contemporary Skin Barrier Wall Design and Water Leakage," *The Construction Specifier,* May 1998.

8. Kimball J. Beasley, "Failure Investigation," *The Construction Specifier,* April 1998.

9. Kimball J. Beasley, Howard Greenspan, James O'Kon, and Joseph Ward, *Failure Investigation,* American Society of Civil Engineers, New York, 1989.

10. ASTM C856-95, *Standard Practice for Petrographic Examination of Hardened Concrete,* American Society for Testing and Materials, West Conshohocken, PA, 1995.

11. ASTM C1218/C1218M-97, *Standard Test Method for Water-Soluble Chloride in Mortar and Concrete,* American Society for Testing and Materials, West Conshohocken, PA, 1997.

12. ASTM E447-92, *Standard Test Method for Compressive Strength of Masonry Prisms,* American Society for Testing and Materials, West Conshohocken, PA, 1992.

13. Donald V. Roberts, *Expert,* American Society of Forensic Engineers, Silver Spring, MD, 1995.

14. *Minimum Design Loads for Buildings and Other Structures,* ASCE 7-95. American Society of Civil Engineers, New York, 1996.

15. *The BOCA National Building Code,* Building Officials and Code Administrators International, Inc., Country Club Hills, IL, 1996.

16. AAMA/NWWDA 101/I.S.2-97, *Voluntary Specifications for Aluminum, Vinyl (PVC) and Wood Windows and Glass Doors,* American Architectural Manufacturers Association/National Wood Window and Door Association, 1997.

17. AAMA 1503.1-98, *Voluntary Test Method for Thermal Transmittance and Condensation Resistance of Windows, Doors, and Glazed Wall Sections,* American Architectural Manufacturers Association, Schaumburg, IL, 1998.

18. ASTM E 330-97e1, *Standard Test Method for Structural Performance of Exterior Windows, Curtain Walls, and Doors by Uniform Static Air Pressure Difference,* American Society for Testing and Materials, West Conshohocken, PA, 1997.

19. ASTM E 1105-96, *Standard Test Method for Field Determination of Water Penetration of Installed Exterior Windows, Curtain Walls, and Doors by Uniform and Cyclic Static Air Pressure Difference,* American Society for Testing and Materials, West Conshohocken, West Conshohocken, PA, 1996.

20. "AAMA 501.1-94, Standard Test Method for Exterior Windows, Curtain Walls and Doors for Water Penetration Using Dynamic Pressure," *Methods of Test for Exterior Walls: Publication No. AAMA 501-94,* American Architectural Manufacturers Association Technical Information Center, Palatine, IL, 1994.

21. "AAMA 501.2-94, Field Check of Metal Storefronts, Curtain Walls and Sloped Glazing Systems for Water Leakage," *Methods of Test for Exterior Walls: Publication No. AAMA 501-94,* American Architectural Manufacturers Association Technical Information Center, Palatine, IL, 1994.

22. "AAMA 501.3-94, Field Check of Water and Air Leakage through Installed Exterior Windows, Curtain Walls and Doors by Uniform Air Pressure Difference," *Methods of Test for Exterior Walls: Publication No. AAMA 501-94,* American Architectural Manufacturers Association Technical Information Center, Palatine, IL, 1994.

23. *Secretary of the Interior's Standards for Rehabilitation and Guidelines for Rehabilitating Historic Structures,* Department of the Interior, National Park Service, Preservation Assistance Division, Washington, revised 1992.

CHAPTER 15
TIMBER STRUCTURES

Donald W. Neal, P.E.

ENGINEERING PROPERTIES OF WOOD

Wood and brick and stone have been the construction materials of choice since antiquity. Development of wood as an engineered material based upon known design properties, rather than rules of thumb and artisans' judgment, is more recent. The 20th century has seen virtually all this development with an accelerating pace toward the end of the century.

Three Distinct Grain Orientations. Wood fibers are formed in the living tree with their long dimension approximately parallel to the axis of the tree trunk. Wood is classified as anisotropic in that it has distinct and different mechanical properties in the three major axes. (See Fig. 15.1.)

Longitudinal	Parallel to grain
Radial	Normal to annual rings and perpendicular to grain
Tangential	Tangent to annual rings and perpendicular to grain

Wood grain direction is the wood fiber orientation. For engineering purposes, design properties are referred to as parallel or perpendicular to the grain. This means *approximately* parallel or perpendicular to the faces of finished lumber or timbers. The wood fiber is not precisely parallel or perpendicular to the faces of finished lumber because of natural growth characteristics or sawmill tolerances. The angle between wood fiber orientation and the faces of finished lumber is termed the *slope of grain,* and its impact upon strength and stiffness is addressed in the lumber-grading rules. The annual rings are formed radially owing to wood density differences in the growth seasons. In a finished piece of lumber, the orientation of annual ring lines is not necessarily parallel to the wood fiber or grain orientation. Checking that develops as wood dries will be parallel to the grain orientation.

Anyone who has split firewood understands that wood is anisotropic, not isotropic, like many other materials. Since the difference between radial and tangential annual ring orientation in a given piece of lumber is normally random and the difference in properties between radial and tangential orientation is relatively

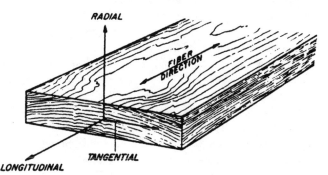

FIGURE 15.1 The three principal axes of wood with respect to grain direction and growth rings. Longitudinal: parallel to grain; radial: normal to annual rings and perpendicular to grain; tangential: tangent to annual rings and perpendicular to grain. (From *Wood Handbook*, USDA Forest Service.)

small, the engineer needs only to consider properties perpendicular or parallel to the grain for design purposes. Distinctly different properties between perpendicular and parallel to the grain include the modulus of elasticity (MOE), shear, tension, compression, and dimensional change due to wood moisture content variation.

Establishing Design Values.   Traditionally the basic allowable stress design (ASD) values for lumber and timbers have been determined per the clear-wood procedure. Small, clear, straight-grained specimens of a given species are tested in bending, tension parallel to grain and compression parallel to grain in sufficient quantity for statistical analysis. A series of factors are then applied which include adjustment for size effect, moisture content, safety factor, a strength ratio between the value for clear wood and the grade for which a basic allowable stress is desired, and other adjustment factors where applicable.

Basic allowable stress design values for solid sawn timbers are still established using the clear-wood procedure. Following an extensive testing program, allowable design values for dimension lumber (nominal 2- to 4-in thickness) are now established by the in-grade procedure. This program consisted of more than 70,000 pieces of full-sized lumber from production runs tested in bending, tension and compression parallel to grain, and allowable design properties subsequently determined per American Society for Testing and Materials (ASTM) procedures. This large data set was used to develop a model to assign design values for North American dimension lumber. Tabular stresses resulting from the in-grade program reflect actual lumber in the marketplace rather than statistical theory. The program also addressed the current status of the material source from large log to small log mills and old growth to second-growth resource which has changed over time. The 1991 National Design Specification[1] (NDS) first presented allowable dimension lumber stresses based upon the in-grade procedure.

Over the past several years, industry trade and professional associations have worked to produce a *Load Resistance Factor Design (LRFD) Manual of Wood Construction,* coordinated by the American Forest and Paper Association/American Wood Council. The manual is essentially an LRFD version of the National Design Specification. Evolution of concrete design from ASD to ultimate strength design occurred over a considerable period, and evolution of steel design from ASD to LRFD is ongoing. Acceptance of LRFD for wood construction by code jurisdictions and the design community is not yet determined.

Glulam timber is a sandwich of bonded laminates whose design properties are dependent upon the properties of these component laminates. Since most glulam is bonded from dimension lumber sizes, the basic design values were initially those of its dimension lumber laminates. In the late 1960s, an ongoing testing program was initiated by the American Institute of Timber Construction and the Forest Products Laboratory, using full-sized glulam members. Basic design values in bending and tension were back-calculated from these test data, causing a reduction in allowable stresses. The current design procedure incorporating the back-calculated test results is based upon statistical procedures in accordance with ASTM D 3737.[2] A procedure is published by the American Institute of Timber Construction (AITC) in AITC-500,[3] which is based upon ASTM D 3737. This procedure permits computation of basic allowable design values for virtually any combination of laminates within a glulam member. While both ASTM D 3737 and AITC-500 documents are available, the computation of allowable design values using this procedure is both time-consuming and tedious. These computations have been computerized by the trade associations servicing the glued laminated timber industry.

Bending. A majority of timber structural members are used primarily in bending, so bending is often considered the defining design property. Basic bending stress is often used to label the grade for both solid sawn and glulam members. Within the elastic range, the flexural stress block is considered to be a straight line, and extreme fiber bending stresses are calculated as M_C/I. The *modulus of rupture* (MOR), by definition, is the value of M_C/I calculated using the bending moment M at ultimate load. The MOR is not the maximum fiber stress at failure since the stress block beyond the elastic range is not a straight line. However, the MOR is a useful index and is often used for test comparisons.

Tension Parallel to Grain. Until recent years, test equipment was not readily available to pull full-sized pieces of lumber to failure in tension, so only small strip-tension tests were used. Older tabulated allowable design values for both solid sawn timbers and glulam grouped bending and tension parallel to grain together on the theory that pure tension stress would behave the same as the tension portion of bending stress. The 1968 NDS was the first to provide separate columns of allowables with different design values for bending and tension.

Tension Perpendicular to Grain. Tension perpendicular to grain, also called *cross-grain tension,* describes stress perpendicular to the wood fiber. This may result from an applied gravity load at the lower edge of a member, or from a lateral load such as that applied to a ledger. When tension perpendicular to grain is induced by an increase in radius, straightening the arc of a curved beam, it is commonly termed *radial* tension.

Cross-grain tension is the property of timber least understood among design professionals. Cross-grain tension is not presently tabulated in allowable design tables. Allowable values for radial tension are covered in the body of NDS and in AITC specification 117.[4] The basic radial tension allowable stress is 15 lb/in^2 for Douglas fir-larch, Douglas fir-south, hem-fir, western woods, and Canadian softwood species subjected to gravity loading. The low value of 15 lb/in^2 was assigned on the basis of judgment and field experience. The allowable radial tension stress has historically been one-third of the allowable horizontal shear stress for the above species subjected to lateral loading and for southern pine subjected to all types of loading. (See Case Study 11, Lucky Strike Lanes, and Case Study 15, Hood River Valley High School Theater.)

Compression Parallel to Grain (Short Compression). This is termed precisely *crushing strength* under the provisions of ASTM Standard D 198[5] and is defined as the maximum stress sustained in compression parallel to the grain by a specimen having a ratio of length to least dimension of less than 11. Compression parallel to grain tests are often possible to obtain during forensic evaluation, as a relatively small test specimen is required and the test setup is simple. From this test compressive MOE, proportional limit and ultimate compression data may be obtained. While useful as comparative data in evaluation, allowable stresses in compression parallel to grain are of limited value to the design engineer as most compression member capacity is limited by buckling.

Buckling (Long Compression). Buckling strength of timber members in compression is defined by the Euler critical buckling stress and the slenderness ratio l/d, where l is the distance between points of lateral support and d is least cross-sectional dimension. From the 1950s until the 1977 NDS, the allowable column stress was the lesser of the crushing strength or the following Euler buckling equation, which is adjusted for factor of safety:

$$F_c = \frac{0.3\,E}{(l/d)^2}$$

where E = modulus of elasticity (MOE). From the 1977 NDS until the 1991 NDS, columns were classified as short, intermediate, and long.

Short columns	Columns with an l/d ratio of 11 or less used an allowable stress based upon crushing strength.
Long columns	Columns with an l/d ratio greater than a K factor, defined in the specification, used the adjusted Euler buckling stress design equation.
Intermediate columns	Columns with an l/d ratio between 11 and K used a formula representing interaction between crushing and the adjusted Euler buckling stress design equation.

The 1991 NDS incorporated the single continuous column formula, often referred to as the *Ylinen formula,* for all ranges of slenderness ratio with interaction between crushing and Euler buckling failure modes. The continuous column formula is a refinement of the Euler equation with different input constants dependent upon the type of timber member (sawn lumber, glulam, etc.)

$$F_c' = F_c^* \, C_p$$

$$= F_c^* \left[\frac{1 + F_{CE}/F_c^*}{2c} - \sqrt{\left(\frac{1 + F_{CE}/F_c^*}{2c} \right)^2 - \frac{F_{CE}/F_c^*}{c}} \right]$$

where F_C^* = tabulated compression design value multiplied by all applicable
adjustment factors except C_p

F_{CE} = critical buckling design value for compression members

$$= \frac{K_{CE} E'}{(l_e/d)^2}$$

K_{CE} = Euler buckling coefficient for columns
   = 0.3 for sawn lumber
   = 0.418 for glulam

c = 0.8 for sawn lumber
   = 0.9 for glulam

l_e = effective column length

Compression Perpendicular to Grain.   Compression perpendicular to the grain is used primarily to size the required bearing area of beams over supports or under concentrated loads. Failure in compression perpendicular to the grain cannot be as well defined as with other modes of failure. Excessive compression perpendicular to grain loading causes wood cells to collapse and crush but rarely causes member collapse or catastrophic failure. Prior to the 1982 NDS, allowable stresses were based upon a proportional limit approach. Starting with the 1982 NDS, the basis for the allowable design value in compression perpendicular to the grain was revised and now is tabulated as the mean stress at a stated deformation. Deformation limits of 0.04 and 0.02 in are commonly used. The time-dependent load duration factor C_D is not applicable to a property defined by the deformation limit and is not used with compression perpendicular to grain calculations.

Shear.   Tabulated allowable shear stresses are for the shear plane parallel to the faces of finished lumber and approximately parallel to wood fiber orientation. Since most timber members are beams oriented horizontally, this is commonly termed *horizontal shear.* For the most part, allowable shear stress is unchanged between grades of a given specie. Data obtained by shear testing of glulam per ASTM D 198 resulted in increased allowable shear stresses being adopted in 1994 and additional increases in 1998. The 1994 revisions are incorporated in the 1997 NDS, and both 1994 and 1998 revisions are available as addenda to AITC Specification 117 *Design.* It may be some time before all these revisions find their way to the structural design community by way of incorporation into the model building codes.

Stiffness (MOE).   *Young's modulus,* or the modulus of elasticity (MOE), is the slope of the stress-strain curve and may be measured in the testing laboratory when members are loaded in flexure or axial tension or compression. The tabulated MOE included in tables of allowable design stresses is an average value. MOE in bending is included with all design property tables for dimension lumber, timbers, and glulam. Glulam design tables include MOE in bending for both axes of the laminations, and MOE in axial loading. Machine stress-rated (MSR) grades of dimension lumber have

MOE measured for each piece at the point of manufacture. The MOE rating and an accompanying allowable bending stress are used for member identification, and tabular values are listed in table 4C of the NDS Supplement.

CODES, SPECIFICATIONS, STANDARDS, AND REFERENCE PUBLICATIONS

Model Building Codes. The three model U.S. building codes—*UBC, BOCA,* and *Standard*—are scheduled for merger in the near future. Each city, county, or state jurisdiction selects and adopts a given code as of a given date. The code typically incorporates specifications already developed, such as the NDS, but differences may exist on key points. For example, the 1994 UBC adopted the 1991 NDS except for a difference in the load duration factor C_D for lateral wind loading. It is common for a given jurisdiction to add or revise portions of the model code, tailoring it to specific climatic or site conditions such as permafrost, hurricanes, expansive soils, and snow. It is imperative in forensic evaluation to know the specific code and code revisions that a structure must be evaluated against. The building code is the legal document for structural compliance, and if differences exist between the code and other specifications or standards, the code prevails. The code is a minimum standard, and the prudent engineer may incorporate more conservative criteria of which he/she has knowledge, if those criteria have not yet been adopted into the code.

National Design Specification (NDS). The National Design Specification for Wood Construction may be obtained from the American Forest & Paper Association at 1111 19th Street N.W., 7th floor, Washington DC 20036. This is the source document for design with solid sawn timber and its connections. It was first published during World War II and was periodically updated with editions in 1944, 1957, 1960, 1962, 1968, 1971, 1973, 1977, 1982, 1986, 1991, and 1997. The main volume contains design provisions and equations for design of solid sawn and glulam members, plus provisions and design allowables for connections. The Supplement contains section properties and allowable design values for both solid sawn and glulam members. The Commentary provides a historical overview and explanation behind the specification provisions.

AITC Standards. American Institute of Timber Construction (AITC) [at 7012 S. Revere Parkway #140, Englewood, CO 80112] publishes the following standards, designated by AITC number and title:

104   *Typical Construction Details*

108   *Standard for Heavy Timber Construction*

109   *Standard for Preservative Treatment of Structural Glued Laminated Timber*

110	*Standard Appearance Grades for Structural Glued Laminated Timber*
111	*Recommended Practice for Protection of Structural Glued Laminated Timber During Transit, Storage and Erection*
112	*Standard for Tongue-and-Groove Heavy Timber Roof Decking*
113	*Standard for Dimensions of Glued Laminated Structural Members*
114	*Structural Glued Laminated Timbers for Electric Utility Framing and Crossarms*
117	*Standard Specifications for Structural Glued Laminated Timber of Softwood Species*
119	*Standard Specifications for Hardwood Glued Laminated Timber*

All the standards are potentially valuable to the forensic engineer. The most commonly used of the standards, and the source document for design with softwood glulam timber, is Specification 117, *Design,* which provides allowable design values and design examples. The latest edition was in 1993 with addenda in 1994 and 1998. The 117 specification is issued in two documents, Design and Manufacturing. The manufacturing document showing lamstock grade requirements and layup zones for the various glulam combinations is of interest primarily to those in glulam manufacture.

AITC Timber Construction Manual (TCM). The AITC *Timber Construction Manual*[6] is published by John Wiley & Sons, Inc. At the time of this writing the latest volume is the 1994 fourth edition, which was preceded by editions in 1966, 1974, and 1985.

ANSI/AITC Standard 190.1 and AITC 200-92 Inspection Manual. ANSI/AITC Standard 190.1[7] for wood products, *Structural Glued Laminated Timber,* is a consensus standard concerned primarily with the nuts and bolts of glulam manufacture. The standard is revised periodically, the current edition being 1992. The AITC 200, *Inspection Manual,*[8] available from the same source, describes all the tests and procedures for qualification, production, and testing of glulam timber, and is based upon ANSI/AITC 190.1.

Grading Rules—Lumber and Timber. Rules-writing agencies have evolved which develop lumber grades for specific species within a geographic area. Lumber mills producing graded lumber join an appropriate grading agency, and their products carry that agency's stamp.

Wood Handbook: Wood as an Engineering Material. The *Wood Handbook*[9] is available from Forest Products Society at 2801 Marshall Court, Madison, WI 53705. The handbook contains a wealth of technical data on wood not found elsewhere. The 1999 edition was preceded by editions in 1935, 1955, 1974, and 1987, all by the U.S. Government Printing Office. The 1999 edition is published by the Forest Products Society.

Evaluation, Maintenance, and Upgrading of Wood Structures. The American Society of Civil Engineers (ASCE) published this in 1982.

Western Woods Use Book. This is published by Western Wood Products Association (WWPA) in 1996.

STRUCTURAL TIMBER CHARACTERISTICS AND STRESS ADJUSTMENTS

The basic design strengths in structural timber are influenced by numerous factors which include natural growth characteristics, wood moisture content, temperature, duration of design load, size/volume effect, loading orientation, and lateral stability. Adjustment factors have been developed to adjust the basic tabular design stresses for these conditions when applicable. (See Table 15.1.)

Organic Material—Moisture Content. Wood is a natural-growth organic material with a cellular structure, which retains water. Water is a living tree's best friend and lumber products' worst enemy. Wood moisture content is expressed as a

TABLE 15.1 Applicability of Adjustment Factors

	Load duration factor	Wet-service factor	Temperature factor	Beam stability factor[a]	Size factor[b]	Volume factor[a, c]	Flat-use factor[d]
$F_b' = F_b$	C_D	C_M	C_t	C_L	C_F	C_V	C_{fu}
$F_t' = F_t$	C_D	C_M	C_t	—	C_F	—	—
$F_v' = F_v$	C_D	C_M	C_t	—	—	—	—
$F_{c\perp}' = F_{c\perp}$	—	C_M	C_t	—	—	—	—
$F_c' = F_c$	C_D	C_M	C_t	—	C_F	—	—
$E' = E$	—	C_M	C_t	—	—	—	—
$F_g' = F_g$	C_D	—	C_t	—	—	—	—

[a]The beam stability factor C_L shall not apply simultaneously with the volume factor C_v for glued laminated timber bending members. Therefore the lesser of these adjustment factors shall apply.
[b]The size factor C_F shall apply only to visually graded sawn lumber members and to round timber bending members.
[c]The volume factor C_v shall apply only to glued laminated timber bending members.
[d]The flat-use factor C_{fu} shall apply only to dimension lumber bending members 2 to 4 in (nominal) thick and to glued laminated timber bending members.
[e]The repetitive-member factor C_r shall apply only to dimension lumber bending members 2 to 4 in thick.

weight percentage of the water present to the dry weight of wood. Water is retained in the cell walls to saturation, and additional free water may be retained within the cell cavity. The fiber saturation point of most wood species occurs in the middle 20 percent range with Douglas fir about average at 25 to 26 percent. Additional moisture above the fiber saturation point may be retained as free water within the cells. Since water softens the cellular wall, strength and stiffness increase as moisture content is reduced below the fiber saturation point. Design values for solid sawn softwood lumber are based upon wood moisture content of 15 percent described as an average of 19 percent or below, with a wet-service factor C_M reduction applied where moisture content will exceed 19 percent. Glulam is usually produced in a moisture content range of 12 to 15 percent. Design values for glulam are based upon wood moisture content of 12 percent with a wet-service factor C_M reduction applied where moisture content will exceed 16 percent.

Wood in use and not subject to free water will come to equilibrium at a moisture content as a function of temperature and humidity. An oven-dry laboratory test in which all moisture is driven off can accurately determine the weight of water in a specimen, from which the wood moisture content may then be calculated. A simpler but not quite so precise method employs an electric resistance wood moisture meter. A moisture meter and probe, such as the G-30 by Delmhorst Instrument Co., should be in the forensic engineer's tool kit. Adjustments for specie and temperature are provided by the instrument supplier. Wood moisture content in the higher ranges provides an environment favorable to wood-eating

Incising factor	Repetitive-member factor[e]	Curvature factor[f]	Form factor	Column stability factor	Shear stress factor[g]	Buckling stiffness factor[h]	Bearing area factor
C_i	C_r	C_c	C_f	—	—	—	—
C_i	—	—	—	—	—	—	—
C_i	—	—	—	—	C_H	—	—
C_i	—	—	—	—	—	—	C_b
C_i	—	—	—	C_P	—	—	—
C_i	—	—	—	—	—	C_T	—
—	—	—	—	—	—	—	—

The curvature factor C_c shall apply only to curved portions of glued laminated timber bending members.
[g]Shear design values parallel to grain F_v for sawn lumber members shall be permitted to be multiplied by the shear stress factors C_H.
[h]The buckling stiffness factor C_T shall apply only to 2-in × 4-in or smaller sawn lumber truss compression chords subjected to combined flexure and axial compression when $3/8$-in or thicker plywood sheathing is nailed to the narrow face.
Source: American Forest & Paper Association, Washington, D.C.

organisms, fungi, termites, etc. A softwood moisture content of 20 percent is considered the approximate threshold at which primitive forms of life that cause decay become active. Many of the problems a forensic engineer is asked to investigate with wood structures are moisture-related.

Variability.   All structural materials have characteristic variability from one member to another. Wood has natural growth characteristics that contribute to its variability. Allowable design stresses are based upon adjustments for safety factor and load duration that are applied to 5th percentile strength values, thus accounting for the variability.

Glulam may have an allowable bending stress nearly double that of solid sawn lumber of the same species. By dispersion of defects and reforming the wood using graded laminates, the variability of the end product is reduced. Structural members of smaller glued veneer-size laminates, such as laminated veneer lumber (LVL) and parallel-strand lumber (PSL), further reduce variability. The coefficient of variation (COV) for MOE of wood products is approximately as listed:

0.40   ungraded solid sawn lumber

0.25   visually graded solid sawn lumber

0.11   machine stress-rated solid sawn lumber

0.10   Glulam

0.06   LVL, PSL, etc.

A frequency histogram for MOE would consist of a bar chart with the Y axis height of bars indicating the frequency of occurrence of each increment of MOE which is plotted on the X axis. The histograms shown in Fig. 15.2 for the five COVs listed above are a smoothed-out version of the bar charts.

Time-Dependent Relationship.   A unique property of structural wood is its ability to sustain higher loads for a short time than under extended or permanent loading. Tabulated allowable design stresses are for normal loading duration defined as a 10-year period. Design stress adjustments must be applied for other loading durations, as shown in Table 15.2. Be aware that building codes for some jurisdictions may require a different load duration factor C_D for wind loading than that listed in the NDS and that the building code always governs.

The *load duration* is the accumulated time the design load is applied during the life of the structure. For example, the usual duration factor for snow loading is 1.15 for a 2-month duration. This does not mean 2 months of snow loading per year or 2 months of continuous snow loading, but rather 2 months of *design* snow loading during the life of the structure. If the design snow load could reasonably be applied for more than 2 months, such as at a high elevation or a ski resort, then the 1.15 factor is not appropriate and should be reduced.

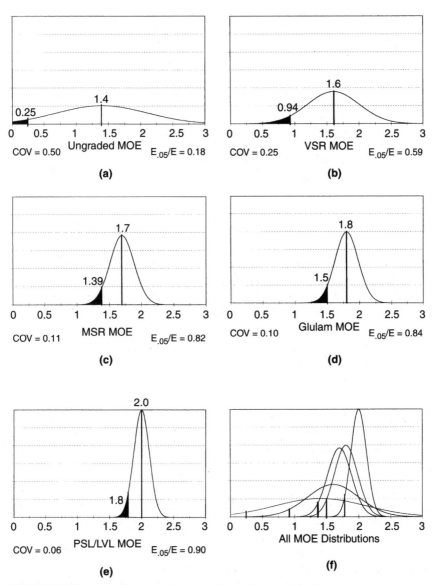

FIGURE 15.2 Frequency histograms for various structural wood products.

Size/Volume Effect. Testing over a long time confirms that smaller wood members have a higher modulus of rupture (MOR) than larger members. This appears to be true across the full range of member sizes. Research at the Forest Products Laboratory resulted in a depth factor formula as a function of depth only in use until the middle 1960s. In 1966 a size factor C_F as a function of depth only was adopted as a modifier to allowable bending stress for both solid sawn lumber and timbers plus glulam:

TABLE 15.2 Frequently Used Load Duration Factors

Load duration	C_D	Typical design loads
Permanent	0.9	Dead load
10 years	1.0	Occupancy live load
2 months	1.15	Snow load
7 days	1.25	Roof live load
1 day	1.33	Wind/seismic load
10 min	1.6	Wind load
Instantaneous	2.0	Impact load

$$C_F = \left(\frac{12}{d}\right)^{\frac{1}{9}}$$

The size factor remains in effect for solid sawn timbers as a modifier to bending, tension parallel and compression parallel tabular stresses and is also used as a modifier to bending for LVL and PSL products. In 1991 the volume factor C_v as a modifier to bending stresses was adopted for glulam which is a function of depth, width, and length. The basic formula shown below is further modified for support and loading conditions by a K_L factor:

$$C_V = K_L \left(\frac{21}{L}\right)^{1/x} \left(\frac{12}{d}\right)^{1/x} \left(\frac{5.125}{b}\right)^{\frac{1}{x}}$$

where x = 20 for southern pine
  = 10 for other species
 L = beam length, ft
 d = beam depth, in
 b = beam width, in
 K_L = loading condition coefficient furnished in NDS

The volume factor is more conservative for larger glulam members than the previous size factor.

Temperature. The tabular design stresses for wood are based upon a temperature of approximately 20°C with higher strengths at low temperature and lower strengths at high temperature. No allowable stress increase is permitted for low-temperature use, but Table 15.3 from NDS provides reduction factors for wood used at elevated temperatures. Up to approximately 150°F for short exposure times the temperature effect is reversible. At temperatures above 150°F or at temperatures above 100°F for repeated or prolonged periods, some of the strength loss is permanent.

Adjustment Factors. A common error in design or evaluation of structural timber is the use of tabulated design values without adjustment of those values for specific

TABLE 15.3　Temperature Factor C_t

Design values	In-service moisture conditions	C_t		
		$T \leq 100°F$	$100°F < T \leq 125°F$	$125°F < T \leq 150°F$
E_t, E	Wet or dry	1.0	0.9	0.9
F_b, F_v	Dry	1.0	0.8	0.7
F_c, and $F_{c\perp}$	Wet	1.0	0.7	0.5

Source:　American Forest & Paper Association, Washington, D.C.

use conditions. The list of adjustment factors for design values has grown over time, and use of the adjustment factors is often perceived as a confusing complication in timber design. All have a rational basis in design refinement. In practice, most designs use only one to three adjustment factors. Several factors are used only in specialized applications. The Applicability of Adjustment Factors table from the NDS, furnished here as Table 15.1, provides a quick review of the adjustment factors required for a specific design. A similar table is provided in NDS for applicability of adjustment factors required for connection design in timber.

Load Duration Factor C_D.　This factor addresses the time-dependent property of timber to sustain a given loading. (See Table 15.2.) Factor C_D is applied to all tabulated design values except MOE, which is not time-dependent, and compression perpendicular to grain which is based upon a deformation limit. The load duration factor is used in virtually all design and evaluation calculations. (See the paragraph Time-Dependent Relationship.)

Wet-Service Factor C_M.　(See paragraph entitled Organic Material—Moisture Content.) The wet-service factors are furnished at the front of design tables in the NDS for solid sawn lumber and timbers. The wet-service factors are furnished at the lower edge of tabular design tables for glulam in AITC Specification 117.

Temperature Factor C_t.　The temperature factor is rarely used in design as it applies only to members subjected to temperatures above 100°F for repeated and prolonged periods. It should be considered in forensic evaluation of members subjected to elevated heat such as plywood dryers, papermills, industrial or food processing applications, and attics in hot climates. (See paragraph entitled Temperature and Table 15.3.)

Beam Stability Factor C_L.　The beam stability factor was introduced with the 1991 NDS and is applied only to allowable bending stress. It addresses the buckling tendency of beams where the compression edge is not laterally stabilized. In the design of solid sawn lumber, C_L is applied simultaneously with the size factor C_F. In the design of glulam, C_L, which is a function of the compression edge, is not applied simultaneously with volume factor C_V, which is a function of the tension edge. The lesser of the two factors applies.

Size Factor C_F. The size factor applies to bending, tension and compression parallel to grain, for solid sawn lumber and timbers. The factors are furnished at the front of design tables in the NDS. (See paragraph entitled Size/Volume Effect.)

Volume Factor C_V. The volume factor applies only to bending stress for glulam. The volume factor is not applied simultaneously with the beam stability factor C_L. The lesser of the two factors applies. (See paragraph entitled Size/Volume Effect.)

Flat-Use Factor C_{fu}. The flat-use factor applies to bending stress for members with load applied to the wide face of member. The factors for dimension lumber are furnished at the front of design tables in the NDS. In glulam members a flat-use factor is applied when loading is parallel to the wide face of the lamination. The factors are furnished in AITC Specification 117.

Repetitive-Member Factor C_r. The repetitive-member factor applies only to bending stress for dimension lumber to account for load sharing by sheathing elements. The 1.15 factor may be applied to a system of at least three members spaced at not more than 24-in centers.

Curvature Factor C_c. The curvature factor applies only to bending stress at curved glulam members per the formula

$$C_c = 1 - 2000 \, (t/R)^2$$

where t = lamination thickness and R = radius of curvature.

Form Factor C_f. This rarely used factor is applied only to bending stress. It converts round or diamond-shaped cross-section bending members to the same moment capacity as a square member of the same cross-sectional area.

Column Stability Factor C_p. Similar to the beam stability factor and introduced with the 1991 NDS, the factor addresses buckling tendency and is applied only to compression parallel to grain design stresses.

Shear Stress Factor C_H. The allowable shear stress of solid sawn lumber is lower than glulam to account for separations such as splits, checks, and shake. Factors at the front of NDS design tables for dimension lumber and timbers permit increases in allowable shear stress dependent upon the measured size of separation in a specific member. This factor should not be used for design, but is of value to the forensic engineer for evaluation of specific members.

Incising Factor C_i. When sawn lumber is incised with incisions parallel to grain to increase treatment penetration, an adjustment to MOE and allowable design values is required.

STRUCTURAL MEMBER TYPES

Beams. A majority of structural lumber and timber products find use as bending members such as girders, stringers, beams, purlins, joists, rafters, and decking. Virtually all solid sawn and most glulam bending members are prismatic, having a constant cross section. The development of glulam enlarged the possibilities of deeper, wider, and longer sections in straight, cambered, or curved shapes. See Fig. 15.3 for timber beam profiles.

Tapering the cross section to a nonprismatic shape is done to form the straight tapered or the popular curved pitched and tapered beam profiles. Since wood is composed of longitudinal fibers, tapering of the cross section severs stressed wood fibers and causes a readjustment of stresses carried by those fibers. The AITC *Timber Construction Manual* (TCM) contains a design procedure for both straight tapered and curved pitched and tapered beams which is substantially more complex than the design of prismatic beams. Severing of wood fibers stressed in tension is particularly harmful structurally, so any tapering should be confined to the compressive edge of members. In a glulam member, the laminations should be parallel to the nontapered edge. Since glulam is a structural sandwich normally laid up with higher grades of material near its top and bottom flanges, a reduction in allowable stress may be required if the taper cut removes the higher-grade zone, exposing the lower-grade core material to maximum bending stress. Custom layup combinations can provide higher-grade laminates throughout the tapered portion.

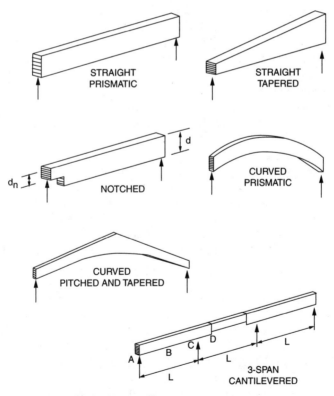

FIGURE 15.3 Timber beam profiles.

Notching of timber structural members also severs stressed wood fibers. A combination of section loss, stress concentrations at the notch, and interaction of tension perpendicular to grain and shear stresses create a complex situation for analysis. Knowledge of fracture mechanics and stress concentrations beyond that possessed by most practicing structural engineers is required to understand the complex situation created by notching timber flexural members. The following formula for shear stress at a tension face notch has been used since early versions of the NDS:

$$f_v = \left(\frac{3v}{2bd_n}\right)\left(\frac{d}{d_n}\right)$$

where v = shear at notch location
   b = member width
   d = full member depth
   d_n = member depth at notch

The formula is based upon testing of short, relatively deep beams with a span-to-depth ratio of 9. Caution should be used in reliance on the above formula, which does not address characteristics and sharpness of the notch, the possibility of separations or low strength perpendicular to grain in the shear plane, or beam profiles with a span-to-depth ratio greater than 9. Over the years due to service problems with notched beams, more restrictions have been added. The NDS limits notch depth at the tension face for solid sawn members to $d/4$ at a support and to $d/6$ elsewhere. The AITC *Timber Construction Manual* limits notch depth at the tension face to $d/10$ for glulam beams. The *Uniform Building Code* prohibits sawn taper cuts on the tension face of glulam beams. In-service problems suggest that beams tapered or notched at the tension face should be avoided. (See Case Study 4, First Nazarene Church.)

Cantilever beam systems are commonly used for roof framing of warehouse-type structures. Negative bending moment, caused by downward force of the link span at the end of a cantilever beam, permits a smaller more economical beam section (see Fig. 15.3). Published tables and formulas usually give optimum cantilever length, assuming balanced loading. Unbalanced span loading should be checked in design or evaluation of cantilever beam systems. (See Case Study 1, Port of Longview Warehouse No. 1.) The optimum cantilever length is that at which bending moment at support C for the balanced-load condition is equal to maximum moment near midspan B for the unbalanced-load condition (see Fig. 15.3). Experience with cantilever beam systems suggests that the economic benefits often vanish when analyzed for unbalanced span loading. Deflection should be checked as the reduced section, based upon bending criteria alone, may result in a beam too flexible and subject to ponding. (See Case Study 1, Port of Longview Warehouse No. 1.) The portion of beam past the inflection point where compression is at the lower portion of beam should be considered in regard to buckling stability. One problem with cantilevered glulam beams is that the deflected shape is complex, and it may be preferable to use a straight beam, rather than attempting to camber. A recent development in glulam technology utilizes high-strength composite fibers bonded into the tension zone of a glulam beam. The fiber panels are fiberglass, kevlar, or similar-type material. The composite panel is bonded to the beam tension face with a wood coverboard for cosmetic purposes. Strength of the tension zone is increased with the goal of reducing member size. Addition of the composite reinforcing may alter the member sizing from strength-controlling to stiffness-controlling. Availability of composite-reinforced glulam at this point is through proprietary suppliers.

Columns. Timber is a good material for columns in that allowable stresses are high in compression and the relatively larger cross section compared to steel limits the buckling tendency. Column design is based upon the continuous column formula, which is an interaction between crushing strength of pure compression and Euler buckling.

Trusses. Wood trusses may be roughly divided into heavy truss and light truss categories. Heavy trusses are typically spaced from 12 to 20 ft apart, have intermediate joist or purlin framing between them, and are designed by a structural engineer and custom-built. Light trusses are typically spaced from 12 to 48 in apart, are covered with sheathing, and may have the benefit of load sharing. They are typically designed and manufactured as proprietary products. Failure at any chord, web member, or joint in a truss can cause failure of the full truss, so a more detailed analysis is required than for a beam. Older truss designs, which the forensic engineer is often called upon to evaluate, usually ignored joint and heel eccentricity and chord continuity which could not be addressed by approximate precomputer methods of analysis.

Bowstring trusses are among the most efficient truss forms in timber. Almost a variation of a curved tied arch, the web forces are very small for balanced loading. Top chord bending is also relatively small because the positive moment from gravity loading is partially offset by the negative Pe moment, which is the product of top chord compression force and the eccentricity due to curvature. Web-to-chord connection forces are relatively small. Most of the in-service problems with bowstring trusses involve lack of safety factor for overloading or state-of-the-art reductions in allowable tension stresses at the lower chord. (See Case Study 9, Hughes Aircraft Building, and Case Study 10, Sheridan High School Gym.) By contrast, heavy parallel chord trusses have large web forces, large web members, and large web-to-chord connections.

Most trusses are unstable alone and require bracing, both during construction and in service, to remain structurally viable. In most cases the roof diaphragm of the building stabilizes the truss top chord against lateral buckling. Removal of such bracing elements without replacement bracing can create serious problems. A case in point is a bowstring truss framed industrial building investigated by the author where roof framing at one-half of the span had been removed and raised to provide natural lighting via a clerestory. It lasted several years until compression caused by a heavy snow loading buckled the unsupported portion of the truss top chords, collapsing the entire building.

Arches.   One advantage of glulam is that it may be produced in curved shapes at a reasonable and competitive cost. A primary application of curved glulam is arches of which the three-hinged Tudor profile is most common (see Fig. 15.4). Although often tapered throughout its full length, the arch is in combined bending and compression so the maximum bending stress is at the compression side of the stress block. As such, it does not usually suffer from the problems of tapering the tension face discussed earlier in this chapter. A graphical equilibrium polygon analysis, considered archaic today for most analysis, provides a rapid procedure for an approximate arch analysis. A precise analysis is complicated by the tapered profile. A full design procedure is provided in the AITC *Timber Construction Manual.*

Domes.   Glulam timber has distinct advantages as a framing material for spherical domes. Most steel-framed domes are formed with straight members creating a series of flat facets on the dome surface. Glulam dome members may be produced to the great-circle radius of the dome, producing a smooth, spherical surface which is less costly to sheathe and roof. Domes of the reticulated-type pattern are a series of triangles on the domical surface—a three-dimensional truss. Curved glulam members carry primarily compression with bending relatively small, as the positive moment from gravity loading is partially offset by the negative *Pe* moment. Most dome analysis consists of a three-dimensional space truss approach where roof sheathing is considered only to provide lateral buckling restraint to the primary members. Shell action of the sheathing is usually ignored and provides some additional safety factor. Connections are designed per the analysis, with joint tension caused by concentrated or unbalanced loading. Any pattern of space truss members on the dome surface, which may be defined, analyzed, designed, and connected, may be used to frame a dome. The designer strives for a pattern pleasing to the eye, which is efficient and

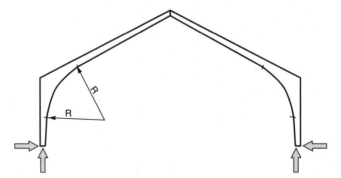

FIGURE 15.4   Tudor arch profile.

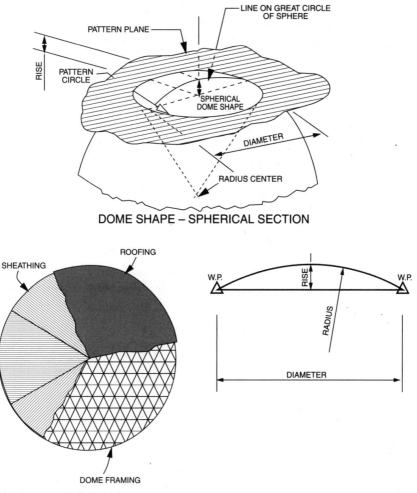

DOME SHAPE – SPHERICAL SECTION

FIGURE 15.5 Reticulated domes.

repetitive to design. In a common pattern, a series of equilateral triangles in the plane of supports is projected from the radius center to the dome surface. See Fig. 15.5.

METHODS OF TESTING

Standard tests for strength and stiffness in bending, tension parallel to grain, compression parallel to grain, shear and compression perpendicular to grain are specified by ASTM. ASTM D 143[10] applies to small specimens, and ASTM D 198 and D 4761[11] apply to large members. Use of standard tests is strongly recommended.

Wood Moisture Content.   Wood moisture content is expressed as a percentage of the wood moisture weight to the dry weight of wood. A precise measurement of wood moisture content is a destructive test in which a specimen is weighed before and after all moisture is driven off in an oven per ASTM D 4442.[12] A nondestructive approximation of wood moisture content may be obtained easily by using a calibrated electric resistance moisture meter where the electric resistance between two needles driven into the wood is measured parallel to grain per ASTM D 4444.[13]

Coring.   AITC shear test T-107, per *Inspection Manual AITC 200-92,* is used to evaluate face bonding adhesive quality and allows two specimen options, one of which is a 1-in-diameter core. To be of value for testing adhesive bond, the cylindrical core must be taken perpendicular to the glue lines. This test is extensively used for in-plant quality control, but is also useful for existing structures when the core may be extracted at a noncritical location. The cores may also be used to calculate material density if it is measured accurately with dial calipers and weighed on a gram scale. Coring or boring with a $3/8$- or $1/4$-inch bit is a crude, but effective way of quickly determining if advanced decay or deterioration, is present. Lack of drill resistance indicates advanced wood deterioration, and inspection of the shavings indicates if the wood is sound. Powdery or discolored shavings indicate decay or deterioration. Preservative-treated tapered wood plugs are available to seal the coring hole.

Stress Wave.   Modulus of elasticity is the slope of the stress-strain curve in a static load test. A dynamic MOE may also be determined by the formula

$$\text{MOE} = \frac{DV^2}{g}$$

where D = material density
     V = wave velocity through material
     g = constant of gravity, 32.2 ft/s^2

Instruments are available with sensors and timers which can measure the elapsed time of a stress wave induced into the material in either a test laboratory or an in-place structure. The wave may be induced with a hammer-type object. If both wave velocity and density can be measured, then dynamic MOE may be calculated. A calibrating factor with static MOE measured by physical testing and dynamic MOE measured by stress wave testing of the same specimen is necessary in order to estimate static MOE using the stress wave procedure. When used to estimate MOE for comparison with design tables, the stress wave is induced parallel to grain.

A valuable diagnostic tool for detecting decayed wood is stress wave testing with the wave induced perpendicular to grain. Decayed wood slows the wave velocity, and the location of deteriorated wood may be mapped, using a series of stress wave tests in a gridwork pattern. (See Case Study 7, Hayward Field Grandstand.)

Chemical Testing.   Wood is more resistant to chemical action than most construction materials but is not free from chemical deterioration. Acids, acid salts, and alkalines may cause permanent strength loss in wood. Fire-retardant treatment (FRT) chemicals are commonly borates, ammonium sulfate, and ammonium phosphate, which cause wood degradation by acid hydrolysis. During an evaluation, questions often arise regarding the presence of preservative treatment, wood specie, etc. Testing for presence of chemicals is nondestructive as very small test specimens are required.

Testing for the presence of preservative treatment is a common and inexpensive procedure. Wood specie identification is available from laboratories or consultants in wood technology. A spectrometer analysis may be utilized to determine the elemental breakdown of retained chemicals. Penetration depth of the chemical in wood is important, and a chemical indicator applied to the specimen is commonly used for that purpose. Some chemicals, such as those used for fire-retardant purposes, are more detrimental near the wood surface due to their interaction with atmospheric moisture.

Slope of Grain. The angle of wood fiber to the longitudinal axis of member, known as the *slope of grain,* ranks with knots as a natural-growth strength reducer considered when lumber or timber is graded. Electronic instruments are available which can detect slope of grain. A simpler device is a stylus made for this purpose with a sharp needle which follows the wood fiber when pulled by hand in a general parallel to grain direction with the stylus embedded slightly in the wood. The slope of wood fiber should not be confused with the annual ring orientation. The *Wood Handbook,* in chapter 4, Mechanical Properties of Wood, gives thorough coverage of this topic. (See the paragraph entitled Three Distinct Grain Orientations.)

Bending. A static bending test in a laboratory provides a measure of member strength more easily visualized by a client than a ream of calculations. Properly instrumented, it can provide both modulus of elasticity and modulus of rupture. Occasionally a full-sized member is available as a test specimen where one member is sacrificed; or one end of a beam may be available following damage to the other end. More commonly secondary members or strips cut from the member are available as test specimens. Commonly the test setup consists of concentrated loading of the specimen at one-third points, creating uniform bending across the middle one-third of the test beam. AITC test T114, per *Inspection Manual AITC 200-92,* is a bending test extensively used in the past for testing end joints in individual laminates used for glulam manufacture. Test equipment is now more commonly available for testing end joints in tension.

Tension. In the past, strips cut from a specimen were usually tested in tension. Equipment is now more commonly available which is capable of pulling specimens in the 2 × 6 size range to failure in tension. AITC test T119 per *Inspection Manual 200-92* is a procedure for pulling a full-size lamination in tension for end joint testing. Where end joint strength is questioned in a glulam forensic inspection and a specimen is available for testing, end joints may be sawn out of the glulam specimen and pull-tested per this procedure.

Compression. Short column compression crushing strength testing is available from virtually any test laboratory and requires only a small specimen for testing. While compression members rarely function structurally as short columns, this test is inexpensive and can provide compressive MOE in addition to ultimate compressive strength data.

Shear. AITC test T107, per *Inspection Manual 200-92,* for glulam members permits the option of stairstep type of block shear tests or core shear tests as specimen options for evaluating shear strength along the face bonding adhesive line. Test machines using a calibrated hydraulic cylinder shear the specimen along the adhesive line. The adhesive bond is evaluated based on adhesive shear strength and an estimate of wood failure percentage in the shear plane. Accurate calibration of the complete system of cylinder and gauge to be used is imperative for meaningful results. Do not accept secondhand information that the test machine is calibrated. Recalibrate rented or borrowed test equipment prior to use. Shear testing presented in a forensic report should be confined to ASTM or industry standard tests.

Delamination. AITC test T110, per *Inspection Manual 200-92,* is a cyclic delamination test used for glulam in-plant quality control but is useful for forensic evaluation when possible delamination is under investigation. The test involves several cycles of impregnating a glulam specimen with water in a pressure vessel and rapidly drying in an oven. This test simulates repeated wetting-drying cycles and tests glue line adequacy by placing stress on the glue line.

Modulus of Elasticity. Machine stress-rated (MSR) lumber requires measuring the MOE of each piece at the point of manufacture and assigning design properties based upon MOE with visual grading restrictions using high-speed production equipment. In test specimens MOE may be measured by plotting the stress-strain curve from bending, tension, or compression load tests or by stress wave testing.

Connector Testing. The presence of corroded bolts or other fasteners may become the focus of a forensic evaluation, and testing the connector may be required. It may be necessary to determine if a bolt is mild steel or one of the hardened-steel grades. A bolt test for tensile and yield is available at reasonable cost from most test laboratories. ASTM or industry standard tests are recommended.

Full-Structure in Situ Load Testing. Full-structure load testing is often proposed following evaluation and/or repair of a distressed structure. It is easily visualized, and the structure either passes or fails. Caution should be employed in use of full-structure load testing for the following reasons:

1. Costs may be substantial.
2. How much load should be applied and for what duration? The load duration factor C_D is based upon the assumption that the reserve capacity of the member can withstand a specified load in excess of the design allowable for a specified

duration during the life of the structure. It is often difficult to determine what percentage of overload to use in a performance test without risking yield or damage to structural elements.

3. It may be difficult to isolate the structure being tested from nonstructural elements fastened to the structure. May elastic deflection be isolated from nonelastic deflection? What if the structural frame tests are satisfactory, but nonstructural walls, gypboard, windows, etc., are damaged—who pays for the damage?

4. When testing is done, be cautious about agreeing to an unrealistic criterion of acceptance. Early in the author's career his company designed and constructed a timber domed structure for a university. The specification required a load test representing full dead plus unbalanced live load, and the criterion of acceptance was that deflection under full load be measured and 80 percent deflection recovery be achieved upon removal of the test load. The structure performed very well under test load. Deflection under full-design loading was substantially less than calculated, but 80 percent recovery was not achieved, as some of the initial deflection was nonelastic due to small amounts of crushing as the connectors seated. As such, the structure did not pass the acceptance criterion, and some negotiation was required prior to acceptance.

TYPES AND CAUSES OF NONPERFORMANCE AND FAILURE

Evolution of Engineered Timber Design

State-of-the-art changes resulting from research and testing caused revisions in the procedure for establishing tabular design stresses, in the magnitude of the tabular stresses, in stress adjustments, and in the analysis procedures. Virtually all these revisions tended to reduce allowable design stresses. Based upon present knowledge, the older tabular stresses for tension and the tension portion of flexural members were nonconservative for an appropriate safety factor.

War Production Directive. In August 1943, the U.S. War Production Board issued Directive No. 29[14] as an emergency specification, which was simply a revised NDS specifying higher working stresses for lumber, timbers and timber connectors, and defined rules for their use. Issued to help in the war effort, some of the measures were arbitrary and most lacked adequate test data backup. One justification for the measures was short-term use of 5 to 10 years, but many of these World War II structures remain in use today. Lumber and timber working stresses and connector values were increased from previously used values by approximately 20 percent with MOE unchanged. Designs were often based on a roof snow load of 15 lb/ft^2 regardless of location. Many of the engineered structures were designed using an allowable bending stress $F_b = 1200$ lb/in^2, but the lumber volume required was so large that non-stress-graded lumber was used without design revision. Structures designed with $F_b = 1800$ lb/in² lumber were often built with $F_b = 1200$ lb/in² material.

Construction with timber was extremely heavy during this window of time. The wartime directive increase, coupled with the fact that most allowable stresses in timber were higher than current use for tension and bending, is a historical situation the forensic engineer should be aware of when evaluating World War II structures. (See Case Study 9, Hughes Aircraft Building.)

Radial Tension. Tension perpendicular to grain is induced in a curved bending member when the bending moment increases the radius. The equation for calculating radial tension was derived theoretically from mechanics as an analogy to a pressure vessel:

$$f_r = \frac{3M}{2Rbd}$$

where M = bending moment
      R = radius at member middepth
      b = member width
      d = member depth

It was not well understood among design engineers that the above formula was applicable only to prismatic members of constant cross section. The curved pitched and tapered glulam beam was widely used, and tension perpendicular to grain separations developed in a small percentage of these beams, but enough to be of great concern to the glulam industry. Separations developed in beams where radial tension was analyzed using the above formula, and stresses were within published allowables. An extensive research program in the 1960s provided both a reduction in allowable cross-grain tension stresses for western softwoods and a revised design approach for tapered curved members. The iterative design procedure resulting from that approach is presented in the AITC *Timber Construction Manual.* Reinforcing perpendicular to grain, where required per the design approach for nonprismatic members, solved the problem of beam separations and has been in common use since the late 1960s.

Curved glulam beams require steel reinforcing, as do reinforced-concrete beams. Two common reinforcing methods are the installation of full thread lag bolts or the placement of epoxy-embedded deformed reinforcing bars perpendicular to grain. Since radial tension stresses are a function of radius, reinforcing is required in the curved portion only. A side effect of radial reinforcing is that member dimension is locked in perpendicular to grain when it is fastened or bonded to the steel dowel. This prevents slight expansion and contraction of the timber due to moisture cycling. When the wood does shrink due to moisture loss but is restrained, checking occurs in the reinforced portion.

Allowable Design Stress. Clear-wood procedures were initially used to establish allowable design stresses for dimension lumber (2- to 4-in nominal thickness), timbers (5-in and greater nominal thicknesses), and glulam.

Beginning in the late 1960s, the glulam timber industry initiated an ongoing program of testing full-size glulam beams for stiffness and to destruction for bending stress. Here are highlights from that testing:

- Beam strength limitation in flexure is predominately triggered by the tension face.
- Natural-growth characteristics, such as knots and slope of grain, have greater impact upon strength at the edges of the tension laminations in the tension zone than at the interior portion of the lamination.
- The older clear-wood procedure was nonconservative for the larger beam sizes. A size/volume relationship exists across the full range of member sizes such that larger members have a lower MOR than smaller members.

The following revisions in glulam design and manufacture resulted:

- Special grades were developed for the tension face laminates with closer tolerances on natural-growth characteristics.
- New bending stress combinations were developed requiring the special laminate grades at the tension face.
- In the early 1990s a volume factor, which is a function of beam width, depth, and length, replaced the former size factor, which is a function of depth only. The volume factor reduces the allowable bending stress of larger glulam beams as compared to the former size factor.

Tabular bending and tension stresses for solid sawn dimension lumber and timbers were also adjusted. Over time there was a gradual downward trend in allowable bending and tension stresses for commonly used glulam combinations and dimension lumber grades in Douglas fir and other softwood species.

Knowledge of the above state-of-the-art design revisions is imperative in evaluating older flexural or tension members. These members, originally designed in accordance with the building code in effect at the time, often do not meet current criteria. While failure is rare, many of the flexural or tension members designed to older criteria have infringed upon their safety factor. An example is a recent evaluation of glulam beam roof framing at a textile mill designed in 1959. The beam was originally designed to full allowable bending stress. Criteria changes included reduction of allowable bending stress, introduction of the volume factor, and a snow load increase from 40 to 100 lb/ft² due to more recent snow load history. (See Case Study 13, Guilford of Maine Textile Mill.)

Loading/Overloading

Dead Load. Dead load is more easily defined and calculated than the more capricious wind and seismic loadings. In forensic design review, the dead load must be accurately estimated. This is relatively simple for conventional construction where the components may be seen. However, in some instances not all the construction is visible. Where poured decks of gypsum or lightweight concrete cannot be measured for depth, it may be necessary to remove portions of the structure or take a roof core. A competent roofer can remove a roof core and patch the roof, preserving the roofing bond. (See Case Study 8, Robert Frost School, and Case Study 9, Hughes Aircraft Building.)

Snow and Snow Drifting. Snow loading for design review is specified by each local city, county, or state building jurisdiction. The snow load specified is usually ground snow load. Codes permit adjustment of ground snow load for roof snow load and pitch of roof dependent upon conditions. The building codes extensively cover calculation of specific snow load conditions such as drifting, sliding surcharge, overhangs, and valley design.

A forensic inspection where snow load is known or suspected should consider snow weight measurement a top priority. Measuring snow depth is not adequate. The measurement should be precise and well documented. Shoveling snow into a bucket for weighing is not acceptable. Extracting a core of snow down to and including ice against the roof is the most accurate method of measurement. While specialized snow coring equipment is available, the author prefers sections of 6- or 8-in stovepipe available at most hardware stores. The extracted core may be weighed wherever convenient and the snow density calculated. It is valuable to measure snow weight on both the roof and an adjacent undisturbed area of the ground. (See Case Study 12, Albertsons Grocery Warehouse.)

Ponding. Water ponding on flat or nearly flat roofs may be caused by inadequate roof slope, drainage obstructions, frozen drain pipes, or deflection due to lack of stiffness in the roof framing members. Ponding problems are more common in areas where roof live loads, rather than snow loading, control the design. Under *UBC* the roof live load may be reduced to 12 lb/ft^2 for flat roofs with tributary loaded area of 600 ft^2 or more. This leaves little reserve for water ponding compared to a northern area requiring 25 lb/ft^2 or more of snow load for design. Water ponding is a chicken-and-egg type of progressive-deflection problem. Weight of water accumulation causes roof beams to deflect, roof beam deflection creates a deeper pond with greater water weight, causing more deflection, causing more water weight and more deflection. This continues until balanced by beam resistance, the water escapes or the beam fails. (See Case Study 1, Port of Longview Warehouse No. 1.)

Wind Load. Wind load requirements of the building code are derived from various available sources but primarily from extensive work and documents published by ASCE culminating in ASCE Standard 7-95.[15] Wind is a capricious force whose maximum intensity may last for only a few seconds. Wind force is not distributed uniformly over a given area. It is a common occurrence, following a major windstorm, to find a wind-damaged structure standing adjacent to one which is intact. Most older buildings were designed without consideration for tying elements of the structure together, such as roof to column, column to footing, etc. An initial step in a forensic investigation of wind load damage should be wind gauge records from the National Climatic Data Center or other sources. (See Case Study 4, First Nazarene Church.)

Unbalanced Load. Simple span beams do not require checking for unbalanced loading, but multiple-span and cantilever beam systems are sensitive to unbalanced loading. The model building codes all have some language requiring consideration of unbalanced loading where it creates a more severe design situation than balanced loading. The 1997 *Uniform Building Code* (*UBC*)[16] in section 1607 requires unbalanced loading where such loading will result in larger members or connections. However, an exception is included in the code where alternate span loading need not be considered if the uniform roof live load is 20 lb/ft^2 or more. The author's design review experience has shown that unbalanced loading is often not considered in the design of cantilever beam systems. Most, if not all, cantilever beam systems will be controlled by unbalanced live load at alternate spans, and the author's experience is counter to the above code exception which tends to sanitize cantilever beam system design without provision for unbalanced loading. (See Case Study 1, Port of Longview Warehouse No. 1.) For trusses, unbalanced loading may control web design and web-to-chord connections. Spherical dome members are primarily in compression except that unbalanced or concentrated loading may reverse them to tension.

Deterioration

Decay, Termites, and Marine Borers. Under conditions favorable to their growth, fungi will attack wood, causing decay and seriously reducing the structural integrity of timber members. These organisms require four essentials to survive: food, air, moisture, and a favorable temperature. Wood decay cannot progress when the organisms lack any of these four essentials. Wood is the food source. Lacking air, continuously submerged wood will not decay from most wood-eating organisms although in saltwater it may be attacked by marine borers. The wood-eating organisms are dormant at temperatures below the middle 30°F range. In normal use three of these essentials are usually present, requiring only moisture as the catalyst to induce decay. Coring and stress wave testing, as described under Methods of Testing, are useful in situ methods to determine the extent and limits of decay in structural members. (See Case Study 7, Hayward Field Grandstand.)

Termite activity is a function of temperature, being more prevalent in warmer climates such as Florida, with reduced activity as temperature decreases. Termites are virtually nonexistent in the northern heartland states away from the tempering effect of oceans. Subterranean termites maintain ground colonies with mud tunnels to the wood structure above.

Wood exposed to saltwater environments is subject to a family of wormlike marine borers which burrow below the wood surface. As with termites, their activity is a function of temperature, and unprotected woods in tropical waters have become nonfunctional due to marine borers within a period of a few months.

Chemical Deterioration. Wood is considered superior to many other materials of construction in resistance to chemical action but is not totally free from chemical deterioration. While working in the wet environment of the Aleutian Islands, the author saw untreated timber bridge members in good condition where the steel bolts had disintegrated to rust traces due to corrosion caused by sea salt. He once designed a timber domed roof covering a chemical coking operation so corrosive that the previous steel roof had collapsed after a reasonably short period of service.

Wood structures are used for bulk storage of chemicals such as urea fertilizer which corrodes unprotected steel rapidly. The heartwood of many species is more resistant to chemical action than sapwood. Water and some organic liquids such as alcohol cause wood to soften and swell, causing a temporary strength reduction. Acids and acid salts cause permanent strength loss due to chemical changes in the cell structure. Alkalines cause permanent strength loss due to destruction of lignins which bind wood fibers together.

Heat. Wood strength decreases with higher temperature and increases with lower temperature. Tabular design values are set at approximately 20°C. Temporary strength reduction occurs at temperatures to approximately 150°F, and permanent strength reduction occurs beyond that level. (See paragraph entitled Temperature.)

Lateral Buckling

Columns, arches, and truss members stressed in compression are usually controlled by buckling or the interaction of buckling and compression, rather than by pure compression. Trusses and arches are rarely stable alone until secured into a diaphragm or some type of lateral bracing system; therefore buckling problems with these structural systems are most likely to occur during construction. Inadequate bracing has been the primary cause of truss problems that the author has investigated. Causes include inadequate temporary bracing, diaphragm construction lagging behind truss or arch placement, and pressure to release expensive rented cranes. (See Case Study 2, McMinnville Town Center; Case Study 3, Lighter than Air Hangars; and Case Study 5, Rosemont Horizon Arena.)

Notching or Tapering Tension Face

Notching or tapering the tension face of a stressed timber member severs stressed wood fibers and sets up a potential distress situation that is difficult to analyze accurately. A good rule of thumb is to never notch or taper the tension side of a highly stressed timber member. (See Case Study 4, First Nazarene Church, and paragraph entitled Beams.)

Eccentricity

Older bowstring trusses were often constructed using double chords with single webs in the plane between chords. In this case the webs could not be connected concentrically because of web-to-web interference. Bowstring trusses with small web forces were usually able to tolerate this eccentricity. Older precomputer structural analyses by graphic analysis or the method of joints assumed pinned concentric joints and ignored web-to-chord eccentricity. Truss heel eccentricity where centroid intersection of heel members is eccentric with the truss reaction induces a torque into the heel connection that may create distress in trusses not designed for this condition. Internal truss member eccentricity where centroid intersections of adjacent web members are eccentric with chords creates the same condition. For bowstring trusses, distress due to heel eccentricity is more likely than distress due to internal web eccentricity as the member forces at the heel are much higher. (See Fig. 15.6 and Case Study 6, Rainier Beach Library, and Case Study 10, Sheridan High School Gym.)

Secondary Effects

Secondary effects and particularly the effect of nodal rotation on trusses should be considered in design or forensic evaluation. Ideally, web-to-chord truss joints should be as designed—i.e., welded if designed fixed, or frictionless pins if designed pinned. Most web connections in timber trusses are designed as pinned, but have partial fixity due to restraints in the connection. If long, rigid steel side plates, designed to transfer axial loads only, are used for web-to-chord connections and the truss is flexible with considerable nodal rotation, then the connectors will resist that rotation by creation of moment couples in the web members. In severe cases these couples create a cross-grain tension force which can split the truss member. See Case Study 6, Rainier Beach Library, in which the outer truss web split due to a combination of nodal rotation and truss heel eccentricity. See Case Study 15, Hood River Valley High School Theater, where nodal rotation at a wood chord-wood web truss with glued connections failed due to cross-grain tension stresses induced at the web-to-chord connections.

State-of-the-Art Design Changes

The state of the art in timber design has changed substantially over time, but many structures the forensic engineer is retained to evaluate are older and designed to a less rigorous code standard. The safety factor is usually adequate to keep older structures viable, but effective reduction of the safety factor due to evolution of design criteria leaves these structures less able to carry additional or unexpected loading. Understanding state-of-the-art changes in tabular stresses and design procedure during the life of the structure being evaluated is vital to a forensic evalu-

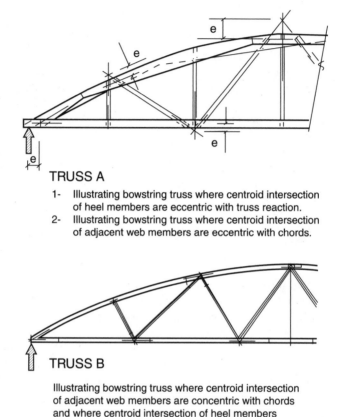

TRUSS A

1- Illustrating bowstring truss where centroid intersection of heel members are eccentric with truss reaction.

2- Illustrating bowstring truss where centroid intersection of adjacent web members are eccentric with chords.

TRUSS B

Illustrating bowstring truss where centroid intersection of adjacent web members are concentric with chords and where centroid intersection of heel members are concentric with truss reaction.

FIGURE 15.6   Truss member eccentricity.

ation. (See paragraph entitled Evolution of Engineered Timber Design and Case Study 1, Port of Longview Warehouse No. 1; Case Study 9, Hughes Aircraft Building; Case Study 10, Sheridan High School Gym; Case Study 11, Lucky Strike Lanes; and Case Study 13, Guilford of Maine Textile Mill.)

Compatibility of Analysis and Structural Performance

All structural analyses involve assumptions such as fixed or pinned, support conditions, etc. Analyses also involve simplifications on account of constraints of time and economics. Most of the assumptions and simplifications are conservative. In lateral analysis the engineer may use only those stiffening elements for which design values are available. Lateral bracing is analyzed on contributions from shear walls, diaphragms, cross-bracing, rigid frames, etc. Not considered are contributions from interior partitions, friction, and other structural and nonstructural elements which contribute to bracing. Timber dome analysis usually ignores the shell action of roof sheathing.

The fact that structures may perform somewhat differently than the analysis assumptions may not always be on the conservative side and could be a factor in nonperformance. An old engineering expression says, "Structures are smarter than the engineers who design them," meaning structures find their own way to function. In reviewing nonperformance, one possibility to keep in mind is that the structure is performing in a manner different from the assumptions used in the analysis.

STRUCTURAL EVALUATION OF IN-SITU TIMBER STRUCTURES

Forensic structural evaluation of timber structures in place requires a strong engineering background and judgment tempered by experience. It is elementary that the physical data relating to a member or structure in question must be documented in regard to specie, grade, age, loading history, dimensions, site conditions, wood moisture content, member condition, etc. Some of this may be found in archives of the owner or the building department. The remainder must be determined on site or from documents. This may involve inclement weather, unpleasant site conditions, and inconvenient time frames. Avoid undocumented second-hand information. Structures do not become distressed or fail without a reason. A forensic engineer must identify and document in a report to his or her client the reasons for a structural problem.

Knowledge of the subject matter, in particular engineering properties of wood and timber characteristics, is necessary to evaluate structural timber members. Access to older, out-of-date codes and standards is of great value as evaluation often involves older structures. All possible in situ plus laboratory testing within budget constraints should be performed and guesswork minimized. Nondestructive tests such as wood moisture content readings and stress wave testing are possible on most structures. Where specimens are available, bending, strip tension, compression, and MOE tests from a laboratory are invaluable. Test data enhance a forensic report by reducing speculation in the conclusions. Full-size load testing of bridges and buildings, if done at all, should be used with caution because of the problems of isolating the variables and possible damage to adjacent members or nonstructural elements. It is difficult to know what percentage of the design load may be applied without damage to some of the members or connections.

The tenacity and inquiring mind of a detective are a great asset for a forensic engineer. Keep an open mind and be prepared to learn something from every commission. Expect the unexpected. (See Case Study 14, Church of Christ.)

TEMPORARY AND PERMANENT REMEDIAL REPAIRS

Simply stated, any structural repair must satisfy the results of the structural analysis. The repair of members and connections must satisfy the shear, bending moment, tension compression, etc., from the analysis plus any condition such as eccentricity introduced by the repair. As such, the repair engineer must have analysis data available prior to final repair design.

Shoring. When a condition of structural distress is first identified, the situation is usually a state of emergency. Shoring may be required to prevent collapse before there is time for detailed analysis. Emergency shoring usually consists of what is readily available. Wood members have an advantage in that they may be easily field-trimmed to length. Round wood poles and square or rectangular timbers work well. If only dimension lumber is available, it may be nailed into T, H, or box-shaped members to resist buckling. Wood or steel wedges may be used to bring shoring tight under a distressed member. Engineered tubular steel shoring with known load capacity is ideal, if available.

When trusses from the lower chord are shored, it is usually necessary to shore all panel points. This is particularly true at bowstring trusses where web-to-chord connections are relatively small due to axial web forces which are small compared to axial chord forces. The shore becomes a truss reaction, and webs fastening to the lower chord close to the shore tend to act as the top chord of a reconfigured truss. Partial shoring of a bowstring truss will cause substantial increase in web compression adjacent to the shore and may cause web-to-chord failure and possible truss collapse. Shoring under the top chord of a distressed truss is preferable to lower chord shoring but more difficult to accomplish. In a recent truss failure investigation by the author, the analysis showed that placing a crosswall tight under a bowstring truss lower chord increased compression at one web from 3 to 78 kips and caused progressive web failure and subsequently truss chord failure.

In the case of overloaded beams, placing additional columns to shorten the span may be the most favorable solution. (See Case Study 13, Guilford of Maine Textile Mill.)

Replacement. Replacement of a distressed member inside a structure is usually not feasible owing to adjacent members and interference with other building elements. In those situations where replacement is possible, it is usually more economical to replace a member than to design and install a repair, as most repairs are labor-intensive. Replacement of deteriorated truss members is feasible where the full truss may be stress-relieved by top chord shoring.

Sistering. Addition of a new structural member where the original member is physically left in place is often a solution for reinforcing a distressed member in an industrial structure where appearance is not crucial. The new *sistering* member should be designed to carry all the load and should be fastened so as to transfer forces from the original members if required. (See Case Study 3, Lighter than Air Hangars.) Sistering members of like materials are preferred for ease of connection, but steel channel or plate may be used for sistering timber members.

Bolt Tightening. Sawn timber structures fastened with bolts and shear plates or split rings should have bolts tightened after moisture equilibrium is achieved, and periodically if bolts loosen. Large sawn timbers are too large to be kiln-dried and are usually installed wet with shrinkage occurring after installation. Shrinkage at connections fastened with shear plates or split-ring timber connectors may cause a separation between timbers at the load transfer point, which reduces the bearing area of wood against the plate or ring, thereby reducing connector capacity. Glulam is kiln-dried and more dimensionally stable, so it is less in need of periodic bolt tightening.

Clamps and Stitch Bolts. Clamps and stitch bolts are particularly useful to prevent propagation of timber separations in truss chords and webs. Usually a stitch bolt of $1/2$-in diameter with washers is adequate to close a separation. Stitch bolts should only be used at stressed members if the loss of section by the additional bolthole may be tolerated. A vertical stitch bolt adjacent to truss lower chord-web connections may be used to resist the cross-grain tension stress created by ceiling loading on the lower chord below the connection. Clamps consisting of steel plate, angle, or channel above and below a member and fastened by bolts each side of the member may be used to close separations or resist cross-grain tension forces without loss of section.

"Beam Stretcher" Moment Connections. A flexural member may be spliced providing that the connection accounts for all the shear, axial force, and bending moment felt by the member. Moment splice connections are used in original designs in glulam arches to shorten the member for shipment. They are also used at knees of glulam rigid frames. Moment connections may also be used in repair to replace a portion of a flexural member. Decayed or damaged arch legs may be repaired by removing the damaged portion and fitting a new moment-connected base shoe. (See Case Study 14, Church of Christ.) In a recent investigation by the author at a papermill, a glulam beam end supported at a column had decayed in the wet environment. The decayed ends were removed and fitted with steel moment connected caps which fit the original beam seat. The beam was salvaged without full beam replacement.

Post Tensioning. Post tensioning of beams involves application of an external compression force into the member, preferably at a location causing bending moments which counter those due to the supported loads. Because this force is usually applied by a steel rod or cable strand in tension, it is termed *post tensioning.* Numerous tensioning strand configurations are possible, the most common being a tension strand at or near the beam soffit to create maximum negative moment due to the lever arm distance between the tension strand and the beam neutral axis. Tension strands below the beam soffit may use a vertical spreader member to increase the tension strand lever arm, creating a sort of king post truss.

Since strand tension may be quite high, anchorage of strand to beam is critical. Mild steel shapes, mild steel threaded rod, and cable have been used successfully as tension strands. Turnbuckles may be used to apply tension to steel rod tension strands. Cable of the type used for prestressed concrete has an advantage in that inexpensive "button" type of end anchors may be fastened to the cable and a predetermined amount of tension applied using a calibrated hydraulic jack. The author prefers this system over use of threaded rods for tensioning, as the amount of force applied may be accurately controlled without risk of overtensioning.

Post tensioning of trusses may be utilized to counteract overloading or calculated overstress due to changes of criteria. Post tensioning of trusses usually consists of a tension strand at middepth of the lower chord applying an axial force to the chord without inducing moment. Truss post tensioning will reduce lower chord tension and reduce the possibility of lower chord distress.

Radial Tension/Cross-Grain Tension Reinforcement. Wood separations due to radial tension induced by bending of curved glulam members are rarely seen today as radial reinforcing has become a typical design procedure installed during manufacture. Field repairs of unreinforced beams containing radial tension separations may be engineered using a lag bolt field installed to carry the tension perpendicular to grain force. The beam section must be adequate to sustain section loss from the repair dowel. To close the separation, the lag bolt may be installed from below in holes $1/16$ in oversize below the separation and above the separation in undersize lead holes as prescribed in the NDS for lag bolts in withdrawal for the wood specie present.

Stitch bolts perpendicular to grain may be used to resist tension perpendicular to grain forces in ledgers resisting lateral loads and at truss lower chords at web connections.

Shear Reinforcement. Load-induced shear separations are rare in wood as a rather large safety factor separates actual ultimate shear strength and tabular design stresses in horizontal shear. If delamination occurs in glulam, reinforcing against a potential shear failure may be appropriate. The potential failure mode for this situation is separation of the beam into two segments along a horizontal plane and subsequent flexural failure due to reduced section modulus.

If a separation parallel to grain due to delamination, checking, etc., has the potential for shear failure of the member, then shear reinforcing is appropriate. The reinforcing must transfer shear between the separated segments, which may be accomplished by embedded dowels or exterior side plates. The dowel shear transfer or side plate connectors must be engineered to transfer the calculated shear. Lag bolts or epoxy-embedded dowels, placed perpendicular to grain, may be used with the added advantage of the dowel's being able to resist any perpendicular to grain forces. A precise evaluation of beam net section containing reinforcing dowels would be with a transformed section using full section for the compression side of the neutral axis, and the full section less dowel area removed for the tension side of the neutral axis. A quicker, more conservative assumption would be the full dowel area removed from the entire net section. Data sufficient for an engineer to design either a lag or epoxy-embedded dowel reinforcing are covered in AITC 404-92, which is an appendix to *Inspection Manual AITC 200-92*.

Steel side plates on each side of a beam connected with timber rivets may also be used to transfer shear between separated wood segments. The total shear transfer required may be calculated and the repair designed per the procedure outlined in the NDS.

EXAMPLES AND CASE STUDIES

Several case studies are included to illustrate examples of distress, forensic evaluation, and repairs discussed in the body of this chapter. All the case studies included here were forensic investigations or evaluations conducted by the author's firm.

Case Study 1. Port of Longview Warehouse No. 1 Longview, Washington

This case study illustrates

- Ponding
- Unbalanced loading at cantilevered beams
- State-of-the-art criteria revisions

A glulam framed cantilevered beam warehouse roof framing system was designed in 1965 per the following criteria: Glulam combination A with allowable bending stress of 2600 lb/in², 20 lb/ft² roof snow load, and 12 lb/ft² roof dead load.

Using balanced loading for the full beam length, including 16-ft overhangs on each side, the beams were acceptable for shear and bending per the original design criteria, and deflection was within $L/240$.

The author's firm was retained for forensic evaluation in 1973 following collapse of a portion of the roof after a heavy rainstorm. See Fig. 15.7.

Several factors contributed to the overstressed condition leading to collapse, some of which alone were of relatively minor significance. A 20 lb/ft² roof snow load was permitted by the building code in 1965, but by 1970 it had been raised to 25 lb/ft². The design dead load of 12 lb/ft² was about 1 lb/ft² low, which is about the weight of the sprinkler system. By 1973 the glulam A combination at

FIGURE 15.7 Collapse of cantilever beam system due to water ponding. Port of Longview
Warehouse No. 1, Longview, Washington.

F_b = 2600 lb/in² had been discontinued, and the 24F combination was widely
used. Based upon present criteria, the A combination should be used at approximately 2200 lb/in² for an appropriate safety factor.

A plan sketch of roof framing in Fig. 15.8 shows that the four building corners
were notched in plan view; i.e., overhangs were not present at the corners of the
building. This caused the overhang portion of the end beams to carry only one-half
the roof load of comparable interior beams. Reduction of roof load at overhangs
caused bending moments in the end beams to be higher than in interior beams. The
beams appear to have been sized for the less severe case. The beams appear to have
been sized without consideration for unbalanced loading.

Cantilevered beam systems are relatively flexible because of reduced beam
moments due to cantilever action and the resulting smaller beam size. The roof
was constructed flat or close to flat. Bracing of beams in the negative moment portion was inadequate but did not appear to contribute to the collapse. Calculations
by the author showed the following:

4,100,000 in·lb   maximum moment with unbalanced snow load and reduced
                   tributary area at roof overhang portion for end beams per
                   1995 criteria

2,850,000 in·lb   maximum moment with balanced snow load and no consid-
                   eration for reduced tributary area at roof overhang portion
                   per 1965 criteria

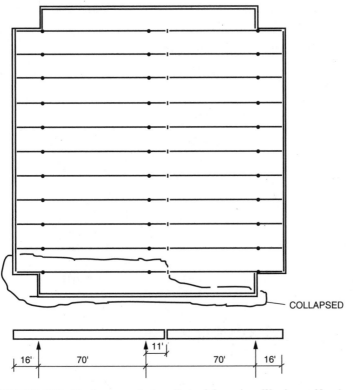

FIGURE 15.8 Warehouse roof plan. Port of Longview Warehouse No. 1, Longview, Washington.

9-in × 27⁵/₈-in glulam beams: $A = 247.5 \text{ in}^2$ $S = 1134 \text{ in}^3$

The original 1965 design condition using 1965 design criteria and use of balanced snow load (SL) plus dead loading at beam overhang yields

$$f_b = \frac{2{,}850{,}000 \text{ in·lb}}{1134 \text{ in}^3} = 2513 \text{ lb/in}^2$$

$$f_b' = (2600 \text{ lb/in}^2)(1.15)(0.86) = 2571 \text{ lb/in}^2$$
$$\phantom{f_b' = (2600 \text{ lb/in}^2)}\uparrow \quad\; \uparrow$$
$$\phantom{f_b' = (2600 \text{ lb/in}^2)}C_D \quad\, C_F$$

$$\frac{f_b}{F_b'} = \frac{2513 \text{ lb/in}^2}{2571 \text{ lb/in}^2} = 0.98$$

$$\text{Maximum SL deflection} = \frac{L}{262}$$

Use of 1965 design criteria with unbalanced snow load and reduced tributary area at roof overhang yields:

$$f_b = \frac{4{,}100{,}000 \text{ in}\cdot\text{lb}}{1134 \text{ in}^3} = 3616 \text{ lb/in}^2$$

$$\frac{f_b}{F_b'} = \frac{3616 \text{ lb/in}^2}{2571 \text{ lb/in}^2} = 1.41$$

$$\text{Maximum SL deflection} = \frac{L}{210}$$

Use of 1973 design criteria with unbalanced snow load and reduced tributary area at roof overhang yields:

$$f_b = \frac{4{,}100{,}000 \text{ in}\cdot\text{lb}}{1134 \text{ in}^3} \cdot \frac{38 \text{ lb/ft}^2}{32 \text{ lb/ft}^2} = 4293 \text{ lb/in}^2$$

$$F_b' = (2400 \text{ lb/in}^2)(1.15)(0.86) = 2324 \text{ lb/in}^2$$
$$\quad\quad\quad\quad\quad\quad \uparrow \quad\;\; \uparrow$$
$$\quad\quad\quad\quad\quad\quad C_D \quad C_F$$

$$\frac{f_b}{F_b'} = \frac{4293 \text{ lb/in}^2}{2324 \text{ lb/in}^2} = 1.81$$

Use of 1998 design criteria with unbalanced snow load and reduced tributary area at roof overhang yields:

$$C_V = 0.746$$

$$F_b' = (2200 \text{ lb/in}^2)(1.15)(0.746) = 1880 \text{ lb/in}^2$$
$$\quad\quad\quad\quad\quad\quad \uparrow \quad\;\; \uparrow$$
$$\quad\quad\quad\quad\quad\quad C_D \quad C_V$$

$$\frac{f_b}{F_b'} = \frac{4293 \text{ lb/in}^2}{1880 \text{ lb/in}^2} = 2.28$$

Conclusion. In this case the beam was initially undersized for good design practice and had too many strikes against it with water ponding creating the failure trigger. The actual water loading at failure is unknown, but the above calculations show the beam substantially overstressed without ponding considerations. Examination of the failed beam showed classical flexural failure of a properly manufactured beam.

Case Study 2. McMinnville Town Center
McMinnville, Oregon

This case study illustrates lateral buckling.

FIGURE 15.9 Collapse of light timber trusses during construction. McMinnville Town Center, McMinnville, Oregon. (Photo courtesy of McMinnville News Register.)

A series of one-story wood-framed buildings forming a retail sales strip mall was under construction in 1977. Proprietary wood chord-wood web, parallel chord roof trusses 42 in deep were used with 32-in truss spacing and 68-ft truss span.

Truss collapse had occurred at a portion of the complex while some trusses remained standing. See Fig. 15.9. The forensic evaluation was conducted in June and July of 1977. The position of the collapsed trusses on the ground indicated top chord buckling and truss rollover. No bracing was apparent. No detailed structural analysis was performed by the author. The problem was not a strength deficiency, as the trusses at time of collapse were carrying approximately 7 percent of their total design load.

The truss supplier had designed and furnished bracing elements consisting of bridging and plywood shear panels between trusses. None of this bracing or the roof diaphragm had been installed. All the trusses were installed by the contractor, who was planning to add bracing later in order to save crane time.

The forensic evaluation determined the collapse was caused solely by lateral buckling of truss top chords due to inadequate bracing. Litigation between the contractor and truss supplier was decided in favor of the truss supplier. The structure was rebuilt with identical, properly braced trusses.

Case Study 3. Lighter than Air Hangars
Moffett Field Naval Air Station
Moffett Field, California

This case study illustrates lateral buckling.

During the early portion of World War II, Germany waged a devastating sea war in the Atlantic, using its U-boats against Allied shipping. To counter this, the U.S. Navy was charged with developing a lighter-than-air (LTA) blimp patrol program, as the blimp could stay aloft for extended periods, spot submarines, and escort ship convoys.

To house the blimp squadrons, a total of 17 LTA hangars were constructed of fire-retardant treated solid sawn timbers. Two of these hangars were constructed at Moffett Field, California. Among the largest structures ever built of timber, the hangars are 1040 ft in length. The two-hinged trussed frames span 296 ft 6 in and rise to 170 ft 4 in in height.

Among the problems identified in the forensic evaluation were 36 buckled frame chords. The immense height placed some restrictions upon the repair procedures considered. The frames are constructed of double chords, double diagonal webs, and single vertical webs. The repair procedure selected consisted of placing solid glulam blocking between the double buckled chords with glulam strong-back sistering members on each side to realign buckled chords. The repair procedure was simple in concept, but more complex in execution.

Buckling of frame chords was a problem of the original design in selecting chord sizes of inadequate thickness or *l/d* ratio. About one-half of the 17 hangars constructed utilized 4-in nominal chords, and the remainder used 3-in nominal chords. Little or no buckling occurred at the 4-in nominal chords. Buckled chords at the Moffett Field hangar were confined to the 3-in nominal chords. A more detailed description of the forensic evaluation is contained in *Proceedings of the ASCE Structures Congress,* New Orleans, LA, 1986.[17]

The lower edges of frame lower chords have been covered with nailed blocking to discourage pigeon nesting. Figure 15.10 shows buckled lower chords with

FIGURE 15.10   Repair of timber frame lower chords at LTA hangar. Moffett Field Naval Air Station, Moffett Field, California. (*a*) Buckled frames with bird blocking present. (*b*) Buckled frames with bird blocking removed. (*c*) Repaired frames.

bird blocking in place, buckled lower chords with bird blocking removed, and repaired lower chords.

Following closure of the base by the Navy, the hangars were transferred to NASA. The 1989 Loma Prieta earthquake caused extensive damage to one of the hangars, and the author's firm was retained by NASA for forensic evaluation and development of structural repairs relating to the seismic damage.

Case Study 4. First Nazarene Church
Portland, Oregon

This case study illustrates notching and tapering of the tension face of the beam.

The roof structure of a large church was designed using glulam roof framing. Two beams $14\frac{1}{4}$ in $\times$ $88\frac{1}{2}$ in spanning 118 ft supported the entire roof system with glulam beam and light truss subframing. To satisfy architectural constraints the tension faces of beams were tapered 30 ft at each end. To facilitate the upper column seat, a notch was located within the upper taper cut. See roof framing plan and beam elevation sketches in Figs. 15.11 and 15.12.

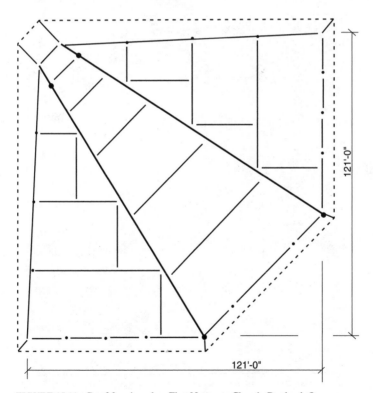

FIGURE 15.11 Roof framing plan. First Nazarene Church, Portland, Oregon.

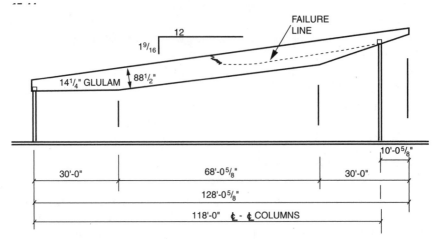

FIGURE 15.12 Roof beam elevation. First Nazarene Church, Portland, Oregon.

FIGURE 15.13 Collapsed structure. First Nazarene Church, Portland, Oregon.

The church had been occupied approximately one year when total collapse of the roof occurred on September 9, 1981. Approximately 20 min elapsed between the time failure was recognized and the time when total collapse occurred. Sticking doors and other building deformations had been occurring for a period of weeks or months preceding collapse, but were not initially recognized as a failure in progress. The author's firm was retained for forensic evaluation by the beam supplier. See Fig. 15.13.

The collapse occurred under mild weather conditions with no snow or other roof live loads present. The collapse was triggered by a separation at the notch located in the upper taper cut near the beam middepth. The separation progressed toward the midspan of the beam, separating the beam into two segments.

FIGURE 15.14 Beam following recovery from collapse. First Nazarene Church, Portland, Oregon.

Flexural failure occurred when bending stress exceeded resistance at the top portion of the separated beam. The two beams failed in identical fashion. See Fig. 15.14. Forensic evaluation determined that failure was solely due to effects of the notch and taper cut. The beam was otherwise sized in accordance with code requirements.

The church suffered substantial additional damage when a windstorm collapsed some of the remaining unbraced walls. Broken water pipes from the collapsed walls caused additional damage to what remained of the building. The church was rebuilt to the same configuration, using moment connected steel girders to replace the two failed beams. With the structure in place, a replacement timber beam was too heavy to lift by crane.

Case Study 5. Rosemont Horizon Arena
Rosemont, Illinois

This case study illustrates lateral buckling.

The sports and general-purpose arena was constructed in 1979 adjacent to Chicago's O'Hare Field. A total of 14 glulam barrel arches, spaced at 24-ft centers and spanning approximately 288 ft, frame the sports arena structure. The building footprint is approximately 288 ft × 382 ft in plan. Arches are $10^3/_4$ in × $73^1/_2$ in 24F glulam. Radius at top of barrel arch is 431 ft 8 in. The glulam arches were supplied in three segments, connected by two moment connections. Framing between arches consisted of glulam purlins at 4-ft centers with wood decking/diaphragm over.

On August 13, 1979, at a point when 12 of the 14 arches were in place, collapse occurred rapidly, killing five workers and injuring 19 others. Initially, several collapse theories were discussed in the extensive media coverage including vibration and wingtip vortex from low-flying aircraft.

Placement of purlins and decking/diaphragm was following well behind erection of the arches. Causes were attributed to lack of workers available, lack of coordination between the two operations, and schedule pressure. Every sixth purlin at 24-ft centers was of a larger size and designed as a tie beam bolted in place between arches. Investigation revealed that about one-third of these bolts were in place, and no bolts secured the last arch set.

Compressive buckling of the unrestrained arch, due to inadequate bracing, is considered to be the sole cause of failure. Arches ahead of the decking/diaphragm placement had inadequate or nonexistent lateral bracing. The rapid collapse also suggests buckling, whereas flexural failure is usually accompanied by noise and incremental movements over a period of time. The arena was rebuilt per the original design.

Case Study 6. Rainier Beach Library
Seattle, Washington

This case study illustrates

* Nodal rotation of fixed truss connections
* Secondary effects

A branch of the Seattle Public Library system was constructed in 1980, framed with timber roof trusses. Parallel chord trusses were designed using glulam chords and webs and connected with bolted steel plates. Truss span is 46 ft, and overall truss depth is 5 ft. See Fig. 15.15. Chords are continuous, and web-to-chord con-

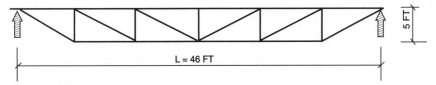

FIGURE 15.15   Truss profile. Rainier Beach Library, Seattle, Washington.

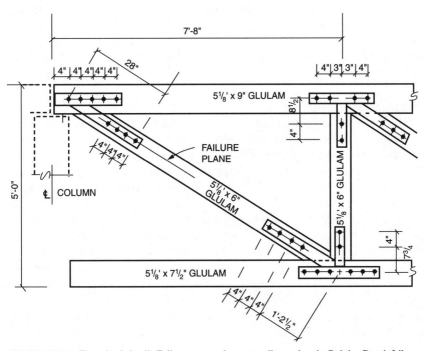

FIGURE 15.16   Truss heel detail. Failure occurred at outer diagonal web. Rainier Beach Library, Seattle, Washington.

nections were analyzed as pinned. Member sizing and bolt capacity were adequate for the primary loading condition.

The web-to-chord connections consisted of welded 3-in $\times$ 1/4-in steel fin plates on each side of truss following the profile of truss members. All connectors were 1-in bolts. The welded truss connection plates created partial fixity at truss joints. When the truss deflected under loading and nodal joints rotated, the multiple bolts in a row resisted that rotation by creation of moment couples in the glulam truss members, inducing a force perpendicular to grain and thereby stressing the glulam member in cross-grain tension. (See Fig. 15.16.)

In 1985, one outer diagonal web separated during a snow loading condition due to the moment couple induced by truss joint rotation. At the truss heel the distance from intersection of top chord and outer bolt of web connection is 28 in. The truss was shored and the split web replaced, including stitch bolts to resist perpendicular to grain forces.

The web failure was caused by a combination of nodal rotation and torque induced from heel eccentricity causing cross-grain tension in web members. (See Figs. 15.6 and 15.16.) This is an example of an adequate design for primary forces, but failure of a truss member caused by secondary effects of joint rotation as the truss deflected under loading. The moment couple induced in truss members was high due to a relatively flexible truss and a long moment arm caused by the rigid steel plate connection.

Case Study 7. Hayward Field West Grandstand
University of Oregon
Eugene, Oregon

This case study illustrates decay.

The University of Oregon has traditionally fielded a strong track and field program, and the Hayward Field facility is the heart of that program. The west grandstand, framed in glulam timber, was constructed in 1974.

Column-supported cantilevered glulam frames carry both the roof and the grandstand seating. The grandstand contains 11 glulam frames. The outer frame at each end is preservative-treated with pentachlorophenol in light solvent, and the inner 9 frames are untreated. Glulam beams spanning between the primary frames form treads and risers supporting the grandstand seating. These treads and risers restrain but do not prevent passage of free water from the grandstand to the glulam frames below.

Free water is present at the front portion of the grandstand from wind-blown rain and throughout the grandstand from power washing the underside of the seats following an event in the arena. Small amounts of moisture escaping through the grandstand wetted the glulam frame below and tended to accumulate in the steel base shoe supporting the frame. The problem was not recognized until substantial decay damage had occurred.

A forensic evaluation was conducted, examining the lower leg of all 11 frames in the spring of 1998, using nondestructive stress wave testing. The outer frames

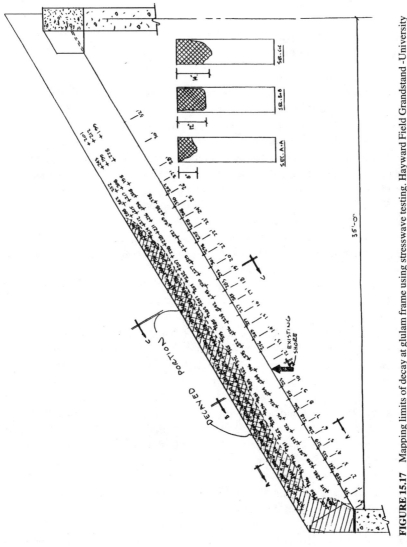

FIGURE 15.17 Mapping limits of decay at glulam frame using stresswave testing. Hayward Field Grandstand -University of Oregon, Eugene, Oregon.

containing preservative treatment were in nearly new condition. The nine untreated interior frames were in various stages of decay. Stress wave testing located the limits of decay, which were mapped to scale. Figure 15.17 illustrates stress wave mapping of decay at one of the glulam frames. Repair design is under way by the owner's structural engineer.

Case Study 8. Robert Frost School
Arlington Heights, Illinois

This case study illustrates overloading.

The school classroom and gymnasium roof structure is framed with glulam roof beams. The original building dates to 1964 for which southern pine glulam was furnished. A major addition in 1966 utilized Douglas fir glulam.

In February 1990, the author's firm was retained to conduct a forensic evaluation of distressed glulam roof beams at several classrooms. Six glulam beams were found to have failure of the tension lamination at or adjacent to the end joint. Those beams were shored, and no roof collapse occurred. All the beams appeared to be deflected in excess of what would be expected for the conditions of span, beam size, and apparent loading.

Stress wave testing was conducted to measure MOE, and cores were extracted to check material density and shear-tested for face bonding adhesive strength. End joints were examined carefully. The material stiffness was normal, and the adhesive strength and wood condition were good, except for the distress locations. Most beams had lost their initial camber and showed residual deflection which, in the absence of significant snow load, suggested long-term heavy dead load.

The original roof deck design consisted of 2-in poured gypsum on $1/2$-in gypsum formboard on steel bulb tees with 1-in rigid insulation, built-up roofing, and gravel. The school had recently been reroofed, and the roof level modified to improve roof drainage. Original gravel, roofing, and insulation were removed, and over the original gypsum deck was placed a leveling coat of insulating concrete, 1-in styrene insulation, and new roofing. Our firm was issued a letter indicating 20 lb/ft² total roof dead load including beams. Original design data were not available, but calculations showed the combination B glulam beams ($F_b = 2400$ lb/in²) were designed to carry approximately this amount of loading with code-prescribed 30 lb/ft² snow loading. Due to the uncertainty of calculating dead load with tapered elements or this type of construction, roof cores were requested. The request was initially rejected due to constraints of time, cost, and reluctance to bore holes in a new roof. The company installing the reroof was eventually retained for roof coring, but these cores were of roofing only, indicating a roofing weight of approximately 17 lb/ft². The cores did not penetrate the gypsum decking. A request was made for cores through the full roof and decking. Later an independent test laboratory was retained for coring of the full roof and decking. Roof weight varied due to tapering of the original gypsum decking and tapering of the reroof to achieve drainage, but a design dead load of 55 lb/ft^2 was recommended by the owner's structural engineer based upon the core data.

Beams designed for 20 to 25 lb/ft^2 dead load had initial dead load in excess of this amount due to gypsum deck thicker than specified. The reroof added more dead load to 55 lb/ft^2. The glulam beams performed exceptionally well under 25 years of substantial overload. Steel flitch plate beam reinforcing was designed by the owner's structural engineer.

Case Study 9. Hughes Aircraft Building
El Segundo, California

This case study illustrates

- Overloading
- War production directive
- State-of-the-art criteria revisions

The Hughes R-5 building covers approximately 11 acres, and the roof framing consists of approximately 540 timber bowstring trusses spanning 40 ft and spaced at 20-ft centers. The building was constructed during World War II and is located on Nash Street adjacent to the Los Angeles International Airport. At one time it was used as an assembly facility for Nash automobiles.

FIGURE 15.18 Roof mounted HVAC equipment. Hughes Aircraft Company, El Segundo, California.

The author's firm was retained in 1992 to evaluate approximately 20 percent of the roof structure following several truss failures. The bowstring trusses of solid sawn timber showed evidence of considerable weathering. A design review indicated the trusses were probably designed for 7 lb/ft² roof dead load, no ceiling load, and 12 lb/ft² live load using elevated allowable stresses per the War Production Directive. A variety of patching, splicing, and repair work showed evidence of past truss distress. The top chord was not fastened directly to a diaphragm and was stabilized only by the continuity of vertical truss webs to the roof above.

An analysis and design check showed the truss adequate for 9.9 lb/ft² dead load and no live load per the 1991 *UBC*. Although the trusses were initially marginal and well overstressed by current criteria, it is probable they would have performed without distress in the absence of roof overloading. The failure trigger for the distress observed was substantial overloading from roof-mounted HVAC equipment, as shown in Fig. 15.18. The roof surface is a maze of pipes, walkways, and mechanical equipment, which includes chilled water lines, ductwork, cooling and ventilating units, walkways, and platforms. The mechanical equipment loading created an extreme situation of roof overloading. From a structural standpoint, the simplest repair option was a new beam under each distressed truss, as the span was only 40 ft. The client elected to utilize new steel sistering trusses fastened on each side of the distressed original trusses.

Case Study 10. Sheridan High School Gym
Sheridan, Oregon

This case study illustrates

- Truss heel eccentricity
- State-of-the-art criteria revisions

The high school gym was constructed in 1949 using sawn timber bowstring roof trusses spanning 68 ft and spaced at 20-ft centers. A review of the truss supplier's documents indicates the trusses were designed to carry 640 lb/ft total dead plus snow load per 1949 design criteria. When investigated, the trusses were carrying dead load which added to the code-prescribed snow load amounting to 1040 lb/ft.

The author's firm was retained in 1994 to evaluate the trusses following extensive splitting at both top and lower chords near the vicinity of truss heels at several trusses. An analysis and design check showed the lower chord in tension to be 85 percent overstressed by present criteria. The overstress resulted from state-of-the-art criteria revisions over time, and additional ceiling dead load beyond that considered in the original design.

The failure trigger for splitting and distress of chords at truss heels was heel eccentricity of approximately 6 in. It is not known whether truss heel eccentricity resulted from not considering heel eccentricity significant initially or whether the columns were set too far apart. Heel eccentricity creates a torque induced into the heel joint which is the product of the eccentricity and the support reaction. This style of truss was not designed to resist heel eccentricity, and for full design load at the east truss heel, torque was nearly one-quarter million inch-pounds. (See Fig. 15.6.)

The factors contributing to the distress at truss heels were added ceiling load, state-of-the-art criteria changes, and heel eccentricity, with heel eccentricity having the greatest impact upon the distressed truss heels. The school district elected to demolish the building rather than repair the trusses.

Case Study 11. Lucky Strike Lanes
Tucson, Arizona

This case study illustrates

* Cross-grain tension at web-lower chord connection
* State-of-the-art criteria revisions

The bowling alley structure was constructed in about 1954. The roof is framed with solid sawn timber bowstring monochord trusses with a span of 120 ft and spacing of 19 ft 6 in. Ceiling framing supported by the truss lower chord carries HVAC equipment and the finish ceiling. The author's firm was retained in 1995 to evaluate separations in the truss lower chords. Of the seven trusses inspected, one contained an old lower chord separation, subsequently repaired, and three others showed unrepaired lower chord separations. The most severe location of distress amounted to a full severing of the lower chord, and that truss was shored.

The cause of lower chord separations was cross-grain tension due to the component of web members at the chord connection acting perpendicular to grain at the truss chord and the weight of the ceiling acting downward. Truss analysis assumes members to be line or bar elements and connections to be point nodes. The actual lower chord is an 8×12 timber member with the web connection near the top edge of chord and ceiling supported by framing near the lower edge of the chord. The ceiling load created cross-grain tension stress acting continuously upon the chord over its service life and eventually pulled the lower chord apart perpendicular to grain.

A simple clamp or stitch bolt on each side of each web-to-chord connection to resist this relatively small perpendicular to grain force could have prevented this type of problem.

Truss repair design was performed by the owner's structural engineer.

Case Study 12. Albertsons Grocery Warehouse
Portland, Oregon

This case study illustrates snow drifting.

Albertsons Inc. maintains a grocery warehouse in Portland, Oregon, servicing retail stores in Oregon and Washington. The 14-acre warehouse built in 1987 is framed with glulam timber beams and a panelized timber roof system. Attached to the primary building was a small 60-ft × 80-ft recycling and salvage building. Walls of the primary building were 11 ft higher than the roof of the salvage building at the location where they joined.

The 1994 *UBC* provides a design procedure for calculating the triangular surcharge of drifted snow load against an adjacent structure. Using that procedure, the calculated uniform snow load is 134.5 lb/ft² adjacent to the building, tapering to the minimum snow load of 25 lb/ft² in 25.5 ft, as shown in Fig. 15.19. Previous editions of the building code carried slightly different formulas yielding similar results.

The roof of the adjacent building was apparently designed without snow drift consideration. During the winter of 1994–1995, wind-driven snow accumulated at the wall adjacent to the higher building, which acted as a snow fence. The full 11-ft elevation filled with snow to the point where workers could walk from lower to upper roof level on the snow. This occurred in an area where snowfall is typically light but winds can be high.

The excessive loading fractured one purlin and several subpurlins, overstressing the entire area, and they were shored. The forensic evaluation was conducted in July 1995, and a repair procedure was developed. Subsequently it was learned

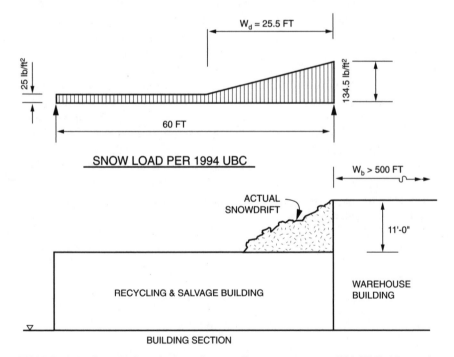

FIGURE 15.19 Snow load surcharge against an adjacent structure per 1994 UBC. Albertson's Grocery Warehouse, Portland, Oregon.

that Albertsons planned a major expansion which would require removal of the recycling and salvage building. As such, the shoring was retained and the building occupied until demolished by the facility expansion.

Case Study 13. Guilford of Maine Textile Mill
Newport, Maine

This case study illustrates

- State-of-the-art criteria revisions
- Beams in bending

The textile mill structure was built in 1959 with a major addition in 1962. The building footprint is approximately 228 ft $\times$ 176 ft. The roof structure is framed with 38 glulam beams 9 in $\times$ 45^1/$_2$ in size. Allowable bending stress of the combination 11 glulam beams was 2600 lb/in^2 per the 1957 NDS. Beam span is 85.5 ft with 12-ft beam spacing. The original loading criteria were 20 lb/ft^2 dead load and 40 lb/ft^2 snow load. A design check per the original design criteria showed the following:

$$\text{Size factor } C_F = 0.862$$

$$F_{b_{DL+SL}} = \frac{7,895,000 \text{ in·lb}}{3088 \text{ in}^3} = 2557 \text{ lb/in}^2$$

where the snow load, SL, is 40 lb/ft^2

$$F_b' = (2600 \text{ lb/in}^2)(1.15)(0.862) = 2577 \text{ lb/in}^2$$
$$\uparrow \quad \uparrow$$
$$C_D \quad C_F$$

$$f_b/F_b' = \frac{2557 \text{ lb/in}^2}{2577 \text{ lb/in}^2} = 0.992$$

Flexural distress of one beam occurred in February 1998. The beam was shored and did not collapse. The author's firm was retained for forensic evaluation in March 1998. The allowable bending stress for combination 11 glulam was adjusted to 2050 lb/in^2 based upon current allowable stress values for the grades of material present in the original beam layup. The dead load of 20 lb/ft^2 was verified. The ground snow load increased to 100 lb/ft^2 in this jurisdiction, adjusted to 70 lb/ft^2 for roof snow load. A design check of the existing beam per present criteria showed the following:

$$\text{Volume factor } C_V = 0.719$$

$$f_{b_{DL+SL}} = \frac{11,840,000 \text{ in·lb}}{3088 \text{ in}^3} = 3835 \text{ lb/in}^2$$

where the snow load, SL, is 70 lb/ft^2

$$F_b' = (2050 \text{ lb/in}^2)(1.15)(0.719) = 1695 \text{ lb/in}^2$$
$$\qquad\qquad\qquad\uparrow\qquad\uparrow$$
$$\qquad\qquad\qquad C_D\qquad C_V$$

$$\frac{f_{b\text{DL}+\text{SL}-40}}{F_b'} = \frac{2557 \text{ lb/in}^2}{1695 \text{ lb/in}^2} = 1.51$$

$$\frac{f_{b\text{DL}+\text{SL}-70}}{F_b'} = \frac{3835 \text{ lb/in}^2}{1695 \text{ lb/in}^2} = 2.26$$

Based upon 1998 design criteria, the beam capacity remaining for snow loading is 19.8 lb/ft^2. The distressed beam will be shored permanently, and post tensioning or intermediate support was recommended for the remaining beams.

Case Study 14. Church of Christ Spokane, Washington

This case study illustrates

- Arch repair with moment connections
- The unexpected

The Church of Christ roof structure was framed with glulam Tudor arches of the type commonly used for small church sanctuaries. The arch bases measured 5^1/$_8$ in $\times$ 15 in. A deranged person with a vendetta against churches vandalized numerous churches in eastern Washington over time. The person gained entry to the church at night and attempted to destroy the building by fire. A propane torch was wired to the base of several arches and lighted. The bases of three arches were severely charred in the vicinity of the torches, but the full building did not burn. The remaining cross section of the most severely burned arch was approximately equivalent to a 4 $\times$ 4 member.

For repair, the arch was shored against vertical load plus horizontal thrust. The lower 1^1/$_2$ ft of arch leg was cut off and fitted with a steel shoe. The shoe acted as a moment connection in that compression was confined to a bearing plate at the inside edge of the arch, and tension was taken with a steel strap fastened to the back of the arch with shear plates and lag bolts. The steel replacement shoe was narrower than the 5^1/$_8$-in-wide arch so that strips cut from a glulam beam could be fit on each side covering the steel and provided a cosmetic match with the glulam arch above.

Case Study 15. Hood River Valley High School Theater Hood River, Oregon

This case study illustrates

- Secondary effects
- Cross-grain tension at web-chord truss connections

The theater structure was designed and built in 1977 with walls of tilt-up concrete and roof framing of light timber trusses. Truss length is 64 ft 11^1/$_2$ in, truss depth is 45 in, and truss spacing is 32 in. The wood chord wood web trusses were of a unique design where web-to-chord and web-to-web connections consisted of glued finger joints.

Roof collapse occurred on January 12, 1979, under snow loading well below the design snow load. Initial forensic investigation centered on the strength of adhesive bond at web-to-chord finger joints. The author's firm was retained for forensic evaluation by the school district. Several undamaged trusses were removed from the structure and tested to destruction on a test rack.

Failure of the three trusses tested occurred well below design load with an average of dead load plus 56 percent of design snow load. The failure mode could be observed in the test rack. Failure occurred not in the adhesive but as cross-grain tension in the wood at web-to-chord finger joints. Nodal rotation of the truss connection caused a triangular-type tension distribution across the finger joint connection. The outer web connection failed, followed by inner web connections in rapid succession.

REFERENCES

1. *National Design Specification for Wood Construction (NDS)*, American Forest & Paper Association, Washington, DC, ANSI-AF & PA NDS-1997 and previous editions.
2. ASTM D 3737-89a, *Standard Method for Establishing Stresses for Structural Glued Laminated Timber*, American Society for Testing and Materials, Philadelphia, PA.
3. AITC 500-91, *Determination of Design Values for Structural Glued Laminated Timber in Accordance with ASTM D 3737-89a*, American Institute of Timber Construction, Englewood, CO.
4. AITC 117-93 Design, *Standard Specification for Structural Glued Laminated Timber of Softwood Species*, American Institute of Timber Construction, Englewood, CO, AITC 117-93 with 1994 and 1998 addenda.
5. ASTM D 198-94, *Standard Methods of Static Tests of Lumber in Structural Sizes*, American Society for Testing and Materials, Philadelphia, PA.
6. *Timber Construction Manual*, American Institute of Timber Construction (AITC), Wiley, New York, 1994.
7. *ANSI/AITC Standard A 190.1-1992 for Wood Products—Structural Glued Laminated Timber*, American Institute of Timber Construction, Englewood, CO.
8. *Inspection Manual AITC 200-92 for Structural Glued Laminated Timber*, American Institute of Timber Construction, Englewood, CO.
9. *Wood Handbook: Wood as an Engineering Material*, Reprinted from Forest Products Laboratory, General Technology Report FPL-GTR-113, Forest Products Society, Madison, WI.

10. ASTM D 143-83, *Standard Methods of Testing Small Clear Specimens of Timbers,* American Society for Testing and Materials, Philadelphia, PA.

11. ASTM D 4761-96, *Standard Test Methods for Mechanical Properties of Lumber and Wood-Base Structural Material,* American Society for Testing and Materials, Philadelphia, PA.

12. ASTM D 4442-92, *Standard Test Methods for Direct Moisture Content Measurement of Wood and Wood-Base Material,* American Society for Testing and Materials, Philadelphia, PA.

13. ASTM D 4444-92, *Standard Test Methods for Use and Calibration of Hand-Held Moisture Meters,* American Society for Testing and Materials, Philadelphia, PA.

14. Directive No. 29, *National Emergency Specification for the Design, Fabrication and Erection of Stress Grade Lumber and Its Fastenings for Buildings,* Conservation Division, War Production Board, Washington, August 9, 1943.

15. ASCE Standard 7-95, *Minimum Design Loads for Buildings and Other Structures,* American Society of Civil Engineers, Reston, VA, 1998.

16. *Uniform Building Code,* vol. 2, International Conference of Building Officials (ICBO), Whittier, CA, 1997.

17. Donald W. Neal, "Restoration of Navy LTA (Lighter Than Air) Hangars, Evaluation and Upgrading of Wood Structures," Session of ASCE Structures Congress, New Orleans, LA, 1986.

CHAPTER 16
STRUCTURAL FOUNDATIONS AND RETAINING WALLS

Robert W. Day, P.E.

ALLOWABLE FOUNDATION MOVEMENT

A foundation is defined as that part of the structure that supports the weight and loads acting on the structure and transmits this load to underlying soil or rock. Foundations are commonly divided into two categories: shallow and deep foundations. Table 16.1 presents a list of common types of foundations. The most frequently encountered conditions that cause damage to foundations and structures are settlement, expansive soil, lateral movement, and deterioration. Table 16.2[1] presents a list of the typical types of problems that affect foundations.

Because of the great diversity of foundation types (Table 16.1), there is no single code or standard in the United States that specifies the allowable movement of foundations. However, there is a considerable amount of data available on the subject (e.g., Refs. 2 through 7). For example, it has been stated that the allowable differential and total settlement should depend on the flexibility and complexity of the structure, including the construction materials and type of connections.[8]

In terms of the allowable foundation settlement, Coduto[9] states that it depends on many factors, including the following:

- *The type of construction.* For example, wood-frame buildings with wood siding would be much more tolerant than unreinforced brick buildings.

- *The use of the structure.* Even small cracks in a house might be considered unacceptable, whereas much larger cracks in an industrial building might not even be noticed.

- *The presence of sensitive finishes.* Tile or other sensitive finishes are much less tolerant of movements.

- *The rigidity of the structure.* If a footing beneath part of a very rigid structure settles more than the other footings, the structure will transfer some of the load away from the footing. However, footings beneath flexible structures must settle much more before any significant load transfer occurs. Therefore, a rigid structure will have less differential settlement than a flexible one.

TABLE 16.1 Common Types of Foundations

Category	Common types	Comments
Shallow foundations	Spread footings (also called pad footings)	Spread footings are often square in plan view, are of uniform reinforced-concrete thickness, and are used to support a single-column load located directly in the center of the footing.
	Strip footings (also called wall footings)	Strip or wall footings are often used for load-bearing walls. They are usually long, reinforced-concrete members of uniform width and shallow depth.
	Combined footings	Reinforced-concrete combined footings are often rectangular or trapezoidal in plan view, and carry more than one column load.
	Conventional slab-on-grade	A continuous reinforced-concrete foundation consisting of bearing wall footings and a slab-on-grade. Concrete reinforcement often consists of steel rebar in the footings and wire mesh in the concrete slab.
	Post-tensioned slab-on-grade	A continuous post-tensioned concrete foundation. The post-tensioning effect is created by tensioning steel tendons or cables embedded within the concrete. Common post-tensioned foundations are the ribbed foundation, California slab, and PTI foundation.
	Raised wood floor	Perimeter footings that support wood beams and a floor system. Interior support is provided by pad or strip footings. There is a crawl space below the wood floor.
	Mat foundation	A large and thick reinforced-concrete foundation, often of uniform thickness, that is continuous and supports the entire structure. A mat foundation is considered to be a shallow foundation if it is constructed at or near ground surface.

TABLE 16.1 Common Types of Foundations (*Continued*)

Category	Common types	Comments
Deep foundations	Driven piles	Driven piles are slender members, made of wood, steel, or precast concrete, that are driven into place by using pile-driving equipment.
	Other types of piles	There are many other types of piles, such as bored piles, cast-in-place piles, or composite piles.
	Piers	Similar to cast-in-place piles, piers are often of large diameter and contain reinforced concrete. Pier and grade beam support are often used for foundation support on expansive soil.
	Caissons	Large piers are sometimes referred to as caissons. A caisson can also be a watertight underground structure within which construction work is carried on.
	Mat or raft foundation	If a mat or raft foundation is constructed below ground surface or if the mat or raft foundation is supported by piles or piers, then it should be considered to be a deep foundation system.
	Floating foundation	A special foundation type where the weight of the structure is balanced by the removal of soil and construction of an underground basement.
	Basement-type foundation	A common foundation for houses and other buildings in frost-prone areas. The foundation consists of perimeter footings and basement walls that support a wood floor system. The basement floor is usually a concrete slab.

Note: Shallow and deep foundations in this table are based on the depth of the soil or rock support of the foundation.

16.4

TABLE 16.2 Problem Conditions Requiring Special Consideration

Problem type	Description	Comments
Soil	Organic soil, highly plastic soil	Low strength and high compressibility
	Sensitive clay	Potentially large strength loss upon large straining
	Micaceous soil	Potentially high compressibility
	Expansive clay, silt, or slag	Potentially large expansion upon wetting
	Liquefiable soil	Complete strength loss and high deformations caused by earthquakes
	Collapsible soil	Potentially large deformations upon wetting
	Pyritic soil	Potentially large expansion upon oxidation
Rock	Laminated rock	Low strength when loaded parallel to bedding
	Expansive shale	Potentially large expansion upon wetting; degrades readily upon exposure to air and water
	Pyritic shale	Expands upon exposure to air and water
	Soluble rock	Rock such as limestone, limerock, and gypsum that is soluble in flowing and standing water
	Cretaceous shale	Indicator of potentially corrosive groundwater
	Weak claystone	Low strength and readily degradable upon exposure to air and water
	Gneiss and Schist	Highly distorted with irregular weathering profiles and steep discontinuities
	Subsidence	Typical in areas of underground mining or high groundwater extraction
	Sinkholes	Areas underlain by carbonate rock (Karst topography)
Condition	Negative skin friction	Additional compressive load on deep foundations due to settlement of soil
	Expansion loading	Additional uplift load on foundation due to swelling of soil
	Corrosive environment	Acid mine drainage and degradation of soil and rock
	Frost and permafrost	Typical in northern climates
	Capillary water	Rise in water level which leads to strength loss for silts and fine sands

Source: Reproduced with permission from *Standard Specifications for Highway Bridges,* 16th ed., AASHTO, 1996.

Coduto[9] also states that the allowable settlement for most structures, especially buildings, will be governed by aesthetic and serviceability requirements, not structural requirements. Unsightly cracks, jamming doors and windows, and other similar problems will develop long before the integrity of the structure is in danger. Because the determination of the allowable settlement is so complex, engineers often rely on empirical correlations between observed behavior of structures and the settlement that results in damage.

Another major reference for the allowable settlement of structures is the 1956 paper by Skempton and MacDonald entitled "The Allowable Settlement of Buildings."[10] As shown in Fig. 16.1, Skempton and MacDonald defined the maximum angular distortion δ/L and the maximum differential settlement Δ for a building with no tilt. The angular distortion δ/L is defined as the differential settlement between two points divided by the distance between them less the tilt, where tilt equals the rotation of the entire building. As shown in Fig. 16.1, the maximum angular distortion does not necessarily occur at the location of maximum differential settlement.

Skempton and MacDonald studied 98 buildings, of which 58 had suffered no damage and 40 had been damaged in varying degrees as a consequence of settlement. From a study of these 98 buildings, they concluded in part the following:

- The cracking of the brick panels in frame buildings or load-bearing brick walls is likely to occur if the angular distortion of the foundation exceeds $1/300$. Structural

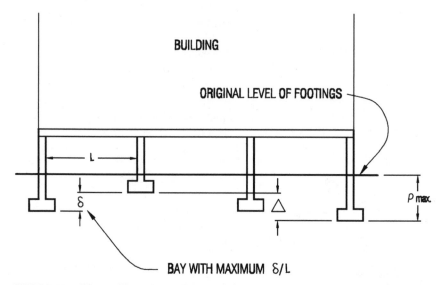

FIGURE 16.1   Diagram illustrating the definitions of maximum angular distortion and maximum differential settlement.

damage to columns and beams is likely to occur if the angular distortion of the foundation exceeds $1/150$.

- By plotting the maximum angular distortion δ/L versus the maximum differential settlement Δ, such as shown in Fig. 16.2, a correlation was obtained that is defined as $\Delta = 350\delta/L$ (note that Δ is in inches). Using this relationship and an angular distortion δ/L of $1/300$, cracking of brick panels in frame buildings or load-bearing brick walls is likely to occur if the maximum differential settlement Δ exceeds $1^{1}/4$ in (32 mm).

- The angular distortion criteria of $1/150$ and $1/300$ were derived from an observational study of buildings of load-bearing wall construction, and steel and reinforced-concrete-frame buildings with conventional brick panel walls but without diagonal bracing. The criteria are intended as no more than a guide for day-to-day work in designing typical foundations for such buildings. In certain cases they may be overruled by visual or other considerations.

The 1974 paper by Grant et al.[11] updated the Skempton and MacDonald data pool and also evaluated the rate of settlement with respect to the amount of damage incurred. Grant et al. in part concluded the following:

- A building foundation that experiences a maximum value of deflection slope δ/L greater than $1/300$ will probably suffer some damage. However, damage does not necessarily occur at the point where the local deflection slope exceeds $1/300$.

- For any type of foundation on sand or fill, new data tend to support Skempton and MacDonald's suggested correlation of $\Delta = 350\delta/L$ (see Fig. 16.2).

- Consideration of the rate of settlement is important only for the extreme situations of either very slow or very rapid settlement. Based on the limited data available, the values of maximum δ/L corresponding to building damage appear to be essentially the same for cases involving slow and fast settlements.

Data concerning the behavior of lightly reinforced, conventional slab-on-grade foundations have also been included in Fig. 16.2. These data indicate[12] that cracking of gypsum wallboard panels is likely to occur if the angular distortion of the slab-on-grade foundation exceeds $1/300$. The ratio of $1/300$ appears to be useful for both wood-frame gypsum wallboard panels and the brick panels studied by Skempton and MacDonald.[10] The data plotted in Fig. 16.2 would indicate that the relationship $\Delta = 350\delta/L$ can also be used for buildings supported by lightly reinforced slab-on-grade foundations. By using $\delta/L = 1/300$ as the boundary where cracking of panels in wood-frame residences supported by concrete slab-on-grade is likely to occur and substituting this value into the relationship $\Delta = 350\delta/L$ (Fig. 16.2), the calculated differential slab displacement is $1^{1}/4$ in (32 mm). For buildings on lightly reinforced slabs-on-grade, cracking of gypsum wallboard panels is likely to occur when the maximum slab differential exceeds $1^{1}/4$ in (32 mm).

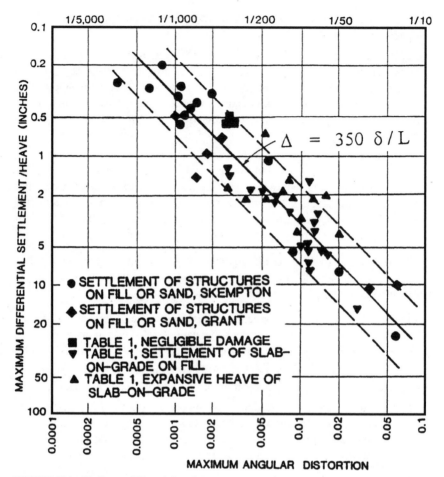

FIGURE 16.2 Maximum differential settlement versus maximum angular distortion. (Initial data from Skempton and MacDonald 1956, Table 1 in Day 1990.)

Another example of allowable settlements for buildings is Table 16.3.[13] In this table, the allowable foundation displacement has been divided into three categories: total settlement, tilting, and differential movement. Table 16.3 indicates that those structures that are more flexible (such as simple steel-frame buildings) or have more rigid foundations (such as mat foundations) can sustain larger values of total settlement and differential movement.

Figure 16.3 presents data from Ref. 14. Similar to the studies previously mentioned, this figure indicates that cracking in panel walls is to be expected at an angular distortion δ/L of $^1/_{300}$ and that structural damage of buildings is to be expected at an angular distortion δ/L of $^1/_{150}$. This figure also provides other limiting values of angular distortion, such as for buildings containing sensitive machinery or overhead cranes.

FOUNDATION MOVEMENT AND SEVERITY OF DAMAGE

Table 16.4 summarizes the severity of cracking damage versus approximate crack widths, typical values of maximum differential movement Δ and maximum angular distortion δ/L of the foundation.[15–17] The relationship between differential settlement Δ and angular distortion δ/L was based on the equation $\Delta = 350\delta/L$ (from Fig. 16.2).

When the severity of damage for an existing structure is assessed, the damage category (Table 16.4) should be based on multiple factors, including crack widths, differential settlement, and the angular distortion of the foundation. Relying on only one parameter, such as crack width, can lead to inaccuracy in cases where cracking has been hidden or patched, or in cases where other factors (such as concrete shrinkage) contribute to crack widths.

TABLE 16.3   Allowable Settlement

Type of movement	Limiting factor	Maximum settlement
Total settlement	Drainage	15–30 cm (6–12 in)
	Access	30–60 cm (12–24 in)
	Probability of nonuniform settlement:	
	Masonry-walled structure	2.5–5 cm (1–2 in)
	Framed structures	5–10 cm (2–4 in)
	Smokestacks, silos, mats	8–30 cm (3–12 in)
Tilting	Stability against overturning	Depends on H and W
	Tilting of smokestacks, towers	$0.004L$
	Rolling of trucks, etc.	$0.01L$
	Stacking of goods	$0.01L$
	Machine operation—cotton loom	$0.003L$
	Machine operation—turbogenerator	$0.0002L$
	Crane rails	$0.003L$
	Drainage of floors	0.01–$0.02L$
Differential movement	High continuous brick walls	0.0005–$0.001L$
	One-story brick mill building, wall cracking	0.001–$0.002L$
	Plaster cracking (gypsum)	$0.001L$
	Reinforced-concrete building frame	0.0025–$0.004L$
	Reinforced-concrete building curtain walls	$0.003L$
	Steel frame, continuous	$0.002L$
	Simple steel frame	$0.005L$

Notes: L = distance between adjacent columns that settle different amounts, or between any two points that settle differently. Higher values are for regular settlements and more tolerant structures. Lower values are for irregular settlement and critical structures. H = height and W = width of structure.
Source: From Sowers, 1962.[13]

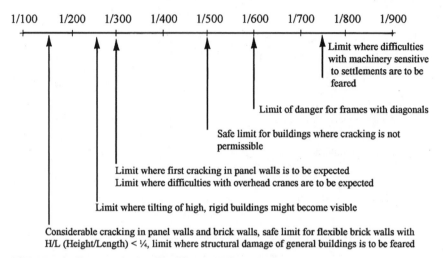

FIGURE 16.3   Damage criteria. (After Bjerrum 1963.)

Foundations subjected to settlement can be damaged by a combination of both vertical and horizontal movements. For example, a common cause of foundation damage is fill settlement. Figure 16.4 shows an illustration of the settlement of fill in a canyon environment. Over the sidewalls of the canyon, there tends to be a pulling or stretching of the ground surface (tensional features), with compression effects near the canyon centerline. This type of damage is due to two-dimensional settlement, where the fill compresses in both the vertical and horizontal directions.[18,19]

Another common situation where both vertical and horizontal foundation displacement occurs is at cut-fill transitions. A cut-fill transition occurs when a building pad has some rock removed (the cut portion), with a level building pad being created by filling in (with soil) the remaining portion. If the cut side of the building pad contains nonexpansive rock that is dense and unweathered, then very little settlement would be expected for that part of the building on cut. But the fill portion could settle under its own weight and cause damage. For example, a slab crack will typically open at the location of the cut-fill transition, as illustrated in Fig. 16.5. The building is damaged by both the vertical foundation movement (settlement) and the horizontal movement, which manifests itself as a slab crack and drag effect on the structure (Fig. 16.5).

In the cases described above, lateral movement is a secondary result of the primary vertical movement due to settlement of the foundation. Table 16.4 can therefore be used as a guide to correlate damage category with Δ and δ/L. In cases where lateral movement is the most predominate or critical mode of foundation displacement, Table 16.4 may underestimate the severity of cracking damage for values of Δ and δ/L.

TABLE 16.4 Severity of Cracking Damage

Damage category	Description of typical damage	Approx. crack width	Δ	δ/L
Negligible	Hairline cracks.	< 0.1 mm	< 3 cm (1.2 in)	< 1/300
Very slight	Very slight damage includes fine cracks that can be easily treated during normal decoration, perhaps an isolated slight fracture in building, and cracks in external brickwork visible on close inspection.	1 mm	3–4 cm (1.2–1.5 in)	1/300 to 1/240
Slight	Slight damage includes cracks that can be easily filled and redecoration would probably be required; several slight fractures may appear, showing on the inside of the building; cracks that are visible externally and some repointing may be required; and doors and windows may stick.	3 mm	4–5 cm (1.5–2.0 in)	1/240 to 1/175
Moderate	Moderate damage includes cracks that require some opening up and can be patched by a mason; recurrent cracks that can be masked by suitable linings; repointing of external brickwork and possibly a small amount of brickwork replacement may be required; doors and window stick; service pipes may fracture; and weathertightness is often impaired.	5–15 mm or a number of cracks >3 mm	5–8 cm (2.0–3.0 in)	1/175 to 1/120

TABLE 16.4 Severity of Cracking Damage (*Continued*)

Damage category	Description of typical damage	Approx. crack width	Δ	δ/L
Severe	Severe damage includes large cracks requiring extensive repair work involving breaking out and replacing sections of walls (especially over doors and windows); distorted windows and door frames; noticeably sloping floors; leaning or bulging walls; some loss of bearing in beams; and disrupted service pipes.	15–25 mm but also depends on number of cracks	8–13 cm (3.0–5.0 in)	$1/120$ to $1/70$
Very severe	Very severe damage often requires a major repair job involving partial or complete rebuilding; beams lose bearing; walls lean and require shoring; windows are broken with distortion; and there is danger of structural instability.	Usually >25 mm but also depends on number of cracks	>13 cm (>5 in)	$>1/70$

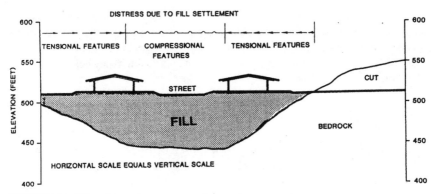

FIGURE 16.4 Fill settlement in a canyon environment.

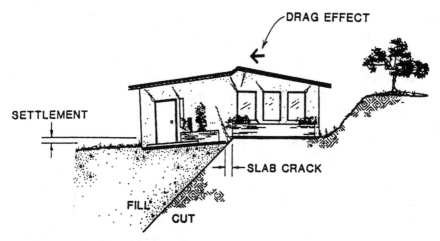

FIGURE 16.5 Cut-fill transition lot.

FIELD OBSERVATION, INSTRUMENTATION, TESTING, AND ANALYSIS

Field Observation

The purpose of the field observation is to evaluate the scope and nature of the failure. The initial site visit should be performed by the forensic engineer, who may be accompanied by assistants. For those structures having sudden damage or collapse, it is important to perform the initial site visit immediately after the assignment has been accepted. This is because evidence may be lost or disturbed as time goes by. It is important to take photographs of the observed damage and to collect samples at the initial site visit if it is likely that the samples will be lost or destroyed before the investigation can be completed.

Numerous photographs should be taken of the damaged structure. It may be appropriate to take a professional photographer who has the proper equipment for long-range and close-up photographs of the site. Sequentially numbering and marking the location of the photographs on a site plan sketch may help refresh recollection of where the pictures were taken.

Instrumentation

There are many types of monitoring devices used by forensic engineers. Some of the more common monitoring devices are as follows:

Inclinometers. The horizontal movement preceding or during the movement of slopes can be investigated by successive surveys of the shape and position of flexible vertical casings installed in the ground.[20] The surveys are performed by lowering an inclinometer probe into the flexible vertical casing. The inclinometer probe is capable of measuring its deviation from the vertical. An initial survey (base reading) is performed, and then successive readings are compared to the base reading to obtain the horizontal movement of the slope. Figure 16.6[21] shows a sketch of the inclinometer probe in the casing and the calculations used to obtain the lateral deformation.

Piezometers. Piezometers are routinely installed to monitor pore water pressures in the ground. Several different types are commercially available, including borehole, embankment, or push-in piezometers. Figures 16.7 and 16.8 (from Ref. 21) show examples of borehole piezometers.

Settlement Monuments or Cells. Settlement monuments or settlement cells can be used to monitor settlement or heave. Figure 16.9[21] shows a diagram of the installation of a pneumatic settlement cell and plate. More advanced equipment includes settlement systems installed in borings that not only can measure total settlement, but also can measure the incremental settlement at different depths.

Crack Pins. A simple method to measure the widening of a concrete or masonry crack is to install crack pins on both sides of the crack. By periodically measuring the distance between the pins, the amount of opening or closing of the crack can be determined.

Other crack-monitoring devices are commercially available. For example, Fig. 16.10 shows an Avongard crack-monitoring device. There are two installation procedures: (1) The ends of the device are anchored by the use of bolts or screws, or (2) the ends of the device are anchored with epoxy adhesive. The center of the Avongard crack-monitoring device is held together with clear tape, which is cut once the ends of the monitoring device have been securely fastened with bolts, screws, or epoxy adhesive.

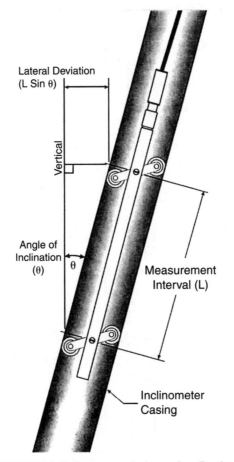

FIGURE 16.6 Inclinometer probe in a casing. (Reprinted with permission from the Slope Indicator Company.)

Other Monitoring Devices.   There are many other types of monitoring devices that can be used by the forensic engineer. Some commercially available devices include pressure and load cells, borehole and tape extensometers, soil strainmeters, beam sensors and tiltmeters, and strain gauges.

Testing

There are two general categories of field testing for the forensic investigation of foundation failures: nondestructive testing and destructive testing.

Nondestructive Field Testing.   After the initial site visit, there are usually follow-up visits in order to prepare field sketches and field notes, conduct interviews,

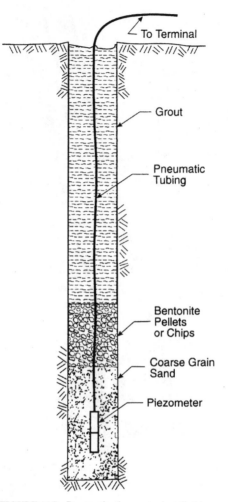

To Terminal

Grout

Pneumatic
Tubing

Bentonite
Pellets
or Chips

Coarse Grain
Sand

Piezometer

FIGURE 16.7 Pneumatic piezometer installed in a
borehole. (Reprinted with permission from the
Slope Indicator Company.)

perform nondestructive testing, and install monitoring devices such as piezometers and inclinometers.

As the name implies, nondestructive testing does not cause any damage or disruption to the site. An example of nondestructive testing is geophysical techniques that can be used to locate underground voids or buried objects, such as oil tanks. Similar to geophysical techniques is acoustic emission, which uses high-frequency sound waves to detect flaws in engineering structures. For example, Kisters and Kearney[22] state that "acoustic emission is presently being used to monitor crack propagation in bridges. This technique can be easily adapted to steel

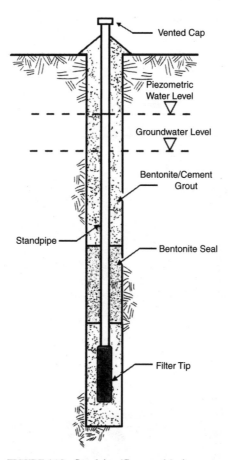

FIGURE 16.8   Standpipe (Casagrande) piezometer installed in a borehole. (Reprinted with permission from the Slope Indicator Company.)

lock and dam structures." According to Rens et al.,[23] other nondestructive testing includes thermal, ultrasonic, and magnetic methods. Thermal techniques have been applied to several civil engineering projects such as asphalt and pavement condition assessments.[23]

Another example of nondestructive testing is a manometer survey, which is also referred to as a floor-level survey. It is a nondestructive means of finding flaws or design defects in foundations. A manometer survey is commonly used to determine the relative elevation of a concrete slab-on-grade or other foundation element. The survey consists of taking elevations at relatively close intervals throughout the interior floor slab. These elevation points are then contoured, much like a topographic map, to provide a graphical rendition of the deformation condition of the foundation. Soil movement can cause displacement of the foundation,

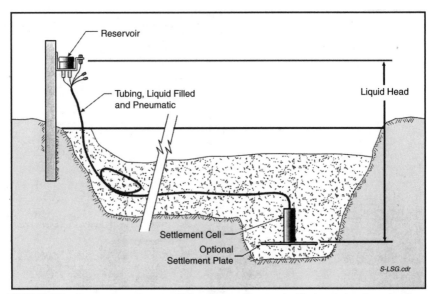

FIGURE 16.9 Pneumatic settlement cell installation. (Reprinted with permission from the Slope Indicator Company.)

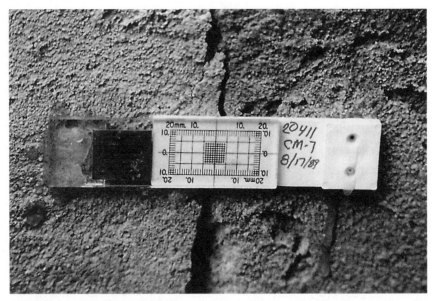

FIGURE 16.10 Avongard crack monitoring device.

and the manometer survey can detect this deformation. For example, if one side or corner of a concrete slab is significantly lower than the rest of the foundation, this could indicate settlement or slope movement in that area. Likewise, if the center of the foundation bulged upward, it would be detected by the manometer survey and this could indicate expansive soil. Other soil phenomena or slab conditions can also be detected by the manometer survey. For example, close deformation contours indicate a high angular distortion, which in many cases corresponds to the location of foundation cracks.

Destructive Field Testing. Concerning destructive testing, Miller[24] states:

> To document and cover the extent of resultant damages, it is often necessary to perform extensive destructive testing to determine the source and extent of the damage. Destructive testing can involve removing limited sections of the building so that access may be gained to concealed areas. If destructive testing is undertaken, it is imperative that it be performed in a logical and methodical fashion. Extensive documentation should be made during all portions of the destructive testing because it is a costly process, and repetition should be avoided if at all possible.

Examples of destructive testing include subsurface exploration, such as the excavation of test pits and borings.

The test pits or borings are used to determine the thickness of soil and rock strata, estimate the depth to groundwater, obtain soil or rock specimens, and perform field tests such as sand cone tests or standard penetration tests (SPTs). The Unified Soil Classification System (USCS) can be used to classify the soil exposed in the borings or test pits.[25] The subsurface exploration and field sampling should be performed in accordance with standard procedures, such as those specified by the American Society for Testing and Materials[26-28] or other recognized sources.[29-32] An example of field exploration and testing is shown in Fig. 16.11, where a test pit has been excavated into an airport runway and a sand cone test is being performed on the runway base material.

Another common type of destructive testing is the coring of foundations. By coring the foundation, the thickness of concrete, reinforcement condition, and any deterioration can be observed. Also, soil samples can be obtained directly beneath the foundation. Figure 16.12 shows a photograph of a slab-on-grade foundation that has been cored.

Numerous other types of destructive testing can be performed by the forensic engineer. Examples include field load tests, cone penetration testing, and in-place testing, such as determining the shear strength of in-place soil or rock.

Laboratory Testing. Laboratory tests are commonly used to determine the classification, moisture and density, index properties, shear strength, compressibility, and hydraulic conductivity of the soil. Soil, groundwater, or foundation samples recovered from the site visits can be sent to the laboratory for testing.

FIGURE 16.11   Test pit excavation.

FIGURE 16.12   Coring of a concrete slab-on-grade.

Usually at the time of the laboratory testing, the forensic engineer will have developed one or more hypotheses concerning the cause of the foundation failure. The objective of the laboratory testing is to further investigate these failure hypotheses. It is important that the forensic engineer develop a logical laboratory testing program with this objective in mind. The laboratory tests should be performed in accordance with standard procedures, such as those recommended by the American Society for Testing and Materials (ASTM) or those procedures listed in standard textbooks or specification manuals (e.g., Refs. 33 to 36).

For some foundation investigations, it may be important to determine the potential for future soil movement and damage. In these cases, the laboratory testing should model future expected conditions so that the amount of movement or stability of the ground can be analyzed.

For forensic investigations involving civil litigation, samples that are not irrecoverably damaged or destroyed during the laboratory testing should be saved and preserved so that they do not become contaminated. This is because other forensic experts involved in the case may want to observe or test the specimens. Also, at the time of trial, the specimens may need to be admitted as evidence.

Document Search

Table 16.5 presents a list of typical documents that may need to be reviewed for a forensic investigation. The following is a brief summary of these types of documents:

Reports and Plans.   The reports and plans that were generated during the design and construction of the project may need to be reviewed. The reports and plans can provide specific information on the history, design, and construction of the project. These documents may also provide information on maintenance or alterations at the site.

As part of the discovery process for projects dealing with civil litigation, attorneys commonly subpoena, or the judge may order, that the entire records of the owner, designers, and contractors be placed in a document depository. Once the documents are submitted to the document depository, they will be available to all parties involved in the lawsuit.

The judge assigned to the case will normally issue an order detailing the procedures to be followed concerning the document depository. Once documents have been submitted to the document depository, the depository coordinator will place a "bate-stamp," which is a prefix code and number, on each individual page or map. (The bate-stamp is named after the person who invented the sequential-numbering apparatus.) Many documents in the depository will be irrelevant in terms of the cause of the failure, and the forensic engineer must be able to distinguish the important applicable documents from useless data. For example, Matson[37] describes a case where the opponents flooded the document depository with irrelevant papers:

TABLE 16.5 Typical Documents That May Need to Be Reviewed for a Forensic Investigation

Project phase	Type of documents
Design	Design reports, such as geotechnical reports, planning reports, and feasibility studies Design calculations and analyses Computer programs used for the design of the project Design specifications Applicable building codes Shop drawings and design plans
Construction	Construction reports, such as inspection reports, field memos, laboratory test reports, mill certificates, etc. Contract documents (contract agreements, provisions, etc.) Construction specifications Project payment data or certificates Field change orders Information bulletins used during construction Project correspondence between different parties As-built drawings (such as as-built grading plans and foundation plans) Photographs or videos Building department permits and certificate of occupancy
Postconstruction	Postconstruction reports, such as maintenance reports, modification documents, reports on specific problems, and repair reports Photographs or videos
Technical data	Available reports such as weather reports and seismic activity Reference materials, such as geologic and topographic maps and aerial photographs Technical publications, such as journal articles that describe similar failures

The approach was the "needle in the haystack" in which the opponents supplied tons of paper so overwhelming that my eyes became bloodshot reading only box labels. I spent all my time searching for meaningful documents in the flood of paper.

Building Codes.   A copy of the applicable building code in effect at the time of construction should be reviewed. It has been argued that the standard of care is simply to perform work in accordance with the local building code. While performing work in accordance with building codes may reduce potential liability, it is still possible that in a court of law a design engineer will be held to a higher standard. For example, Shuirman and Slosson[38] state that, in many jurisdictions, the building codes and code enforcement may not meet current professional standards, and design engineers cannot rely on building codes to indemnify them from liability.

Technical Documents.   During the course of the forensic investigation, it may be necessary to check reference materials, such as geologic maps or aerial photographs. Other useful technical documents can include journal articles that may describe a failure similar to the one under investigation. For example, the *ASCE Journal of Performance of Constructed Facilities* deals specifically with construction-related failures or deterioration.

Analysis

Calculations or computer analyses may be needed to help evaluate different failure hypotheses or the potential for future damage. It may even be appropriate to model the failure, such as by using finite-element analyses (e.g., Refs. 39 and 40). A thorough analysis is especially important with projects involving lawsuits because one objective is usually to determine proportional responsibility. Based on the cause of the failure, the forensic engineer will be able to offer an opinion on who is responsible for the failure and proportion the responsibility between different parties.

In performing the analysis and in the development of conclusions, the forensic engineer may need to rely on the expertise of other forensic specialists. For example, geological studies are often essential in the investigation of landslides, rockfall, and seismic activity.[41]

There can be many different causes of failure. Some of the more common causes of failure are related to inadequate subsurface exploration and laboratory testing, technical deficiencies or design errors, specification mistakes, improper construction, and defective materials.[42] The failure theory must be well thought out and based on the facts of the case. It is not unusual that the forensic engineers involved in a case will disagree on the cause of the failure. Common reasons for a disagreement on the cause of the failure include the loss of evidence during the failure, the presence of conflicting test data, substantially differing eyewitness accounts of the failure, or just differences of engineering opinions.

TYPES AND CAUSES OF COMMON NONPERFORMANCE AND FAILURE

As previously mentioned, the most frequently encountered geotechnical conditions that cause damage to foundations and structures are settlement, expansive soil, lateral movement, and deterioration. Each is discussed in this section.

Settlement

Settlement can be defined as the permanent downward displacement of the foundation. There are two basic types of settlement:

- *Settlement due directly to the weight of the structure.* For example, the weight of a building may cause compression of an underlying sand deposit or consolidation of an underlying clay layer.

- *Settlement due to secondary influences.* This may develop at a time long after the completion of the structure. This type of settlement is not directly caused by the weight of the structure. For example, the foundation may settle as water infiltrates the ground and causes unstable soils to collapse (i.e., collapsible soil). The foundation may also settle due to movement of adjacent excavations, or due to the collapse of limestone cavities or underground mines and tunnels. Other causes of settlement that would be included in this category are natural disasters, such as settlement caused by earthquakes or undermining of the foundation resulting from floods.

Subsidence is usually defined as a sinking down of a large area of the ground surface. Subsidence could be caused by the extraction of oil or groundwater which leads to a compression of the underlying porous soil or rock structure. Since subsidence is due to a secondary influence (extraction of oil or groundwater), its effect on the structure is included in the second basic type of settlement described above.

A special case of vertical movement is the downward displacement of the foundation due to the drying of underlying wet clays. Often this downward displacement of the foundation caused by the desiccation of clays is referred to as settlement. But upon the introduction of moisture, such as during the rainy season, the desiccated clay will swell and the downward displacement will be reversed. The foundation could even heave more than it initially settled. When dealing with expansive clays, it is best to consider the downward displacement of the foundation as part of the cyclic heave and shrinkage of expansive soil, and not as permanent settlement.

In terms of forensic engineering, settlement is defined as vertical or differential movement of the failed facility resulting in distress or collapse.[42] The determination of settlement can be made through field and laboratory testing. When one is investigating settlement of structures, it is important to compare the actual applied loading that caused failure with the design or expected loading. Settlement of the structure could be due to increased or unanticipated loading or problems with the bearing soil or rock.

The majority of foundations are adequately constructed and perform as designed; however, there are many instances where settlement can cause damage and foundation failure. Common causes of settlement are consolidation of soft and/or organic soil, settlement from uncontrolled or deep fill, and the development of limestone cavities or sinkholes.[43] Foundations can also experience settlement due to natural disasters, such as earthquakes or the undermining of the foundation from floods. There have been reports of widespread ground subsidence caused by the extraction of oil or groundwater as well as the collapse of underground mines and tunnels.

When investigating damage due to settlement, the forensic engineer should also evaluate the foundation design and construction process, which could be contributing factors in the damage. There are many excellent references, such as *Foundation Analysis and Design,*[44] that present the methods and procedures for the analysis and design of foundations.

Settlement of the Foundation Caused by Collapsible Soil. In the southwestern United States, probably the most common cause of foundation settlement is collapsible soil. For example, Johnpeer[45] states that ground subsidence from collapsing soils is a common occurrence in New Mexico. The category of collapsible soil would include the settlement of debris, uncontrolled fill, deep fill, or natural soil, such as alluvium or colluvium.

Collapsible soil can be broadly classified as soil that is susceptible to a large and sudden reduction in volume upon wetting. Collapsible soil usually has a low dry density and low moisture content. Such soil can withstand a large applied vertical stress with a small compression, but then experience much larger settlements after wetting, with no increase in vertical pressure.[46]

In general, there has been an increase in damage due to collapsible soil, probably because of the lack of available land in many urban areas. The scarcity of land causes development of marginal land, which may contain deposits of dumped fill or deposits of natural collapsible soil. Also, substantial grading can be required to develop level building pads, which results in more areas having deep fill.

Fill. Deep fill has been defined as fill that has a thickness greater than 6 m (20 ft).[43] Uncontrolled fills include fills that were not documented with compaction testing as they were placed; these include dumped fills, fills dumped underwater, hydraulically placed fills, and fills that may have been compacted but there is no documentation of testing or the amount of effort that was used to perform the compaction.[43] These conditions may exist in rural areas where inspections are lax, or for structures built many years ago when the standards for fill compaction were less rigorous.

For collapsible fill, compression will occur as the overburden pressure increases. The increase in overburden pressure could be due to the placement of overlying fill or the construction of a building on top of the fill. The compression due to this increase in overburden pressure involves a decrease in the void ratio of the fill due to expulsion of air. The compression usually occurs at constant moisture content. After completion of the fill mass, water may infiltrate the soil due to irrigation, rainfall, or leaky water pipes. The mechanism that usually causes the collapse of the loose soil structure is a decrease in negative pore pressure (capillary tension) as the fill becomes wet.

For a fill specimen submerged in distilled water, the main variables that govern the amount of one-dimensional collapse are the soil type, compacted moisture content, compacted dry density, and vertical pressure.[47-51] In general, the one-dimensional collapse of fill will increase as the dry density decreases, the moisture content decreases, or the vertical pressure increases. For a constant dry density and moisture content, the one-dimensional collapse will decrease as the clay fraction increases once the optimum clay content (usually a low percentage) is exceeded.[52]

Alluvium or Colluvium. For natural deposits of collapsible soil in the arid climate of the southwest United States, a common mechanism involved in rapid volume reduction entails breaking of bonds at coarse particle contacts by weakening of fine-grained materials brought there by surface tension in evaporating water. In other cases, the alluvium or colluvium may have an unstable soil structure which collapses as the wetting front passes through the soil.

Laboratory Testing. If collapsible soil is the suspected cause of damage at a site, then soil specimens should be obtained and tested in the laboratory. One-dimensional collapse is usually measured in the oedometer.[53] After the soil specimen is placed in the oedometer, the vertical pressure is increased until it approximately equals the in situ overburden pressure. At this vertical pressure, distilled water is added to the oedometer to measure the amount of collapse of the soil specimen. Percent collapse $\%C$ is defined as the change in height of the specimen due to inundation divided by the initial height of the specimen.[53]

Figure 16.13 presents the results of a one-dimensional collapse test performed on a fill specimen. The fill specimen contains 60 percent sand-size particles, 30 percent silt-size particles, and 10 percent clay-size particles and is classified as a silty sand (SM). To model field conditions, the silty sand was compacted at a dry unit weight of 92.4 lb/ft³ (14.5 kN/m³) and moisture content of 14.8 percent. The silty sand specimen, having an initial height of 1.0 in (25.4 mm), was subjected to a vertical stress of 3000 lb/ft² (144 kPa) and then inundated with distilled water. Figure 16.13 shows the amount of vertical deformation (collapse) as a function of time after inundation. The equations that are used to determine the percent collapse $\%C$ are shown in Fig. 16.14. For the collapse test on the silty sand (fill type number 1, Fig. 16.13), the percent collapse $\%C = 2.62$ mm/25.4 mm $\times$ 100% = 10.3 percent.

The collapse potential CP of a soil can be determined by applying a vertical stress of 2 tons/ft² (200 kPa) to the soil specimen, submerging it in distilled water, and then determining the percent of collapse which is designated the collapse potential CP. This collapse potential can be considered as an index test to compare the susceptibility of collapse for different soils. In Fig. 16.14, the collapse potential versus severity of the problem has been listed in tabular form.

As previously mentioned, the triggering mechanism for the collapse of fill or natural soil is the introduction of moisture. Common reasons for the infiltration of moisture include water from irrigation, broken or leaky water lines, and an altering of surface drainage which allows rainwater to pond near the foundation. Another source of moisture infiltration is from leaking pools. For example, Fig. 16.15 shows a photograph of a severely damaged pool shell which cracked due to the collapse of an underlying uncompacted debris fill.

Settlement of the Foundation due to Limestone Cavities or Sinkholes. Settlement related to limestone cavities or sinkholes will usually be limited to areas having karst topography. *Karst topography* is a type of landform developed in a region of easily soluble limestone bedrock. It is characterized by vast numbers of depressions of all sizes, sometimes by great outcrops of limestone, sinks and other solution passages, an almost total lack of surface streams, and larger springs in the deeper valleys.[54]

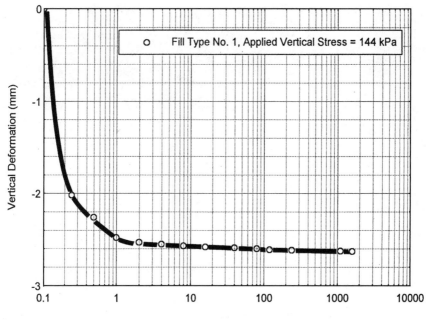

FIGURE 16.13   Laboratory test results from a collapsible soil.

Percent collapse (%C) defined as:

$$\%C = \frac{100\ \Delta e_c}{1 + e_o} \quad \text{or} \quad \%C = \frac{100\ \Delta H_c}{H_o}$$

Δe_c = Change in void ratio upon wetting, e_o = Initial void ratio
ΔH_c = Change in height upon wetting, H_o = Initial height

Collapse Potential Values (Based on ASTM D 5333-92, 1998)*

Collapse Potential (CP) (1)	Severity of Problem (2)
0	No problem
0.1 to 2%	Slight
2.1 to 6%	Moderate
6.1 to 10%	Moderately severe
>10%	Severe

*Note: For collapse potential, the vertical pressure upon inundation must equal 200 kPa.

FIGURE 16.14   Equations and collapse potential values.

FIGURE 16.15 Damage to a pool shell due to collapse of underlying uncompacted fill (arrows point to cracks in the pool shell).

Identification techniques and foundations constructed on karst topography are discussed by Sowers.[55] Methods to investigate the presence of sinkholes are geophysical techniques and the cone penetration device.[56,57] A low cone penetration resistance could indicate the presence of raveling, which is a slow process whereby granular soil particles migrate into the underlying porous limestone. An advanced state of raveling will result in subsidence of the ground, commonly referred to as sinkhole activity.

Settlement of the Foundation due to Consolidation of Soft and/or Organic Soil. Most soil mechanics textbooks have an in-depth discussion of the subsurface exploration, laboratory testing, and engineering analysis required to identify and evaluate the settlement potential of soft clay and/or organic soil.[58–61] The settlement of saturated clay or organic soil can have three different components: immediate (or initial), consolidation, and secondary compression.

Immediate or Initial. In most situations, surface loadings causes both vertical and horizontal strains, and this is referred to as two- or three-dimensional loading. Immediate settlement is due to undrained shear deformations, or in some cases contained plastic flow, caused by the two- or three-dimensional loading.[62] Common examples of three-dimensional loading are from square footings and round storage tanks. Such a loading of a saturated clay can result in distress or collapse due to vertical and horizontal strains caused by immediate settlement of the clay.

Consolidation.   The typical one-dimensional case of settlement involves strain in only the vertical direction. Common examples of one-dimensional loading include the lowering of the water table or a uniform fill surcharge applied over a very large area. Consolidation is a time-dependent process that may take many years to complete.

Secondary Compression.   The final component of settlement is due to secondary compression, which is that part of the settlement that occurs after essentially all the excess pore water pressures have dissipated. Secondary compression occurs at constant effective stress and can constitute a major part of the total settlement for peat or other highly organic soil.[60] Figure 16.16 shows two examples of the settlement of peat at the "Meadowlands," which is a marshy area in New Jersey (west of New York City). Piles are often used to support structures at the Meadowlands, but as shown in Fig. 16.16, the floor slab is typically unable to span between piles and it breaks off from the pile caps or deforms around the pile caps as the peat settles.[63]

Settlement of the Foundation due to Collapse of Underground Mines and Tunnels.
According to Gray,[64] damage to residential structures in the United States caused by the collapse of underground mines is estimated to be between $25 and $35 million each year, with another $3 to $4 million in damage to roads, utilities, and services. There are approximately 2 million hectares of abandoned or inactive coal mines, with 10 percent of these hectares in populated urban areas.[65] It has been stated that ground subsidence associated with long-wall mining can be predicted fairly well with respect to magnitude, time, and areal position.[66] Once the amount of ground subsidence has been estimated, there are measures that can be taken to mitigate the effects of mine-related subsidence.[67–70] For example, in a study of different foundations subjected to mining-induced subsidence, it was concluded that post tensioning of the foundation was most effective, because it prevented the footings from cracking.[66]

Similar to the discussion of fill in a canyon environment, the collapse of underground mines and tunnels can produce tension- and compression-type features within the buildings. Figure 16.17[71] shows that the compression zone will be located in the center of the subsided area. The tension zone is located along the perimeter of the subsided area. These tension and compression zones are similar to fill settlement in a canyon environment (Fig. 16.4).

Besides the collapse of underground mines and tunnels, there can be settlement of buildings constructed on spoil extracted from the mines. Mine operators often dispose of other debris, such as trees, scrap metal, and tires, within the mine spoil. In many cases, the mine spoil is dumped (no compaction) and can be susceptible to large amounts of settlement. For example, Cheeks[72] describes an interesting case of a motel unknowingly built on spoil that had been used to fill in a strip-mining operation. The motel building experienced about 3 ft (1 m) of settlement within the monitoring period (5 years). The settlement and damage for this building actually started during construction, and the motel owners could never place

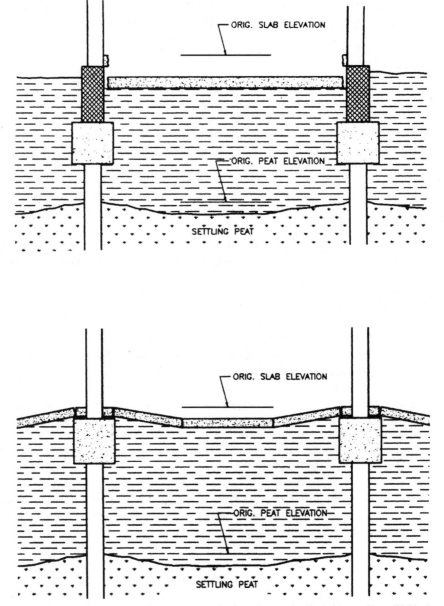

FIGURE 16.16   Common slab displacement mechanisms due to subsoil subsidence. (From Whitlock and Moosa 1996, reprinted with permission from the American Society of Civil Engineers.)

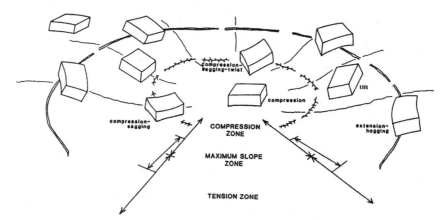

FIGURE 16.17   Location of tension and compression zones due to collapse of underground mines. (From Marino et al. 1988, reprinted with permission from the American Society of Civil Engineers.)

the building into service. The outcome of the subsequent lawsuit was that the cost of litigation exceeded $1 million, which approached the value of the final monetary award.[72] Litigation expenses that approach or even exceed the final judgment are a common occurrence.

Settlement of the Foundation due to Ground Subsidence from Extraction of Oil or Groundwater.   Large-scale pumping of water or oil from the ground can cause settlement of the ground surface over a large area. The pumping can cause a lowering of the groundwater table which then increases the overburden pressure on underlying sediments. This can cause consolidation of soft clay deposits. In other cases, the removal of water or oil can lead to compression of the soil or porous rock structure, which then results in ground subsidence.

Lambe and Whitman[58] describe two famous cases of ground surface subsidence due to oil or groundwater extraction. The first is oil pumping from Long Beach, California, which affected a 25-mi^2 (65-km^2) area and caused 25 ft (8 m) of ground surface subsidence. Because of this ground surface subsidence, the Long Beach Naval Shipyard had to construct special seawalls to keep the ocean from flooding the facilities. A second famous example is ground surface subsidence caused by pumping of water for domestic and industrial use in Mexico City. Rutledge[73] shows that the underlying Mexico City clay, which contains a porous structure of microfossils and diatoms, has a very high void ratio (up to $e_o = 14$) and is very compressible. Ground surface subsidence in Mexico City has been reported to be 30 ft (9 m) since the beginning of the 20th century.

Besides ground surface subsidence, the extraction of groundwater or oil can cause the opening of ground fissures. For example, Fig. 16.18 shows the ground surface subsidence in Las Vegas Valley between 1963 and 1987 due primarily to groundwater extraction. It has been stated[74] that the subsidence has been focused on preexisting geologic faults, which serve as points of weakness for ground movement. Figure 16.19 shows one of these fissures that ran beneath the foundation of a home.

Expansive Soil

Expansive soils are a worldwide problem, causing extensive damage to civil engineering structures. Jones and Holtz[75] estimated in 1973 that the annual cost of damage in the United States due to expansive soil movement was $2.3 billion. Although most states have expansive soil, Chen[76] reported that certain areas of the United States, such as Colorado, Texas, Wyoming, and California, are more susceptible to damage from expansive soils than others. These areas have large surface deposits of clay and have climates characterized by alternating periods of rainfall and drought.

Expansive Soil Factors.   There are many factors that govern the expansion behavior of soil. The primary factors are the availability of moisture, and the amount and type

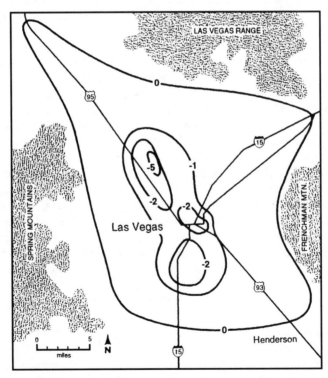

FIGURE 16.18 Land surface subsidence (in feet) in Las Vegas Valley between 1963 and 1987. (From Purkey et al. 1994, reprinted with permission from the Nevada Bureau of Mines and Geology.)

FIGURE 16.19 Fissure, widened by erosion, running beneath the foundation of an abandoned home near Simmons St. in North Las Vegas. (From Purkey et al. 1994, reprinted with permission from the Nevada Bureau of Mines and Geology.)

of the clay particles in the soil. For example, Seed et al.[77] developed a classification chart based solely on the amount and type (activity) of clay particles (see Fig. 16.20). Other factors affecting the expansion behavior include the type of soil (natural or fill), the condition of the soil in terms of dry density and moisture content, the magnitude of the surcharge pressure, the amount of nonexpansive material (gravel or cobble-size particles), and the amount of aging.[78–81] In general, expansion potential increases as the dry density increases and the moisture content decreases. Also, the expansion potential increases as the surcharge pressure decreases.

As shown in Fig. 16.20, the more clay particles of a particular type a soil has, the more swell there will be (all other factors being the same). Likewise, as shown in Fig.

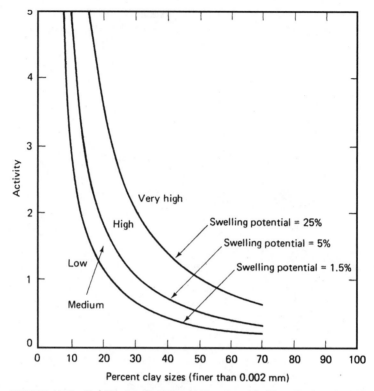

FIGURE 16.20 Classification chart for swelling potential. (From Seed et al. 1962, reprinted with permission from the American Society of Civil Engineers.)

16.20, the type of clay particles significantly affects the swell potential. Given the same dry weight, kaolinite clay particles (activity between 0.3 and 0.5) are much less expansive than sodium montmorillonite clay particles (activity between 4 and 7). Using such factors as the clay particle content, Holtz and Gibbs[82] developed a system to classify soils as having a low, medium, high, or very high expansion potential. Table 16.6 lists typical soil properties versus the expansion potential.[83,84]

Laboratory Testing.   The forensic engineer can determine the presence of expansive soil by performing subsurface exploration and laboratory testing. One common laboratory test used to determine the expansion potential of the soil is the expansion index test. The test provisions are stated in the *Uniform Building Code*,[83] titled "Uniform Building Code Standard 18-2, Expansion Index Test," and in ASTM,[85] which has a nearly identical test specification (D 4829). The purpose of this laboratory test is to determine the expansion index, which is then used to classify the soil as having a very low, low, medium, high, or very high expansion potential, as shown in Table 16.6.

Other laboratory tests, such as hydrometer analyses and Atterberg limits, can be used to classify the soil and estimate its expansiveness. Those soils hav-

TABLE 16.6 Typical Soil Properties versus Expansion Potential

	Expansion potential				
	Very low	Low	Medium	High	Very high
Expansion index	0–20	21–50	51–90	91–130	130+
Clay content	0–10%	10–15%	15–25%	25–35%	35–100%
Plasticity index	0–10	10–15	15–25	25–35	35+
% Swell @ 2.8 kPa (60 lb/ft^2)	0–3	3–5	5–10	10–15	15+
% Swell @ 6.9 kPa (144 lb/ft^2)	0–2	2–4	4–7	7–12	12+
% Swell @ 31 kPa (650 lb/ft^2)	0	0–1	1–4	4–6	6+

Note: Percent of swell for specimens at moisture and density conditions per HUD criteria.

ing a high clay content and plasticity index, such as clays of high plasticity, CH, will usually be classified as having a high to very high expansion potential (see Table 16.6).

The most direct method of determining the amount of swelling is by performing a one-dimensional swell test by utilizing the oedometer apparatus. The undisturbed soil specimen is placed in the oedometer, and a vertical pressure (also referred to as surcharge pressure) is applied. Then the soil specimen is inundated with distilled water, and the one-dimensional vertical swell is calculated as the increase in height of the soil specimen divided by the initial height, often expressed as a percentage. Such a test offers an easy and accurate method of determining the percent of swell of the soil. After the soil has completed its swelling, the vertical pressure can be increased to determine the swelling pressure, which is defined as that pressure required to return the soil specimen to its original (initial) height.[76]

Surcharge Pressure. The bottom three rows of Table 16.6 list typical values of percent of swell versus expansion index. Note in Table 16.6 the importance of surcharge pressure on percent of swell. At a surcharge pressure of 650 lb/ft^2 (31 kPa), the percent of swell is much less than at a surcharge pressure of 60 lb/ft^2 (2.8 kPa). For example, for "highly" expansive soil, the percent of swell for a surcharge pressure of 60 lb/ft^2 (2.8 kPa) is typically 10 to 15 percent, while at a surcharge pressure of 650 lb/ft^2 (31 kPa), the percent of swell is 4 to 6 percent. The effect of surcharge is important because it is usually the lightly loaded structures, such as concrete flatwork, pavements, slab-on-grade foundations, or concrete canal liners, that are significantly impacted by expansive soil.

Lateral Movement

The most common cause of lateral movement of foundations is slope movement. The most common types of slope movement that damage foundations are as follows:

1. *Gross slope failure.* A gross slope failure involves shear displacement of the entire slope. Terms such as *fill slope failures* and *earth* or *rock slumps* have been used to identify similar processes.

2. *Landslides.* The gross failure of a slope could be referred to as a landslide. However, landslides in some cases may be so large that they involve several different slopes.

3. *Debris flow.* Debris flow is commonly defined as soil with entrained water and air that moves readily as a fluid on low slopes. Debris flow can include a wide variety of soil-particle sizes (including boulders) as well as logs, branches, tires, and automobiles. Other terms, such as *mud flow, debris slide, mud slide,* and *earth flow,* have been used to identify similar processes. While categorizing flows based on rate of movement or the percentage of clay particles may be important, the mechanisms of all these flows are essentially the same.[86]

4. *Creep.* Creep is generally defined as an imperceptibly slow and more or less continuous downward and outward movement of slope-forming soil or rock. Creep can affect both the near-surface (surficial) soil or deep-seated (gross) materials. The process of creep is frequently described as viscous shear that produces permanent deformations, but not failure, as in landslide movement.

Table 16.7 presents a checklist for the study of slope failures and landslides (adapted from Ref. 87). This table provides a comprehensive list of the factors that may need to be considered by the forensic engineer when investigating slope failures.

As compared to the settlement of buildings, there is less work available on the allowable lateral movement. To evaluate the lateral movement of buildings, a useful parameter is the horizontal strain ε_h, defined as the change in length divided by the original length of the foundation. Figure 16.21 shows a correlation between horizontal strain, ε_h and severity of damage.[16,88] Assuming a 20-ft (6-m) wide zone of the foundation subjected to lateral movement, Fig. 16.21 indicates that a building can be damaged by as little as 0.1 in (3 mm) of lateral movement. Figure 16.21 also indicates that a lateral movement of 1 in (25 mm) would cause "severe" to "very severe" building damage.

It should be mentioned that in Fig. 16.21, Boscardin and Cording[88] used a "distortion factor" in their calculation of angular distortion β for foundations subjected to settlement from mines, tunnels, and braced cuts. Because of this distortion factor, the angular distortion β by Boscardin and Cording in Fig. 16.21 is different from the definition δ/L used in the previous section.

The severity of building damage caused by lateral movement will depend on the tensile strength of the foundation. Those foundations that cannot resist the tensile forces imposed by the slope movement will be the most severely damaged. For example, Figs. 16.22 and 16.23 (from Ref. 89) show damage to a tilt-up building. For a tilt-up building, the exterior walls are cast in segments upon the concrete floor slab; then once they gain sufficient strength, they are tilted up into position. The severe damage shown in Figs. 16.22 and 16.23 was caused by slope movement,

TABLE 16.7 Checklist for the Study of Slope Failures and Landslides

Main topic	Relevant items
Topography	Contour map, consider landform and anomalous patterns (jumbled, scarps, bulges)
	Surface drainage, evaluate conditions such as continuous or intermittent drainage
	Profiles of slope, to be evaluated along with geology and the contour map
	Topographic changes, such as the rate of change by time and correlate with groundwater, weather, and vibrations
Geology	Formations at site, consider the sequence of formations, colluvium (bedrock contact and residual soil), formations with bad experience, and rock minerals susceptible to alteration
	Structure: evaluate three-dimensional geometry, stratification, folding, strike and dip of bedding or foliation (changes in strike and dip and relation to slope and slide), and strike and dip of joints with relation to slope. Also investigate faults, breccia, and shear zones with relation to slope and slide
	Weathering, consider the character (chemical, mechanical, and solution) and depth (uniform or variable)
Groundwater	Piezometric levels within slope, such as normal, perched levels, or artesian pressures with relation to formations and structure
	Variations in piezometric levels due to weather, vibration, and history of slope changes. Other factors include response to rainfall, seasonal fluctuations, year-to-year changes, and effect of snowmelt
	Ground surface indication of subsurface water, such as springs, seeps, damp areas, and vegetation differences
	Effect of human activity on groundwater, such as groundwater utilization, groundwater flow restriction, impoundment, additions to groundwater, changes in ground cover, infiltration opportunity, and surface water changes
	Groundwater chemistry, such as dissolved salts and gases and changes in radioactive gases

TABLE 16.7 Checklist for the Study of Slope Failures and Landslides (*Continued*)

Main topic	Relevant items
Weather	Precipitation from rain or snow. Also consider hourly, daily, monthly, or annual rates
	Temperature, such as hourly and daily means or extremes, cumulative degree-day deficit (freezing index), and sudden thaws
	Barometric changes
Vibration	Seismicity, such as seismic events, microseismic intensity, and microseismic changes
	Human induced from blasting, heavy machinery, or transportation (trucks, trains, etc.)
History of slope changes	Natural processes, such as long-term geologic changes, erosion, evidence of past movement, submergence, or emergence
	Human activities, including cutting, filling, clearing, excavation, cultivation, paving, flooding, and sudden drawdown of reservoirs. Also consider changes caused by human activities, such as changes in surface water, groundwater, and vegetation cover
	Rate of movement from visual accounts, evidence in vegetation, evidence in topography, or photographs (oblique, aerial, stereoptical data, and spectral changes). Also consider instrumental data, such as vertical changes, horizontal changes, and internal strains and tilt, including time history
	Correlate movements with groundwater, weather, vibration, and human activity

Note: Reprinted with permission from *Landslides: Analysis and Control, Special Report 176.* Copyright 1978 by the National Academy of Sciences. Courtesy of the National Academy Press, Washington, DC.
Source: Adapted from Sowers and Royster, 1978.[87]

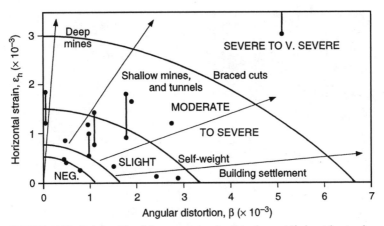

FIGURE 16.21   Relationship of damage to angular distortion and horizontal extension strain. (From Boscardin and Cording 1989, reprinted with permission from the American Society of Civil Engineers.)

which affected the tilt-up building because it was constructed near the top of the slope. Figure 16.22 shows lateral separation of the concrete floor slab at the location of a floor joint. Figure 16.23 shows separation at the junction of two tilt-up panels. Because of the presence of joints between tilt-up panels and joints in the concrete floor slab, the building was especially susceptible to slope movement, which literally pulled apart the tilt-up building.

Those foundations that have joints or planes of weakness, such as the tilt-up building shown in Figs. 16.22 and 16.23, will be most susceptible to damage from lateral movement. Buildings having a mat foundation or a post-tensioned slab would be less susceptible to damage because of the high tensile resistance of these foundations.

Earthquakes

Earthquakes throughout the world cause considerable death and destruction. Much as diseases will attack the weak and infirm, earthquakes damage those structures that have inherent weaknesses or age-related deterioration. Those buildings that are nonreinforced, poorly constructed, weakened from age or rot, or underlain by soft or unstable soil are most susceptible to damage.

Surface Fault Rupture.   Surface fault rupture caused by the earthquake is important because it has caused severe damage to buildings, bridges, dams, tunnels, canals, and underground utilities.[90–95] Fault displacement is defined as the relative movement of the two sides of a fault, measured in a specific direction. Example of large surface fault rupture are the 35-ft (11-m) vertical displacement in the Assam earthquake of 1897[96] and the 29-ft (9-m) horizontal movement during the Gobi-Altai earthquake of 1957.[97] The length of the fault rupture can be quite significant.

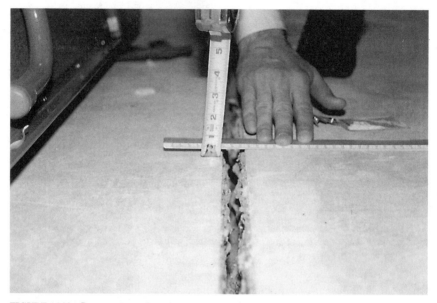

FIGURE 16.22 Damage due to lateral movement. (From Day 1997, reprinted with permission from the American Society of Civil Engineers.)

For example, the estimated length of surface faulting in the 1964 Alaskan earthquake varied from 600 to 720 km.[98,99]

A recent (geologically speaking) earthquake caused the fault rupture shown in Fig. 16.24. The fault is located at the base of the Black Mountains, in California. The vertical fault displacement caused by the earthquake is the vertical distance between the two arrows in Fig. 16.24. The fault displacement occurred in an alluvial fan being deposited at the base of the Black Mountains. Most foundations would be unable to accommodate the huge vertical displacement shown in Figure 16.24.

In addition to fault rupture, there can be ground rupture away from the main trace of the fault. These ground cracks could be caused by many different factors, such as movement of subsidiary faults, auxiliary movement that branches off from the main fault trace, or ground rupture caused by the differential or lateral movement of underlying soil deposits.

Liquefaction. The typical subsurface condition that is susceptible to liquefaction is a loose sand, that has been newly deposited or placed, with a groundwater table near ground surface. During an earthquake, the ground shaking causes the loose sand to contract, resulting in an increase in pore water pressure. The increase in pore water pressure causes an upward flow of water to the ground surface, where it emerges in the form of mud spouts or sand boils. The development of high pore water pressures due to the ground shaking and the upward flow of water may turn the sand into a liquefied condition, which has been termed liquefaction. Structures

FIGURE 16.23 Joint separation between wall panels. (From Day 1997, reprinted with permission from the American Society of Civil Engineers.)

on top of the loose sand deposit that has liquefied during an earthquake will sink or fall over, and buried tanks will float to the surface when the loose sand liquefies.[100]

Liquefaction can also cause lateral movement of foundations and create flow slides.[101] Seed[100] states, "If liquefaction occurs in or under a sloping soil mass, the entire mass will flow or translate laterally to the unsupported side in a phenomena termed a flow slide. Such slides also develop in loose, saturated, cohesionless materials during earthquakes and are reported at Chile (1960), Alaska (1964), and Niigata (1964)."

Another example of lateral movement of liquefied sand is shown in Fig. 16.25.[102] This damage occurred to a marine facility at Redondo Beach King Harbor

FIGURE 16.24 Fault rupture at the base of the Black Mountains (arrows indicate the amount of vertical displacement caused by the earthquake).

during the 1994 California Northridge earthquake. The 18 ft (5.5 m) of horizontal displacement was caused by the liquefaction of an offshore sloping fill mass that was constructed as a part of the marine facility.

There can also be liquefaction of seams of loose saturated sands within a slope. This can cause the entire slope to move laterally along the liquefied layer at the base. These types of gross slope failures caused by liquefied seams of soil created extensive damage during the 1964 Alaskan earthquake.[103,104] It has been observed that slope movement of this type typically results in little damage to structures located on the main slide mass, but buildings located in the graben area are subjected to large differential settlements and are often completely destroyed.[100]

Slope Movement and Settlement.   Besides loose saturated sands, other soil conditions can result in slope movement or settlement during an earthquake. For example, Grantz et al.[105] described an interesting case of ground vibrations from the 1964 Alaskan earthquake that caused 2.6 ft (0.8 m) of alluvium settlement. Other loose soils, such as cohesionless sand and gravel, will also be susceptible to settlement due to the ground vibrations from earthquakes.

Slopes having a low factor of safety can experience large horizontal movement during an earthquake. Types of slopes most susceptible to movement during earthquakes include those slopes composed of soil that loses shear strength with strain (such as sensitive soil) or ancient landslides that can become reactivated by seismic forces.[106]

Deterioration

In terms of deterioration, the National Science Foundation[107] states:

> The infrastructure deteriorates with time, due to aging of the materials, excessive use, overloading, climatic conditions, lack of sufficient maintenance, and difficulties encountered in proper inspection methods. All of these factors contribute to the obsolescence of the structural system as a whole. As a result, repair, retrofit, rehabilitation, and replacement become necessary actions to be taken to insure the safety of the public.

There are many different types of deterioration that can affect foundations. Two of the more common causes of foundation deterioration are sulfate attack and frost action.

Sulfate Attack of Concrete Foundations. Sulfate attack of concrete is defined as a chemical and/or physical reaction between sulfates (usually in the soil or groundwater) and concrete or mortar, primarily with hydrated calcium aluminate in the cement-paste matrix, often causing deterioration.[108] Sulfate attack of concrete occurs throughout the world, especially in arid areas, such as the southwestern United States. In arid regions, the salts are drawn up into the concrete and then deposited on the concrete surface as the groundwater evaporates, such as shown in Figs. 16.26 and 16.27.

FIGURE 16.25 Damage to marine facility, 1994 California Northridge earthquake. (From Kerwin and Stone 1997, reprinted with permission from the American Society of Civil Engineers.)

FIGURE 16.26 Concrete sidewalk deterioration, Mojave Desert (salts were deposited on concrete surface from evaporating groundwater).

There has been considerable research, testing, and chemical analysis of sulfate attack. Two different mechanisms of sulfate attack have been discovered: chemical reactions and the physical growth of crystals.

Chemical Reactions. The chemical reactions involving sulfate attack of concrete are complex. Studies[109,110] have discovered two main chemical reactions. The first is a chemical reaction of sulfate and calcium hydroxide (which was generated during the hydration of the cement) to form calcium sulfate, commonly known as gypsum. The second is a chemical reaction of gypsum and hydrated calcium aluminate to form calcium sulfoaluminate, commonly called ettringite.[109] As with many chemical reactions, the final product of ettringite causes an increase in volume of the concrete. Hurst[111] indicates that the chemical reactions produce a compound of twice the volume of the original tricalcium aluminate compound. Concrete has a low tensile strength, and thus the increase in volume fractures the concrete, allowing for more sulfates to penetrate the concrete, resulting in accelerated deterioration.

Physical Growth of Crystals. The physical reaction of sulfate has been studied by Tuthill[112] and Reading.[113] They conclude that there can be crystallization of the sulfate salts in the pores of the concrete. The growth of crystals exerts expansive forces within the concrete, causing flaking and spalling of the outer concrete surface. Besides sulfate, the concrete, if porous enough, can be disintegrated by the expansive force exerted by the crystallization of almost any salt in its pores.[112,113] Damage due to crystallization of salt is commonly observed in areas where water is migrating through the concrete and then evaporating at the concrete surface. Examples include the surfaces of concrete dams, basement and retaining walls that lack proper waterproofing, and concrete structures that are partially immersed in salt-bearing water (such as seawater) or soils.

The forensic engineer can recognize sulfate attack by the physical loss of concrete (Fig. 16.28) or the unusual cracking and discoloration of concrete, such as shown in Fig. 16.29. When investigating concrete deterioration, the forensic engineer should be aware of the factors that cause sulfate attack. In general, the degree of sulfate attack of concrete will depend on the type of cement used, quality of the concrete, soluble sulfate concentration that is in contact with the concrete, and surface preparation of the concrete.[114]

FIGURE 16.27 Concrete patio deterioration, Mojave Desert (arrows point to deterioration of concrete surface).

FIGURE 16.28   Physical loss of concrete due to sulfate attack.

1. *Type of cement.* There is a correlation between the sulfate resistance of cement and its tricalcium aluminate content. As previously discussed, it is the chemical reaction of hydrated calcium aluminate and gypsum that forms ettringite. Therefore, limiting the tricalcium aluminate content of cement reduces the potential for the formation of ettringite. It has been stated that the tricalcium aluminate content of the cement is the greatest single factor that influences the resistance of concrete to sulfate attack, where, in general, the lower the tricalcium aluminate content, the greater the sulfate resistance.[115] Of the types of portland cements, the most resistant cement is type V, in which the tricalcium aluminate content must be less than 5 percent. Both the ACI[108] and the Portland Cement Association[116] have identical requirements for normal-weight concrete subjected to sulfate attack. Depending on the percentage of soluble sulfate in the soil or groundwater, a certain cement type is required. In an investigation of damage due to sulfate deterioration, the forensic engineer should compare the requirements of ACI with the actual cement type used for the concrete.

2. *Quality of concrete.* The condition of the concrete in terms of its permeability should be evaluated by the forensic engineer. In general, the more impermeable the concrete, the more difficult for the waterborne sulfate to penetrate the concrete surface. To have a low permeability, the concrete must be dense and have a high cement content and a low water-cement ratio. Using a low water-cement ratio decreases the permeability of mature concrete.[116] A low water-cement ratio is a requirement of ACI[108] for concrete subjected to soluble sulfate in the soil or groundwater. For example, the water-cement ratio must be equal to or less than 0.45 for concrete exposed to severe or very severe sulfate. There are many other conditions that can affect the quality of the concrete. For example, a lack of proper consolidation of the concrete can result in excessive voids. Another condition is the corrosion of reinforcement, which may crack the concrete and increase its permeability. Cracking of concrete may also occur when structural members are subjected to bending stresses. For example, the tensile stress due to a bending moment in a footing may cause the development of microcracks, which increases the permeability of the concrete.

3. *Soluble sulfate concentration.* When investigating sulfate attack of concrete, the forensic engineer should determine if the soil or water in contact with the concrete was tested to determine the soluble sulfate content. In some cases, the soluble sulfate may become concentrated on crack faces. For example, water evaporating

FIGURE 16.29 Cracking and discoloration of concrete due to sulfate attack

through cracks in concrete flatwork will deposit the sulfate on the crack faces. This concentration of sulfate may cause accelerated deterioration of the concrete.

4. *Surface preparation of concrete.* An important factor in concrete resistance is the surface preparation, such as the amount of curing of the concrete. Curing results in a stronger and more impermeable concrete,[116] which is better able to resist the effects of salt intrusion.

Frost. There have been extensive studies done on the detrimental effects of frost.[117–120] Two common types of damage related to frost are (1) freezing of water in cracks and (2) formation of ice lenses. In many cases, deterioration or damage is not evident until the frost has melted. In these instances, it may be difficult for the forensic engineer to conclude that frost was the primary cause of the deterioration.

Freezing of Water in Cracks. There is about a 10 percent increase in volume of water when it freezes, and this volumetric expansion of water upon freezing can cause deterioration or damage to many different types of materials. Damage to the concrete foundation could be caused by freezing during the original placement of the concrete or after it has hardened. To prevent damage during placement, it is important that the fresh concrete not be allowed to freeze. Air-entraining admixtures can be added to the concrete mixture to help protect the hardened concrete from freeze-thaw deterioration.

Formation of Ice Lenses. Frost penetration and the formation of ice lenses in the soil frequently damage shallow foundations and pavements. The frost penetration will cause heave of the structure if moisture is available to form ice lenses in the underlying soil. The spring thaw will then melt the ice, resulting in settlement of the foundation. It is well known that silty soils are more likely to form ice lenses because of their high capillarity and sufficient permeability that enables them to draw up moisture to the ice lenses. When dealing with buildings possibly damaged by frost action, the forensic engineer should determine if the outside columns or walls of the building are located below the level to which frost could have caused perceptible heave.

Feld and Carper[121] describe several interesting cases of foundation damage due to frost action. At Fredonia, New York, the frost from a deep-freeze storage facility froze the soil and heaved the foundations upward 4 in (100 mm). A system of electric wire heating was installed to maintain soil volume stability.

Another case involved an extremely cold winter in Chicago, where frost penetrated below an underground garage and broke a buried sprinkler line. This caused an ice buildup which heaved the structure above the street level and sheared off several supporting columns.

TEMPORARY AND PERMANENT REMEDIAL REPAIRS

It is not possible to cover every type of foundation repair, and the purpose of this section is to provide examples of commonly used repair methods.

The most expensive and rigorous method of repair would be to entirely remove the foundation and install a new foundation. This method of repair is usually reserved for cases involving a large magnitude of soil movement. Common types of new foundations are the reinforced mat or reinforced mat supported by piers.[9]

Reinforced Mat

Figure 16.30 shows the manometer survey of a building containing two condominium units at a project called Timberlane in Scripps Ranch, California. The building shown in Fig. 16.30 was constructed in 1977 and was underlain by poorly compacted fill that increased in depth toward the front of the building. In 1987, the amount of fill settlement was estimated to be 4 in (100 mm) at the rear of the building and 8 in (200 mm) at the front of the building. As shown in Fig. 16.30, the fill settlement caused 3.2 in (80 mm) of differential settlement for the conventional slab-on-grade and 3.9 in (99 mm) for the second floor. The second floor had greater differential settlement because it extended out over the garage. Note in Fig. 16.30 that the foundation tilts downward from the rear to the front of the building, or in the direction of deepening fill. Typical damage consisted of cracks in the slab-on-grade, exterior stucco cracks, interior wallboard damage, ceiling cracks, and racked door frames. By using Table 16.4, the damage was classified as severe. Due to ongoing fill settlement, the future (additional) differential settlement of the foundation was estimated to be 4 in (200 mm).

To reduce the potential for future damage due to the anticipated fill settlement, it was decided to install a new foundation for the building. The type of new foundation for the building was a reinforced mat, 15 in (380 mm) thick, and reinforced with no. 7 bars, 12 in (305 mm) on center, each way, top and bottom.

To install the reinforced mat, the connections between the building and the existing slab-on-grade were severed, and the entire building was raised about 8 ft (2.4 m). Figure 16.31 shows the building in its raised condition. Steel beams, passing through the entire building, were used to lift the building during the jacking process.

After the building was raised, the existing slab-on-grade foundation was demolished. The formwork for the construction of the reinforced mat is shown in Fig. 16.32. The mat was designed and constructed so that it sloped 2 in (50 mm) upward from the back to the front of the building. It was anticipated that with future settlement, the front of the building would settle 4 in (100 mm) such that the mat would eventually slope 2 in (50 mm) downward from the back to the front of the building.

After placement and hardening of the new concrete for the mat, the building was lowered onto its new foundation. The building was then attached to the mat, and the interior and exterior damages were repaired. Flexible utility connections were used to accommodate the difference in movement between the building and settling fill.

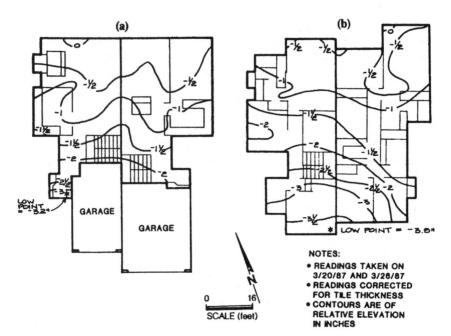

FIGURE 16.30 Manometer survey: (*A*) first floor; (*B*) second floor.

FIGURE 16.31 Raised building.

FIGURE 16.32 Construction of mat foundation.

Reinforced Mat with Piers

A common foundation repair for structures subjected to settlement and/or slope movement is to remove the existing foundation and install a mat supported by piers. The mat transfers building loads to the piers, which are embedded in a firm bearing material. For a condition of soil settlement, the piers will usually be subjected to down-drag loads from the settling soil.

The piers are usually at least 2 ft (0.6 m) in diameter to enable downhole logging to confirm end bearing conditions. Either the piers can be built within the building, or the piers can be constructed outside the building with grade beams used to transfer loads to the piers. Given the height of a drill rig, it is usually difficult to drill within the building (unless it is raised). The advantages of constructing the piers outside the building are that the height restriction is no longer a concern and a large, powerful drill rig can be used to quickly and economically drill the holes for the piers.

Figure 16.33 shows a photograph of the conditions at an adjacent building at Timberlane. Given the very large magnitude of the estimated future differential settlement for this building, it was decided to remove the existing foundation and then construct a mat supported by 2.5-ft (0.76-m) diameter piers. The arrow in Fig. 16.33 points to one of the piers.

To construct the mat supported by piers, the building was raised and then the slab-on-grade was demolished. With the building in a raised condition, a drill rig

FIGURE 16.33 Construction of mat supported by piers (the arrow points to one of the piers).

was used to excavate the piers. The piers were drilled through the poorly compacted fill and into the underlying bedrock. The piers were belled at the bottom in order to develop additional end bearing resistance. After drilling and installation of the steel reinforcement consisting of eight no. 6 bars with no. 4 ties at 1-ft (0.3-m) spacing, the piers were filled with concrete to near ground surface. Figure 16.34 shows a close-up of the pier indicated in Fig. 16.33. Note the bent steel reinforcement (no. 6 bars) at the top of the pier which is connected to the steel reinforcement in the mat.

Besides piers, the structure can be underpinned with piles or screw or earth anchors.[122] Greenfield and Shen[43] present a list of the advantages and disadvantages of pier and pile installations.

Partial Removal and/or Strengthening of Foundations

A second type of foundation repair is the partial removal of the damaged foundation and/or the strengthening of the foundation. This is usually a less expensive and rigorous method of repair than total removal and replacement of the foundation. The amount of soil movement is usually less for the case of partial removal and/or strengthening than for the case of total removal and replacement. The main objective of this type of repair is to fix the damaged foundation and then strengthen the foundation so that the damage does not recur. Partial removal and/or strengthening of the foundation is a common type of repair for damage caused by expansive soil.

Figure 16.35[123] shows a cross section of a typical design for a deepened perimeter footing. The advantage of this type of repair is that the perimeter footing is strengthened and deepened. This can mitigate seasonal moisture changes and hence movement of the perimeter footings when founded on expansive soil. The construction of the deepened perimeter footing starts with the excavation of slots in order to install the hydraulic jacks. After the hydraulic jacks have been installed (Fig. 16.35), the entire footing is exposed. Steel reinforcement is then tied to the existing foundation by using dowels. The final step is to fill the excavation with concrete. The jacks are left in place during the placement of the concrete.

For isolated interior concrete foundation cracks, one method of repair is the strip replacement repair. Figure 16.36 shows a cross section of this type of repair. The construction of the strip replacement starts by saw-cutting out the area containing the concrete crack. Figure 16.36 recommends that a distance of 1 ft (0.3 m) on both sides of the concrete crack be saw-cut. This is to provide enough working space to install reinforcement and the dowels. After the new reinforcement (no. 3 bars) and dowels are installed, the area is filled with a new portion of concrete.

For those foundations that have unacceptable differential movement or are too badly damaged to be repaired by the strip replacement method, the entire interior foundation can be removed and replaced. For example, Fig. 16.37 shows a photograph where the foundation has been removed, except for the interior bearing wall footings. As seen in Fig. 16.37, the exposed expansive soil subgrade has been flooded to allow the clay to expand prior to construction of the new slab.

FIGURE 16.34 Close-up view of Figure 16.33.

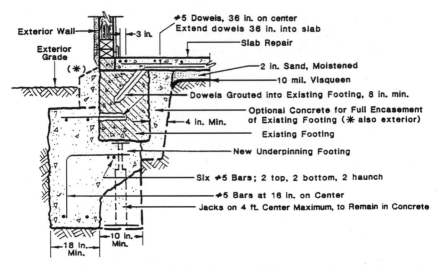

FIGURE 16.35 Deepened perimeter footings. (From Day 1996, reprinted with permission from the American Society of Civil Engineers.)

Concrete Crack Repairs

The third type of repair is to patch the existing cracks in the concrete. Of the three general categories of repair, this is the least expensive repair method. This repair is usually recommended if the foundation has not excessively deformed (i.e., the foundation does not require releveling) and the foundation can accommodate the estimated future soil movement. The objective of this type of repair is to return the foundation to a satisfactory appearance and to provide structural strength at the cracked areas. It has been stated[124] that a patching material must meet the following requirements:

1. Be at least as durable as the surrounding concrete

2. Require a minimum of site preparation

3. Be tolerant of a wide range of temperature and moisture conditions.

4. Be noninjurious to the concrete through chemical incompatibility

5. Preferably be similar in color and surface texture to the surrounding concrete

Figure 16.38 shows a typical detail for concrete crack repair. If there is differential movement at the crack, then the concrete may require grinding or chipping to provide a smooth transition across the crack. The material commonly used to fill the concrete crack is epoxy. Epoxy compounds consist of a resin, a curing agent or hardener, and modifiers that make them suitable for specific uses. The typical range [500 to 5000 lb/in^2 (3400 to 35,000 kPa)] in tensile strength of epoxy is similar to its range in compressive strength.[125] Performance specifications for epoxy have been developed (e.g., Ref. 126). In order for the epoxy to be effective, it is important that the crack faces be free of contaminants (such as dirt) that could

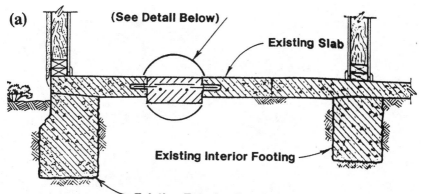

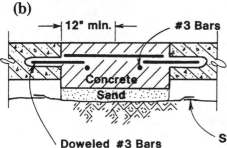

Saw–Cut 12" Each Side of Crack, Dowel #3 Bars 6"(min.) Into
Existing Slab. Provide 5" Concrete Section with #3 Bars, 12"
O.C. Both Ways . Underlay with 2" Moist Sand.   Where Visqueen
Exists,   Splice/Seal in a Replacement Section

FIGURE 16.36 Concrete crack repair: (*a*) strip replacement of floor cracks; (*b*) strip replacement
detail. (From Day 1996, reprinted with permission from the American Society of Civil Engineers.)

prevent bonding. In many cases, the epoxy is injected under pressure so that it can
penetrate the full depth of the concrete crack.

Other Foundation Repair Alternatives

The previous sections dealt with the strengthening or underpinning of the foundation in order to resist soil movement or bypass the problem soil. There are many

FIGURE 16.37 Slab removal and replacement.

other types of foundation repair or soil treatment alternatives.[127,128] In some cases, the magnitude of soil movement may be so large that the only alternative is to demolish the structure. For example, movement of the Portuguese Bend landslide in Palos Verdes, California, has destroyed about 160 homes. But a few homeowners refuse to abandon their homes as they slowly slide downslope. Some owners have installed steel beams underneath the foundation which are supported by hydraulic jacks that are periodically used to relevel the house. Other owners have tried bizarre stabilization methods, such as supporting the house on huge steel drums.

A more conventional repair alternative is to treat the problem soil. For example, fluid grout can be injected into the ground to fill in joints, fractures, or underground voids in order to stabilize settling structures.[129,130] Another option is mudjacking, which has been defined as a process whereby a water and soil-cement or soil-lime cement grout is pumped beneath the slab, under pressure, to produce a lifting force which literally floats the slab to the desired position.[122]

A commonly used in-place treatment alternative for foundation soils is compaction grouting, which consists of intruding a mass of very thick-consistency grout into the soil, which both displaces and compacts the loose soil.[131,132] Compaction grouting has proved successful in increasing the density of poorly compacted fill, alluvium, and compressible or collapsible soil. The advantages of compaction grouting are less expense and disturbance to the structure than foundation underpinning, and it can be used to relevel the structure. The disadvantages of compaction grouting are that it is difficult to analyze the results, it is usually ineffective near slopes or for near-surface soils because of the lack of confining pressure, and there is the danger of filling underground pipes with grout.[131]

For expansive soil, mitigation options can include horizontal or vertical moisture barriers to reduce the cyclic wetting and drying around the perimeter of the structure.[133-135] Drainage improvements and the repair of leaky water lines are also performed in conjunction with the construction of moisture barriers. Other expansive soil stabilization options include chemical injection (such as a lime slurry) into the soil below the structure. The goal of such mitigation measures is to induce a chemical mineralogical change of the clay particles which will reduce the soil's tendency to swell.

RETAINING WALLS

A *retaining wall* is defined as a structure whose primary purpose is to provide lateral support for soil or rock. In some cases, the retaining wall may also support vertical loads. Examples include basement walls and certain types of bridge abutments.

Cernica[136] lists and describes varies types of retaining walls. Some of the more common types of retaining walls are gravity walls, counterfort walls, cantilevered walls, and crib walls. Gravity retaining walls are routinely built of plain concrete or stone, and the wall depends primarily on its massive weight to resist failure from overturning and sliding. Counterfort walls consist of a footing, a wall stem, and intermittent vertical ribs (called counterforts) which tie the footing and wall stem together. Crib walls consist of interlocking concrete members that form cells which are then filled with compacted soil.

Although reinforced earth retaining walls have become more popular in the past decade, cantilever retaining walls are still probably the most common type of retaining structure. There are many different types of cantilevered walls, with the common features being a footing that supports the vertical wall stem. Typical cantilevered walls are T-shaped, L-shaped, or reverse L-shaped.

To prevent the buildup of hydrostatic water pressure on the retaining wall, clean granular material (no silt or clay) is the standard recommendation for backfill material. Import granular backfill generally has a more predictable behavior in terms of earth pressure exerted on the wall. A back-drain system is often constructed at the heel of the wall to intercept and dispose of any water seepage in the granular backfill.

Common Causes of Failure

There are many different reasons for retaining wall failures, such as bearing capacity failure, sliding failure, or failure by overturning of the retaining wall. Common causes include inadequate design, improper construction, or unanticipated loadings. Other causes of failure are listed below:

1. *Clay backfill.* A frequent cause of failure is that the wall was backfilled with clay. As previously mentioned, clean granular sand or gravel is usually recommended as backfill material. This is because of the undesirable effects of using clay or silt as a backfill material. When clay is used as backfill material, the clay backfill can exert swelling pressures on the wall.[137,138] The highest swelling pressures develop when water infiltrates a backfill consisting of a clay that was compacted to a high dry density at a low moisture content. The type of clay particles that will exert the highest swelling pressures are montmorillonite. Because the clay backfill is not free-draining, there could be additional hydrostatic forces or ice-related forces that substantially increase the thrust on the wall.

2. *Inferior backfill soil.* To reduce construction costs, soil available on site is sometimes used for backfill. This soil may not have the properties, such as being a clean granular soil with a high shear strength, assumed during the design stage. Using on-site available soil, rather than importing granular material, is probably the most common reason for retaining-wall failures.

3. *Compaction-induced pressures.* Larger wall pressures typically will be generated during compaction of the backfill. By using heavy compaction equipment in close proximity to the wall, excessive pressures can be developed that damage the wall.

4. *Failure of the back-cut.* There could also be the failure of the back-cut for the retaining wall. The back-cut can fail if it is excavated too steeply and does not have an adequate factor of safety.

EXAMPLES OF CASE STUDIES OF NONPERFORMANCE AND FAILURE

Example 16.1 Slab-on-Grade Foundation

The following is a case study of damage to a house caused by fill settlement. A level building pad was created in 1973 to 1974 by filling in a deep canyon. The house was then constructed, and it contains a lightly reinforced, conventional slab-on-grade foundation. The depth of fill underneath the house, based on the original grading plans and subsurface exploration, varied from 25 ft (7.6 m) up to 45 ft (13.7 m). Figure 16.39 shows a sketch of the house and indicates the location of the shallowest and deepest fill.

By 1987, the house had experienced 7.9 in (20 cm) of differential foundation movement Δ. This movement caused very severe damage, such as foundation cracks, interior wallboard cracks, racked door frames, and a near complete separation of the house from the originally attached garage. The fill settlement caused both functional and structural damage. A picture of typical observed damage is shown in Fig. 16.40.

A benchmark had been established by the city on a nearby sidewalk in 1975. This benchmark recorded 12.6 in (32 cm) of settlement from 1975 to 1987.

A large-diameter boring excavated adjacent to the residence (see Fig. 16.39) revealed clayey sand to sandy clay fill underlain by very dense bedrock. Based on

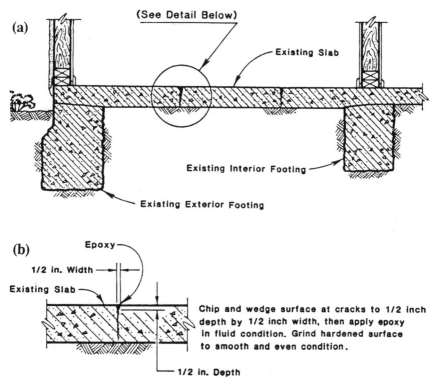

FIGURE 16.38 Concrete crack repair: (*a*) epoxy repair of floor cracks; (*b*) detail of crack repair with epoxy. (From Day 1996, reprinted with permission from the American Society of Civil Engineers.)

the results of the subsurface exploration and laboratory testing, it was concluded that the relative compaction was so low that negligible compaction effort was used during construction.

Example 16.2 Post-Tensioned Slabs-on-Grade

Post-tensioned slab-on-grade foundations are common in southern California and other parts of the United States. They are an economical foundation type when there is no ground freezing or the depth of frost penetration is low. The most common uses of post-tensioned slab-on-grade are to resist expansive soil forces or when the projected differential settlement exceeds the tolerable value for a conventional (lightly reinforced) slab-on-grade. For example, post-tensioned slabs-on-grade are frequently recommended if the projected differential settlement is expected to exceed 0.75 in (2 cm).

Installation and field inspection procedures for post-tensioned slab-on-grade have been prepared by the Post-Tensioning Institute.[139] Post-tensioned slab-on-

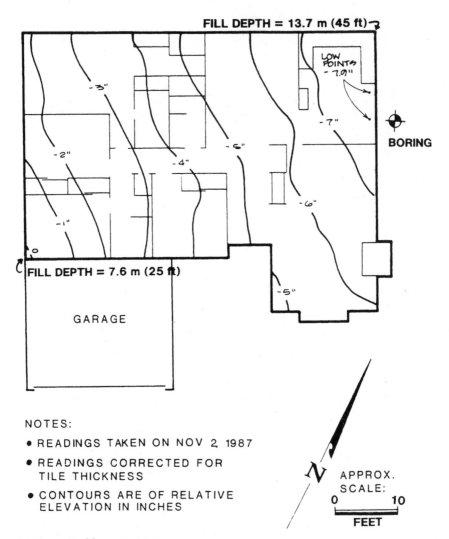

FIGURE 16.39 Manometer survey.

grade consists of concrete with embedded steel tendons that are encased in thick plastic sheaths. The plastic sheath prevents the tendon from coming in contact with the concrete and permits the tendon to slide within the hardened concrete during the tensioning operations. Usually tendons have a dead end (anchoring plate) in the perimeter (edge) beam and a stressing end at the opposite perimeter beam to enable the tendons to be stressed from one end. However, the Post-Tensioning Institute[139] does recommend that the tendons in excess of 100 ft (30 m) be stressed from both ends. The Post-Tensioning Institute also provides typical anchorage details for the tendons.

FIGURE 16.40 Cracking to exterior stucco at garage door.

This second case study deals with fill settlement that affected a post-tensioned slab-on-grade for a single-family house having an attached garage located in Oceanside, California. The house was constructed in 1987 using typical wood-frame construction with interior wallboard and an exterior stucco facade. A post-tensioned slab-on-grade was recommended because the site had alluvium and colluvium that could not be removed due to the presence of a shallow groundwater table.

The post-tensioned slab-on-grade was not designed as a "ribbed" (or waffle) type of foundation having stiffening beams projecting from the bottom of the slab in both directions. Instead, the post-tensioned slab-on-grade was designed so that it consisted of a uniform-thickness slab with an edge beam at the entire perimeter, but no intersecting interior stiffening beams. This type of post-tensioned slab-on-grade is commonly referred to as the "California slab" or the "California foundation."[139]

The post-tensioned slab-on-grade consisted of an 18-in (0.46-m) thick perimeter edge beam and a 5-in (13-cm) slab. The edge beam and slab were placed at the same time in order to create a monolithic foundation. The post-tensioning tendons were 0.5-in (1.3-cm) diameter cables having seven strands and an ultimate capacity of 270 ksi (1.9 GPa). The tendons were spaced 5.5 ft (1.7 m) on-center (both ways), and each tendon was tensioned with a force of approximately 25 kips (110 kN). Based on the tendon spacing, tendon force, and thickness of slab, the compressive stress in the slab due to the post-tensioning is about 75 lb/in^2 (0.5 MPa).

Figure 16.41 presents a manometer survey performed on the post-tensioned slab-on-grade. Including measurements taken on the attached garage stemwall, the maximum slab differential Δ is about 3.0 in (7.6 cm), and the maximum angular distortion δ/L is about $^1/_{120}$. If the maximum slab differential Δ of 3.0 in (7.6 cm) versus maximum angular distortion δ/L of $^1/_{120}$ is plotted in Fig. 16.2, the data point is consistent with the data from other types of foundations. As shown in Fig. 16.41, there is a distinct tilt in the post-tensioned slab-on-grade. It was observed that about one-half of the post-tensioned slab-on-grade tilted downward in the direction of deepening fill. There was up to about 10 ft (3 m) of poorly compacted fill that settled beneath the east side of the house and caused the foundation displacement shown in Figure 16.41.

Figure 16.42 is a photograph of the observed post-tensioned slab crack. The slab crack was relatively linear, and the location is indicated by the two arrows on Fig. 16.41. The slab crack appeared to act as a hinge point, with the most signifi-

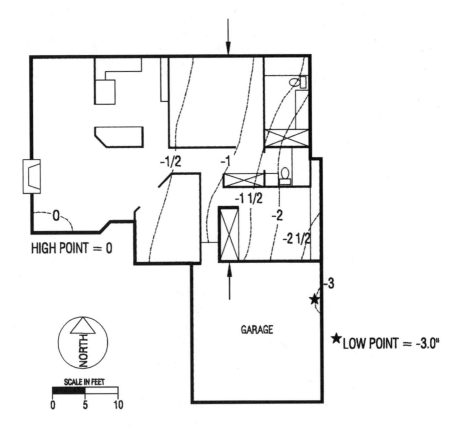

CONTOURS ARE OF RELATIVE ELEVATION IN INCHES

FIGURE 16.41 Manometer survey. (From Day 1998, reprinted with permission from the American Society of Civil Engineers.).

FIGURE 16.42 View of post-tensioned slab crack. (From Day 1998, reprinted with permission from the American Society of Civil Engineers.)

cant wallboard and ceiling cracks located in an area approximately parallel to the slab crack. Considering the magnitude of foundation displacement, the width of the crack was relatively small [0.06 in (1.5 mm)]. This was attributed to the post-tensioning compression effect, which prevented the foundation from pulling apart when it settled.

Although the slab crack was relatively small (Fig. 16.42), there was significant cracking to the house including wallboard, ceiling, and exterior stucco cracks. Based on the observed interior and exterior cracking to the house, and using Table 16.4 as a guide, the damage could be classified as moderate, with functional (or serviceability) damage.

In summary, the width of the slab crack was relatively small due to the post-tensioning (compression) effect on the slab. However, because of the development of a hinge point, the post-tensioned slab deformed to such an extent that there was moderate damage to the interior and exterior wood-framed walls.

Example 16.3 Post-Tensioned Slab-on-Grade

Example 16.3 is similar to Example 16.2 in that the site consists of a single-family house having a post-tensioned slab-on-grade (California slab) that was affected by settlement. The site is located in San Clemente, California. The site originally consisted of a deep canyon which required substantial cut-and-fill operations to create a level building pad. The original geotechnical engineer for the site recognized that there would be postconstruction settlement of the fill due to its own weight and variations in moisture content. Given the likelihood of settlement of the deep canyon fill, in 1985 the geotechnical engineer recommended that the structural engineer design a post-tensioned slab-on-grade that would be compatible with a maximum angular distortion δ/L on the order of $1/300$. For a fill thickness of 60 ft (18 m) the geotechnical engineer estimated a long-term fill settlement ρ_{max} of 2 in (5 cm).

As in Example 16.2, the house was built using wood-frame construction with interior wallboard and an exterior stucco facade. Also, the construction details for the post-tensioned (California slab) were similar for both cases. For example, the slab thickness was 5 in (13 cm), there were perimeter edge beams, and the tendon spacing was 5 ft (1.5 m) on-center, both ways.

Figure 16.43 presents the manometer survey performed on the post-tensioned slab-on-grade. Including measurements taken on the attached garage stemwall, the maximum slab differential Δ is about 4.7 in (12 cm), and the maximum angular distortion δ/L is about $1/115$. If the maximum slab differential Δ of 4.7 in (12 cm) versus maximum angular distortion δ/L of $1/115$ is plotted in Fig. 16.2, the data point is consistent with the data from other types of foundations. Elevation surveys of the top of curbs indicated that the site had indeed settled and that the deformation shown in Fig. 16.43 represented actual downward movement of the house foundation.

As shown in Fig. 16.43, there is a distinct tilt in the post-tensioned slab-on-grade. It was observed that the post-tensioned slab-on-grade tilted downward in the direction of deepening fill. In Fig. 16.43, the depths of fill have been indicated at the corners of the house. There is about 23 ft (7 m) of fill at the southeast corner of the house, and the fill uniformly increases to about 61 ft (19 m) at the northwest corner of the house. Results of the subsurface exploration and laboratory testing indicated that the fill settlement was mainly restricted to the deeper zones of fill. The main process of fill settlement was due to infiltration of water into the fill which caused soil collapse.[48,49]

As indicated in Table 16.4, a maximum differential settlement Δ of 4.7 in (12 cm) and a maximum angular distortion δ/L of $1/115$ for the foundation should result in

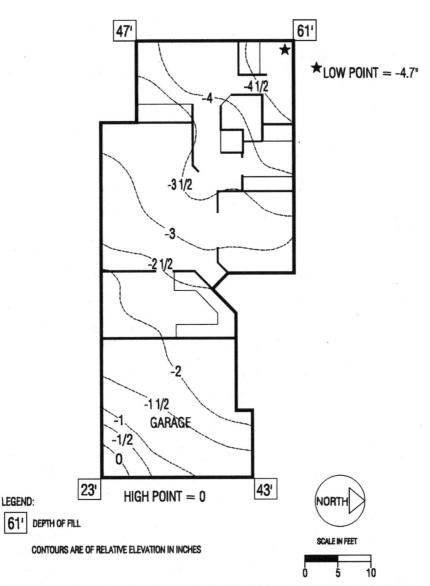

FIGURE 16.43   Manometer survey; Example 3. (From Day 1998, reprinted with permission from the American Society of Civil Engineers.)

severe damage. But based on observed damage, the damage classification was only *slight* and consisted of architectural damage. For example, cracking to the house included minor interior wallboard cracks and a few exterior stucco cracks at the corners of window and door openings. There was a 0.03-in (0.8-mm) wide crack in the garage portion of the post-tensioned slab-on-grade. The most significant damage was to exterior utilities and appurtenances. For example, there was a pipe leak under the sidewalk located at the front of the house. When the pipe break was exposed, there was apparently a 3-in (8-cm) offset of the ends of the broken pipe. In addition, there were separations on the order of 0.5 in (1.3 cm) between the concrete driveway and the house and up to 0.3 in (0.8 cm) separation of the rear patio from the house.

As previously mentioned, these tension-type features are common for fill settlement over the sidewalls of a filled-in canyon (Fig. 16.4). Because of the post tensioning (compression) of the foundation at the site, the tension effects were not present and mainly developed in the exterior appurtenances.

The damage was only slight because the post-tensioned slab-on-grade was able to resist the tension effects of the fill settlement. Also, a hinge point did not develop in the slab. Instead, there was a tendency for the post-tensioned slab-on-grade to tilt uniformly, similar to rigid-body movement, in the direction of deepening fill.

In summary, Examples 16.2 and 16.3 indicate that the amount of damage to the structure depends on how the post-tensioned slab-on-grade deforms. For Example 16.2, the width of the foundation crack (Fig. 16.42) was relatively small due to the post-tensioning (compression) effect of the slab, which prevented the foundation from pulling apart when it settled. However, the post-tensioned slab nevertheless deformed to such an extent that there was moderate damage to the interior and exterior walls. The slab crack appeared to act as a hinge point, with the most significant wallboard and ceiling cracks located in an area approximately parallel to the slab crack. The hinge point developed because about one-half of the post-tensioned slab-on-grade was unaffected by soil movement and remained relatively level, while the remaining one-half of the slab settled. For this case study, the Skempton and MacDonald[10] criterion that cracking is likely to occur if the angular distortion of the foundation exceeds $1/300$ seems reasonable. Also Table 16.4, which correlates the damage category with crack widths, maximum differential settlement Δ, and maximum angular distortion δ/L, was applicable.

Once again, for Example 16.3, the width of the slab crack was relatively small due to the post-tensioning (compression) effect which enabled the slab to resist the tensional forces due to fill settlement over the sidewall of a preexisting canyon. For Example 16.3, the post-tensioned slab-on-grade was able to adjust to the deep settlement. For example, there was a tendency for the post-tensioned slab-on-grade to tilt uniformly (no hinge point). Table 16.4 did not accurately correlate the damage category with crack widths and maximum differential settlement Δ for the post-tensioned slab-on-grade (California slab) subjected to foundation displacement for Example 16.3.

These case studies indicate the importance of the foundation type (conventional lightly reinforced versus post-tensioned slab-on-grade) and mode of foundation deformation (development of a hinge point) in the magnitude of damage to the structure.

Example 16.4 **Retaining Wall**

The case study involves a retaining-wall failure in San Diego, California. The wall was constructed as a basement wall for a large building. In 1984, the building was demolished, and the site was turned into a parking lot.

As originally constructed, the basement wall received lateral support from the foundation, a bowstring roof truss, and perpendicular building walls. When the building was demolished, the retaining wall essentially became a cantilevered wall with no lateral support except from the footing.

The retaining wall is about 8 to 9 ft (2.4 to 2.7 m) high, 8 in (20 cm) thick, with thickened pilasters that originally supported the bowstring roof truss. Figure 16.44[141] shows a photograph of the wall after demolition of the building. The area behind the wall belonged to an adjacent property owner, who experienced damage when the wall moved due to the loss of lateral support. Figure 16.45 shows a photograph of cracks that opened up in the concrete flatwork located behind the retaining wall.

The movement of the wall was monitored by installing brass pins on opposite sides of the flatwork cracks. By measuring the distance between the pins, the opening of the cracks (lateral movement) was calculated and plotted versus time, as shown in Fig. 16.46. The horizontal axis in Fig. 16.46 is time after installation of the crack pins.

Note in Fig. 16.46 that the movement of the wall versus time is not at a constant rate, but rather intermittent. The data indicate that the wall moves forward,

FIGURE 16.44 Photograph of retaining wall. (From Day 1997, reprinted with permission from the American Society of Civil Engineers.)

FIGURE 16.45   Area behind retaining wall (arrows point to cracks opening up in the flatwork). (From Day 1997, reprinted with permission from the American Society of Civil Engineers.)

the cracks open up, and then lateral movement ceases for awhile. This is because the soil thrust is reduced when the wall moves forward, and it takes time for the soil to resume its original contact with the back face of the wall. In Fig. 16.46, crack pin (CP) 3 did record a closing of the crack at a time of 0.9 to 1.2 years, but this is due to settlement of the backfill and flatwork as the soil resumed contact with the back face of the wall. Figure 16.47 shows the voids that developed beneath the flatwork due to lateral movement of the wall.

As illustrated by this case study, most retaining-wall failures are gradual, and the wall slowly fails by intermittently tilting or moving laterally. It is possible that a fail-

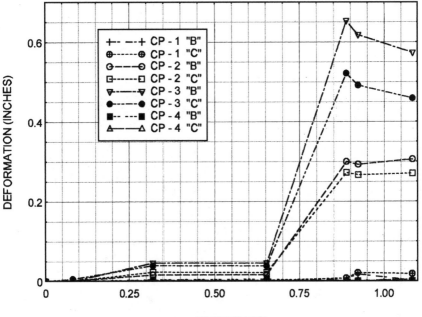

FIGURE 16.46   Wall deformation versus time. (From Day 1997, reprinted with permission from the American Society of Civil Engineers.)

ure can occur suddenly, such as when there is a slope-type failure beneath the wall or when the foundation of the wall fails due to inadequate bearing capacity. These rapid failure conditions could develop if the wall foundation is supported by clay.[61]

Another example of sudden wall failure could occur during an earthquake. It is difficult to accurately predict the additional lateral forces that will be generated on a retaining wall during an earthquake. Some factors affecting the magnitude of earthquake forces on the wall are the size and duration of the earthquake, the distance from the earthquake epicenter to the site, and the mass of soil retained by the wall. Many retaining walls are designed for only the active earth pressure and then fail when additional forces are generated by the earthquake.

FIGURE 16.47   Voids that developed below flatwork as result of wall movement. (From Day 1997, reprinted with permission from the American Society of Civil Engineers.)

REFERENCES

1. AASHTO, *Standard Specifications for Highway Bridges,* 16th ed., American Association of State Highway and Transportation Officials, Washington, 1996.

2. G. A. Leonards, *Foundation Engineering,* McGraw-Hill, New York, 1962.

3. ASCE, *Design of Foundations for Control of Settlement,* American Society of Civil Engineers, New York, 1964.

4. J. Feld, "Tolerance of Structures to Settlement," *Journal of Soil Mechanics,* ASCE, vol. 91, no. SM3, 1965, pp. 63–77.

5. R. B. Peck, W. E. Hanson, and T. H. Thronburn, *Foundation Engineering,* 2d ed., Wiley, New York, 1974.

6. E. N. Bromhead, *Ground Movements and Their Effects on Structures,* chap. 3, "Slopes and Embankments," P. B. Attewell and R. K. Taylor, eds., Surrey University Press, London, 1984, p. 63.

7. H. E. Wahls, "Tolerable Deformations," *Vertical and Horizontal Deformations of Foundations and Embankments, Geotechnical Special Publication No. 40,* ASCE, New York, 1994, pp. 1611–1628.

8. H. F. Winterkorn and H. Fang, *Foundation Engineering Handbook,* Van Nostrand Reinhold, New York, 1975.

9. D. P. Coduto, *Foundation Design, Principles and Practices,* Prentice-Hall, Englewood Cliffs, NJ, 1994.

10. A. W. Skempton and D. H. MacDonald, "The Allowable Settlement of Buildings," *Proceedings of the Institution of Civil Engineers, Part III,* London, no. 5, 1956, pp. 727–768.

11. R. Grant, J. T. Christian, and E. H. Vanmarcke, "Differential Settlement of Buildings," *Journal of Geotechnical Engineering,* ASCE, vol. 100, no. 9, 1974, pp. 973–991.

12. R. W. Day, "Differential Movement of Slab-on-Grade Structures," *Journal of Performance of Constructed Facilities,* ASCE, vol. 4, no. 4, 1990, pp. 236–241.

13. G. F. Sowers, "Shallow Foundations," chap. 6 in *Foundation Engineering,* G. A. Leonards, ed., McGraw-Hill, New York, 1962.

14. L. Bjerrum, "Allowable Settlements of Structures," *Proceedings of European Conference on Soil Mechanics and Foundation Engineering,* vol. 2, Wiesbaden, Germany, 1963, pp. 135–137.

15. J. B. Burland, B. B. Broms, and V. F. B. DeMello, "Behavior of Foundations and Structures: State of the Art Report," *Proceedings of the 9th International Conference on Soil Mechanics and Foundation Engineering,* Japanese Geotechnical Society, Tokyo, 1977, pp. 495–546.

16. S. T. Boone, "Ground-Movement-Related Building Damage," *Journal of Geotechnical Engineering,* ASCE, vol. 122, no. 11, 1996, pp. 886–896.

17. R. W. Day, Discussion of "Ground-Movement-Related Building Damage," *Journal of Geotechnical and Geoenvironmental Engineering,* ASCE, vol. 124, no. 5, 1998.

18. E. C. Lawton, R. J. Fragaszy, and J. H. Hardcastle, "Stress Ratio Effects on Collapse of Compacted Clayey Sand." *Journal of Geotechnical Engineering,* ASCE, vol. 117, no. 5, 1991, pp. 714–730.

19. R. W. Day, Discussion of "Collapse of Compacted Clayey Sand," *Journal of Geotechnical Engineering,* ASCE, vol. 117, no. 11, 1991, pp. 1818–1821.

20. K. Terzaghi and R. B. Peck, *Soil Mechanics in Engineering Practice,* 2d ed., Wiley, New York, 1967.

21. *Slope Indicator. Geotechnical and Structural Instrumentation,* prepared by Slope Indicator Company, Bothell, WA, 1996.

22. F. H. Kisters and F. W. Kearney, "Evaluation of Civil Works Metal Structures," *Technical Report REMR-CS-31,* Department of the Army, Army Corps of Engineering, Washington, 1991.

23. K. L. Rens, T. J. Wipf, and F. W. Klaiber, "Review of Nondestructive Evaluation Techniques of Civil Infrastructure," *Journal of Performance of Constructed Facilities,* ASCE, vol. 11, no. 4, 1997, pp. 152–160.

24. T. E. Miller, *California Construction Defect Litigation, Residential and Commercial,* 2d ed., Wiley, New York, 1993.

25. A. Casagrande, "Classification and Identification of Soils," *Transactions,* ASCE, vol. 113, 1948, p. 901.

26. ASTM, "Special Procedures for Testing Soil and Rock for Engineering Purposes," *ASTM Special Technical Publication 479,* Philadelphia, PA, 1970.

27. ASTM, "Sampling of Soil and Rock," *ASTM Special Technical Publication 483,* Philadelphia, PA, 1971.

28. ASTM, *Annual Book of ASTM Standards,* vol. 04.08, *Soil and Rock (I).* Standard No. D 420-93, *Standard Guide to Site Characterization for Engineering, Design, and Construction Purposes,* West Conshohocken, PA, 1997, pp. 1–7.

29. M. J. Hvorslev, *Subsurface Exploration and Sampling of Soils for Civil Engineering Purposes,* Waterways Experiment Station, Vicksburg, MS, 1949.

30. ASCE, "Subsurface Investigation for Design and Construction of Foundations of Buildings," Task Committee for Foundation Design Manual, *Journal of Soil Mechanics,* ASCE, part I, vol. 98, no. SM5, pp. 481–490; part II, no. SM6, pp. 557–578; parts III and IV, no. SM7, 1972, pp. 749–764.

31. ASCE, *Subsurface Investigation for Design and Construction of Foundations of Buildings,* Manual No. 56, American Society of Civil Engineers, New York, 1976.

32. ASCE, *Site Characterization & Exploration,* Proceedings of the Specialty Workshop at Northwestern University, C. H. Dowding, ed., New York, 1978.

33. T. W. Lambe, *Soil Testing for Engineers,* Wiley, New York, 1951.

34. A. W. Bishop and D. J. Henkel, *The Measurement of Soil Properties in the Triaxial Test,* 2d ed., Edward Arnold, London, 1962.

35. Department of the Army, *Engineering and Design, Laboratory Soils Testing (Engineer Manual EM 1110-2-1906),* prepared at the U.S. Army Engineer Waterways Experiment Station, published by the Department of the Army, Washington, 1970.

36. *Standard Specifications for Public Works Construction,* published by Bni Building News, Los Angeles, CA, commonly known as the "Green Book," 1991.

37. J. V. Matson, *Effective Expert Witnessing,* 2d ed., Lewis Publishers, Boca Raton, FL, 1994.

38. G. Shuirman and J. E. Slosson, *Forensic Engineering—Environmental Case Histories for Civil Engineers and Geologists,* Academic Press, New York, 1992.

39. T. Y. Poh, I. H. Wong, and B. Chandrasekaran, "Performance of Two Propped Diaphragm Walls in Stiff Residual Soils," *Journal of Performance of Constructed Facilities,* ASCE, vol. 11, no. 4, 1997, pp. 190–199.

40. J. M. Duncan, "State of the Art: Limit Equilibrium and Finite-Element Analysis of Slopes," *Journal of Geotechnical and Geoenvironmental Engineering,* ASCE, vol. 122, no. 7, 1996, pp. 577–596.

41. R. M. Norris and R. W. Webb, *Geology of California,* 2d ed., Wiley, New York, 1990.

42. H. F. Greenspan, J. A. O'Kon, K. J. Beasley, and J. S. Ward, *Guidelines for Failure Investigation,* ASCE, New York, 1989.

43. S. J. Greenfield and C. K. Shen, *Foundations in Problem Soils,* Prentice-Hall, Englewood Cliffs, NJ, 1992.

44. J. E. Bowles, *Foundation Analysis and Design,* 3d ed., McGraw-Hill, New York, 1982.

45. G. D. Johnpeer, "Land Subsidence Caused by Collapsible Soils in Northern New Mexico," *Ground Failure,* vol. 3, National Research Council, Committee on Ground Failure Hazards, Washington, 1986.

46. J. E. Jennings and K. Knight, "The Additional Settlement of Foundations due to a Collapse of Structure of Sandy Subsoils on Wetting," *Proceedings of the 4th International Conference on Soil Mechanics and Foundation Engineering,* vol. 1, London, England, 1957, pp. 316–319.

47. J. H. Dudley, "Review of Collapsing Soils," *Journal of Soil Mechanics and Foundation Engineering Division,* ASCE, vol. 96, no. SM3, 1970, pp. 925–947.

48. E. C. Lawton, R. J. Fragaszy, and J. H. Hardcastle, "Collapse of Compacted Clayey Sand," *Journal of Geotechnical Engineering,* ASCE, vol. 115, no. 9, 1989, pp. 1252–1267.

49. E. C. Lawton, R. J. Fragaszy, and M. D. Hetherington, "Review of Wetting Induced Collapse in Compacted Soil," *Journal of Geotechnical Engineering,* ASCE, vol. 118, no. 9, 1992, pp. 1376–1394.

50. R. Tadepalli and D. G. Fredlund, "The Collapse Behavior of Compacted Soil during Inundation," *Canadian Geotechnical Journal,* vol. 28, no. 4, 1991, pp. 477–488.

51. R. W. Day, Discussion of "Evaluation and Control of Collapsible Soil," *Journal of Geotechnical Engineering,* ASCE, vol. 120, no. 5, 1994, pp. 924–925.

52. K. M. Rollins, R. C. Rollins, T. D. Smith, and G. H. Beckwith, "Identification and Characterization of Collapsible Gravels," *Journal of Geotechnical Engineering,* ASCE, vol. 120, no. 3, 1994, pp. 528–542.

53. ASTM, *Annual Book of ASTM Standards,* vol. 04.09, *Soil and Rock (II), Geosynthetics.* Standard D 5333-92, *Standard Test Method for Measurement of Collapse Potential of Soils,* West Conshohocken, PA, 1997, pp. 225–227.

54. W. C. Stokes and D. J. Varnes, *Glossary of Selected Geologic Terms,* Colorado Scientific Society Proceedings, vol. 116, Denver, CO, 1955.

55. G. F. Sowers, *Building on Sinkholes: Design and Construction of Foundations in Karst Terrain,* ASCE Press, New York, 1997.

56. *Earth Manual,* A Water Resources Technical Publication, 2d ed., U.S. Department of the Interior, Bureau of Reclamation, Denver, CO, 1985.

57. J. Foshee and B. Bixler, "Cover-Subsidence Sinkhole Evaluation of State Road 434, Longwood, Florida," *Journal of Geotechnical Engineering,* ASCE, vol. 120, no. 11, 1994, pp. 2026–2040.

58. T. W. Lambe and R. V. Whitman, *Soil Mechanics,* Wiley, New York, 1969.

59. G. F. Sowers, *Soil Mechanics and Foundations: Geotechnical Engineering,* 4th ed., Macmillan, New York, 1979.

60. R. D. Holtz and W. D. Kovacs, *An Introduction to Geotechnical Engineering,* Prentice-Hall, Englewood Cliffs, NJ, 1981.

61. J. N. Cernica, *Geotechnical Engineering: Soil Mechanics,* Wiley, New York, 1995.

62. C. C. Ladd, R. Foote, K. Ishihara, F. Schlosser, and H. G. Poulos, "Stress-Deformation and Strength Characteristics," *State-of-the-Art Report, Proceedings, 9th International Conference on Soil Mechanics and Foundation Engineering,* vol. 2, International Society of Soil Mechanics and Foundation Engineering, Tokyo, Japan, 1997, pp. 421–494.

63. A. R. Whitlock and S. S. Moosa, "Foundation Design Considerations for Construction on Marshlands," *Journal of Performance of Constructed Facilities,* ASCE, vol. 10, no. 1, 1996, pp. 15–22.

64. R. E. Gray, "Coal Mine Subsidence and Structures," *Mine Induced Subsidence: Effects on Engineered Structures, Geotechnical Special Publication 19,* ASCE, New York, 1988, pp. 69–86.

65. R. C. Dyni and M. Burnett, "Speedy Backfilling for Old Mines," *Civil Engineering Magazine,* ASCE, vol. 63, no. 9, 1993, pp. 56–58.

66. G. Lin, R. M. Bennett, E. C. Drumm, and T. L. Triplett, "Response of Residential Test Foundations to Large Ground Movements," *Journal of Performance of Constructed Facilities,* ASCE, vol. 9, no. 4, 1995, pp. 319–329.

67. *Subsidence Engineers Handbook,* National Coal Board Mining Department, National Coal Board, London, 1975.

68. H. Kratzsch, *Mining Subsidence Engineering,* Springer-Verlag, Berlin, Germany, 1983.

69. S. S. Peng, *Coal Mine Ground Control,* 2d ed., Wiley, New York, 1986.

70. S. S. Peng, *Surface Subsidence Engineering,* Society for Mining, Metallurgy and Exploration, Inc., Littleton, CO, 1992.

71. G. G. Marino, J. W. Mahar, and E. W. Murphy, "Advanced Reconstruction for Subsidence-Damaged Homes," *Mine Induced Subsidence: Effects on Engineered Structures,* H. J. Siriwardane, ed., ASCE, New York, 1988, pp. 87–106.

72. J. R. Cheeks, "Settlement of Shallow Foundations on Uncontrolled Mine Spoil Fill," *Journal of Performance of Constructed Facilities,* ASCE, vol. 10, no. 4, 1996, pp. 143–151.

73. P. C. Rutledge, "Relation of Undisturbed Sampling to Laboratory Testing," *Transactions,* ASCE, vol. 109, 1944, pp. 1162–1163.

74. B. W. Purkey, E. M. Duebendorfer, E. I. Smith, J. G. Price, and S. B. Castor, *Geologic Tours in the Las Vegas Area,* Nevada Bureau of Mines and Geology, Special Publication 16, Las Vegas, NV, 1994.

75. D. E. Jones and W. G. Holtz, "Expansive Soils—The Hidden Disaster." *Civil Engineering,* vol. 43, Nov. 8, 1973.

76. F. H. Chen, *Foundations on Expansive Soil,* 2d ed., Elsevier Scientific, New York, 1988.

77. H. B. Seed, R. J. Woodward, and R. Lundgren, "Prediction of Swelling Potential for Compacted Clays," *Journal of Soil Mechanics and Foundations Division,* ASCE, vol. 88, no. SM3, 1962, pp. 53–87.

78. C. C. Ladd and T. W. Lambe, "The Identification and Behavior of Expansive Clays," *Proceedings, 5th International Conference on Soil Mechanics and Foundation Engineering,* vol. 1, Paris, France, 1961.

79. G. Kassiff and R. Baker, "Aging Effects on Swell Potential of Compacted Clay." *Journal of the Soil Mechanics and Foundation Division,* ASCE, vol. 97, no. SM3, 1971, pp. 529–540.

80. R. W. Day, "Expansion of Compacted Gravelly Clay," *Journal of Geotechnical Engineering,* ASCE, vol. 117, no. 6, 1991, pp. 968–972.

81. R. W. Day, "Effective Cohesion for Compacted Clay," *Journal of Geotechnical Engineering,* ASCE, vol. 118, no. 4, 1992, pp. 611–619.

82. W. G. Holtz and H. J. Gibbs, "Engineering Properties of Expansive Clays," *Transactions,* ASCE, vol. 121, 1956, pp. 641–677.

83. *Uniform Building Code,* International Conference of Building Officials, three volumes, Whittier, CA, 1997.

84. R. L. Meehan and L. B. Karp, "California Housing Damage Related to Expansive Soils," *Journal of Performance of Constructed Facilities,* ASCE, vol. 8, no. 2, 1994, pp. 139–157.

85. ASTM, *Annual Book of ASTM Standards,* vol. 04.08, *Soil and Rock (I).* Standard D 4829-95, *Standard Test Method for Expansion Index of Soils,* West Conshohocken, PA, 1997, pp. 866–869.

86. A. M. Johnson and J. R. Rodine, "Debris Flow," *Slope Instability,* Wiley, New York, 1984, pp. 257–361.

87. G. F. Sowers and D. L. Royster, "Field Investigation," chap. 4 of *Landslides, Analysis and Control, Special Report 176,* Transportation Research Board, National Academy of Sciences, R. L. Schuster and R. J. Krizek, eds., Washington, 1978, pp. 81–111.

88. M. D. Boscardin and E. J. Cording, "Building Response to Excavation-Induced Settlement, *Journal of Geotechnical Engineering,* ASCE, vol. 115, no. 1, 1989, pp. 1–21.

89. R. W. Day, "Soil Related Damage to Tilt-up Structures," *Practice Periodical on Structural Design and Construction,* ASCE, vol. 2, no. 2, 1997, pp. 55–60.

90. A. C. Lawson et al., *The California Earthquake of April 18, 1906—Report of the State Earthquake Investigation Commission,* Carnegie Institution of Washington, Publication 87, 1908, vol. 1, part 1, pp. 1–254; part 2, pp. 255–451.

91. N. N. Ambraseys, "On the Seismic Behavior of Earth Dams," *Proceedings of the Second World Conference on Earthquake Engineering,* vol. 1, Tokyo and Kyoto, Japan, 1960, pp. 331–358.

92. C. M. Duke, "Foundations and Earth Structures in Earthquakes," *Proceedings of the Second World Conference on Earthquake Engineering,* vol. 1, Tokyo and Kyoto, Japan, 1960, pp. 435–455.

93. California Department of Water Resources, "Earthquake Damage to Hydraulic Structures in California," *California Department of Water Resources, Bulletin 116-3,* Sacramento, CA, 1967.

94. M. G. Bonilla, "Surface Faulting and Related Effects," chap. 3 of *Earthquake Engineering,* Robert L. Wiegel, ed., Prentice-Hall, Englewood Cliffs, NJ, 1970, pp. 47–74.

95. K. V. Steinbrugge, "Earthquake Damage and Structural Performance in the United States," chap. 9 of *Earthquake Engineering,* Robert L. Wiegel, ed., Prentice-Hall, Englewood Cliffs, NJ, 1970, pp. 167–226.

96. R. D. Oldham, "Report on the Great Earthquake of 12th June, 1897," India Geologic Survey Memorial, *Publication 29,* 1899.

97. N. A. Florensov and V. P. Solonenko, eds., "Gobi-Altayskoye Zemletryasenie," *Iz. Akad. Nauk SSSR.*; also 1965, *The Gobi-Altai Earthquake,* U.S. Department of Commerce (English translation), Washington, 1963.

98. J. C. Savage and L. M. Hastie, "Surface Deformation Associated with Dip-Slip Faulting," *Journal of Geophysical Research,* vol. 71, no. 20, 1966, pp. 4897–4904.

99. G. W. Housner, "Strong Ground Motion," chap. 4 of *Earthquake Engineering,* Robert L. Wiegel, ed., Prentice-Hall, Englewood Cliffs, NJ, 1970, pp. 75–92.

100. H. B. Seed, "Soil Problems and Soil Behavior," chap. 10 of *Earthquake Engineering,* Robert L. Wiegel, ed., Prentice-Hall, Englewood Cliffs, NJ, 1970, pp. 227–252.

101. K. Ishihara, "Liquefaction and Flow Failure During Earthquakes," *Geotechnique,* vol. 43, no. 3, London, England, 1993, pp. 351–415.

102. S. T. Kerwin and J. J. Stone, "Liquefaction Failure and Remediation: King Harbor Redondo Beach, California," *Journal of Geotechnical and Geoenvironmental Engineering,* ASCE, vol. 123, no. 8, 1997, pp. 760–769.

103. Shannon and Wilson, Inc., *Report on Anchorage Area Soil Studies, Alaska, to U.S. Army Engineer District, Anchorage, Alaska,* Seattle, WA, 1964.

104. W. R. Hansen, *Effects of the Earthquake of March 27, 1964 at Anchorage, Alaska,* Geological Survey Professional Paper 542-A, U.S. Department of the Interior, Washington, 1965.

105. A. Grantz, G. Plafker, and R. Kachadoorian, *Alaska's Good Friday Earthquake, March 27, 1994,* Department of the Interior, Geological Survey Circular 491, Washington, 1964.

106. R. W. Day and D. M. Poland, "Damage due to Northridge Earthquake Induced Movement of Landslide Debris," *Journal of Performance of Constructed Facilities,* ASCE, vol. 10, no. 3, 1996, pp. 96–108.

107. National Science Foundation (NSF), "Quantitative Nondestructive Evaluation for Constructed Facilities," *Announcement Fiscal Year 1992,* Directorate for Engineering, Division of Mechanical and Structural Systems, Washington, 1992.

108. *ACI Manual of Concrete Practice,* Part 1, *Materials and General Properties of Concrete,* American Concrete Institute, Detroit, MI, 1990.

109. F. M. Lea, *The Chemistry of Cement and Concrete,* 1st American ed., Chemical Publishing Company, New York, 1971.

110. P. K. Mehta, Discussion of "Combating Sulfate Attack in Corps of Engineers Concrete Construction," by Thomas J. Reading, *ACI Journal Proceedings,* vol. 73, no. 4, 1976, pp. 237–238.

111. W. D. Hurst, "Experience in the Winnipeg Area with Sulphate-Resisting Cement Concrete," *Performance of Concrete, Resistance of Concrete to Sulphate and Other Environmental Conditions,* University of Toronto Press, Canada, 1968, pp. 125–134.

112. L. H. Tuthill, "Resistance to Chemical Attack-Hardened Concrete," *Significance of Tests and Properties of Concrete and Concrete-Making Materials,* STP-169A, ASTM, Philadelphia, PA, 1966, pp. 275–289.

113. T. J. Reading, "Combating Sulfate Attack in Corps of Engineering Concrete Construction," *Durability of Concrete, SP47,* American Concrete Institute, Detroit, MI, 1975, pp. 343–366.

114. B. Mather, "Field and Laboratory Studies of the Sulphate Resistance of Concrete," *Performance of Concrete, Resistance of Concrete to Sulphate and Other Environmental Conditions,* University of Toronto Press, Canada, 1968, pp. 66–76.

115. B. P. Bellport, "Combating Sulphate Attack on Concrete on Bureau of Reclamation Projects," *Performance of Concrete, Resistance of Concrete to Sulphate and Other Environmental Conditions,* University of Toronto Press, Canada, 1968, pp. 77–92.

116. *Design and Control of Concrete Mixtures,* 13th ed., Portland Cement Association, Stokie, IL, 1988.

117. A. Casagrande, Discussion of "A New Theory of Frost Heaving," by A. C. Benkelman and F. R. Ohlmstead, *Proceedings of the Highway Research Board,* vol. 11, 1932, pp. 168–172.

118. C. W. Kaplar, "Phenomenon and Mechanism of Frost Heaving," *Highway Research Record 304,* 1970, pp. 1–13.

119. R. N. Yong and B. P. Warkentin, *Soil Properties and Behavior,* Elsevier Scientific, New York, 1975.

120. M. A. Reed, C. W. Lovell, A. G. Altschaeffl, and L. E. Wood, "Frost Heaving Rate Predicted from Pore Size Distribution," *Canadian Geotechnical Journal,* vol. 16, no. 3, 1979, pp. 463–472.

121. J. Feld and K. L. Carper, *Construction Failure,* 2d ed., Wiley, New York, 1997.

122. R. W. Brown, *Foundation Behavior and Repair, Residential and Light Commercial,* McGraw-Hill, New York, 1992.

123. R. W. Day, "Repair of Damaged Slab-on-Grade Foundations," *Practice Periodical on Structural Design and Construction,* ASCE, vol. 1, no. 3, 1996, pp. 83–87.

124. Transportation Research Board, *Rapid-Setting Materials for Patching Concrete,* National Cooperative Highway Research Program Synthesis of Highway Practice 45, National Academy of Sciences, Washington, 1977.

125. R. J. Schutz, "Properties and Specifications for Epoxies Used in Concrete Repair," *Concrete Construction Magazine,* published by Concrete Construction Publications, Inc., Addison, IL, 1984, pp. 873–878.

126. ASTM, *Annual Book of ASTM Standards: Concrete and Aggregates,* vol. 04.2. Standard C 881-90, *Standard Specification for Epoxy-Resin-Base Bonding Systems for Concrete,* West Conshohocken, PA, 1997, pp. 436–440.

127. R. W. Brown, *Design and Repair of Residential and Light Commercial Foundations,* McGraw-Hill, New York, 1990.

128. E. C. Lawton, "Nongrouting Techniques," *Practical Foundation Engineering Handbook,* Robert W. Brown, ed., McGraw-Hill, New York, 1996, section 5, pp. 5.3 to 5.276.

129. E. D. Graf, "Compaction Grouting Techniques," *Journal of the Soil Mechanics and Foundations Division,* ASCE, vol. 95, no. SM5, 1969, pp. 1151–1158.

130. J. K. Mitchell, "In-Place Treatment of Foundation Soils," *Journal of the Soil Mechanics and Foundation Division,* ASCE, vol. 96, no. SM1, 1970, pp. 73–110.

131. D. R. Brown and J. Warner, "Compaction Grouting," *Journal of the Soil Mechanics and Foundations Division,* ASCE, vol. 99, no. SM8, 1973, pp. 589–601.

132. J. Warner, "Compaction Grouting—The First Thirty Years," *Proceedings of the Conference on Grouting in Geotechnical Engineering,* W. H. Baker, ed., ASCE, New York, 1982, pp. 694–707.

133. J. Nadjer and M. Werno, "Protection of Buildings on Expansive Clays," *Proceeding of the Third International Conference on Expansive Soils,* vol. 1, Haifa, Israel, 1973, pp. 325–334.

134. D. R. Snethen, *Technical Guidelines for Expansive Soils in Highway Subgrades,* Report FHWA-RD-79-51, U.S. Army Engineering Waterway Experiment Station, Vicksburg, MS, 1979.

135. A. A. B. Williams, "The Deformation of Roads Resulting from Moisture Changes in Expansive Soils in South Africa," *Moisture Equilibria and Moisture Changes in Soils Beneath Covered Areas,* G. D. Aitchison, ed., Symposium Proceedings, Butterworths, Australia, 1965, pp. 143–155.

136. J. N. Cernica, *Geotechnical Engineering: Foundation Design,* Wiley, New York, 1995.

137. A. B. Fourie, "Laboratory Evaluation of Lateral Swelling Pressures," *Journal of Geotechnical Engineering,* ASCE, vol. 115, no. 10, 1989, pp. 1481–1486.

138. E. T. Marsh and R. K. Walsh, "Common Causes of Retaining-Wall Distress: Case Study," *Journal of Performance of Constructed Facilities,* ASCE, vol. 10, no. 1, 1996, pp. 35–38.

139. Post-Tensioning Institute, *Design and Construction of Post-tensioned Slabs-on-Ground,* 2d ed., Phoenix, AZ, 1996.

140. R. W. Day, "Settlement Behavior of Post-Tensioned Slab-on-Grade," *Journal of Performance of Constructed Facilities,* ASCE, vol. 12, no. 2, 1998, pp. 56–61.

141. R. W. Day, "Design and Construction of Cantilevered Retaining Walls," *Practice Periodical on Structural Design and Construction,* ASCE, vol. 2, no. 1, 1997, pp. 16–21.

CHAPTER 17
TEMPORARY STRUCTURES

Robert T. Ratay, Ph.D., P.E.

INTRODUCTION

To architects, engineers, lawyers, and even some contractors, temporary structures in construction are not as familiar as permanent structures, such as buildings and bridges. For the engineer to design effective, economical, and safe temporary access or support structures, he or she has to have an understanding of not only loads, strength, and stability; but also the business and practice of temporary works in order to know where, when, how, why, and by whom temporary works are used. For the forensic engineer to conduct an intelligent investigation of a construction failure involving temporary structures, she or he, too, has to have an understanding of not only loads, strength, and stability; but also the business and practice of temporary works in order to recognize the possible sources and nature of problems. Therefore, it was decided to devote much of this chapter to design philosophies, to an overview of the design-construction processes as they relate to temporary structures, and to the applicable design and construction codes, standards, and regulations. The rest of the chapter includes presentations of several case histories.

CONSTRUCTION FAILURES

Disturbingly large numbers of structural failures during construction occur in the United States, as well as throughout the world. Advances in construction technology, newly developed materials, increasingly fine-tuned designs, and the construction of more daring structures, as well as the pressure of time- and cost-cutting driven by competition, are all contributing factors. But the most frequent direct causes of failures are human factors: oversight; carelessness; incompetence; breakdown of organization; poor management and communication; disregard of codes, standards, and specifications; and general nonadherence to good practice.

There appears to be a mismatch of the practice of one group, the designers-of-record who by necessity distance themselves from the construction of the project, and the objectives and capabilities of the other group, the constructors who by contract must perform under the constraints of agreed time and money.

More structures fail during construction than in service after completion; and many, if not most, of the construction disasters occur as the result of the failure of temporary structures. A tacit attitude seems to prevail in the design-construction industry: "These things" are temporary only, hence generally less important, therefore greater risks are acceptable than in permanent structures. But a dollar or a life lost at a construction site is no less valuable or less tragic than its loss elsewhere. More than 1000 construction workers lose their lives and many others are injured each year in the United States. (A 1989 ABC News broadcast on construction accidents reported that 6 workers die each day in construction accidents in the United States.) According to some estimates, the direct and indirect cost of construction injuries in this country is more than $17 billion annually. No one appears to have estimated and published the total of property losses in construction failures. These occurrences are not unique to the United States but are prevalent in all other countries as well.

Failures of unbraced excavations, scaffolding, falsework, formwork, excavation supports, and temporary erection shoring, bracing, and guying (in approximately this order) are the most frequent occurrences of temporary structure failures. Often the total absence of some of these, such as excavation supports, shoring, bracing, or guying, is the proximate cause of a disaster.

Reasonable and clearly written codes, standards, and regulations would improve construction safety, but the best ways to mitigate temporary structure failures obviously are competent designs, good construction practices, utmost care, strict inspection, and unwavering enforcement of high standards.

WHAT ARE TEMPORARY STRUCTURES?

Young engineer: Sir, what is a temporary structure in construction?

Old contractor: Whatever it takes, sonny.

Indeed, although there is a long list of temporary structures identified by name or function, anything that is erected and used to aid in the construction of a permanent project should fall under the designation of temporary structure in construction. As defined in the McGraw-Hill *Encyclopedia of Science and Technology,*

> Temporary structures are those structures that are erected and used to aid in the construction of a permanent project. They are used to facilitate the construction of buildings, bridges, tunnels and other above and below-ground facilities by providing access, support, and protection for the facility under construction, as well as to assure the safety of the workers and the public. Temporary structures are either dismantled and removed when the permanent works become self-supporting or completed, or they are incorporated into the finished work. In addition to new construction, some temporary structures are also used in inspection, repair and maintenance work.
>
> The long list of temporary structures includes: cofferdams; earth-retaining structures; tunneling supports; underpinning; diaphragm/slurry walls; roadway decking; construction ramps, runways and platforms; scaffolding; shoring; falsework; concrete formwork; bracing and guying; site protection structures such as sidewalk bridges, fall protection boards and nets, barricades and fences, and signs; and all sorts of unique structures that are specially conceived, designed and erected to aid in a construction operation.
>
> These temporary works have a primary influence on the quality, safety, speed and profitability of all construction projects. More failures occur during construction than during the lifetime of structures, and most of those construction failures involve temporary structures.
>
> Many aspects of temporary structures (such as design philosophy, loads, allowable stresses, materials, methods, workmanship, tolerances, field inspection and control) are different from those of permanent structures. The reference literature on temporary structures is scant. [At the time of this writing the *Handbook of Temporary Structures in Construction,* 2d ed., is the only book on the subject in the United States.] Codes and standards do not provide the same scrutiny as they do for

permanent structures. Typical design and construction techniques and some industry practices are well established, but responsibilities and liabilities remain complex
and present many contractual and legal pitfalls.

For an extensive treatment of the subject of temporary structures with detailed
descriptions, illustrations, and discussions of their design, construction, maintenance, and removal, see *Handbook of Temporary Structures in Construction,* 2d
ed., Robert T. Ratay, ed., McGraw-Hill, 1996.

UNDERSTANDING THE DESIGN-CONSTRUCTION PROCESS AS IT RELATES TO TEMPORARY STRUCTURES

Temporary structures are the concern of the designer, the contractor, the building
official, and the insurer, as well as the workers on the job and the general public.
Yet, this most important component of the construction process is not a "field" of
practice but a neglected stepchild, at times claimed, at other times disclaimed by
both designers and contractors, and almost totally neglected by researchers and
educators. Surprisingly little guidance exists in the civil engineering profession
for their design, erection, maintenance, and removal.

A tacit attitude seems to prevail in the design-construction industry: These
things are temporary and generally less important, therefore greater risks are
acceptable than in permanent structures. Certainly, less care and control is exercised with temporary than with permanent structures. Possibly as a result, far more
failures and loss of life occur during construction than in completed projects.

The literature is scant: mostly manufacturers' promotional pamphlets; a few
public authority, government, and military manuals; isolated specifications; and a
handful of journal papers, although slowly more and more publications have been
appearing in recent years. OSHA (Office of Safety and Health Administration)
regulations are just that: regulations—they do not provide technical information.
The first and so far the only comprehensive book known to exist on the subject is
Handbook of Temporary Structures in Construction, Robert T. Ratay, ed., published by McGraw-Hill in 1984, and the second edition in 1996.

Many, perhaps most, construction disasters occur as a result of the failure of
temporary structures. Is that due to poor construction practices, or poor designs,
or improper temporary design loads and allowables?

Design Philosophies and Practices.   It is an axiom among some designers that for
temporary works during construction, lower safety factors may be applied than for
completed permanent structures. In light of the uncertainties with temporary structures and their history of failures, this is an inappropriate and even dangerous attitude if applied indiscriminately. If we put aside the notion that "these things" are
temporary and generally less important (i.e., if we do not allow greater risk to life

and property at a construction site), then the design loads should perhaps be even more severe, the allowables even lower, and the calculated safety factors higher than those for permanent structures.

On the other hand, a school of thought persists that short-term construction loads are more closely predictable and can be more effectively controlled than the live loads during the decades of use—and who knows what alternate uses—of the permanent structure. Therefore, indeed, lower design safety factors may be acceptable on temporary structures and on permanent structures during their construction.

Several factors are inherently involved in the establishment of design loads, allowable stresses, and safety factors that are used for the design of any structure. These include the following:

Intended function of the structure

Nature of loads

Predictability of occurrence of loads

Certainty in the magnitudes of loads

Possibility of simultaneous occurrence of loads

Strength and deformation characteristics of the material

Reliability of the rated strength of the material (or member)

Possible secondary stresses, redundancy, and instability

Condition of the member and its material (new, used, damaged, deformed)

Acceptable behavior of the structure (such as tolerable deflections, vibrations)

Allowable degree of unacceptable behavior

Acceptable probability of total failure

Consequences of failure

Construction tolerances

Workmanship in the construction

Inspection standards

Protection of the structure against damage, deterioration, and extremities of weather

Intended life span of the structure with increasing probability of occurrence of maximum loads, abnormal loads, damage, and deterioration with time

Probably not all these factors were explicitly weighed in the establishment of a particular design load or allowable stress, but they were inherent in the evolution of the values used by the engineering profession today.

A discussion of these factors is beyond the scope of this chapter. The reader is urged to make a column alongside the above list and mark the equalities and differences of the items between permanent structures (such as a building) and temporary structures (such as falsework and shoring). The differences will outnumber the equalities.

Clearly, at least some of the design criteria should be, and indeed are, different for temporary and permanent structures. (For that matter, at least some of the design criteria for a structure during its construction phases should be different from the criteria used for its completed form.) The numbers—the values of the design loads—may work out to be the same even if the criteria for their development are different. But we do not know that until we do it.

The most complete and up-to-date public document outlining a design philosophy and specifying design loads and load combinations for temporary works is the (at the time of this writing: proposed) *Design Loads on Structures During Construction Standard*, developed over the last 11 years by the ASCE Design Loads on Structures During Construction Standards Committee, chaired by the author. (The ASCE standard is expected to undergo public balloting and publication for use in the year 2000.)

Drawings. Who performs the design of a temporary structure, who makes the drawings, and the detail required in the specifications vary depending on the temporary structure under consideration. In an extremely complex job involving such temporary work as a coffer dam for bridge piers or a method of driving shafts for a tunnel, the design of the temporary structures will often be done, and the drawings prepared, by the designer of the permanent project. It will then be the responsibility of each contractor to build the temporary work in strict accordance with those drawings. On the other hand, for simpler types of temporary structures, such as a temporary ramp that might be used by an excavation contractor for a building, the excavation contractor will likely do the designing.

Between the extremes is the type of temporary structure in which specialty contractors, who make a business of doing a specific type of temporary structure, will be employed. Examples of this include concrete forms using patented panels. The drawings by the specialty contractor will look more like shop drawings with lots of specific details.

It is well established that the contractor who builds in accordance with the design that is provided by another party is not responsible for the adequacy of the design or for bringing about the result for which the design was intended, provided that the design is strictly followed in the field. However, the contractor who does provide the design is responsible for both the adequacy of the design and its fitness for the intended use.

In the provision of a temporary structure for sheeting and shoring of an excavation, as an example, the project design engineer for the permanent structure might merely indicate that sheeting or shoring is required for that particular embankment. This general directive may be required by code and/or may be incorporated on the plans or in the specifications. On the other hand, the project design engineer may provide the design on the contract drawings.

In the first instance, the contractor in all likelihood will be required to have her or his detailed plan checked and signed by a licensed professional engineer. The adequacy of the sheeting and shoring will be the responsibility of the contractor together with the licensed professional engineer. This may also require that the contractor submit the design for the proposed sheeting and shoring to the project design engineer.

If, on the other hand, the designer of the permanent structure shows the details of the sheeting and shoring and the contractor follows this design in the execution of the work, then the responsibility for adequacy will rest with the original designer. Should the contractor deviate from this design, and should it be shown that the deviation from the design resulted in a failure of the sheeting and shoring to properly perform its function, then the contractor is responsible for the damages which result from this deviation.

Specifications. The specifications for the temporary structures are usually drawn up by the temporary structure contractor. In most cases, architects or engineers designing a permanent structure will not provide a design drawing or even specifications for the temporary structure work. For example, a temporary structure contractor working on concrete formwork will have to specify the type of plywood, framing, form ties, snap ties, braces, and other form accessories that are required for the work. The responsibility for the adequacy of the specified material and for its quality will be the temporary structure contractor's.

In the case of a design which is prepared by a temporary structure contractor for the approval of the architect or engineer, the specifications which are part of that design must also be the responsibility of the temporary structure contractor. The specifications may have to be reviewed by the project's engineer or architect for their adequacy and for the durability and strength of the materials. Should there then be a question about any of these qualities, the temporary structure contractor will have to justify the appropriateness of the specified material.

Shop Drawings. In a temporary structure, the shop drawing and its preparation are somewhat different from a shop drawing prepared by a subcontractor or supplier for a permanent structure. The shop drawing for a temporary structure may, in fact, be a completely original design which does not appear in any way on the contract drawings. An example of this might be a shop drawing prepared for the dewatering system using well points. In this case, it is the responsibility of the subcontractor of the dewatering work not only to prepare the details of where the dewatering system will be located and the type of piping and pumping equipment that would be used, but also to incorporate in the shop drawings or its specifications the calculations made by the subcontractor to ensure the adequacy of the system being installed.

Reviews and Approvals. If the temporary structure subcontractor has provided the calculations for the work to be done, the question is, Who will be responsible for those calculations? Normally an engineer or architect checks shop drawings for "compliance only" with the original contract drawings and specifications. In this case, however, since there are no original contract drawings of the material or equipment being shown on the shop drawings, it is necessary for the project's engineer or architect to decide whether the shop drawings have to be reviewed and approved at all. In most cases the engineer or architect will merely review the shop drawings for interferences or for conditions which might affect the permanent works.

The following question sometimes arises when a shop drawing is submitted for approval by a temporary structure subcontractor and is, in fact, checked and approved by the architect or engineer: Is the temporary structure subcontractor now relieved of any further responsibility for the adequacy of this temporary structure?

In any event, it is clear that shop drawings for temporary structures have an important difference in the legal sense from shop drawings for the permanent structure. It is also evident that shop drawings for temporary structures sometimes require a great deal more design work than is normally required for shop drawings for permanent structures.

In a forensic engineering investigation and litigation after a failure, the history of the preparation, review, and approval of the drawings and specifications can be important.

Permits.   The temporary structure contractor is required to obtain permits for the work to be done. These permits may be issued after approval of the plans for the temporary work by the building department, when this type of approval is required. Such approvals, as an example, might be for shoring or sheet-piling work, or for equipment that the contractor may be required to use in performing the work. The equipment may consist of cranes or hoists to be placed in the street or on the sidewalk. Other permits may be required for sidewalk crossings and for storage of materials in the street. In general, the cost of the permits must be borne by the temporary structure contractor. When a permit requires a submission of a drawing prepared by a licensed professional engineer, the drawing is the responsibility of the temporary structure contractor. If the temporary structure contracting company does not have a licensed professional engineer on its staff, then it is necessary for it to obtain such a qualified individual for the preparation of the plans.

Materials and Workmanship.   Temporary structures are often constructed of reusable manufactured elements. Although such elements are designed and made to be reused, their repeated transportation, assembly, loading, disassembly, storage, exposure to weather, and rough handling result in their damage and deterioration. They should be inspected, their existing strength and stability verified before use, and allowances made for their lost strengths, if any.

Contractors, especially on smaller projects, often use used materials for temporary structures. These materials may or may not be visibly damaged, but their strengths may well be inferior to what is required by the design. If the required member or element is not available at the site, a contractor may substitute or make it up from other pieces, sometimes even from scraps. If their adequacy is not verified, these materials may precipitate the failure of the temporary structure.

Except for specially designed and controlled major temporary structures, the workmanship in their installation is generally inferior to the workmanship in permanent construction. The required tolerances are usually more relaxed; the "looks" are generally unimportant; the overall attitude is that "these things" are temporary only and will come down anyway. This is all understandable as long as it does not compromise the proper performance and safety of the temporary structure.

In the absence of strict control of the materials and standards of workmanship, these practices of used materials and possibly inferior workmanship should be anticipated and reflected in the design through more generous factors of safety. The forensic engineer should not be influenced by the looks of temporary structures, but should recognize sloppy and unsafe work when he or she sees it.

Supervision. Supervision of a temporary structure installation includes not only its initial installation but also its adequacy during the entire period during which it is performing its function. The contractor must maintain adequately trained superintendents and supervisors who are on the site at all times when work is under way.

A qualified supervisor is one who has training and experience in the type of work which is being done. Obviously, a supervisor who has only a general background in construction but who has never been directly involved in the supervision of a temporary structure, such as the one which is being built, is not as qualified to do this work as one who has many years of experience directly or indirectly related to the work on hand.

Concrete formwork for multistory high-rise reinforced-concrete buildings, e.g., requires many intricate details of bracing, posting, strutting, and tying so that they not only will be adequate to sustain the load of the wet concrete and the embedded reinforcing bars but also will be able to undergo the impact of motorized buggies and jolting of temporary hoppers and to sustain the weight of workers, and will have the necessary clearances required for cranes and hoists. Even after the concrete is poured, it is necessary to continue proper supervision for such activities as winter heating, timing of stripping, and reshoring.

Improperly trained or inexperienced supervisors can endanger workers' lives, and the neglect of good practices can cause structural failures.

Inspection. The responsibility for inspection of the work of the contractor for temporary structures is shared by three entities:

1. *The temporary structure subcontractor* whose own supervisors or engineers must inspect the work as it is being installed, such as when a temporary structure contractor is installing shoring. As the work is being placed, the supervisor and supervisory personnel of the shoring contractor must be alert to all the requirements of safe and adequate practice and be certain that shop drawings or permits that specified the methods of performing the work are being adhered to.

2. *The general contractor* who is responsible for the entire finished structure, both temporary and permanent. The second required inspection is by the general contractor to see that the installation of the temporary structure contractor is being performed safely and adequately. The general contractor has to ascertain that the temporary structure is not interfering with other portions of the work that may be a part of the permanent structure, and that it is not interfering with other contractors or subcontractors who may be working simultaneously or subsequent to the work of the temporary structure contractor. The inspection will also cover such things as quality of the materials being installed and compliance with plans and specifications and shop drawings to the extent that they pertain to the temporary structure contractor.

3. *The party whose responsibility it is to perform the ultimate inspection* of the work. This third required inspection may be made by either an architect or an engineer who has the inspection responsibility, or her or his designate. It may also be made by a government official such as a member of a building department or government financing agency. This third inspector is the one whose inspection must be the most comprehensive, painstaking, and flawless. It is the responsibility of this inspector to be absolutely sure that all necessary compliance is being taken with building codes, safe structural practices, OSHA requirements, and any other procedure for good construction which is a part of the contract, as well as with the plans, specifications, and shop drawings for the temporary structure.

Unfortunately, there is often the tendency by some of or all these parties to concentrate on the permanent construction to the detriment of the temporary works.

The inspection and enforcement of OSHA regulations are performed by regional offices. OSHA inspectors are generally allowed to enter any construction site at reasonable times and without undue delay. An OSHA inspector who is refused admission can obtain a search warrant. Inspections can also be initiated by accidents, collapses, or employee complaints. In addition to federal OSHA, compliance checks of construction sites are often made by state or local agencies, most insurance carriers, and some private consultants.

Licensed Site Professionals and Controlled Inspection.   In recent years, some state and local governments have initiated requirements for licensed site professionals and/or controlled inspection. These regulations have imposed the requirement that a licensed professional certify compliance with statutory and regulatory enactments for all or specified portions of the construction. These requirements gained favor in the aftermath of construction failures such as the one that occurred in 1987 at L'Ambiance Plaza in Connecticut.

Familiarity with the ins-and-outs of inspection can be of great benefit to the forensic engineer in the attempt to sort out the origins and timing of many construction errors.

Monitoring and Maintenance.   Most temporary structures need periodic or continuous monitoring and maintenance during the construction work. Connections, members, or entire sections may loosen, deform, move, or fail since they are not fixed "permanently." Well-designed and properly built temporary structures have failed because they were not monitored and maintained.

Removal. Disassembly and removal of temporary works may be critical phases of the work, especially if they functioned as temporary supports. The time and method must be clearly specified and controlled, so as to avoid overstress and excessive deflections in the permanent work.

It is important to understand how the temporary structure works so as not to impair its own stability and cause its collapse during the disassembly, or to cause damage to the permanent facility by the sudden removal of the temporary structure.

Both the designer of the temporary structure and the contractor need to look ahead in the planning of the project and consider this terminal phase of the temporary work.

RESPONSIBILITIES AND LIABILITIES

The contractual responsibilities and legal liabilities for temporary structures may be more complex than those for the permanent facility that is being constructed. Temporary structures present as many contractual and legal pitfalls as technical challenges. The contractual and legal positions can become especially complex when problems or disputes occur.

Who does the design? Who prepares the drawings? How detailed and tight should the specifications be? Who is responsible and liable for what? What are the various legal positions of the owner, designer, general contractor, subcontractor, and construction manager? There are no universal industry standards covering these matters in relation to temporary structures. The answers often depend on the particular temporary structure, the contract(s) among the involved parties, local laws and regulations, and sometimes the specific circumstances.

Apart from negligence or strict liability standards, the rights and duties of parties involved in temporary construction work are most often detailed in the contract documents, i.e., in the general, supplementary, and special conditions. These generally start with one of several standard forms, such as those provided by the American Institute of Architects (AIA), the Engineers Joint Contract Documents Committee (EJCDC), or the Associated General Contractors of America (AGC), and then include modifications tailored to meet the specific needs of a particular project.

The responsibilities and liabilities of the various participants on a construction project, as related to temporary structures, are outlined in the following paragraphs. The forensic investigator must be knowledgeable about these, in addition to technical matters, if he or she is called upon to opine as to the assignment of the responsibilities for a construction failure.

All Parties

All parties on a construction project have responsibilities to one another and to the public. They have obligations to the other contracting parties and to a wide range of third persons as well, such as workers, pedestrians, and adjoining property owners. As regards the contracting parties, their responsibilities to each other are governed by the contract. These include the duty not to interfere with the work of the trades and the duty to cooperate with all other parties to allow proper progress of the work.

All contracting parties potentially can be held liable to third persons who are injured or damaged as a result of the contracting parties' failure to exercise the standard of care required by either common or statutory law. For example, the designer or builder of a sidewalk bridge may be liable to pedestrians if the bridge collapses. Similarly, an excavation contractor who fails to adequately underpin an adjacent structure will be liable to the owner of that adjacent structure for any damage caused by the contractor's neglect. In some states, the violation of a statutory duty (e.g., to adequately underpin) is, in and of itself, conclusive proof of negligence. The practical effect of this is that the injured party has only to establish the amount of damages in order to recover—there can be no issue as to fault or liability. In other states, violation of a similar statute is considered merely as evidence of negligence to be considered with all other evidence, so that the injured party's prospect for recovery is far less certain.

The Owner

The owner is concerned with temporary structures only insofar as they are necessary to the construction of the permanent product. Therefore, the construction contract documents will often simply provide what must be done rather than detailed instructions on how to do it, e.g., "earth banks shall be adequately shored" or "adjoining structures shall be adequately protected." Under this performance-type specification, the involved contractors are responsible for meeting the required result, and they, not the owner, are responsible for the means and methods used to achieve it. This is in contrast to the technical or detailed specification wherein the owner or the designer specifies the method to be used and is deemed implied to warrant its adequacy. The difference in the owner's responsibilities can be seen as follows: If a proper performance specification is being used, then the owner bears no responsibility if the contractor's work fails unless the owner was negligent in hiring the contractor or, notwithstanding the written documents, the owner undertook direction or control of the contractor's work. If, however, a detailed specification is utilized, then the owner bears full responsibility for any deficiencies in the contractor's work, as long as the contractor performs that work strictly as specified.

An owner's responsibility to third persons is usually secondary in that most lawsuits arising out of temporary construction work, while naming the owner as a party, are attributable to negligent performance by the contractors or to the design deficiencies by the responsible architect or engineer. Thus, even in the absence of a contractual indemnity provision, the owner can shift the liability to the party ultimately responsible, assuming that party has the financial resources to shoulder the responsibility. In other words, although the owner is primarily liable to the injured party, the owner has a right of indemnity or contribution from the party who was negligent.

However, by statue or legal precedent an owner may assume strict liability, regardless of fault, for such things as worker safety or ultrahazardous activity conducted on the owner's property.

The Designer

The design professional is responsible for the accuracy and adequacy of her or his plans and specifications. By distributing these documents for use, the design professional impliedly warrants to both the owner and contractor that a cohesive structure will result, provided the plans and specifications are followed. But the designer does not guarantee perfection, only that he or she exercised ordinary care. When a contractor who properly follows the designer's documents experiences a problem, liability will ultimately rest with the architect or engineer. The designer would be responsible for all additional costs of construction attributable to faulty design: the cost of redesign and all resultant damage. This includes liability to third parties for injuries, death, and property damage.

A design professional has no duty to supervise, inspect, or observe the performance of the work she or he designed, absent a duty which the design professional has assumed by contract, by statute, or by having filed plans with a local building department. Once some duty has been assumed, however, state courts are in wide disagreement as to the extent of responsibility and liability. Some courts have found that design professionals have a nondelegable duty to regularly supervise the means and methods of construction. At the very least, the architect or engineer will be responsible for making occasional visits to the site to verify technical compliance with the contract documents.

Designers should be wary of so-called routine sign-offs of the contractor's work. The sign-off may include a certification by the designer that the contractor has complied with the plans and specifications and with applicable codes. Such a certification could impose on the designer liability equal to the contractor's in the event of a failure.

An engineer of record should be particularly careful in requiring submission of and in "approving" the contractor's detailed plan for temporary construction. Exculpatory language is often placed on the engineer's "approval" stamps to the effect that the engineer has assumed no responsibility by having reviewed the submission. In the event the design was not adequate and there was injury to person or property, it is likely that the engineer's stamp would not be sufficient to exculpate him or her from liability to injured third parties. The engineer of record should, but often does not, have adequate familiarity with the materials, hardware, and equipment, or the experience with methods of installation of temporary structures. If the engineer of record does not have the necessary expertise, or does not intend to carefully review each and every submission, the submission should not be required at all. "Don't ask for it, if you don't know what to do with it."

The Contractor

The ambit of the contractor's responsibility is far-reaching. The contractor is responsible for performing all required work in accordance with the contract documents, generally accepted construction practices, and governing legislative enactments. In sum, no matter what goes wrong, the contractor stands suspected, accused, and delayed and eventually is likely to pay or at least share the resulting costs.

It is important to stress that it is not necessarily enough that the contractor has performed to the best of her or his own ability. When assessing liability, the courts do not simply accept at face value what the contractor did, but measure that against what an ordinary contractor of similar experience would have done under similar circumstances. Consequently, when determining whether a contractor exercised ordinary or reasonable care in doing the work, the court will look at how that work compares to the degree of skill prevalent in the industry at the time the work was performed.

The Construction Manager

The construction manager, although not involved in the performance of any actual construction work, may assist the owner in choosing the contractors who will perform work, coordinating the work of these trades, and approving requisitions for payment. The construction manager ordinarily does not assume any design responsibility, which remains with the owner's architect or engineer. However, construction managers should be wary of contractual assumption of responsibility for the contractor's performance. They should be careful with sign-offs or certifications related to the work. For example, by approving payment, the construction manager tacitly declares that the portion of the work for which the payment is requested by the contractor has been completed satisfactorily. Note the hidden risks.

CODES, STANDARDS, AND REGULATIONS

Temporary structures do not receive the same intense scrutiny and protection of building codes and design standards as do permanent structures. Indeed, codes and standards are mostly silent on the subject or give such general statements as "proper provisions shall be made..." and "adequate temporary bracing shall be provided...." Even these statements refer to the permanent structure during its short-term construction phase rather than to the temporary support or access structures themselves. *Temporary works* or other synonymous terms do not even appear as entries in the indexes and tables of contents of many building codes and design standards.

The federal government, many states, municipalities, and public authorities have safety codes concerning construction activities. However, they do not give technical information that would aid in the actual design of temporary structures. The regulations of the Occupational Health and Safety Administration (OSHA) are regulations which, as important as they are for the safety of workers and protection of the public, do not provide technical assistance.

For a rather extensive discussion and up-to-date list of codes and standards which address temporary structures, the reader is directed to chapter 4, "Codes, Standard and Regulations," by John Duntemann, in *Handbook of Temporary Structures in Construction,* 2d ed., Robert T. Ratay, ed., McGraw-Hill, 1996.

Despite the long list of publications, and the important bits and pieces of data in them, the information is highly fragmented. In the author's opinion, no one document is complete enough to carry one through the design and construction of a temporary structure without consulting other documents.

Design Codes, Standards, and Specifications

As pointed out earlier, the structural design codes, standards, and specifications in the United States deal rather superficially, if at all, with temporary structures. With increasing importance being attributed to construction site safety, and the consequent attention paid to the design and construction of temporary works, however, more and more guidance is becoming available. Some of the foreign codes and standards are more focused than those in the United States with specific design criteria. The forensic engineer should be familiar with at least the existence, if not the contents, of the guides and requirements for temporary structures.

The most extensive specifications of temporary structure design criteria, loads, and load combinations are in a currently developing ASCE, and in a recently published FHWA document: *Design Loads on Structures During Construction Standard,* and *Guide Design Specifications for Bridge Temporary Works,* by J. R. Duntemann et al., FHWA Report FHWA-RD-93-032, Washington, November 1993. (The ASCE standard is expected to undergo public balloting in the year 2000 and publication for use in 2001.)

Some state and municipal design manuals, such as those by CALTRANS and the NYC Transit Authority, are good sources for local conditions. Some of the foreign design codes and standards that have criteria specific to temporary structures are the various Canadian Standards, the Construction Safety Codes of the various Canadian provinces, the British Code of Practice for Falsework and the one for Scaffolds, the Australian standard for formwork, the "Design for Construction and Temporary Structures" section of the Australian State Road Authorities' Bridge

Design Specifications, the New Zealand Code of Practice for Falsework, the Japanese Bridge Standards, the Israeli Standard on Formwork, the former USSR (now Russian) State Standard Specifications for scaffolding, erection, platforms, etc., and others.

Two recent conference proceedings papers contain good information on where to find design requirements for temporary structures: J. R. Duntemann and R. T. Ratay, *Review of Selected U.S. and Foreign Design Specifications for Temporary Works,* Part 1, and A. Chini and G. Genauer, *Technical Guidance Available to Designers of Temporary Structures.* Both papers are in the *Proceedings of the SEI/ASCE Structures Congress,* Portland, OR, April 13–16, 1996.

Construction Standards, Regulations, and Recommended Practices

Occupational Safety and Health Administration regulations and several American National Standards Institute (ANSI) standards are aimed at ensuring safe construction practices, and most of them address temporary structures. They are, with very few exceptions, qualitative rather than quantitative requirements. The OSHA regulations are mandatory (see Chap. 3 of this handbook). The ANSI and other standards are voluntary compliance standards that become mandatory when adopted by "the authority having jurisdiction."

OSHA's *Safety and Health Standards Regulation* 29CFR, Part 1926, *Safety and Health Regulations for Construction,* defines mandatory requirements to protect employees from the hazards of construction operations. Part 1926 has 24 subparts, or subdivisions, which include Subpart L, *Scaffolding*; Subpart P, *Excavations*; Subpart Q, *Concrete and Masonry Construction*; Subpart R, *Steel Erection*; and Subpart S, *Underground Construction, Caissons, Cofferdams and Compressed Air.* Chapter 3 of this book includes a good overview of the OSHA regulations for the construction industry.

A few of the OSHA regulations may necessitate engineering analysis and design, but most do not.

OSHA's existing and proposed standards for the construction industry contain stated and implied requirements for contractors to assign professional engineers to perform or inspect job site activities for the assurance of safety. The role of engineers is being changed in construction as a result of the government's emphasis on *performance* rather than the traditional *prescriptive* standards, and the development of new enforcement strategies. A good, up-to-date discussion of these important developments is by Jim E. Lapping, *OSHA Standards that Require Engineers,* in the recent ASCE/SEI *Proceedings, Construction Safety Affected by Codes and Standards,* Robert T. Ratay, ed., October 1997. The paper, indeed all five articles in the *Proceedings,* are highly recommended reading for the engineer engaged in temporary structures work.

Although most states in the United States administer their own occupational safety and health programs, they generally adopt the federal OSHA regulations.

Because three sets of regulations may apply to the same project at the federal, state, and local levels, contractors are advised to follow the strictest requirement when the codes merely supplement each other, and forensic investigators are advised to review all three for any given case. When there is a direct conflict between state, federal, or city regulations, the federal code should take precedence, followed by the state and finally the municipal regulations.

ANSI issued standards, designated as safety requirements, for scaffolding (ANSI A10.8), concrete and masonry work (ANSI 10.9), steel erection (ANSI A10.13), and others, all of which include the relevant temporary structures.

The *Construction Handbook for Bridge Temporary Works* by J. F. Duntemann et al., FHWA Report FHWA-RD-93-034, by the Federal Highway Administration, is a credible guide on the subject.

Building Codes

In the United States, most local building codes are patterned after the so-called model building codes, which include the *National Building Code* (NBC) by the Building Officials and Code Administrators (BOCA), the *Uniform Building Code* (UBC) by the International Conference of Building Code Congress (ICBC), and the *Southern Standard Building Code* by the Southern Building Code Congress (SBCC). (A joint effort is under way by the code organizations to combine all the model codes into one national building code in the next very few years.) Provisions related to construction safety and temporary works in these model codes are generally minimal or nonexistent—they do not intend to place controls on construction. The provision in section 1612.5, construction loads and erection stresses, of the BOCA *National Building Code 1996*—"Provisions shall be made for temporary construction loads which occur during the erection of the building; and all structural members and connections shall be designed and erected so as to prevent overstressing during construction"—is typical of the superficial treatment of temporary structures in building codes. What provisions shall be made? For what magnitudes of temporary erection loads? What is considered overstressing? Where does one find guidance?

The model codes, however, do adopt many of the national design standards developed by organizations such as the American Concrete Institute (ACI), the American Institute of Steel Construction (AISC), and the National Forest Products Association (NFPA), all of which make some reference to temporary structures. The model codes also adopt by reference many of the American Society for Testing and Materials (ASTM) standards as the recognized test procedures to ensure construction quality. *ASTM Standards in Building Codes* is a compilation of these standards. ASCE's consensus standards, developed under the rules of the American National Standards Institute, will soon find their way into the model codes as well.

State, city, and other local building codes (or ordinances), such as the *Massachusetts State Building Code* and the *New York City Building Code,* include certain requirements for temporary structures. State labor laws, such as the New York State Labor Law, set out rather general but remarkably strict requirements to ensure the safety of workers and the general public.

Recommended Practices, Guidelines, and Manuals

Sources of selected information related to the design, erection, and construction of temporary structures are the publications produced by various industry groups. These include the American Institute of Steel Construction, the American Concrete Institute, the American Association of State Highway Transportation Officials (AASHTO), the Precast/Prestressed Concrete Institute (PCI), the American Institute of Timber Construction (AITC), the Truss Plate Institute (TPI), the Scaffolding Industry Association (SIA), and the Scaffolding, Shoring, and Forming Institute (SSFI). Private industry groups, such as the U.S. Steel Corporation, also produce related publications. In addition, there are federal organizations, such as the Federal Highway Administration (FHWA), the Department of Commerce, the Army and Navy, and state and city agencies, such as CAL-TRANS and the New York City Transit Authority, that publish some noteworthy manuals.

Some of the more helpful structure or material-specific publications are the AISC *Code of Standard Practice,* the AASHTO *Standard Specification for Highway Bridges,* the ACI 347-88 *Guide to Formwork for Concrete,* the ACI Publication SP-4 *Formwork for Concrete,* the new AISC *Erection Bracing of Low-Rise Structural Steel Frames,* the PCI *Design Handbook,* the PCI *Recommended Practice for Erection of Precast Concrete,* the AITC *Timber Construction Manual,* the TPI *Commentary and Recommendations for Handling and Erecting Wood Trusses,* the SIA *Directory and Handbook* for scaffolding, the *Steel Sheet Piling Design Manual* by U.S. Steel Corporation, the *California Falsework Manual* by CALTRANS, the NYC Transit Authority *Field Design Manual,* and the FHWA *Guide Design Specification for Bridge Temporary Works.* The Center for Excellence in Construction Safety of West Virginia University publishes a quarterly newsletter, *Excel,* that often contains very informative articles on temporary structure–related items.

ASCE's Manual of Professional Practice: *Quality in the Constructed Project, a Guideline for Owners, Designers and Constructors,* 1988, includes some guidelines for the responsibilities of design professionals and makes some rather inconsequential references to temporary works.

DESIGN CRITERIA

The forensic structural engineer should be familiar with the design criteria for temporary works. It is, however, not possible to list a set of universally accepted criteria for the design of all temporary structures in construction. The functions, types, materials, uses, and abuses of temporary structures are very wide ranging. The concerns and interests of owners, designers, constructors, authorities having jurisdiction, and the general public are in parts different and often conflicting. Most structural design engineers are ignorant of the intricacies of temporary works, hence are not well qualified and not interested in the subject, and gladly use the familiar design criteria that exist for permanent structures. Many contractors handle the temporary works to give them the "competitive edge" in their business, hence are not interested in uniform criteria that might limit their inventiveness and eliminate that competitive edge. Many other engineers and contractors do hold that the economy and safety of construction projects would be improved by well-thought-out standardized design criteria, hence they are supporting and indeed working on their development.

After some 11 years of deliberation and discussion, the ASCE Design Loads on Structures During Construction Standards Committee, made up of dozens of designers, contractors, and regulators, is just coming to a consensus on the level of safety that should be ensured by the design of a temporary structure. In its present form the Committee's 12/99 draft of the proposed ASCE *Design Loads on Structures During Construction Standard* requires that "The design loads shall provide for a level of safety of partially completed structures, and temporary structures used in construction, that is comparable to the level of safety of completed structures."

We are in a transition and development mode. Evidence of that is the appearance of more and more articles, design guides, and regulations on temporary structures.

To be sure, one can use the *ASCE-7 Minimum Design Loads on Building and Other Structures,* the *AISC Specifications for the Design of Structural Steel Buildings,* the *ACI 318 Building Code Requirements for Concrete,* the *NFPA National Design Specifications* for wood, and other well-known documents to determine loads and allowable or ultimate stresses in the design of temporary structures. But those design loads and design stresses were not established with the conditions of temporary works in mind; therefore they may not be the most appropriate for temporary works, to which not only strength and serviceability but a gamut of other criteria as well have to be applied, as is apparent from reading the section Understanding the Design-Construction Process in this chapter.

The writer recommends that the reader consult the following recent publications for guidance as to where to find design criteria for temporary structures as well as for permanent structures during construction:

John Duntemann, "Codes, Standards and Regulations," Chap. 4 in *Handbook of Temporary Structures in Construction,* 2d ed., R. T. Ratay, ed., McGraw-Hill, New York, 1996.

J. R. Duntemann et al., *Guide Design Specifications for Bridge Temporary Works,* FHWA Report FHWA-RD-93-032, Washington, November 1993.

A. Chini and G. Genauer, "Technical Guidance Available to Designers of Temporary Structures," *Proceedings of the 1996 SEI/ASCE Structures Congress,* Portland, OR, April 13–16, 1996.

J. R. Duntemann and R. T. Ratay, "Review of Selected U.S. and Foreign Design Specifications for Temporary Works, Part 1," *Proceedings of the 1996 SEI/ASCE Structures Congress,* Portland, OR, April 13–16, 1996.

D. O. Dusenberry, "Environmental Loads on Structures During Construction," *Proceedings of the 1996 SEI/ASCE Structures Congress,* Portland, OR, April 13–16, 1996.

C. J. Carter and T. J. Schlafly, "What the SER (Structural Engineer of Record) Can Do to Improve Erection Safety and Reduce Erection Costs," *Construction Safety Affected by Codes and Standards,* R. T. Ratay, ed., ASCE, 1997.

A. D. Fisher, "ASD—The Design Method of Choice for Engineered Temporary Structures," *Proceedings of the 1999 SEI/ASCE Structures Congress,* New Orleans, LA, April 19–21, 1999.

CASES OF TEMPORARY STRUCTURE FAILURES

There is no shortage of construction failures caused by the nonperformance or complete absence of temporary structures in construction. Just about every step along the design-construction process includes hidden risks and has been shown to be prone to errors or omissions that resulted in subsequent construction failure.

Failures of excavation supports, scaffolding, falsework, formwork, and temporary shoring, bracing, and guying (in approximately this order) are the most frequent occurrences of temporary structure failures. Often the total absence of some of these, such as excavation supports, shoring, bracing, and guying, is the proximate cause of a disaster.

With very few exceptions that involve large fatalities, temporary structure failures do not make as much news as the collapse of a building or bridge. They may happen away from the public eye, at an isolated construction site, or behind solid fences, and they are often kept hidden—for everyone's benefit. The author has observed that whenever a construction failure is reported in *ENR, Engineering News-Record,* in books, or in other technical publications, it is nearly always the permanent structure that is described, with little or no discussion of the details of the temporary structure even if *it* was the thing that actually failed.

It is the author's opinion that one of three reasons is the underlying cause of all temporary structure failures: one is the willingness, indeed deliberate choice, to accept greater risks, another is error or omission out of oversight, carelessness, or ignorance, and the third is an unanticipated confluence of events or conditions. All are human failings and all can be averted. Therefore—at the risk of being simplistic—failures can be prevented.

An interesting fallout from failures and their investigations is that regardless of what is found to have been the proximate cause of the failure, and who is found to have the immediate responsibility, often several other errors or defects related or unrelated to the cause of the failure are discovered as well, which would never have come to light if not for the failure. If you scratch hard enough, you find many problems and several culprits—often more than first meet the eye.

It is believed by some that the best way to learn how to prevent future failures is by studying past failures. In this author's opinion such studying is superficial and largely useless unless one delves deeply into the design and construction details of the project. Few construction failures are so simple that all the pertinent information can be discussed adequately in a paragraph, in a page, or even in two or three pages. Nevertheless, for the sake of illustration of the extent of temporary structure failures, and at the risk of leaving questions hanging in the air, 15 cases of temporary structure failures are described very briefly. It is pointed out that the conclusions offered are those that have been formulated and/or published by one or more investigators, and appear to have "carried the day." Different investigators may come to divergent conclusions for the same event from the same data, and even trials by jury can come to surprising decisions.

Some of these cases were well-known catastrophies with tragic fatalities, others were obscure events known only to those involved. They were selected for inclusion here to illustrate the kinds of errors, omissions, and goofs that can cause temporary structure failures. Some were extracted in part from publications, such as the *ENR, Engineering News-Record*; some others were extracted in part from books, such as *Construction Failure*, 2d ed., by Feld & Carper; *Design and Construction Failures,* by Kaminetzky; *Why Buildings Fall Down,* by Levy and Salvadori; and *Handbook of Temporary Structures in Construction,* 2d ed., by Ratay. Several were summarized from reports of investigations by NBS (now NIST) and OSHA; two from the records of the Worker's Compensation Board of British Columbia; two were contributed by individuals; and four came from the author's job files of his own consulting practice.

It is noted once again that reciting the highlights of failures and the summaries of conclusions of their investigations in such rudimentary fashion may be meaningless, and may even be misleading, because the details and circumstances, and even the participants of a project, are usually very important in evaluating and understanding the causes and assigning the responsibilities. The reader, if interested, is encouraged to find the complete reports and follow-up discussions, if available, on these cases for the pertinent details.

It is also noted that the causes of failures cited in these case histories may not have been agreed upon by all the investigators. In some failures, there is no concensus even years or decades later.

Case History 1: Skyline Plaza at Bailey's Crossroads Falsework/Shoring

Fourteen construction workers were killed and 35 others injured in the progressive collapse of the 27-story Skyline Plaza apartment building at Bailey's Crossroads in Fairfax, Virginia, on March 2, 1973. Investigators of the NBS and engineering

SHORES

NO SHORES
OR RESHORES

(a)

FIGURE 17.1   Skyline Plaza. (*a*) View of collapse. (From Dov Kaminetzky, *Design and Construction Failures,* McGraw-Hill, New York, 1991.)

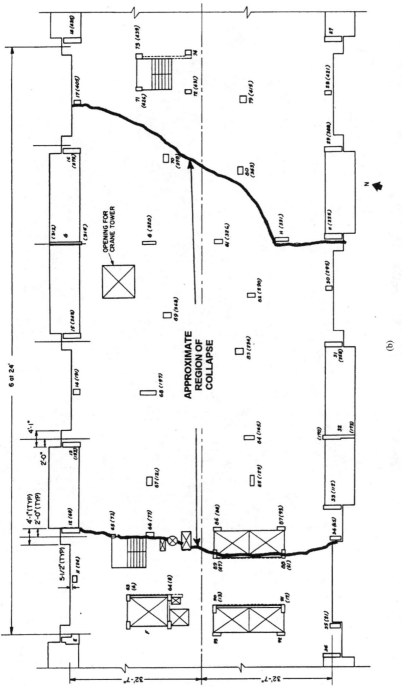

FIGURE 17.1 Skyline Plaza. (*Continued*) (*b*) Plan of 22d and 23d floor slab showing approximate region of collapse. (From *NBS Building Series 94,* February 1977.)

17.23

(c)

FIGURE 17.1 Skyline Plaza. (*Continued*) (*c*) Upper floors of the east end of the collapsed region. Note shoring below the 24th and reshoring under the 23d floors only. (From *NBS Building Science Series 94,* February 1977.)

firms concluded that premature removal of falsework was the proximate cause of the failure.

Construction of the 8-in flat-plate slabs on 27-ft 9-in maximum column grids had proceeded at the rate of one floor per week, and accelerated to one per 5 days before the collapse. On the day of the collapse, concrete placement on the 24th floor was completed at noon. Removal of formwork below the 23d floor started after lunch. Soon a big sag became apparent in both the 23d and 24th floors. The reshores directly under the 22d floor fell over as the 22d floor was unloaded by the removal of the shores on top of it. The collapse was triggered most likely by punching shear failure in the 23d-floor slab which now carried its own weight plus the weight of the fresh concrete of the 24th-floor slab. The weight of falling debris, and a crane that had been at the 24th floor, initiated the progressive collapse of the floors, tearing a wide gap in the building from top to bottom.

Concrete cores from the upper slabs tested to between 700 and 1400 lb/in^2, which was well below the expected 5- to 7-day strength. There were no preconstruction plans of concrete placement, no formwork drawings, no formwork removal and reshoring schedules.

The failure was clearly the result of mismanaged temporary structure procedures: bad field practice exacerbated by substandard material and lack of effective review and inspection of the temporary works.

Another aspect of this case was the engineer's responsibility. While the contract of the engineer of record specifically stated that he had no responsibility for field inspection, the trial jury found him negligent because the pertinent code required that a "competent architect or engineer" must provide supervision where requested by the building official.

Case History 2: Willow Island Jump Formwork and Scaffolding

The worst construction accident in U.S. history occurred on April 27, 1978, on the construction of a cooling tower at the Willow Island power plant in West Virginia. The top 5 ft of the shell around the entire circumference of the tower broke off and fell inward, taking with it the jumpform erection system and 51 workers who fell nearly 170 ft to their deaths. (Or did the erection system anchorage fail, weakening and taking with it the top 5 ft of the shell?)

The temporary structure consisted of a complex combination of formwork and scaffolding. As construction advanced, the system traveled up the tower, always supported on the partially matured concrete of the previously completed portion of the tower. In essence, at any one time the formwork system was anchored to the tower, and the four-level access scaffolding was suspended from the formwork system. Jacking took place at both the inside and outside jumpform beams simultaneously at all 96 beam locations around the tower.

An investigation by the NBS concluded that the most probable cause of the failure was the "imposition of construction loads on the shell before the concrete…gained adequate strength to support the loads." It was also alleged that the anchorage of the formwork was inadequate, i.e., too few anchor bolts, for the construction loads. NBS further concluded that "the collapse did not initiate due to any component failure of the hoisting and scaffolding systems."

Some details, such as the continuity of the forming system all around the tower

(a)

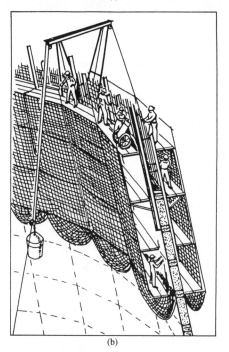

(b)

FIGURE 17.2   Willow Island. (*a*) Completed and uncompleted cooling towers. (From *NBS Building Science Series 148*, February 1982.) (*b*) Artist's sketch of a view of the scaffolding system and work in progress. (From *NBS Building Science Series 94*, February 1977.)

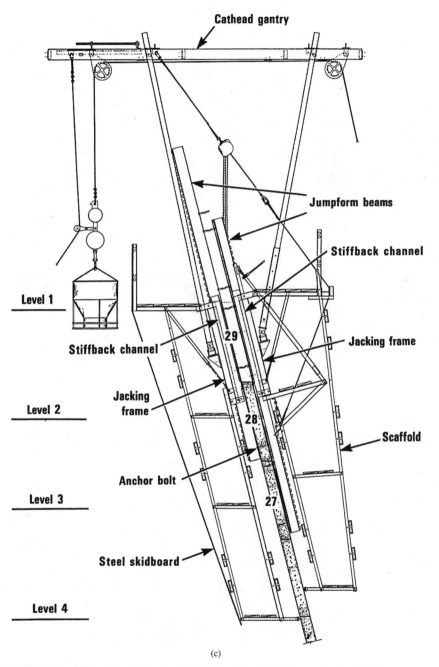

FIGURE 17.2 Willow Island. (*Continued*) (*c*) Section through the formwork and scaffolding system. (From *NBS Building Science Series 94,* February 1977.)

(d)

(e)

FIGURE 17.2   Willow Island. (*Continued*) (*d*) Close-up of the formwork and scaffolding. (From *NBS Building Science Series 94*, February 1977.) (*e*) Fallen debris inside the cooling tower. (From *NBS Building Science Series 94*, February 1977.)

without isolation of circular segments, contributed to the totality of the collapse that was initiated by a local failure. So it seems to have been a construction error which combined with a poor design approach. The latter might never have surfaced without the former.

Case History 3: Riley Road Interchange Falsework

Three spans of an elevated highway, the Riley Road Interchange Ramp C (also known as the Cline Avenue Bridge) in East Chicago, Indiana, failed during its construction on April 15, 1982. The entire 180 ft of one span, and 160 and 135 ft, respectively, of two adjoining 180-ft spans, collapsed, killing 13 and injuring 18 workers. On the day of the collapse, workers had been casting concrete in one of the spans. The failure occurred before post-tensioning of the cast-in-place concrete superstructure when all the construction loads were still carried by the falsework/shoring.

(a)

FIGURE 17.3 Riley Road Interchange (a) Shoring towers before failure. (From John Duntemann, Wiss, Janney, Elstner Associates, Inc., Northbrook, IL.)

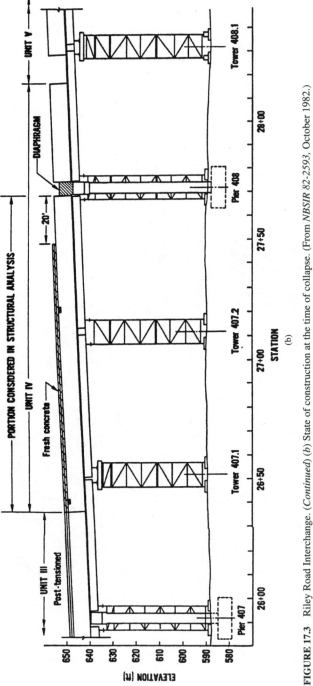

FIGURE 17.3 Riley Road Interchange. (*Continued*) (*b*) State of construction at the time of collapse. (From *NBSIR 82-2593*, October 1982.)

17.30

(c)

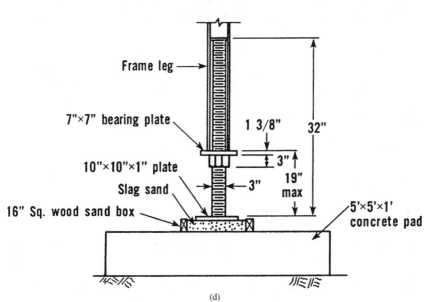

(d)

FIGURE 17.3   Riley Road interchange. (*Continued*) (*c*) View of base of shoring towers. (From John Duntemann, Wiss, Janney, Elstner Associates, Inc., Northbrook, IL.) (*d*) Typical shoring tower screwleg. (From *NBSIR 82-2593,* October 1982.)

(e)

FIGURE 17.3 Riley Road interchange. (*Continued*) (*e*) Failed concrete foundation pad. (From John Duntemann, Wiss, Janney, Elstner Associates, Inc., Northbrook, IL.)

At the request of OSHA, NBS conducted an investigation to determine the most probable cause of the collapse. NBS researchers concluded that the collapse most likely was triggered by the cracking of a concrete pad under a leg of one of the shoring towers which were to support the ramp during construction. This initial failure occurred because the pads did not have an adequate margin of safety to support the loads.

The initial failure of the pads caused additional tower components to fail, leading to the collapse of the support system as well as major segments of the partially completed ramp. The support tower location where the collapse most likely began was pinpointed by NBS engineers, who also reported the most likely sequence of failure.

Three other deficiencies were identified that did not trigger the collapse but contributed directly to it:

- Specified wedges that were to have been placed between steel crossbeams and stringer beams at the top of the support system (or falsework) to compensate for the slope of the roadway were omitted, thus increasing the load on critical pads.

- The tops of the shoring towers were not adequately stabilized against the longitudinal movement which occurred when the concrete pads cracked and the tower frames dropped slightly.

- The quality of welds in the U-shaped supports for the falsework's crossbeams at

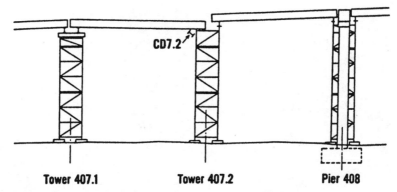

Tower 407.1   Tower 407.2   Pier 408

Cross-beam CD7.2 falls down, U-heads are broken off.

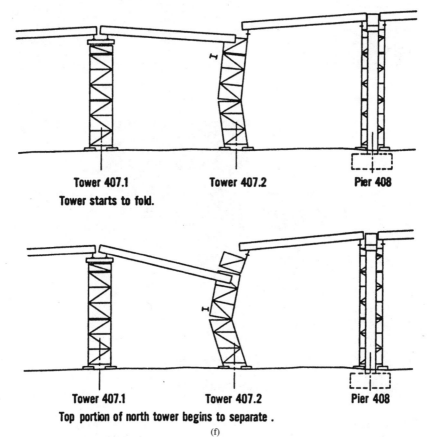

Tower 407.1   Tower 407.2   Pier 408
Tower starts to fold.

Tower 407.1   Tower 407.2   Pier 408
Top portion of north tower begins to separate .

(f)

FIGURE 17.3 Riley Road interchange. (*Continued*) (*f*) Possible collapse sequence of falsework at Tower 407.2. (From *NBSIR 82-2593*, October 1982.)

(g)

(h)

FIGURE 17.3 Riley Road interchange. (*Continued*) (*g*) View of collapsed unit IV from the south-east. (From John Duntemann, Wiss, Janney, Eltsner Associates, Inc., Northbrook, IL.) (*h*) View of top of pier 407 and buckled shoring towers from the northwest. (From John Duntemann, Wiss, Janney, Eltsner Associates, Inc., Northbrook, IL.)

the top of the towers was poor, thus making them unable to resist the forces resulting from the longitudinal movement.

"Had any one of these deficiencies not existed, it is unlikely that the collapse would have occurred," the NBS report concludes.

Additional deficiencies contributed to the collapse of an adjacent ramp unit which failed about 5 minutes after the first unit:

- Specified 1-in bolts to connect certain stringer beams to crossbeams were not used; frictional clips were used instead.
- Special overlap beams at the ramp's supporting piers were not constructed as specified.
- The construction sequence deviated from that specified in the construction drawings, so that concrete for one span was placed before it should have been.

Case History 4: L'Ambiance Plaza Lift Slab

In many respects the "mostest" U.S. construction failure was the collapse of the two buildings of L'Ambiance Plaza under construction in Bridgeport, Connecticut, on April 23, 1987. It was probably the most investigated, most analyzed, most written about, most argued about (and, interestingly, one of the least

(a)

FIGURE 17.4   L'Ambiance Plaza (a) "Parked" slabs during construction. (From John Ruddy.)

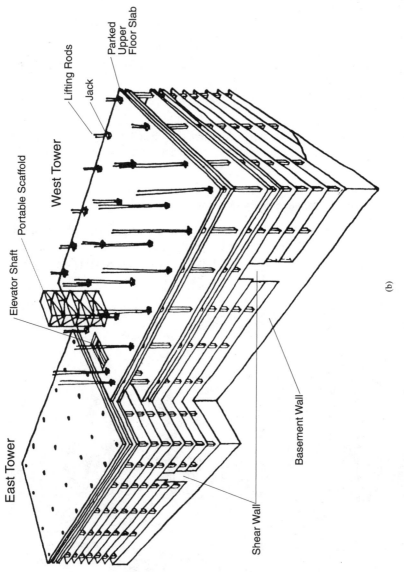

FIGURE 17.4 L'Ambiance Plaza.(*Continued*) (*b*) Isometric drawing of buildings just prior to collapse. (From M. Levy and M. Salvadori, *Why Buildings Fall Down.*)

(b)

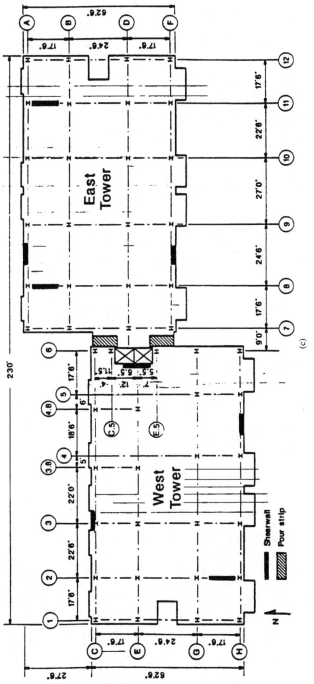

FIGURE 17.4 L'Ambiance Plaza. (*Continued*) (c) Plan showing column and shear wall locations. (From *NBSIR 87-3640*, September 1987.)

17.37

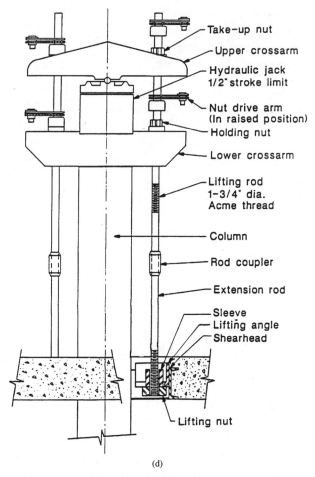

Take-up nut
Upper crossarm
Hydraulic jack
1/2" stroke limit
Nut drive arm
(In raised position)
Holding nut
Lower crossarm
Lifting rod
1-3/4" dia.
Acme thread
Column
Rod coupler
Extension rod
Sleeve
Lifting angle
Shearhead
Lifting nut

(d)

FIGURE 17.4 L'Ambiance Plaza. (*Continued*) (*d*) Slab lifting assembly. (From *NBSIR 87-3640*, September 1987.)

litigated) major construction disaster. It had far-reaching effects on construction site safety, particularly related to lift-slab construction.

The building was to be a 13-story structure constructed using the lift-slab method. The floor slabs were cast one on top of the other and post-tensioned in two orthogonal directions while still at ground level. After post-tensioning, the slabs were lifted by hydraulic jacks and secured to the columns at their respective floor levels. At the time of the collapse, lifting of the slabs was more than one-half completed. The collapse occurred during placement of wedges under a package of three slabs being "parked" in a temporary position during erection of the building. In the collapse, all the floor slabs fell, killing 28 workers.

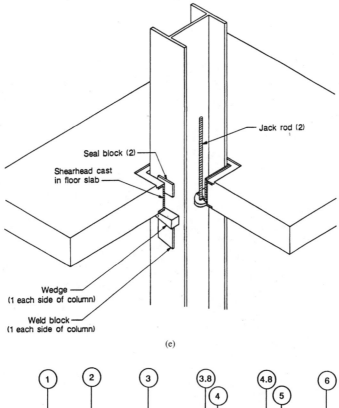

(e)

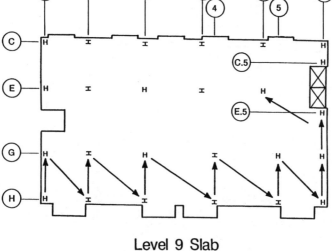

Level 9 Slab
(f)

FIGURE 17.4 L'Ambiance Plaza. (*Continued*) (*e*) Detail of slab-to-column initial/temporary wedge connection. (From *NBSIR 87-3640,* September 1987.) (*f*) Sequence of placement of wedges in west tower levels 9, 10, 11 immediately prior to collapse. (From *NBSIR 87-3640,* September 1987.)

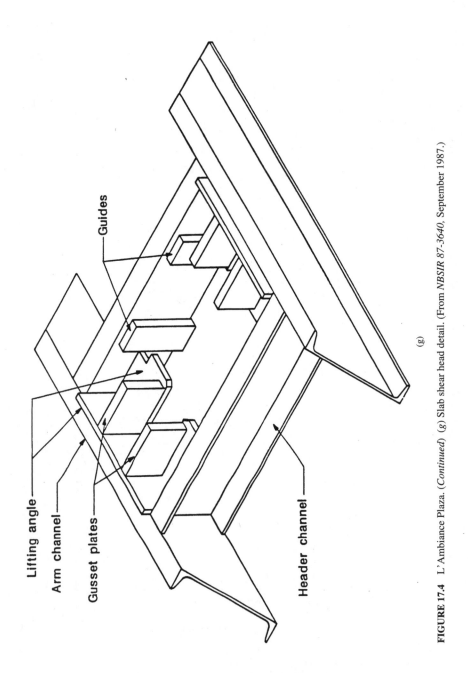

Guides

Lifting angle

Arm channel

Gusset plates

Header channel

(g)

FIGURE 17.4 L'Ambiance Plaza. (*Continued*) (*g*) Slab shear head detail. (From *NBSIR 87-3640*, September 1987.)

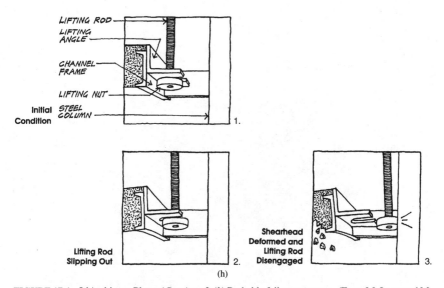

FIGURE 17.4 L'Ambiance Plaza. (*Continued*) (*h*) Probable failure sequence. (From M. Levy and M. Salvadori *Why Buildings Fall Down.*)

NBS and several engineering firms and consultants, including the author, investigated the failure as experts for various parties. It was agreed by nearly all that the most likely trigger of the failure was a condition in a shear head (a four-sided steel collar cast into the concrete slab and sleeved around the column, providing for the permanent anchorage of the slab to the column): either the rolling out of a temporary wedge between the column face and the shear head, or the slipping of a temporary lifting rod from a slotted angle welded on the sheer head. The same or similar incident occurred once, or possibly twice, before on other lift-slab projects of the same contractor but was considered only a glitch and had not resulted in collapse. It was and still is the author's opinion, shared by at least some of the other investigators, that the reason for the catastrophic collapse, following the localized failure, was the absence of temporary bracing or guying, hence the lack of lateral stability of the entire structure. Sheet S-301 of the contract drawings carried the following note: "Contractor shall be responsible for temporary bracing required until shear walls are placed and cured..." At the time of the collapse the shear walls were not placed and cured above the third floor, and there was no temporary bracing or guying at all—clearly a temporary structure failure by virtue of the complete omission of the temporary structure. A glitch turned into a catastrophe.

It is worthwhile to note that had the contractor decided to install temporary bracing or guying, how would he or she have known what lateral loads to resist? What code, standard, specification, or other source would the contractor have consulted? On what basis would an engineer have approved or disapproved a proposal?

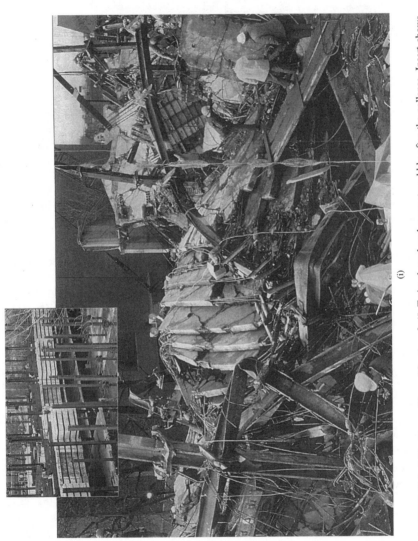

(i)

FIGURE 17.4 L'Ambiance Plaza. (*Continued*) (*i*) Twisted steel and concrete rubble after the collapse. Insert shows "parked" slabs. (From *Civil Engineering,* January 1988.)

Case History 5: Baltimore-Washington Expressway Shoring Towers

A highway bridge built to carry Maryland Route 198 over the Baltimore-Washington Expressway collapsed during construction on August 31, 1989, injuring 5 workers and 9 motorists. The structure was designed as five contiguous post-tensioned box girders spanning 100 ft between simple-support abutments. The bottom slab was cast in July, and the box girder webs were cast between July 21 and August 4. On the day of the collapse, workers were pouring the 8-in deck slab. The collapse occurred 5 h into the pour, when 120 of the 160 ft^3 total was in place. The shoring collapsed "in a flash" without warning, landing all the formwork and concrete on the roadway below. The formwork had been used earlier to cast the westbound structure.

FHWA and private investigators found that the most likely factor causing the failure of one of the shoring towers was the use of 10-kip rather than 25-kip screw jacks, shown on the approved drawings, on the tops of the shoring towers supporting the bridge. A review board found no evidence that the FHWA (the owner) had not lived up to its contract responsibilities, and ruled that the assembly of the falsework system in accordance with the approved design was the responsibility of the contractor. The FHWA requires a contractor's engineer to certify that falsework has been assembled according to approved drawings before it is loaded. A fine of more than $900,000 was levied by the state against the contractor.

The FHWA report also said that "the top screw jacks were rusty" and that much of the cross-bracing had "large amounts of rust and heavy pitting." In one section, the cross-brace pieces were connected by nail instead of the required bolt.

Case History 6: Lake Street Bridge Shoring

One of four 23-ft-tall, 200-ft-long temporary trusses supporting formwork in the construction of a concrete arch in a multispan bridge collapsed and fell into the Mississippi River on April 24, 1990. One worker was killed when he fell 90 ft with the falsework at the Lake Street/Marshall Avenue Bridge construction site in Minneapolis/St. Paul, Minnesota. The bridge was to have two twin concrete box-section arches, each spanning 555 ft over a navigation channel. At the time of the collapse, one arch over shallow water had been completed, and the contractor was casting the top section of the second arch over the navigation channel. The first arch was built on falsework/shoring towers, but the second arch needed the temporary trusses to allow for unobstructed clearance over the navigation channel. The trusses were supported at each end on three structural steel temporary towers on piles driven into the riverbed. Falsework was built on top of the trusses to support the arch's formwork.

As a result of an unusual screeching noise, the trusses were inspected an hour or so before the collapse. No broken welds or bolts were found, but the web of a short deep beam that was designed to support the top chord of the truss was discovered buckled. The deformed beam allowed the truss to drop more than 2 in. This appeared to have caused a redistribution of the shoring loads on the truss,

(a)

(b)

FIGURE 17.5 Baltimore-Washington Parkway. (*a*) Aerial view of collapse. (From *The New York Times,* September 1, 1989.) (*b*) Collapsed falsework previously supported construction of bridge's twin. (From Kate Patterson, Springfield, VA, and *ENR*, September 7, 1989.)

which exacerbated the conditions. Although temporary in its function, this was a rather complex structural system involving piles, steel shoring towers, 200-ft long-span trusses, falsework, and formwork rising 100 ft in severe exposure. One can appreciate the experience needed in both the design and construction of the system and the attention to be paid to the details.

(c)

FIGURE 17.5 Baltimore-Washington Parkway. (*Continued*) (*c*) End view of collapsed falsework. (From Kate Patterson, Springfield, VA, and *ENR*, September 7, 1989.)

It is the author's understanding that a report on the investigation of the failure is not available to the public, although a report was prepared by Construction Technology Laboratories, Inc., for the Minnesota Department of Transportation. According to hearsay, there appears to have been a great deal of conflict and adversity between the state and some of the parties involved, which may be the reason for the dearth of published information on the failure.

Case History 7: 14th & H Streets, Washington, Excavation Supports

Portions of a 150-ft × 208-ft × 47-ft deep braced open excavation for an office building in Washington, DC, collapsed on November 19, 1990. Since it occurred in the late evening, after construction work stopped, no one was injured, although there was significant potential for casualties.

Due to the size of the excavation, external support with wales and tiebacks was more economical than internal support with wales, struts, diagonals, and rakers. However, the adjacent UPI Building basement, the existing utility lines, and the underground right-of-way permit constraints prohibited the installation of tiebacks

(a)

FIGURE 17.6 Lake Street Bridge. (*a*) Collapsed falsework arch truss. (From Conrad Bloomquist/Scenic Photo, Minneapolis, MN and *ENR,* May 3, 1990.)

in certain locations. Thus, the west portion of the excavation was supported by an external tieback system, while the east portion was supported by an internal structural steel bracing system consisting of diagonal struts, cross-lot and cross-corner bracing. Based on the original design drawings, both the tiebacks and the bracing were at three levels, or three tiers.

For the protection of adjacent building foundations and utilities, the support system was designed to maintain a preload in the system and to minimize the stress change in the adjacent ground mass in order to limit its deformation until the permanent structural concrete gained sufficient strength to maintain this preload force. Thus, any tier of the internal support system could not be removed before the adjacent concrete gained sufficient strength. In addition, to build the basement wall to coincide with the property line to obtain the maximum usable space, it was elected to place the temporary soldier beam and lagging wall just outside the property line, and use this wall as the outside half of the formwork for concrete. To accomplish these two goals, sufficient clearance (3 ft) had to be maintained (by 3-ft-long spacers or "outlookers") between the soldier beam and wale, to accommodate the thicknesses of the perimeter wall of the permanent basement between the lagging and the wales, and to provide for removing the wale and cutting off the protruding outlookers from inside the finished basement wall when the concrete wall gained adequate strength. The outlookers were welded to the inside face of the soldier beams and the outside face of the wales.

(b)

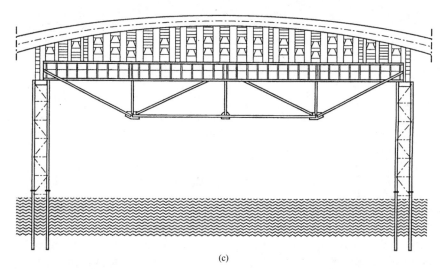

(c)

FIGURE 17.6 Lake Street Bridge. (*Continued*) (*b*) Shoring tower underneath the collapsed falsework arch truss. (From Conrad Bloomquist/Scenic Photo, Minneapolis, MN and *ENR*, May 3, 1990.) (*c*) Schematic diagram of arch falsework system. (From *Report to Minnesota DOT, Evaluation of Collapse of Lake Street/Marshall Avenue Bridge Replacement*, By Construction Technology Laboratorie, Inc., September 1990.)

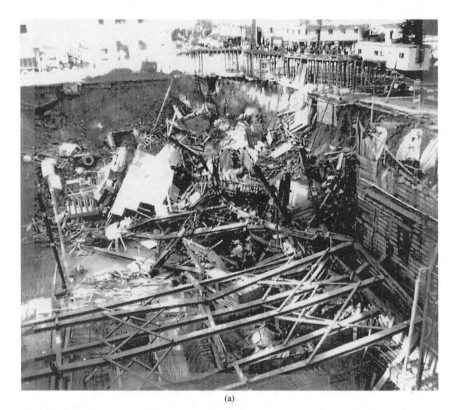

(a)

FIGURE 17.7 Washington excavation. (*a*) Overall view of the collapsed site—looking toward the east. (From OSHA *Investigation of November 19, 1999 Excavation Collapse at 14th & H Streets, N.W., Washington, D.C.*, report, May 1991.)

The initial collapse was followed 17 h later by a second additional collapse of a portion adjacent to the first one, resulting in a great deal of damage in and around the excavation.

OSHA investigators concluded that the collapse of the excavation occurred due to the failure of certain structural members of the internal support system along the north and south walls, and that the external support tieback system did not fail. They also found that the failure load, the soil pressure immediately preceding the collapse, was lower than the load for which the temporary structure was designed by the shoring subcontractor. It was apparently overlooked in the design and/or in the detailing that the force component of a 45° corner brace which was in the direction of the longitudinal axis of the wale in the north and south wall did not have a physical reaction in the system. The "outlookers" could transmit the bracing force component (earth pressure) *across* the plane of the wall, but had no ability to resist the east-west force component *in* the plane of the wall and just "folded" over like a two-hinged linkage in a horizontal direction.

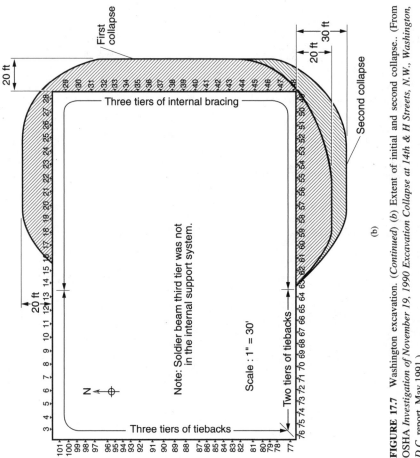

FIGURE 17.7 Washington excavation. (*Continued*) (*b*) Extent of initial and second collapse.. (From OSHA *Investigation of November 19, 1990 Excavation Collapse at 14th & H Streets, N.W., Washington, D.C.* report, May 1991.)

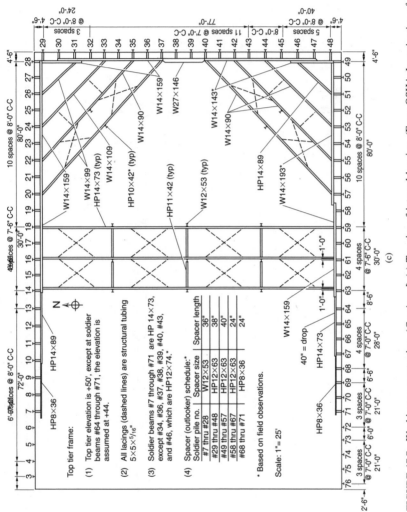

FIGURE 17.7 Washington excavation. (*Continued*) (*c*) Top tier of internal bracing. (From OSHA *Investigation of November 19, 1990 Excavation Collapse at 14th & H Streets, N.W., Washington, D.C.* report, May 1991.)

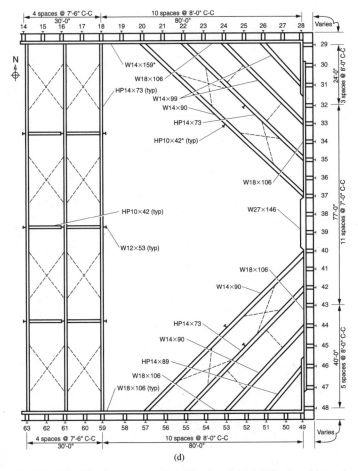

FIGURE 17.7 Washington excavation. (*Continued*) (*d*) Middle tier of internal bracing. (From OSHA *Investigation of November 19, 1990 Excavation Collapse at 14th & H Streets, N.W., Washington, D.C.* report, May 1991.)

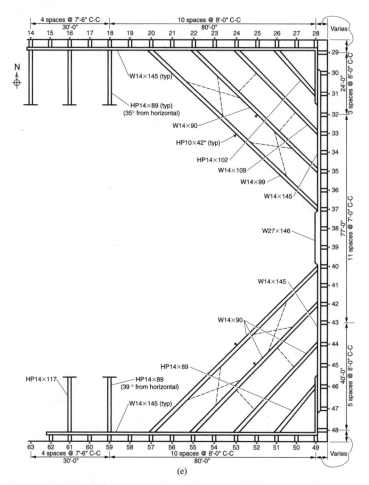

FIGURE 17.7 Washington excavation. (*Continued*) (*e*) Bottom tier of internal bracing. (From OSHA *Investigation of November 19, 1990 Excavation Collapse at 14th & H Streets, N.W., Washington, D.C.* report, May 1991.)

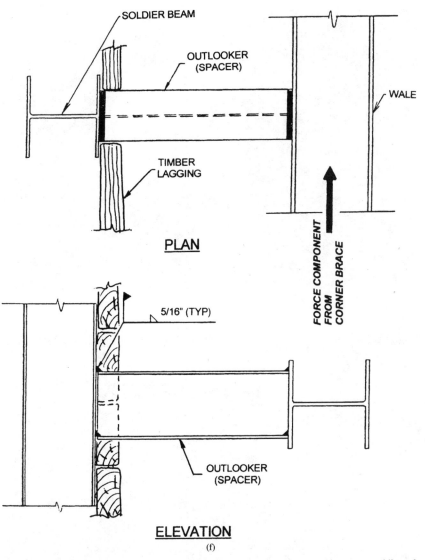

FIGURE 17.7 Washington excavation. (*Continued*) (*f*) An "outlooker/spacer" between a soldier column and a wale. (Based on OSHA *Investigation of November 19, 1990 Excavation Collapse at 14th & H Streets, N.W., Washington, D.C.* report, May 1991.)

Case History 8: Denver I-70 Overpass Scaffolding/Shoring Tower

A scaffolding/shoring tower collapsed, and 2 workers were badly injured in 1986 at the construction of the Wadsworth exit overpass bridge over Interstate I-70 in Denver, Colorado. The portion of the bridge under which the tower collapsed was to be of three horizontally curved steel tub girders running side by

(g)

(h)

FIGURE 17.7 Washington excavation. (*Continued*) (*g*) End view of a bottom-tier wale, outlooker, and soldier beam. (From OSHA *Investigation of November 19, 1990 Excavation Collapse at 14th & H Streets, N.W., Washington, D.C.* report, May 1991.) (*h*) A toppled middle-tier outlooker welded to a wale and a soldier beam. (From OSHA *Investigation of November 19, 1990 Excavation Collapse at 14th & H Streets, N.W., Washington, D.C.* report, May 1991.)

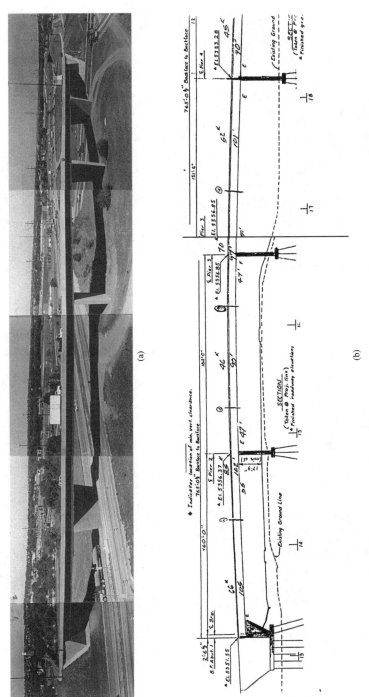

(a)

(b)

FIGURE 17.8 Denver I-70 overpass. (a) View of completed interchange overpass. (From R. T. Ratay Engineering, P.C.) (b) Longitudinal section with weights of girder segments. (From R. T. Ratay Engineering, P.C.)

(c)

(d)

FIGURE 17.8   Denver I-70 overpass. (*Continued*) (*c*) Part of collapsed scaffolding/shoring tower toppled over the embankment. (From R. T. Ratay Engineering, P.C.) (*d*) Close-up of collapsed scaffolding shoring tower toppled over the embankment. (From R. T. Ratay Engineering, P.C.)

(e)

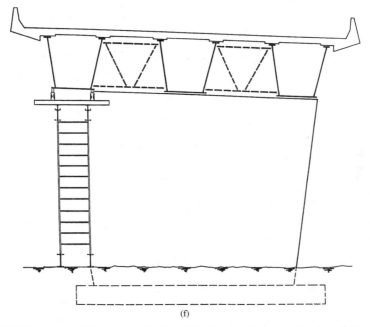

(f)

FIGURE 17.8 Denver I-70 overpass. (*Continued*) (*e*) Reassembled upper tier of scaffolding/shoring tower. (From R. T. Ratay Engineering, P.C.) (*f*) Schematic cross-section of bridge with scaffolding/shoring tower in place. (From R. T. Ratay Engineering, P.C.)

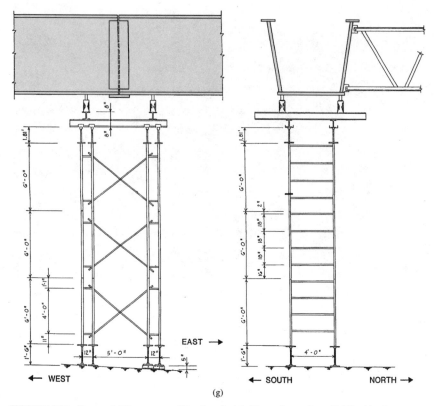

EAST →

← WEST

← SOUTH   NORTH →

(g)

FIGURE 17.8 Denver I-70 overpass. (*Continued*) (*g*) Dimensions of scaffolding/shoring tower. (From R. T. Ratay Engineering, P.C.)

side and connected to each other with vertical diaphragm braces, working in composite action with the cast-in-place concrete deck on top of them. The girders were continuous over three spans of 150, 180, and 160 ft. The average radius of horizontal curvature of the bridge in the middle span, under which the shoring tower collapsed, was about 800 ft. As a tub girder was lifted into place, it was connected at its end to the previously set girder with the permanent bolts but only finger-tight, and the diaphragms were installed. When all the girders over the three continuous spans were in place, the formwork for the concrete deck was erected on top of them. Prior to pouring the concrete deck, the elevations of all the girder end-to-end splice connections had to be adjusted and the bolts tightened, or "driven home." This was done with the aid of a 22-ft-tall temporary scaffold/shore tower erected on the ground directly below the connection.

The tower was assembled from standard 4-ft-wide by 6-ft-high scaffold frames: four parallel planes of frames stacked three-high, with screw jacks at the base and

(h)

FIGURE 17.8   Denver I-70 overpass. (*Continued*) (*h*) Presentation
board showing tower and two workers prepared for the jury trial. (From
R. T. Ratay Engineering, P.C.)

at the top, connected by diagonal braces, so that the assembled tower measured 4
ft by 7 ft in plan. A rectangular grid of four 8-in wide flange beams was placed on
top of the screw jacks on the top of the tower to receive the hydraulic jacks. Four
hydraulic jacks were placed between the top of the tower and the underside of the
two butting tub girders.

Two men positioned themselves on a work platform near the top. Each man was
pumping a pair of jacks, one pair under each of the two abutting girder ends, until
the steel reached the proper elevation signaled by a surveyor. Several of the con-

nections had already been completed when, during the jacking of a connection (Marked 3 in Fig. 17.8b), the tower collapsed and, with the two men and all equipment, fell to the ground. The connection being jacked when the collapse occurred was in the middle span of a three-span outside girder.

Investigators for the plaintiffs (the injured workers) and the defendant (the scaffold/shoring rental company) never came to an agreement on the cause of the collapse. An out-of-court settlement was made between the defendant and the more seriously injured worker; a significant award after trial by jury was made to the other plaintiff.

It is important to know that the contractor did not specify the type, size, or shape of the tower, but showed the bridge structural drawings to the rental agency's engineer and asked him to furnish whatever was needed.

Plaintiffs' expert, the author, found that both the rated and the calculated capacities of the tower were less than the load to be lifted at the collapse location. (The actual mode of initial failure of the tower could not be determined from the wreckage, so all possible modes of failure had to be evaluated.) He further found, from the calculations of the rental agency's engineer, that the engineer calculated the load to be lifted as the weights of the girders from the connection to halfway to the next bridge pier, as if the girders were simply supported at both ends. That is, he did not consider resistance against lifting that would be created by the continuity of the girder into the neighboring span. Nor did the rental agency's engineer consider loads on the lifted girder from the weight of the adjacent parallel girder tied to it through the connecting diaphragm. The difference between the assumed simple-beam and the real continuous-beam reactions against jacking was very significant.

Defendant's expert contended that the reason for the collapse was not the miscalculation of the load and the consequent inadequacy of the tower but the workers' uneven pumping of the jacks, hence unbalanced loading of the tower legs. He built a full-size replica of the tower and load-tested it under various top support conditions.

Defendant's expert further contended that the rental agency's young engineer, even though a licensed professional engineer, should not be expected to have the sophistication of all these experts with doctorates to understand all the complexities arising from continuous, curved, interconnected, composite beam action. Plaintiff's expert contended that a licensed professional engineer must be expected to at least recognize when there is so much complexity that he is getting in over his head and needs to seek competent advice. Based on its verdict, the jury appears to have agreed with the plaintiff.

An interesting question in the forensic investigation and litigation was whether the tower was scaffolding, because it provided access for the workers, or shoring, because it supported superimposed loads, or both a scaffolding and a shoring at different times. Design safety factors and allowable height-to-width ratios are different for scaffolding and shoring, as per OSHA regulations.

(a)

FIGURE 17.9 A West coast hotel. (*a*) Collapsed scaffolding. (From R. A. LaTona Simpson, Gumpertz & Hager, Inc., San Francisco, and *Civil Engineering,* April 1998.)

Case History[1] 9: West Coast Hotel Scaffolding

During the 1992 construction of a west coast hotel, 3 construction workers were seriously injured when a scaffold collapsed, causing them to fall about 30 ft along with hundreds of pounds of scaffold parts and building materials. The

---

[1]This case history was contributed by Raymond W. LaTona, Simpson Gumpertz & Hager, Inc., San Francisco, CA.

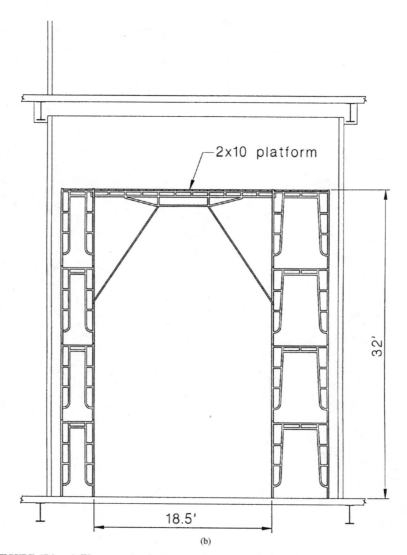

FIGURE 17.9   A West coast hotel. (*Continued*) (*b*) Typical elevation of the scaffolding. (From Raymond A. LaTona, Simpson Gumpertz & Hager, Inc. San Francisco.)

scaffold platform was erected in the lobby of the hotel to provide access for the installation of the gypsum wallboard ceiling and lighting fixtures. The platform was 32 ft above the lobby floor and covered a 30-ft by 80-ft area. The structure included two towers constructed from pipe frame scaffolding, with a platform using steel putlogs spanning between the towers. The putlogs spanned 18.5 ft and had knee braces at their third points; 2 × 10 wood planks spanned between putlogs to form the platform.

(c)

FIGURE 17.9   A West coast hotel. (*Continued*) (*c*) Break at a
defective repair weld in the bottom chord. (From Raymond A.
LaTona, Simpson Gumpertz & Hager, Inc. San Francisco.)

On the day of the collapse, 80 to 100 sheets of gypsum wallboard were stacked
in four or five piles at various locations on the platform. On the morning of the collapse, four workers were on the platform. One of them approached a stack of gypsum wallboard that was near the middle of the platform. As he got close to the
stack, a sound similar to a gunshot rang out, and the center of the platform dropped
2 to 3 in. The initial sag was followed quickly by the total collapse of a central putlog. Within seconds, the four center sections of the platform were on the lobby
floor along with several seriously injured workers among the pile of scaffold parts,
planks, and gypsum wallboard.

The postcollapse investigation associated with the litigation initiated by the
injured parties included observations of hundreds of photos, hours of videotape,
and samples of the scaffold parts; metallurgical studies of the metal at the failure
location; and analyses of forces in the structure, stresses at the failure location, and
progression of the collapse. The review of the photos and videotape that were
taken after the collapse immediately identified shortcomings including missing
ties between the scaffold towers and the building and missing or incorrectly
installed braces between adjacent putlogs. The photos of the arrangement of the
fallen structure and the order of the pieces in the pile on the floor also helped to
identify the region where the collapse initiated.

The photos showed that one putlog near the center of the platform had an
end sheared off. This was the only scaffold member that broke; almost all the
other collapsed members were bent and twisted without breaking. In addition,

the putlogs and towers collapsed in toward the center of the platform, suggesting that the collapse initiated in the general area of the putlog that sheared off during the collapse.

Visual inspection of the failed scaffold members revealed that the broken putlog had one location on the bottom chord which had a welded repair prior to use on this job. The weld metal was deposited on the outside surface of the pipe, but it was not fully fused to the metal of the pipe wall. Metallurgical studies showed that the section at the point of the break had been broken previously, and the bottom chord pipe had cracked around 75 percent of its circumference. The weld that was intended to repair the putlog only covered the crack and did little to reestablish the strength of the cross section. The metallurgical examination also revealed that the repaired bottom chord location failed in a brittle manner (consistent with the sound like a gunshot and the platform dropping a few inches while the loads transferred from the putlog bottom chord to the top chord), and that the top chord of the broken putlog failed in a ductile manner (consistent with the pause between initial failure and total collapse while the top chord yielded).

Analysis of the platform using the scaffolding supplier's load tables showed that the dead weight alone resulted in the putlogs being loaded to the published capacity. Therefore, based on the supplier's tables, the allowable superimposed loading on the platform supported by the putlogs was essentially zero, and the platform was grossly underdesigned for its intended use. Even though the platform was improperly designed, that condition did not explain the failure because the published capacities appropriately include factors of safety. A structural analysis showed that although loaded beyond the allowable loadings, these putlogs should still take the additional load of the gypsum wallboard and a worker without failing. The putlogs under the stacks of gypsum wallboard were nearly at yield stress under the applied load. Using the reduced capacity for the damaged putlog based on the conclusions of the metallurgical analysis and the computational results for the applied loads, the repaired putlog was loaded to the ultimate strength of the repaired location under the weight of the gypsum wallboard. The weight of the worker approaching the stack of gypsum wallboard was enough additional load to break the repaired putlog.

In conclusion, the combination of the seriously underdesigned scaffold platform and the weight of the stack of gypsum wallboard plus the worker on an area supported by a poorly repaired putlog caused the failure. The collapse spread to a larger area beyond the broken putlog because the platform was not properly braced and tied into the building.

How did this happen? The platform design was inappropriate; the scaffolding supplier and the contractor never discussed the intended purpose of the platform, so the scaffolding supplier did not know what load the platform was to carry. Also, the supplier's designer said the design was based on "experience," and he never looked at load tables or performed calculations of any kind. This resulted in a scaffold platform with no capacity for any superimposed loads. Another contributing factor for the collapse was that some of the scaffold components were not properly handled and maintained. The supplier's policy stated that damaged components were to be discarded and not repaired; consequently, the putlog with the broken chord should have been discarded. Finally, the scaffold supplier did not follow the company bracing and tie requirements, which led to a general collapse of the temporary structure.

Case History 10: Masons' Scaffold

A seven-frame-high masons' scaffold collapsed during construction of a multistory brick veneer facing on a building in British Columbia, Canada. Three workers who were working on the fifth scaffold level rode down with the frames and other materials. At the time of the failure in addition to the three workers and their materials on the fifth level, bricks were stockpiled on the seventh level. The weight of the stockpiled materials was approximately double the safe working load of the scaffold. Investigators of the Worker's Compensation Board of British Columbia (similar to a state OSHA in the United States) found that the horizontal bracing members of the scaffold were incomplete and the scaffold's ties to the permanent structure were inadequate. In addition, they indicated that the contractor was not aware of the maximum allowable load that could be placed on the scaffold, nor did he have manufacturer's documentation available to perform reasonable assessment of the maximum allowable superimposed load.

Case History[2] 11: Indianapolis Structural Steel Frame Guying

A major section of the structural steel frame collapsed during erection of a large warehouse-type building in Indianapolis, Indiana, in April 1992. There was no loss of life, but there were injured ironworkers, subsequent lawsuits, and out-of-court settlements. As a result of the settlements, there were no trials and neither side's case was fully developed or challenged. The case, however, is instructive because of the relationships among the various parties, the allegations made, the expert opinions offered, and some pertinent temporary structure information that was "lost in the shuffle."

The essentially one-story structure with extensive mezzanine areas was approximately 220,000 ft^2 T-shaped in plan, with two expansion joints separating the arms of the T from the stem. It was one of the approximately 60,000-ft^2 arms which collapsed during erection.

The structure consisted of steel roof deck on steel joists and joist girders supported by hot-rolled structural steel beams, girders, and columns on shallow spread footings. Lateral load resistance was provided by the steel deck diaphragms, rigid frames, and precast concrete shear walls.

---

[2]This case history was contributed by Michael A. West, Computerized Structural Design, S.C., Milwaukee, WI.

(a)

FIGURE 17.10   Mason's Scaffold. (*a*) Aerial view of collapsed scaffold. (From Jozef Jakubowski, Workers' Compensation Board of British Columbia, Vancouver, BC, Canada.)

(b)

FIGURE 17.10   Mason's Scaffold. (*Continued*) (*b*) Collapsed scaffold. (From
Workers' Compensation Board of British Columbia, Vancouver, BC, Canada.)

(a)

(b)

17.11 Indianapolis Steel Frame. (*a*) "Orderly line-up" of structural steel framing. (From A. West, Computerized Structural Design, Milwaukee, WI.) (*b*) Partially toppled steel (From Michael A. West, Computerized Structural Design, Milwaukee, WI.)

(c)

FIGURE 17.11 Indianapolis Steel Frame. (*Continued*) (*c*) Pulled-out and broken column base anchor bolts. (From Michael A. West, Computerized Structural Design, Milwaukee, WI.)

The project was a design-build type with a construction manager. The architect retained a structural engineer to design the foundations and exterior walls. A steel fabricator was responsible for the structural design, fabrication, and erection of the steel frame, but subcontracted both its design and erection. Because of this division of design responsibilities, the designer of the steel frame had to communicate essential features of the design, such as foundation and shear wall reactions, to others. In addition to providing memoranda listing these reactions, a diagram of diaphragm reactions was provided on the structural steel construction documents. Following the *AISC Code of Standard Practice for Structural Steel Buildings,* the structure was identified as "non-self-supporting." This means that elements not characterized as being of structural steel (such as precast concrete shear walls) are needed for the lateral stability of the completed structure. The column reactions furnished to the foundation designer were identified as being only those associated with the behavior of the completed building.

At the time of the collapse, the steel columns, joist girders, and nearly all joists had been set. The joists between those on the column lines had been spread out in each bay but not yet welded to their supports. The columns were resting on leveling nuts beneath the base plates; the base-plate grout had not yet been installed. There was little temporary cable guying in place. It was reported that there was a significant increase in wind velocity prior to the collapse.

The expert retained by the injured worker plaintiffs cited insufficient guying as contributing to the collapse, but also named design and construction conditions as contributors. Some of the expert's contentions are listed below. [Positions of the defense are shown in brackets.]

- The designer of the steel frame was responsible for the design of its temporary support. [Such design was excluded by contract. The *AISC Code of Standard Practice* in paragraph 7.9.1 states that "Temporary supports such as temporary guys, braces, falsework, cribbing or other elements required by the erection operation will be determined and furnished and installed by the erector."]
- The notices of "non-self-supporting" frame in the construction documents were not explicit enough.
- The method of temporary support of the columns on four leveling nuts was improper, and pregrouted leveling plates should have been used. [The use of leveling nuts was a common practice in the industry.]
- The anchor bolts and piers should have been designed for loads resulting from erection operations. [It was the steel erector's responsibility to make this analysis.]
- In at least one instance the concrete pier was constructed too low, resulting in a relatively long projection of the anchor bolts. This condition was directly contributing to the collapse.
- The owner and construction manager had responsibility for site safety. They failed to observe the long anchor bolt projection and the lack of temporary guying of the steel frame.

Although there were differing and unresolved expert opinions as to the cause of the collapse, it was the structural designer's belief that the collapse could have been prevented by the erector's preparation and implementation of a proper temporary erection bracing and guying system. This would have resulted in the necessary temporary bracing and guying materials being on site as they were needed, and in instructions for their timely installation and removal as the permanent lateral load-resisting systems were completed.

Case History 12: Brooklyn Wall Bracing

A 15-ft-high, 93-ft-long, 12-in-thick load-bearing unreinforced-concrete masonry block wall collapsed during its construction in Brooklyn, New York, on March 23, 1990. The wall was being built as the south side of a second-floor addition to a one-story commercial building. The wall toppled away from the mason's scaffold, fell onto and broke through the roof of the adjacent one-story building, killing 2 and injuring 14 people below. The mason's scaffold was not connected to the wall, so rather grotesquely it remained standing in the middle of nowhere.

(a)

FIGURE 17.12   Brooklyn wall. (*a*) Unbraced second-story masonry wall collapsed during construction, breaking through adjacent roof. (From *ENR*, April 5, 1990.)

Several improprieties and violations were alleged by OSHA and other investigators soon after the collapse. These included no building permit, no seal on the architectural/structural drawings, no shop drawings for the wall support beams, inadequate and unstable support at the base of the wall, no inspection, and, perhaps most importantly for construction safety, no temporary lateral bracing of the wall. Because of the fatalities and the obvious negligence, criminal proceedings were started against the contractor, and the engineering investigations were halted. OSHA did complete its report but has not released it for the public.

While this appears to be an extreme case, collapses of masonry walls during construction are chronic occurrences, and the cause is nearly always the total absence of temporary bracing.

Note, however, that a contractor wanting to actually design temporary wall bracing would have a difficult time determining what the required lateral design load should be. Where would she or he find that information?

Case History 13: Huntington Wall Bracing

An unfinished 18-ft-high, 180-ft-long hollow-core concrete masonry bearing wall collapsed on February 25, 1996, several months after construction had been halted in Huntington, New York. The wall had Durowall horizontal wire reinforcement at every third course, 16-in-wide by 8-in-deep unreinforced pilasters at 18-ft intervals, and the wall was standing on an 8-in-wide reinforced-concrete foundation

(b)

FIGURE 17.12   Brooklyn wall. (*Continued*) (*b*) Remnant of concrete block wall built on widened top flange of wide flange beam. (From R. T. Ratay Engineering, P. C.)

wall. The 180-ft length was broken into three segments by two vertical control joints that separated the wall from the adjacent pilaster at those two locations.

Prior to the collapse, the wall was allegedly braced, probably from one side only, by an unknown number of 16-ft-long (or so), 9-in by 2-in wood planks.

During the night of the collapse, the fastest-mile wind speed, according to the National Weather Service records, was 45 mi/h (creating a calculated stagnation pressure of 5.4 lb/ft^2). The 50-year design wind speed by the *New York State*

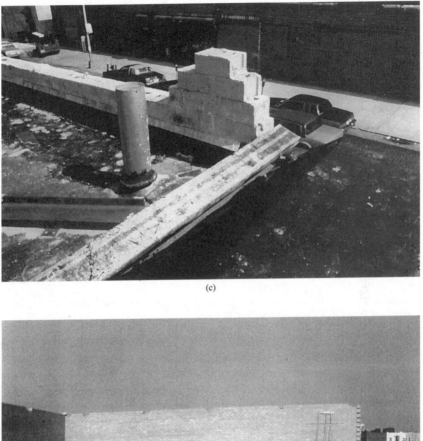

(c)

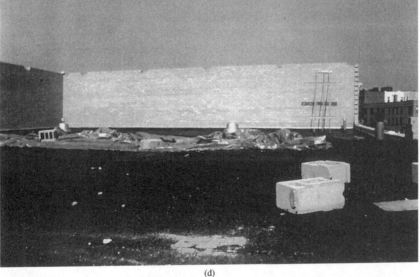

(d)

FIGURE 17.12   Brooklyn wall. (*Continued*) (*c*) Web of wide flange beam bent and top flange rotated under the wall. (From R. T. Ratay Engineering, P. C.) (*d*) Another wall received temporary lateral bracing after the catastrophic collapse. (From R. T. Ratay Engineering, P. C.)

(a)

FIGURE 17.13   Huntington wall. (*a*) Inadequately braced unfinished masonry block wall toppled in strong wind. (From R. T. Ratay Engineering, P. C.)

Building Code for the subject location is 75 mi/h (translating to 15 lb/ft² stagnation pressure).

According to the engineering investigator retained by the insurance company, while the 9-by-2 diagonal bracing planks when straight would provide some support, they were bent so much (about 2-in snag at midlength), hence having so little axial stiffness, as to be ineffective to restrain lateral movement of the top of the wall.

Case History 14: Wood Truss Erection

Dozens of 42-ft-span wood trusses collapsed during construction of a major addition to a church in British Columbia, Canada. One worker fell with a truss and was slightly injured. The trusses were approximately 5 ft deep with sloping parallel chords peaking at midspan, spanning north-south 42 ft between two 22-ft-high load-bearing stud walls of 2-by-6 studs at 8 in on center. The causes of the collapse appeared to have been inadequate temporary bracing of the trusses and the incomplete construction of the load-bearing stud wall on the south side of the building. The wall was not fully sheathed, the sheathing that was in place was only partially nailed, and it is likely that this wall was not adequately braced. No truss drawings were available at the site. According to the workers, "the bracing didn't make any sense, the other guys on the other site were responsible for the bracing."

(b)

FIGURE 17.13 Huntington wall. (*Continued*) (*b*) Remnant of collapsed wall. (From R. T. Ratay Engineering, P. C.)

Case History 15: Column Reinforcing Steel Bracing

A tall reinforcing bar cage for a concrete column collapsed in Vancouver, British Columbia, in the morning of November 2, 1993, seriously injuring one worker. The column rebar cage consisted of 44 bars of 25-mm diameter and 38-ft length each from the ground up, to which an additional 40 bars of 25-mm diameter and 24-ft length were spliced starting at 9 ft aboveground, or 16 in above the top of the previous pour. The collapsed cage was reported as weighing approximately

(c)

FIGURE 17.13   Huntington wall. (*Continued*) (*c*) "Orderly line-up" of collapsed masonry on the ground. (From R. T. Ratay Engineering, P. C.)

(a)

FIGURE 17.14   Wood trusses. (*a*) Wood roof toppled over during construction. (From Jozef Jakubowski, Workers' Compensation Board of British Columbia, Vancouver, BC, Canada.)

(b)

FIGURE 17.14 Wood trusses. (*Continued*) (*b*) Close-up view of collapsed wood trusses. (From Jozef Jakubowski, Workers' Compensation Board of British Columbia, Vancouver, BC, Canada.)

(a)

FIGURE 17.15 Column reinforcing steel. (*a*) Tall reinforcing steel cage collapsed before erecting formwork. (From Jozef Jakubowski, Workers' Compensation Board of British Columbia, Vancouver, BC, Canada.)

(b)

FIGURE 17.15   Column reinforcing steel. (*Continued*) (*b*) Column rebar
cage bent over at top of previously poured concrete. (From Jozef Jakubowski,
Workers' Compensation Board of British Columbia, Vancouver, BC, Canada.)

14,000 lb. The column was to be part of a ductile moment-resisting frame. The
reinforcing steel requirements and lap locations were detailed on the structural
engineering drawings. Five guy cables were stabilizing the cage. At the time of the
accident, the injured worker was on top of a previously poured concrete wall, rigging a section of gang form to be moved by a tower crane. He was positioned such
that two of the five guylines were on either side of him, to his east and west.

Two possible scenarios were developed by investigators of the Worker's
Compensation Board of British Columbia: "Either the moving gang form panel
tripped the guyline to the west of the worker, initiating the rebar cage's collapse,
or someone had undone one of the guylines to the east, which sent the cage over
in a northwesterly direction."

They further opined, "Either scenario could have caused the other guylines to
go down, with the one behind the worker (to the east) catching and flinging him

approximately 32 ft across the site. Had the rebar cage been adequately braced, it would not have collapsed."

Following this incident, and others in which reinforcing steel or its temporary supports had collapsed, the Worker's Compensation Board issued a Technical Commentary, stating that "The contractor is required to address the support and stability of reinforcing steel in concrete structures..." and suggested to "consider retaining an engineer to design the temporary support and stability of rebar column cages, wall panels and [elevated] reinforcing steel mats in [thick] foundation slabs."

HOW TO AVOID TEMPORARY STRUCTURE FAILURES

Take them seriously: Consider them just as important as the permanent facility they help build!

ATTRIBUTION

The "What Are Temporary Structures?" part of this chapter is, in part, reproduced from the article "Temporary Structures" that the author wrote for the McGraw-Hill *1999 Encyclopedia of Science and Technology.* The section "Understanding the Design-Construction Process" relies heavily on chapter 1, "Technical and Business Practices," by Robert F. Borg, in *Handbook of Temporary Structures in Construction,* 2d ed., Robert T. Ratay, ed., McGraw-Hill, New York, 1996, and on papers and presentations the author had made in the past. "Responsibilities and Liabilities" was extracted from chapter 2, "The Legal Positions," by Robert A. Rubin, in *Handbook of Temporary Structures in Construction.* "Codes, Standards, and Regulations" is loosely based on chapter 4, "Codes and Standards," by John F. Duntemann, also in *Handbook of Temporary Structures in Construction,* and on a paper that Duntemann and the author recently wrote. Portions of this chapter appeared before as proceedings of the invited lectures the author presented at professional seminars of the Boston Society of Civil Engineers in 1997, and of the New York Met Section of the American Society of Civil Engineers in 1998.

INDEX

ABOUT THE EDITOR

Robert T. Ratay, Ph.D., P.E., is a highly regarded structural engineer and former university professor with an extensive background in both design and failure analysis. His nearly four decades of professional experience is divided almost equally between structural engineering practice, and combined teaching and consulting. Dr. Ratay worked with such prominent firms as Le Messurier Associates, Severud Associates, and HNTB. He was professor and Chairman of the Civil Engineering Department, then Dean of the School of Engineering at Pratt Institute, and a professor at Polytechnic University (formerly Brooklyn Polytech). His current practice in forensic structural engineering is directed toward the investigation of structural and construction failures, providing expert consultant services to architects, engineers, contractors, owners, attorneys, insurance companies, and government agencies. Dr. Ratay is a fellow of the American Society of Civil Engineers, has chaired several of its technical committees, and currently serves on the Executive Committee of its Structural Engineering Institute. He is also the Editor-in-Chief of the authoritative *Handbook of Temporary Structures in Construction* published by McGraw-Hill.